Incarnation and Resurrection

D1561482

Incarnation and Resurrection

Toward a Contemporary Understanding

Paul D. Molnar

WILLIAM B. EERDMANS PUBLISHING COMPANY
GRAND RAPIDS, MICHIGAN / CAMBRIDGE, U.K.

Published 2007 by
Wm. B. Eerdmans Publishing Co.
2140 Oak Industrial Drive N.E., Grand Rapids, Michigan 49505 /
P.O. Box 163, Cambridge CB3 9PU U.K.

Library of Congress Cataloging-in-Publication Data

Molnar, Paul D., 1946-
    Incarnation and Resurrection: toward a contemporary understanding / Paul D. Molnar.
        p.   cm.
    Includes bibliographical references.
    ISBN: 978-0-8028-0998-8 (pbk.: alk. paper)
    1. Incarnation — History of doctrines — 20th century.
    2. Jesus Christ — Resurrection — History of doctrines — 20th century.
    3. Incarnation — History of doctrines — 21st century.
    4. Jesus Christ — Resurrection — History of doctrines — 21st century.   I. Title.

    BT220.M65   2007
    232′.1 — dc22

                                                                2007004073

www.eerdmans.com

Contents

Preface

In a fascinating article entitled "Interpreting the Resurrection," David Fergusson asks: "What do we mean when we say that 'Jesus is risen'?"[1] For the sake of a coherent Christology he outlines "three rival interpretations . . . [the] radical, liberal and traditional." He equates the radical view with the position represented by Bultmann, Marxsen and others who, for a variety of reasons, reduce the resurrection to the rise of faith in the disciples. Classically stated in the words of Bultmann:

> If the event of Easter Day is in any sense an historical event additional to the event of the cross, it is nothing else than the rise of faith in the risen Lord, since it was this faith which led to the apostolic preaching. The resurrection itself is not an event of past history.[2]

Willi Marxsen's thesis rests on his conviction "that the activity of Jesus of Nazareth goes on after his death in the lives of his followers" so that "the resurrection stories are imaginative ways of expressing Christian faith."[3]

Fergusson equates the liberal view with the thought of Hans Küng, Edward Schillebeeckx, James Mackey and others who, despite distinct differences, nevertheless seem to suggest that the resurrection is created within or realized through the faith of the disciples.

> Its characteristics include a dissatisfaction with the radical view, an emphasis upon the appearance stories as explanation, a historical scepticism about the empty tomb, and an uneasiness about any notion of the miraculous.[4]

The last two characteristics of course overlap with those of the radical view. Representing this position, Schillebeeckx argues on the one hand that the resurrection, that is, "the stimulus to faith" could be best described as

> a set of resurrection visions disclosing the continuing activity of Jesus. . . . From out of these experiences arises the conviction that Jesus is risen. . . . The way in which [Schillebeeckx] interprets the narratives suggests that they refer primarily to the religious experiences of the disciples. They are experiences of divine grace and forgiveness. . . . On the other hand, his language about 'renewed fellowship' with Jesus seems to imply that the resurrection is an event in the personal destiny of Jesus.[5]

The basic ambivalence of the liberal position is well expressed, according to Fergusson, by James Mackey who suggests, in answer to the question of whether the resurrection is an event in the destiny of Jesus or in the believer, that it seems to be both. Mackey speaks of the resurrection as "the Christian experience of Jesus as Spirit or Lord in the lives of his followers" and concludes that the resurrection "is *the* myth of the death of Jesus. It is *the* statement, in the form of narrated symbols, of the deep significance for human kind of the death of this man."[6] Fergusson rightly concludes that the liberal view, thus explicated, actually collapses back into the radical position because the resurrection is presented as no more than an event in the life of the believer.

Finally, Fergusson equates the traditional view that the resurrection was an event in the life of Jesus that gave rise to the faith of the disciples, with the Pauline tradition of 1 Cor. 15. As Fergusson puts it:

> The language [of 1 Cor. 15] suggests that Jesus' significance for faith is a consequence of his being personally raised from the dead. Its reference is to an event in the destiny of Jesus which makes possible his subsequent appearance for faith. The resurrection is here construed as the condition of the rise of faith rather than being assimilated to the latter.[7]

In this position the empty tomb functions as

> a necessary condition which enables us to make sense of a personal resurrection of Jesus prior to the rise of faith. As a necessary or negative condition the empty tomb, in conjunction with some appropriate account of the appearances, has the function, not so much of verifying faith, as contributing to its overall shape and balance.[8]

I believe that the radical and liberal interpretations of the resurrection are still alive and well today in contemporary systematic theology while the traditional view is also still alive and well, even though it has become something of a minority view at present. In this book I propose to explore the thinking of a number of prominent contemporary theologians to show that wherever and whenever the starting point for interpreting the resurrection is not Jesus himself, the incarnate Son of the Father, then Christology and soteriology are undermined precisely because they are not properly rooted in a plausible doctrine of the Trinity. In other words whenever it is thought that the statement, "Jesus is risen" is merely a description of the disciples' experience of faith instead of a description of an event in the life of Jesus that gave meaning to their faith and to ours, then the objective meaning of the person and work of Jesus Christ has been lost. Such thinking, I will contend, is possible only to the extent that a proper doctrine of the immanent Trinity is ignored or compromised at the outset.

In the course of this discussion I hope to develop the thesis that the incarnation and resurrection are so closely related that if one is compromised in the slightest way then so too is the other. It will be my contention that the same unique subject who was active in the incarnation remains active in the resurrection and beyond as the ascended Lord of the church and world. Importantly, then, it will be demonstrated that any Christology that begins with the resurrection in abstraction from the incarnation undermines the very meaning of the incarnation and thus also of the resurrection itself. I will contend that any approach to Christology which claims that the incarnation can only be the conclusion and not the starting point for Christology also damages the connection between the resurrection and incarnation and causes difficulty for other doctrines as well.[9]

I will also argue that there are ethical implications to any compromise of these doctrines because where the person and work of Jesus Christ are undermined by historicist, existentialist or mythological thinking, it is then thought that salvation becomes a work that we must perform in some fashion in order to save society in some way or another. But any form of self-justification in ethics or in theology proper represents a failure to see and to understand the intimate connection between the doctrines of the incarnation and the resurrection. Further, any form of self-justification ultimately represents a failure to understand that the incarnation and resurrection, as free acts of God within history on behalf of the entire human race, are grounded within the inner life of God himself so that they are not "necessary" to God and cannot be read off logically from any experience or set of experiences within the economy of salvation. My aim then is to show how and why dogmatic thinking is necessarily interrelated and is important in very practical ways. Hence those who deny or ignore the significance of a doctrine of the immanent Trinity and those who ignore the importance of recognizing Jesus as the Word of God incarnate, weaken the theological basis for the comfort and truth of the Christian faith; they also lead people astray and create unnecessary anxiety with the idea that they must somehow contribute to their own salvation and the salvation of the world by virtue of what they think and do. Nothing could be further from the truth and nothing, as will be seen, could be less helpful to people in their times of deepest need.

Specifically, I hope to show how important issues involved in the three positions mentioned above develop in the theology of three influential theologians: Karl Barth, Karl Rahner and Thomas F. Torrance. From there I will widen the discussion to explore the thinking of many other contemporary proposals in order to make my case that wherever and whenever the resurrection is interpreted in a liberal or radical way, such theology also has misconstrued the meaning of the incarnation and the doctrine of the Trinity. And I intend to show that there are always practical theological and ethical results to such misunderstanding so that any such compromise will always lead to uncertainty rather than to the certainty promised by Christ himself to those who abide in the truth which is identical with his very person and work. Perhaps most importantly I believe that this book can establish a context for ecumenical agreement between Reformed and Roman Catholic theology centered in these important doctrines. If Reformed and Roman Catholic theology could consistently allow their thinking to begin and end with Jesus Christ himself as the Word incarnate, then the union of churches would be based on something more than merely formal declarations that could be explained by both sides in ways that perpetuate the divisions that continue to exist, in spite of those formal declarations of unity.[10]

Acknowledgments

I would like to thank the Very Reverend Professor Iain R. Torrance not only for his unwavering support, encouragement and friendship, but also for his enthusiastic assistance in bringing this manuscript to publication with William B. Eerdmans Publishing Company. It is not too much to say that without his help this work might never have reached this final form.

Thanks are also due to Bill Eerdmans for his encouragement, good humor and kind assistance with this book from the very beginning. I am grateful as well to all of the editors at Eerdmans who have been so helpful, especially Jennifer Hoffman.

I am indebted to Iain Taylor for taking time out of his busy schedule to read and comment on the Pannenberg material contained in Chapter Eight of this book. His interaction was extremely helpful to me in thinking through some of the more complex issues related to Wolfhart Pannenberg's theology. I am grateful to St. John's University for providing me with a research leave during the spring of 2003 to work on this book.

Thanks are also due to my good friends, Professors John Webster and George Hunsinger for many helpful conversations that have contributed invaluably to my thinking over these last several years. And I must also acknowledge a debt to Professor David Fergusson for providing a very clear view of how to interpret the resurrection with his article on the subject in the *Scottish Journal of Theology* over twenty years ago. In addition I am grateful to members of the Barth Society and T. F. Torrance Fellowship, too numerous to mention here for providing important interaction that has helped my thinking during recent years as well.

Also, I would like to express my deep gratitude to John J. McCormick who gave up much valuable time and expended a good deal of effort to read and re-read several versions of this manuscript, including the final proofs, and to offer both encouragement and his important editorial suggestions along the way.

Additionally, I would like to express my sincere appreciation to the Very Reverend Professor Thomas F. Torrance whose profound insights regarding the important connection between the doctrines of the resurrection and the incarnation inspired me to pursue the line of thought expressed in this book in the first instance.

Finally, I am grateful to Blackwell Publishers for permission to reprint the following previously published material: Paul D. Molnar, "Incarnation, Resurrection and the Doctrine of the Trinity: A Comparison of Thomas F. Torrance and Roger Haight" *International Journal of Systematic Theology* 5 (2003), 147-67.

1. Incarnation and Resurrection in the Theology of Karl Barth

Let us begin by employing the categories developed by David Fergusson and ask whether Barth believes the resurrection is an event in the life of Jesus that gives meaning to the faith of the disciples and to ours or if he believes it is created by or realized within the faith of the disciples and our faith. Barth's answer to this question is about as unequivocal as one could get. He insists that the resurrection is an event in the life of Jesus that gives meaning to the disciples' faith and to ours today through the power of the Holy Spirit and thus through faith. And he insists that the power of the resurrection, which is the very power of God himself, acting within history for our benefit is not at all contingent on human belief. Instead it is the very factor that enables belief. For that reason Barth asserts that the resurrection refers to a specific event that took place once upon a time and included the forty days of the Easter appearances; it most definitely does not refer to a timeless truth or timeless event. And it does not describe the disciples' experience of faith. Rather it describes the object of their faith who actually rose bodily from the dead and appeared to them in specific circumstances. In this chapter I shall explore exactly what Barth has to say about the resurrection and its connection with the incarnation and ultimately with his view of the Trinity. Further, I shall explore how this thinking has ethical implications with respect to the doctrine of justification. Because Barth's understanding of the resurrection is tied to his view of the incarnation it will be helpful to indicate briefly what Barth means by the incarnation and how his view opposes any sort of Ebionite or Docetic Christology before exploring his specific view of the resurrection.

Barth's View of the Incarnation

Barth understood the incarnation as a real act of becoming flesh, sinful flesh, on the part of God's eternal Word.[1] The Word was the subject of that event; it was not something that befell him in accordance with the evolutionary trend of world events or the nature of God's love. It was certainly not something that could be understood as the supreme form of a theology of the symbol as Rahner does.[2] Hence, "This becoming cannot be brought into connexion with creation. It cannot be regarded as one of its evolutionary possibilities. . . . God's Word becoming a creature must be regarded as a new creation . . . it is a sovereign divine act, and it is an act of lordship different from creation" (*CD* I/2, 134, see also 151ff. and 160ff.).[3] As a free act of the Word it did not rest on "any necessity of the divine nature or upon the relation between Father, Son and Spirit, that God becomes man. . . . God acts with inward freedom and not in fulfilment of a law to which He is supposedly subject" (*CD* I/2, 135).[4] Hence, "The Father and the Son are not two prisoners. They are not two mutually conditioning factors in reciprocal operation. As the common source of the Spirit, who Himself is also God, they are the Lord of this occurrence. God is the free Lord of His inner union" (*CD* IV/2, 345).

The incarnation did not mean a diminution of his divinity but a concealment of it and all for the sake of his mercy toward us. Barth preferred to speak of an assumption of flesh by the Word because it implied that what took place in the incarnation was a miracle, that is, a special new direct act of God in history[5] that meant that the Word remained the Word and did not cease to be God while truly becoming flesh.[6] This did not mean that some third reality arose from the union of natures because that in itself would suggest the cessation of both his divine and human being;[7] the fact that the Word assumed our flesh meant that "The *kenosis,* passion, humiliation which He takes upon Himself by becoming man, signifies no loss in divine majesty but, considered in the light of its goal, actually its triumph" (*CD* I/2, 37).[8] Here Barth distinguishes between the servant form of revelation in which God is hidden in the "externalization" of the incarnation of the Word and the "divine form" "in which God knows Himself, in which the Father knows the Son and the Son the Father. It is in this veiling — which after all is a veiling in a form familiar to man — that the Majesty can meet men and so far make knowledge of itself possible through men" (*CD* I/2, 37-38). But in this "externalization" the Word become flesh is exposed to the possibility that we might not recognize him. "Knowledge of it becomes real to men only in virtue of a special unveiling through Jesus' resurrection from the dead, or through all the sayings and acts of His life so far as they were signs of His resurrection" (*CD* I/2, 38). In all of this, however, there is no lessening of his divinity:

> That it is only veiling, not abandonment nor yet lessening of His divinity, is shown by the unveiling, which is not only the result but from the start — it is revelation we are concerned with — its goal. He who the third day rose from the dead was no less true God in the manger than on the cross. (*CD* I/2, 38)

There can thus be no hint of a two-stage Christology in Barth's thought:

> It was neither a 'historical Jesus' nor a 'Christ of faith' which they [the apostles] knew and proclaimed, neither the abstract image of one in whom they did not yet believe nor the equally abstract image of one in whom they afterward believed. Instead, they proclaimed concretely the one Jesus Christ who had encountered them as the one who he was, even when they did not yet believe in him. Having their eyes opened by his resurrection, they were able to tell who he was who had made himself known to them *before* the resurrection. A twofold Jesus Christ, one who existed *before* and another who existed *after* Easter, can be deduced from the New Testament texts only after he has been arbitrarily read into them.[9]

Barth's starting point for Christology, namely, Jesus Christ himself as truly God and truly human, excludes from the outset and at each point along the way even the slightest implication of Ebionite or Docetic Christology. Jesus was neither the highest human creature nor the content of our idea of divinity confirmed in experience. Rather "He the eternal Subject now exists — a stumbling-block to all Jewish ears and foolishness to all Greek ears — just as anything else or as anyone else exits. That is the meaning of ὁ λόγος ἐγένετο . . ." (*CD* I/2, 159).

For these reasons revelation for Barth is identical with the person and work of Jesus Christ. "Jesus *is* the revelation of the Father and the revelation of the Father *is* Jesus. And precisely in virtue of this 'is' He is the Son or Word of the Father." Barth insists that the apostolic thinking about Jesus "always ended with the knowledge of Christ's deity because it had already begun there" (*CD* I/1, 412). Hence Barth insists that Jn. 1:14 must be accepted as a genuine statement about Jesus Christ as truly divine and human: "One cannot subsequently speak christologically, if Christology has not already been presupposed at the outset, and in its stead other presuppositions have claimed one's attention" (*CD* I/2, 123). But none of this is under our control:

"The knowability of the Word of God stands or falls, then, with the act of its real knowledge, which is not under our control" (*CD* I/1, 224). Real knowledge of God must find its assurance not in itself but in the Word of God so that "His assurance is his own assurance, but it has its seat outside him in the Word of God . . ." (*CD* I/1, 224-25). That is why Barth rejected the idea that Jesus was the revealer in his humanity as such: "Not of its own activity but in virtue of the Word united with it did the flesh of the Lord do what was divine; by the same means the Word proved His own divineness" (*CD* I/2, 137).

And this is also why Barth rejected any quest of the "historical Jesus" as well as Catholic devotion to the Sacred Heart. Each in their own way made the human Jesus the object of their inquiry or devotion and in that way sought to evade the Word so that

> by direct glorification of Christ's humanity as such the divine Word is evaded and camouflaged. For when we are speaking of Jesus Christ, this Word . . . is God's revelation to us in Its human-ness: inseparable from it, but in such a way that this human-ness is not only inseparably linked with the Word on its own account, but also receives its character as revelation and its power to reveal solely from the Word and therefore certainly cannot in itself, abstractly and directly, be the object of faith and worship. (*CD* I/2, 138)

Additionally, for Barth, revelation is offensive to us precisely because we resist the divine act of lordship evident in God's fulfillment of time in Jesus Christ.[10] No human *a priori* is admissible here because we have no vantage point from which we may judge the validity of the revelation of God in Jesus Christ. Even as a historical event, revelation is not open to human appraisal. That is why Barth argues that a proper view of revelation sees "'fulfilled time' from the standpoint of the fulfilment, not of the time . . . history is what it is, entirely and altogether in virtue of the Subject who acts here" (*CD* I/2, 60). Sin, according to Barth, is exposed in its true proportions only over against Jesus Christ. In its very hiddenness, revelation is resisted by us — we fight against it.

> It is primarily only at revelation that one can — and inevitably must — be 'offended.' 'God in time,' 'God in history' — that is the offending thing in revelation. God in Himself is not offending. Time in itself is also not offending. But God in time is offending because the order of rank mentioned is thereby set up, because we are thereby gripped by God, as it were, in our very own sphere, namely in the delusion that we possessed time. Fulfilled

time in our midst is the enemy who has forced himself in, the center of confusion which, driven by necessity, we want to destroy or at least render innocuous or conceal from our sight. (*CD* I/2, 61)

We are offended by the fact that our time, the time of Adam, has come to an end in Jesus Christ so that "the disposal of our days is taken from us by the revealed God, that our time is really in his hands" (*CD* I/2, 67; see also *CD* IV/2, 406).

Barth's View of the Resurrection

When we turn to Barth's understanding of the resurrection we can see that, as in his view of the incarnation, so here he systematically excludes any sort of Ebionite or Docetic view of the resurrection. Resurrection, incarnation and atonement are tightly knit together in Barth's thinking and the truth of these events and occurrences of God acting for us in the history of salvation is contingent on Barth's belief in the fact that each of these actions of God is an action of the eternal Father, Son and Holy Spirit as the one who loves in freedom. Barth's theological method itself is dictated by his view of the resurrection as a miracle that gives meaning to every aspect of dogmatic theology, as we shall see. This is why he maintains that "Because it is an event which took place for the apostles in their encounter with the living Christ, the knowledge of it will necessarily be ordered by their witness and continually orientated by it" (*CD* IV/2, 149).

There is no doubt that the resurrection plays a decisive role in every facet of Barth's theology. On the one hand Barth equates revelation and resurrection underlining rather than undermining Christ's uniqueness and the need for faith:

the function of the resurrection is to make the passion of Christ, in which the incarnation of the Word of God was consummated, clearly and unmistakably revelation, the realisation of the covenant between God and man, God's act for us, as reconciliation. . . . The resurrection is the event of the revelation of the Incarnate, the Humiliated, the Crucified. Wherever He gives Himself to be known as the person He is, He speaks as the risen Christ. The resurrection can give nothing new to Him who is the eternal Word of the Father; but it makes visible what is proper to Him, His glory. (*CD* I/2, 111)

On the other hand Barth insists that the resurrection is an event in the life of the historical Jesus that gives meaning to the disciples' faith and to ours.

So Barth maintains that in the incarnation and resurrection there is no lessening of the eternal Word but rather a veiling of the eternal Word which leads to an unveiling in his resurrection (*CD* I/2, 38f.). But this resurrection is not simply a way of thinking about the life of Jesus and it is not just an expression describing the disciples' experience of faith. It is rather an objective event within history whose meaning is always tied to Jesus himself as subject and object and thus requires faith in him to be understood. Speaking of Mark's account of the empty tomb Barth writes: "Everything else related by this story can be heard and believed in the very literalness in which it stands, but can really only be believed, because it drops out of all categories and so out of all conceivability" (*CD* I/2, 115). This is the case because the NT does not supply a description of the resurrection itself and could not, since it was presenting the recollection "of the pure presence of God, recollection of a time which cannot be the past and has no future before it, recollection of eternal time" (*CD* I/2, 115). This is why Barth argues that the Easter story does not speak eschatologically but of

> a present without any future, of an eternal presence of God in time.... The Easter story, Christ truly, corporeally risen, and as such appearing to His disciples, talking with them, acting in their midst — this is, of course the recollection upon which all New Testament recollections hang, to which they are all related, for the sake of which there is a New Testament recollection at all. (*CD* I/2, 114)

From Barth's point of view then the NT rests upon the recollection of a specific event in time and space, a datable event that was the object of the OT expectation, that is, the coming of the Messiah. The NT recollection is not just a look backward at a once for all happening because this particular event does not just belong to the past. It is the recollection of what Barth calls "eternal time" because the Messiah has come. Without this and without the 40 days Barth says we would just have a bit of "docetic philosophy" (*CD* I/2, 116). But for the NT and for us this recollection must also be expectation because in his revelation to come our own being will be revealed. "If we confess that Christ is risen and risen bodily, we must also confess to our own future resurrection" (*CD* I/2, 117). Hence "if recollection does not actually become expectation" then the NT is "simply a bit of ebionite tradition" (*CD* I/2, 117).

Because of this eschatological trend of the NT we must also note the "distinction in unity between Christ and ourselves" (*CD* I/2, 118). Thus, NT faith is "not a continuation of Christ's faith and still less a kind of prolongation of the existence of Christ Himself, but it is faith in Christ" (*CD* I/2, 118) and

"Revelation remains identical with Christ and Christ remains the object of Christian faith, even though He lives in Christians and they in Him. . . . What Christ is in us, that He is for us and therefore in His difference from us. This is what is assured by the eschatological trend of New Testament faith" (*CD* I/2, 118).[11] This is why faith in Christ really is hope in Christ: "Faith has Christ as it hopes in Him. So in hope in Christ . . . it has the Spirit as the surety for its hidden sonship to God, it has peace with God. . . . Hope describes the manner or mode of faith" (*CD* I/2, 118-19). Barth insists that the foundation of hope is Christ himself and only him because it is in him that our justification and sanctification have taken place, it is in him that the world is reconciled to God. But this recollection is also a looking forward in hope to Christ's second coming. Christian hope is distinguished from any other kind of hope in Barth's thought:

> Let us be clear that . . . we are again speaking of the Second Coming of *Jesus Christ*. Christian Eschatology is different from all other expectations for the future, whether they be worldly or religious or religious-worldly, in that it is not primarily expectation of something, even if this something were called resurrection of the flesh and eternal life, but expectation of the Lord.[12]

In Barth's thinking all aspects of theology are determined by the way one interprets Jesus' resurrection. Any hint of the liberal or radical view would undermine the meaning of the incarnation, atonement and redemption and would ultimately signify a misunderstanding of the eternal nature of the Tri-une God who has acted, now acts as God for us in his Word and Spirit and will act for us in the future. For these reasons it is important to explore just what Barth means by the resurrection so that we can see how and why theology must be grounded in the person and work of Christ and ultimately in a proper understanding of the doctrine of the Trinity.

In his theological anthropology Barth's understanding of Jesus as "a man in His time" (*CD* III/2, 441) reflects his anti-docetic view that it is because Jesus lives out his human life in time that he shares our humanity to the full. Yet he lives this human life "as the One He is in virtue of His unity with God" (*CD* III/2, 439). Hence he acts as our representative and judge by living for God and for us. As Jesus lives out his own time, he is as such the Lord of time. For that reason "His time acquires . . . the character of God's time, of eternity, in which present, past and future are simultaneous" (*CD* III/2, 440). How do we know this? The answer is to be found in his resurrection. While Jesus' own lifetime in history was the "time of salvation" (*CD* III/2, 441) and while it ended at a particular time on the cross and in the grave, Jesus had a second history in contrast to others. That second history is the "Easter history," namely, the forty days between his resurrection and ascension. The man Jesus (the historical Jesus) is seen in this light and thus Jesus is seen as the Lord of all time. All of Jesus' words and deeds are understood in light of the particular event of his resurrection. But this resurrection itself took place at a particular time and as such "irradiated" his entire life in time. Barth's view here depends upon acknowledging that the apostolic proclamation regarding Jesus "derives from the fact that Jesus was among them even in this particular time, the Easter time" (CD III/2, 442).

One can clearly see the connection between incarnation, resurrection and atonement in Barth's thinking here. Because Jesus is uniquely a man of his time as the eternal Son of God who is Lord of time, Jesus is the unique savior of the world. Yet he is this savior only as the man who was among them in a second specific time, the time of the Easter history. Take away the historicity of these events and both incarnation and resurrection become no more than myth. This is why Barth insists that Christ's resurrection took place in time and history and was not a "timeless idea, a kind of *a priori*" through which his earthly life was interpreted. The very man Jesus who died on the cross and was buried existed in this "later time" (CD III/2, 442). For that reason Barth insists, in his doctrine of reconciliation, that it is the unity of God with this man that gives justification its significance (CD IV/1, 306).

Resurrection and Atonement

And Barth also argues that Jesus' human suffering is not dissimilar from other human suffering because what makes it unique cannot be found

> in the human passion as such. . . . The mystery of this passion, of the torture, crucifixion and death of this one Jew which took place at that place and time at the hands of the Romans, is to be found in the person and mission of the One who suffered there and was crucified and died. His person: it is the eternal God Himself who has given Himself in His Son to be man, and as man to take upon Himself this human passion. His mission: it is the Judge who in this passion takes the place of those who ought to be judged. . . . (CD IV/1, 246)

Hence for Barth the problem posed here is not the problem of theodicy, namely, how can God will or permit this to happen in a world that he created good. Rather this is "a matter of the humiliation and dishonouring of God Himself, of the question which makes any question of a theodicy a complete anticlimax" (*CD* IV/1, 246).

Did God abdicate his deity in surrendering to human folly? Can God really die and be dead? These questions are all rendered irrelevant by the fact that "in this humiliation God is supremely God, that in this death He is supremely alive, that He has maintained and revealed His deity in the passion of this man as His eternal Son" (*CD* IV/1, 246-47). Indeed this is what makes his mission one of reconciliation: "There takes place here the redemptive judgment of God on all men" (*CD* IV/1, 247). As with the resurrection, Barth insists that everything depends upon the fact that this happens as an act of God for us and that it is "not simply imagined and presented as a true teaching of pious and thoughtful people, but that it happened in this way, in the space and time which are those of all men . . . it is the passion of Jesus Christ itself and as such which has to be believed and proclaimed as the act of God for us" (*CD* IV/1, 247-48). Here Barth insists, against the tendency of much contemporary theology,[13] that

> we cannot be content to define the passion of Jesus Christ as the act of God for us, however true that may be, but we must go on to define the act of God for us as the passion of Jesus Christ. In this, and in this alone, is it the act of God for us. With this there stands or falls the truth of Christian experience. (*CD* IV/1, 249)

Barth wishes to stress that the truth of God's action for us takes place in a way that does not depend in the slightest on our experience, insight or cooperation because "its authenticity, its validity and its force are in itself" (*CD* IV/1, 250). That is why, for Barth, our reconciliation with God is not some general or repeatable occurrence. "There is no other reconciliation of the world with God for any other man than that which took place in this One. . . . In Him the world is converted to God. In Him man is the friend of God and not His enemy" (*CD* IV/1, 251). The certainty of faith, then, is grounded in the truth which is identical with Jesus himself who "is the truth. . . . To be of the truth means to hear His voice in encounter and confrontation with Him: not to hear first the voice of that which God will give us in Him but to hear His voice. To be of the truth means first to believe in Him . . ." (*CD* IV/1, 252). That is why Barth insists that the essence of faith is that "we are no longer expected to live in our own strength, because we see ourselves and act as those who have thankfully found the centre of their being in the faith that God lives for them" (*CD* II/1, 392).

Two important things must be kept in mind here. First, it is proper, Barth argued, to say that God is love, but only in the context of 1 Jn. 4, which stresses that God's love was identical with the "completed act of divine loving in sending Jesus Christ" (*CD* II/1, 275). This thinking also must be linked with Jn. 3:16 which states that "For this is how God loved the world: he gave his only Son, so that everyone who believes in him may not perish but may have eternal life." Therefore one could never say, as did Angelus Silesius that "I know that without me God cannot an instant be. He needs must perish at once were death to come to me." Barth rejected any thinking that implied mutual necessity between God and us and rejected the "pious blasphemies" of Angelus Silesius, wondering whether the bishop who gave Silesius's *Cherubinischer Wandersmann* an imprimatur "was an imbecile or whether he had a secret understanding with the modern rogue" (*CD* II/1, 282).[14]

Speaking of the importance of Christ's death on the cross for the reconciliation of the world Barth insists it is not the case that a "possibility" was created on Golgotha "the setting up of a model and example, an extraordinary offer of dying, or quite simply the institution of a law: 'Die and become,' the reality of which will come only when it is followed" (*CD* IV/1, 295). This is an extremely important point because, as we shall see throughout this book, far too many Protestant and Catholic theologians adopt some form of this conditional thinking in order to stress the soteriological significance of Jesus for the church today. But it is just this emphasis that is dogmatically and ethically misguided, as I hope to show. Such thinking pulls the ground out from under the Gospel. In answer to the question *Cur Deus homo?* Barth finally answered: Christ took our place as Judge (as the Priest who represented us — not as the priests of the Old Testament who also had to act for themselves) but as *the* Priest because "As the Son of God He acts exclusively on behalf of the people and not for Himself" (*CD* IV/1, 275), as the judged, he was judged and he acted justly in our place. But this means that

> we cannot add anything to this — unless it is an Amen. . . . All theology, both that which follows and indeed that which precedes the doctrine of reconciliation, depends upon this *theologia crucis*. . . . Everything depends upon the fact that the Lord who became a servant, the Son of God who went into the far country, and came to us, was and did all of this for us; that He fulfilled, and fulfilled in this way, the divine judgment laid upon Him. (*CD* IV/1, 273)

Second, Barth stresses the unity of God's mercy and righteousness while insisting on the priority of God's mercy. What is the meaning of God's righteousness and mercy in this context? The divine mercy is understood as "a determination of the love and grace of God manifested in time as God's effectual participation in the misery of another, a participation prompted by his inmost being" (*CD* II/1, 377). Does this imply that God has lost his freedom and is now subject to his inmost being rather than the free subject of his inmost being? That is certainly the way a number of contemporary theologians actually think about God's love and mercy. For instance Jürgen Moltmann argues that only that which suffers is divine and that God had to become incarnate to be truly God. And while Wolfhart Pannenberg is far more careful than Moltmann, he does argue that "the divine essence overarches each personality"[15] and he claims that "love is a power which shows itself in those who love. . . . Persons do not have power over love. It rises above them and thereby gives them their self-hood. . . . This applies especially to the trinitarian life of God" (*Systematic Theology*, 1: 426f.). And when he corrects Cremer's idea of God's love with the idea of the true infinite and concludes that "God himself is characterized by a vital movement which causes him to invade what is different from himself . . ." (*Systematic Theology*, 1: 400), Pannenberg is led by his philosophy to compromise God's freedom since the God who actually loves in freedom is not caused by anything to create, reconcile and redeem the world; he is the free divine subject of these events.[16]

But that is certainly not how Barth thinks about it. Barth insists that God does not have to do so but that "He can, take to Himself the suffering of another in such a way that in doing so, in founding and accomplishing this fellowship, He does what corresponds to His worth" (*CD* II/1, 377). There is, however, no "necessity of logic" here. While we know from revelation that God's holiness, "the self-affirmation of the will of God which takes place in His founding and accomplishment of fellowship with another" (*CD* II/1, 377), is indeed his righteousness (the fact that what he does in realizing fellowship with us "corresponds to His worth"), that does not mean that we can logically deduce his righteousness from his holiness or his mercy from his righteousness. What distinguishes God from a tyrant who one day loves and the next day strikes out in anger is the fact that God's will is good; it is "worthy of Himself and therefore really righteous" (*CD* II/1, 379). Barth's argument depends upon the fact that Jesus is uniquely God's incarnate Son. Hence, Barth asserts that the reason why the "No" of Good Friday is so terrible,

> But why there is already concealed in it the Eastertide Yes of God's righteousness, is that He who on the cross took upon Himself and suffered the wrath of God was no other than God's own Son, and therefore the eternal

God Himself in the unity with human nature which He freely accepted in His transcendent mercy. (*CD* II/1, 397)

It is clear then that Barth's understanding of the incarnation as an act of God's free mercy, grounded in the antecedent existence of the eternal Son of the Father, determines not only his view of the cross and the resurrection but also his view of justification. And of course this has ethical implications. All of our attempts to obey the law, important as they actually are, can only express our trust in God who is righteous to effect his promise to perfect us in and through our participation in the new humanity of Jesus Christ himself through the Holy Spirit.

As noted above, Barth does not think of the incarnation as God's assumption of some idealized human nature. Rather it is our sinful flesh that the Son of God assumed so that "He took this conflict [between us as God's enemies and God himself] into His own being" (*CD* II/1, 397). It cost God something to maintain his righteousness and to love us in Christ. That is why for Barth the full implications of sin are disclosed only here in the events of the cross and resurrection. What really had to happen for the salvation of the human race could happen only here because here God's Son took our place. Does this mean that since Jesus is God's Son that he was somehow pre-programmed or magically able to avoid sin and suffering? Not for Barth. In his opinion Christ actually became sin for us. And while he did not in fact sin — that is the miracle of the incarnation as reconciliation and redemption — he did indeed experience the alienation and God-forsakenness of our lost condition even to the point of genuinely feeling our pain by taking it into the very heart of his being in order to spare us the need to continue down the road toward eternal death. All other suffering can only be a token of God's judgment which Jesus himself actually experienced and could withstand precisely because he was God's Son. In him therefore we have been freed from the divine anger and judgment. Following the Heidelberg catechism Barth asserts that

> Without any diminution of His divine majesty, in the exercise of the divine majesty of His love He could enter into this 'likeness of sinful flesh' to bear, in the same majesty, the judgment of divine wrath without annihilation, to be and to reveal Himself supremely as divine majesty even in His humiliation, to rise from the dead as conqueror of the judgment to which He had subjected Himself. . . . Only God's mercy could so feel this pain as to take it into the very heart of His being. And only God's mercy was strong enough not to be annihilated by this pain. (*CD* II/1, 400)

This is how God's righteousness triumphed in the death of Christ.

Because the Son of God, God himself incarnate in Jesus Christ, suffered and died for us on Good Friday, the destruction of the suffering and death caused by human disobedience which took place there was able to satisfy and fulfill the righteousness of God. By remaining true to himself and without surrendering his righteousness God remained true to us by coming into conflict with our unfaithfulness in his faithfulness; if God had surrendered his honor by not opposing our sinfulness, his faithfulness would have been no help to us. Still, God's faithfulness here meant that he did not allow us to fall victim to eternal death and destruction. Barth's thinking here is powerful and effective and stands in stark contrast to those who are less careful. Moltmann, for instance, resolves God's sovereignty into his suffering for us arguing that God's sole omnipotence is the omnipotence of his suffering love.[17] By contrast Barth argues that

> it did not have to happen in this way if we mean by that that God was under an obligation to clothe His righteousness in mercy and therefore in fulfillment of His righteousness to give His only Son to die for us. God could have been true to Himself without giving His faithfulness the determination of faithfulness to us. It could easily have been God's good-pleasure to express His righteousness in quite another way, namely in the form of our destruction. God would not have been any less God if this had happened. (*CD* II/1, 401)

The only reason why we can say that God had to exercise his righteousness as mercy is because that is how it in fact was exercised in Jesus Christ. We have no other claim here. It is based only on the factual necessity of its occurrence in this way and in this person. It is only because it was the eternal God himself who entered into this situation in Christ that he could be our representative and guarantor toward God and God's guarantor toward us.

Does Barth's emphasis on the divinity of the man Jesus in explaining God's mercy and righteousness tend toward Docetism? That is the opinion of a number of contemporary theologians. But I'm afraid they haven't paid sufficient attention to all that Barth says here. Barth insists that because Jesus is God's Son "He could take humanity to Himself in such a way that in it He was the Advocate for God to us and to God for us all — this one man for every man. . . . He really suffered our distress as the distress in the heart of God Himself" (*CD* II/1, 402).[18] We do not have here some raging indignation on God's part against an innocent man so that the rest of us can hide behind him as those saved but "unchanged in themselves." That, Barth says, is the ridiculous way it is often put. Christ's suffering is not the motive of God's expression of his righteousness here. Rather

> it is God's own heart which moves in creation on the basis of His own good-pleasure. It suffers what the creature ought to suffer and could not suffer without being destroyed. It suffers it with omnipotent vicariousness in virtue of the fact that it is the heart of the almighty Lord and Creator, who, since it is His good-pleasure, cannot be prevented from Himself sustaining His creature. . . . (CD II/1, 402)

This analysis shows that for Barth it is impossible to understand the meaning of the resurrection or the incarnation in abstraction from the reconciliation accomplished by God in the history of Jesus himself. That is why Barth insists that the resurrection is God's answer to Jesus' life of obedience; it is our justification:

> By virtue of His resurrection from the dead, by virtue of the righteousness revealed in His life, in Him and from Him we have a future and hope, the door has been opened, and we cross the threshold from wrong to right, and therefore from death to life. Risen with Him from the dead, we do this, or rather it takes place for us. (CD IV/1, 557)

The resurrection actually means that the man Jesus received and lived his eternal life on our behalf so that it is neither our faith nor our hope that provides the horizon for understanding the resurrection. Rather that understanding comes from the risen Lord himself and through faith in him. And this faith is real only as the Holy Spirit unites us to the risen Christ. This insight provides the positive focus for the thesis I wish to advance in this book. Because it is the risen Lord himself who, through the power of the Holy Spirit, gives meaning to Christian faith and hope, our starting point for a theology of the resurrection in its essential union with the incarnation can be none other than the risen Lord himself. It can never be or become our experiences of faith, hope or love without undercutting our constant need for Jesus himself as the Word of God incarnate.

With respect to the resurrection in particular, Barth believes that the time of the forty days gave content to the early apostolic preaching. The truth of Jesus' Easter history Barth writes "does not depend on our own acceptance or rejection of the Easter story . . ." (CD III/2, 442). Whatever we may think of this second history, Barth insists that all must agree that for the NT it is "essential and indispensable" (CD III/2, 443); it is the starting point for the NT portraits of Jesus and thus it is the key to the whole NT. But, again, the resurrection has no meaning if it is not tied indissolubly to the incarnation and the atonement. That is why Barth insists that because of sin we live in a "monstrous situation" (*CD* III/2, 517) which we can neither solve nor ignore, a situation in which we are alienated from God and our true human nature because of our lost time. The reason for this is that we are not left to ourselves

> but that in the existence of the man Jesus with His very different being in time a divine protest is made against his perverted and disturbed reality. . . . It is an effective protest, upsetting all our attempts to call black white. . . . In the existence of the man Jesus it is decided and revealed that God did not at all create man in the state of falling 'from cliff to cliff.' . . . (*CD* III/2, 517f.)

In Jesus, God "has come to save us" (*CD* III/2, 518). That is why Barth actually equates revelation and reconciliation:

> The work of the Son or Word is the presence and declaration of God which, in view of the fact that it takes place miraculously in and in spite of human darkness, we can only describe as revelation. The term reconciliation is another word for the same thing. (*CD* I/1, 409)[19]

And salvation is accomplished effectively no matter how much we "whine and turn" because the monstrosity of sin is really overcome in the man Jesus who is Lord of time. Still, it is important to realize that Jesus could rectify the situation only because he was the eternal Word or Son of the Father who had become the man Jesus of Nazareth for our sakes. That is precisely what makes his death a saving death. And that, as we have just seen, is indeed what is revealed in his resurrection from the dead.

Barth and Bultmann

In case one might have missed Barth's decisive and realistically objective understanding of the resurrection as an event in the life of Jesus that gave meaning to the community's faith then, and now gives meaning to ours, he sharply distinguishes his position from Bultmann's insisting that faith "springs from His historical manifestation" rather than "from the rise of faith in Him" (*CD* III/2, 443). If the Easter happening is limited to the development of the disciples' faith then that might mean there was "a kind of parthenogenesis of faith without any external cause" (*CD* IV/1, 339).[20] That is why, in his doctrine of reconciliation, Barth also insists that in the NT there is a foundation for faith and that it takes the form of God's act in raising Jesus from the dead and includes "a series of appearances and sayings of Jesus Christ risen from the dead and raised from the tomb" (*CD* IV/1, 340).[21]

Barth is also critical of Kümmel and Cullmann for not presenting the resurrection as something that is essential and indispensable. And he is unhappy with any idea (including Cullmann's) that the NT authors had an idea of timeless truth into which they inserted Jesus as the center. No, their thinking was specifically shaped by the particular history of Jesus. But that is not the end of it. Barth analyzes the implications of Bultmann's thinking in some depth insisting that Bultmann offers an interpretation of the resurrection as "the revelation of the meaning of the cross" and so Bultmann can even say there is "'a self-manifestation of the risen Lord'" and thus an "'eschatological event of redemption'" (*CD* III/2, 444) that is the foundation of faith and preaching. In Bultmann's thinking not only are the cross and resurrection, thus understood, included but also included is the apostolic preaching that originated in the event of Easter as part of the eschatological event. By eschatological, Bultmann means "a verifiable event in history and time which also has a supra-temporal significance accessible only to faith. Thus the eschatological event includes the death of Jesus, the faith of the first disciples, their preaching, the Church, the sacraments and the Christian life" (*CD* III/2, 444). But for Bultmann the objective fact of Jesus' return to history during the forty days "is not a part of this eschatological event" because it is a "nature-miracle" and a proof that must be demythologized since it cannot be accepted as an event in time and space. Hence

> An 'Easter event' in this sense can be regarded only as an objectifying of primitive Christian Easter faith in terms of the mythical world-view of the time, and it is no longer valid for those who have ceased to hold this view. The real Easter event, which belongs to that eschatological occurrence, is the rise of the Easter faith of the first disciples. This was not based on any event in time, but only on the supra-historical, supra-temporal act of God. (*CD* III/2, 444)

Here Barth observes that Bultmann himself seems on the verge of relapsing into mythology but reassures himself with the view that this particular event is not traditional mythology since it is not a "'miraculous, supernatural event,'" but "'an historical event wrought out in space and time'" (*CD* III/2, 444).

At this point Barth himself makes the connection between the resurrection and the incarnation for us by arguing that if Bultmann's interpretation is correct then there are two ways of understanding Jn. 1:14 and 1 Jn. 1:1. "Either we must deny that these texts have anything whatever to do with the One who manifested His life during the forty days, or we must dismiss these statements (though both of them are fundamental in this context) from the sphere of the relevant content of primitive Christian faith" (*CD* III/2, 444-45) as mythology. On this view Barth contends both the Easter history and Easter time would be seen as the beginning of the history and time of faith. The decisive factor here would be the disciples who made up their minds about Jesus in this time and history and especially his death; it could not be the risen Jesus himself. Jesus' own work and activity after his death was identical with the faith of his disciples. In other words

> The 'self-declaration' of the 'Resurrected' is staged in the minds of the disciples and nowhere else. Nothing happened between Him and them. There was no new, and in its novelty decisive and fundamental, encounter between Him and them to give rise to their faith. . . . They were quite alone. . . . Their faith had no object distinct from itself, no antecedent basis on which to rest as faith. . . . The 'act of God' was identical with their faith. And the fact that . . . they believed, is the real content of the Easter history and the Easter time . . . the basis of the existence of the Church and sacraments. Jesus Himself had not risen. (*CD* III/2, 445)

Barth unequivocally rejects this thinking and maintains the exact opposite view. For Barth

> Jesus Himself did rise again and appear to His disciples. This is the content of the Easter history, the Easter time, the Christian faith and Christian proclamation, both then and at all times. This is the basis of the existence of the Church and its sacraments. This — if we may call it so — is the 'eschatological event' in its manifest form which it acquired at Easter. This is the act of God — the act in which He appeared objectively in the glory of His incarnate Word, encountering first their unbelief and then, when this was overcome, their faith. Hence they were not alone with their faith. It was established, awakened and created by God in this objective encounter. (*CD* III/2, 445)

By making a clear and sharp distinction between the objective event that gave rise to their faith and the disciples' faith itself, Barth was able to stress that Jesus himself was present with them in time and history during the forty days before the ascension. His thinking is clearly in line with what David Fergusson characterizes as the traditional view. Notice too that Barth's anti-docetic and anti-ebionite stance, evident in his Christology, is in full view here as well. Barth argues that this risen Jesus is the very same Jesus who was and remains the Word incarnate. Barth will not think of Jesus as a mere man even for a moment because that is not the Jesus of the Gospels. The man Jesus was the eternal Word even before Easter.[22] As already noted, there is no two-stage Christology in Barth's mind.[23] And it is precisely because the man Jesus existed as the one assumed into unity with the Word in the incarnation that there was and could be a genuine encounter between him and the disciples and a genuine establishment of faith, the church and the sacraments. As we shall see, it is the freedom that comes from this unique action of God in time and space that enables our life as children of God rather than as sinners.

Resurrection, Incarnation and the Trinity

Barth rejects Bultmann's exegesis primarily because it is distorted by his own systematic theological presupposition that statements cannot be theologically true if they are not depictions of human existence. But Barth insists that none of the major affirmations of the creed actually fulfill this demand. They can be adjusted to become descriptions of human existence, but that is not what they are in the first instance, and to do so would be to surrender to the anthropological emphases already seen in Herrmann, Ritschl and Schleiermacher. "Primarily, they [the major affirmations of the creed] define the being and action of the God who is different from man and encounters man; the Father, the Son and the Holy Ghost. For this reason alone they cannot be reduced to statements about the inner life of man" (CD III/2, 446). This is an extremely important insight and it sets Barth's theology apart from much contemporary trinitarian theology. For Barth it is because God exists in eternity as the one who loves in freedom that God is none other than the eternal Father, Son and Holy Spirit. These are not just freely chosen symbols describing our experience of salvation in Barth's thought. These categories really describe who God is based on God's own disclosure of himself in Jesus Christ and through the Holy Spirit. For Barth the immanent Trinity is thus an indispensable premise of all that is said about God's economic trinitarian actions in history as creator, reconciler and redeemer. Take away or weaken the doctrine of the immanent Trinity and trinitarian theology becomes little more than our discussion about communion, relationality and temporality which we experience humanly and then project onto the divine. It is this understanding of the Trinity which gives Barth's understanding of the resurrection, incarnation and atonement its strength. These are divine actions in the history of Jesus Christ which refer us away from ourselves and toward our justification by faith. Indeed Jesus' own resurrection is the justification of humanity. There is no other. And the search for some other justification is just another indication of the predicament of human sin.

As this book proceeds we shall see that it is precisely the failure of many contemporary theologians to make a clear and sharp distinction between the immanent and economic Trinity without separation (as Barth does) that leads them to compromise not only the resurrection as an event in time and history that gives meaning to faith, but also to compromise the objectively real actions of God within time and history in the incarnation, grace and glory (without ceasing to be God). And that compromise opens the door to the panentheistic or pantheistic dissolution of divine into human activity. The end result of such dissolution once again is that theological categories are used to describe our inner experiences, but leave us without any genuine savior, creator, lord and redeemer. But beyond this, such thinking opens the door to the idea that righteousness is something that we can achieve either through ethical perfection or through spiritual experience of some other sort.

This, as we shall see, has decisive ethical implications because such thinking always requires a form of self-justification and self-sanctification that is at odds with our actual justification by faith and sanctification through the Holy Spirit. Interestingly, it is precisely Barth's clear distinction between the immanent and the economic Trinity that enables him to present a Christology that does justice to both Jesus' divinity and humanity in his account of the resurrection. And that is not mere idle chatter or pointless theological speculation. Barth really believed that

> We cannot say anything higher or better of the 'inwardness of God' than that God is Father, Son and Holy Spirit, and therefore that He is love in Himself without and before loving us, and without being forced to love us. And we can say this only in the light of the 'outwardness' of God to us, the occurrence of His revelation. (*CD* I/2, 377)[24]

But it is precisely because God loved us in Christ while we were still sinners that the truth of our behavior is both called into question and made possible. That is why Barth insists that living by God's forgiving grace enacted in the history of Jesus Christ means that we must seek God in Christ (love God) and love our neighbor as well. Right human behavior is not a condition for God's loving us but is that action that takes place as one lives by the promise of forgiveness. All ethics then is nothing more than our human response as it follows from and corresponds with what God has done and is doing for us in Jesus himself.

Barth makes a number of other interesting points that should be noted here. First, can the resurrection of Jesus, as an event in history, be proven to be a historical fact in the modern sense? And if it cannot, does that mean that it was not a historical event? That of course is Bultmann's view since he rejects the idea that there was a real history of Jesus in the forty days. But Barth argues that such history "may well have happened. We may well accept as history that which good taste prevents us from calling 'historical fact,' and which the modern historian will call 'saga' or 'legend' on the ground that it is beyond the reach of his methods, to say nothing of his unavowed assumptions" (*CD* III/2, 446). Barth compares the Easter history to the creation narratives of Genesis 1 and 2 as history in the higher sense because, while it speaks of history, its aim is speak of an occurrence that escapes "historical proof" and Barth contends that "It is sheer superstition to suppose that only things which are open to 'historical' verification can have happened in time" (*CD* III/2, 446).

Second, Barth asks if Bultmann is correct in suggesting (following W. Herrmann) that those who accept the resurrection as historical fact have blindly accepted a piece of mythology or have committed a dishonest *sacrificium intellectus* and descended from faith to works. Here Barth's objectively realistic view of the matter is in evidence:

> For the New Testament at any rate the resurrection is good news in which we may believe. And this faith, as those who accepted it were gratefully aware, was made possible only by the resurrection itself. They were not able to accept it because the prevailing mythical world-view made it easier to accept it then than it is supposed to be to-day. Even in those days the Easter message seems to be utterly 'incredible.' (*CD* III/2, 446-47)

Barth insists that if the resurrection is not presented as something to be joyfully accepted, then there is something wrong with the presentation.

Third, Barth wonders whether all modern thought is shaped by modern science as Bultmann contends and asks if there is a modern world-picture that is incompatible with the "mythical world-view and superior to it" (*CD* III/2, 447). Barth cites Bultmann's famous statement that "It is impossible to use electric light and the wireless and to avail ourselves of modern medical and surgical discoveries, and at the same time to believe in the New Testament world of demons and spirits" and asks "Who can read this without a shudder?" (*CD* III/2, 447). Why? Because Barth astutely notes that the modern world-view may very well not be as final as the "Marburg Kantians" with their complete lack of any sense of humor seemed to think. Indeed Barth saw the decisive point, that is, that no world-view of any age can be normative for understanding the message of the New Testament. Hence he opposes to Bultmann's view the simple observation that it may well be that contemporary people would find themselves able to give a free and joyous factual assent to the resurrection and not to some "*fides implicita* in a world of spirits and demons" (*CD* III/2, 447).

Fourth, and finally, Barth wonders whether it is the job of Christianity to accept or reject world-views at all. Indeed he believes that there is no reason why we would need to accept the ancient world's mythical world-view. Nonetheless he notes that the early church very cautiously used elements of this world-view in its witness to Jesus Christ while the world-view accepted today has either lost these elements or features or allowed them to slip into the background. Thus, in Barth's mind, "we have every reason to make use of 'mythical' language in certain connexions" (*CD* III/2, 447) without a guilty conscience. For if we go to extremes with demythologizing, then we could not bear witness to Jesus Christ at all. That is what happens to Bultmann when he dismisses the NT connection between sin and death and the relation of death and resurrection and the concept of substitution because he thinks they are offensive and obsolete. Barth notes that it makes sense to speak of the rise of faith in the disciples but that it is folly to suggest that this can be substituted for Christ's actual resurrection and appearances. And so he decisively maintains "we must still accept the resurrection of Jesus, and His subsequent appearances to His disciples, as genuine history in its own particular time" (*CD* III/2, 447).

Implications of the Resurrection for Barth

What then are the positive implications of Christ's actual resurrection for Barth's thinking? First, Barth emphasizes the fact that "the *man* Jesus was manifested among them in the mode of *God*. It is essential to a true understanding that both his humanity and his deity should be kept in view" (*CD* III/2, 448; emphasis in original). In Barth's opinion the man Jesus was present among them and was seen, touched and heard by them and ate and drank with them as the "Resurrected." He was before them "as true man, *vere homo*" (*CD* III/2, 448). As he did in his Christology and elsewhere in the *Church Dogmatics* Barth insists here that if anyone refused to see and accept this first of all, then that person would not only misunderstand but would fall directly into Docetism.[25] In addition to the reference to 1 Jn. 1:1 mentioned above, Barth here cites two important NT texts that explicitly refute any Docetic understanding of the resurrection (Lk. 24:36f. and Jn. 20:24).

And of course Barth is able to do this precisely because, in his Chalcedonian Christology, he had already carefully indicated that the mystery of Jesus Christ, as the revelation and salvation of God, could never be understood in an Ebionite or Docetic way. In other words, for Barth, Jesus Christ in his true and essential divinity and his true humanity is the one who enables us to know and to love God. But his divinity is the divinity of the antecedently existing Son of the Father and not any other sort of naturally recognizable deity.[26] Hence, he had to be acknowledged in his uniqueness before he could be understood just as the recognition that we are forgiven sinners which "is not an insight of abstract anthropology" implies that we can only know we are God's enemies from the fact that God has established a relationship with us in Jesus, the Reconciler (CD I/1, 407).

Docetic Christology, as noted above and as I have discussed at length elsewhere,[27] is any Christology which finds in Jesus the confirmation of its prior idea of divinity and can thus more or less dispense with the man Jesus from Nazareth as the one who gives meaning to Christology, as well as to other important Christian doctrines. By contrast, Ebionite Christology refers to any Christology which supposes that Jesus' divinity is simply the product of the community's expression of faith. His divinity then would just be a way of speaking of the significance of his humanity. For Ebionitism, in all its forms, Jesus is really no more than an important human figure who was described as a God because of the impression he made on his followers. Barth rejects these two false approaches to Christology because he wants to allow Jesus himself, truly God and truly human, to dictate the meaning of revelation, salvation and ultimately of our knowledge of the Trinity. Indeed this same Jesus Christ sets the parameters for an ethics of true human freedom as well. It is significant that in treating the incarnation in CD I/2 Barth sorts through the key insights by attempting to avoid both Ebionite and Docetic Christology. Hence he describes the incarnation as "the decisive contradiction to any ebionite Christology" (CD I/2, 23).

For Barth the Synoptic emphasis on Jesus' human history is meant to serve "the anti-ebionite thesis of the God-man" (CD I/2, 23) while the spiritual emphasis of John and Paul is meant to counter any sort of Docetism: "Docetism cannot be countered adequately in any other way than that used by the Fourth Evangelist and Paul" (CD I/2, 19). "That anyone should deliberately and frequently mention John and Paul in the same breath with the idea of Docetism because of their undoubtedly spiritual view of the human life of Jesus, belongs to the very worst kind of misunderstandings of the New Testament" (*CD* I/2, 19). For Barth the NT authors recognize in Jesus

> what they had nowhere believed or recognised before, namely 'the life which was with the Father,' the reality of divine sending and divine work as the real presence of God Himself, i.e., the Word or the Son of God. They thus derived their conception of the Son or Word of God from no other source than Jesus Himself. (*CD* I/2, 17)[28]

This thinking is anti-docetic because it excludes any idea that the notion of Jesus' divinity was acquired from a conception of God derived elsewhere than from the Son of God himself. This is what was disclosed in Christ's resurrection. And that is why Barth argued that for the early Christians the revelation of Jesus as God's Son is the starting point of the Evangelists "as witnesses of the resurrection" (*CD* I/2, 22). Before them was the "problem" of Jesus' humanity even though the problem is now solved and offered to the readers in that sense: "The solution is the divinity of Christ, but it has to be achieved again and again" (*CD* I/2, 22).

Second, Barth insists equally that "the man Jesus appeared to them during these days in the mode of God" (*CD* III/2, 448). The disciples came to see that Jesus "had always been present among them in His deity, though hitherto this deity had been veiled" (*CD* III/2, 448). While the disciples could now understand the preliminary manifestations of Jesus' glory they had witnessed "with unseeing eyes" during his earthly life, Barth stresses that these events in Jesus' earthly life nonetheless always had their particular importance in themselves. In other words they did not become significant by virtue of the insight now acquired by the disciples in light of the resurrection. The truth that dawned on the disciples during the forty days was that "'God was in Christ' (2 Cor. 5:19)" (*CD* III/2, 449 and *CD* IV/1, 301). This is not to be understood dialectically in this context, Barth insists. Jesus is not here veiled and unveiled to them. Rather he was veiled before but now is completely manifest to them. Yet it is imperative to note that in Barth's mind "this was not a self-evident truth [for the disciples], nor a discovery of their own, but a conviction that went utterly against the grain" (*CD* III/2, 449).

Later in this book we shall see that this insight, which differentiates Barth's thinking from much contemporary resurrection theology, indicates the difference between a theology that accepts the incarnation, resurrection and atonement as miraculous new acts of God within history and those that see the resurrection, incarnation and atonement as ways of describing human existence. According to the resurrection narratives, when the disciples are exhorted by Jesus to be believing rather than unbelieving (cf. Jn. 20:27f.) Barth maintains "that this is not just pious exhortation, but a word of power" to which Thomas gives the appropriate response, that is, "My Lord and my God" (CD III/2, 449). Barth then insists "God Himself, the object and ground of their faith, was present as the man Jesus was present in this way. That this really took place is the specific content of the apostolic recollection of these days" (CD III/2, 449). It is just for this reason that proper theology cannot be grounded in our experience of salvation; such an approach would displace God at the outset or might seek God apart from his presence as the risen Lord and thereby miss him as God.

Barth's reasoning here is nuanced and is extremely important because he is able to see and to maintain a realistically objective account of the resurrection without compromising Jesus' divinity or humanity and without confusing the event in Jesus' life with the faith or perceptions of the disciples. This of course is in keeping with his realistically objective view of the incarnation in which he stressed that while the Word assumes flesh in Jesus Christ in order to reconcile the world to God, the Word was not transformed into the man Jesus and Jesus in his humanity as such was not the Word.[29]

Hence, in contrast to many recent interpretations, Barth argues that faith itself was created in this Easter history. And this faith

> did not consist in a reassessment and reinterpretation *in meliorem partem* of the picture of the Crucified, but in an objective encounter with the Crucified and Risen, who Himself not only made Himself credible to them, but manifested Himself as the ἀρχηγὸς τῆς σωτηρίας αὐτῶν (Heb. 2:10) and therefore the καὶ ἀρχηγὸς καὶ τελειωτής of their πίστις (Heb. 12:2). This being the case, he was among them as God Himself. (CD III/2, 449)

Barth thus takes seriously Matt. 28:18ff., arguing that Jesus' missionary charge is not only issued with binding authority but itself creates the effectiveness that will be needed to carry it out. In other words the risen Lord is neither dependent on the disciples' resources or accomplishments nor is he thwarted by their incapacity for the task. Apart from their capacities or endowments they are, in the words of 1 Pet. 1:3, "begotten . . . again . . . by the resurrection of Jesus Christ from the dead." The recollection of the NT then is of a real fact, a mighty act of God and "not just an intellectual notion of perception" (CD III/2, 450). All of their thinking and knowledge is grounded in this fact, namely, the fact that God was present among them and revealed among them in this way.

This memory leads the disciples to call Jesus *Kyrios.* But this does not mean that they were just offering their appraisal or interpretation of this man based on their experience of him. If that had been the case then we might wonder if they had perhaps overestimated this man and argue for a more modest interpretation of his existence. No, Barth insists that because God had spoken, that is, "here is a *Deus dixit* spoken in the existence of Jesus during these days" therefore this "is a decision which the apostolic Church cannot discuss or revise" (*CD* III/2, 450). He did not give himself this name. God did it precisely by exalting him in the sense of Phil. 2:9. And thus they were "compelled to do so" (*CD* III/2, 451). Though he was once known after the flesh (2 Cor. 5:16), now he is known, after the resurrection, as *Kyrios.* All the Gospels in fact were written in light of this decision and thus at least indirectly in light of the resurrection. Hence, "If we try to bypass this decision, concentrating our attention upon a human Jesus who is not the *Kyrios* because He is not risen, we simply show that we have failed to take note of what they really say, and intend to say" (*CD* III/2, 450). As we shall later see, this is an extremely important point that is either contested by or ignored by much contemporary theology. The trend today to begin Christology "from below" frequently attempts to understand Jesus from within a perspective that sees the historical Jesus through the eyes of the disciples as it is supposed that they might have perceived him before Easter. This very thinking, however, distorts the NT presentations because it assumes the existence of a Jesus who is not yet the Lord because he is not yet risen. And the reality is that the Gospels, written from the vantage of the resurrection, stress the fact that this man Jesus was the Lord from the very beginning in virtue of the miracle of Christmas. It is here that we can observe why it is so important to hold the incarnation and resurrection together as Barth does. For if the man Jesus was the incarnate Word, then as the bearer of a hidden glory that would be effective for us by being disclosed, "everything had to happen as it did according to the Easter Story in its simple, literal sense" (*CD* III/2, 451).

Third, in answer to the question of how Jesus was present among them Barth offers the straightforward answer "that the Jesus who three days earlier had been rejected by the Jews and put to death by the Gentiles and buried by His disciples was among them again as a living man" (*CD* III/2, 450). Barth links this insight directly to the incarnation:

If the man Jesus was the incarnate Word of this God, if as such he was the Bearer of a hidden glory, of an initially inapprehensible declaration of His nature, and if finally this hidden declaration of His nature was to be effective as well as operative, if it was not to remain hidden . . . then everything had to happen as it actually did according to the Easter story in its simple, literal sense. (*CD* III/2, 451)

This man, the Word incarnate, was seen and understood to be the triumphant justification of both God and humanity, of God's sovereign overcoming of death and as one who now exists in the "eternal time of God" (*CD* III/2, 451). This is what Jesus was in his "real and therefore physical resurrection from the dead, in His appearances as the One who was really and therefore physically resurrected. This is the way in which He was 'manifested in the mode of God' to His disciples" (*CD* III/2, 451).

While Barth insists (against Bultmann) that the resurrection of Jesus included his body and was therefore a physical event in nature, this is not what made it what it was in fact. What then was it that made it the unique event it was? For Barth the answer to this question is that it was because God himself, the creator, who was hidden in this man's lowliness and death on the cross "was now manifested in His resurrection, that it was absolutely necessary for this event genuinely and apprehensibly to include nature, and therefore to be physical" (*CD* III/2, 451). The early Christian community was not interested in resurrection in general or other possible resurrections. They were only interested in the resurrection of this man and the resurrection of everyone else that began with his resurrection. This was the mystery that called forth adoration from the early community.

This explains why the evidence for the resurrection in the NT is so fragmentary and even contradictory. Barth is well aware of the differences between the accounts offered by Matthew and Luke; by the Synoptics and John; and by the Synoptics and Paul in 1 Cor. 15. It is impossible, Barth argues, to find a "nucleus of genuine history" (*CD* III/2, 452) in these accounts. And Barth notes that the reference to the forty days in Acts 1:3 is clearly connected with the forty days of the flood (Gen. 7:4) and also with Ez. 4:6 and Jon. 3:4 as well as with the forty days of temptation faced by Jesus at the start of his ministry (Matt. 4:2 and Lk. 4:2). Indeed Barth explains that there may even be a connection here with the forty days spent in Canaan by the spies who preceded the Israelites (Num. 13:25) and with the forty days and nights that it took Elijah to get to Horeb. All of this leads Barth to observe that "the forty days are not to be taken literally but typically" (*CD* III/2, 452).

Both the chronology and topography depicted in the narratives, Barth says, are vague and any attempt to harmonize the accounts would be futile. The narratives, including 1 Cor. 15, read very differently than myths because they deal with a real man of flesh and blood. But they are not to be taken as "history" in our sense of the word either. It is because the stories are couched in what Barth terms the "poetic style of historical saga" (*CD* III/2, 452) that they are marked by obscurity. They are in fact describing an event that is beyond the reach of normal historical inquiry. That is why they cannot be analyzed and harmonized. Still

> There can be no doubt that all these narratives are about the same event, and that they are agreed in substance, intention and interpretation. None of the authors ever even dreamed, for example, of reducing the event to 'the rise of the Easter faith of the first disciples.' (*CD* III/2, 452)

The Empty Tomb and Ascension

Barth regards these stories as indispensable to the NT witness because they mark the limits of the Easter history in two ways. Both the empty tomb and the ascension are "indicated rather than described" (*CD* III/2, 452) as introduction and conclusion to the Easter history.[30] Barth admits that the ascension is spoken of in the strict sense only in Acts 1:9f. and that there are reasons for this.

> The content of the Easter witness, the Easter event, was not that the disciples found the tomb empty or that they saw Him go up to heaven, but that when they had lost Him through death they were sought and found by Him as the Resurrected. (*CD* III/2, 453)

As the Virgin birth was a sign of the miracle of the incarnation, so the empty tomb and the ascension were signs of the Easter event. These are important signs that Barth insists cannot be omitted.

The empty tomb functioned by pointing to the fact that the man Jesus who died and was buried was set free from the grave by the very power of God and that, as Lk. 24:5 indicates, he was not to be sought among the dead because he was alive. And according to Mk. 16:6, Lk. 24:6 and Matt. 28:6 he had arisen and was not in the tomb. Barth notes that it is the angels who say this. And that is their first active role in the narrative since the nativity and temptations. By only pointing to the empty tomb the angels indicate that there is no going back. The center of attention, however, is not the empty tomb but the fact that Jesus is risen. Thus, while the empty tomb itself "was obviously a very ambiguous and contestable fact (Mt. 27:62f.; 28:11f.) . . . [it] is not the same thing as the resurrection. It is not the appearance of the living; it is only is presupposition" (*CD* III/2, 453). Still, Barth argues that this does not mean we can actually trust in the living Christ without accepting the empty tomb. Is the empty tomb merely a legend? Barth insists that it does not matter because

> It still refers to the phenomenon ensuing the resurrection, to the presupposition of the appearance of Jesus. It is the sign which obviates all possible misunderstanding. It cannot, therefore, but demand our assent, even as a legend. Rejection of the legend of the empty tomb has always been accompanied by rejection of the saga of the living Jesus, and necessarily so. Far better, then, to admit that the empty tomb belongs to the Easter event as its sign. (CD III/2, 453)

Barth applies similar thinking to the ascension noting that it is less prominent in the NT, but has nonetheless found a place in the creed and in the church calendar. The positive function of this sign is to point forward and upward instead of backward and downward as did the empty tomb. As the beginning of the Easter time and history was marked by the women's discovery of the empty tomb, so the end of this Easter time and history is marked by Matt. 28:16 in Galilee and Acts 1:12 at the Mount of Olives. It is important to realize that Barth's understanding of Jesus' being taken up into heaven (Acts 1:11) means that Jesus has entered into that part of the created world which is "inaccessible and incomprehensible . . . and cannot be disclosed except on His initiative" (CD III/2, 453). But again the ascension is not identical with the risen Lord; it is rather the sign of the risen Jesus. Hence

> There is no sense in trying to visualise the ascension as a literal event, like going up in a balloon. . . . The point of the story is not that when Jesus left His disciples he visibly embarked upon a wonderful journey into space, but that when He left them He entered the side of the created world which was provisionally incomprehensible, that before their eyes He ceased to be before their eyes. (CD III/2, 453-54)

Barth insists, however, that he did not cease to be a creature because of the ascension but that he clearly showed himself to be a man who lives now "on the God-ward side of the universe, sharing his throne, existing and acting in the mode of God, and therefore to be remembered as such" (CD III/2, 454). Jesus is provisionally distinct from all other human beings and he is to be seen as the "exalted man" to all eternity. Barth believes that when Acts 1:9 says that a cloud received Jesus out of the sight of the disciples this signified not only God's hiddenness but his "hidden presence and the coming of revelation which penetrates this hiddenness" (*CD* III/2, 454). This is therefore not an occasion for sorrow because Jesus is revealed "as the One who according to Mt. 28:20 will be with them in this heavenly mode of existence all the days, even to the consummation . . . of the age, but also as the One who will come again to usher in this consummation" (*CD* III/2, 454). Because of Jesus' impending future revelation, the ascension is a joyous occasion and an indispensable sign pointing us to Jesus' second coming and not to some hiddenness other than the very hiddenness of God himself.[31]

Resurrection and Christian Hope

Barth's eschatological perspective plays itself out in *CD* IV/1 in his understanding of Christian hope. He argues that the "teleological determination" of those who are justified and sanctified in Jesus Christ, that is, of those who live by faith and love in relation to God, is hope. This means that, as "Christian faith is the human response to God's justifying sentence, so Christian love is the human response to His direction" (*CD* IV/1, 102). Conversion to God takes place in Jesus Christ alone so that in the power of the Holy Spirit "in Jesus Christ man is directed by God to awakening and life in the freedom for which He has made him free" (*CD* IV/1, 102). Barth insists that the obedience of faith is followed by the obedience of love (though in practice the one may precede the other). That is why sanctification is indissolubly united with justification in Barth's thought. Faith necessarily involves not only love of God but love of neighbor and cannot really exist without it. The possibility of loving God and neighbor is itself "the work of the Holy Spirit which makes man a Christian" (*CD* IV/1, 103). The love of God is expressed in the fulfillment of the covenant in Jesus Christ: in him the love of God "is decisively, fundamentally and comprehensively His coming together with all men and their coming together with him. . . . It embraces *realiter* both the world and the community, non-Christians and Christians. But the knowledge and proclamation of it is a matter only for the Christian community" (*CD* IV/1, 103). Even this is controlled by God's freedom in the sense that all is dependent on the Holy Spirit:

> That God did not owe His Son, and in that Son Himself, to the world, is revealed by the fact that He gives His Spirit to whom He will. The hand of God the Reconciler is over all men. Jesus Christ was born and died and rose again for all. The work of atonement, the conversion of man to God was done for all. The Word of God is spoken to all. God's verdict and di-

rection and promise have been pronounced over all. To that extent, objectively, all are justified, sanctified and called. But the hand of God has not touched all in such a way that they can see and hear, perceive and accept and receive all that God is for all and therefore for them. . . . To those who have not been touched in this way by the hand of God the axiom that Jesus Christ is the Victor is as such unknown. It is a Christian and not a general axiom; valid generally, but not generally observed and acknowledged. Similarly, they do not know their sin or even what sin is, since it can be known only in the light of that axiom. And naturally they do not know their justification, sanctification and calling as they have already taken place in Jesus Christ. (CD IV/1, 148)[32]

The human acts of faith and love are acts of pure gratitude because they demonstrate that we have no claim on the fact that God has freed us to live in fellowship with him and with each other. The human existence of Christians then is characterized by their loving God and neighbors. Loving neighbors is not the condition for loving God because its possibility resides in our justification by faith so that "it can as little contribute to the setting up of that fellowship and therefore to justification as can faith itself as the human recognition that it has been set up" (CD IV/1, 105). One cannot therefore equate the commandments to love God and neighbor without confusing God and creatures and without suggesting some form of self-justification.[33] Barth insists that "If we are to be justified by faith, in faith we will not look either at our works or our sins" (CD IV/1, 105). But that means that "No one can and will love God who does not believe." This means that love to God expresses a freedom given to us in Christ and would be lost if "we tried to burden it with the, in itself, impossible and superfluous task of accomplishing or actualising or even completing the justification of man" (CD IV/1, 105). In this sense Christian ethics is determined by our justification so that love can only be an expression of our faith in God's freely reconciling us with himself and can never be a work of ours by which we think we can or must justify ourselves before God.

In this context Barth interprets Matt. 25:31ff. as follows. Jesus Christ himself is the king, ruler, lawgiver and judge of every person. Along with his known people, however, "this King has also a much larger unknown people, which, according to Heb. 2:11, He, the only Son of the Father, is not ashamed to call His brethren even down to the most lowly members" so that the criterion of his judgment will be "the question what we have done or not done to Him in the person of the least of His brethren" (CD IV/1, 106). But Barth insists that while they are witnesses (whom we cannot overlook) to the poverty embraced by Jesus himself in order to give us the wealth (secretly to the world and openly to Christians) in their fellowship with him, they still are not identical with Jesus Christ. This is important because Barth wants to say that, as witnesses in this way, they represent Jesus Christ as the neighbor

> as the one who fell among thieves, and as the Good Samaritan who took him and poured oil into his wounds and brought him to the inn at his own expense. They are not identical with Him. But He cannot be had without them. And that means that God cannot be had without them, nor can reconciliation with Him nor conversion to Him. He cannot be had without gratitude for their witness and a willingness to be witnesses to them, without love to them, without their indispensability to each one whom God loves, without that one seriously setting out and never ceasing to seek and to find them, both in the community and therefore in the world as well, Christian and also non-Christian neighbours. Christian love is at one and the same time love to God and love to the neighbour — and it is love to neighbour because it is love to God. This is the test whether it is the response to God's own love, whether it is the work of the Holy Spirit. (*CD* IV/1, 106)

It is crucially important to note here, however, that because Barth does not equate love of God with love of neighbor, but instead sees them as indissolubly united in Christ and through the Spirit, he insists that our love of God and neighbor does not contribute in the least to our justification and sanctification. Hence "Even neighbourly love cannot look away to anything that might be won or attained from God by means of it. Just as love to God can envisage and seek and love only God, and for His own sake, so love to the neighbour can envisage and seek and love only the neighbour, and for his own sake. As in the vertical, so in the horizontal dimension, it is free and pure love" (*CD* IV/1, 107). This is why Barth describes love as a pure act of obedience — it is exercised without any ulterior motive — it is an act of freedom which acknowledges that all people are members of the "people of which Jesus Christ is the King, because this King willed that those who recognise Him should recognise Him again in the members of His people in the narrower and wider sense" because fellowship with Christ the King "carries with it unconditionally and without reserve and therefore with genuine force the work of bringing together man and man" (*CD* IV/1, 107). It is here finally, that Barth introduces Christian hope as the final form of our justification and sanctification because it is the "moment of the promise given to man in Jesus Christ, and therefore Christian hope, and therefore the calling of man side by side with his justification and sanctification" (*CD* IV/1, 108). Hope is determined by its object: Jesus Christ who has reconciled the world to God and who, in his Holy Spirit sanctifies the world for God, gives the world direction in his promise of eternal life. Of course only God gives eternal life — but that is exactly what he does give in seeking and creating "fellowship" between himself and us in Christ himself. Eternal life is our future fellowship with God which is a completed reality in Christ's life, death and resurrection which took place on our behalf.

Barth distinguishes the Christian view of eternal life from "pagan conceptions" (*CD* IV/1, 112) which see God as a "supreme being with neither life, nor activity, nor history, in a neutrality which can never be moved or affected by anything, a being with which man can ultimately be united only in rest or in some kind of passive enjoyment or adoring contemplation" (*CD* IV/1, 112). The God who is Father, Son and Holy Spirit is not anything like this because he is a living and active God who is revealed in Jesus Christ — what is revealed is that God not only has a history in himself but that he has one in relationship to us:

> He is the Lord of His kingdom, deciding, acting, ruling, doing good, creating peace, judging, giving joy, living in His will and acts. And that kingdom is not merely a kingdom which He possesses in the cosmos created by Him. It is the kingdom which He sets up in the course of a historical movement which has a beginning, a middle and an end. (*CD* IV/1, 112)

Our future is given in Jesus Christ as the "unveiled depth of fellowship with God" so that the content of the promise is our future with God. Our future with God can be with God because in Jesus Christ his kingdom has come and we may serve his eternal righteousness "as He is risen from the dead and lives and reigns to eternity" (*CD* IV/1, 113). Our future with God is to participate in the being and life of God by willing what God wills and doing what he does. But what is it that gives hope its content and meaning?

For Barth,

> Jesus Christ is the divine pledge as such — its effective and authentic proclamation. In Him that to which it refers has already taken place. It is already present. He is the man who lives not only under the verdict and direction of God but also in the truth of His promise. . . . He Himself as the eternally living God is also the eternally living man. The world is reconciled and converted to God in Him in the fact that He is this man, not merely in distinctness and antithesis in relation to God, but also in participation in

His being and work. . . . No one beside Him is man in this way, just as no one beside Him is as man the same divine Son of the Father. (*CD* IV/1, 115)

The world itself is not without hope then because a promise is given absolutely by God "that in Him [Jesus Christ] its own future is already present, that in Him even in its present life it is already seized and determined by its future being" (*CD* IV/1, 116). This is the eschatological aspect of the Christian. Not only does a Christian necessarily live by faith and love. A Christian must also hope — but it is not some general hope for some kind of life after death — it is a very specific hope grounded in and determined by God's promise revealed and apprehended or as Barth says "seized" in Jesus Christ himself. Christian hope

> derives from Jesus Christ, i.e., as he hears and understands the pledge which God has given in Him, making it his own, letting his life be shaped by this promise and opened up for the future. . . . Jesus Christ is also the content of the divine pledge, the One in whom the Christian is summoned to hope. (*CD* IV/1, 116)

This is the meaning of freedom — Christ through his Spirit frees us to live by hope so that "the Christian hopes in Jesus Christ, in Him alone, but in Him confidently. For He alone, but dependably, is the origin, theme and content of his hope, as of his faith and love" (*CD* IV/3, 921f.). In the specific expectation of the risen Lord coming again, the Christian "has the freedom not to fear his end . . . but to rejoice in it" (*CD* IV/3, 928).[34] The future promised to us cannot in any way be separated from our life in Christ:

> He is the eternally living man who as such is the future of the world and of every man, and the hope of the Christian. By His coming to His disciples after His resurrection in the revelation of the forty days He pointed to Himself as their hope and future. In so doing He showed them and the whole community that their own hope and future and that of the world are to be found in His own coming. (*CD* IV/1, 117)

It is his final coming which will be the redemption of the world; it will be the consummation of his promise of eternal life and of the reconciliation accomplished in Jesus Christ. Even now it is our service of God that is our eternal life here below. We do not have this present or future in ourselves — but we do have it in Jesus Christ. That is the hope of Christians — they have eternal life in him alone and because of this "Christians will never find that they are called to anything other than hope — for themselves and the world" (*CD* IV/1, 118).[35] If Christians were to seek their present or future in themselves, then they would demonstrate thereby that they did not really have hope in their Savior and would to that extent cease to be Christians. Hence "Jesus Christ and their future in Him is their own personal hope, the hope of their own personal redemption and consummation" (*CD* IV/1, 119). For this reason Barth insists that what makes a person a Christian is "his derivation from the resurrection of Jesus Christ and his present in the sphere of the power of the Holy Spirit" (*CD* IV/3, 907). This hope of Christians comes alive in people's lives through the action of the Holy Spirit which makes them Christians — in the act of hope "the objective becomes subjective" because Christians strive after and seize "the goal and future given" to them in Jesus Christ. "In the act of Christian hope that which is promised (as promised and therefore future) is already present. Jesus Christ as the (promised and coming) eternally living One is already present. Not merely virtually and effectively, but actually and actively in the person of the Christian" (*CD* IV/1, 119). In this sense Christians do not merely see things differently from others; they actually are different because in their lives of faith, love and hope they "are different from others" (*CD*, IV/1, 120).

The most important point to be made here, however, is that hope is completely tied to Jesus Christ himself: "He, the content of the promise and the object of hope, cannot be replaced by any other" (*CD* IV/1, 121). Were that to happen our hope would be without foundation and without reality: "It is He alone in His futurity, and to that extent as the One who is beyond, who gives hope to the present, the life of man in this world where otherwise there is no hope" (*CD* IV/1, 121). Thus, "To be sure, if we do not believe in Him as the One who came then, nor love Him as the One who is present now, we cannot hope in Him as the One who will come one day" (*CD* IV/3, 911f.). Whatever smaller hopes we have in this life exist then for the sake of this great hope so that "If man does not seriously wait for Jesus Christ, at bottom he will not wait for anything else. Daily hope can persist only where in basis and essence it is itself eternal hope" (*CD* IV/1, 121). But it must also be said that Christian hope means being seized by God's promise and called to the promise of this future with God.

> If a man does not seize this hope, apprehend it, conform himself to it here and now as a man who belongs to the future, he is not one who has Christian hope. Rather, it will be revealed that he does not genuinely hope for the perfection and wholeness of His being in the service of God, for eternal life in its futurity, that he does not wait for Jesus Christ as the coming One.

> If he waits for Him here and now, then the here and now cease to be future-less. He looks for Him, the coming One, to-day, and to-morrow, that is, in the decisions in which he has to live to-day and to-morrow as long as time and space are given him. He does not make them without direction or into a future which is empty, but in obedience to his calling, towards that future promised him by God. (*CD* IV/1, 121)

Here finally it is important to realize that Christian hope is completely tied to the fact that it is the resurrection of Jesus Christ that gives us insight into our future with God:

> The verdict of God pronounced in His resurrection tells us that He not only was and is but also will be, not only at the end of time, but as Himself the end of time. He is not, therefore, just one future of men and the world behind and after which there might be others. He is the absolute and final future. (*CD* IV/1, 324)[36]

This is why Barth insists that we cannot base and understand NT hope on "a state of things in the time after the end of the forty days" (*CD* IV/1, 325). It must always remain based and understood from the one himself who comes again and him alone. While we live in the limitation associated with the fact that the time between Christ's resurrection and ascension and his second coming does not give clear evidence of what was actually accomplished in these events, the fact remains that if we do not detach our hope from the One who comes, we will see that he is our only sure hope. To focus on the limitations of the community directs us away from this hope which must be in him, as the early community prayed "Even so, come, Lord Jesus" (*CD* IV/1, 326).[37] The early community did not hope in Jesus as a last resort in order to get beyond this limitation; rather

> They certainly expected the removal of that limitation at His return. But they did not postulate and prove His return because they wanted that limitation removed. . . . They lived with a burning longing for the sight denied them in this time, for the liberation and redemption which are still to come . . . they had this burning longing because they looked for Jesus Christ Himself. And they looked for Him because He Himself in His present as the Crucified and Resurrected as He encountered them in this time showed Himself to them as the One He once was, as the One who was with them and indeed in them but also as the One who stood before them as the eternally future. (*CD* IV/1, 326-27)

Hence for Barth

> The eschatological perspective in which Christians see the Crucified and Resurrected and the alteration of their own situation in Him is not the minus-sign of an anxious 'Not yet,' which has to be removed, but the plus-sign of an 'Already,' in virtue of which the living Christ becomes greater to them and altogether great, in virtue of which they here and now recognise in Him who is the first word the final word, in Him who is the subject and object of the basic act of God the subject and object of the consummating act of God which reveals that basis, so that believing in Him and loving Him they can also hope in Him; in Him — and because in Him in the removal of that limitation. (*CD* IV/1, 327)

The resurrection therefore opened the eyes of the disciples to who Jesus was in his earthly life. "God the Creator had not merely been present to them in the man Jesus, but He had actually appeared in this post-history. This is what illuminated and explained the whole history of this man in His time" (*CD* III/2, 454). It is precisely this that Barth insists made the community

> immune from Docetism, from the possibility of a faith in Christ detached from the existence and knowledge of the man Jesus. The glory of the risen Christ was identical with the glory of the Jesus of Nazareth who went up from Galilee to Jerusalem to be crucified. It was identical with the glory of His human person, his human words and works. That this Jesus was the appearance of God, the salvation of the world, was what the disciples remembered as they looked back upon that post-history. (*CD* III/2, 455)

Resurrection and Reconciliation

We have already seen that Barth sees revelation as reconciliation in Christ. "He died, the just for the unjust, to bring us to God" (*CD* IV/1, 252). Our access then to reconciliation is in the cross of Christ. Why the cross? Because sin has disrupted our relationship with God and with all creation, the atonement is necessary. Sin must be removed and overcome if our relations with God and creation are to be normalized. The wages of sin is death (Rom. 6:23). And this refers not only to physical death but to eternal death. Hence for Barth "The very heart of the atonement is the overcoming of sin," namely, "rebellion of man against God" and also our hopeless destiny in eternal death. Jesus himself who, "by completing our work in the omnipotence of the divine Son, by treading the way of sinners to its bitter end in death . . . fulfils this judgment by suffering the punishment which we have all brought on ourselves" (*CD* IV/1, 253). While Barth notes that the term punishment here comes from its use in Is. 53, he also insists that it should not be understood in accordance with Anselm's theory of satisfaction. That idea, says Barth, is foreign to the NT.

So, for Barth, the emphasis here is on the fact that Jesus Christ made atonement with God and peace between creator and creature by killing and burying the man of sin, the first Adam on the cross. By bearing our sin on the cross he was our Representative. In that way,

> not by suffering our punishment as such, but in the deliverance of sinful man and sin itself to destruction, which He accomplished when He suffered our punishment, He has on the other side blocked the source of our destruction. . . . He has saved us from destruction and rescued us from eternal death. (*CD* IV/1, 254)

This is not an act of vengeance or retribution on God's part but occurs because of "the radical nature of the divine love, which could 'satisfy' itself only in the outworking of its wrath against the man of sin, only by killing him, extinguishing him, removing him" (*CD* IV/1, 254). But the relevance of our atonement rests on the fact that this man Jesus is God incarnate: "As the passion of the Son of God who became man for us it is the radical divine action which attacks and destroys at its very root the primary evil in the world" (*CD* IV/1, 254). As a result of the atonement or the peace restored by the man Jesus as the Son of God acting in our place and on our behalf Barth can argue that our justification is "the immediate consequence of that divine human action" (*CD* IV/1, 283). Also included in Barth's thinking is the community as the provisional form that corresponds to this and the life of faith which apprehends it.

In sum we have seen that Barth's view of the resurrection fits within the traditional position described by David Fergusson. For Barth Jesus' bodily resurrection is the starting point and decisive factor that gives meaning to the faith of the disciples' and to ours. Barth takes seriously the empty tomb tradition and Barth's understanding of the atonement and incarnation is dictated by the fact that the man Jesus from Nazareth and he alone is the unique savior of the world precisely because he was eternally the unique Son of the Father who became incarnate out of love for us. The strength of Barth's position is that it is firmly rooted in the immanent Trinity as disclosed through the economic Trinity. Thus, his position is seriously bound to history in that it is the historical Jesus himself as the Word incarnate who gives meaning to all Christian theology and not the experience, faith or hope of the community. This leads Barth to argue that any form of self-justification means the failure to recognize and live the freedom of the children of God which was established and is real in Christ and through the Holy Spirit.

For Barth human freedom means obedience to the God revealed in Jesus Christ. But that means that we are never truly free if we think we can or should do something to save ourselves. It means that salvation is in no way conditional. And it means most of all that because Jesus took the burden of humanity, in its attempt to make the decisions of God, away from us, we no longer have to worry about being the judge of our own behavior. In other words because Jesus lived a life of perfect obedience on our behalf, we no longer have the burden of trying to find our way to God and to eternal life and happiness by means of our ethical choices. This way exists because God in Christ has found his way toward us and continues to do so. The decisive ethical implication here is that right behavior is the behavior that takes place in obedience to the revelation of God in Jesus Christ. Hence any abstract attempt to define Christian ethics, any attempt to understand right behavior that bypasses or ignores the risen Lord, will inevitably end in some form of legalism or license and thus far from the comfort that comes from the forgiving grace of God that is the promise of Christian faith. Barth's theology of the resurrection leads him away from legalism and license (lawlessness) precisely because his understanding of the divine command is structured on the freedom of God exercised in the life, death, resurrection and ascension of Jesus, the Son of God. Hence for Barth the divine command which meets us in Christ always takes the form of freedom or permission to obey the will of God by loving Christ. Let us explore very briefly some of the ethical implications of Barth's view of the incarnation and resurrection in their essential unity.

Ethical Implications of Barth's Theology

What then would be some ethical implications of Barth's understanding of the relationship between the incarnation and the resurrection? First, it is just because Barth never deviates from acknowledging that Jesus Christ is both "the holy God and sanctified man in One" that he sees ethics as an interpretation of the "Law as the form of the Gospel" and thus as God's sanctification of the creation through his electing grace. This means that in Jesus Christ God has made himself completely responsible for us by claiming us in him. And because ethics witnesses to God's act for us in Jesus Christ, it witnesses to the grace of sanctification that reaches us in Christ and through the Spirit (*CD* II/2, 509). Thus faith in Christ is decisive because it is only in him that we may stand in a way that avoids anxiety and fear on the one side and legalism and lawlessness on the other (*CD* II/2, 598ff.). Because God's command always means liberation or permission and obligation only in light of that permission, the law is the form of the Gospel. Beyond that, faith acknowledges that this command of God in his Word is a spiritual command and so it always remains incomprehensible in a certain sense because when it reaches us, it is always a miraculous act of the Holy Spirit. Hence, "It is His Spirit which drives the children of God into the freedom which as such is real obedience" (*CD* II/2, 605).[39]

Second, Barth not only includes ethics within the doctrine of God because God is not alone since he claims us for himself in and through the covenant of grace, but Barth believes that even knowledge of God, which he discusses at length in *CD* II/1, involves ethics precisely because true knowledge of God can only take place through the miraculous grace of God without in any way abrogating our full sinful humanity, which becomes sanctified through the Holy Spirit, and certainly without in any way obscuring the sovereignty of grace. In fact it is the sovereignty of God's grace that is revealed in the cross and resurrection. God is not prevented by his nature or our sin from having a genuine relationship with us in Christ and through the Holy Spirit — a relationship that upholds our freedom and relative independence from God as creatures reconciled and destined to be redeemed in him. This is why he describes knowledge of God as a miracle and as an event enclosed in the mystery of the divine Trinity.[39] And this is why he describes knowledge of God only as obedience, that is, our free choice to believe and to acknowledge God's choice of us in Christ through the Spirit. The gist of the *analogia fidei* is that we can truly know God but only if and when we acknowledge that such knowledge is not a human work but rather is an expression of our justification by faith. Barth himself sums this up in his doctrine of election:

> This is something which ought to have been apparent for some time. For who can possibly see what is meant by the knowledge of God, His divine being, His divine perfections, the election of His grace, without an awareness at every point of the demand which is put to man by the fact that this God is his God, the God of man? How can God be understood as the Lord if that does not involve the problem of human obedience? (*CD* II/2, 512)

This is certainly why Barth so strongly opposed natural theology as that attempt to know God outside the circle of obedience. It was, in his mind, an attempt by "ethical man" to know good and evil as God knows them.[40] The only possible result of such an enterprise is anxiety and fear or legalism and lawlessness, according to Barth.[41]

One of the great differences between Barth and much contemporary theology is the fact that he takes sin seriously. Hence he rejects any thinking that assumes it must reckon with the fact that we possess "a kind of moral nature, with a knowledge of good and evil which is peculiar to [us], and of which [we are] capable apart from the fact that [we are] under the overlordship of the divine command" (CD II/2, 522-23). Barth therefore insists that theological ethics must be "on its guard against a retrospective reinterpretation of the fall, as though the presumption of man in wishing to know of himself what is good and evil were only a natural inclination to do the will of God" (CD II/2, 523).[42] Hence "It will not, then, make the disastrous, traitorous use of 'natural' theology, which is the only use that can be made of it" (CD II/2, 523). Barth of course is not denying the possibility of a general ethics. He is simply asserting that theological ethics must live exclusively by the grace of God and never allow that general ethics to define what is good and righteous, since God alone did that and does that now in Christ. This is the danger he sees in the Roman Catholic approach to ethics which attempts to coordinate moral philosophy and moral theology in a way that presumes a basic harmony between "nature and super-nature, reason and revelation, man and God" (CD, II/2, 530). When this happens grace can no longer be seen as grace and the command can no longer be seen as the divine command. For Barth the command of God is distinguished from all other commands by the fact that it is permission.[43] The problem here, once again, is that sin is not taken seriously so that in the Roman Catholic view

> the fall does not alter the fact that man's imitative knowledge is capable and to that extent partakes of true being even without grace, and therefore — analogia entis — of communion with the supreme essential being, with God, and therefore with the supreme good, although on account of the fall a special illumination by the grace of revelation is needed actually to prevent it from falling into error. (CD II/2, 530)

Barth objects to three things here: first, the grace of God revealed in Jesus Christ cannot be thought of in such a way that is has to share its power "with a force of nature." Such grace is no longer grace and cannot be recognized as the grace of God; second, "revelation which has from the very outset a partner in the reason of the creature, and which cannot be revelation without its co-operation, is no longer revelation"; third, any such revelation does not recognize that God opens himself to us in pure goodness so that "He does not find an existing partner in man, but creates a partner; in which even the fact that God is known and knowable is the work of his freedom" (*CD* II/2, 531). Hence, when man is co-ordinated with God "on the basis of this analogy — not in the humanity of Jesus Christ and therefore on the basis of God's own free decree, but simply in his metaphysical being as a rational creature — God is no longer God" (*CD* II/2, 531).

Barth is adamant then in respecting God's action as decisive. He insists that the truth and reality of the divine command cannot be translated "into a necessary element of man's spiritual life, or the realisation of human reason, or the realisation of the good as achieved by man himself, or a value-position anchored in the transcendent" (*CD* II/2, 522). Because the command of God is God's act alone, we cannot explain its why or whither from some human or other vantage point — we can only accept it and live by it obediently. It is because the command of God is neither founded on nor derived from anyone or anything else and it is because its validity cannot be tested by anyone or anything other than itself that Barth insists

> man cannot say this command to himself, but can only have it said to him. He has not invented this principle of theological ethics, and he cannot evade or even so much as conceal it. He has not given it its offensive character, and he cannot try to take it away. (*CD* II/2, 522)

Third, because the Christian doctrine of God does not just have God as its content but God who became incarnate in Jesus Christ, it must also have humanity as its content "to the extent that in Jesus Christ man is made a partner in the covenant decreed and founded by God" (*CD* II/2, 509). This relationship between God and us, however, is not "essential, indispensable, and inalienable," Barth insists, because it is a covenant of grace that has its foundation only in God's free choice to be God for us. To this extent Barth maintains that humanity in itself and as such does not have a place in the doctrine of God — but since Jesus Christ does — therefore we do. And it is a mark of Barth's doctrine of election that he understands humanity in its freedom and righteousness only as it is included by grace in the sanctification of Christ himself. This is the sense in which election is the sum of the Gospel; "God elects Himself to be gracious toward man, to be his Lord and Helper, and in so doing He elects man to be the witness to His glory" (*CD* II/2, 510). God determines to be our Lord and Helper and ethics concerns our free personal responsibility that "corresponds to this determination." It is not the sort of freedom, Barth repeatedly insists, as exercised by Hercules at the crossroads choosing between two possibilities — good and evil so that the person who chooses between these is "good on the basis of His choice of the good" (*CD* II/2, 517);[44] it is rather the freedom to obey God's righteous choice of us executed in Christ who is himself electing God and elected man and is as such our helper and friend. Hence for Barth

> The Son, who is obedient to the Father, could not possibly want to ask and decide what is good and evil. He could not possibly regard as the good that which He had chosen for Himself as such. No, it is as He is elected by the grace of God that the good is done. As this Elect, quite apart from any choice of His own between good and evil, He is concerned only with obedience. He does not crave to be good of and for Himself. And so in all His acts He is subject only to the will and command of the God who alone is good. This is how the good is done here. (*CD* II/2, 517)

This divine ethics is what answers the ethical question. To go behind this to some generally understood problem of ethics is precisely what the sinner does. Divine ethics is not "one disputant in debate with others" (*CD* II/2, 519). The problem of the truth and knowledge of the good of general ethics is no problem at all for theological ethics because the divine command as the form of God's electing grace is the starting point of "every ethical question and answer" (*CD* II/2, 519). It can never be "surpassed or compromised." But our actual human situation in which we are confronted with the question of the goodness of our behavior, our actual distance from the good and the overcoming of that distance which is no problem for general ethics is the "burning problem" for Christian ethics. Here Jesus Christ is seen as the solution to the problem of Christian ethics because he himself is the one who not only acts for us as God in the incarnation and resurrection but because he acts obediently for us as the only man who truly and completely obeyed God's will.

Fourth, because God in Jesus Christ makes himself responsible for us, he also makes us responsible. Hence "Ruling grace is commanding grace. The Gospel itself has the form and fashion of the Law. The one Word of God is both Gospel *and* Law" (*CD* II/2, 511). This means that this work of God is a "prior decision concerning man's self-determination. It is the claiming of his freedom. It regulates and judges the use that is made of this freedom" (*CD* II/2, 511). Our task is to be witnesses of Jesus Christ. But we can never assume his role of judge, i.e., he is the one who alone decides the worth of our behavior (*CD* IV/3, 921). Hence "the goal of the freedom in which He makes a man genuinely free — free to believe in Him — is the freedom to be His witness" (*CD* IV/1, 776). That is why the goal of faith is confession of Jesus Christ as the basis and meaning and future of human life. That is why Barth can sum up his view of ethics by saying that

> what God wants of us and all men is that we should believe in Jesus Christ. Not that we should believe *like* Jesus Christ — that aspect is better left on one side seeing that He is God and we are only men — but that we should believe in Jesus Christ, in the gracious action of God actualised and revealed in Him. The essence of faith is simply to accept as right what God does. . . . In the last resort, the apostles had only one answer to the question: 'What are men to do?' This was simply that they should believe, believe in Jesus Christ. All the answers of theological ethics to the same question can only paraphrase and confirm the imperative: 'Seek those things which are above.' (*CD* II/2, 583)

Finally, it is because Jesus really is who he is in his uniqueness that we not only can, but we are forbidden to fear death; not because we put in its place some false beyond or some false present; but because as the "resurrection and the life" (Jn. 11:25) he is our hope. And he is this because "in the resurrection of this man Jesus Christ, He then revealed Himself to be the hope of man, to be the manifest hope of all those who look to Jesus Christ and are ready to live by faith in Him" (*CD* III/4, 594). Jesus Christ has completely destroyed death, Barth asserts. He has not just destroyed dying but all the nothingness that threatens human existence and he has brought life and immorality to light (2 Tim. 1:10). He himself as the risen Lord takes from us all our fear and anxiety. "He does this who by His dying and rising again is Himself our hope in face of our dying — God for us where we can no longer in any sense be for ourselves" (*CD* III/4, 594).

We have now seen how Barth's understanding of the resurrection is distinctly tied to his view of the incarnation, atonement and the Trinity and how that influences his understanding of Christian hope and ethics. Now let us explore the thinking of Karl Rahner to see how his thinking about the resurrection affects and is affected by his understanding of God, the incarnation, salvation and the nature of Christian hope and what some of the ethical implications of his dogmatics might be.

2. Incarnation and Resurrection
   in the Theology of Karl Rahner

Employing the categories developed above with the help of David Fergusson we may begin by asking how Rahner would respond to the question of whether or not the resurrection is an event in the life of Jesus or an event realized by or within the faith of the disciples. In this chapter I will show that Rahner actually endeavors to hold both views simultaneously. And of course because the resurrection and incarnation are intrinsically related, any such viewpoint exhibits Rahner's failure to allow the incarnation of God in Jesus of Nazareth to dictate his understanding of both doctrines, especially with his idea that the incarnation should be seen as the conclusion rather than as the starting point for Christology. To the extent that Rahner will not begin his Christology with the incarnation, Jesus' humanity is not taken seriously as the locus of God's revelation in history. Instead of focusing on the Word of God incarnate in the man Jesus to understand Christian revelation, Rahner focuses on the revelation he finds in transcendental experience and then in Jesus of Nazareth. In this way he coordinates transcendental experience with the events attested in the NT in such a way as to blur the distinction between the objective events in the life of Jesus which give meaning to faith and faith itself.

Returning first to the resurrection we may note that on the one hand Rahner repeatedly speaks of Christ as risen and of the risen Lord. That would seem to indicate that he believes that the resurrection is an event in the life of Jesus that gives meaning to the disciples' faith and to ours. On the other hand Rahner frequently suggests that there would be no resurrection of Christ without the belief of the disciples and even accepts a modified version of Willi Marxsen's view that Jesus rose into the faith of the disciples.

And when he explains the meaning of Jesus' resurrection, it is not at all clear that he envisions a specific Easter history lived by Jesus and lived in such a way that what happened in that history is now made available to us in a particular and recognizable encounter with that risen Lord through the witness of scripture.

Matters are seriously complicated by Rahner's transcendental method which leads him to ascribe the meaning of the resurrection to our transcendental experience of hope and to what he calls the disciples' Easter experience. The result, unfortunately, is that he undermines his own desire to maintain the uniqueness of Jesus' person and work by attempting to deduce the meaning of the resurrection from transcendental experience instead of from the risen Lord himself as attested in the NT. This is further complicated by his understanding of grace, faith and revelation and by his symbolic ontology, as will be shown. In this chapter I plan to present the kind of doctrine of the incarnation and view of the Trinity that undergirds Rahner's thought about the resurrection. Because of the complexity and sheer volume of Rahner's work, I will limit my discussion of the ethical implications of his theology only to one point which cannot be discussed at length but only mentioned in this chapter. That point is that Rahner equates human ethical behavior with salvation. This equation fits the overall pattern of his transcendental theology. But, as I shall argue, it also opens the door to a kind of self-justification and universalism that Rahner undoubtedly thought he avoided.

Fundamental and Dogmatic Theology

Karl Rahner wanted to see fundamental and dogmatic theology united so that people could believe in Christianity precisely from the very content of Christian dogma itself. Rahner says fundamental theology in the past had been formal and did not consider individual dogmas.[1] But it must be remembered that for Rahner fundamental theology is not just that area of theology which deals with the most basic introductory questions such as revelation, faith, authority, the ways of knowing God and the nature and task of theology itself.[2] For Rahner fundamental theology is still a kind of apologetic theology.[3] That is why Rahner sees three mutually conditioning moments involved in the study of fundamental theology: (1) we reflect on ourselves as the universal question that we are; (2) we reflect on the transcendental and historical conditions that make revelation possible; and finally, (3) we reflect on the assertion that Christianity is the answer to the question that we as human beings are. This view of fundamental theology determines what Rahner thinks about the resurrection and the incarnation and their relation to atonement and the Trinity.

It must be acknowledged that Rahner properly wished to overcome a formally extrinsicist notion of theology which was espoused in the past. Such theology believed that by appealing to miracles as proofs of revelation one could then assert that revealed truths, demonstrated by formal reasoning, would be presented to individuals with the proviso that "this is revealed truth; you must believe it; it does not matter whether you understand it or not, or whether you find any interior, personal access to it" (*TI* 16: 4). Of course I agree with Rahner's rejection of this approach to theology. But that does not mean that we should search, as Rahner believes, for the "interior foundation of faith" (*TI* 16: 4).[4] If Jesus Christ is the foundation for the Christian faith, as I believe he is, then it will be true that one will discover the meaning of the Christian faith in him and in him alone and through the Holy Spirit (1 Cor. 12:3). But if it is through the Holy Spirit that this discovery takes place, then that means if we have the Holy Spirit, we have the Spirit only insofar as the Spirit unites us to Christ, so that our lives are lived from him and in him and toward him alone and therefore through faith in him alone. It is Rahner's search for that interior foundation that shapes his particular understanding of the resurrection and incarnation as well as all other doctrines. Instead of beginning and ending his theology with Jesus Christ as the first and final Word of God incarnate in Jesus of Nazareth, Rahner argues "In order to provide grounds for belief we can begin quite happily with man" (*TI* 16: 9). Rahner insists that this will not mean a fall into subjectivism or reductionism.

Still, the cornerstone of his fundamental theology, with its apologetic concern to commend Christianity to people from within their own deepest experiences of life, causes him to argue that there is a "complementary relationship existing between the anthropological starting point and the theological answer" (*TI* 16: 9). This thinking shapes his entire theology because it leads him to think that there is a relationship of mutual conditioning between knower and known,[5] between Christology and anthropology[6] and between natural knowledge of God and knowledge of God based on revelation.[7] This is why Rahner asserts that

> Man is essentially a questioner; indeed he is an absolute question . . . a person is endowed, even before he begins to ask questions, with the grace of the Holy Spirit, which is rooted in the centre of his personal being . . . we experience ourselves in the concrete situation of salvation as a question which can only find an answer in the self-communication of God in the Holy Spirit and in Christian revelation. (*TI* 16: 9)

Is it really possible to ascribe the Holy Spirit to us in our experience in this way without falling into subjectivism and reductionism; without implying that God's self-communication is little more than the theoretical seal of approval of what we have already discovered within our own self-experience? That will be the crucial question to be considered as we present Rahner's understanding of the resurrection and incarnation. Could it be that Rahner's starting point in human experience is what leads him to believe that "The basic human hope and the experience of Jesus sustain and justify each other" (*TI* 16: 15)? Does Jesus really need our human hope to be sustained in his life as the Lord of history? That is the question. Two more preliminary remarks are in order.

First, in attempting to unite fundamental and dogmatic theology Rahner maintains that their unity can be held on the Thomistic presupposition that fundamental theology is done under the light of faith and "is a justification of faith by faith." Hence Rahner contends we must reflect on the reality believed in and not on "the formal event of revelation as such" (*FCF*, 12-13). That is why Rahner cautions against a *"too narrowly Christological approach"* (*FCF*, 13). While he admits that Vatican II proposed that "theologians should be introduced to the mystery of Christ right at the beginning" he also says that the same Council declares that "this mystery of Christ affects the whole history of the human race" (*FCF*, 13). For that reason

> a too narrow concentration of the foundational course on Jesus Christ as the key and the solution to all existential problems and as the total foundation of faith would be too simple a conception. It is not true that one has only to preach Jesus Christ and then he has solved all problems. Today Jesus Christ is himself a problem . . . in what sense may one risk his life in faith in this concrete Jesus of Nazareth as the crucified and risen God-Man? This is what has to be justified. Hence we cannot begin with Jesus Christ as the absolute and final datum, but we must begin further back than that. (*FCF*, 13)

And of course this belief, coupled with Rahner's conviction that it is not impossible to go behind the "late" New Testament Christologies of John and Paul "to ask about a more original and somewhat more simple experience of faith with the historical Jesus, in his message, his death, and his achieved finality that we describe as his resurrection,"[8] leads Rahner to his starting point in human experience and this dictates the content of Rahner's theology as, for example, when he argues that "God's self-revelation in the depths of the spiritual person is an a priori determination coming from grace and is in itself unreflexive. It is not in itself an objective, thematic expression; it is not something known objectively, but something within the realm of consciousness" (*FCF*, 172). While Rahner insists that this *a priori* revelation is always mediated categorically because human transcendence has a history, it is hard to avoid the conclusion that it is the *a priori* and not the historical object that determines the truth of what is later said, especially when he argues that God is experienced as the "innermost dynamism of our spirit, which we call God. That experience is a grace. . . . When and where this innermost self-communication of God, which is already revelation . . . is objectivated in words, there we have that which one calls . . . revelation."[9]

Indeed, revelation itself means that "historical experience and the innermost dynamism of human beings toward God meet each other and confirm each other. From this unity of the historical experience of Jesus Christ and of the innermost experience of grace emerges what we call God's revelation accepted in faith in the full sense of the word" (*Rahner in Dialogue*, 77). Let it be stated here as clearly as possible: any idea that we could possibly justify belief in Jesus from a point outside Jesus Christ himself must necessarily mean a compromise of Jesus' unique lordship and thus a compromise of the essential meaning of resurrection and incarnation, as well as a compromise of grace and revelation. It can only mean that we are no longer justifying faith within faith as Rahner intended because faith by its very nature lives from its object alone and that means faith is justified only because Jesus Christ himself is our justification.

Second, in chapter six of *Foundations*, Rahner begins his Christology first by stressing the importance of anonymous Christianity which would imply that people accept the "offer" of grace which in fact is already an existential of their existence because, in Rahner's view, God has communicated himself to each person "as an offer to man's freedom" (*FCF*, 176).[10] And this offer is itself "a moment in the self-communication of God to the world which reaches . . . its climax in Jesus Christ" (*FCF*, 176). For Rahner then transcendental theology "must develop in a general ontology and anthropology an a priori doctrine of the God-Man" in order to formulate the conditions that enable a "genuine capacity to hear the historical message of Jesus Christ, and an insight into the necessity of hearing it" (*FCF*, 176-77). And this task, according to Rahner, stands in radical tension with the task of uncovering plain historical testimony about Jesus as the basis of salvation itself; thus "what is most historical is most essential" (*FCF*, 177).

There is a deep ambiguity in Rahner's thought here that runs through his entire theology. On the one hand he insists that no *a priori* doctrine of the God-Man could actually be developed "prior to the actual encounter with the

God-Man. We always reflect upon the conditions of possibility for a reality which we have already encountered" (*FCF*, 177). But on the other hand Rahner insists that transcendental Christology cannot say that the absolute savior has been found precisely in Jesus of Nazareth[11] and he also argues that everyone, whether Christian or not, lives what he calls a "searching Christology" even though they have not had any explicit contact with Jesus, the God-Man.[12] Yet, if one had actually encountered the God-Man, then the fact that Jesus is the savior of the world would have been no secret from Rahner's transcendental Christology in the first place and any idea that one could be searching for Jesus as the savior of the world without an actual encounter with Jesus of Nazareth would be self-contradictory.[13] Such thinking leaves one with the impression, once again, that Jesus is little more than the stamp of approval for whatever *a priori* one constructs from one's own spiritual hopes and wishes. This, as we shall see shortly, explains why Rahner actually believes he can make sense of Christ's resurrection from an analysis of our human experience of hope. And of course such a view, as we shall also see, is far from the NT or traditional view of Jesus' resurrection.

More importantly, an actual encounter with the Jesus of the NT faith renders impossible any attempt at an *a priori* Christology. Any such attempt would be essentially a Docetic Christology (which Rahner himself theoretically rejects) in which the determining element was not Jesus of Nazareth, God incarnate, but one's *a priori* idea of a savior or of a God-Man projected from one's own spiritual experience. And that brings me to the point I wish to make here. At the very beginning of chapter six in *Foundations*, Rahner unintentionally sets the stage for a combination of Ebionite and Docetic Christology.

Rahner insists that he will begin with the "history" of Jesus and thus with an "ascending Christology" (*FCF*, 177).[14] This Ebionite starting point sounds innocuous enough until one hears his conclusion: the expressions "incarnation of God" and "incarnation of the eternal Logos" Rahner contends must be the "end and not the starting point of all Christological reflection" (*FCF*, 177). And yet if this is in any sense true, then the incarnation cannot be seen as a unique act of God that is its own validation. The very idea that one does not need to begin theological thinking from the incarnate Lord means that some criterion other than Christ himself has been introduced. Naturally, it could hardly be otherwise, given what was said above about the fact that Rahner wished to begin with experience for apologetic reasons and not in some narrow way with Jesus Christ. And the matter does not end there.

Faithful to these insights, Rahner's Christology offers an almost classically Docetic conclusion as when he argues that if Jesus as the Christ has ever encountered someone "the idea of a God-Man, of God coming into our history, and hence a descending Christology, also has its own significance and power" (*FCF*, 177).[15] These insights suggest that we begin Christology in Ebionite fashion with the man Jesus (why else would Rahner say that the incarnation of God is the end and not the starting point of the incarnation doctrine?) and then infer in Docetic fashion that an encounter with that man produces in us (in an *a priori* way perhaps) the idea of a God-Man. But what is it that determines the truth of one's reflections in this scenario? The answer quite obviously is to be found in combining our *a priori* idea of a God-Man with what we find attested about Jesus in the NT as the answer to the quest for an absolute savior. That is why Rahner places much weight on what he calls "searching Christology" or "questing Christology" which everyone lives out in their lives whenever they make profound moral judgments and whenever they are faithful to their consciences.[16] This is what makes them anonymous Christians. And this very thinking leads Rahner to equate ethical judgments made in obedience to conscience with salvation in the Christian sense, as we shall see. Before answering the question of how this general approach to Christology shapes Rahner's view of the resurrection I will briefly note three extremely important related concepts that structure all of Rahner's theology, that is, (1) his ontology of the symbol, (2) his concept of an obediential potency and (3) his notion of a supernatural existential.

Rahner's Ontology of the Symbol, Incarnation and the Trinity

There are, for Rahner, two principles of symbolic ontology: (1) "all beings are by their nature symbolic, because they necessarily 'express' themselves in order to attain their own nature"[17] and (2) "The symbol strictly speaking (symbolic reality) is the self-realization of a being in the other, which is constitutive of its essence" (*TI* 4: 234). The concept of expression plays a fateful and decisive role in Rahner's thinking here and elsewhere. Rahner believes

> Being *as* such, and hence *as* one *(ens* as *unum),* for the fulfillment [in the case of the Trinity "*on account of* its being perfect"] of its being and its unity, emerges into a plurality — of which the supreme mode is the Trinity. (*TI* 4: 228)

Hence,

> each being, as a unity, possesses a plurality — implying perfection — formed by the special derivativeness of the plural from the original unity:

the plural is in agreement with its source in a way which corresponds to its origin, and hence is 'expression' of its origin by an agreement which it owes to its origin. (*TI* 4: 228)

Two important issues arise here. First, is the Trinity the supreme mode of being as such? And if the Trinity is considered such a supreme mode, does Rahner run the risk of defining the unique trinitarian relations by his general ontology of the symbol? I have argued at length elsewhere that this is exactly the reason Rahner tends to collapse the immanent into the economic Trinity.[18] Second, when Rahner thinks of plurality emerging from an "original unity" and then applies that thinking to the Trinity, does that not invariably lead toward some form of adoptionism in Christology, despite Rahner's explicit denials?[19] In my opinion, it does indeed lead to problems in Christology, because it encourages Rahner to think of God's primal unity by identifying that with the Father as Unoriginate origin, whereas the primal unity of God, according to Rahner's own reckoning, is identical with the fact that the one God is eternally three as Father, Son and Spirit.[20] Beyond that, does not such an idea necessarily compromise divine and human freedom with the thought that the plural is the "expression" of the original unity and is in agreement with it by virtue of its origin? Such thinking leads Rahner to underplay the problem of sin and the need to distinguish sharply between the immanent and the economic Trinity. Most importantly it leads Rahner to believe he can reflect on human experience and by virtue of an *analogia entis* describe the existence of the triune God. My purpose here is not to go into all the details of this but rather to illustrate that Rahner's ontology of the symbol causes problems for his view of the incarnation and of the Trinity.

For Rahner "the whole of theology is incomprehensible if it is not essentially a theology of symbols" (*TI* 4: 235). In fact Rahner argues that "the thought of the mystery of the *Trinity*" is what gives meaning to his understanding of symbolic reality so that he can say that in a study of general ontology we may assert that "each being bears within itself an intrinsic plurality, without detriment to its unity and perfection — which may eventually be supreme — precisely as the perfection of its unity" (*TI* 4: 235). Rahner declares that his "ontology of the symbol" was worked out in such a way that "it would be immediately applicable to the theology of the Trinity in blameless orthodoxy" (*TI* 4: 235). Hence for Rahner the "theology of the Logos is strictly a theology of the symbol, and indeed the supreme form of it" (*TI* 4: 235). How then does this thinking cause problems in connection with the incarnation and the Trinity and ultimately with Rahner's view of the resurrection? How do Rahner's principles of symbolic ontology create difficulties for this theology?

First, when Rahner applies these principles to the Trinity he reaches the following conclusions: "the Logos is the 'symbol' of the Father . . . the inward symbol which remains distinct from what is symbolized, which is constituted by what is symbolized, where what is symbolized expresses itself and possesses itself" (*TI* 4: 236). Hence "It is because God 'must' 'express' himself inwardly that he can also utter himself outwardly; the finite, created utterance *ad extra* is a continuation of the immanent constitution of 'image and likeness' — a free continuation, because its object is finite" (*TI* 4: 236-37). But if the immanent constitution of the Trinity is the result of God's necessary expression of himself in conformity with the principles of symbolic ontology, where exactly is the line to be drawn between God's internal expression and his free actions *ad extra?* The very notion of symbolic expression makes it virtually impossible for Rahner to recognize and uphold God's freedom in any realistic sense. That is why he can describe the creature as at once the paradigm of a possible utterance of God[21] and a continuation of the immanent constitution of the Trinity. This is especially true because he seems to equate God's actions *ad extra* with the very expression of the Logos *ad intra.*

Second, applying his symbolic ontology to the incarnation Rahner argues, following Jn. 14:9 that "He that sees me, sees the Father"[22] because the Logos is the image "filled with all the fullness of the Godhead" (*TI* 4: 237). Therefore

> the incarnate word is the absolute symbol of God in the world, filled as nothing else can be with what is symbolized. . . . He is the expressive presence of what — or rather, who — God wished to be, in free grace, to the world, in such a way that this divine attitude, once so expressed, can never be reversed, but is and remains final and unsurpassable. (*TI* 4: 237)

Therefore Christ's humanity "is really the 'appearance' of the Logos itself, its symbolic reality in the pre-eminent sense, not something in itself alien to the Logos and its reality" (*TI* 4: 238).

The principal question that arises here is whether or not Rahner has been misled by his ontology of the symbol into confusing Jesus' divinity and humanity by means of the notion of symbolic expression. Rahner wants to forge a deeper unity between Christ's divinity and humanity than he believes is expressed in the classical Christologies.[23] But he is unable to acknowledge that God could have remained fully who he is in eternity without creating and saving the world and so he writes: "The humanity is the self-disclosure of the Logos itself, so that when God, expressing himself, exteriorizes himself, that very thing appears which we call the humanity of the Logos" (*TI* 4: 239). If, however, all symbolic reality must express itself to attain its own nature and the incarnation is merely the exteriorization of that internal expression, what happened to God's freedom to exist without the world and without saving the world? Are they not blended together into the symbolic self-expression of the divine being? And that is not the end of it.

Rahner then argues, following his symbolic ontology, that "the Logos, as Son of the Father, is truly, in his humanity as such, the revelatory symbol in which the Father enunciates himself, in this Son, to the world — revelatory, because the symbol renders present what is revealed" (*TI* 4: 239). But if Jesus, in his humanity as such, is the revealer because the symbol renders present what is revealed then Rahner has in fact confused the power of the Word with his humanity in this very thinking precisely by applying his symbolic ontology to the incarnation. Jesus cannot be the revealer in his humanity as such unless his humanity itself is his divinity. And Jesus' humanity does not have the power in itself to reveal God to us because the Word was not transformed into the man Jesus in the incarnation as Rahner himself would admit. That power remains the power of the Word that is spoken in and through his humanity. It is this very thinking that, against all of Rahner's intentions to avoid Idealism, leads directly to the Idealist conclusion that the natural symbolic depth of all things "now in ontological reality [has] received an infinite extension by the fact that this reality has become also a determination of the Logos himself or of his milieu" (*TI* 4: 239).

It is exactly this idea of an infinite extension that leads Rahner to assign revelation and grace to our transcendental experiences and to search there for the meaning of Christology and the resurrection itself. It is Rahner's ontology of the symbol that leads him to insist that a symbol does not merely indicate an object but rather contains it. Hence "the symbol is the reality, constituted by the thing symbolized as an inner moment of moment of itself, which reveals and proclaims the thing symbolized, and is itself full of the thing symbolized, being its concrete form of existence" (*TI* 4: 251). This very thinking is confirmed in Rahner's treatise on the Trinity when he writes "what Jesus is and does as man reveals the Logos himself; it is the reality of the Logos as our salvation amidst us . . . here the Logos with God and the Logos with us, the immanent and the economic Logos, are strictly the same."[24]

This statement certainly seems to suggest that Jesus' humanity is the Logos present among us. And at least one Rahnerian actually interprets Christ's humanity as his divinity under the rubric "theandric"[25] while another explains that when Christ's humanity is thought of as the very expression of the Logos, the idea is conveyed that "the symbol not only renders the symbolized present, but is its very reality."[26] This makes it impossible to dis-

tinguish either Christ's divinity and humanity or the immanent and economic Trinity, in spite of Rahner's desire to do both. Here Rahner applies his
notion of quasi-formal causality[27] and believes that the doctrine of the Trinity can be properly grasped only "by going back to the history of salvation
and of grace, to our *experience* of Jesus and the Spirit of God, who operates in
us, because in them we really already possess the Trinity itself as such."[28]

But it is just here that Rahner's symbolic ontology has caused many of
the problems that have begun to arise and will be discussed throughout this
chapter. Is it the *experience* of Jesus and the Spirit that is the basis of belief in
Christ and the Trinity? Or is it Jesus himself now risen from the dead and
present to us in the power of the Spirit in and through our experiences? It is
this focus on experience, as we shall see, that leads Rahner to many ambiguities in his understanding of the resurrection. Much of what he says is dictated by his ontology of the symbol. For instance, as we shall see shortly, his
belief that the resurrection would not be complete without the disciples' experience of faith; his belief that a clear and sharp distinction cannot be made
between the disciples' experience and the event of Jesus' resurrection; his belief that the horizon for understanding the resurrection is our transcendental
experience of hope; his idea that the meaning of the resurrection can be understood by analyzing our own experiences of hope; his belief that the resurrection is not something totally new and unexpected; and finally his belief
that Jesus' resurrection can be vaguely expressed by saying that he achieved
definitiveness, rather than saying, that because he rose bodily from the dead,
he therefore appeared to the disciples in his glorified existence during the
forty days. But before we specifically discuss the resurrection and its connection with the incarnation let us very briefly highlight what Rahner means by
obediential potency and supernatural existential.

Obediential Potency and Supernatural Existential

Following his view of the relationship between fundamental and dogmatic
theology Rahner contends that the concept of mystery does not describe
something senseless and unintelligible but the "horizon of human existence
which grounds and encompasses all human knowledge."[29] Theological science actually is "the 'science' of mystery."[30] Hence, in Rahner's view, creatures have a positive affinity, given by grace, to the Christian mysteries of
faith which he conceptualizes as our obediential potency and supernatural
existential. The former refers to our openness to being (as spirit in the
world) and as such it refers to our openness to God's self-communication,

at least as a possibility. "This potency is . . . our human nature as such. If the divine self-communication did not occur, our openness toward being would still be meaningful . . . we are by nature possible recipients of God's self-communication, listeners for a possible divine word."[31] The latter refers to

> a basic structure which permeates the whole of human existence; it is not a localized part or region of our being, but a dimension pertaining to the whole. Our being in the world, or our being with others, could serve as examples . . . this existential . . . is not given automatically with human nature, but is rather the result of a gratuitous gift of God. . . . Because of the supernatural existential, grace is always a part of our actual existence.[32]

The Christian mysteries that Rahner has in mind include "the self-communication of God in the depths of existence, called grace, and in history, called Jesus Christ, and this already includes the mystery of the Trinity in the economy of salvation and of the immanent Trinity."[33] It is clear from this brief description that the concepts of the obediential potency and supernatural existential allow Rahner to focus on experience in such a way that he claims for humanity that which humanity was supposed to receive by grace and faith through Christ alone. In other words this thinking, which follows the logic of his symbolic ontology, opens the door to the universalism Rahner thinks he has avoided. The very idea that humanity has an obediential potency for grace compromises our need for Christ at the outset while the idea of a supernatural existential, as far as I can tell, basically ascribes grace to human nature while simultaneously denying it is doing so.

According to one Rahner commentator the supernatural existential means "it belongs to the very essence of concrete human nature to be called to grace, to be able to find God in the particularities of all history . . . the history of salvation and revelation are coextensive with the history of the human race."[34] Thus, "the offer and the possibility of grace is given with human nature itself as . . . historically constituted . . . the supernatural existential wants to affirm something about the reality of grace, namely, that it is a constituent part of our historical human existence."[35] But I think Stanley Grenz and Roger Olson have correctly evaluated this important Rahnerian concept as follows:

> the supernatural existential is a highly unstable concept. If the theologian emphasizes the universal aspect denoted by the term *existential*, the concept may easily fall into intrinsicism and become little more than another

religious a priori like Schleiermacher's God-consciousness. If one puts forward the supernatural aspect, the supernatural existential may easily fall
into extrinsicism and become little more than another theological assertion about the transcendence of God's self-revelation . . . [the supernatural
existential] is highly ambiguous and of dubious value in solving the dilemma of transcendence and immanence in contemporary Christian theology.[36]

That is why the universal aspect allows Rahner and many who follow him to
claim that God's universal offer of salvation is given in transcendental experience rather than exclusively by God's Word and Spirit. This necessitates the
idea that reason and revelation exist in a mutually conditioning and mutually
conditioned relationship. Such thinking has affected the theological land-
scape today perhaps more than any of Rahner's other insights. In this chapter
we are seeing how it affects his view of the incarnation and now we shall see
how it affects his view of the resurrection.

Rahner's View of the Resurrection

Even though his method centers on human experience, Rahner certainly asserts that Christ is risen: "For in fact he is risen in that which we call his human nature."[37] Indeed Rahner insists we can say with the first disciples "that
because Christ is risen, I believe" (*FCF*, 242) and the "risen and exalted Lord
must be the permanent and ever-active access to God."[38] But what exactly
does Rahner mean by this? He considers Jesus' resurrection "a borderline
problem between exegesis and dogmatic theology" (*TI* 11: 210) and hence he
will not confine himself to the NT accounts of the resurrection to understand
its meaning. Actually he begins to understand the resurrection from us,
thinking about our own resurrection and what that might mean, and then
applying what we discover to Jesus. One of the first peculiar conclusions that
he reaches is that

> we can never adequately separate this 'for us' aspect of the risen Lord from
> the 'in himself' aspect of him. I cannot work out for myself whether or not
> the glorified wounds of the physical side of Jesus actually exist in the 'in
> himself' dimension which belongs to him as risen. I do not even know
> whether one who has been glorified has a head. I have no positive grounds
> for denying it, but ultimately speaking I do not know it, and, moreover, it is
> a matter of indifference. (*TI* 11: 210)

What was, for the NT, a matter of pivotal concern, namely, that Jesus rose bodily from the dead and appeared to the disciples eating breakfast with them (Jn. 21:9-14), breaking bread with them (Lk. 24:30), and even inviting Thomas to touch his wounds (Jn. 20:27ff.) has been transformed by Rahner into a rather amorphous description of what he imagines eternal life for us might look like. And the most he can say is that it will have some sort of eternal validity for us and thus for Jesus. Why? Partially because Rahner fears that a whole series of what he would consider mythological questions would arise if one were to believe in Jesus' literal bodily resurrection (not the resuscitation of a corpse, of course, which Rahner and all theologians agree did not take place in Jesus' resurrection).

That is why Rahner says that when doubts are raised about whether or not his understanding of the resurrection is "sufficiently Christian" because he says "it is nothing other than the absolute fulfillment and the salvation of the concrete human person" he cannot "see what more [his] critic can imagine in regard to the resurrection" (*Rahner in Dialogue,* 130). Anything more would raise questions about whether people in heaven eat, what their hairstyle might be, whether they are tall, short, fat or thin and Rahner clearly does not want to have to confront these questions. To solve this problem Rahner asks "what Jesus might have done with his body after the resurrection if there were no 'address' in heaven" and then declares

> Fulfillment in our case takes place at death. Heaven is not a 'salad' made up, on the one hand, of those who have already experienced the bodily resurrection and of 'fluttering' souls on the other. . . . If someone says: I will get there, I will be saved, and in doing so does not distinguish, or rather while distinguishing does not separate what are ordinarily called body and soul, then I would say that person believes in the resurrection. (*Rahner in Dialogue,* 130-31)

This is why Rahner explains the "original experience" on the part of the disciples that "'Jesus is alive'" as a secondary "literary and dramatic" embellishment with the result that "it is to be explained after the manner of our experience of the powerful Spirit of the Living Lord rather than in a way which either likens this experience too closely to mystical visions of an imaginative kind in later times, or understands it as an almost physical sense experience" (*FCF,* 276).[39] Hence "Faith is not taking cognizance of a fact which by its nature could exist just as well without being taken cognizance of" (*FCF,* 267). Rather the disciples' "*faith* in his resurrection is an intrinsic element of this resurrection itself" (*FCF,* 267) so that God's eschatological victory which took place in Jesus' resurrection not only cannot be grasped without faith in it as "freely arrived at" but "it is only in this faith that its own essential being is fully realized" (*FCF*, 268).[40] It is in this sense that Rahner accepts a modified version of Willie Marxsen's view that

> Jesus is risen into the faith of his disciples. But this faith into which Jesus is risen is not really and directly faith in this resurrection, but is that faith which knows itself to be a divinely effected liberation from all the powers of finiteness, of guilt and of death, and knows itself to be empowered for this by the fact that this liberation has taken place in Jesus himself and has become manifest for us. (*FCF*, 268)[41]

For Jesus' free manifestation of himself to the disciples "to imply sense experience, everything would have to belong to the realm of normal and profane sense experience" (*FCF*, 276). That is why Rahner insists that "the risen Jesus himself gives witness that he is alive *in* the successful and inseparable correspondence between transcendental hope in resurrection and the categorical and real presence of such a resurrection" (*FCF*, 275; emphasis mine). Both of these, Rahner believes, reinforce each other just as "the transcendental experience of the expectation of one's own resurrection, an experience man can reach by his very essence, is the *horizon* of understanding within which and within which *alone* something like a resurrection of Jesus can be expected . . ." (*FCF*, 273-74; emphasis mine). Hence our hope and the experience of faith in Jesus' resurrection mutually condition each other — thus, according to Rahner, one can only experience Jesus' resurrection if one has had this experience of hope (*FCF*, 274).[42] That is why Rahner also insists that "we do not learn something which is totally unexpected and which lies totally outside of the horizon of our experience and our possibilities of verification" (*FCF*, 275).

It is hard to escape the conclusion once again that for Rahner, Jesus is no more than an instance, a necessary one in his view, of our own hope for some definitive existence for ourselves. That is why Rahner argues that in faith and hope we acquire the courage to stand beyond death by "gazing upon the risen Jesus who comes before us in the apostolic witness" (*FCF*, 275). Part of the difficulty in this reasoning, however, is the fact that Rahner's focus is on the experience of the disciples and our experience so that his main concern is that we should believe that we are not just transitory elements in this world but that the physical as well as the spiritual side of our existence "is destined to endure, for which [we are] answerable to God, and which will have an eternal validity" (*TI* 11: 210). This is why Rahner finds it difficult, if not impossible, to distinguish the disciples' "Easter experience" from the risen Lord himself:

There is such a thing as Easter faith. Those possessing it are beyond all reckoning. It is present first in the disciples of Jesus, and the witness *which they bear to their Easter experience* and their Easter faith is to acknowledge him who was crucified. . . . It may be that we of today cannot draw any clear distinction within the Easter event as understood here between Easter itself (precisely the fact of the risen Christ) and the Easter experience of the disciples. . . . In the case of Jesus' disciples their Easter faith and their Easter experience (their belief and the grounds for that belief) are already blended into each other indissolubly.[43]

This blending of experience and the object of faith (the risen Lord) results from Rahner's method and is manifested in his belief that there is a mutually conditioning and mutually conditioned relationship between subject and object and between knower and known, as noted above. For example, with respect to our knowledge of God and in accordance with his belief that natural theology and revealed theology mutually condition each other, Rahner writes:

We have discussed both the holy mystery, which exists absolutely and which we call by the familiar name 'God,' and our transcendence to this holy mystery together. In the original unity of this transcendental experience, the two are *mutually dependent* on each other for their intelligibility. (*FCF*, 68; emphasis mine)

Consequently, Rahner contends that "In any act of cognition it is not only the object known but also the knowing subject that is involved" (*TI* 11: 87). Indeed "It [knowledge] is dependent not only upon the distinctive characteristics of the object, but also upon the essential structure of the knowing subject . . . the *a priori* transcendental subjectivity of the knower on the one hand and the object of knowledge . . . on the other are related to one another in such a way that they *mutually condition* one another" (*TI* 11: 87; emphasis mine).[44]

Rahner insists that the risen Lord "does not belong to the world of our experience" (*TI* 11: 211) and thus he could not be photographed and could not be interviewed by reporters. So what then was the nature of the disciples' experience? First, Rahner asserts that if they had been able to touch Jesus as we ordinarily touch things in everyday experience then this would "in fact not have constituted the true experience of the definitive state which this man Jesus had attained to at all" (*TI* 11: 211). Second, he insists that the more they might have had such a "solid" experience within the dimensions of this world "the less they would have experienced that in which the essence of resurrection in fact consists: the fact that this man is he who has been definitively delivered" (*TI* 11: 211). Third, the most we can maintain, Rahner says, is that the disciples had this experience and described it but that this experience was not merely something subjective because its point of departure was "him and not their own subjectivity" (*TI* 11: 211) and that it was not just a visionary experience. At this point Rahner explicitly rejects the radical understanding of the resurrection as espoused by Bultmann:

> The disciples do not create the Resurrection of Jesus *by* their experience. Rather they experience (this is a witness that we must accept from them if we are willing to believe at all) the Resurrection of Jesus. The Catholic interpreter of the apostles' experience of the Resurrection says, 'What I accept from them is that they had experience of one who had risen.' (*TI* 11: 212)

But Rahner's focus on experience, as we already have been seeing, will not allow him to maintain this insight in any realistic sense and with any consistency. So when he explains the meaning of what he had just affirmed Rahner says

> we can uncompromisingly state that Jesus properly and radically became he who had risen from the dead only when he had attained precisely to *that* point towards which everything tends as its goal, and at which he is present in my faith too as he who has risen from the dead. . . . Whether we refuse to accept the apostles' witness to this experience of theirs or not — that is a matter for ourselves. (*TI* 11: 212-13)

But were the apostles really witnessing to their experience? Were they not witnessing unequivocally to an event in the life of Jesus that gave meaning to their experience? Again Rahner rejects, as uncritical rationalism, the idea that the disciples were merely projecting the idea of the resurrection because of their own religious inclinations. But he pulls the ground out from under his own assertion simply because he is unable to make a clear and sharp distinction between subject and object at this point. He insists that if anyone would understand the resurrection properly

> if at the centre of his own existence, he yearns for his own 'resurrection' since on any true anthropology, he can only understand himself as a man who hopes for that which is described in terms of resurrection, then, in my belief, he has also achieved an *a priori* perspective such that, while it cer-

tainly does not excuse him from the *free decision* of faith in the Resurrection of Jesus, still at the same time it does justify him in believing in such a thing as the Resurrection of Jesus, i.e. in accepting the Easter experience of the disciples as a matter of his own intellectual honesty. (*TI* 11: 213)[45]

But what is the determining element here that justifies this intellectual honesty? Clearly, that determining element is not exclusively grounded in the risen Lord himself but is at least partially grounded in our personal yearning for some sort of definitive validity for our own lives. It is our *a priori* perspective, our horizon, that drives our hope here and this perspective stands in a mutually conditioning relationship with the Easter experience of the disciples so that this perspective is what justifies belief in the risen Lord while at the same time Rahner asserts the need for a free decision of faith concerning Jesus' resurrection. This is why, in another context, Rahner insists that

> we are not saying . . . that this witness handed down through history of the Resurrection of Jesus is exclusively, or taken in isolation, the sustaining basis for the witness of faith of subsequent generations and of Christian belief. For the credibility of this historical witness ('the Lord is risen indeed') is itself sustained by the transcendental expectation of resurrection which is inherent in man's basic attitude. It is because (whether he explicitates it to himself or not) he entertains a hope for himself . . . that he has 'ears' to hear this witness to an historical fact.[46]

This thinking then represents an almost classic explication of what David Fergusson labeled the liberal position regarding the resurrection which, in the end, collapses back into the radical position. And this thinking creates a serious problem because it would appear that one does not need to believe in a specific historical occurrence in the life of Jesus *in order* to make this particular decision; one might even have an anonymous faith in the resurrection of Jesus himself. Rahner's espousal of an anonymous faith in the resurrection of Jesus is the tell-tale sign that, despite his own intentions, he has in fact reduced the Easter event to the experience of hope on the part of the disciples and on our part. Hence, while he does indeed admit we depend on the disciples' testimony to connect our experience of the Spirit with Jesus, he also insists, in a way that undermines any real need for the risen Lord himself, that

> wherever and whenever we experience the unshakeableness of our own hope of a final victory of our existence, there takes place, perhaps anonymously, that is, without reference to the name of Jesus, an experience that

he has risen. For this power of the spirit that we experience in this way as life's victorious defiance of all forms of death is the power of the Spirit which raised Jesus from the dead and thereby displays its victorious power to the world in history.[47]

Enough has been said at this point to illustrate that while Rahner sincerely believes in Christ's actual resurrection from the dead, his explanation of the meaning of the resurrection is substantially shaped by his transcendental method which presumes that we can and must develop an *a priori* understanding not only of the God-Man but of our own hope as the horizon within which contemporary Christology and a theology of the resurrection will make sense to modern people without falling into mythology. This leads him to conclude that (1) the starting point for understanding Christ's resurrection is our experience of hope; (2) Jesus' resurrection and our faith exist in a mutually conditioned and mutually conditioning relationship; (3) the resurrection actually is not realized without the faith of the disciples and without our faith; (4) the resurrection of Jesus is not a historical fact existing independently of the disciples' faith and ours; (5) the resurrection can and must be verified by means of our experience of hope; (6) the resurrection is not something unexpected and entirely new within the realm of human experience; (7) the disciples witnessed to their experience of faith; and (8) one can have an anonymous experience of the risen Lord.

Therefore it is not surprising that in *Our Christian Faith: Answers for the Future*, Rahner says he is choosing one of several possible starting points to explain the resurrection by asking the question: "Do I wish for my resurrection?" asserting that he "probably" would not have asked the question that way if the doctrine of Jesus' resurrection and ours did not exist (*Our Christian Faith*, 109-10). So he begins with experience noting that my wish for my resurrection exists always and everywhere provided I maintain that my existence has meaning (*Our Christian Faith*, 110). This abstract understanding of the resurrection corresponds with Rahner's belief that the expression "resurrection" is equivalent to belief in immortality of the soul as belief in life beyond death.[48] While Rahner consistently wishes to eschew any sort of dualism between body and soul which might suggest that only the soul continues to exist after death, he nonetheless will use the expression "immortality of the soul" to designate what he means by resurrection. That is why Rahner can say that resurrection means "the irrevocable claim that my existence shall be saved and acquire definitive form" and this "implies a claim to resurrection" (*Our Christian Faith*, 110) even though I might be unable to portray or imagine this existence. Here his method is in full view:

If one has a radical hope of attaining a definitive identity and does not be-lieve that one can steal away with one's obligations into the emptiness of non-existence, one has already grasped and accepted the resurrection in its real content. . . . The absoluteness of the radical hope in which a human be-ing apprehends his or her total existence as destined and empowered to reach definitive form can quite properly be regarded as grace, which per-meates this existence always and everywhere. This grace is revelation in the strictest sense . . . this certainly is revelation, even if this is not envisaged as coming from 'outside.' (*Our Christian Faith*, 110-11)

And in a very important article in his *Theological Investigations,* Rahner be-gins his analysis of Jesus' resurrection saying:

It is possible to enquire about Jesus' resurrection today . . . only if we take into account the whole of what philosophy and theology have to say about man. Here we must start from the assumption that the hope that a person's history of freedom will be conclusive in nature . . . already includes what we mean by the hope of 'resurrection' . . . this hope must include knowl-edge of what is really meant by resurrection.[49]

And for Rahner "the knowledge of man's resurrection given with his tran-scendentally necessary hope is a statement of philosophical anthropology even before any real revelation in the Word" (*TI* 17: 18). By the time Rahner appeals to grace and scripture they can only describe something which every-one already knows and experiences without faith in Christ and the Spirit.

This ambiguity in Rahner's understanding of the resurrection is also present in his view of death and is problematic since he insists that Christ's death and resurrection must be held together. One wonders how seriously Rahner accepts death as an end of human existence as when he argues that it is myth to say "that the one resurrection of men and women takes place *after* a period of complete non-existence on the part of the dead" (*TI* 17: 17). Such thinking in Rahner's view would make it impossible to identify the dead per-son with the one who is raised. That is why Rahner insists that resurrection means "the acquiring of a final and ultimate form by the whole, individual person in his own history of freedom; it applies to his 'body' only in a second-ary and derivative sense" (*TI* 17: 17). And he believes that "death is the birth of life set free" (*TI* 4: 129) and the final fulfillment of life so that what follows death is the definitive thing that took place in death. Resurrection therefore is an "element in *this* death" (*TI* 4: 131). Indeed Rahner also maintains that in death "man does not perish but is transformed into a new manner of exis-

tence" (*TI* 4: 347). Of course Rahner does not mean that our material existence simply continues in another form just as he does not think of eternity as
the continuation of time.

Rather, as eternity grows out of time (*TI* 4: 351; *FCF,* 271), so our lives and
Jesus' life are saved by becoming definitively valid as a result of our and his
free decisions and obedience to God. What comes to be in and through death
is the "hard-won and untrammelled validity of what was once temporal" (*TI*
4: 348). Hence Rahner can ask: "Does not he who really faces his end *calmly*
show that he is more than time" (*TI* 4: 349) and it is only "because we have become immortal in our life that death . . . is for us so deadly" (*TI* 4: 349). But
how can it really be deadly if, in it, we already experience our immorality? According to Rahner it is in our moral decisions that we are constituted as having a valid end so that when we love another person for instance "something
eternal happens" (*TI* 4: 350).[50]

Rahner thus understands eternity as a mode of spirit and freedom and
thinks that revelation presupposes that every man "achieves so much spiritual and personal eternity in his life, that the possibility inherent in his spiritual substance is realized in fact as eternal life" (*TI* 4: 351). In that sense death
makes definitive the basic attitude of a person so that there is a "ripening of
the whole man 'after' death" (*TI* 4: 353). Rahner rejects séances and false spiri-
tualism as ways of communicating with the dead because they do not enable
us to meet the dead as they really are now in "the definitive kernel of their being" (*TI* 4: 353). Rather, according to Rahner,

> we meet the living dead . . . in faith, hope and love, that is, when we open
> our hearts to the silent calm of God himself, in which they live; not by call-
> ing them back to where we are, but by descending into the silent eternity of
> our own hearts, and through faith in the risen Lord, creating in time the
> eternity which they have brought forth for ever. (*TI* 4: 353-54)

If, however, death does not mean the end of human existence but merely
its transformation in the manner described by Rahner, in what sense can we
really regard death as that final enemy to be done away with (1 Cor. 15:26) that
the apostle Paul believed was overcome in Jesus' resurrection from the dead
and would be overcome for us finally with his second coming (1 Cor. 15:24)?
In what sense can we believe with Paul that the dead are asleep in Christ? In
what sense can we believe that our new spiritual bodies will come into existence when Christ returns to raise us from the dead? To be asleep in Paul's
language is to be dead and thus to await Christ's return and the fulfillment of
his promise of eternal life in the form of our own resurrection from the dead.

If we already live in the sense described by Rahner, what could it possibly mean to say that we die believing in eternal life because Christ, risen from the dead, has promised to raise us from the dead on the last day as well? In 1 Cor. 15 the apostle Paul does think some people will be alive when Christ returns and that they will be changed "in the twinkling of an eye" (1 Cor. 15:52) when the last trumpet sounds. But at that time he says "the dead will be raised imperishable, and we shall be changed."

Rahner's thinking, with its focus on our experience, tends to blur the distinction between Christ's own resurrection and ours and so underplays the fact that death is a real cessation of existence with the result that we can *only* live now by faith and hope in Jesus himself. But that would mean that we could never claim eternal life as something that grows out of our free moral decisions since it would always be that life we live by faith in, through and from the risen Lord himself. Our lives would be hidden with Christ in God. Even in death we would, as those who have died, be in God's hands to be sure. But we would still be dead. And eternal life, as the gift of God given in and through Christ, would then be our new life which remains to be received when, according to his promise Christ raises us to eternal life. I agree with Rahner that all dualism between body and soul is to be rejected. But I wonder whether, in place of a belief in the immortality of the soul, Rahner has substituted a holistically imagined existence which persists between the period of our death and the time of our resurrection.

The Meaning of Jesus' Resurrection

What then is the meaning of Jesus' own resurrection? Rahner insists not only that the possibility of belief in Jesus' resurrection takes place "within this transcendentally necessary hope of resurrection" but that its meaning is determined by this transcendentally necessary hope of ours (*TI* 17: 18). And he insists that "*because* Jesus is risen, I believe in and hope for my own resurrection" (*TI* 17: 18). But what meaning does he assign to the risen Lord? First, he argues that Jesus' resurrection means "the final and conclusive form of this person and his actual history before God and with him. The statement 'he lives in the glory of God' is therefore more primal and basic than the individual accounts of the visions and 'appearances' of the risen Jesus" (*TI* 17: 19). Second, Rahner insists

> what is really at stake is an experience of faith in the Spirit — the experience that Jesus is alive. And this experience is fundamentally open to every Christian. He has only to accept believingly and trustingly his own transcendental hope of resurrection. (*TI* 17: 19)

Third, Rahner believes that one who has this hope must implicitly or explicitly be on the lookout for "a specific event in his own history, on the basis of which his hope can be believed in, as something that has been realized in another person" (*TI* 17: 19). Fourth, the empty tomb for Rahner, while a tradition that belongs to the oldest tradition of the NT, should be understood as "an expression of a conviction which had already spread for other reasons — the conviction that Jesus was alive" (*TI* 17: 20).[51] Fifth, the "facts" of Jesus' resurrection "must simply be determined in the light of what we have to understand by our own 'resurrection'" (*TI* 17: 20). Sixth, the actual meaning of Jesus' resurrection then is

> the ultimate deliverance of actual human existence by God and before him. This means that human history acquires its real validity for the first time; it neither simply goes on continuing into vacuity, nor is it simply destroyed . . . death, without which this ultimate conclusiveness is impossible . . . is the essential and radical renunciation of every concept of the 'how' of this conclusiveness, whether it applies to 'the body' or to 'the soul' of any human life. (*TI* 17: 20-21)

Resurrection therefore does not mean any kind of continuance of human existence that "would be neutral towards man's salvation." Rather, it means

> that [human] existence's acceptance and deliverance by God. That is why a person cannot be separated from the activity or 'cause' that animated his earthly life. . . . The real activity or 'cause' . . . is always whatever is brought to fulfilment in the actual existence of the human person. Consequently in saying that this is what has permanent validity, we are saying that what is permanently valid is the validity of the person himself. (*TI* 17: 21)

And this means to Rahner that because Jesus' cause (which was to act as savior) did not come to an end in death or merely continue in the form of an idea (Willi Marxsen's view), this "person-cause does not simply mean that some man or other and his history go on existing, but that the *victory* of his special claim to be the absolute mediator of salvation is endorsed once and for all" (*TI* 17: 21-2). Because of that, "*faith* in his resurrection is an inner aspect of that resurrection itself. It does not simply mean registering a certain fact, which by its very nature could just as well exist even if we did not register it at all" (*TI* 17: 22). And finally, for Rahner Jesus' resurrection

> does not mean the beginning of a new period in the life of Jesus, a further

extension of time filled with new and different things. It means rather and precisely the permanent, redeemed, final and definitive validity of the single and unique life of Jesus who achieved the permanent and final validity of his life precisely through his death in freedom and obedience. (*FCF*, 266)

Given what was said above, it goes without saying that it is not because Jesus *is* the eternal Son of the Father that he is savior of the world in this schema. Rather, it is because his human life has reached a definitive validity so that his cause is confirmed. That is why, for Rahner, the resurrection is not a *fact* existing in itself that gives meaning to faith. Rahner's inability to describe the resurrection as an event in the life of Jesus that gives meaning to faith stems directly from his failure to accept the incarnation as the starting point for his Christology. Making the incarnation the end and not the starting point for Christology means that someone or something other than Jesus himself as the Word incarnate must become the theological criterion. What kind of theology of the incarnation and view of the Trinity then undergirds this view of the resurrection?

Rahner's View of the Incarnation

As seen above Rahner believes the incarnation cannot be the starting point but rather must be seen as the conclusion of our christological reflections. This methodological judgment affects his view of the incarnation. It will be my contention that this weakness in Rahner's Christology is precisely what led to his liberal understanding of the resurrection and his subsequent confusion of resurrection and faith by viewing them within a relationship of mutual conditioning. This is not a small issue or a minor quibble. The whole Christian faith stands or falls with the fact that Jesus is who he is quite independently of our experiences and that what happened to him in the resurrection is the precondition for all Christian theology whatsoever.

Both of these pivotal insights are blurred and compromised by Rahner's transcendental method which begins with experience rather than with Jesus himself. Subsequently, of course, Rahner insists that Jesus himself is the true foundation for all Christology and knowledge of God, just as he insists that Jesus' resurrection is the only way to the Father. But because of his starting point in transcendental experience he is unable to maintain those insights with any consistency; he regularly undercuts the need for Christ before arriving at his theological explanations; and so he unintentionally compromises the traditional meaning of both doctrines. Such a compromise has very practical and devastating theological consequences. When Jesus is not the starting point for theological reflection, then no matter how strongly one may afterward stress his importance and significance, the fact is that he no longer has the significance he had for the NT and for the faith of the church through the ages or for today. He is no longer absolutely necessary. At best he is seen as a model we may wish to use to validate our experiences of faith, hope and love. At worst he is seen as a historical instance of what we think we have already discovered in the depth of our own experiences of faith, hope, love or freedom. What follows such thinking always is some variation on a theme of self-justification, with the result that in the end we are alone with our experiences of faith, hope and love, trusting in ourselves and using Jesus Christ as our historical choice to validate those experiences. Let us see how these issues play out in Rahner's understanding of the incarnation and of the Trinity.

Rahner's Christology has been characterized, at least in part, as a type of degree Christology by Colin Gunton.[52] What is degree Christology? Perhaps John Robinson expressed it best when he said: "If one had to choose, I should side with those who opt for a 'degree Christology' — however enormous the degree. For to speak of Jesus as different in kind from all other men is to threaten, if not to destroy, his true solidarity with other men."[53] While Gunton notes that one of the functions of Christology is to show how Jesus shares our humanity to the full but without sin, degree Christology wants to do more than this. It wants to say that "Jesus's especial or divine significance is grounded in or demonstrated by his supreme human qualities."[54] Therefore Gunton identifies the chief weakness of this Christology with its apparent proposal "that to be divine (or unique in the way a Christology asserts) is the same thing as to be successfully human." Beyond this, such Christology seems to suggest that if we can discover certain qualities of the man Jesus that allow him to "exceed" other human beings, "we can present him as a source of salvation or model for behaviour." And Gunton believes there may be another tacit assumption at work in degree Christology, that is, "in some sense already to be human is to share in divinity. . . . Jesus, then, would be seen to be the one who brought this innate quality to perfection." In that sense he would be divine "as the supreme *degree* of what we are already, and is therefore not *in principle* different. In this way a crudely docetic Christology, in which Jesus is simply a god dressed in human guise, is avoided."[55]

But, according to Gunton, one of the earliest Christologies as expressed in Heb. 1:2 and 4:15 stresses both the "high" and "otherworldly" fact that Jesus is the Son through whom the world was created while simultaneously emphasizing that he was a human who could, as high priest, sympathize with our weaknesses. Nonetheless, "A Christology from below whose *only* resource is some kind of transcendental anthropology seems logically bound either to [take Jesus out of our sphere] or to concede the content of traditional Christology." Why? Because Christology from below (ascending Christology in Rahner's thinking) seeks "to rise from below, by using a logical ladder from the human to the divine."[56] Degree Christology then is distinguished by the view that Jesus is different from us not in kind but in the degree of self-transcendence which he experienced in his life and this view results from Rahner's attempt to reconcile traditional Christology with what he calls an evolutionary view of the world in his "neo-Chalcedonian"[57] Christology. Rahner certainly attempts to uphold Jesus' uniqueness in kind by stressing that he also is different from us as the Logos or Word. But even his explanation of that difference, as we shall see, does not convincingly overcome the appearance that Rahner has fallen prey to a type of degree Christology by conceiving Jesus as a uniquely divinized human being. This issue, as we shall see shortly, leads him and a number of his followers to equate Jesus' divinity with his humanity. But let us not get ahead of ourselves.

Incarnation/Evolution

Rahner insists that he will not fall into any kind of rationalism by allowing evolution to dictate the meaning of Christology and thus of the incarnation. But there is little doubt that it is his very idea of evolution that leads him to his degree Christology precisely by conceiving the incarnation and hypostatic union as events that receive their meaning from developments within history rather than as unique actions of God coming into history from outside. Hence, Rahner first explores the meaning of human nature to understand what happened in the incarnation:

> if this is what human nature is, the poor, questioning and in itself empty orientation towards the abiding mystery whom we call God, then we do understand more clearly what it means to say: God assumes a *human* nature as his own. If this indefinable nature, whose limit, that is, its 'definition,' is this unlimited orientation towards the infinite mystery of fullness, is assumed by God as *his own* reality, then it has reached the very point toward which it is always moving by virtue of its essence. (*FCF,* 217)

Second, Rahner asserts that

> The very thing which necessarily takes place in man in an initial way and which places him before the question whether he wants to have anything

... to do with it, this takes place in an unsurpassable way and in the strictest and most radical sense when this nature of man as so understood so gives itself to the mystery of fullness and so empties itself that it becomes the nature of God himself. (*FCF*, 218)[58]

Third, Rahner draws the conclusion that "the Incarnation of God is the unique and *highest* instance of the actualization of the essence of human reality, which consists in this: that man is insofar as he abandons himself to the absolute mystery whom we call God" (*FCF*, 218). This is what Rahner calls an "obediential potency for the hypostatic union" (*FCF*, 218).

Rahner notes, however, that this union of God and man cannot be said to have taken place in every one just because he has described it as "the most radical culmination of man's essence" (*FCF*, 218). This thinking, Rahner says, would overlook the fact that "historicity" and "personhood" cannot be reduced to the level of nature, that is, to what exists always and everywhere. "The truth of a divine humanity," Rahner writes, "would be mythologized if it were simply a datum of every person always and everywhere" (*FCF*, 218). Furthermore such an idea would ignore the fact that Jesus' humanity, as the humanity of God, is graced with a closeness to God in the same way as all other humanity, even though the God-Man "as individual exists for every individual person" (*FCF*, 218).

Still, the weight of his own transcendental anthropology leads Rahner almost immediately to contradict this quite proper assertion with the belief that "God and the grace of Christ are present as the secret essence of every reality we can choose" (*FCF*, 228). How can such thinking avoid mythologizing Jesus' uniqueness as God incarnate precisely by blending God's grace with every reality we can choose? Indeed it is exactly at this point in his reflections that Rahner argues that self-acceptance is the same as accepting Christ:

> anyone who, though still far from any revelation explicitly formulated in words, accepts his existence in patient silence (or, better, in faith, hope and love), accepts it as the mystery which lies hidden in the mystery of eternal love and which bears life in the womb of death, is saying 'yes' to Christ even if he does not know it. . . . Anyone who accepts his humanity fully . . . has accepted the Son of Man because in him God has accepted man. (*FCF*, 228)

This conclusion is certainly the tell-tale sign that, although Rahner sincerely wishes to maintain the uniqueness of Christ in the incarnation, his belief that evolution and Christology have "an intrinsic affinity" and perhaps also "a reciprocal correlation" (*FCF*, 179) causes him to be unable to do so. That would explain why, in order to avoid a view of the incarnation that would alienate people today, Rahner chooses as his starting point an evolutionary view of the world (FCF, 180). Rahner says he will try to avoid the theories of Teilhard de Chardin, but that if he reaches the same conclusions as Teilhard, then that would be acceptable.

It is this starting point then that affects Rahner's transcendental method. First, it leads him to argue "the essence of man himself can be seen within a fundamental and total conception of the world" (FCF, 181) and thus in terms of self-transcendence into God. Second, it leads him to say that the permanent beginning and absolute guarantee that this ultimate self-transcendence will succeed has begun "with what we call the 'hypostatic union'" (FCF, 181). Hence Rahner insists that in the first instance the hypostatic union "may not be seen so much as something which distinguishes Jesus from us, but as something which must occur once and only once when the world begins to enter upon its final phase" (FCF, 181). That is why Rahner actually describes the hypostatic union as the highest instance of human self-transcendence.[59]

What, however, dictates whether or not the world is entering its final phase? Is it the evolutionary process? Or is it the unique act of God becoming man in the history of Jesus of Nazareth? The very fact that Rahner refuses to acknowledge Jesus' uniqueness at the start of his reflections, with his methodological proposal that the incarnation is the end and not the starting point for Christology and with his idea that theology cannot begin exclusively with Jesus himself, suggests that the evolutionary process and not Jesus himself is dictating the meaning here. That is why Rahner understands the incarnation in this context as "the necessary and permanent beginning of the divinization of the world as a whole" (FCF, 181). Indeed Rahner insists that the notion of an absolute savior does not mean that God's self-communication to the world in its spiritual subjectivity must begin with him in a temporal sense. Instead Rahner says it is "co-existent with the whole spiritual history of the human race" (FCF, 194).

Third, Rahner conceptualizes God's self-communication to creatures as something that "is still in its historical process" (FCF, 190) so that "the entire dynamism which God has implanted in the process by which the world comes to be in self-transcendence" is intrinsic to it but not a constitutive element of its own essence (FCF, 192). It is Rahner's belief, of course, that God's self-communication can be intrinsic to us without being an element of our essence. But there is every reason to believe that his conceptions of an obediential potency on the one hand and a supernatural existential on the other suggest otherwise as noted above. When Rahner argues that God becomes the innermost life of the world which then receives God into itself (FCF, 190-91) his thinking verges on the pantheism he sincerely believes he overcomes with his distinctions between grace and nature by means of his concepts of obediential potency and supernatural existential.

Fourth, it is precisely at this point that Rahner's thinking bypasses Christ and assigns God's self-communication directly to the freedom of cosmic subjects (*FCF*, 193).[60] Hence he argues that God's self-communication necessarily exists "either in the mode of its acceptance, which is usually called justification, or in the mode of its rejection, which is called disbelief and sin" (*FCF*, 193). The problem here of course is that Rahner ascribes God's self-communication and thus God's grace to the freedom of each and every individual and it is that ascription which leads to the universalism Rahner intends to avoid. And this happens once again because he refuses to begin his Christology by acknowledging Jesus' uniqueness and instead begins an ascending Christology with Jesus' humanity conceived in an evolutionary context. It is hardly surprising that in the end he can only describe Jesus as the climax of humanity's self-transcendence into God.

This thinking is linked to the fact that Rahner thinks that God's immediacy to us "must be embedded in this world to begin with" (*FCF*, 87) as "a moment in and a modality of our transcendental and at the same time historically mediated immediacy to God" (*FCF*, 87). That is why Rahner insists that every genuine intervention of God in the world, free though it is, "is always only the becoming historical and becoming concrete of that 'intervention' in which God as the transcendental ground of the world has from the outset embedded himself in this world as its self-communicating ground" (*FCF*, 87).[61] It is hard to escape the conclusion that it is Rahner's evolutionary view of the world that leads him to believe that revelation itself is simply "the becoming historical" of something that is already "embedded" in the world. Such thinking makes it extremely difficult to maintain a clear and sharp distinction between God and the world as Rahner certainly wanted to do. It also creates problems for Rahner's conception of Jesus' pre-existence.

Was Jesus the eternal Word of God before creation and without it? As noted above Rahner would say that Jesus is the Word in the sense that

> historical experience and the innermost dynamism of human beings toward God meet each other and confirm each other. From this unity of the historical experience of Jesus Christ and of the innermost experience of grace emerges then what we call God's revelation accepted in faith in the full sense of the word. (*Rahner in Dialogue*, 77)

Even Rahner's conception of Jesus as the Word, however, is tainted by his evolutionary view of the world. Rahner insists that Jesus is the Word insofar as he is unsurpassable in what he does. A mere prophet can never be the last in this sense Rahner insists. Only a history which is lived out in divine and human freedom that determines him once and for all and hence becomes irrevocable can describe an absolute "eschatological" event of salvation (*FCF,* 301). Rahner believes his initial approach to Christology from below is objectively identical with the classical Christologies because he reaches the *idea* of an absolute savior from transcendental experience *and* historical considerations. In that way Rahner contends Christology has already reached a Christology of Christ's eternal and divine Sonship (*FCF,* 301). Rahner claims a Son or a Logos Christology is already implied in the notion of an absolute Savior. But is this the eternal Son of the Father, begotten before all worlds, or is this Son or Logos determined by Rahner's philosophy and theology of the symbol together with his evolutionary view of the world?

Interestingly, when Rahner does finally consider Johannine Christology in *Foundations,* he insists that Christ's pre-existence must be treated "more explicitly and more cautiously" than before (*FCF,* 304) and this means for Rahner that

> if Jesus Christ is the absolute and eschatological expression and offer of God's own self, and without this Christology is not Christian, and if along with this he is the free and created acceptance of this offer, an acceptance effected by the offer in a formal predefinition, and it is only then that he can be the absolute event of salvation, then the one who expresses himself and offers himself, namely God, is 'pre-existent.' Indeed he is so in a radically different way than is the case when God is pre-existent to some other temporal creature which is not his own self-expression. (*FCF,* 304)

This thinking, however, is a far cry from the classical Christologies. On the one hand, in this context, Rahner never actually says that Jesus *is* the eternal Son of the Father, begotten before all worlds simply because he is who he is from all eternity. On the other hand, Rahner also says that it is only when Jesus humanly accepts this offer of God, through God of course, that he can be the absolute event of salvation. Further, in another context discussed above (51ff.), Rahner conceptualizes Jesus' pre-existence in terms of his symbolic ontology as the expression of God that conforms to the principles of symbolic expression that govern all reality: "This man is, as such, the self-utterance of God in its self-emptying, because God expresses *himself* when he empties himself" (*TI* 4: 116). Then he argues that the incarnation is God's expression of himself into the void:

when this God utters himself as himself into the *void,* this expression speaks *out* this immanent Word, and not something which could be true of another divine person . . . we could now define man . . . as that which ensues when God's self-utterance, his Word, is given out lovingly into the void of god-less nothing. . . . If God wills to become non-God, man comes to be, that and nothing else, we might say . . . Christology is the end and beginning of anthropology. And this anthropology, when most thoroughly realized in Christology, is eternally theology. It is the theology which God himself has taught, by speaking out his Word, as our flesh, into the void of the non-divine and sinful. (*TI* 4: 115-17)

While Rahner clearly wishes to accord something specific to the Word, his concept of symbolic expression operates in such a way as to suggest that since symbols must express themselves to exist, therefore God must express himself *ad intra* and *ad extra* as well, especially when he contends that "God's creative act always drafts the creature as the paradigm of a possible utterance of himself. And he cannot draft it otherwise, even if he remains silent" (*TI* 4: 115). And, as suggested above, since Rahner thinks the expression of God's Word *ad extra* is the continuation of his necessary symbolic expression *ad intra* it is difficult if not impossible for him to maintain a clear and sharp distinction between the immanent and economic Trinity and between God's free existence *ad intra* and his free act of creation *ad extra.*

By contrast, the traditional Christologies insisted that Jesus was the absolute savior just because he himself was the eternal Son or Word of the Father who became flesh for us and our salvation. In other words the classical Christologies refer to the virgin birth as the miracle pointing to the work of the Holy Spirit by which the Word assumed flesh from Mary in order to become one with us in our humanity. The incarnation was not seen as the expression of God into the void. It was not seen as a symbolic expression at all in Rahner's sense. It was rather a miraculous divine act which is inevitably denied or distorted the moment it is conceived in an ascending line within a Christology from below. Rahner even suggests that exegetes may discover that what Jesus meant by "Son" may not only imply that the Son is identical with the God who "expresses himself in time" but may also contain "an element which is not identical with this God and hence is not 'pre-existent'" (*FCF,* 304). This last point, Rahner says, does not exclude pre-existence in the classical christological sense.

This is a trinitarian rather than a christological problem, Rahner believes, because it concerns our ability to speak of the three persons or if by persons we understand three modes of subsistence in the one God, and the second of these is exactly identical with God's *ability* to express himself in history, which ability precisely as such belongs immanently and essentially to God and is inner-trinitarian, then we can and also have to speak of a pre-existence of the subject who expresses himself in Jesus Christ. (*FCF*, 304)

But that is precisely the problem Rahner has created by conceptualizing the Trinity from within his symbolic ontology as noted above. Instead of maintaining that the Son eternally pre-exists as begotten of the Father before all worlds and that the Son has become incarnate for the sake of our salvation Rahner refers to an inner-trinitarian ability on the part of God to express himself in history. To put the matter pointedly: when Rahner says we have to speak of a pre-existence of the subject who expresses himself, which subject is he referring to? Better, what is determining Rahner's thought at that point? Of course no theologian, including me, would oppose speaking of the Son or Word as the eternal expression of the Father. My objection is to the idea that what pre-exists in Rahner's thought appears mainly as the projection of his notion of symbolic expression into the deity. Among other things (some of which were discussed above) this line of reasoning leads Rahner to understand love of God and neighbor "in the direction of a radical identity of the two loves"[62] so that "the love of God and the love of neighbour are one and the same thing" (*TI* 6: 233). Thus

> wherever a genuine love of man attains its proper nature and its moral absoluteness and depth, it is in addition always so underpinned and heightened by God's saving grace that it is also love of God, whether it be explicitly considered to be such a love by the subject or not . . . this is the direction in which the understanding of the thesis of identity as it is meant here leads . . . wherever man posits a positively moral act in the full exercise of his free self-disposal, this act is a positive supernatural salvific act . . . wherever there is an absolutely moral commitment of a positive kind in the world . . . there takes place also a saving event, faith, hope and charity. . . . (*TI* 6: 237, 239)

And as we have just seen this leads Rahner to assert that "Christology is the end and beginning of anthropology . . . this anthropology, when most thoroughly realized in Christology, is eternally theology" (*TI* 4: 117) so that "for all eternity such an anthropology is really theo-logy" (*TI* 9: 28). Indeed, as noted above, for Rahner "anthropology and Christology mutually determine each other within Christian dogmatics if they are both correctly understood" (*TI* 9: 28). The ethical implication of Rahner's inability to maintain a clear and sharp distinction between the immanent and economic Trinity and between the humanity and divinity of Christ is the idea that our moral commitments can be equated with salvation itself. On the one hand this conclusion is precisely the Idealism Rahner thinks he has avoided because it makes salvation a universal that can be described as part of all human experience quite apart from any explicit reference to and dependence upon Jesus of Nazareth. On the other hand this conclusion is at the very least an espousal of some form of self-justification. And such a notion once again calls into question the relevance and significance of Christ's incarnation and resurrection as events in which God has decisively acted for us in history.

Ethical Implications of Rahner's Theology

There can be no doubt that Rahner's transcendental method shapes his ethics just as it shaped his view of the incarnation, resurrection and the Trinity. Rahner's view of ethics takes shape within the natural law tradition which saw morality as designed and implied according to "natural structures built into human being" with the result that if one is faithful to those structures one is good and if one is unfaithful to them one is evil.[63] The difference between Rahner's view and the older natural law theology is that Rahner seeks to be less "objective" in the sense that he wanted to incorporate the free human subject into his reflections and so for Rahner "The structures of nature are to be found not primarily by empirical observation but by looking *within* the immediacy of conscious self-experience" (*A World of Grace,* 173). Thus, instead of finding those structures which provide the moral ideal within nature, Rahner seeks to find them within the "the human person's immediate experience of the self acting morally, within subjectivity" (*A World of Grace,* 173).

By situating the locus of reflection within the human person Rahner can understand freedom without specifically adverting to the revelation of God in Jesus Christ, the Word incarnate. Of course, as we have already seen, it is part of his transcendental method to include his belief that human beings are open to God as the term, horizon or goal of the experience of self-transcendence and thus toward what he calls "holy mystery." But the problem with this is the predicament of natural theology itself — the holy mystery that is the term of the experience of self-transcendence is not and cannot be identical with the God revealed in Jesus Christ and through his Holy Spirit for the simple reason that this naturally known God can be recognized apart from faith in Jesus and thus apart from any specific relationship of reconciliation with Jesus himself. Such thinking will always lead to an "ideal" God and not to the real God who exists eternally and in time as Father, Son and Holy Spirit.

In other words, it is this starting point that allows and even requires Rahner to explore the meaning of human freedom in abstraction from the incarnation and resurrection, and then to conclude that good moral action, even without any specific advertence to Jesus Christ, is salvific action.[64] It is hard to imagine how, from the point of view of the Gospel, such thinking can escape the appearance of being a form of self-justification precisely because it seeks and finds human freedom within the human subject and not specifically in Jesus Christ and through the Holy Spirit. No doubt Rahner ascribes all of this to grace and not to nature. But again, we have seen that in virtue of his ideas of an obediential potency and supernatural existential, Rahner is compelled to ascribe grace and God's self-communication to us in our transcendental dynamisms.

It is in his ethics then that his dogmatics, while certainly tied to the doctrine of God, displays the weaknesses of Rahner's own peculiar natural theology. Instead of appealing directly to the risen Lord acting in the power of his Spirit to enable us to live our justification by faith, Rahner defines human freedom by reference to our "dynamic drive toward incomprehensible Holy Mystery" so that "this structure of being makes the actual performance of self-conscious and objective thinking and acting possible" (*A World of Grace*, 174). According to this analysis freedom means (1) the responsibility to shape oneself and to strive to do so; (2) "to do this in accordance with the other structures of nature or to refuse to do so" (*A World of Grace*, 174); (3) the capacity for moral action. The important point to be made here is that freedom means the ability to choose the good or perhaps even to choose evil. But if we have the capacity to choose the good, then it is our choices for good or ill that determine who we are and not Jesus Christ himself as our savior, helper and friend. We have already seen that in Barth's theology freedom means that we are actually set free by the Word of grace to obey the command of God which is our justification and sanctification in and through the Holy Spirit. This means that although our lives certainly are shaped in relation to God in and through our free decisions and actions, it is Christ himself through his Holy Spirit who is decisive.

Here then is a very basic difference that arises from and can be seen in their respective starting points for interpreting both the incarnation and the resurrection. For Barth the starting point is Jesus himself who is the Word of God incarnate and who thus is both the source and creator or re-creator of human freedom which is enslaved by sin. For Rahner the starting point is

transcendental experience and freedom defined in relation to our human actions relative to moral ideals formulated in relation to our human experiences of choice. For Barth this picture of human freedom is not the freedom
that comes to us in Christ because we do not in reality have the capacity to
obey God; this can only come to us in the miracle of justification and sanctification and thus through faith which necessarily includes love and hope as
each of these is tied to the unique object that is the subject which gives meaning to them, namely, the risen Lord himself in his personal presence between
the time of his ascension and second coming through the power of his Spirit.
We may be good humanly speaking, but that cannot be equated with salvation, because righteousness comes to us only through faith in Christ and not
through our choices *per se.*

Rahner's objection to the traditional natural law approach to ethics was
that it did not allow for the fact that human action shares in the divine creative action. "In no real sense was freedom a risk-taking venture participating
in God's own risk of creating a world of persons who are able to respond to
God and who respond not merely by producing good or evil acts but by making themselves good or evil" (*A World of Grace,* 173). But that is just the problem of discussing ethics in abstraction from revelation: a properly Christian
ethics is one that begins and ends with our justification by faith and our sanctification by the Holy Spirit. Such a Christian ethics, while certainly acknowledging that we do create our history in a certain sense through our actions,
will nevertheless clearly insist that we are not "co-creators" with God and that
it is in reality only God and not our good activity that makes us good in God's
eyes. Here it is important to see that the outcome of Rahner's approach to
theology and thus also to ethics is a picture of the human person choosing for
or against himself or herself and thereby being or becoming a Christian.[65]
This is part and parcel of Rahner's view of the "fundamental option." One answers the call of the "holy Mystery" when one says yes "to the very structure
of the person, to the innermost grounding of freedom itself, to the nature of
person as such. The self co-creates itself with Holy Mystery" (*A World of
Grace,* 178).

While the fundamental option is designed to avoid a legalistic and overly
objectivist natural law style of morality which should indeed be overcome, it
unfortunately sets the question of human freedom and responsibility in the
context of our own transcendental dynamisms and so can actually speak of us
justified and saved apart from any specific relationship to Jesus Christ and the
Holy Spirit. This is the weakness of this particular ethical solution. And the
most important results of this weakness are that salvation is seen to be conditional upon our moral behavior and then is universalized by being equated

with our moral behavior itself and particularly with our love of neighbor. By equating our love of neighbor, as Rahner does, with our love of God, Rahner subverts our need for repentance and belief in the risen Lord as the only one who can actually free us for the responsibility required of us by God himself.

Instead, by defining God as a naturally known holy mystery, Rahner is able to present freedom and morality in a way that encompasses both Christians and non-Christians and thus ascribes salvation to whoever is faithful to his or her conscience.[66] He also insists repeatedly that salvation is "offered" to everyone in the depths of their human experiences of freedom. But this of course implies that we must seize that offer for it to become effective for us. Yet the Gospel suggests that salvation is not merely offered to us in Christ but becomes a reality in his life, death and resurrection; a reality in which we may participate by faith. If this is the case, however, then the reality of salvation is not in any sense conditional on what we do, nor is it offered to us within our own spiritual dynamisms. It is, rather, given and effected in Christ himself so that by his resurrection and after his ascension the Lord himself enables us to say yes to him and thus to live lives of obedience which we were incapable of living before. That is the essential weakness of Rahner's ethics. It properly overcomes what is perceived to be the older natural law ethics, but does so improperly with a new more subjectivist view that actually leads to a kind of universalism and self-justification that is at variance with the Gospel. It is important then to note in this context that it is just because of Rahner's method that he is led not only to a liberal view of the resurrection but to a view of ethics that leaves the responsibility of freedom tied to what we do or fail to do instead of to what Christ has done for us on the cross and through his resurrection and is doing for us now through the Spirit as the ascended Lord and thus as the one mediator between the Father and us.

3. Incarnation and Resurrection in the Theology of Thomas F. Torrance

The thesis of this book is that there is a definite relationship between the doctrines of the incarnation and resurrection so that any theology of the resurrection which does not begin with Jesus Christ himself as the Word of God incarnate will always present a view of the resurrection that is more than a little ambiguous. It will never allow the risen Lord himself and him alone to determine what is said, but instead will espouse a liberal or radical view of the resurrection just because its understanding of the incarnation is dictated not by who Jesus was and is as God incarnate, but by our Christian experiences of faith and hope. In addition, such a theology will invariably underplay Jesus' pre-existence as the eternal Son of the Father and consequently tend to blur the distinction between the immanent and economic Trinity. Ultimately such a theology will offer an inadequate account of our knowledge of God himself, for as T. F. Torrance notes,

> It is in and through Jesus Christ . . . that we creatures of space and time may know God the Father, in such a way as to think and speak truly and validly of him, even in such a way that the forms of our thought and speech really terminate objectively on God himself. . . . Apart from the resurrection we could not say this.[1]

Further, such a theology will customarily espouse an ethics of self-justification by equating our moral behavior with our salvation or damnation, instead of arguing that true human freedom can only be experienced in obedience to Christ through the Spirit with the result that salvation always is and remains an act of God in Christ on which we continually depend in prayer and thanksgiving.

If one were to ask T. F. Torrance whether he believed the resurrection was an event in the life of Jesus that gave meaning to the faith of the disciples and to our faith or if it was an event that was realized in or by the faith of the disciples, I believe Torrance would answer unequivocally that it is just because the resurrection was an event in Jesus' life that Christian faith has meaning at all. And he meant to uphold a strong realistic sense that Jesus rose from the dead bodily and appeared to the disciples, thus enabling their faith. In fact Torrance insists that the resurrection must be the starting point for all Christian theology:

> *The raising of the Christ* is *the* act of God, whose significance is not to be compared with any event before or after. It *is the primal datum of theology, from which there can be no abstracting,* and the normative presupposition for every valid dogmatic judgment and for the meaningful construction of a Christian theology. (*STR*, 74)

This starting point, however, only makes sense in light of Torrance's strong emphasis on the *unity* of the incarnation and resurrection, which of course means his consistent material and methodological rejection of any sort of Ebionite or Docetic Christology.[2] Because the NT holds together Jesus' humanity and divinity from the start, any implication of adoptionism with "an approach from below upwards" (Ebionite Christology) (*TF*, 112) or any implication of Apollinarianism with "an approach from above downwards" (Docetic Christology) (*TF*, 113) inevitably meant that neither approach

> had really started from the fundamental datum of the Gospel: that in Jesus Christ, who was born of Mary and suffered under Pontius Pilate, God himself has come to be with us and reveal himself to us, and that in the one Person of Jesus Christ God and man are inseparably united for us and our salvation. (*TF*, 114, 163f.)

In his last conversation with Karl Barth in 1968 Torrance responded to Barth's assertion that Christ's resurrection must be the starting point of theology by insisting that "unless that starting point was closely bound up with *the incarnation,* it might be only too easy . . . to think of the resurrection after all in a rather docetic way, lacking concrete ontological reality" (*STR*, x-xi).[3] At that Barth responded: "Mark well, bodily resurrection" (*STR*, xi). Indeed, Torrance believes that taking the resurrection seriously means treating the resurrection "as of the same nature . . . as his birth and death" (*STR*, xv). "It is in the resurrection" wrote Torrance "that God's incarnate and redeeming purpose for us is brought to its triumphant fulfilment" (*STR*, 13). But in order to understand this it is important to realize that, from the very first, the incarnation means that God is revealing himself in Jesus Christ and reconciling a world gone wrong through the entirety of Christ's life from his birth, through his ministry and then in and through his death and resurrection. That is why Torrance argues that the objective meaning of the Bible which concerns theologians

> is bound up with the incarnation of the Son of God to be one with us in our physical human existence within the world of space and time in such a way that through his vicarious life and passion he might redeem human being and creatively reground it in the very life of God himself, and therefore it is also bound up with the resurrection of Jesus Christ in body, or the physical reality of his human existence among us. (*STR*, 13)[4]

Hence, while the incarnation and resurrection are intimately related in Torrance's thought, they cannot be understood apart from the doctrines of the atonement and the Trinity either. Whenever Torrance speaks about incarnation and resurrection, atonement and the Trinity are implicitly and explicitly present because it is for us and for our salvation that the Word became incarnate and it is the *homoousion* between the Father and Son in eternity that gives meaning to his *homoousion* with us in the history of salvation.

Fundamental and Dogmatic Theology

Interestingly, while Torrance explicitly ruled out any *a priori* theological knowledge (*STR*, 4), his thinking exhibited his own attempt to harmonize fundamental and dogmatic theology. Hence he actually begins his book on the resurrection recalling another part of his last conversation with Barth about the error of constructing an "independent" natural theology; he says both agreed that when Barth rejected natural theology as a *"praeambula fidei"* he was rejecting the idea that natural theology could function epistemologically prior to the actual knowledge of God that takes place in faith. Torrance therefore insists that a true scientific method will "allow all our presuppositions and every preconceived framework to be called in question by what is actually disclosed in the process of inquiry" (*STR*, x).

Torrance's view of natural theology then differs from traditional natural theology and can be seen as his attempt to relocate natural theology within the sphere of revelation by not detaching it from its material content.[5] For

Torrance, natural theology "constitutes the epistemological structure of our knowledge of God" (*STR*, x) and thus it has no independent standing and cannot be detached from our actual knowledge of God that takes place in encounter with Christ and the Spirit. Yet it is open to philosophical analysis. In his last conversation with Barth, Torrance used the analogy of geometry to suggest that when geometry is idealized and detached from experience (as happens in traditional Euclidean geometry), it becomes an independent conceptual system that becomes a rigid framework for the interpretation of physics. This leads to a distortion of physics, as Einstein himself pointed out, because geometry should be "brought into the midst of physics where it changes and becomes a kind of natural science (four-dimensional geometry) indissolubly united to physics" (*STR*, ix). Torrance frequently uses this analogy to emphasize that just as Euclidean geometry is abstract and incomplete without physics, so natural theology is abstract and incomplete without revelation.[6]

Still, Torrance does think geometry can function independently of physics in a certain limited way. Hence, applying this analogy to natural theology, he proposes to explore the formal structure of our human understanding of God "apart from the divine side of the bi-polar relationship which knowledge of God involves." This amounts to an artificial methodological separation akin to "converting four-dimensional geometry back into three-dimensional Euclidean geometry, or physical geometry back into *a priori* geometry."[7] Such an enterprise, Torrance insists, can only have "quasi-validity" because of the artificially imposed limits (*RST*, 60). This methodological move, however, leads to an ambiguity in Torrance's reformulated natural theology with the result that while Torrance very clearly wishes to avoid any idea that natural theology can operate independent of revelation, part of his thinking suggests that because it can, there may be some validity to the content of natural theology. Thus Torrance says that for Barth there can be no independent natural theology because such thinking does not terminate upon the Trinity but upon "some being of God in general" (*Karl Barth*, 151). But then in a very subtle but revealing statement Torrance asks "Does it [an independent natural theology] not really miss the mark, by abstracting his existence from his act, and so by considering one aspect of his being apart from other aspects?" (*Karl Barth*, 151). Here Torrance presumes that natural theology actually knows an "aspect" of God's being, while Barth unequivocally insists that it does not know God at all.[8] For Barth natural theology cannot know even an aspect of God's being because

> God is who He is, the Father, Son and Holy Spirit, Creator, Reconciler and Redeemer, supreme, the one true Lord; and He is known in this entirety or

he is not known at all. There is no existence of God behind or beyond this entirety of His being. Whatever we can know and say about the being of God can only be a continual explanation of this entirety. (*CD* II/1, 51)

Torrance goes on to say that when natural theology is included within our actual knowledge of God through revelation it must be trinitarian in structure. And by this he clearly means that our thinking must correspond to the being and act of God disclosed in and by Christ and the Spirit.[9] But if this is the case, then we no longer have a natural theology at all in any traditional sense. And when Torrance applies the doctrine of justification to say that all our natural goodness and natural knowledge is called into question so that both must find their true meaning only in Christ, it would appear that his positive intention is simply to say that human nature marked by sin is not destroyed but fulfilled by God's grace revealed and active in Christ.[10]

Nevertheless, on this issue Barth and Torrance remain divided because, for Barth, natural theology could only lead to idolatry just because we do not even know God in part without his revelation. What difference does this make in Torrance's theology? As far as I can tell it makes no real difference in his understanding of the incarnation, resurrection, atonement and the Trinity. But it does make a difference in his thinking about the relation of theology and natural science where he occasionally seems to revert to a subtle form of the old natural theology, against his own intentions. This is not the place to discuss this in detail. But some brief indication of what I mean is in order.

While Torrance believes the universe cannot provide an answer to the question of its ultimate intelligibility, he nonetheless contends that "it does more than raise a question for it seems to *cry silently* for a transcendent agency in its explanation and understanding" (*RST*, 58).[11] He also argues that we cannot coerce God by our questions "rather does He coerce us by this silence or emptiness to listen to Him."[12] But is it by this silence that God "coerces" us to listen to him or by the encroachment of his Word and Spirit? And when Torrance says "the combination of unpredictability and lawfulness in nature found in its capacity spontaneously to generate richer and more open-structured forms of order . . . may be regarded as something like the signature of the Creator in the depths of contingent being"[13] his thinking seems to be in conflict with his own conviction that, while God can reveal himself through nature, that does not mean that an examination of nature can actually produce knowledge of God.[14]

Here then is the issue: Torrance maintains that natural theology can only function properly within the sphere of revelation but at the same time says it can and should be artificially bracketed from the material content of theology temporarily as a methodological device to achieve clarity.[15] But therein lies the problem. On the one hand Torrance insists that a proper natural theology cannot be bracketed at all, but must function within the sphere of revelation. But on the other hand his thinking suggests that creation itself cries for an explanation grounded in the Christian God and he believes that this "silent" cry is a touchstone for discussion between theology and science.

Unfortunately, however, he cannot have it both ways. A choice is required here. Either the universe cries silently for the Christian God and that is the locus for scientific theology in relation to natural science or the universe lacks sufficient intelligibility and we must turn to the Christian God and not to its silent cry to understand both its limit and its ultimate intelligibility. Either natural theology functions *solely* within revelation (in which case of course it is no longer natural theology) or it may function prior to and/or apart from revelation, perhaps with its silent cry. But one cannot say that natural theology must function within revelation as Torrance does and then claim that we can achieve clarity by bracketing the material content of theology as Torrance also does. Of course what Torrance really seems to have intended, despite this ambiguity, is a theology of nature in light of revelation; to that extent it would be a mistake to think that he was advocating any sort of traditional natural theology as a touchstone for theology.

That is why there can be little doubt that Torrance's attempt to unite fundamental and dogmatic theology with his new or reformulated natural theology escapes two problems that afflict Rahner's theology. First, Torrance is adamant about the fact that no "logical bridge" can be built from our knowledge of the world to knowledge of God.[16] Indeed, Torrance insists that knowledge of the world is precisely that — knowledge of a world created from nothing by God and existing in true contingence in its dependence upon God for its existence and continuance. That is the difference between natural science and the science of theology. Both deal with distinct objects and each science must operate in accordance with the nature of the object being investigated. Science deals with the world of nature. Theology deals with the God who created nature but who also became incarnate within nature in order to redeem it and did indeed redeem it in and through Christ's resurrection. This self-same God continues to relate with us in space and time as the risen, ascended Lord who will return to complete the redemption at his second coming, without altering created nature in its distinction from God. For Torrance natural theology has its proper place in the "overlap" between theology and science because both approach nature with a unitary view of reality and a view of contingence and freedom originally contributed by Christian theology.[17]

Second, Torrance insists that there can be no *a priori* knowledge of God, revelation or grace and thus no *a priori* understanding of the resurrection or incarnation either. Any such thinking, for Torrance, would represent an attempt by us to create God in our own image either mythologically or existentially. This rejection of *a priori* knowledge in theology is a crucial indication that Torrance really allows the God of Christian revelation to dictate what he has to say about the relationship between the incarnation and the resurrection, as we shall see. And the results are quite interesting because he conveys a startling amount of information that remains more than a little ambiguous in Rahner's thinking just because he believed the incarnation and resurrection disclosed something entirely new and unimaginable to human insight.

Torrance, like Rahner, has forged a unity between fundamental theology and dogmatic theology, and with the exception of these few ambiguities, he unflinchingly moves forward thinking about the resurrection and incarnation as well as space and time from a center in God provided by God in Jesus Christ rather than from a center in human experience or in nature. Unlike Rahner, Torrance insists on allowing the incarnation and the resurrection to interpret themselves to us because, for him, that is the nature of scientific theology. Such theology thinks in accordance with the nature of the reality it is investigating. And since Jesus Christ is utterly unique and cannot be understood outside a specific relationship with him, his uniqueness as God become man dictates the meaning of the resurrection and of our concepts of space and time. It is this starting point that allows Torrance consistently to present a Christology that avoids both the Ebionite and Docetic pitfalls that afflict much contemporary Christology.[18] Let us now consider Torrance's understanding of these doctrines.

Resurrection and Incarnation in the Theology of T. F. Torrance

Torrance wrote his book on the resurrection with his last conversation with Barth in mind because he wanted to stress the centrality of the resurrection for Christian theology and he saw that the connection between the incarnation and the resurrection actually overcame any sort of dualistic interpretation of the theoretical and empirical or of ground and experience. Therefore Torrance seeks to give an account of the resurrection "in the light of its own intrinsic significance which has thrown its integrating light upon the whole of the New Testament" (*STR*, xii). But just how does Torrance envision the relation between systematic theology and NT studies? How does the incarnation shape Torrance's view of space and time?

Allowing his thought to be shaped by the incarnation of the Word into space and time, Torrance begins his analysis by rejecting what he calls "non-cognitive" revelation which he rightly says is detached from the objective structures of space and time.[19] This is why Torrance insists that

> Even though God transcends all that we can think and say of Him, it still holds good that we cannot have experience of Him or believe in Him without conceptual forms of understanding — as Anselm used to say: *fides esse nequit sine conceptione.*[20]

This thinking reflects Torrance's practical avoidance of any sort of Ebionite or Docetic approach to Christology once again because for him Christology is dictated by the unique nature of Jesus Christ himself as disclosed to faith. And if Reformed and Roman Catholic theology could find a way to agree here, then the possibility for wide-ranging agreement would become feasible. But, as we shall see in the next chapter, it is just here that Barth and Torrance stand diametrically opposed to the thinking of Karl Rahner with methodological and practical consequences. In anticipation of such a comparison let us first explore some of the key features of Torrance's view of the incarnation with a view toward seeing why he thinks the container notion of space and time has been and remains so damaging for Christian theology.

Torrance's View of the Incarnation

It is very important to realize that for Torrance the incarnation means the entry of God himself into the sphere of space and time without ceasing to be God.

> By the Incarnation Christian theology means that at a definite point in space and time the Son of God became man, born at Bethlehem of Mary, a virgin espoused to a man called Joseph, a Jew of the tribe and lineage of David, and towards the end of the reign of Herod the Great in Judea. Given the name Jesus, He fulfilled His mission from the Father, living out the span of earthly life allotted to Him until He was crucified under Pontius Pilate, but when after three days He rose again from the dead the eyes of Jesus' disciples were opened to what it all meant: they know Him to be God's Son, declared with power and installed in Messianic Office.[21]

For this reason it is extremely important for Torrance to emphasize both the fact that Jesus Christ, the incarnate Word, is *homoousion* with the Father in his divinity and with us in our humanity. The entire Gospel would lose its saving significance if Jesus were not both truly and fully divine and truly and fully human. Torrance relies on Athanasius to stress that "while everything pivots upon the downright act of God himself in Christ, that act of God takes the concrete form of the actual historical man Jesus" (*TF*, 148). Just as there is one God, so there is one mediator, the man Jesus and his mediation "involved a twofold movement, from God to man and from man to God . . . both divine and human activity in Christ must be regarded as issuing from one Person" (*TF*, 149). Unless Jesus Christ is truly God, we are not in fact saved; unless he is truly human, then salvation has nothing to do with our actual human condition.

That is why Torrance insists "that the incarnation is to be understood as *God really become man.* Jesus Christ is not just man participating in God but is himself essential Deity (οὐσιώδης Θεότης)" (*TF*, 149). God became fully and completely human and dwelt among us as a man but "without of course ceasing to be God the Son" (*TF*, 150).[22] This was a real becoming on God's part so that we must say that God came "*as man* and acts *as man,* all for our sake" (*TF*, 150). This is an important point. God did not become man because of some law of generativity that had to be fulfilled in God or in God's relations with creation. Rather, God loved the world in such a way that he freely condescended to become one of us for our sake, that is, in order to save us from sin, corruption and death itself. In fact his incarnation was "an act of utter self-abasement and humiliation in which he assumed our abject servile condition, our state under the slavery of sin" (*TF*, 153) so that he could reconcile us fully with God the Father.

Kenosis did not mean that there was a "contraction, diminution or self-limitation of God's infinite being" but rather that he loved us in such a "self-abnegating" way that he freely suffered abasement for our sakes (*TF*, 153). And Jesus' humanity was not merely an "instrument" he used to achieve his purposes but his entire human life from birth to death must be understood "in a thoroughly personal and *vicarious* way" (*TF*, 150-51). Here Rahner and Torrance agree that there can be no mythological understanding of the incarnation. If Jesus is just an instrument used by God then there is no real incarnation of God for our sakes. But for Torrance it is Jesus himself, the incarnate Word, and not some symbolic philosophy that dictates his understanding here. For that very reason Torrance eschews both Ebionite and Docetic Christology from the outset and at each point in his reflections and he never separates incarnation from atonement or resurrection.

Significative/Symbolic Understanding
and the Container Concept of Space

For Torrance the Nicene Creed was carefully constructed so that statements of the Nicene fathers could not vary with each person's perspective but rather signified realities they intended in their statements. In other words their statements were "controlled by the reality intended" (*STI*, 2). That raises the question of how to interpret the spatial statements of the Creed. If they are merely symbolic, then there is no difficulty in interpreting them metaphorically; but then, according to Torrance, they would not actually signify or describe God's nature and so would not offer us any definite understanding of God himself. So Torrance wishes to understand the spatial statements of the Creed by beginning with God the Father almighty, the creator. Because God transcends creation "It follows that the relation between God and space is not itself a spatial relation" (*STI*, 2).

This is an extremely important point because it enabled Athanasius to respond to the Arian questions about whether God was in a place or without a place by saying that such questions were "nonsensical" because they supposed that "God can be thought of in a way parallel with ourselves" (*STI*, 2). In a similar way then when the Creed says the Son came down from heaven this is not to be understood as "a journey through space" (*STI*, 2). It is instead to be understood relationally and theologically in accordance with the statements that the Son is God from God and Light from Light. What this means above all is that the relation between the incarnate Son and the Father "cannot be spatialized . . . even if we could conceive of a heaven of heavens we could not think of this as containing God. . . . God is the transcendent Creator of the whole realm of space and stands in a creative, not a spatial or a temporal relation, to it" (*STI*, 3).

Therefore, God cannot be included within space and time as we creatures exist in space and time; this was the error that developed in the second and third centuries when God was mythologically synthesized with the cosmos so that a conception of "intervening space between God and man" arose in conflict with the thinking espoused at Nicaea. For the Nicene theologians God personally interacted with us in space and time with the result that "what [the Son] was towards us in His incarnate activity He was inherently, and therefore antecedently and eternally, in Himself" so that his condescension did not indicate a finite imperfection but rather expressed his self-humiliation for our sakes. Hence "He was not creaturely or space-conditioned in His own eternal Being" (*STI*, 3). Further, when the Creed asserts that his Kingdom will have no end it really means that the Son's assumption of human nature was not "merely economic" or temporary but that his genuine involvement in our humanity must be maintained "without reserve" after his resurrection, ascension and *parousia.*

This relational concept of space that was crucial for Nicene theology came into conflict with the dominating view of Greek thought which was to conceive of space as a *"receptacle* or a *container" (STI,* 4). We cannot get into all the details and nuances of how this concept arose in early Greek philosophy and how it took shape among Plato, the Stoics and Aristotelians. A detailed account of this can be found in chapter 1 of *Space, Time and Incarnation.* Suffice it to say that for Torrance, Aristotle misunderstood Plato and developed a "predominantly volumetric conception of space" according to which space or place "was the vessel . . . into which and out of which things pass and which not only contains them but exercises a certain force or causal activity . . . in relation to them" *(STI,* 7). Thus arose a "receptacle notion of space in which there is a relation of interdependence between the container and its contents" *(STI,* 7) while place was defined as "the immobile limit within which a body is contained" *(STI,* 8) so that there could be no void or empty space. According to Torrance, Aristotle's view of space was static because it was determined by the idea of a point of absolute rest in accordance with his doctrine of the "unmoved Mover." Volume was then equated with a spatial magnitude so that space became isolated from time and the concept of space became so rigid that Aristotle had to introduce "a highly artificial disjunction of substance and accidents" that led to the endless difficulties of Western medieval theology *(STI,* 8-9).[23] The most important point to be made here is that the Aristotelian concept of space "found no place at all in the Nicene theology. Its rejection meant also the rejection of a strict receptacle view of space and the cataphatic conceptualism that went along with it" *(STI,* 11).

It is in light of the *creatio ex nihilo* that theologians could say that God does not participate in being since everything else participates in him to exist. "God Himself, then, cannot be conceived as existing in a temporal or spatial relation to the universe" *(STI,* 11). God cannot be contained by anything but rather he contains everything by his power — not however in the manner of a bodily container. When the incarnation is seen in its proper relation to creation then it will also be seen that in the incarnation Christ cannot have the same space relation to the Father that we have. Because Athanasius never accepted the dualistic separation of the sensible and intelligible worlds he also refused to think of the incarnate Son and the Father in terms of a receptacle notion of space. That would lead to what Torrance calls false kenoticism, namely, theories that fail to think of the Father and Son "in accordance with their natures" as fully divine in their mutual indwelling; in other words such thinking inevitably fails to take seriously the fullness or the perfection of the Son and Father together. This thinking allows Torrance to maintain a number of crucial christological insights.

First, instead of thinking of space and time from a "point of absolute rest" Nicene theology started with Christ who is the eternal Word through whom both the visible and invisible were made and who guides the entire universe and holds it in being. Second, while Christ was not far off from creation before the incarnation, "He is fully present with us in space and time and yet remains present with the Father" (STI, 14). But of course this can never obscure the fact that incarnation was something new for God in that just as God was always Father, but not always creator, so God was always Son, but was not always incarnate.[24] Third, the Word was outside all created things in essence, but in all events and things by virtue of his power. Fourth, "He did not activate the body He assumed from us in such a way as to cease to deploy Himself actively throughout the universe in all its dimensions" (STI, 14). Fifth, since the Word is the unique occupant of space in the incarnation we are obliged to say that he shared our physical space with us; but he did so in such a way that he never ceased being the eternal Word that he always was. This means that

> the spatial ingredient in the concept of the Incarnation must be interpreted from the side of His active and controlling occupation of bodily existence and place. Space is here a predicate of the Occupant, is determined by His agency, and is to be understood in accordance with His nature. (STI, 14-15)

It is this all-important point that is decisive also for Torrance's understanding of the resurrection: the subject of the resurrection for Torrance is a

> a divine-human subject, and therefore [Christ's resurrection is] a unique happening defined by the nature of the unique Agent. Other human agents were involved in the life of Jesus . . . but because we have here a different Subject, the Son of God incarnate in human existence in space and time, we have to understand the inner movement of his history in a way appropriate to his nature — that applies to his birth, to the whole of his life, and to his resurrection. (STR, 94)

And that is why Torrance insists that "It is through the Spirit that we may understand the resurrection of Jesus in accordance with its own inner and free happening, as the sovereign act of its Subject" (STR, 95). That is why the resurrection must be understood enhypostatically and anhypostatically; but if it is only understood anhypostatically then it will not be seen as historical.

What all of this means is that our ordinary use of the concepts of place and space had to be changed in light of who Jesus was as the incarnate Word. While the Word is "in" the Father and "in" us by virtue of the incarnation, we can only understand what this means when we allow our creaturely concepts to point beyond themselves to the reality of God in Christ without blurring the distinction between the creaturely and the divine. Following Athanasius, Torrance opts for analogies that find their basis in Christ and are not arbitrarily chosen by us. Thus all concepts of space as "infinite receptacle or infinite substance, or as extension conceived as the essence of matter, or as a mere necessity of our human apprehension, and certainly the concept of space in terms of the ultimate immobile limit of the container independent of time, all fall away" in favor of a relational concept grounded in the incarnation (*STI*, 17-18). When the receptacle notion of space is dropped, then the incarnation is understood in a way which does not confine the Son in the limit of his body in such a way that "the universe was left empty of His government" (*STI*, 18). Here Torrance stresses the familiar theme that if our terms are to have a meaning beyond their ordinary use in human experience, then they must "have a transcendental reference to what is really beyond them," but this "must be given them by God Himself" (*STI*, 19).

How then do we speak of the incarnation without projecting the limitations of creaturely time into God who transcends time? For instance we say that after the incarnation God was at work in space and time in a way that he was not previously. There are elements of time even in that statement. Our thinking can never be cut loose from its moorings in time and space and so for Torrance the only way it can refer to the transcendent God who is not part of space and time is if it points beyond itself to God. But our language can only do that "on the ground of His interaction with the world He has created and within the relation that He has established between it and Himself" (*STI*, 55). This is why it is imperative in Torrance's thinking to understand incarnation and creation together just as it is vital to understand incarnating, resurrection and ascension together. What specifically is to be gained by rejecting a receptacle notion of space and time and replacing it with the Nicene relational concept? Before answering this question, it will be important to describe Torrance's view of the matter.

There are two forms of the receptacle notion that have been influential in the course of history and today, namely, the idea of the finite receptacle and the idea of the infinite receptacle. In Greek thought both primarily had to do with space, according to Torrance. The former (space as finite receptacle) implies that space was not independent of what went on within it since anything other than a determinate existence was thought to be unintelligible. According to Torrance, in Aristotelian and Stoic thought, this meant that both the universe and God were conceived as finite. This concept of space was rejected by Patristic theology but re-entered Western thought under the category of magnitude "apart from the conception of time" and so led simultaneously to a pantheistic and dualistic view of God's relation with the world (*STI*, 56-57). The latter (space as infinite receptacle) implies that space was independent of what happened within it and so was conceived as "'the great void.'" This view was held by both Atomists and Pythagoreans and "tended either towards materialism and atheism or to a conception of a detached unknowable deity calling for mystical, non-rational communion" (*STI*, 57). This receptacle notion had also been rejected by the church Fathers but re-entered Western thought through the Florentine Academy and was adopted and elaborated by Newton with the result that a dualistic view of space and matter became the order of the day. Newton's view of God then tended both toward pantheism, with the idea that God and the world had space and time in common and toward dualistic separation of God and the world, with the deistic idea that God was separate from the world. This led to a new and more rigid natural theology which attempted to overcome pantheism and deism.

When we follow Patristic theology and think of creation and incarnation in relational terms and drop the receptacle notion of space and time in both its forms, several positive implications follow. First, the Christian doctrine of creation from nothing means that God has made the universe out of nothing and made it with an inherent intelligibility that is knowable. God the creator remains distinct from the world and so cannot be known in the way created things are known just as the world of nature, in its distinction from God, can be known "in its natural processes only out of itself" (*STI*, 59). From a theological point of view the world is to be seen as subsisting in God's creative Word since God freely maintains the world in existence and is free to be present in it and to realize its reality in relation to his purposes. From a natural point of view, we can understand the world in accordance with its natural intelligibility from within itself. Because of this relationship between God and nature Torrance can say that "nature by itself speaks only ambiguously of God, for while it may be interpreted as pointing intelligibly beyond itself to God, it does not permit any necessary inferences from its contingence to God" (*STI* 59-60). Second, this means that space and time cannot be included with God as in Newton's thinking because the doctrine of creation "excludes any mythological synthesis between God and the universe, God and nature, or between the divine reality and this-worldly reality. God stands in a transcendent and creative, not a spatial or temporal, relation to the creaturely world" (*STI*, 60). Third, the relation between the incarnate Son in space and time and his Father cannot be spatialized or temporalized. Fourth, any retreat into spaceless and timeless relations to explain God's relations with us in space and time would only lead to pantheism and dualism.[25]

What then is gained in Christology and in our concept of the hypostatic union if the container or receptacle notions of space and time are discounted and the Nicene understanding is embraced? First, we will no longer think of the incarnation as the Son entering a finite receptacle. Any idea that the humanity of Christ should be seen as the earthen vessel into which the Son of God "emptied himself" is to be rejected. Ultimately such thinking opens the door to Monophysitism and gives rise either to the idea that Christ's deity is restricted or to the idea that Jesus is simply another object of history; under the influence of Kantian thought this latter difficulty became worse when the receptacle idea was seen to reside in the human mind. Second, we must reject the idea that God himself should be seen as "the infinite receptacle, *infinitum capax finiti*" (*STI*, 63). This inherently dualistic view meant that it would be impossible to take the incarnation seriously "for if God is the infinite container of all being He can no more be one of the particular beings He contains than a vessel can at the same time be one of the things contained in it" (*STI*, 63). This view led directly to Arianism and deism. And that deism, which is a form of dualism, has influenced contemporary views of history and of God's relations with the world along Kantian lines. That is why Torrance insists that "both forms of the receptacle idea of space and time must be rejected" (*STI*, 63).

According to Torrance another way of thinking of the incarnation must also be avoided and that is the approach offered by Origen and adopted in modern theology by E. A. Milne. Briefly, this view holds that since God has endowed the world with a created intelligibility we may know God within space and time through the medium of history and we may then be delivered from a sense of meaninglessness since the world's ultimate meaning could be found in God. But for Origen this implied the "eternal coexistence of the universe in the mind of God" (*STI*, 64). He tried to guard against that idea by asserting God's priority even over his own intelligence. But in the thought of E. A. Milne this thinking implied "a necessary relation between them" and so compromised the contingent nature of the universe and came to mean a "limitation of God since he is not free from a relation of necessity between His transcendent rationality and that of the material universe" (*STI*, 64). This ultimately leads to a kind of pantheistic confusion of divine and created objectivity.

Finally, Torrance advocates a view that he traces from Patristic theology, through Anselm, Duns Scotus, Pascal and Karl Barth: God remains free from any sort of necessity in his relationship with creation. With respect to the incarnation this means that he assumes "created truth and rationality" and while making them his own, he distinguishes himself from them as well. One of the hazards in this view is the Occamist danger that would suggest that God remains finally inscrutable because knowledge of God was made to be completely dependent on his will and was not connected with the truth of his Being. This was not a danger for Anselm who held that while God remains transcendent and free over all our conceptions of him, nonetheless, when we do conceive God in truth we do so "under the compulsion of the divine Being. Created rationalities thus embody an element of necessity, i.e. their impossibility of being other than they are, in relation to the Supreme Truth of God" (*STI*, 65). Torrance accepts Anselm's approach and argues that there is a closer connection between theological concepts and those of natural science than could be found in Barth's thinking.

Ultimately what Torrance wants to affirm then is that while there is no necessary relation of God with the world that can be discovered through any *a priori* conceptualities, nevertheless, we must understand the incarnation

> as the chosen path of God's rationality in which He interacts with the world and establishes such a relation between creaturely being and Himself that He will not allow it to slip away from Him into futility or nothingness . . . while the Incarnation does not mean that God is limited by space and time, it asserts the reality of space and time for God in the actuality of His relations with us, and at the same time binds us to space and time in all our relations with Him. (*STI*, 67)

That is the sense in which the incarnation is necessary. It is not necessary for God to be God. It is only necessary in the sense that once it has taken place there is no way for God or for us to go back on the reality of that unique expression of divine love. Hence there is no way to try to relate with God in a way that would ignore space and time and the path (incarnation in Christ) that God himself has chosen to love us and to have communion with us. This then is the reason why Torrance rejects any form of non-conceptual theological knowledge.

Resurrection and the Trinity

At the same time Torrance also rejects any notion of faith that is not correlated with God's objective revelation as this can be apprehended by us in a rational manner (*STR*, 2). It is precisely some sort of non-cognitive notion of revelation, with its corresponding view of faith, that is behind what Torrance calls the "fatal deistic disjunction" between God and the world that refuses to allow for the fact that God's Word "can cross the gulf between God and the creature" and "permit man in space and time any real knowledge of God as he is in himself" (*STR*, 2). This is a crucial point in all of Torrance's theology but it is significant that the question of our knowledge of God arises here in connection with his consideration of the resurrection. Torrance insists that apart from the resurrection we could not say that "we creatures of space and time may know God the Father, in such a way as to think and speak truly and validly of him" (*STR*, 71). It is because the resurrection enables us to understand that "Jesus Christ is himself the Truth" and as the risen Lord "remains Truth, uncreated Truth and created truth in one. He is not simply the eternal Logos of God, but that Logos become flesh . . . not simply Word of God addressed to man, but answering word of man addressed to God in the unity of his one Person" (*STR*, 70-71). Here, in the incarnate Word, our knowledge of God finds a center in God and in creaturely reality that guarantees the validity of our knowledge of God as he is in himself (the immanent Trinity) without leaving the sphere of space and time.

For Torrance our knowledge of God is actually a sharing in Jesus' human knowledge of God and also a sharing in the very being of God.[26] That is what guarantees its objectivity. Hence

> The resurrection is therefore our pledge that statements about God in Jesus Christ have an objective reference in God, and are not just projections out of the human heart and imagination, objectifying forms of thought in which we fashion a God in terms of the creaturely content of our own ideas. (*STR*, 72-73)

Here then is the all-important connection between the resurrection and incarnation that enables contemporary theology to avoid any sort of agnosticism that might open the door to the destructive and dangerous idea that we can and should name God from our experiences in order to make theology relevant.[27]

Any denial of Christ's bodily resurrection then would be a clear indication of a denial of the reality and importance of the immanent Trinity, which for Torrance, undergirds the entire truth of theology, including the theology of the incarnation and resurrection. That is why he places strong emphasis upon the *homoousion*. Unless the Son is one in being with the Father from all eternity and unless our knowledge of the Spirit is governed by that unique relation of the Father and Son so that the Spirit too is one in being with the Father and Son from all eternity, we have neither true knowledge of God nor genuine reconciliation with God nor eternal life. For this reason, as already seen in connection with the incarnation, Torrance repeatedly insists that what God is toward us in Jesus Christ and the Holy Spirit he is eternally in himself.[28] This does not represent an arbitrary reading back of human experience into God. For that is what the Arians did. Rather it represents an understanding of God from a center in God provided in Christ and the Spirit and therefore not from a center in ourselves. That is why the Trinity is so central to Torrance's thinking. But the doctrine is not a description of human experience. Instead it is a description of the eternal God who is Father, Son and Holy Spirit and who by virtue of the incarnation and resurrection meets us within the sphere of space and time without ceasing to be God so that he can heal and overcome the effects of sin and bring about a new creation that will be fully manifest when the ascended Christ returns to complete the redemption. This is why Torrance believes, correctly, that knowing God through God alone and thus through his self-revelation

> does not mean that the doctrine of the Trinity is a postulate of revelation, as if it could be argued that because God reveals himself in this way he must be a Trinity in himself, for that would mean that the Trinity is not itself part of the divine revelation but only an inference from it. . . . God reveals himself to us in a three-fold form and a three-fold way, as he who reveals himself, as he who is the content of his revelation.[29]

It is in this sense that Jesus Christ is the guarantee of our knowledge of God and our participation in God's own self-knowledge and love. We become, in the words of 2 Pet. 1:4, "partakers of the divine nature" in such a way that our difference from the Son in his unique relation with the Father is not compromised:

> for he is God the Son in the unity of the Holy Trinity, but the resurrection of our human nature in him implies a reconciliation or oneness with God which is not identity, yet a real sharing in the union of the incarnate Son with the Father, through a sharing not only in his human nature but in the life and love of God embodied in him. (*STR,* 70)[30]

Torrance means what he says here. He is willing to interpret Athanasius' "unfortunate"[31] statement that "He became man that we might be made divine" (*De Inc.* 54) to mean that we "partake of God" through Christ who "is himself fully and wholly God." Christ is not divine because he participates in God but because he is one in being with the Father. This Word incarnate acts on us in a creative and divine way to enable this partaking. Θεοποίησις or θέωσις describes

> the unique act of God incarnate in Jesus Christ, but act which inheres in his divine being and is inseparable from it. . . . Jesus Christ *is* in his incarnate Person the unique act of God whereby we are saved and made new, but . . . we are not saved or renewed by the activity of Christ without being united to him and partaking of him. (*TF,* 139)

Torrance clearly stresses that Christ alone is true God of true God and therefore the Lord and that we "are adopted and made sons of God in him." For that reason and in that way we are partakers of the divine life through union with Christ and by the grace of the Holy Spirit. Torrance therefore rejects ideas of divinization which do not maintain this clear distinction in union and tend to identify human and divine being.[32] That is why Torrance insists that grace is no created medium between us and God. Rather grace is God's act in Jesus Christ so that it must be acknowledged that Gift and Giver are one. Grace cannot be regarded as "a detachable and transferable quality which may inhere in or be possessed by the human being to whom it is given in virtue of which he is somehow 'deified' or 'divinised'" (*TF,* 140).

Torrance maintains that the grace of Christ must be understood in the same way that we understand the Holy Spirit as Lord and giver of life. Citing Athanasius, Torrance writes: "The Holy Spirit is always the same, and does not belong to those who partake, but all things partake of him" (*TF,* 140). Because grace as God's self-giving cannot be separated from him in any way: "This self-giving of God in grace is no more divisible than the one being and activity of the Holy Trinity" (*TF,* 141). Therefore there can be no suggestion that human or divine nature changes through *theopoiesis* because in the incarnation the Word was not less divine by becoming human and we are not less human by being enabled to partake of his human and divine natures. What makes us "divine" in the sense of Athanasius' "unfortunate" statement mentioned above is that "the Word of God has come to us and acts directly upon us, or more concretely the fact that in Jesus Christ the Son of God has become man and thus brought us into kinship with himself" (*TF,* 189). This notion of "deification" "more than recreates our lost humanity, for it lifts us up in Christ to enjoy a new fullness of human life in a blessed communion with divine life" (*TF*, 189).

Further, Torrance makes an extremely important point here noting that *theopoiesis* means that it is the Holy Spirit dwelling within us that enables us to be "partakers of God beyond ourselves." Because of the atonement that took place through Christ's incarnation this has become possible. According to Irenaeus it is because of the incarnation that the Holy Spirit "descended upon man in Christ and became accustomed to dwell in humanity" so that humanity could dwell in God. In Athanasius' view, Christ sanctified himself by receiving the Holy Spirit — he literally gave himself the Spirit in the incarnation so that "the Spirit's descent on him in Jordan was a descent upon us because of his bearing our body. This did not take place for the promotion of the Word himself, but for our sanctification, that we might share in his anointing" (*TF*, 190). This twofold giving and receiving of the Spirit is, according to Torrance, the actualizing of atonement in the depths of human being. It is in this sense that Pentecost is not something added on to the atonement but rather "the actualisation within the life of the Church of the atoning life, death and resurrection of the Saviour" (*TF*, 190).

Ethical Implications of Our Justification by Faith

Because of this Torrance is adamant that salvation cannot be understood properly if there is even the slightest hint of self-justification or self-sanctification. Because Christ's priesthood arises out of his Sonship he makes true atonement and as the risen and ascended Lord he not only completed our redemption in time and place once and for all but his priestly sacrifice and oblation of himself "are taken up eternally into the life of God, and remain prevalent, efficacious, valid, or abidingly real" (*STR*, 114-15). That is part of the significance of the ascension. Because Christ has ascended in his divinity and humanity he represents us eternally and this rules out any Pelagian idea of us offering an immolated Christ to the Father or of us offering ourselves in addition to Christ in the Lord's Supper. By its very nature Christ's sacrifice is offered on our behalf and in our place "so that it is not we but Christ himself who here stands in for us as our Mediator and Advocate, while we take refuge in his sole sacrifice, finding shelter in his prayer and intercession and not in our own" (*STR*, 117). But it is important to realize that the ascension itself points us to the historical Jesus attested in scripture for a true understanding of all this.

Torrance thus strongly opposes all notions of conditional salvation: "if divine forgiveness were conditional on our responses, we would never be saved."[33] It is precisely because Christ died for us while we were still sinners that

> we must think of him as having died for all people while they are yet sinners irrespective of their response. Just as the cross is proclaimed to all, so the total forgiveness and the total judgment it involves are proclaimed to all, whether they believe or not. (*PCT,* 36)

Hence both the judgment enacted and exhibited on the cross and the grace of forgiveness disclosed in Christ's resurrection are not "offered" to us or given to us based on "some condition being met by us." Rather Christ's unconditional grace is proclaimed as the summons to repent and believe. But in repenting and believing we too come under God's judgment, according to Torrance, so that even our most fervent prayers and our strongest faith and worship are shown to be "unclean in God's sight." This, because our free-will is marked by our *self*-will and so there is a "subtle Pelagianism of the human heart, that comes under the judgment of Christ's unconditional forgiveness" (*PCT,* 36). Even in our faith and worship we are trapped within ourselves so that we "are cast wholly and unreservedly upon the unconditional forgiveness of Christ Jesus . . . we are thrown upon Christ alone and are saved by grace alone" (*PCT,* 36). This is no cheap grace in Torrance's view but a costly grace because our free will which we so cherish is taken from us by being exposed as a kind of self-will which no one is free to escape. Torrance argues that this costliness of grace is what people resent. The cost is our entire selves. We must hand ourselves over to Christ. There can be no self-reliance at all. Torrance abhors contemporary preaching and teaching that suggest some sort of "co-redemption" which occurs when people are told that they will not be saved

> *unless* they make the work of Christ real for themselves by their own personal decision, or that they will be saved *only if* they repent and believe, for this is to make the effectiveness of the work of Christ conditional upon what the sinner does, and so at the crucial point it throws the ultimate responsibility for man's salvation back upon himself. (*God and Rationality,* 58)[34]

That, Torrance believes, is very far from the NT picture of salvation. For if we are thrown back on ourselves in any sense, then we are truly lost because then salvation in the end depends on our adding our last "weak link" to the chain of salvation. And that is exactly what we are unable to do just because of the nature of sin. That is hardly good news! For Torrance, however, the NT message is quite different. It proclaims that Christ's work of atonement and reconciliation is finished and "*therefore* it calls for repentance and the obedience of faith, but never does it say: This is what God in Christ has done for you, and you can be saved on condition that you repent and believe" (*God and Rationality*, 58). This, for Torrance, is another Gospel because "It is not faith that justifies us, but Christ in whom we have faith" (*God and Rationality*, 58).[35]

Because of this Torrance emphasizes that Christian ethics is determined by God's free unconditional forgiveness exercised in Christ so that it is neither the law nor our behavior that justifies us but Christ himself, with the result that ethics can never be seen as "a prolongation of man's already existing experience, and a reduction of it to what his previous knowledge includes" (*God and Rationality*, 62).[36] Justification means that God himself has intervened in our "ethical predicament" and thus has overcome our free-will which is our self-will; hence while we cannot overcome the vicious circle created by our self-will in order to be free for God and our neighbor, God in Christ has already done this and thus has enabled our human freedom once again. Because of Christ's death and resurrection we are now free to obey God without worrying about our motives and we are also free from self-concern and self-understanding so that we "may love both God and our neighbour objectively for their own sakes" (*God and Rationality*, 63). This involves a "moral revolution" that places all our ethical relations on an entirely new basis. This happens when Christ occupies the center of human existence.

Here Torrance stresses his all-important point that when Christ is allowed to disappear behind his benefits, that is, when God for us is reduced to what he did for us in Christ, then the person of Christ is determined by our value judgments and he ceases to be the unique God acting for us *as* man. The atonement then is no longer rooted ontologically in Christ or in God, and salvation is then detached from his person, being and action and located in timeless events having no relation to history. This thinking requires that we are thrown back on ourselves so that in interpreting our own existence we "read out of it only what we have first read into it" (*God and Rationality*, 64). And Torrance rightly insists that everything depends on who Jesus was so that his death in itself did not constitute the atonement, but his death as the Son of God sacrificing himself for us did. Therefore "we must allow the Person of Christ to determine for us the nature of His saving work, rather than the other way round. The detachment of atonement from incarnation is undoubtedly revealed by history to be one of the most harmful mistakes of Evangelical Churches" (*God and Rationality*, 64). Among other things such thinking leads to the idea that it is perhaps our orthodoxy that saves us, whereas Torrance insists that even in our orthodoxy we are in "untruth." Hence, to boast of our orthodoxy is to claim that we are somehow already in the truth and do not have to be placed there by God's grace. In Torrance's words,

> It is a form of self-justification in which we claim that we are able to verify and justify our own beliefs and statements, whereas he who really knows the grace of God knows that he is unable to compel God to be the truth of what he says about Him. (*God and Rationality*, 67)

The epistemological significance of justification then is that we are directed unequivocally to Christ for the truth of our existence and this means that the criterion of truth can never be found within the knower. Justification therefore is cheap, Torrance says, because it is given to us without a price or condition. But it is also difficult or costly because it devalues our own moral self-understanding or religious self-understanding as a basis for our salvation. Torrance argues that we today want "cheap grace," that is, grace that does not cost us anything or ask us to deny ourselves to take up our cross and follow Christ. Because we do not want a grace that breaks in upon us "from beyond all human possibility" (*God and Rationality*, 71), we think it is the task of the church to make grace comprehensible on the basis of our religious and moral self-understanding. But for Torrance the Gospel cannot be commended to people within the framework of their existing natural knowledge (*God and Rationality*, 72).

This is why Torrance stresses that the resurrection takes place as the redemption of time: "it takes place within the nomistic character of our existence, and yet emancipates us from it into a new relationship with God the Father" (*STR*, 96). What Torrance means by our nomistic existence is our existence in fallen time marked by the law, i.e., *nomos*. The curse of the law of which St. Paul speaks refers to our existence in fallen time which is marked by sin and death in which our lives once lived cannot be undone. We therefore need to be redeemed from this curse of the law; and that is why redemption took the form of justification "under the law" and yet "apart from the law" (Rom. 7:8ff. and Gal. 4:4-5). It is in this sense that Torrance believes we are prisoners of "an ethical or legal order" (*STR*, 97) from which we cannot extricate ourselves just because we cannot do the one thing necessary for our existence, that is, obey God unequivocally. It is important to realize here that it is because of the resurrection that time is actually redeemed. It is recreated and not annihilated "for it is taken up in Christ, sanctified in his human life and transformed in his resurrection as man" (*STR*, 98). There is in the hypostatic union of Christ's divine and human natures a hypostatic union between eternity and time and thus between eternity and new time or redeemed time. Jesus' resurrection and exaltation to the Father's right hand means that our human time is taken up into God. Hence "In Christ the life of human being is wedded to eternal life" (*STR*, 98). What is disclosed in the ascension is that the time of the new creation "is hidden from us" and "held back until in the mercy of God Jesus Christ comes again to judge and renew all his creation" (*STR*, 98). Still, Torrance insists that our creaturely and temporal human nature is redeemed, renewed and established by being taken up into the life of God himself.

Torrance thinks of our participation in new creation and redeemed time eschatologically by stressing that the church is the body of the crucified, risen and ascended Christ. Even though the church is on earth and within history it participates in "his risen power" and thus lives in two times: the time of this passing world and ongoing history "but also in the time of the risen Saviour and of the new creation that is already a perfect reality in him. This happens through the *koinonia* of the Spirit" (*STR*, 99). For this reason the church continues to live on earth by being crucified with Christ to this world's time form while yet fulfilling its mission within the temporal and nomistic structures of this world. Thus,

> though risen with Christ and already a partaker through the Spirit in the new creation, the Church is sent like Christ into the world as the servant of the Lord, humbling itself and containing itself in *kenosis* within the limits and laws of this world in order to proclaim the Gospel of reconciliation and to live out reconciliation within the conditions of fallen human existence . . . to keep vigil as those who are already risen with Christ and wait his coming for their final release . . . into the fullness of our inheritance in the new creation. (*STR*, 99)

Resurrection and Biblical Interpretation in Torrance

It is important to realize that Torrance begins his treatment of the resurrection by rejecting non-cognitive revelation and faith because when such thinking is applied to the study of the Bible then

> the Bible is treated, and interpreted, in such a way as to bracket off the surface text and the phenomenal events it may describe from the objective, intelligible depth of God's active self-revelation, as though it were not

academically respectable to take God or his self-revelation into account! (*STR*, 3)

When such thinking is employed, then the Bible is thought to embody whatever people believe based on the particular cultural standards in effect at the time. Torrance rightly insists that such thinking imagines that we have no access to "standards of truth and falsity" which transcend particular times and cultures and "might limit imaginative construction or subjective fantasies!" (*STR*, 3). Accordingly, it is thought that the Bible has to be re-translated into our modern cultural context in order to be understood and made relevant. In that way the Bible becomes "a nose of wax" which can be bent according to whatever interpretation we may wish to impose upon it. Torrance is distinctive among contemporary theologians for insisting that the ontological objectivity of the biblical witness cannot be supplied by our cultural, historical, existential or idealistic pursuits but rather by "the living, acting, revealing, judging, reconciling God" (*STR*, 3).[37] He certainly does not deny that the Gospel must make sense to modern culture in its own idiom; he only denies that this can happen properly if we consider scripture without its theological content.

Accordingly, Torrance objects to employing the historical-critical method in historicist fashion or in a "phenomenalist" or "positivist" way. He refuses to base his biblical analysis on the "assured results" of research that is determined or predetermined by "uncritical epistemological assumptions." Torrance believes that it is just the "pseudo-assumption" that there can be no objective standards transcending culture and time that leads to the consecration of "spurious ideas . . . in the name of 'historico-critical scholarship'" (*STR*, 3). While not rejecting historical criticism, Torrance rejects the attempt to make historical analysis the key to biblical interpretation apart from faith, that is, apart from the ontological objectivity supplied by God himself in his revelation.[38] Torrance recognizes the complexity of the resurrection narratives, including their difficulties and contradictions. He is no fundamentalist. But he quite properly refuses to allow any social, cultural or philosophical *a priori* assumptions to dictate the meaning of the biblical texts. He wants to allow the texts to interpret themselves to us. And they can do this only if they are allowed to present both the history and the theology they intend to convey. History detached from theology results in historicism while theology detached from history results in mythology. Hence,

> we can interpret the resurrection only if we interpret it theologically as well as historically. It will not do, however, to interpret it merely 'theologically'

as if it could be done apart from history, for that would mythologize and docetize it, and then we would have nothing to interpret. Nor can we interpret it merely 'historically' in the sense that we interpret other historical events . . . for that would be tantamount to insisting that all we have here is an ordinary historical happening, and so to rejecting from the start the claim that the Agent is the Son of God. (*STR*, 94)

That is why Torrance notes that the "quest of the historical Jesus" invariably involves just this falsification of Jesus' person and so amounts to an unscientific approach to the NT (*STR*, 95).

What then is the standard of truth to which Torrance appeals when reading the reports of the NT? Torrance insists that theologians must understand the NT reports "in the light of the reality which they claim to indicate" and try to "understand that reality in its own right, independent of the reports, by letting his mind fall under the power of its intrinsic significance" (*STR*, 5). In a manner reminiscent of Barth's interpretation of Hilary, Torrance asserts that the theologian should interpret the reports "not by subjecting the reality they indicate to the reports but by subjecting the reports to the reality" (*STR*, 6).[39] In this regard Torrance wants to avoid any kind of nominalism or extreme realism that would equate the realities spoken of in scripture with the linguistic forms used to refer to them. Torrance will not accept the results of historical criticism if those results have been reached by tearing apart the empirical and theoretical components in the reports; additionally he rejects the idea that kerygmatic material can be separated from the didactic material with the idea that the later material arose from within the church rather than from the Gospel itself. If the facts are not disconnected from their ontological foundation in the reality of God's self-revealing activity attested in the texts, then there will be no need to construct an artificial framework to connect "kerygma" and "dogma" once again.

An example of what Torrance objects to here is the refusal of many scholars, "irrespective of textual evidence, to accept the commission of the risen Lord to baptize in the Name of the Father and of the Son and of the Holy Spirit as belonging to the original evangelical tradition, not to mention its derivation from Jesus himself" (*STR*, 7).[40] Torrance believes that the connection between that and Jesus' baptism, along with the word of the Father and the descent of the Spirit, clearly suggests just the opposite to theologians who do not disjoin the empirical from the theoretical.[41] Clearly Torrance wants to oppose any sort of fundamentalism that would equate the reality of revelation with the words used to express that revelation and any sort of liberalism that supposes that revelation simply refers to the content of one's faith experience and nothing more.[42] For Torrance scientific theology is not primarily concerned with thinking thoughts but with "thinking realities through thoughts and statements" that are "objectively and ontologically controlled by the intrinsic connections of God's *self*-communication as Father, Son and Holy Spirit" (*STR*, 8).

Torrance also rejects the dualistic approach that would attempt to deduce doctrine or dogma from "observational data" regarded as "raw" or "'uninterpreted' facts." Such thinking Torrance believes is the consequence of a type of "observationalist" view of science indebted to Newton's belief that his hypotheses were not invented because they were deduced "from appearances or phenomena" (*STR*, 8). Torrance rejects this dualistic conception of science that supposes there are "raw facts" with no interpretation from which science then makes its "direct" observations. Such thinking disjoins scientific constructs from being or ontology and leads people to impose their thinking onto reality rather than to recognize reality through their thinking. When such thinking was applied to history in the nineteenth century by Collingwood and Dilthey, a "positivist notion of natural science" was juxtaposed "with a somewhat idealist notion of history" with the result that historical investigation "became inevitably trapped within the fatal disjunction and artificial connection of the empirical and theoretical components of knowledge" (*STR*, 9). Because "historical criticism," necessary though it was and is, arose out of this historicizing of the human sciences "it was developed and employed in forms which carried with them the basic errors and limitations that beset nineteenth-century thought from which historical criticism has not yet broken free" (*STR*, 9). The way forward is to be found by theology following the scientific method of Einstein and allowing the real to manifest itself without carving it up into "analytic particulars."[43] Theologians cannot derive genuine concepts from "analytical particulars" and thus cannot accept the results of historical criticism that ignore the real in its depth by equating it with observed raw facts.[44]

Furthermore, Torrance rejects source-critical claims to establish a "basic layer," whether written or oral, that is "stripped clear of 'later dogmatic accretions'" from which theology must work (*STR*, 10). This type of what Torrance labels "Q fundamentalism" would ignore the fact that certain ontological factors associated with God's self-revealing activity attested in the traditions were involved in the development of these traditions. Theologians are concerned with the different layers of tradition "only as they are integrated with a bearing on the saving acts of God in Jesus Christ" (*STR*, 10). This is an extremely important point and it leads Torrance to assert that not only can we not explain how our insights are controlled by God's self-revelation, but we cannot say exactly how ideas are related to the realities we experience and apprehend . . . for this is a relation of an ontological kind which by its very nature eludes . . . analytical explicitation and formalization; yet it is in and through that very relation alone that we can attain genuine knowledge of the realties concerned. (*STR*, 11)

By dwelling on the semantic focus of the NT, theologians gradually understand by allowing their thinking to be guided by "the intelligible power of those events and realities" intended by the words of scripture. Theologians thus understand the biblical message and reports "under the self-evidencing force and intrinsic significance of their objective content, i.e. the self-revelation and self-communication of God through Jesus Christ and in the Holy Spirit" (*STR*, 11).

Finally, theologians interpret scripture within the frame of objective meaning that gave rise to the layers of tradition. Hence they do not separate God's self-revealing activity in Jesus Christ from the apostolic proclamation of Christ on the one hand and on the other hand they recognize that "The framework of objective meaning which concerns the theologian here is bound up with the incarnation of the Son of God to be one with us in our physical human existence within the world of space and time" (*STR*, 13). Moreover, because the incarnation is intimately connected with the atonement, theological knowledge must also take account of the fact that the incarnation involves Christ's creative regrounding of our human existence "in the very life of God himself." For that exact reason objective theological meaning is also "bound up with the resurrection of Jesus Christ in body, or the physical reality of his human existence among us, for it is in the resurrection that God's incarnate and redeeming purpose for us is brought to its triumphant fulfilment" (*STR*, 13).[45] Here then is the theme of this book: for Torrance both the incarnation and the resurrection of Jesus, including his whole life and activity,

constitute together the basic framework within which the New Testament writings, for all their rich diversity, are set, and which gives them their deep underlying unity in which Jesus Christ the incarnate and risen Lord is himself the dynamic centre and the objective focus of their creative integration. (*STR*, 14)

In other words if anyone were to undermine theoretically or practically the incarnation or the resurrection of Jesus Christ in their unity and ontological depth, that person would also undermine any possible scientific understanding of the New Testament. And, as already seen above, once scientific under-standing of the NT is undermined in this way, so too is any objective knowl-edge of the transcendent God. Beyond that, all Christian theology and its practical significance would then become questionable because whenever Christ is ignored or discounted, some form of self-justification or some form of self-sanctification immediately follows. And those ethical implications of the unity of the incarnation and resurrection have enormous significance be-cause, as we have seen, any sort of self-justification would undercut the only possible foundation for ethical behavior that is truly free because genuinely free human activity is grounded in the atonement made by Jesus himself as the incarnate Son of the Father.

Torrance freely admits his thinking operates in circular fashion here, but he contends this is not a vicious circle because it is not arbitrarily imposed on the subject matter. Rather the subject matter itself dictates meaning here; but the meaning is finally grounded in ultimate beliefs "which cannot be derived or justified from any other ground than that which they themselves consti-tute" (*STR*, 15). We are faced with a decision then according to Torrance: will we "commit ourselves to belief in the ultimates which are constitutive of the system"? (*STR*, 15). Scientists too are committed to certain ultimate beliefs such as the belief in the order of the universe without which science would be impossible.[46] But he insists that we can accept as ultimate "only what is objec-tively forced upon us by the intrinsic intelligibility, truth and authority of the subject-matter" (*STR*, 16). What happens if something utterly new occurs? How do we fit that into the framework of our knowledge? According to Torrance we cannot and should not. We would have to commit ourselves to a radical reconstruction of our knowledge in light of the new event or occur-rence. A conversion would be required.

This is how in fact the incarnation and the resurrection came to be ac-cepted in the early church and by classical Christian theology.

> They forced themselves upon the minds of Christians from their own em-pirical and theoretical ground *in sharp antithesis* to what they had believed about God and *in genuine conflict* with the framework of secular thought or the world view of their age. That God himself had become man was an offence to the Jew and folly to the Greek; that Jesus Christ rose from the dead was deemed to be utterly incredible. Yet the incarnation and the res-urrection forced themselves upon the mind of the Church against the grain of people's convictions, as ultimate events bearing their own intrinsic but shattering claims in the self-evidencing reality and transcendent rationality of God himself. (*STR*, 17)

This is why Torrance adamantly rejects Bultmann's assertion that the objective form of the NT presentations of the incarnation and resurrection "was the result of mythological objectifying shaped by a primitive and unscientific world-view" (STR, 17). Why? Because for Torrance the early Christians were very well aware of the fact that the Gospel was in serious conflict with the prevailing world-view. For Torrance it is Bultmann's own dualist world-view along with its obsolete scientific preconceptions, that make him mythologize the NT and then demythologize it in terms of his own "mistaken exaltation of self-understanding, which transfers the centre of reference away from the action of God in the historical Jesus to some spiritual event of 'resurrection' in man's experience" (STR, 18).

Knowledge of the Incarnation and Resurrection

Torrance's all-important point then is that the difficult Christology of the ancient church, along with its revised concept of God and of human life itself, "could not be derived or inferred from anything conceived by man before" and yet became the basis for the church's self-understanding as this was indeed rooted in the incarnation and resurrection of Jesus himself (STR, 18). How then do we know and understand the incarnation and resurrection today? For Torrance the answer lies in the fact that both the incarnation and the resurrection as objective realities are the means of God's self-communication which

> force themselves upon our minds, within the vastly changed cultural and scientific outlook of our own times. In the life and work of Jesus Christ we are confronted with an ultimate self-revelation of God into the truth of which there is no way of penetrating from what we already know or believe we know, far less of establishing or verifying it on grounds that are outside of it. (STR, 18)

No blind act of faith is required of us "divorced from any recognition of credibility" (STR, 18) because the reality of the incarnation and resurrection itself creates the conditions for its recognition and acceptance. In other words our faith represents the "subjective pole of commitment to objective reality . . . which is to be grasped only through a repentant rethinking and structural recasting of all our preconceptions" (STR, 19).

That is why theology is knowledge of faith: we must allow our minds to "yield to the intrinsic claims of God's cognitive self-revelation in Jesus Christ" if we are ever to understand the actual meaning of the incarnation and resurrection. While faith is indeed correlated with God's objective self-revelation in the incarnation and resurrection, that does not mean faith is the basis of our belief in these events because "The only proper ground of faith is the reality to which it is correlated as its objective pole" (*STR*, 19). Torrance unequivocally opposes Bultmann's reduction of the objective reality of the resurrection to the "Easter faith" and affirms instead that

> 'Easter faith' is not at all intelligible or reasonable apart from the actual event of the resurrection of Jesus himself; nor can it be consistently interpreted in association with the crucifixion, as Bultmann rightly wants, if the resurrection is denied the same kind of mundane palpability as is conceded to the crucifixion. (*STR*, 19)

Without the incarnation and resurrection then Christianity would be something entirely different. The incarnation and resurrection *together* supply the basic framework within which God's relations with us in space and time can be understood. They are *ultimates*, however, and that means they have their own authority in themselves and call for belief in the sense of Anselm's *fides quaerens intellectum* and *credo ut intelligam*. This faith rests on the truth itself and would not be true faith without resting on things as they really are, as Irenaeus also believed. As *ultimates* they simply must be accepted or rejected because they cannot be verified or validated "on any other grounds than those which they themselves provide" (*STR*, 22). These are the *miracles* upon which the entire Gospel rests. As such they cannot be verified by means of natural science which observes nature; if they were verifiable in that way they would be neither *miracles* nor *ultimates*. Nonetheless, since incarnation and resurrection are acts of God within space and time, their meaning can be explored through human scientific approaches but they can never be fully understood except as ultimates whose meaning is grounded in God himself and not within the natural order. Instead of understanding incarnation and resurrection as interruptions of the natural order or a violation of its laws Torrance insists that they are acts of God that restore order in a world damaged by sin and evil.

To sum up, for Torrance the incarnation means that the eternal Word and Reason of God has become human flesh. This enables us to have communion with God and personal knowledge of God that is grounded in the very being of God himself. The resurrection is the fulfillment of the incarnation in the sense that God's love for us in the reconciling and revealing actions of his incarnate Son was completed in the destruction of death, decay and corruption.

This means that Christ's sacrifice for the sins of the world, his vicarious suffering and the communion established between God and us in the incarnate life of the Son "are finally actualized and remain valid beyond death, as eternally prevailing reality for man as well as for God" (*STR*, 21).

Resurrection in Torrance's Theology

What then is the nature of the resurrection event according to T. F. Torrance? Torrance argues that while there is mention of resurrection in the Old Testament, there is nothing there that compares to the resurrection of Jesus; that is why, in spite of the "deep continuity" between the Old and New Testaments, the NT message can only be presented "with a profound revolution in the tradition of Judaism in which basic categories of thought have to be creatively reconstructed" (*STR*, 30).[47] In this regard Torrance says the resurrection is an event that takes place in history but it is "an act that breaks into history with the powers of another world. It is akin to the creation in the beginning" (*STR*, 31). And for Torrance the resurrection is the "resurrection of the incarnate Word of God" (*STR*, 31) and as such the beginning of the new creation. He never separates Jesus' humanity and divinity and in no way allows the resurrection to be defined by people's experiences of faith.

The resurrection for Torrance is a miracle that is inexplicable from the human side. As a miracle, the resurrection is connected to the virgin birth so that "the whole life of Jesus is to be regarded as downright miracle, the raising up of the Saviour and Servant out of the dry ground" as an act of God drastically altering the world in those events by "inaugurating a new creation" which was "quite unexpected" from the human side (*STR*, 33-34). Torrance believes that we are included corporately: "The New Humanity is already raised up in Christ" (*STR*, 34) with the result that every aspect of human life is affected. "Our resurrection has already taken place and is fully tied up with the resurrection of Christ" so that it is a "manifestation" of what has happened instead of just an "effect" of it (*STR*, 37). In other words "in Christ we are already living 'in the end time'. Through Christ the very fullness . . . of God, which resides in him, already overflows to us (Col. 2:9-10)" (*STR*, 37). Immortality does not come from some interior principle of creation such as an immortal soul, but is conferred by God in fulfillment of his covenant mercies in the incarnation and resurrection. Hence "Christ only has immortality and we receive out of his fullness" (*STR*, 35). Here atonement is intrinsically connected with incarnation and resurrection: "He was put to death for our trespasses and was raised for our justification. In the resurrection of Jesus an objective and vicarious act has been carried out in our human nature in which we are already implicated" (*STR*, 35). In contrast to Rahner's belief in an anonymous experience of the resurrection that can be read off our transcendental experiences of hope and faith, Torrance contends that the saving power of the resurrection "is applied to us through the preaching of the Gospel. He who responds to that message by faith discovers that he has already been involved in the resurrection, and is already included in the objective reality of Jesus Christ risen from the dead" (*STR*, 35).

According to the NT witness Jesus did not rise to his old condition which would then be followed by death as it did with Lazarus; rather Jesus died and rose "in such a way as never to die again" (*STR*, 36). This meant that while the risen Jesus was the same Jesus born of Mary and crucified under Pilate, he was also different because when he rose from the grave "something had taken place akin to the original creation, and indeed transcending it. It was not just a miracle within the creation, but a deed so decisively new that it affected the whole of creation and the whole of the future" (*STR*, 36). Christ's resurrection must transform our whole understanding of God's relation with the world.

Torrance asserts that the evidence for the resurrection will look different to believers and unbelievers because it will appear only in a distorted and mutilated way to those who refuse to allow themselves to be affected by its power or refuse to listen to the message of the resurrection. This does not mean that faith is the only evidence for the resurrection, but that believers will be capable of understanding the message only because they have already been raised up by Christ and have been included in the new creation. Hence "there is a corresponding subjective counterpart in us which as such belongs to the whole integrated reality of the resurrection event" (*STR*, 39).

This sounds dangerously close to the subjectivist thinking Torrance resolutely denies. But in fact it is about as far from subjectivism as one could possibly get because Torrance maintains that we cannot simply identify or resolve Christ's resurrection into that subjective "counterpart" as happens with those who reduce the Easter event to the Easter faith of the disciples. For Torrance "a clear distinction is drawn between the event of Christ's rising and its counterpart or coefficient in the believing community" (*STR*, 39). Torrance stresses that the appearances are to be seen as objective in their own way, even as they are distinguished from the actual events of the resurrection, crucifixion and burial.

This is where Torrance applies his thinking mentioned above, that those who would reduce the Easter event to the Easter faith as the only real historical event are trapped in dualistic thinking that is in fact unscientific because it separates the empirical and theoretical. Why? Because subjectivism of this type derives from the idea that some things which are unknowable in themselves must be radically separated from the way they "appear" to people. By imposing a "phenomenalist" framework onto the NT, such thinking distorts the meaning of the NT, because its very presuppositions prevent hearing its actual message. It is here that German New Testament scholarship made a fatal distinction between history "rooted in objective empirical reality" and history "rooted in the inner life and experience of men" which is spaceless and timeless and therefore at best tangentially related to concrete history (STR, 40). This allows people to think that interpretation is somehow "put upon" facts "by way of valuation" using symbolic imagery rather than being intrinsically related to the facts in an ontological way. Such interpretations, since they are spaceless and timeless, can be detached from the facts and have a life of their own. That is what happens when the resurrection is interpreted in abstraction from the "revelation of Jesus Christ in his objective and personal reality as incarnate Son of God, the Lord of history and of creation" (STR, 41). Torrance therefore insists that the NT stressed Jesus' bodily resurrection precisely in order to maintain the integrity of "the humanity of the Incarnate Son" against the dualistic conceptions of Docetism and adoptionism. As we have seen, that is why Torrance characteristically rejects Ebionite and Docetic Christology as forms of unscientific thinking.[48]

Here Torrance connects the resurrection with the doctrine of God by insisting that if resurrection and incarnation are held together in a non-dualist sense "deriving from Israel" then that would mean "a radical revision of the concept of God himself" (STR, 42). Jesus would be seen as Son of God, justified by his Father and installed with power; indeed it would also be seen that "God himself was directly present and personally active in the resurrection of Jesus" (STR, 42). But of course that meant that he was seen to be present and active in his passion as well. That the crucified Jesus could forgive sins, judge the living and the dead and stand at God's right hand all implied that Jesus shared the prerogatives of God himself. According to Torrance this was the great stumbling block that was offensive to Judaism so that "it was unwilling to go forward with the Christian Church in accepting the full implication of the resurrection of Christ" (STR, 43).

It is here and on this basis that the concept of God which had been more or less fixed in late Judaism had to be changed. Instead of seeing God as namelessly remote or detached and operating through intermediaries, now "God himself must be thought of as having visited his people" so that the whole doctrine of God and his covenant relation with Israel had to be "reconstructed in face of the crucifixion and resurrection of Jesus" (STR, 43). Here

Torrance contends that all dualism was forever rendered inappropriate for understanding God because of the resurrection of Jesus "in Body." It is just here that "a new understanding of the living God whose very being and life are accessible to human knowing and participating" became a reality (*STR*, 43). This is why Torrance has a strong sense of the immanent Trinity that is echoed in his frequently repeated assertion that what God is toward us in Jesus Christ and the Holy Spirit he is eternally in himself.[49] As seen above, the key to the doctrine of the Trinity is found in the fact that Jesus as eternal Son of the Father is *homoousios* with the Father from eternity and *homoousios* with humanity by virtue of the incarnation and resurrection. If the ground is pulled out from under the reality of either the incarnation or the resurrection by any sort of Ebionite or Docetic view, or if they are separated in any way as happens in Nestorian and Eutychian Christologies, then the very meaning of the doctrine of the Trinity is called into question as well. We can know God with truth and certainty, according to Torrance, just because God has provided us with the possibility to think from a center in God in and from his incarnate Son and through the Holy Spirit. Because Jesus, the incarnate Son, is now risen from the dead and lives, he can, in the power of his Holy Spirit, enable us to know God as God really is, in a way that avoids projecting our mythological concepts into the divine being. God, of course, remains incomprehensible in his utter transcendence; but it is precisely that incomprehensible God who has made himself known and knowable in Christ and the Spirit. This knowledge of faith is real only in, from and through Jesus himself.

The Nature of the Resurrection Event

What then does all this suggest about the nature of the resurrection event itself? Is the resurrection an event in history or not? Torrance answers with an unequivocal yes. "Certainly it is an event datable in history" (*STR*, 87). Unless this is so our atonement and redemption are called into question as well. And so is the very possibility of thinking about God the Father, Son and Holy Spirit. All Docetic conceptions of the resurrection then are irrelevant to us because we are flesh and blood. Eschatology too is meaningless without the resurrection because then there is no on-going life of the world. Accordingly "Everything depends on the resurrection of the body, otherwise all we have is a Ghost for a Saviour" (*STR*, 87). But as we have just seen, the resurrection is not merely a historical event because, as an event of redemption and new creation, it "bursts through the structures and limitations of space and time" (*STR*, 88). It is because Christ is the redeemer who delivers us from sin, guilt and evil and the structures determined by them that the resurrection event "is not something that can be caught within the framework of those structures or interpreted by the secular historian who can only work within it" (*STR*, 88). That is why Torrance believes that the intersection of the order of creation by the order of redemption in the incarnation and resurrection means that "the basic structure of what emerges in the Easter event is absolutely new: a reality which is not only entirely unknown to us but entirely unknowable in terms of what we already know or think we know, and only knowable through a radical reconstruction of our prior knowledge" (*STR*, 175).

This is an enormously important point. By connecting incarnation, resurrection, atonement and redemption as acts of God within history Torrance explains why the methods and canons of credibility that apply for secular historians cannot apply here. In the case of the risen Lord we are not dealing with history marked by sin, evil and death. We are instead dealing with "a *new kind of historical happening*" which rises from the grave and continues to exist (*STR*, 88; emphasis in original). This is a fully real historical happening, Torrance insists, but one that never runs down or decays and dies, for the risen Jesus

> is not dead but alive, more real than any of us. Hence he does not need to be made real for us, because he does not decay or become fixed in the past. He lives on in the present as real live continuous happening, encountering us here and now in the present and waiting for us in the future. (*STR*, 89)

This allows Torrance continually and consistently to argue that all theological interpretation must find its truth in the Truth itself, namely, in the risen and ascended Lord who is himself prophet, priest and king even now. While the resurrection happened once for all in history "it remains continuous live happening within history" (*STR*, 90). In the liturgy and in ethics alike Jesus Christ must remain the active Lord who enables prayer, thanksgiving and right behavior by virtue of his free and gracious love. This, once again, excludes any sort of self-justification, whether epistemological or ontological.

Empty Tomb

What about the empty tomb? Just as the resurrection was a resurrection of the body of Jesus within history so, for Torrance, the empty tomb was absolutely central:

> Everything in the Christian Gospel, now regarded in the light of Easter, was
> seen to pivot finally upon the *empty tomb* — that Jesus arose in body, arose
> as very man in the fullness and integrity of his human nature, but human
> nature which through the Spirit of holiness had been stripped of corroding
> forces of corruption and clad in the incorruptible garment of deathless-
> ness. (*STR*, 83)[50]

Torrance agrees with W. Künneth who explains that while the empty tomb
cannot be identified with the miracle of the resurrection, it is recorded in all
the Gospels and is inseparably bound up with the resurrection. Therefore the
empty tomb is the strongest expression of concern for Jesus' bodily resurrection and also "the clear safeguard against every spiritualizing tendency to
evaporate the central declaration of the resurrection" (*STR*, 83). Here especially there is a connection between the incarnation and the resurrection: because God actually became incarnate in space and time, Christian theology
cannot ignore the "empirical correlates" of God's actions in history. To do so
would lead to an image of Christ not rooted in history and thus it would be "a
vehicle of our fantasies." That is precisely why the empty tomb is so important for Torrance: "cut that away and it [the Christian doctrine of the resur-
rection] becomes nonsensical" (*STI*, 90). Hence for Torrance "It is *the empty
tomb* that constitutes the essential empirical correlate in statements about the
resurrection" (*STR*, 141).

It is worth noting that here too Torrance's thinking is inherently opposed
to both Ebionite and Docetic Christology because for him Jesus does not receive his significance from our value judgments based on our experience of
him; rather he *is* the Truth because he is the eternal Son of the Father now incarnate for our sakes. And because he truly lives a full human life in space and
time in order to heal and redeem us, he is the one place where we may know
God with truth and certainty without compromising space and time or the
historical or limited nature of our knowledge and without projecting space
and time into God and re-defining God by history.[51]

> This relation established between God and man in Jesus Christ constitutes
> Him as *the place* in all space and time where God meets with man in the ac-
> tualities of his human existence, and man meets with God and knows Him
> in His own divine Being. That is the place where the vertical and horizontal
> dimensionalities intersect, the place where human being is opened out to a
> transcendent ground in God and where the infinite Being of God pene-
> trates into our existence and creates room for Himself within the horizon-
> tal dimensions of finite being in space and time. (*STI*, 75)

That is why Torrance insists that God takes our hurt and pain into himself in the incarnation so that he cannot be seen as merely impassible; that he has exercised his freedom to share our lot and makes himself poor for our sakes so that we might share in his "invariant" love (*STI*, 75); and that in Christ, God demonstrates that he is both passible and impassible and that this must be understood soteriologically rather than logically (*TF*, 185).[52] Torrance is aware of the contemporary tendency to spiritualize Jesus' bodily resurrection. What is behind this? For Torrance it is the horror that spiritualizers have "for *the being and action of God himself in space and time*" (*STR*, 80). Torrance insists that for the NT "If there is no resurrection, human nature is no longer genuinely human" (*STR*, 82). Hence "any 'resurrection' that is not bodily is surely a contradiction in terms" (*STR*, 82).

Torrance maintains that before the resurrection Jesus, the Son of God incarnate, lived on earth

> not 'in the form of God', not snatching at divine power, not calling in 'supernature' to help him out of the weakness of our nature which he had made his own, not therefore in the condition of his transcendent glory as eternal Son of God which he had with the Father before the world was. (*STR*, 84)

After his resurrection, Jesus lived among us on earth "in the mode of the exalted Son of God, yet in his nature as man" (*STR*, 84). He lived in our history then as the "New Man," the man of the new creation. As such he is beyond the corrupting processes of this passing age and on the other side of death, even as he encountered people and lived among them after his resurrection. He ate with them "to show that he was no ghost but real, physical human being" (*STR*, 84).[53] In his treatment of the ascension Torrance insists that Christ is in heaven, i.e., that side of reality which is inaccessible to human insight, but that because he remains both divine and human to all eternity, we are directed back to the historical Jesus as the place to know God and to participate provisionally in eternity prior to his second coming.

What about our resurrection? When the believer dies, according to Torrance, he goes to be with Christ and is in Christ's immediate presence: "participant in him and made like him" (*STR*, 102). When this is seen, however, from a historical perspective which can only perceive history within the ongoing processes of this fallen world, each believer's death means "that his body is laid to sleep in the earth" and awaits the final redemption of the body and "the recreation of all things at the final *Parousia*" (*STR*, 102). From the perspective of the new creation, however, "there is no gap between the death of the believer and the *parousia* of Christ" (*STR,* 102). But from the perspective of time which is still subject to decay and death there is a gap of time between them. Torrance insists that it is only by thinking of them "exclusively *in Christ,* in the one Person of Christ in whom human nature and divine nature are hypostatically united, and in whom our human existence and history are taken up into his divine life" (*STR,* 102) that we can perceive the truth of our existence in this context.

In Torrance's estimation Augustine may be guilty of spiritualizing here with his idea of "ethereal bodies" (*STR,* 140). Augustine failed to observe a proper theological reserve at the boundary of the eschatological. The fact that we will have a spiritual body at our resurrection does not mean that the body is "resolved away into spirit" (*STR,* 141) any more than by being spiritual now means we are any less human. For Torrance, to be spiritual means to be more fully human and that is why he insists again on taking the empty tomb "quite seriously" (*STR,* 141). "The body of Jesus Christ was raised, certainly a spiritual body, but it was no less body because it was a body healed and quickened by the Spirit in which all corruption had been overcome. It is the empty tomb that constitutes the essential empirical correlate in statements about the resurrection of Christ" (*STR,* 141). Here we can see exactly how the incarnation and resurrection are indissolubly connected in Torrance's thinking. Because it is the incarnate Word who died and rose from the dead in order to reconcile us to the Father, it is absolutely imperative that he should be understood to have risen bodily from the dead. It is just this connection between the incarnation and resurrection that leads Torrance to insist, quite properly, that we cannot spiritualize the body of the risen Lord and we cannot spiritualize his coming again either. The very existence of humanity depends then upon the fact that Jesus, the incarnate Word, is risen bodily from the dead and is coming again.

4. Analysis and Comparison of Barth, Rahner and Torrance with a View toward a Scientific Theology of the Resurrection in Its Intrinsic Relation to the Incarnation

We have seen how three leading theologians understand the resurrection and how that understanding is dictated by their particular views of the incarnation, atonement and the Trinity. We have also briefly indicated how ethics is conceptualized in each perspective. In addition, of course, we have discussed many key issues such as theological method, knowledge of God, the role of faith and experience as well as the all-important intrinsic connection between the incarnation and the resurrection. My argument has been and remains that any Ebionite or Docetic view of the resurrection will mean a corresponding Ebionite or Docetic view of Christ's person and work, along with a weak understanding of the Trinity, which would then lead to some form of self-justification in the ethical sphere. While I have raised questions within each of the previous three chapters, I have resisted the temptation to offer a detailed analysis and comparison of these positions so that the three theologians could speak for themselves as much as possible. Of course I could not resist offering some opinions along the way in accordance with my basic theological vision of these issues. In this chapter my goal will be to offer that detailed analysis and comparison with a view toward refining my basic thesis and clarifying just where the key issues lie in a contemporary theology of the resurrection that takes seriously its inherent connection with the incarnation. This will provide the basis for whatever analysis is to take place throughout the rest of the book.

For the sake of convenience I will proceed by considering six key areas discussed above: (1) method and theological knowledge; (2) the nature of the incarnation; (3) the nature of the resurrection and the role of faith and hope; (4) the nature of and significance of the empty tomb; (5) the importance of the doctrine of the Trinity; (6) the ethical implications of a theology of the resurrection. The framework for our discussion will be the categories developed in the preface and briefly introduced in each chapter, namely, David Fergusson's notions of the radical, liberal and traditional views of the resurrection. It is clear so far that I agree with Fergusson, who holds that the traditional view is the stance that does justice to the scriptural witness to the resurrection. It is also clear that I disagree with the radical view, which reduces the resurrection event to the faith of the disciples and to our faith. And it is equally clear that I disagree with the liberal view, which intends to overcome the obvious weaknesses of the radical view, but tends to collapse back into the radical view because of its inability to distinguish the objective resurrection of the historical Jesus from the experiences of the disciples and ultimately from our own experiences. One of the hallmarks of the radical view was its antipathy toward the concept of miracle; this antipathy also marks the liberal view. That explains why, in the liberal view, attempts are made to explain the resurrection from contemporary experience, usually the experience of interpersonal relationships.

Method and Theological Knowledge

It is no secret that the theological method of Karl Barth and Thomas F. Torrance is quite similar. While Torrance himself believed they both agreed that natural theology could not function independently of revelation, Barth also argued that natural theology had no place at all in positive theology. In this regard Torrance's search for a new natural theology had the positive advantage of providing a theology of nature, but actually adopted certain aspects of the old natural theology that both he and Barth in fact rejected.[1] In any case, they both rejected any sort of *a priori* knowledge of revelation, incarnation, atonement, resurrection or the Trinity. Both of them also agreed that we could not logically argue from this world to the existence and nature of God. While they do differ to the degree that Torrance thinks natural theology provides us with some knowledge of God, there is no doubt that Torrance has no wish to build a traditional natural theology. He wishes only to affirm the fact that it is we creatures in our full human nature, fallen but re-created in Christ, who really may know God as he is in himself without leaving the sphere of space and time in some mystical flight of fancy or through some dualistic deism that ultimately cuts us off from true knowledge of God. Ultimately, Barth would agree with Torrance's "new natural theology" only to the extent that it is really no more than a theology of nature.

That is why we saw that both theologians rejected the idea that a logical bridge could be built from this world of experience to knowledge of God. Both theologians insisted on beginning their theology from Jesus Christ alone because he was the unique Son of God revealed and active as our reconciler and redeemer. Theological knowledge for both theologians is knowledge of faith. But it is not grounded in anyone's faith. Rather, as Torrance says, it is knowledge that takes place from a center in God rather than from a center in ourselves. That center is provided by God's own self-communication in the incarnation and resurrection; it is provided by his condescension to be one of us in order to heal our humanity and in order to overcome our attempts to create God in our own image. Barth describes this process as knowledge that takes place in acknowledgment — acknowledgment of Jesus Christ as *doctor veritatis* who alone can impart knowledge of himself through the Holy Spirit.[2] Both theologians agree that there are no theological concepts that are true in themselves because both of them apply the doctrine of justification to our knowledge of God. And both theologians insist that the doctrine of the Trinity plays a central role in our understanding of God. For that reason neither Barth nor Torrance hold an agnostic view of the immanent Trinity. Both of them accept the fact that it is because God exists from eternity in full self-sufficiency as the eternal Father, Son and Holy Spirit that he can act as creator, reconciler and redeemer without threatening the existence of a world outside of him with its own relative independence and yet also dependent on him for its existence. Both of them therefore insist on a strong doctrine of the incarnation as the presupposition for a traditional view of the resurrection. In the ethical sphere both theologians reject any notion of self-justification and any hint of conditional salvation. Both theologians see right behavior as behavior that is obedient to God in Christ. And that obedient behavior is in no way the cause or guarantee of our freedom because that cause and guarantee always remain identical with the present action of the Holy Spirit enabling us to live the Christian life as a life of free obedience.

When we turn our attention to the thinking of Karl Rahner several crucial methodological differences arise. And these differences are so basic that they affect how each theologian interprets the resurrection, the incarnation, the atonement and the Trinity. This has ethical implications as well. Let me carefully state those differences as they emerge from the presentation of the last three chapters and attempt to show how they work themselves out under the six additional headings mentioned above. This is important, because unless these methodological issues are clearly faced and resolved in an appropriate way, then it will not only become impossible for Reformed and Roman Catholic theology to dialogue with each other on these vital issues in a substantive way, but it will become impossible for any theology to offer an intelligible account of the biblical witness regarding the resurrection and the incarnation. Why? Because and to the extent that the biblical witness is not allowed to speak for itself in its own intrinsic intelligibility (as Torrance puts it) the very nature of the resurrection and incarnation tend to be compromised. And of course any such compromise means that the ground is pulled out from under the Christian faith.

The first and most obvious difference among the three theologians is that Rahner argues that we cannot begin our reflections exclusively with Jesus Christ. It is the simple fact of this starting point that creates almost all the tensions and difficulties that arise among these theologians. We will enumerate those specific difficulties as we treat the dogmatic issues. Here we simply note methodological differences. The second difference is that Rahner believes that it is the prime task of Christology to develop an *a priori* concept of the God-man in order to make Christology comprehensible today. Torrance and Barth, as we have seen, insist that because the only proper starting point for Christian theology is Jesus himself as the incarnate Word, all *a priori* attempts to construct a Christology will always reflect our human attempt to control revelation rather than an actual understanding of it. In the words of Torrance, any such attempt will be unscientific just because it is not dictated by the nature of the reality being considered. Such thinking is always inherently Ebionite or Docetic, but never really Christian. It tends to displace the bodily resurrection of Jesus of Nazareth with the faith and hope of Christians and thus opens the door to the kind of subjectivism that determines the liberal and radical views of the resurrection.

This leads to the third difference, namely, Rahner insists that the incarnation is the result but not the starting point for Christology. For Torrance and Barth that very assumption necessarily means a denial of the miracle of Christmas and a compromise of the fact that what took place in the incarnation and resurrection is something utterly new for which we have no prior categories. It means a denial of the offensive element in revelation. As we shall see throughout the rest of this book, this is perhaps the most widely held and most problematic view of much contemporary Christology. Fourth, Rahner thinks that anthropology and theology mutually condition each other and because of that he argues that we should explore "graced" human experience to understand the meaning of Christian doctrine today. This thinking inevitably opens the door to the liberal interpretation of the resurrection and to additional difficulties discussed above when interpreting the incarnation and the Trinity. And, as noted above, the liberal view inevitably collapses back into the radical view. All of this is complicated by the fact that Rahner seriously wishes to maintain the sense of the traditional doctrines and believes he actually has done so. Fifth and finally, it is Rahner's "transcendental method" that allows him and perhaps even requires him to assign grace and revelation to human experience in such a way that attention cannot be focused exclusively on God's Word and Spirit for theological understanding; this permits Rahner to apply his theology of the symbol to key Christian doctrines with the result that his thinking invariably manifests his attempt to construct his theology by moving logically from experience in this world to knowledge of God. This opens the door to his theory of anonymous Christianity and to a number of other difficulties, as we have already seen.

It will be recalled that both Torrance and Barth unequivocally refused to construct a logical bridge from our experiences in the world to God precisely because such a bridge would mean that our thinking was no longer taking place from a center in God but rather was taking place from a center in our own experience. While all three theologians agree that our knowledge of God begins with our experience of grace and revelation and cannot and should not leave the sphere of history and experience to know the triune God, Torrance and Barth insist that there is no logical bridge from human experience to God. It is this that separates Torrance and Barth from Rahner methodologically and doctrinally.

The Nature of the Incarnation

As I have just noted, one's theological method will affect one's understanding of theology. Hence, given the differences between Rahner on the one side and Barth and Torrance on the other we would expect to see very different understandings of the incarnation. As seen above, Barth understood the incarnation as a real act of becoming sinful flesh on the part of God's eternal Word.[3] Because the Word was the subject of that event; it was not something that befell him and it could not be understood as the supreme form of a theology of the symbol as Rahner does.[4] This is why Barth distinguishes between creation and incarnation. As a free act of the Word, incarnation did not rest on any inner or outer necessity, rather it expressed God's free sovereign act on our behalf.

The incarnation did not mean a diminution of the Word's divinity but a concealment of it and all for the sake of God's mercy toward us. Barth preferred to speak of an assumption of flesh by the Word because it implied that what took place in the incarnation was a miracle, that is, a special new direct act of God in history[5] which meant that the Word remained the Word and did not cease to be God while truly becoming flesh. No third reality arose from the union of natures; any such idea would suggest the termination of both his divine being and human being and a compromise of his sovereignty. It will be recalled that Barth distinguishes between the servant form of revelation in which God is hidden in the incarnation of the Word and the "divine form" "in which God knows Himself, in which the Father knows the Son and the Son the Father. It is in this veiling — which after all is a veiling in a form familiar to man — that the Majesty can meet men and so far make knowledge of itself possible through men" (CD I/2, 37-38). But in the incarnation the Word incarnate is exposed to the possibility that we might not recognize him: "Knowledge of it becomes real to men only in virtue of a special unveiling through Jesus' resurrection from the dead, or through all the sayings and acts of His life so far as they were signs of His resurrection" (CD I/2, 38). In all of this, however, there is no lessening of his divinity:

> That it is only veiling, not abandonment nor yet lessening of His divinity, is shown by the unveiling, which is not only the result but from the start — it is revelation we are concerned with — its goal. He who the third day rose from the dead was no less true God in the manger than on the cross. (CD I/2, 38)

That is why on the one hand Barth unequivocally rejects any sort of two-stage Christology and on the other hand Barth's starting point for Christology, namely, Jesus Christ himself as truly God and truly human, excludes from the outset and at each point along the way even the slightest implication of Ebionite or Docetic Christology.

For these reasons revelation, for Barth, is identical with the person and work of Jesus Christ and Jn. 1:14 must be accepted as a genuine statement about Jesus Christ as truly divine and human: "One cannot subsequently speak christologically, if Christology has not already been presupposed at the outset, and in its stead other presuppositions have claimed one's attention" (CD I/2, 123). But none of this is under our control: "The knowability of the Word of God stands or falls, then, with the act of its real knowledge, which is not under our control" (CD I/1, 224). Real knowledge of God must find its assurance not in itself but in the Word of God so that one's "assurance is his own assurance, but it has its seat outside him in the Word of God" (CD I/1, 224-25). That is why Barth rejected the idea that Jesus was the revealer in his humanity as such: "Not of its own activity but in virtue of the Word united with it did the flesh of the Lord do what was divine; by the same means the Word proved His own divineness" (CD I/2, 137).[6] And, as seen above, this is also why Barth rejected any quest (Neo-Protestant or other) of the "historical Jesus" as well as Catholic devotion to the Sacred Heart. Each in its own way made the human Jesus the object of their inquiry or devotion and in that way sought to evade the Word with the result that each approach implicitly and explicitly separated the Word from his humanity and obscured the fact that Jesus' humanity receives its reality and meaning exclusively from the Word. It is worth noting in this context that Karl Rahner's famous article on the Theology of the Symbol in *TI* 4 was specifically written as an apologetic for his belief in the Sacred Heart.

Additionally, for Barth, revelation is offensive to us precisely because we resist the divine act of lordship evident in God's fulfillment of time in Jesus Christ. No human *a priori* is admissible here because we have no vantage point from which we may judge the validity of the revelation of God in Jesus Christ. Even as a historical event, revelation is not open to human appraisal. That is why Barth argues that a proper view of revelation sees "'fulfilled time' from the standpoint of the fulfilment, not of time . . . history is what it is, entirely and altogether in virtue of the Subject who acts here" (*CD* I/2, 60). Sin, according to Barth, is exposed in its true proportions over against Jesus Christ himself. In its very hiddenness, revelation is resisted by us — we fight against it. This is why revelation inevitably must be offending because in revelation God has acted and acts as our savior without consulting us as to how and when he would do so. We are offended by the fact that our time, the time of Adam, has come to an end in Jesus Christ so that "the disposal of our days is taken from us by the revealed God, that our time is really in his hands" (*CD* I/2, 67).[7]

We have seen that it is because Torrance insists that the Word became incarnate in space and time without ceasing to be divine that he also argues that there is no "non-cognitive" revelation of God. Any such thinking, Torrance argued, could open the door to Tillich's symbolic theology, which compromised the *homoousion* with the idea that our knowledge of God might develop from some aspect of culture rather than from God himself through Christ and in the Spirit. Such thinking would thus make Jesus no more than a symbol of God. It would not actually derive from Jesus who, for Torrance, *was* God among us. This undercuts Rahner's belief in what he calls transcendental revelation, which he equates with the subjective transformation of one's transcendental horizon. It is, he says, "a transcendental divinization of the fundamental subjective attitude, the ultimate horizon of man's knowledge and freedom, in the perspective of which he accomplishes his life."[8] For Rahner such "non-objective and unreflexive self-revelation in grace must always be present as mediated in objective and reflexive knowledge."[9] But it is just this "non-objective" and "unreflexive self-revelation" that allows and requires Rahner to appeal to and to rely on our transcendental experiences in order to explain the meaning of the incarnation. And this causes him to divert his attention from the only possible source of true meaning here, namely, Jesus Christ himself as the Word incarnate. This accounts for Rahner's "universalism" as it leads him to think that

> The person who, in a hope which no longer seeks to reassure itself, relinquishes himself in the depths of the mystery of existence, in which death and life can no longer be distinguished because they can only be grasped together, actually believes in the Crucified and Risen one, even if he is not aware of it (in conceptual terms).[10]

Such thinking clearly dissociates the resurrection from the incarnation by locating its meaning in the depths of existence instead of in the history of Jesus Christ. This illustrates why Torrance insists on conceptual knowledge of revelation that is tied to the historical Jesus as the Word incarnate. Torrance never appeals to any of our transcendental dynamisms in order to justify his position but always insists that theology must find its meaning outside itself and in Christ alone through the power of the Spirit. For Torrance this is the meaning of our justification by faith. And any attempt to explain the incarnation without accepting Jesus for who he was and is as the incarnate Word amounts to a type of self-justification that leads to a form of Ebionite and Docetic Christology.

Rahner's understanding of the incarnation then stands in marked contrast with that of Barth and Torrance. In the first instance we have seen that Rahner believes that the incarnation is the "end and not the starting point of all Christological assertion" (*FCF*, 177). Hence Rahner can argue

> we are not starting out from the Christological formulations of the New Testament in Paul and John . . . we are not assuming the impossibility of going behind such a 'late' New Testament Christology to ask about a more original and somewhat more simple experience of faith with the historical Jesus, in his message, his death, and his achieved finality that we describe as his resurrection.[11]

While this belief is in accordance with his method, in Barth's thinking it compromises the simple truth of Jn. 1:14. And for Torrance the incarnation can only be understood from itself as an *ultimate* and so he too opposes the idea that the incarnation can be grasped as the conclusion and not the starting point of one's reflections. A choice is required here: either one accepts the truth of the incarnation as a miraculous act of God in Christ and thus as the starting point for one's deliberations or one can establish its truth from history and experience. Clearly, Rahner chooses the latter option while at the same time insisting on the importance of the incarnation. This leads him to maintain that transcendental theology "must develop in a general ontology and anthropology an a priori doctrine of the God-Man" in order to formulate the conditions that enable a "genuine capacity to hear the historical message of Jesus Christ, and an insight into the necessity of hearing it" (*FCF,* 176-77), and to claim that none of this would have been possible had the incarnation not taken place. As we have seen, however, this approach leads to deep ambiguities in Rahner's own thought about the incarnation. On the one hand he asserts that the incarnation is central to Christian theology and he stresses the uniqueness of Jesus Christ and the hypostatic union. But on the other hand his thinking is determined more by his method than by Jesus Christ himself and this undercuts his attempt to keep the incarnation central to his own thought.

Among other things this thinking leads to his understanding of revelation and grace as elements within transcendental experience and to the idea that by exploring human experiences of self-transcendence one can come to a deeper understanding of Christology, ideas which we have seen both Barth and Torrance reject, because they believe there is no logical bridge that can be built from our historical self-understanding to God. Hence, Rahner claims that one is living a "searching Christology," perhaps anonymously, when one encounters the transcendental dynamisms of one's spirit in the world and this "lived Christology" forms the basis for understanding the church's traditional Christology and can even be equated with it. Such thinking, however, stands in marked contrast to the starting point for Christology for both Barth and Torrance, which is Jesus Christ and faith in him.

The difference between the theologians is stark: Rahner argues that such searching Christology is operative without asking about the concrete savior, namely, Jesus himself so that "prior to the question about an encounter with the historical, concrete Jesus, it makes sense to ask what is really meant when Christianity speaks of an *incarnation of God*" (*FCF,* 212; emphasis in original). Barth and Torrance, however, unequivocally insist that it is quite impossible to ask about the reality of the incarnation except on the ground of its actual occurrence and from within the circle of faith marked by an actual encounter with Jesus himself. That is precisely why, in contrast to Rahner's stated belief, Torrance rejects any historical-critical method that would seek a Jesus of history behind the Gospel confessions that recognized who he was from the very first. What difference does this make? For Torrance it means that the incarnation of God in Jesus Christ and that alone must prescribe what is said here in accordance with his view of scientific theology that allows the unique nature of the object being considered to dictate theological meaning. Hence the incarnation means that Jesus Christ himself is not just man participating in God but is himself "essential Deity." That is why Torrance explicitly rejects a symbolic view of the incarnation — such a view is not controlled by the reality intended. A symbolic view mistakenly applies the container concept of space to God and God's relations with us and so misses the all important point that God does not stand in a spatial relation with us but relates with us as creator and lord of the universe. And Barth insists that in the incarnation, the Word "assumed" human nature into union with the divine Word in a miraculous act signified by the virgin birth and argued that this meant that the Word was not transformed into a man but remained the sovereign subject of the event.

Barth never thought about the incarnation except in its intrinsic unity with reconciliation (atonement). Hence, for Barth, the incarnation had to be the starting point of one's reflections simply because of its uniqueness, which meant to him that one could not comprehend the truth of Christology by starting from the idea of a God-Man into which Jesus could then be placed and understood. This, for Barth, would represent the approach of what he called Docetic Christology, which in his mind, followed almost necessarily from the Ebionite assumption that Christology could be understood from our transcendental experiences rather than exclusively from the historical Jesus who *was* and *is* the Word incarnate. We have seen that T. F. Torrance's thinking is substantially the same as Barth's on this point since he insists on the unity of incarnation and reconciliation contending that incarnation means "an act of utter self-abasement and humiliation in which he [the Son] assumed our abject servile condition, our state under the slavery of sin" (*TF,* 153) so that he could reconcile us fully with God the Father. He also rejects Ebionite and Docetic Christology both explicitly and implicitly and decisively insists that God became fully and completely human and dwelt among us as a man but "without of course ceasing to be God the Son" (*TF,* 150).[12] Hence, *kenosis* did not mean that there was a "contraction, diminution or self-limitation of God's infinite being" but rather that he loved us in such a "self-abnegating" way that he freely suffered abasement for our sakes. Here Torrance's rejection of the container concept of space and time enables him to remain true to his christological presuppositions.

So while Rahner can say that he was seeking the idea of a God-Man "prescinding from the question whether and where this idea has been realized" and that he was doing this "only because in fact we believe . . . we have found this God-Man in Jesus Christ" (*FCF*, 229), both Barth and Torrance would say that if he had indeed found the God-Man in Jesus Christ, that very fact would have prohibited him from seeking such an idea apart from its actual realization in the history of Jesus Christ himself. For both Barth and Torrance, in any case, it is not our seeking and finding that is decisive here; rather it is the fact that we were sought and found by Christ himself that is decisive. The fact that Rahner thinks this way accounts for his "universalism" in the sense that instead of pointing us consistently and directly to Jesus himself as the way, the truth and the life, Rahner points us to our transcendental experiences and only then to Jesus of Nazareth with the result that the offensive element in revelation is undercut by Rahner's belief that salvation is identical with self-acceptance. Hence

> Anyone therefore, no matter how remote from any revelation formulated in words, who accepts his existence, that is, his humanity . . . in quiet patience, or better, in faith, hope and love — no matter what he calls them, and accepts it *as* the mystery which hides itself in the mystery of eternal love and bears life in the womb of death: such a one says yes to something which really is such as his boundless confidence hopes it to be, because God has in fact filled it with the infinite, that is, with himself, since the Word was made flesh. He says yes to Christ, even when he does not know that he does. . . . Anyone who accepts his own humanity in full . . . has accepted the son of Man. (*TI* 4: 119)[13]

This thinking which, as we have seen above, has major ethical ramifications because it leads Rahner to define human freedom without specific reference to the revelation of God in Jesus Christ, also reflects Rahner's attempt to construct an *a priori* anthropology and to apply his theology of the symbol to the incarnation. Instead of arguing that the incarnation refers to the miraculous assumption of human nature by the Word, Rahner contends that the incarnation refers primarily to the *expression* of the Logos in eternity and in time. We have already seen that Rahner's notion of symbolic expression makes it virtually impossible for him to recognize and uphold God's freedom with the result that he argues that

> God's creative act always drafts the creature as the paradigm of a possible utterance of himself. And he cannot draft it otherwise. . . . The immanent self-utterance of God in his eternal fullness is the condition of the self-utterance of God outside himself, and the *latter continues the former*. (*TI* 4: 115; emphasis mine; 117)

The concept of symbolic expression at work here prevents a sharp distinction between the immanent self-utterance of God and God's action *ad extra*. The result is that while both Barth and Torrance insist that creation and incarnation are free new acts of God that are not necessary except as they have factually occurred in the freedom of God, Rahner sees creation and incarnation continuing God's internal expression which, in accordance with his theology of the symbol, means that "It is because God 'must' 'express' himself inwardly that he can also utter himself outwardly; the finite, created utterance *ad extra* is a continuation of the immanent constitution of 'image and likeness' — a free continuation, because its object is finite" (*TI* 4: 236-37). In this last remark it is clear that Rahner too wishes to maintain God's freedom but is hindered in this because of the logic of his symbolic ontology.

Thus, this seemingly minor or even abstruse point of disagreement is full of significance, since it guides Rahner to say of the incarnation that "God has taken on a human nature, because it is essentially ready and adoptable" (*TI* 4: 110) and that human nature, "when assumed by God as *his* reality, simply arrived at the point to which it always strives by virtue of its essence" (*TI* 4: 109). It also leads him to suggest "all theology is . . . eternally an anthropology" (*TI* 4: 116); "Christology is the end and beginning of anthropology" (*TI* 4: 117); and "anthropology and Christology mutually determine each other within Christian dogmatics if they are both correctly understood" (*TI* 9: 28). By contrast, Barth argued that "There is a way from Christology to anthropology, but there is no way from anthropology to Christology" (*CD* I/1, 131); that while humanity is factually included in a relationship with God by God himself and thus should be included in the Christian doctrine of God because of God's electing grace, one could never say that theology is anthropology in any sense. And to suggest that Christology follows from a consideration of anthropology once more confuses Christ with us in our transcendental experiences from Barth's point of view. The practical contrast between Rahner's thinking and the thinking of both Barth and Torrance is noteworthy: for Barth, "human nature possesses no capacity for becoming the human nature of Jesus Christ. . . . It cannot be the work-mate of God . . . this human nature . . . has of itself no capacity for being adopted by God's Word into unity with Himself" (*CD* I/2, 188-89) while, for Torrance, human nature is marked by sin and death and needs to be healed through the incarnate Word and thus recreated. And when God in Christ assumes human nature, it receives a new point of departure toward which it could no longer strive by virtue of its essence, which is affected by sin. This thinking reflects the fact that both Barth and Torrance hold together incarnation and reconciliation in a way that Rahner cannot, based on his symbolic ontology.

Following his symbolic ontology, Rahner adopts what T. F. Torrance has identified as the container notion of space and time with his argument that God has filled human existence with the infinite, namely, with himself "since the Word was made flesh." But once the weaknesses of the container or receptacle view of space and time are seen with the help of T. F. Torrance's analysis, one can then see quite plainly that it is in this very thinking that Rahner has unintentionally but also unwittingly advanced a view that allows for the Word to be transformed into the man Jesus. The result is that in virtue of the overflow of symbolic reality, the Word in a certain sense, was also transformed into human nature itself in its transcendental dynamisms of spirit: "the finite itself has been given an infinite depth and is no longer a contrast to the infinite, but that which the infinite himself has become" (*TI* 4: 117). Here we see the foundation of Rahner's concepts of an obediential potency and supernatural existential, which of course, both Barth and Torrance would regard as an illegitimate confusion of nature and grace. It is here that Barth and Torrance on the one side and Rahner on the other are separated by the fact that the former stress the particular incarnation of God in Christ and allow that to determine the validity of their thinking, while the latter universalizes the incarnation by conceptualizing it as the highest instance of symbolic expression.

This is the basis of Rahner's assertion that Jesus, in his humanity as such, is the revealer,[14] an idea that Barth rejects[15] because he insists that in the incarnation the Word was not transformed into something else but continued to exercise its sovereignty in the hiddenness of Jesus' humanity and especially on the cross; Torrance rejected such thinking as well by rejecting the idea that Jesus' humanity should be seen as the earthen vessel into which the Son of God "emptied himself" because such thinking tended toward Monophysitism and compromises Jesus' uniqueness. But for Torrance such thinking also means that God cannot really be seen as acting in the history of Jesus because if God is the infinite container he cannot himself become one of the particular beings he contains; this opens the door to the deistic idea that God is "nameless" and that Jesus is different from us in degree rather than in kind. That is why Rahner can argue that anyone who says yes to his or her own humanity says yes to Christ even without having heard of Christ. This universalism is the direct result of Rahner's failure to abide by the fact that the Word remains the subject of the event of the incarnation and that the incarnation must indeed be the starting point and not simply the conclusion of one's christological reflections. This is why both Barth and Torrance reject the idea that Jesus' human nature and ours is "divinized" while Rahner embraces such an idea.

Here it is important to realize that Rahner can speak of grace and revelation as elements within human experience in virtue of his belief that the history of salvation and revelation are "coextensive" with the history of the human race. Rahner thus can look to human experience itself (because of our supposed obediential potency and supernatural existential) for theological insight while Barth and Torrance insist that grace and revelation are identical with Jesus Christ and that theological insight is only possible in and through Jesus, the risen Lord and through no other and thus through faith alone. It is his Holy Spirit who enables this by allowing us to participate in the knowledge of the Father and Son that is actualized within history. That is why Barth insists that we must look away from ourselves and toward Jesus as the way, the truth and the life. For Barth,

> Revelation in fact does not differ from the person of Jesus Christ nor from the reconciliation accomplished in Him . . . we are saying something which can have only an intertrinitarian basis in the will of the Father and the sending of the Son and the Holy Spirit, in the eternal decree of the triune God, so that it can be established only as knowledge of God from God . . . [revelation] has no basis or possibility outside itself [and] can in no sense be explained in terms of man and man's situation. . . . It is Jesus Christ Himself who here speaks for Himself and needs no witness apart from His Holy Spirit and the faith that rejoices in His promise received and grasped. (*CD* I/1, 119-20)

That is why Torrance continually argues that we must think from a center in God provided by God himself in the incarnation, atonement, resurrection and ascension rather than from a center in ourselves. For Torrance,

> It is in fact under the Lordship of the Spirit that we learn what objectivity in knowledge [of God] really is. . . . On the one hand . . . the Holy Spirit . . . brings the very Being of God to bear upon us in our experience . . . but on the other hand, the Spirit through His ineffable and self-effacing nature reinforces the impossibility of our conceiving in thought and expressing in speech how our thought and speech are related to God. (*God and Rationality*, 176)

For Torrance, God of course can be known only through God. Hence "the given Object of our knowledge is actively at work in our knowing of it, creating from outside a corresponding action in which our own being is committed." That is why knowledge of God is a spiritual activity in which we, in our

thinking, correspond to the "movement of the Spirit" and actually participate in God's self-knowledge through the Spirit. We can therefore think
from a center in Christ only through the Spirit (*God and Rationality*, 177).
Thus Torrance concludes that by its nature theological knowledge "has its
objective basis not in itself but in God, and must never presume to find its
truth in itself but only in Him" (*God and Rationality*, 182). It is the Holy
Spirit himself who "excludes from us any possibility of non-objective knowledge" but also confers true objective knowledge upon us as the Lord (*God
and Rationality*, 184). How this happens cannot be explained just because it
is an act of the Holy Spirit uniting us to Christ. "Knowledge of God in the
Spirit is profoundly conceptual, rational knowledge in its own right, knowledge in which we are carried right over to what transcends us, yet which is
apposite to the nature of God as *Spirit*" (*God and Rationality*, 188). But for
Rahner "God's self-revelation in the depths of the spiritual person is an a
priori determination coming from grace and is in itself unreflexive. It is not
in itself an objective, thematic expression; it is not something known objectively, but something in the realm of consciousness" (*FCF*, 172). Hence for
Rahner revelation is

> a modification of our transcendental consciousness produced perma-
> nently by God in grace. But such a modification is really an original and
> permanent element in our consciousness as the basic and original lumi-
> nosity of our existence. And as an element in our transcendentality . . . it is
> already revelation in the proper sense. (*FCF*, 149)

It is just this thinking that causes Rahner to focus on our transcendental experiences rather than exclusively on Christ as the Word of God revealed and
revealing himself now in the power of the Spirit. And it is this divergence with
respect to the incarnation that leads to very different explanations of the resurrection as we shall see.

The Nature of the Resurrection

Here we reach the central theme of this book, namely, that because Christ's
incarnation and resurrection are intrinsically related, one's view of the incarnation will determine one's view of the resurrection and *vice versa*. We have
seen that both Torrance and Barth adamantly insist that the resurrection of
Jesus Christ is a unique miraculous action of God in history that benefits us.
Both theologians stress that it is something utterly new for which we have and

can have no *a priori* knowledge whatsoever, and both theologians stress that these events are miracles, with the idea that if a miracle could be explained by us it would no longer be a miracle. And they argue that the incarnation and resurrection require a radical reconstruction of our concept of God. We have seen that they both argue in the traditional sense, following the apostle Paul, that the resurrection must be understood to mean Jesus' bodily resurrection from the dead — resurrection was an event in the life of Jesus that gave meaning to the disciples' faith and now gives meaning to our faith because the Holy Spirit still acts to unite us to the risen and ascended Lord. In all of their thinking, then, both Torrance and Barth refused to resolve the objective resurrection and appearances of Jesus into the subjective experience of the disciples. It is neither their faith nor their hope that creates or conditions the resurrection event or its significance; rather it is the object of faith that gives meaning to their faith and hope. While the appearances of the risen Jesus could not be identified with the resurrection itself for both Barth and Torrance, the appearances were real because the one who appeared was the risen Jesus himself in his glorified humanity. In other words the appearances were neither developed descriptions of the disciples' experience of faith nor projections of their hope; rather they were descriptions of who it was who encountered them and *enabled* their faith and gave them reason to hope: the man Jesus, risen from the dead, was among them and ate and drank with them as the "Resurrected." Hence, Barth and Torrance both argued that the risen Lord specifically interacted with the disciples during the Easter history and that that particular history was the object of the NT recollections and as such was the object of NT expectation.

It is thus the risen and ascended Lord who is the object who gives meaning to Christian hope as well. Christian hope is not something that can be defined or understood in abstraction from the risen Lord himself since he is the one who gives meaning to hope. Hope and faith are defined by who Jesus is and what he does; they certainly cannot be understood in any general way that might disregard his person and work. Without his actual physical resurrection from the dead and without his definite coming again there is no real basis for hope in the Christian sense. That is why Christian hope cannot be understood in abstraction from Christian faith. Both theologians then insisted that the unique nature of the incarnate Word dictated the unique nature of the event of the resurrection and that the resurrection itself was the very power of the triune God acting within history.

When we turn to the thinking of Karl Rahner we see some striking contrasts. First, while Rahner does express his belief in the traditional meaning of Christ's resurrection from the dead and its centrality for Christian faith and practice, his theological method causes numerous irreconcilable difficulties. He adopts what Fergusson called the liberal view of the resurrection. Hence, as we have seen, he begins thinking about the resurrection with our transcendental experience of hope and not with Jesus himself as the risen Lord, so that Rahner can even say that the meaning of the resurrection can be discerned through a transcendental anthropology quite apart from any revelation in the Word. This is in keeping with his starting point for understanding the incarnation; we could not, Rahner insisted, begin with the incarnate Lord because Jesus himself had become a problem. Instead, we must begin further back with our transcendental experience and construct an *a priori* anthropology within which we then might develop specific christological themes. Thus, Rahner's belief that the resurrection can and should be understood as an instance of our transcendental experience of hope is consistent with the starting point that he chose for understanding the incarnation. But this thinking makes our transcendental experience of hope the criterion for the truth of incarnation and resurrection with the result that it cannot be the risen Lord himself who exclusively dictates the meaning of theological truth. In this sense the Holy Spirit is assimilated to the human spirit. As we have seen, this opens the door to both Ebionite and Docetic Christology and thus fails to lead to a proper understanding of who Jesus really was and is and what the resurrection actually means for contemporary theology. In fact, despite Rahner's insistence on the centrality of Jesus Christ for his theology, his method demonstrates that what is really central is not Jesus himself, but our transcendental experience and the hope derived from that experience. Jesus' importance consists in the fact that he confirms the hope we have of our own resurrection.

Second, because of this starting point, Rahner explicitly maintains that the disciples' experience of the risen Lord cannot be distinguished clearly from the object that gives meaning to their experience: "In the case of Jesus' disciples their Easter faith and their Easter experience (their belief and the grounds for that belief) are already blended into each other indissolubly" (*TI* 7: 164). And so for Rahner "We dare to believe, in hope, in our own history and this enables us to believe in the resurrection of Jesus."[16] That is why Rahner also insists that "we do not learn something which is totally unexpected and which lies totally outside of the horizon of our experience and possibilities of verification" (*FCF*, 275). Instead of allowing the risen Lord himself through his Spirit to dictate meaning here Rahner argues that the enabling condition of belief in Jesus' resurrection is our faith and hope in our own history. But from Torrance's point of view such thinking is unscientific because it does not allow the unique object in question (the risen Lord through his Spirit) to dictate what is said, but rather uses our own experiences of faith and hope as the theological criterion. For Barth the enabling condition of belief in Jesus' resurrection is the Holy Spirit in union with the incarnate Word and thus the risen Lord himself, and therefore it cannot in any sense be our own belief or hope in our own history. This would represent an intolerable form of self-justification from the vantage of both Barth and Torrance. And we have seen that the chief ethical implication of this insight is that both Barth (with much more explicit detail of course) and Torrance contend that the law is the form of the Gospel so that our life in hope is marked by the fact that we explicitly trust in the promise fulfilled in Jesus' resurrection and expected at his second coming.

By contrast, the mutual conditioning associated with all symbolic reality marks Rahner's thinking. As symbols have a mutually causal relation with that which they symbolize[17] so the resurrection and the disciples' experience of the risen Jesus condition each other. Hence for Rahner the "facts" of Jesus' resurrection "must simply be determined in the light of what we have to understand by our own 'resurrection'" (TI 17: 20). And this thinking shapes Rahner's ethics because he defines freedom as basic to human nature in its supposed conjunction with grace in transcendental experience so that he claims we have a basic freedom displayed in our fundamental option with the result that freedom cannot be exclusively defined by who Jesus was and is as the risen Lord and the one who alone enables our freedom. In the end Rahner's view of freedom leads him to believe that self-acceptance is the same as accepting the Gospel. This for Barth and Torrance is the very opposite of true human freedom.

Third, it is not at all clear in Rahner's thinking that the risen Jesus actually existed in his own right in a genuinely objective relationship with the disciples during a specific history. Hence, Rahner can actually express the strange view that "I do not even know whether one who has been glorified has a head" (TI 11: 210). He takes an agnostic position with respect to the body of the risen Lord. He even says that the risen Lord "does not belong to the world of our experience" (TI 11: 211). So while Torrance and Barth insist, with the NT witness, that Jesus rose bodily from the dead and ate and drank with the disciples, Rahner is not quite sure what belongs to the body of the risen Lord. We have seen that Rahner is notoriously vague about the body of the risen Christ and prefers to describe this as "the absolute fulfillment of the concrete human person," of his having been "definitively delivered." It is not that Rahner desires to fall into a kind of subjectivism since he argues that something objective did happen here. It is rather that this objective happening is equated by Rahner with the disciples' own experiences of faith and hope: Rahner sees our human experience of hope as the *a priori* perspective that justifies our belief in the resurrection of Jesus and in that way undercuts the objectivity he actually asserts. Rahner thus thinks of the disciples' "original experience" of the resurrection as a dramatic embellishment, which represents an explanation of an experience of the Spirit of the living Lord instead of understanding it in an "almost physical sense" (*FCF*, 276). That is why Rahner argues, "Faith is not taking cognizance of a fact which by its nature could exist just as well without being taken cognizance of" (*FCF*, 267) and that faith should be seen as an intrinsic element of the resurrection itself.

In a sense Rahner is attempting to uphold the view espoused by Torrance that the disciples' faith and ours belong to the whole integrated event of the resurrection. There are formal similarities to the two perspectives in that regard. But Torrance and Rahner are separated by the fact that Torrance will not allow our subjective inclusion in the resurrection event to determine its objective nature and reality. In other words for Torrance there is a clear distinction in the union of the risen Lord and the faith of his disciples then and now, while for Rahner there is a mutually conditioning relationship between the two — and a mutually conditioned relationship always implies an underlying identity. That is why Rahner can say that the resurrection would not have an essential existence without the disciples' faith (*FCF*, 268) and that Jesus rose into the faith of the disciples.

By contrast Torrance would insist that it is only because the Lord rose from the dead bodily and had a specific existence during the Easter history that the disciples' faith had any significance at all. It is here that Rahner and Barth and Torrance are separated by an enormous chasm: Barth and Torrance insist on Jesus' bodily resurrection while Rahner rejects the idea that the disciples had a "sense experience" of the risen Jesus. Such thinking, in Rahner's view, would mean that everything would then have to belong to the realm of "normal and profane sense experience" (*FCF*, 276). That is why Rahner opts for assigning the meaning of Jesus' resurrection to the "correspondence" between one's transcendental experience of hope and the categorical or real presence of such a resurrection. But how can Jesus' resurrection have a historical and genuinely objective meaning if it is assigned in this way to the mutual relation of our experience and the categories we use to describe that experience in relation to Jesus? The very fact that Rahner cannot imagine a genuinely existing body for the risen Lord is reason enough to suspect a Docetic understanding of the matter, an understanding which undermines the particularity of Jesus for all aspects of Christian dogmatics. This would explain Rahner's inability, noted in Chapter Two above, to take death seriously as well as his belief that resurrection is already part of the experience of death, and his belief that in a sense we create eternity from our experiences of time. Here again the difference between Rahner and Barth and Torrance is enormous: Rahner argues that it is and must be our experience of hope that allows us to understand and accept the resurrection, while Barth and Torrance insist that the resurrection is something that is utterly new and cuts completely against the grain of any of our prior thoughts and/or hopes. It is its own validation and cannot be validated from a point outside the unique existence of the risen Lord himself. Both Torrance and Barth insist that death is a real threat to our existence that cannot be alleviated in any sense whatsoever by us; and they also insist that eternity comes into time to re-create our time and history but for that very reason eternity can never be properly conceived as arising from time and history and certainly is never the creation of our own activities within history. Here, once again, methodological issues dictate the actual understanding of the risen Lord offered by each of these three theologians.

Finally, then, we may say that Torrance and Barth on the one side and Rahner on the other are separated in their views of the meaning of the resurrection on eight key points: (1) the starting point for understanding Christ's resurrection: Rahner insists that the starting point is our transcendental experience of hope in our own resurrection while Torrance and Barth insist that Jesus Christ himself risen from the dead must be the starting point; (2) Rahner sees the relationship between the resurrection and faith as a mutually determined relationship while Torrance and Barth insist that the resurrection is what it is objectively and that while it includes us and our faith in a genuine relationship with the risen Lord, it does so in free grace and thus excludes any sort of mutually conditioning and mutually conditioned relationship; (3) while Rahner thinks the resurrection is not actually realized without the faith of the disciples' and ours, Torrance and Barth insist that it is only because it is indeed realized in the life of Jesus independent of anyone's faith that it can be a sufficient ground for faith then and now; (4) Rahner thinks the resurrection was not a historical fact existing independently of faith while both Torrance and Barth insist that it is such a fact, though not one whose meaning can be ascertained by normal methods of historical investigation, since it is an act of God within history; (5) while Rahner thinks the resurrection can and must be anticipated and verified by our experience of hope, both Torrance and Barth insist that the resurrection itself can and must be its own validation because in Christ we have a unique subject, the God-Man Jesus Christ, and that unique subject must be allowed to determine theological meaning here and elsewhere; (6) Rahner believes that the resurrection is not something unexpected or utterly new within the realm of human experience while Torrance and Barth both insist that unless it is acknowledged as something utterly new we will try to account for it in terms of our prior knowledge and experience and thus fall into a kind of Ebionite or Docetic Christology with the result that we will control its meaning instead of accepting its meaning as an act of God for us; (7) for Rahner the disciples primarily witness to their experience of faith in witnessing to the resurrection while for Torrance and Barth they primarily witness to an event in the life of Jesus that gave meaning to their faith and to ours; (8) Rahner believed that one can have an anonymous experience of the risen Lord while both Barth and Torrance insisted that any such idea meant that the historical Jesus had been ignored or subverted by some sort of Docetic interpretation of the resurrection. And the reason for such a Docetic view always lies in the fact that the incarnation of God in Jesus Christ was not taken seriously enough in its intrinsic unity with Jesus' resurrection from the dead.

The Nature and Significance of the Empty Tomb

As seen above, the empty tomb was considered together with the ascension in Barth's thought, as an indispensable sign of the risen Lord. As such it could not be confused with the reality signified, namely, the risen Lord himself. On the one hand the empty tomb signified that Jesus had been buried and was now free from death through the power of God. On the other hand it signified that Jesus was not to be sought among the dead since he now was alive. We saw that for Barth the angels were re-introduced in the Synoptic accounts for the first time since the birth and temptation stories to indicate the empty tomb. In Barth's thinking one should not focus on the empty tomb but on the risen Jesus. Further, he believes the empty tomb was ambiguous and contestable precisely because it is not the appearance of the risen Lord himself. Nonetheless, Barth contends that we cannot actually trust in the living Christ if we deny the empty tomb. In fact Barth believed that wherever the empty tomb was denied there too the resurrection itself was also denied.

Did Barth believe the empty tomb was a legend? He admits that it may have been a legend but then insists that even if it is, that does not alter the witness of the NT because it still refers to an occurrence that preceded the resurrection as the presupposition for the appearances of the risen Lord. As a sign that obviates all misunderstanding then, Barth argued it demands our assent, even as a legend. And so Barth accepts the empty tomb arguing that it belongs to the Easter event as the sign of the risen Lord.

For Torrance, as we have seen, the empty tomb was absolutely central. The entire Gospel, seen in light of Easter, was seen to pivot upon the empty tomb. Like Barth, Torrance notes that the empty tomb was not identified with

the resurrection itself but since it was recorded in all the Gospels and is inseparably bound up with the resurrection, it must be taken seriously. Torrance
insists that the empty tomb is the clearest expression of Christ's bodily resurrection from the dead and an important safeguard against any spiritualizing
of the event. With the empty tomb Torrance connects the incarnation and the
resurrection by contending that since the Word became incarnate in time and
space therefore the "empirical correlates" of the divine actions of incarnation
and resurrection cannot be ignored. That is precisely why the empty tomb is
so important for Torrance: "cut that away and it [the Christian doctrine of
the resurrection] becomes nonsensical" (STI, 90). The resurrection would
then simply express one's subjective fantasies. For Torrance, we have seen that
the empty tomb functions to avoid an Ebionite or Docetic interpretation of
the incarnation and the resurrection. Torrance insists that if there is no resurrection, then human nature is not truly human, because what makes it truly
human is the incarnation of the Word in space and time. Any resurrection
therefore that is not a bodily resurrection would call into question the incarnation of the Word in space and time and thus also the fact that our humanity finds its meaning in the actions of God's Word and Spirit.

> The body of Jesus Christ was raised, certainly a spiritual body, but it was no
> less body because it was a body healed and quickened by the Spirit in
> which all corruption had been overcome. It is *the empty tomb that consti-
> tutes the essential empirical correlate in statements about the resurrection of
> Christ.* (STR, 141; emphasis in original)[18]

Unlike Barth, the question of whether or not the empty tomb was a legend never arises for Torrance. In Torrance's scientific theology, which explicitly ties the resurrection to the incarnation and thus takes space and time with
utter seriousness, it is essential that the "empirical correlates" of God's actions
within history be taken seriously. So for Torrance the empty tomb is necessarily tied to the bodily resurrection of Jesus himself.

In his book on the resurrection Torrance was critical of Barth for being
too anxious to preserve the resurrection as an act of pure divine grace so that
in *CD* IV/1 Barth tended to play down the idea that Jesus actively rose from
the dead (STR, 32), an idea that Torrance embraces: "he raised himself up
from the dead in perfect Amen to the Father's Will, acquiescing in his verdict
upon our sin but responding in complete trust and love to the Father" (STR,
67-68).[19] Torrance believes it is important to stress this because "the activity
of Christ in the resurrection is essential to the unity of his person as Mediator" (STR, 32). Hence for Torrance

The Empty Tomb certainly implies that it was a whole Christ who died for us and that it is the whole Christ who lives for evermore; that He came to redeem us as whole men, not just a part of us; that the body is part of the human personality; and that contempt for the body and the physical is also contempt for the Creator. (*STR*, 66)

This criticism is in line with Torrance's view that in *CD* IV/3 Barth did not sufficiently emphasize Christ's high-priestly ministry as the ascended Lord and that this opened the door to Docetic readings of the *CD* so that even Hendrikus Berkhof had been misled by Barth into a "Sabellian doctrine of the Spirit" (*Karl Barth*, 134 and 206ff.). This was also the basis of Torrance's criticism of Barth's sacramental theology, especially with regard to his overly sharp distinction between water Baptism and Baptism with the Spirit that, according to Torrance, reflected a reversion to an earlier dualism that Barth had overcome in prior volumes of the *CD* (*Karl Barth*, 134). Does Barth's opinion that the empty tomb could be a legend indicate what could perhaps be seen as a Docetic view of the resurrection? It would, I think, be a mistake to draw that conclusion because on the one hand what Barth sought to avoid was any idea that the empty tomb was a "proof" of the resurrection and on the other hand he wanted to argue that the reality of the empty tomb described by the NT text "is not confirmed or disconfirmed by the latest scholarly speculation on whether the empty tomb is legendary or not."[20] In fact Barth insists "The statement that Christ is risen necessarily implies the assertion that a dead man is alive again and that his grave is empty" (*CD* IV/2, 149). And he goes on to assert, "Because it takes place in the majesty of the will and act of God, the knowledge of it [revelation] cannot derive from knowing man, but only from the One who is revealed in it" (*CD* IV/2, 149). The NT texts, according to Barth, "do not attest only a miracle of believing. . . . They attest Jesus Himself, who, having come back to them miraculously, creates and kindles this recognition. They attest the miraculous consequence of the divine act of His awakening from the dead as it took place for Him and therefore for them" (*CD* IV/2, 148).

As seen above, Rahner does not have a lot to say about the empty tomb. In his *Theological Investigations* he expresses the belief that it is part of the oldest NT tradition and he also says that the empty tomb is "an expression of a conviction which had already spread for other reasons — the conviction that Jesus was alive" (*TI* 17: 20). In *Foundations* Rahner takes a somewhat more detached view of the matter arguing that he will

prescind here from the question to which stratum in the tradition of the resurrection of Jesus the empty tomb belongs, and what significance it has in this tradition. Resurrection does not mean to begin with a salvifically neutral survival of human existence, but means its salvation and its acceptance by God. (*FCF*, 267)

Comparing Torrance and Barth on the one side and Rahner on the other, we notice that for Rahner the empty tomb signifies a "conviction" while for Barth and for Torrance it signifies an event that occurred independent of anyone's convictions. The key question here concerns whether it was the conviction that Jesus was alive that was the focus of the NT witness or whether it was the fact that Jesus was alive and encountered the disciples, enabling their faith that was decisive. That was indeed their conviction but it was not the conviction that was central; rather it was the reality that determined the conviction that was central. We have seen that for Rahner it is virtually impossible for him to maintain that it is the living Jesus Christ himself who physically encountered the disciples and enabled their faith and who can thus encounter us through the power of the Holy Spirit and enable our faith. That would explain why Rahner would take the empty tomb to refer to the salvation and acceptance by God of human existence. This is sufficiently vague as to suggest that it could be experienced whenever and wherever anyone has a transcendental experience of faith or of hope suggesting that human existence will continue beyond death. But such a suggestion is a far cry from the particular testimony of the NT in its mention of the empty tomb. The empty tomb signifies that a particular dead man was alive again and that his particular existence is the reality that gives meaning to Christian faith and hope. So it is with the empty tomb that we can see once again that a proper view of the resurrection is tied inextricably to the fact that any sort of Ebionite or Docetic approach to the matter undermines the reality of the resurrection and our atonement in the person and work of Christ himself.

The Importance of the Doctrine of the Trinity and Ethical Implications

We have seen that for Barth and Torrance the doctrine of the Trinity is intimately connected with Christology so that any implicit or explicit compromise of Christ's deity necessarily means a denial that the God who meets us in the incarnation and resurrection of the man Jesus is the eternal Father, Son and Holy Spirit. Such thinking would of course also undermine any genuine doctrine of atonement exactly because of its failure to acknowledge Jesus Christ as the unique mediator between God and us. And such thinking would then open the door to some sort of self-justification in the ethical sphere with the implication that we must somehow do what is right and good in order to be saved. Or it might suggest that in our right and good ethical behavior we are saved irrespective of our actual relationship to Jesus Christ himself. But for Barth and Torrance it is just the other way around: we can do what is right and good in the ethical sphere only because Jesus Christ himself has acted on our behalf to enable such action in and through his death and resurrection for our sakes. And the ascended Lord continues to do so within history through his witnesses within and without the church. Furthermore, Barth and Torrance would never equate our justification and sanctification with our ethical behavior because they both insist that what makes us righteous and holy is and remains always an act of the triune God and never can be directly seen and described by exploring people's general ethical behavior.

For Barth, as for Torrance, it is because there is an immanent Trinity, namely, an eternal Father, Son and Holy Spirit who exists in unapproachable light that this self-same God can act freely in an effective way for us within the confines of sinful history and thus overcome our sin and self-will in a way that not only respects our human freedom, but establishes it in the power of the risen Lord himself and thus through the Holy Spirit. For both Barth and Torrance then it is imperative that we recognize that what God is toward us in his Word and Spirit he is antecedently and eternally in himself. But it is equally important to realize that God's actions on our behalf as creator, reconciler and redeemer are free actions that are in no way necessitated either by God's nature or by anything outside his own free love and decision to act mercifully toward us in Christ and the Spirit. Both Barth and Torrance therefore argue for a clear doctrine of the immanent Trinity as the manner in which we may grasp God's freedom *in se* and *ad extra* with the result that they both clearly distinguish the immanent and economic Trinity so that they can underline the truth that it is precisely God's sovereign freedom for us that is encountered in the incarnation and the resurrection of Jesus Christ. Take away the immanent Trinity and trinitarian thought and discussion become little more than our use of Christian categories to project our own hopes and wishes onto God in such a way that we would then create God in our image rather than recognizing that it is God who created us in his image. In that case theology would be little more than the projection of theological images onto the God of our own invention in order to accomplish some social, political, ethical or religious goal.[21] For Barth and Torrance, God is the eternal Father, Son and Holy Spirit and there is nothing higher or deeper that can be said of God than that, precisely because God has revealed that to us in and through Christ's resurrection from the dead. That is why they both believe that "Resurrection is revelation, and revelation is resurrection" in its identity with the history of Jesus Christ himself.[22] What gives meaning to all of this is the fact that in the history of Jesus Christ it is the triune God himself who is active in a way that transcends any possibilities we might conjure on our own apart from the risen Lord himself.

When we turn to Rahner's trinitarian theology we see that on the surface it appears that all three theologians hold a similar view of the matter. Rahner insists that the immanent and economic Trinity should be seen as strictly identical and wishes to avoid an abstract view of the Trinity that keeps the triune God detached from our Christian experience. In this sense it would appear that all three theologians agree that what God is toward us in Christ and the Spirit, he is eternally in himself. But how then do we account for the crucial differences that we have seen among the three theologians in their theological methods and in their views of the incarnation, grace, resurrection and ethics?

The answer, I suggest, lies in the fact that although Rahner formally wished to build his theology on and from the economic trinitarian self-revelation of God in Christ and the Spirit, he actually allowed his transcendental method to dictate both his conception of God as the nameless silent term of our transcendental experiences and of our relations with God in the economy. This is what opened the door to his idea that natural theology and revealed theology mutually condition each other, and to the idea that the immanent Trinity is identical with the economic Trinity and *vice versa* — it is the *vice versa* that tends to blur God's freedom to exist in his own right and to remain free even in his relations with us in the sphere of the economy. This is what allowed and even required Rahner to develop and to apply his theology of the symbol to the central doctrines of the Christian faith with disastrous results as noted above.

Ultimately, it is because Rahner does not begin his thinking with Jesus Christ as the Word of God incarnate, but sees the incarnation as the conclusion rather than as the starting point for contemporary Christian theology, that he tends to blur the distinction between the immanent and the economic Trinity. This opens the door to the kind of self-justification that all theologians, including Rahner, recognize is so problematic within a Christian context. Unfortunately, however, Rahner also argues that our moral behavior can actually be equated with salvation, with the result that anyone who accepts his/her existence with a clear conscience is saved whether or not he/she believes in Jesus Christ.[23] Now it is quite true that Christ can save anyone within or without the church because he is the Lord and is not controlled by the church itself. But this acknowledgment of the freedom of God in relation to the church is a far cry from the claim that any good moral behavior can be equated with the divine act of salvation that took place in the incarnation and resurrection. The difference here among these three theologians stems from Rahner's failure to maintain a clear and sharp distinction between the immanent and economic Trinity with the result that he collapsed God's actions *ad extra* into the disciples' experiences of faith and hope and subsequently into ours. This accounts for why Rahner so consistently blurred the distinction between the object of faith and hope and our experiences of faith and hope so that he could even use our experiences of faith and hope to define the meaning of incarnation and resurrection. The result was a form of universalism that undermines the particular meaning of Christianity at every point along the way.

The differences between Barth and Torrance on the one side and Rahner on the other regarding Christian ethics are just as stark as are their different interpretations of the relationship between the incarnation and the resurrection. First, Barth and Torrance would agree that Christian ethics is determined by its specific relation to Jesus Christ himself — Christ really has made himself responsible for us. Our life of freedom is therefore hidden with Christ in God (Col. 3:3). Hence, any attempt to discuss human freedom apart from faith in Jesus himself as truly divine and truly human would necessarily lead to some form of self-justification and thus toward legalism (the idea that somehow it is the law or obedience to the law — either the natural law or the ten commandments or a combination of the two that makes us righteous and sanctifies us) or license (the idea that we are free to do whatever we choose because we are righteous and holy already and belief does not require obedience to Christ alone). Because Rahner begins his theology with an analysis of transcendental experience and will not begin exclusively with Jesus Christ, his view of ethics takes place within the natural law tradition and so he assumes we are free and good when we are faithful to the structures built into human being. It is this idea that leads Rahner to look within human self-consciousness to discover God, revelation, grace and freedom. But it is exactly on this decisive issue that Reformed and Roman Catholic theologies are seriously divided. Rahner's approach to ethics would represent the supreme form of self-justification for Barth and Torrance. Yet in Rahner's mind he is only presenting what for him is the Roman Catholic view of justification, namely, the idea that if we are justified (by faith) then we must be able to look to the justified person to grasp the true meaning of theology and freedom. Barth and Torrance, however, think that since Christ is the one who justifies us and the Spirit is the one who sanctifies us, justification and sanctification, as divine acts, always point us away from ourselves to our true being which is in Christ and through his Spirit. They think it is impossible to discover our new life by looking at ourselves because grace does not become part of our nature in the form of a supernatural existential.

Second, knowledge of God itself is really the first form of Christian ethics because such knowledge is right and true only to the extent that it takes place in obedience, namely, only as it begins and ends with God's movement toward us in the incarnation and resurrection. Hence, natural theology is excluded as a form of self-justification. Both Barth and Torrance would agree on this point. Yet, as we saw, Torrance's attempt to construct a "new natural theology" inadvertently displays vestiges of the difficulties of the old natural theology and is therefore in tension with Torrance's own intentions. There is some difference here between Barth and Torrance in spite of Torrance's belief that they are both in full agreement that natural theology is acceptable when it functions within revelation.[24]

When we turn to Rahner we see that it is precisely his natural theology which leads him to think that because human beings are open to God by being open to the horizon of their experiences and thus to the goal of their transcendental experiences, they are innately in touch with the Christian God. It is just this assumption which presents knowledge of God as something that takes places for all outside of a specific decision of faith in relation to Jesus himself. It is just here, in connection with Rahner's natural theology and his belief that natural theology and revealed theology mutually condition each other that he is misled into thinking that moral action, even without any specific reference to Christ himself, is salvific action. Such thinking always uses Christ in some sense as the historical figure who confirms our moral ideals. But in so doing such thinking always allows us (in the form of our moral ideals) to determine the truth and goodness of our behavior and not Jesus himself. This always means some sort of conditional salvation — that is — our salvation in some sense depends either upon our love of neighbor or upon our response to our conscience or to the moral law. Again this thinking represents a form of self-justification that is directly rooted in a type of Docetic Christology that is determined more by our ideals than by the historical Jesus who is our Lord. Within such thinking, Jesus Christ himself becomes little more than the exemplar of our moral ideals. But in reality, when seen from the vantage offered by Barth and Torrance, Jesus Christ has really taken responsibility for us so that we are truly free to obey him alone and thus we are free from the tyranny of subjecting ourselves to our own moral ideals or those of others in the false hope that these can lead us to salvation when in reality they cannot. And they cannot do so precisely because Jesus himself risen from the dead is our savior and is actively at work through his Spirit directing us away from ourselves and toward our new life in him.

Third, it is here that perhaps the greatest difference between Barth and Torrance on the one side and Rahner on the other concerns the impact of sin on their thought. Barth takes sin seriously in the sense that he consistently recognizes that without the grace of God active and revealed in Christ and through the Spirit we cannot live in right relation with God. Both Barth and Torrance would agree that we cannot say or imply that our human attempts to know what is good and evil are simply our natural inclinations to do God's will. Our will is enslaved by sin and must be freed by God in Christ for us to do God's will. Hence, as we have no obediential potency for revelation and faith, so we have none for knowledge of God, or for being good and holy in the Christian sense. This comes to us as a specific freedom and obligation in Christ and through the Holy Spirit in specific circumstances. Barth and Torrance differ most on the issue of natural theology as we have seen. When we turn to Rahner it is precisely his belief in an obediential potency and a supernatural existential that both Barth and Torrance would consider Pelagian in orientation and design. By making grace part of our self-experience in the form of our transcendental unthematic experience of and knowledge of God, revelation and grace, Rahner makes it difficult if not impossible to distinguish our new life in Christ from our relationship to ourselves and he makes it equally difficult to distinguish the Holy Spirit from our human spirit. That is why he can argue that self-acceptance is the same as accepting Christ. Once again such thinking makes Christ irrelevant because it uses him as a moral ideal for good human behavior instead of seeing him as the only possible source of goodness, truth and freedom and indeed as the only one who can set us free from sin. For Rahner sin is not defined exclusively by our relationship to Jesus Christ but by our relationship to ourselves and thus to Jesus Christ. In that sense he does not take sin or its solution seriously enough from the point of view of both Barth and Torrance. And the very fact that Rahner supposes that one can be a Christian without specifically relating to the risen Lord undercuts the fact that no one can say Jesus is Lord without the Holy Spirit. This means, of course, that the Holy Spirit can never be separated from Jesus the Word incarnate without confusing the Holy Spirit with our human spirit.

Fourth, in no sense can we claim that the divine command can be explained either from the "natural law" or from some other human vantage point. We cannot say this to ourselves; it can only come directly from God to us as grace. It is therefore offensive and can never be reduced to our relationship to ourselves in our transcendental dynamisms. It is just because Rahner has removed the offending element in revelation in his Christology by making the resurrection an inevitable part of our own self-interpretation that he concludes that in the form of our fundamental option we become co-creators with God and save or condemn ourselves. This of course is in complete contrast with the thinking of both Barth and Torrance who stress that we never become co-creators and must always recognize that it is not our options (fundamental or other) that determine our judgment and/or salvation, but God's electing grace which was manifest and is in effect in the very history of the risen, ascended and coming Lord. It is in this context that Rahner repeatedly insists that salvation is "offered" to us in the depths of our spiritual experiences of freedom.

Yet, if salvation is merely offered to us in this way, then it remains conditional upon our response to it. This can never be seen as the freedom of grace from within the thinking of Barth and Torrance because the Gospel presents us with a salvation that is unconditionally in effect and that frees us for the service of God and neighbor. So, while Rahner's vision of ethics does overcome the weaknesses of the old natural law ethic with his view of the fundamental option, it does so, as we have seen, at the expense of the true meaning of freedom as presented in the Gospel. In this context true human freedom means choosing between two possibilities so that on the basis of our choice of the good, it could be said that we are both good and free. For Barth and Torrance there is only one possible choice that is enabled and required by the risen Lord himself, and that is to choose him and thus to exercise free obedience. Rahner will often say that our freedom increases in inverse and not in direct proportion to our dependence on God. And that sounds appealing. But the problem is that his view of God, like his view of morality, is not consistently dictated by the God of the Bible and thus by our justification by faith. Because ruling grace is commanding grace, it becomes clear that what God wants of us is simply that we should believe in Jesus Christ. The essence of faith then is to accept as right what God has done and is doing for us in Christ. This takes place in and through the Holy Spirit acting for us and in us. While Torrance does not develop his thought on this subject explicitly with respect to Christian ethics in any sense as thoroughly as Barth has, he nonetheless would agree that true human knowledge and action are possible because they find their meaning outside themselves and only in Christ. And they are specifically tied to the Holy Spirit as Torrance insists in his book *God and Rationality*. In that sense the doctrine of justification shapes all of Torrance's thinking just as it does for Barth. It is here that Rahner's anonymous Christianity reveals how far apart his thinking is from that of both Barth and Torrance. For Rahner every positively moral act is a salvific act just as every transcendental experience of hope is an experience of the resurrection whether or not one has heard the Gospel and believed in the risen Lord. It is just in this sense that Rahner looks to us in our transcendental relationship to ourselves, with its supposed movement toward the nameless, silent incomprehensibility, that he is forced to look away from the only true source of freedom, the only unconditional source of security — namely — the risen, ascended and coming Lord himself. Instead of looking outside himself and toward Jesus of Nazareth consistently and exclusively, Rahner looks toward himself and his relationship with himself just because he refused to begin and end his thinking exclusively with Jesus. For him the incarnation was the conclusion and not the starting point of Christology just as transcendental experience and not Jesus himself was his starting point for thinking about God. The end result is a view of ethics that leaves us alone with ourselves precisely by equating love of God with love of neighbor instead of seeing the two commands as governed by the love of God revealed in this history of Jesus himself.[25] And the possibility for all of this arises simply because the unity of the Holy Spirit with the Word and with the Father has been ignored so that the Holy Spirit is in reality identified with our experiences of faith, hope and love.

Conclusion and Statement of Thesis

We have seen that there is a very definite relationship between one's view of the incarnation and one's view of the resurrection. Any Ebionite or Docetic view of the one necessarily means an Ebionite or Docetic view of the other. And this is not without practical importance for dogmatic theology and theological ethics because any Christian theological vision that does not begin with the historical Jesus himself who was and is the Word of God incarnate will always argue that salvation is only offered to us on condition that we either repent and believe or on condition that we behave in accordance with the moral law or both. We have seen that such a view fails to denote true human freedom because such freedom is the freedom that exists in the obedient life of Jesus and can be had only to the extent that those who follow him simply and factually live by faith from him and from him alone. In other words Christ promises to share his perfect obedience with us and unless that happens we are still enslaved by the attempt to create God in our own image and thus to create happiness for ourselves instead of finding it in the free action of God on our behalf in Christ and the Spirit. Christian freedom means to live from and in Christ who has set us free to obey him and thus to exercise true human choices. "Ethics," as Barth said, "seeks to form a clear conception of those actions to be performed in Church and world which are essential to and typical of the obedience of faith. Ethics seeks to formulate the practical task assigned to man by the gift of freedom" (*Evangelical Theology*, 118).

Those theologians who offer a liberal interpretation of the resurrection, which inevitably collapses back into the radical view, unavoidably weaken the theological ground on which they stand precisely because the resurrection itself, namely, the risen Lord, really is the one who gave meaning to the disciples' faith and hope there and then and gives meaning to ours here and now. As Paul argued in 1 Cor. 15, unless Christ is truly risen from the dead, our faith is without substance and we are still in our sins; we are indeed hopeless. Yet, whenever it is thought that Jesus' resurrection can be explained *from* our own experience of ourselves, then his bodily resurrection has already been discounted in such a way that it becomes something of an embarrassment to further reflection. Then the biblical accounts of the appearances of the risen Lord are not seen as descriptions of events that took place in history — the Easter history — but rather as embellishments of the disciples' experiences of faith. As such they can be re-interpreted in light of our experiences of personal relationship so that they can make sense to us without offending us in any way. And all of this is possible because the incarnate Word was not taken seriously from the outset. Any discounting of the bodily resurrection of Jesus Christ simply reflects a prior discounting of the fact that the man Jesus of Nazareth was, from the moment of his conception by the Holy Spirit, the Word of God incarnate. Christian theology either begins with Jesus who was the Lord incarnate simply because from all eternity he was the Son of the Father and became flesh for us and our salvation, or it begins elsewhere. Any other beginning, however, already represents a form of self-justification or self-reliance that demonstrates the need for the reconciliation that occurred in Jesus' life history on our behalf. It demonstrates the need for repentance, that is, for a real turning away from ourselves and toward Christ alone through the Spirit.

It is the thesis of this book that unless the starting point of theology is Jesus himself, the incarnate Word, risen from the dead with a body that is now no longer subject to sin, suffering, evil and death (a spiritual body in the sense described by Torrance), then theology has lost its unique object and therefore its true meaning. Then the object of theology and the faith of Christians can no longer be distinguished and theology becomes little more than a religious way of speaking about our deepest experiences such as those of faith and hope. Any such theology, however, cannot express the freedom of God for us because it has failed to see the true basis and meaning of human freedom itself. Self-justification of any kind, especially of the kind that implies that we do not need the Word of God incarnate at the start of our theology and ethics, must always mean that we have inserted ourselves into the mystery of Christology in such a way that it now seems possible and necessary for us to re-construct the meaning of theology and ethics in terms of our most fundamental concerns and decisions. Such thinking, however, neither stems from the freedom we are given in Christ and through his Spirit nor does it engender true human freedom precisely because it is self-reliant in the most blatant way, that is, it really supposes that our experience of faith and our experience of hope, in virtue of God's grace, now enable us to explain the meaning and significance of Jesus' resurrection and incarnation for Christian life today. Nothing could be further from the truth, as we have seen. The difference here is stark: either we accept Jesus for who he was and is or we try to justify belief in him and thus belief in ourselves with the result that in the end we are thrown back upon ourselves epistemologically and ontologically in order to be saved. That is not particularly good news to those who realize that we can in no way save ourselves from our own desire to be lord and master of our own lives. Such thinking always leads to a dead end because it keeps us from seeing that our deepest need is for a righteousness that can only come to us as a free act of God himself from outside the circle of our own analysis and concerns.

With these reflections in place it should now be clear why I accept the traditional view of the resurrection as explicated by David Fergusson and why I reject the liberal and radical views. It is my belief that, despite certain differences that we have seen, Barth and Torrance offer us a clear and unequivocal view of the resurrection as the foundation for Christian theology today. And they do so precisely because they take the incarnation and the Trinity seriously as doctrines that find their meaning in the eternal Father, Son and Holy Spirit. Therefore, in the remainder of this book, I hope to show how and why those liberal and more radical interpretations of the resurrection, which have much in common with Rahner's thinking, have failed to make sense of Christianity today precisely because and to the extent that they have explained away the resurrection of Jesus Christ himself as the starting point and conclusion of faith and hope both in the sphere of systematic theology and in the sphere of ethics. Of course this is not to suggest that there are not certain specific differences between those theologians who intentionally argue against recognizing and maintaining Jesus' uniqueness for Christian faith and practice and Rahner who seriously intends to recognize and maintain Christ's uniqueness, but who is hampered in doing so because of his method. Nonetheless, all of those theologians who fail to begin their thinking explicitly with the risen Lord and thus explicitly with the incarnate Word, do indeed compromise Jesus' uniqueness in one way or another, whether intentionally or not, by the very way they approach the theological enterprise. To this we now turn.

5. Incarnation and Resurrection in the Theology of John Macquarrie and Paul F. Knitter

We have now seen that a proper theology of the resurrection eschews any sort of Ebionite or Docetic thinking at the outset and at each point along the way. It does this precisely because such a theology unashamedly begins with faith in Jesus Christ who is the Word incarnate simply because he is and not because people were impressed with him or thought he confirmed their prior idea of God. Most importantly then, a proper theology of the resurrection makes a clear and sharp distinction between the object of Christian faith and the faith of Christians and thus stresses Christ's bodily resurrection and his appearances as events in the life history of Jesus himself that give meaning to Christian faith and practice. In other words such a theology clearly distinguishes Christ as Lord of the church and the church as the body of Christ exactly because it is aware of the fact that true human freedom has no existence at all in itself but must continually find its reality in Christ and thus in faith and hope. All of this, however, depends upon the fact that Jesus himself, risen bodily from the dead, having appeared to his disciples enabling their faith in specific encounters during the forty days, is still alive and yet interacts with us here and now as the ascended and advent Lord through the power of the Holy Spirit and through the witness of the NT to these specific events.

In this chapter I shall explore the thought of John Macquarrie and Paul Knitter in order to show that when theologians begin their christological reflections in an Ebionite or Docetic fashion they can devise the most sophisticated and alluring contemporary Christologies which are especially alluring in a pluralistic world where it seems so tempting to see other revelations alongside the one unique revelation of God that took place in the history of Jesus Christ. But it will be clear that both of these theologians have something in common, that is, they both hold a Docetic view of the resurrection, expressed differently of course in each instance, precisely because their christological starting point was the Ebionite one that refuses to begin with Jesus' uniqueness as attested in the NT, namely, with the Word of God incarnate.

John Macquarrie intended to maintain Christ's uniqueness just as much as did Barth, Torrance and Rahner and so that intention at least gives his thinking a seriousness that is missing from the thinking of Paul Knitter.[1] Knitter also intended to maintain Christ's uniqueness, although one does not have the sense that he really aimed to maintain it in the same serious way as did the others just mentioned. As we shall see, his thinking is incurably Docetic from the outset because he allows much else besides Jesus of Nazareth to claim his attention from beginning to end. He does, of course, maintain a kind of uniqueness for Jesus, but, as we shall see, that uniqueness is very different from the uniqueness envisioned in Scripture and at Nicaea and Chalcedon.

We have seen that for Barth and Torrance it was imperative that we not separate what God reveals in Jesus from how he reveals it, namely, in Jesus and thus they considered Christ's deity to be "definitive, authentic and essential."[2] Both theologians were critical of Bultmann for focusing on Jesus' sayings and ignoring his miraculous deeds because these must be seen together as in the story of the paralytic in Mk. 2:1-12. Hence, as Barth puts it,

> The New Testament statement about the unity of the Son with the Father, i.e., the deity of Christ, cannot possibly be understood in terms of the presupposition that the original view and declaration of the New Testament witnesses was that a human being was either exalted as such to deity or appeared among us as the personification and symbol of a divine being. (CD I/1, 402)

This statement by Barth, with which Torrance would fully agree, reflects his rejection of Ebionite and Docetic Christology and is based upon the fact that Jesus is Lord simply because he is from all eternity the only begotten Son of the Father. On the one hand it excludes all forms of adoptionism, including the idea that to preserve Jesus' humanity we must begin with the human Jesus in abstraction from his Lordship as the antecedent Son of the Father who became incarnate by the power of the Holy Spirit from the flesh of Mary. On the other hand it rules out any notion that some prior idea of God could lead to an understanding of the God revealed and active in Jesus Christ. For Barth, Jesus Christ himself, the Word incarnate, was the starting point of the NT witness and one could not go behind him or ignore him as the one he was without ignoring or attempting to go behind God himself. Any attempt to by-pass Jesus Christ in his humanity, which could not be separated even momentarily from his divinity, would necessarily mean a distortion of Christology and a reduction of theology to anthropology and thus the attempt to create God in our image rather than accepting the fact that God created us in his image. Let us begin then with John Macquarrie.

John Macquarrie

Macquarrie on Christ's Resurrection

What then is John Macquarrie's view of Jesus' resurrection? Did he believe the resurrection was an event in the life of Jesus that gave meaning to the disciples' faith and to ours? Or did he believe the resurrection was created in or realized by the faith of the disciples and ours? There are scattered references throughout his book *Jesus Christ in Modern Thought* that suggest that Macquarrie believes that the resurrection was a significant event in Jesus' life that gave meaning to the NT faith. For instance Macquarrie writes "any merely adoptionist christology must be completed by an incarnational christology. The rising of a man is made possible only by the condescension of God" (*Jesus Christ*, 63). In addition, Macquarrie writes "it is certainly true that the resurrection of Jesus Christ is a key element in what I have called the 'conventional' story. If it were taken away or even radically demythologized, it would certainly have left a major gap behind it" (*Jesus Christ*, 406). Further, when exploring Mark's Gospel Macquarrie says "he knew that it was only with the resurrection that Jesus was recognized as the Christ" (*Jesus Christ*, 92). And in connection with Paul's thinking he says "Paul may well have been correct when he said that if Christ is not risen, then Christian faith is vain" (*Jesus Christ*, 68).

But even Macquarrie's presentation of Paul's view of the resurrection is more than a little ambiguous: "It is one element in that potentiality for being that was given to the human race as created in the image and likeness of God" (*Jesus Christ*, 66). And he asserts "Paul did not equate the resurrection of Jesus with anything so naive as the belief that the dead body had come alive again" (*Jesus Christ*, 66); rather for Macquarrie resurrection means "the attainment of the goal of human transcendence" (*Jesus Christ*, 66).[3] We shall explore the connection between Macquarrie's Pelagian theological anthropology and his view of the resurrection, incarnation and ethics in more depth later. Here it suffices to indicate that Macquarrie's understanding of Jesus' resurrection is already dictated by his prior view of human transcendence as a mode of self-transcendence which expresses the human possibility for revelation and reconciliation in a manner reminiscent of Rahner. In fact Macquarrie explicitly ties his understanding of the incarnation to Rahner's view of human nature in this way.[4] And for this very reason Macquarrie cannot and will not admit that the resurrection was an actual event in the life of Jesus that gave meaning to the disciples' faith and to ours. This is confirmed by Macquarrie's own thinking when, at the end of his book, after presenting what he calls the "happy ending" (as opposed to what he dubs the "austere ending") of the Christian story, he declares

> Suppose in our account of the career of Jesus we had felt compelled to draw the bottom line under the cross? Suppose we omitted the 'joyful mysteries' that traditionally came after the cross? Would that destroy the whole fabric of faith in Christ? I do not think so, for the two great distinctive Christian affirmations would remain untouched — God is love, and God is revealed in Jesus Christ. These two affirmations would stand even if there were no mysteries beyond Calvary. (*Jesus Christ,* 412)

In this thinking we are a very long way from the insistence evident in the theology of Paul, Barth and Torrance that unless Jesus rose bodily from the dead, then our faith is without substance and our hope is empty as well. Here Christianity has been detached from Jesus Christ himself and God's love and revelation have been defined through general human experience rather than from Jesus Christ himself as the God who loved us while we were still sinners and as the revealer of God who was and is the incarnate Word.

What difference does this make? It makes all the difference in the world because Macquarrie confuses Christ with the experience of Christians at the outset and then concludes that the "happy ending," that is, the story of Easter, resurrection, ascension and the second coming stems from what he calls the "happy ending syndrome. We would not have been satisfied if the story had ended with the cross. The need for a happy ending is natural to us and arises out of our moral sense" (*Jesus Christ,* 404). Before exploring the idea of incarnation that underlies this thinking, let us look at this obvious collapse of the Easter event into our moral sense and natural experience of hope and see what specific conclusions Macquarrie reaches regarding Christ's resurrection.

Macquarrie insists that for the post-Enlightenment mentality the idea of the resurrection is very difficult to accept, as if to imply that perhaps it was easier at the time of the original disciples. It wasn't, of course, as both

Torrance and Barth rightly insisted.[5] In any case Macquarrie begins by claiming that the resurrection does not refer to "an actual rising from the dead" (*Jesus Christ,* 406) because it cannot be considered an event in history in the ordinary sense. He even cites Barth to back up his thinking, though as we have already seen, Barth would certainly reject Macquarrie's reasoning, because Barth accepted the historical fact that Jesus rose from the dead while also stressing that it cannot be perceived, proven and described by ordinary historical investigation. It is here that Macquarrie is forced to substitute the church for the risen Lord himself. Instead of arguing that Jesus actually rose bodily from the dead and appeared to the disciples, he argues that the historical event that needs to be explained is "the rise of the Christian church" (*Jesus Christ,* 406).

And this thinking follows Macquarrie's methodological assumption that neither incarnation nor resurrection can be limited to the "career of Jesus" but rather must be blended together in what he classifies as the "Christ-event." Hence, speaking of the resurrection Macquarrie says "This [the Christian church] is, so to speak, the outward, visible, historically observable aspect of the resurrection, considered as part of the Christ-event and not only something in the career of Jesus" (*Jesus Christ,* 406).[6] Because Macquarrie thinks of Jesus first as an ordinary man who was later transformed into a heavenly being by virtue of the community's faith in him, his Christology is not only explicitly adoptionist, but his thinking overtly detaches the message of the NT from the historical Jesus and transfers it to the community. Thus for Macquarrie "Jesus and the community" must be seen "as together embraced in the Christ-event" since "there is no sharp dividing line between Jesus and the community" (*Jesus Christ,* 21). The Christ-event then refers to "something larger than the career of Jesus of Nazareth. In that larger reality there were joined inseparably the career of Jesus and its impact on the believing community" (*Jesus Christ,* 20). Hence for Macquarrie there are "two sources for the knowledge of Jesus Christ — the testimony of the past and the experience of the present" (*Jesus Christ,* 6). What then is the historical fact that the early Christians described as the risen Lord present among them after his death? It is, according to Macquarrie, "that the birth of the church depended on the belief of the disciples that Jesus had been resurrected . . . only a belief in the resurrection provides anything like a sufficient reason for the rise of Christianity after the death of Jesus" (*Jesus Christ,* 406). Yes, but a belief in the resurrection without the risen Lord actually encountering them and enabling that belief is utterly vacuous. Macquarrie presents the usual evidence for the resurrection, that is, the appearances and the empty tomb. And he is critical of Schillebeeckx's Christology because Schillebeeckx held that belief in the biblical promise of the OT that God would not desert his people led to belief in the resurrection and then to the stories of the appearances and the empty tomb. But for Macquarrie this thinking fails to take account of the fact that something "much more dramatic" must have taken place to "bring about the belief that Jesus had been risen from the dead" (*Jesus Christ*, 408).

So what exactly was it that gave rise to this belief? Here he turns to Paul and asserts that "what is resurrected is not the dead body that has been laid in the grave" since such thinking, in Macquarrie's mind, would necessarily lead to the idea that Jesus' corpse had simply been resuscitated (*Jesus Christ*, 408). True to his method Macquarrie does not allow Jesus himself in his uniqueness to define his thinking here but instead appeals to "our present experience, when people claim to be in communion with one another, though not using words or touching or looking at each other" (*Jesus Christ*, 409). And he concludes that

> Perhaps resurrection is transcendence to a new level in the being of the human person, a level which eludes our understanding so long as we are seeing it only from below. In any case, we are not confined to those visionary experiences recorded in the New Testament. (*Jesus Christ*, 409)[7]

Thus, Macquarrie argues that people throughout history have claimed to encounter the "living Christ" especially within a "eucharistic context" and that these encounters must be added to the NT witness as "evidences that the crucified one lives on today" (*Jesus Christ*, 409).

But is Jesus, the man from Nazareth, really alive today according to this thinking or is this only a mythological way of describing our present experiences of faith? When Macquarrie considers the ascension his thinking becomes even clearer:

> the ascension is perhaps best understood like some of the others [e.g., Jesus' descent into hell], as an event in the consciousness of the disciples rather than in the career of Christ himself. It is his final apotheosis when, in the traditional language, he takes his seat at the right hand of God. (*Jesus Christ*, 409-10)

And what about Christ's second coming? That is suitably docetized by Macquarrie as well: "this would come about by the gradual processes of history, not by the dramatic return of a heavenly judge, which looks like the last kick of the *theios aner* Christology" (*Jesus Christ*, 411). So in answer to the question of whether or not the resurrection was an event in the life of Jesus or an event in the faith of the disciples Macquarrie, following Bultmann, presents what he calls the "Austere Ending" of the Gospel or "Ending B" which can be summarized as follows: "faith in resurrection is really the same thing as faith in the saving efficacy of the cross" (*Jesus Christ*, 413). And Macquarrie cites Bultmann, who says:

> We are compelled to ask whether all this mythological language [about resurrection and ascension] is not simply an attempt to express the meaning of the historical figure of Jesus and the events of his life; in other words, the significance of these as a figure and event of salvation. If that be so, we can dispense with the objective form in which they are cast. (*Jesus Christ*, 413-14)

Does this mean that the resurrection is mainly an event in the life of the disciples and not in Jesus' life? Macquarrie answers with a "yes and no."

> Resurrection is an event in the believers, it is indeed the event of the church, which is Christ's living body.... But the meaning of resurrection is originally in Jesus himself — in the possession and mediation by him of true life, eternal life, which he brought to its highest pitch on the cross. (*Jesus Christ*, 414)

Notice that Macquarrie does not and cannot allow for an actual resurrection and ascension of Jesus himself precisely because his thinking was never structured by who Jesus was and is in the first instance precisely because his method begins with the "testimony of the past and the experience of the present." Starting with Jesus himself as the Word incarnate is trumped by experience of the present, which experience also shapes his reading of the tradition. And he has already claimed that Jesus' "victory over evil was already won in the agonizing hours before his death, and that it would remain decisive even if there were no subsequent events of resurrection and ascension" (*Jesus Christ*, 412).

But beyond this, it is clear that Macquarrie is not talking about the eternal life that comes from the triune God alone and is identical with Jesus' life as the eternal Son of the Father. Rather, he sees Jesus as one mediator among many exactly because his Christology is a degree Christology which refuses to accept Jesus as the unique Son of the Father. And he literally cannot understand why Christians have believed that the incarnation could have happened only once in this "unique" figure, Jesus of Nazareth.[8] Let us briefly explore Macquarrie's rather weak view of the incarnation and his unitarian understanding of God to see just how his thinking is incurably Docetic even though he stresses repeatedly that the most important point of contemporary Christology is that Jesus' humanity must be preserved at all costs.

That is the theme of this book. It is ironic that those who would stress Jesus' humanity while abstracting from the fact that his humanity is the humanity of the Word and cannot be explored independently of his existence as the eternal Son of God who became incarnate for us and for our salvation, always propose some sort of adoptionist Christology that ends with a Docetic view of the resurrection and misses the essential significance of the incarnation. And as I will briefly show, such thinking inevitably presents a Pelagian theological anthropology, which suggests that salvation can and should be equated with our human attempts to live good lives. Such thinking, as I have already mentioned, undermines the true meaning of human freedom which can only be understood to mean that we are actually set free from sin and self-will in all dimensions of our lives by Christ himself and that human thought and action thus can be genuinely free only in specific acts of obedience to Christ himself through the power of his Spirit. This of course requires a trinitarian understanding of our ethical activity rather than the quite unitarian one proposed by Macquarrie.

Incarnation and the Doctrine of God

Like Rahner and following Wolfhart Pannenberg, Macquarrie commits the fatal methodological error of assuming that the incarnation can only be the conclusion and not the beginning of any genuine Christology. Of course we have already seen that Barth and Torrance correctly insisted that unless our thinking begins with the incarnate Word, we will never truly respect Christ's humanity and never actually see how our humanity is reconciled and redeemed in him alone. His humanity exists as the unique point of departure for all Christian reflection exactly because the eternal Son of God has assumed flesh in him for our sakes without ceasing to be divine. This is a mystery and a miracle grounded in and effected by the triune God. And Macquarrie will have none of that. So he rejects any notion of a pre-existent Logos as myth and instead, after assessing a number of "kenotic" Christologies, claims that hundreds of years of Docetic Christology must be stood on its head so that Christology can "begin once more from the humanity of Christ, as indeed it had done in the beginning" (*Jesus Christ*, 250). This was accomplished, he believes, by Pannenberg's more balanced view:

> Methodological reasons do not permit us to work with the incarnation as a theological presupposition. To do so would be to make the humanity of Jesus' life problematic from the very beginning. To be sure, all christological

considerations tend towards the idea of the incarnation; it can, however, only constitute the end of Christology. It if is put instead at the beginning, all christological concepts are given a mythological tone. (*Jesus Christ,* 250)[9]

We have already seen how this thinking led to the many conflicts evident in Rahner's theology. Here we see that this thinking requires some form of Christology "from below" in order to emphasize Christ's humanity. And such Christology tends toward a Pelagian understanding of salvation because it presupposes that there is a potentiality in human life, including the human life of Jesus that is released in the process of his human development so that salvation might then be equated with his successful living out his human life of love of others. Yet the inherent difficulty with all Christologies from below is that they are incurably Ebionite and Docetic in their estimations of Jesus' person and work. Let us explore Macquarrie's view of the incarnation with this in mind.

First, Macquarrie refuses to begin his thinking with the plain fact that Jesus Christ is the incarnate Word simply because he is. Hence he begins agreeing with Schillebeeckx that the starting point for his reflections will be "the man Jesus, in the sense of 'a human person.'" "There are no ghosts or gods in disguise wandering around in our human history," writes Macquarrie, in quoting Schillebeeckx (*Jesus Christ,* 312). That is why Macquarrie will not begin where the classical Christologies began, by asking how God became man in Jesus Christ. Rather, his question is "'How does a man become God?' or 'How does a human life embody or manifest the divine life'?" (*Jesus Christ,* 360). Here Macquarrie also insists, as he does throughout his book, that just because he begins in an adoptionist fashion, that does not mean that he wishes to end there.[10] No, he insists that beginning with Christ's humanity not only does not prohibit an inquiry into God's presence in this man, but might even require it. Thus, Macquarrie begins "with the simple assertion that Jesus Christ was a man, a human being" (*Jesus Christ,* 360).

It is this methodological separation of Jesus' humanity and divinity, however, that compromises the mystery of the incarnation at the outset. And Macquarrie systematically excludes anything from the biblical witness to that effect, including the virgin birth[11] and Christ's pre-existence as the eternal Son of the Father. But most importantly it is this methodological assumption that leads Macquarrie to distort the scriptural witness with the rather odd exegesis of J. D. G. Dunn mentioned above (that we must find a unifying idea for the NT and that a historical figure was transformed into an exalted one) so that the heart of his view of Jesus Christ is a version of degree

Christology which quite clearly is a type of what Barth aptly labeled Ebionite Christology.

One does not have to jettison belief in Jesus' divinity to affirm his full and true humanity. On the contrary, there is no doubt that with the incarnation itself we are presented with a human being who is like us in all things except sin; but this is a human being who is simultaneously God incarnate and his humanity is itself what it is in virtue of the activity of the Word. This then is a mystery and miracle grounded in the eternal being and act of the triune God himself. Against this proper view of the matter, Macquarrie's thinking is in fact dualistic (because he will not allow for the fact that this man really is God incarnate), Ebionite (because he bases the incarnation on the impression Jesus made on his followers), and Docetic (because beginning with his humanity he must then find a unifying idea for the NT and also explain how this man "became divine"). Yet if the incarnation is true, then Jesus is not merely different from the rest of us in degree; he is in reality also different in kind, without ceasing to be a fully human being. Because of this any sort of degree Christology must be seen as a new version of the Arian heresy.[12]

Second, Macquarrie himself explicitly embraces degree Christology:

> Just as I shied away from the doctrine that there is an 'infinite qualitative difference' between God and man, so I would not want to urge some absolute difference between man and the lower animals. It is a difference of degree rather than of kind, just as we said in the case of the difference between Jesus Christ and other human beings, but a difference of degree can be quite decisive, and may be so great as to be virtually a difference in kind. (*Jesus Christ*, 361)

While Macquarrie begins his Christology "with a man, a human being of the same constitution as ourselves" he claims it is obvious that there was something special about him. Yet whatever that was it "does not separate him from the human race . . . he differs from other human beings in degree, not in kind" (*Jesus Christ*, 359). Because his Christology is a degree Christology, Macquarrie thinks he can understand Jesus' human being by exploring human nature in general. Accordingly, asking about what it is that makes Jesus special points us "to a prior question: 'Who or what is a man, a human being?'" (*Jesus Christ*, 360). And it is this thinking that allows him to fit Jesus Christ into the evolutionary movement of the world by claiming, with Schleiermacher, that what happened in his humanity is simply the completion of creation rather than its restoration.[13]

It is this failure to distinguish incarnation, creation and atonement that opens the door to a Pelagian understanding of human nature employing the categories of self-transcendence following Rahner's thinking. Here Macquarrie assumes that

> if humanity contains within itself a principle of transcendence, then there may be a way here that, beginning from the total humanity of Jesus Christ . . . leads to the conception of a transcendent or transcending humanity which, in an older terminology, would have been called 'God-manhood'. (*Jesus Christ,* 363)

Macquarrie considers several types of anthropology and seems enamored of Ernst Bloch's view that "There is a principle of 'hope' in everything, that is to say, a tendency to realize its possibilities for being" (*Jesus Christ,* 366-67). That is why Macquarrie prefers to categorize Bloch as a pantheist rather than as an atheist. Nevertheless, it is to Bloch's philosophical anthropology that Macquarrie appeals to explain Christ's humanity and to avoid the appearance that he has made Jesus "merely" a man:

> if one accepts the principle of transcendence as a basic characteristic of the human being, then it is difficult to speak of a 'mere' man. Any human being who has entered on the path of transcendence is already showing that humanity is always 'more' than we think, and we have still to discover how far the mystery of the human may stretch toward the supreme mystery that we call 'God'. (*Jesus Christ,* 368)

This insight, coupled with Rahner's belief that "There is that in the human being which, so to speak, opens out toward God and finds its completion in God" (*Jesus Christ,* 370), seals the fate of Macquarrie's theological anthropology. It is and remains irresistibly Pelagian because he claims for humanity a potentiality for the divine, instead of recognizing that any human ability to relate with God since the fall can only be a gift given by God's own act in history in Jesus Christ and through his Holy Spirit.

But since Macquarrie has already cut the cord that would allow God to be present as man in Jesus Christ, his own dualism prevents him from recognizing and maintaining the priority of grace and revelation at this crucial juncture. And so Macquarrie claims that there is a

> mystery within the human being, that though finite, there is some vestige of the infinite in this being. . . . The presence in the human being, in virtue of his or her humanity itself, of spirit understood as the principle of tran-

scendence, implies an affinity to God and a capacity for receiving God. (*Jesus Christ*, 370)

Had Macquarrie actually allowed the incarnate Word to be his theological criterion, he could have seen that humanity had lost any affinity to God because of its sin and that the very idea that humanity has a capacity for receiving God is an idea that results from our sinful attempt to create God in our own image. Any capacity we have for God comes from God the Holy Spirit enabling our faith in Jesus Christ so as to permit us to live freely by God's grace and revelation.

Plainly, Macquarrie confuses Christ's humanity with humanity in general because of the Pelagian and Gnostic view of human nature just promoted with the twin ideas that (1) there is some vestige of the infinite in our human being, and (2) in virtue of our human self-transcendence we have a capacity for God. This opens the door to Macquarrie's adoptionist perspective that then leads him to think that there could be many saviors. It is important to realize that by undercutting Jesus' true divinity here, Macquarrie is left with a unitarian view of God; and it is this view of God itself that leads to his polytheism at this point. It is quite evident from Macquarrie's thinking in his book *Jesus Christ in Modern Thought* and elsewhere that his view of God is not at all dictated by who Jesus Christ was and is as the Word of God incarnate.[14] Rather, Macquarrie begins with an idea of God's unity which is derived philosophically and then used to understand Christianity in a way that inevitably leads to the kind of Arian position espoused above. Macquarrie's belief that Jesus' Sonship refers only to his "being man in the fullest sense" (*Jesus Christ*, 91) reflects the fact that his adoptionism, along with his mythological view of the incarnation, rest on a misguided view of the Trinity. By rejecting any personal pre-existence for Jesus and by adopting an overtly Ebionite Christology, Macquarrie in effect excludes any doctrine of the immanent Trinity from his reflections.

As a result, he insists that to speak of Jesus as the Son of God is to use a metaphor that does "not imply deification" (*Jesus Christ*, 42). Notice that Macquarrie's thinking is ineluctably Ebionite here. He cannot accept Barth's idea that Jesus is the Son of God simply because he is. He can only envision a man being deified by the community's use of metaphors.[15] It is significant that Matt. 11:27 and Lk. 10:22 play no decisive role in Macquarrie's thought here. It is also significant that Macquarrie circumvents the kind of explanation of this title offered by Eduard Schweizer who argues, correctly in my view, that this title received its actual meaning from Jesus himself.

Jesus does not use the title 'Servant of God', 'Messiah', or 'Son of God' to indicate his significance; neither, in all probability, does he use a familiar
apocalyptic title of honor. His refusal to use these titles shows that he fits
none of these formulas. Repetition of a pre-existing title, assent to some
definition of Jesus' nature, cannot dispense a man from real encounter
with him. . . . By his very act of avoiding all common labels, Jesus keeps free
the heart of the man who encounters him. He wants to enter into this heart
himself . . . not as an image already formed before he himself has a chance
to encounter that person.[16]

Macquarrie notes that Reginald Fuller held that while Jesus never called himself Son of God, he did have a unique relation with his Father. But he wonders
how unique that relation really was. And he argues that once one becomes a
son or child of God through Jesus Christ, one's relation to the Father is not
different in kind from Jesus' own relation because "the potentiality for becoming a Son of God belongs to humanity as such" (*Jesus Christ*, 43).
Macquarrie insists that this "metaphorical" interpretation of the NT does not
in any way detract from the theological significance of the expression "Son of
God." For Macquarrie, it is acceptable to say that the Son is "one in being"
with the Father only in a metaphorical sense. His understanding is attained
by analyzing human speech and applying that to the description of the Word
in John's Gospel. Thus, as my word expresses me and is an extension of me
while remaining distinct from me, so in that sense Macquarrie accepts the
metaphor that the Word is "of the same being" as the Father (*Jesus Christ*,
109). In Macquarrie's own words:

> When I speak a word, that word acquires a kind of separateness or inde-
> pendence, it has been 'uttered' or externalized, it can be heard and appro-
> priated by others, it can even be written down. It has 'proceeded' from the
> speaker, to use a traditional theological term. Yet in another way that word
> is still an extension or part of the speaker. . . . In this sense a word is, to us
> another traditional term of theology, 'of the same being' *(homoousios)* as
> the one who speaks it. (*Jesus Christ*, 108-9)

But Macquarrie then separates the Word from the Son, something Barth explicitly refused to do, in order to explain that the Word cannot be directly
equated with the being of God:

> I have already suggested that John's use of the paradox, 'The Word was with
> God and the Word was God' hovers somewhere between identity and dif-

ference, and does not permit us to say that God and the Word are simply identical. Thus even if we are correct in speaking of the 'identification' of Jesus with the Word, we could not go on to infer an identification of Jesus with God. (*Jesus Christ*, 109)

This thinking, however, is in complete contrast with the NT because Macquarrie denies Jesus' pre-existence as the Word who was God by insisting that

The Word cannot be identical with God for it has gone forth or been uttered as a distinct entity, yet because it proceeds from God and reveals God, it is still 'one in being' with God, an extension of God, if one may use such language. (*Jesus Christ*, 44)

Macquarrie thus rejects Barth's belief that Jesus Christ is literally God's Word insisting that Barth "is surely mistaken about this" (*Jesus Christ*, 108). Yet, it is my contention that any such rejection necessarily means also a dismissal of the immanent Trinity and thus a denial of God's self-sufficiency or freedom to have existed without the world. This is no mere play on words or set of conceptual acrobatics. It is, rather, an acknowledgment that the God who is Emmanuel is truly God, that is, God for us and can be for us in a decisive way precisely because he is God the Father, Son and Holy Spirit from all eternity and does not act to create and reconcile us out of any need on his part but only out of his pure grace. Unable and unwilling to acknowledge Jesus' personal pre-existence as the eternal Word and his genuine consubstantiality with the Father and Spirit, Macquarrie argues that "it is the whole person and history of Jesus Christ that constitute the Word — the Word which makes known what is in the mind of the Father" (*Jesus Christ*, 108). Indeed, Macquarrie asserts "there never was a time when God was wholly contained within himself. God has always been uttering his Word. That is to say, going forth in self-communication, positing another than himself, yet another who shares the same being as the Father" (*Jesus Christ*, 111).[17] In this remark Macquarrie demonstrates his complete inability to recognize a genuinely existing God in himself and thus he also demonstrates his inability to distinguish the immanent and economic Trinity as would be required by any serious interpretation of this matter.

Had Macquarrie's thinking been shaped by a proper understanding of the eternal Trinity he might have realized and maintained the truth of the NT faith, namely, that the Word or Son was constituted by his unique relation with his Father, that is, he was begotten before all worlds and not made. In other words the Word or Son existed from all eternity and it is the miracle of Christmas that this eternal Word became incarnate for us and for our salvation. Any such view, in Macquarrie's eyes, is mythology and that is why he rejects the idea that the incarnation took place on a particular date at a particular time. Had he acknowledged this, however, he then would never have embraced the Pelagian notion that the potentiality for being a son of God is part of humanity as such. This view is the necessary consequence of failing to accept Jesus' uniqueness as the Word of God incarnate in the first instance as the starting point of Christology.

It is just because of his christological and trinitarian misunderstanding that Macquarrie denies the central importance of the Christian doctrine of atonement and then argues that there are and must be many saviors. Macquarrie insists that "we cannot make an absolute distinction between nature and grace. Because nature is itself given, it is from the beginning infused with grace. Likewise, because the power of knowing is itself a gift, all our knowing is in some measure revelation" (*Jesus Christ*, 184). This is why, as we have already noted, Macquarrie maintains that all natural theology is in a sense revealed theology. This is not surprising given his explicit Docetic Christology which consciously follows the thought of Kant: "We recognize the historical Christ as revelation because we already have in our constitution as human beings an ideal or archetype which, we believe, we see fulfilled in him" (*Jesus Christ*, 183).[18]

This is precisely what Barth correctly labeled as Docetic Christology because the particular figure, Jesus of Nazareth, is dispensable here. What is decisive is the idea of God already present in one's natural theology. Thus, if Jesus is seen to confirm that idea, then he can be called God. Therefore the power of the term God does not come from the eternal Trinity but from each individual's concept of the divine that always exists within that person. And it matters little to Macquarrie if that idea is unitarian or polytheistic in the long run. This Pelagian position (Pelagian because it explicitly confuses nature and grace by equating revelation with our natural knowledge) has disastrous consequences ethically, for it implies that we not only can save ourselves by activating our consciousness of the divine but it also implies that Jesus cannot be the sole revealer of God or the sole savior of the world. This in fact is the polytheism that Christians have always rejected.

Macquarrie then appeals to his degree Christology to assert that Christ cannot be the only savior. He does believe that it made sense for the early Christians to hold this belief. But he contends that this belief is no longer tenable today in our pluralistic world. But this means salvation must be a human work grounded in our self-consciousness of God and the good. Yet if that is the case, then we are alone with ourselves and left to do the good by relying on ourselves. This, unfortunately, is what the Bible means by sin. So it turns out that Macquarrie's supposedly more open view that there can and should be more than one savior figure actually illustrates once again, from an ethical perspective, that any attempt to become righteous that is in any respect self-grounded must necessarily lead to a denial of the very center of the Christian doctrine of atonement, namely, that Christ alone can set us free from self-will and from sin, and when he does, we know that we must think and act from a center in God provided in the incarnation and Christ's personal death and resurrection.

The ultimate irony of Macquarrie's Christology is that while he admits that there are different conceptions of "holy Being" and different conceptions of savior figures, including Confucius, Buddha, Jesus and Krishna, he concludes that

> The difference between Jesus Christ and other human beings, including the saviour figures, is a difference *within* humanity — they have all shared that plastic raw material of the spirit that we call human nature, and each has fashioned it as he or she has been able. (*Jesus Christ*, 420)

This assertion, however, misses our deepest human need, which is for a righteousness that can only come from God precisely by excluding the one decisive point of Christology. Jesus is the savior of the world because he alone is God's unique and only Son who became flesh for us and our salvation. Hence, for Macquarrie, ethical behavior no longer means living a life of faith by being conformed to Christ through obedience; a life shaped by the power of the Holy Spirit in his *perichoretic* union with the Father and Son. Instead, it means that all savior figures "were seeking to realize the highest possibilities inherent in being a human person" (*Jesus Christ*, 420). We can do the same since we share the same humanity as they do.

Here Macquarrie's Docetic Christology leads him to undermine Christ's specific human existence by detaching the eternal Logos from the particular man Jesus of Nazareth and locating it within universal human experience; it also leads him to deny Jesus' actual resurrection from the dead, his eternal pre-existence as well as his incarnate and future existence as the Lord. And it is just this Docetism that leads to the idea that we can be saved not only by Jesus but by any one of a number of religious figures who confirm our natural knowledge of what he calls "holy Being." This is nothing short of a form of self-justification that is excluded by the nature of the incarnation and resurrection. And any argument along these lines calls into question both the reality of humanity in its true freedom as well as the distinct sovereignty of God that enables human being to be the human being he intends it to be.

We may end therefore with Macquarrie's understanding of Jn. 14:6 when it says that Jesus is the way, the truth and the life and that no one comes to the Father except through him. He argues that we cannot hear these words in an exclusively narrow way today. Rather "In John's gospel, let us remember, the words of Jesus are the words of the Logos, not just of the individual human being, Jesus of Nazareth" (*Jesus Christ*, 422). Here then is the catastrophic contention of Docetic Christology. Such Christology detaches the Logos from the man Jesus and finds that Logos in numerous savior figures who in turn receive their significance from the community based on its ideas of divinity. In no case, however, can this thinking allow for the fact that Jesus is utterly unique and must therefore be the point of departure for knowing God and ourselves. That is the difference between Macquarrie's thinking and the thought of Barth and Torrance and any serious Christian theology that accepts Jesus for who he was and is. Macquarrie's thinking confirms the fact that some form of Arianism and Pelagianism is lying in wait for anyone who would choose to think about the triune God by discounting the genuine uniqueness of Jesus as the unique Son of the Father who is and remains *homoousion* with the Father and for that very reason is the unique and exclusive savior of the world. Arianism suffers from its lack of freedom to find the way, the truth and the life in Jesus Christ alone because he is the Word in the same definitive sense in which Yahweh was and is Israel's God.

Paul F. Knitter

Paul Knitter's thinking provides a very interesting example of what happens when one's thinking is not dictated by who Jesus was and what he did but rather by one's religious experience and ideology. Let us begin by exploring Knitter's view of the resurrection in order to see just how his method leads him to deny Christ's actual resurrection, even though he sincerely believes he has presented just what the NT affirmed. From there we will see that it is just his Docetic view of the incarnation that leads to this denial and it is his confusion of nature and grace, as well as his unitarian view of God, that compromises a proper notion of salvation and leads him to the idea that there could and should be many saviors.

Knitter's View of the Resurrection

Knitter's purpose in explaining the resurrection is to present it in a way that allows him to argue that Jesus should be seen as one savior among others in accordance with his nonnormative Christology which asserts that Jesus can be normative for Christians but not for others. He is quite clear about this. And this, as we shall see, shapes what he has to say about the resurrection. In any case Knitter begins his analysis by noting that while a number of scholars including Schillebeeckx, Fuller, Perrin, Küng, Vawter, Mackey and Lane differ in approach and conclusions, they all harmonize in trying to avoid an overly objective or subjective view of the resurrection. Hence Knitter concludes

> The resurrection, one might say, happened both *in* and *to* the disciples. Faith in the risen Lord was not simply caused by an objective event taking place in front of them; neither, however, was it created or concocted by the disciples' personal convictions or wishes or hallucinations.[19]

Nonetheless, Knitter argues that whatever it was that happened objectively to the disciples, it "was dependent on their personal perceptions and response (subjective)" (*No Other Name?* 197). And so instead of allowing the unique object Jesus Christ, the Word incarnate, to determine his thinking in this context, Knitter contends that it was on the basis of their experience that they realized that "something had happened to Jesus after his death" (*No Other Name?* 198). But what exactly was it that happened according to Knitter?

It should not, he says, be understood "only or even primarily as an encounter with a physical person standing 'over there'" (*No Other Name?* 198) because Jesus was not just "seen" by the first Christians but "revealed" to them. With this Docetic starting point in place Knitter proceeds to substitute the disciples' experience of faith for the objective fact that Jesus had risen bodily from the dead and appeared to the disciples in a genuine encounter with them:

> belief in the resurrection originated from a deeply personal faith experience, which can be described as a 'revelation' or 'conversion' experience. Like any authentic faith or conversion experience, it was brought about by the objective reality of grace, the power of God, the Spirit. (*No Other Name?* 198)

But given the fact that the resurrection originated from a personal faith experience and not from the risen Lord himself, it is incumbent on Knitter to explain just what he means by the objective reality of grace, the power of God, the Spirit. Knitter explains that the disciples' previous faith played a role in enabling them to renew their faith in Jesus. In this sense "he was still among them in a new, a transformed, presence" (*No Other Name?* 198). Here Knitter notes that this conversion experience is described by Schillebeeckx as an experience of forgiveness, while Dermot Lane describes it as an experience of "personal reconciliation," and Küng describes it as a "vocation received in faith" to pattern one's life out of the "'power of the life of this Jesus,'" and James Mackey explains that this experience is an experience of the Spirit enabling us to overcome evil (*No Other Name?* 198).

On the basis of these explanations, Knitter concludes that

> However difficult it is to define the originating experiences of the risen Jesus, it is clear from these descriptions that such encounters were not essentially different from what Christians can and should experience today. The first meetings with the Living One were not magical, miraculous intrusions coming from above. Rather, they were intense, originating instances of how believers through the ages can encounter the real presence of Christ as they break bread, recall his story, live his message. (*No Other Name?* 198-99)

Consistently Docetic in his understanding of the resurrection, Knitter follows Rahner to argue that one should not understand it as "an almost physical sense experience" (*No Other Name?* 199). Instead, according to Knitter, the appearance accounts and the empty tomb should be interpreted "as attempts to express and give more tangible form to these conversion experiences rather than as photographic statements of what took place" (*No Other Name?* 199).

Now it is quite obvious that the NT never intended to offer photographic explanations of the resurrection. But it is quite a step from that idea to the notion that the appearance accounts and the empty tomb signified the disciples' own conversion experiences rather than an event in the life of Jesus that gave meaning to their experiences of faith. It is here that Knitter's Docetic understanding of the matter leads him to substitute the disciples' conversion experience for the reality of the risen Lord, thus changing the object of the Christian faith from Jesus in his uniqueness, to an experience or set of experiences that can be universally seen and described without faith in Jesus himself. The object of belief cannot be Jesus, the incarnate Word, but must be the experience of conversion that is open to people of all religions.

Knitter insists that he is not diluting the NT witness but taking it seriously as a "richly mythic account . . . of experiences that could never be photographed." And while Knitter honestly believes that his interpretation does justice to the NT accounts and to the nature of the resurrection itself, it is more than obvious that he has not even recognized the reality described in the NT and has failed to see the actual nature of the resurrection precisely because the starting point and criterion for his reflections was the conversion experience of the disciples and not Jesus himself. As David Fergusson has shown us, this liberal interpretation of the resurrection eventually collapses back into the radical one that reduces the event that took place in the life of Jesus to the faith of the community. Hence Knitter concludes that the resurrection was "not and is not a matter of historico-physical proofs but of deeply personal-communitarian experience and commitment" (*No Other Name?* 199). And it is just here that the reason for this particular interpretation is offered: "If such an understanding of the resurrection is valid — and I think it is — then once again we have a contemporary christological interpretation that makes room for the nonnormative christology proposed by the theocentric model" (*No Other Name?* 199).

Knitter's goal throughout his book is to say that if all religions can agree that God is the center of the theological enterprise then we can all agree that while Jesus is normative for Christians as their unique savior, he is not normative for others. In other words he is a norm only for Christians because that is what they believe. This is what he means by nonnormative Christology. This Ebionite thinking, however, is dictated by Knitter's unitarian conception of God and an idealist view of the incarnation which we shall consider in a moment. In this context the important point to be made is that Knitter's goal in interpreting the resurrection by equating it with the disciples' experience of faith is to say that the reality behind the Easter stories does not have to be limited "only to an experience of Jesus" (*No Other Name?* 200). Why? Simply because "such a conversion or faith experience" is essentially "what countless men and women have felt in their experience of other archetypal religious leaders after the deaths of these leaders" (*No Other Name?* 200).

Knitter is quite literally unable to think objectively and scientifically here because for him the resurrection is "an interpretive myth or model" that he believes enabled the people of Jesus' time to explain their own religious experiences. So he insists that as some early Christians could interpret their experience of the living Jesus "without use of the resurrection model, so might Indians, had the Christ event taken place among them, have interpreted his abiding reality in other models" (*No Other Name?* 200). In Knitter's mind the fact that other religious leaders continued to live on in the memory of their followers is equated with the fact that for Christians Jesus is alive. Here he has missed the entire point of the NT. For he contends that Jesus could be alive for Christians without the resurrection because for him resurrection is simply a model of interpretation. But the only way this could be so is if the resurrection were not an event in the life of Jesus that gives meaning to faith but rather an event in the life of believers which they then interpret according to whatever mythological model suits them at the moment. And that is exactly where Knitter ends his analysis of the resurrection. He contends that what happened to "the early Christians and to Jesus after his death might possibly have happened to other believers and their saviors. The resurrection of Jesus, in all its authentic mystery and power, does not necessarily imply 'one and only'" (*No Other Name?* 200).

There is at least one major flaw in this thinking. And it is that Knitter has not described the resurrection attested in the NT at all. Instead he has posited a universal experience of conversion, a faith experience, and then associated that experience with what countless men and women have experienced with or without faith in Jesus Christ himself. In typically Docetic fashion he has ignored Jesus' humanity as the humanity of the Word and has transferred what was supposed to have happened uniquely and exclusively in his life history to the realm of general religious experience. The result is a presentation in which Knitter honestly believes he has done justice to the meaning of Christ's resurrection while effectively undermining it as a reality by interpreting the resurrection in a liberal and then a radical sense so that the reality that gives meaning to faith is not Jesus himself as the only Son of the Father who became incarnate for our sakes, but people's conversion and faith experiences. Not only does this thinking represent an almost classic case of self-justification in the sense that Knitter unequivocally refuses to allow Jesus Christ to be the justification of Christian faith, but this thinking also has no genuine need for Jesus Christ in the first instance precisely because Knitter's understanding of the incarnation is fully Docetic as well. Let me explain.

Knitter's View of the Incarnation

Just as he regards the resurrection as a myth, so too does he regard the incarnation as a myth. Advocating his "theocentric model" for a theology of religions, Knitter contends that the incarnation should be seen "as a true *myth,* a meaningful *model,* for expressing what Christians have experienced Jesus to be" (*No Other Name?* 191). The myth should be taken seriously but not literally. What exactly does this mean? According to Knitter it means that "Incarnation is not a one-time event. Rather, it is an ideal for all, an ideal rooted in the ancient Christian belief in the one, universal logos or wisdom of God" (*No Other Name?* 191). And this belief, from Knitter's perspective, requires that we admit that there can be other incarnations:

> The Council of Chalcedon stressed that, although the union between the divine and human natures in Jesus was complete, the differences between them remain. That would imply that the Word is free for other incarnations. Also, why must God's full and irrevocable offer of grace be given only once? (*No Other Name?* 191)

It is clear from these statements that Knitter's transparently Docetic Christology prohibits him from taking seriously the intrinsic unity between the Christian doctrine of the incarnation and the doctrine of the resurrection. In fact it is precisely his Docetic Christology that requires him to undermine any genuine understanding of the incarnation and resurrection as events in the life of Jesus that gave and give meaning to the Christian faith. There are several key presuppositions that structure Knitter's thought and lead him to compromise the meaning of Christ's incarnation. And these are intimately tied to his unitarian view of God, a view that replicates the Arian error and confirms Colin Gunton's recent observation that Arianism was probably the favorite and most appealing heresy of the twentieth century.[20]

First, he thinks that the incarnation can and should be equated with panentheism: "Panentheism can be more clearly understood under one of its synonyms: incarnation." A panentheistic view of the God/world relation, Knitter believes, follows from a process perspective and confirms Rahner's transcendental Christology. Hence

> God is not identified with the world (pantheism), but everything and everyone in the world exists *in* God. Such a view is not, I should say, opposed to Rahner's understanding of divinity within us; but it does make for a tighter bond between the infinite and the finite. In the process model, divinity, in a limited but real sense, is dependent on the world for the unfolding of its being. (*No Other Name?* 189)

Second, from this insight Knitter presents the following view of the incarnation: "The world in God and God in the world means that all of creation is the arena of divine incarnation"; hence "everytime there is a 'creative transformation,' whether among molecules or societies, God, in different degrees, has taken on flesh" (*No Other Name?* 189). Third, within this incarnational view, Knitter contends that the enfleshment of God in Jesus stands, not as a historical anomaly, but as a full realization of what is going on throughout history. In the life of Jesus of Nazareth, the process 'worked.' What God is up to in all history and in every life was fully achieved in this man. (*No Other Name?* 190)

Fourth, more recently Knitter has argued for a "sacramental" view of the incarnation in order to say that Jesus can be better understood as "a *representative cause* rather than as a *constitutive cause*" of salvation.[21] In this way one would not have to say he is the only savior or that salvation is a one-time event. Hence "as a sacramental Savior, Jesus can stand with others; as a satisfactory or constitutive Savior, he must stand alone" (*Theologies of Religions,* 154). What can be said to all of this?

Quite obviously, Knitter's starting point is not the man Jesus who was and is the incarnate Word. It is rather the ideal entrenched in a belief in a universal logos or wisdom of God. This is the root of Knitter's Docetic Christology. It refuses to acknowledge that the Logos is the eternal Word of the Father who is one in being with the Father and who became flesh at a particular time in history for us and for our salvation and so describes the Logos as a universal that can be detached from the historical Jesus and thus seen and understood. That is the problem with mythology: it is based on people's experiences which they then describe in religious categories. This is the Ebionite aspect of Knitter's Christology. It cannot acknowledge that the man Jesus was and is the eternal Word incarnate, beside whom there is no other, and so it presents Jesus' deity as grounded in the impression he made on his followers.[22]

From this combination of Ebionite and Docetic thinking Knitter quite logically concludes that the incarnation is not a one-time event, insisting that the Word must be free for other incarnations. And Knitter thinks this is implied by the Chalcedonian understanding of the union of natures. Nothing, however, could be further from the truth. For Chalcedon the difference of natures in the person of Jesus Christ never implied that the Word "was free for other incarnations." That very idea is mythological since it suggests that the incarnation was not a unique historical event that happened once in the history of Jesus of Nazareth for the salvation of the human race. Such thinking respects neither history nor God's actual freedom exercised in his Word and Spirit within history precisely because it ignores how God did indeed exercise his freedom for us. Yes, the Word is and remains free even in the event of the incarnation, as Barth and Torrance insist. But that cannot mean that the Word is free for "other incarnations" because there is only one Word of God and because we cannot get behind the Word of God revealed and active in Jesus himself. In other words revelation can never be detached from Jesus the revealer. Yet detaching the Word from Jesus is the starting point for Knitter's view of the incarnation. This is why Knitter argues that Jesus should be seen as one among many. Why does this happen?

First, it happens because his view of the God/world relation is panentheistic. Knitter literally cannot conceive of God existing in sovereign freedom because panentheism by its very nature holds that God's relations with the world are mutually conditioned. As we have just seen, Knitter himself argues: "In the process model, divinity, in a limited but real sense, is dependent on the world. . . ." The triune God, however, is not dependent on the world, as I have made clear elsewhere.[23] Briefly, a God who is dependent on the world in any sense whatsoever is not God at all. For the Christian, God exists from all eternity as the Father, Son and Spirit and would so have existed even if he never decided to create, save and redeem the world. That God who is free is indeed active within history in his Word and Spirit, but he is active precisely as the God who remains free and never becomes dependent on the world. That is what is meant by a proper understanding of the doctrine of the immanent Trinity. But of course Knitter's thinking does not allow for such a recognition because it is theocentric in a unitarian not a trinitarian sense in order to make Christ nonnormative.

Second, because of his panentheism Knitter concludes that "all of creation is the arena of divine incarnation" so that any creative transformation within the world can then be equated with God's becoming incarnate. Yet, both the biblical faith and the Nicene Creed are quite clear that the incarnation refers to an event in the life of Jesus. The incarnation never has been understood as an event in which God became incarnate in the world in general; such a view ignores the particularity of Jesus Christ and manifests the fact that panentheism does not in the end escape the pantheist dilemma. To speak of God's incarnation in the world rather than exclusively in Jesus necessarily means that God has become part of the world in such a way that there is in fact an underlying identity between them. This is the general idea of Knitter's "unitive pluralism" in which he argues that God and the world are neither one nor two. Knitter's dream for the unity of religions hinges on his understanding of nondualist unitive pluralism. Following the "nonduality" advocated by Frithjof Schuon, Knitter explains that

> Nonduality tries to express . . . the experience of Ultimate Being as it manifests . . . itself in and through everything that is finite. So one can say, with the mystics, that the soul *is* God, but at the same time one must also say that it is not. *God and the world are not one,* but neither are they two. This is

the esoteric mystery of nonduality. . . . The faith of exoterics is real . . . yet they still perceive this God as some kind of Superperson distinct from the world. *They miss the deeper and more satisfying oneness between divinity and humanity.* (*No Other Name?* 48-49; most emphases mine)

But if the soul is God, then there can be no God independent of the soul; they are one and the same by way of synthesis. Hence, while Knitter asserts that God and the world are not one, he simultaneously declares that God's relation with the world is a "more satisfying oneness between divinity and humanity." Yet, if they are neither one nor two, how can there be a "oneness" between two distinct entities at all? There cannot of course be such a oneness under these circumstances exactly because this thinking illustrates the pantheism that Christians have always tried to avoid by acknowledging God's freedom *in se* and *ad extra.* A pantheist perspective will always depict the God/world relation as one of mutual need. Hence Knitter claims that

God and the finite are bonded in a mystical, inexpressible unity beyond 'one' and 'two'; this unity can really be known only in experience. God and the finite have their being in each other (of course in different proportions). Distinct, they cannot, however, really exist without each other. (*No Other Name?* 68)

Of course a God who cannot exist without the world is certainly not the Christian God as Walter Kasper himself rightly explains: "if God needs the world in order to be able to be the one God, then he is not really God at all. The transcendence and freedom of God are perceived only if the world is not necessary for God to be himself."[24]

Third, because Knitter has universalized what was supposed to have happened uniquely in the history of the man Jesus of Nazareth, he logically concludes that the incarnation is not "a historical anomaly" but is to be seen as a full realization of what is going on throughout history. Yet the point of the NT and the Nicene Creed is that the incarnation of God in Jesus Christ is the realization of God's covenant promises to Israel and through Israel to the world and that what happened in Jesus Christ is without parallel. It is utterly unique and it alone provides the only proper basis for what happened in the incarnation. Moreover, as Barth and Torrance correctly indicated, the incarnation was offensive and had to be, because it was neither expected nor could it be confirmed by human experience outside the context of faith in Jesus himself. By contrast Knitter can only conceptualize Jesus as the full achievement of what God is up to in all history. But in fact what God did in

Jesus was never done before or since. God was in Christ reconciling the world to himself. Knitter's degree Christology which explicitly finds a basis in Rahner's transcendental Christology can only envision Jesus as the "realization of the highest possibility of man's being . . . the unique, supreme, case of the total actualization of human reality"; Knitter takes this Rahnerian insight to mean that "Jesus, in other words, is the symbol of what human beings really are" (*No Other Name?* 188). As a symbol Jesus gives us assurance that our hopes and natural strivings are not in vain since in him our dreams have really become possibilities. Hence, Knitter cites approvingly Rahner's rather dubious assertion that

> God's creative act always drafts the creature [human being] as the paradigm of a possible utterance of himself. . . . We could now define man . . . as that which ensues when God's self-utterance, his Word, is given out lovingly into the void of god-less nothing. . . . [The] code-word for God is man. . . . If God wills to become non-God, man comes to be, that and nothing else we might say. (*No Other Name?* 188)

As seen above in Chapter Two, Rahner's own lack of precision here certainly led him to be unable to recognize and uphold God's freedom as the genuine basis of human freedom.[25] And so he fails to acknowledge that it is not the creature who is a paradigm for God's self-utterance; God utters his Word eternally without needing us. And we do not set the limits of a possible self-communication on the part of God in any sense at all. God himself does that.

But Rahner clearly envisions the incarnation as the symbolic self-expression of the Word into the void so that when we encounter "man" we thus encounter God. There is a pantheistic overtone to all of this with the suggestion that humanity comes into being because God has willed to become non-God. There is also a lack of precision, because Rahner does not clearly distinguish the immanent and economic Trinity at this point. While Rahner properly insists that the incarnation only happened and could have happened only once, Knitter cannot understand why, even though he acknowledges that Rahner wanted to avoid mythologizing the incarnation with the idea that it might be "a datum of every person always and everywhere" (*No Other Name?* 188). Knitter has certainly identified, perhaps unwittingly to a certain extent, a major weakness of Rahner's theology, namely, that on the one hand he intended to acknowledge and respect Christ's uniqueness as the basis for Christian faith itself. But on the other hand he had already ascribed revelation and grace to human nature in the form of a supernatural existential with the result that Jesus himself at best could be seen as different from us only in degree but not in kind. Following this latter strand of Rahner's thought, Knitter concludes that

> the divine assumption of human nature in Jesus does not stand as one grand exception in the historical process, if rather it is the (or a) full expression of what God is up to in history, then it follows that grace is given as a constitutive part of nature. (*No Other Name?* 94-95)

But if grace is a constitutive part of nature, where then is the distinction between nature and grace and between Christ and us? Clearly, in Knitter's reasoning, the distinction has vanished into the unitive pluralist ideal that exists beyond the distinction between one and two (God and the finite).

Knitter's View of God

Perhaps the most insidious part of Knitter's thinking has to do with his understanding of God and his subsequent espousal of self-justification. From what has been said so far, it is more than evident that Knitter's view of God is unitarian and not at all grounded in the economic Trinity. Not only does Knitter not take seriously the doctrine of the immanent Trinity; rather he insists with Arians of all generations that we must begin our reflections with God *rather than* with Christ: we should, Knitter says, place "God, not the church or Jesus Christ, at the center of things" (*No Other Name?* 166).[26] We should, in other words, move beyond christocentrism toward theocentrism. And he insists that if we are theocentric then we can agree with other religions that we all depend upon God even though we do not all depend upon Christ.

This will, of course, require of us an "intellectual conversion" that goes beyond Nicaea and Chalcedon to affirm a "complementary uniqueness" for Jesus in which he will be universally normative along with other universally normative religious figures. Only as Christians dialogue with others, Knitter believes, can they come to know Christ's uniqueness (*No Other Name?* 133).[27] This starting point for knowing God stands in stark contrast with the starting point offered by St. Athanasius: "It is more pious and more accurate to signify God from the Son and call him Father, than to name him from his works and call him Unoriginate."[28] For Athanasius one could not be thinking accurately about the Christian God if one's thinking did not begin with Jesus, the Son of God incarnate. Here is where the incarnation and resurrection are inseparable. Because Athanasius respects the fact that Jesus is the Word of God incarnate simply because he is, his thinking about God begins with him and not with a God who could be known without him, beyond him or beside him. It certainly does not begin with an abstract idea that God is Unoriginate and can be known by reflecting on the created world he made. Because Knitter thinks of the incarnation as a myth, he is in no way obligated to begin his thinking with Jesus himself as the incarnate Word. Instead he begins with his "unitive pluralism" and argues for a theocentrism that permits and requires other revealers and saviors. "Jesus *is* unique," Knitter says,

> but with a uniqueness defined by its ability to relate to — that is, to include and be included by — other unique religious figures. Such an understanding of Jesus views him not as exclusive or even as normative but as *theocentric,* as a universally relevant manifestation (sacrament, incarnation) of divine revelation and salvation. (*No Other Name?* 171-72)

Any such suggestion, however, is inherently polytheistic and pantheistic because for Christians, God's oneness really is his being as Father, Son and Spirit. In other words God is eternally three persons, one being. It is the Nicaean *homoousion* that is decisive here. But for Knitter

> unitive pluralism is a unity in which each religion, although losing some of its individualism . . . will intensify its personality. . . . Each religion will retain its own uniqueness, but this uniqueness will develop and take on new depths by relating to other religions in mutual dependence. (*No Other Name?* 9)

Thus, Knitter turns to new perspectives offered by sociology and social psychology in order to understand God. And what does he discover?

First, following the thought of Ernst Troeltsch, Arnold Toynbee and Carl Jung, Knitter argues that Christians can and should be totally committed to Christ but that they should be open to the fact that they can attain a deeper understanding of Christ through

> recognition of other revealers. Such a Christology will also bring about . . . a theology that is more *theo*centric than *christo*centric; a theology that is not limited only to what God has done in Christ but is more open to what God is doing universally in all religions. (*No Other Name?* 47)

Second, and specifically following Jung, Knitter argues that "The encounter with the mystery of the psyche cannot be distinguished from an experience of God" (*No Other Name?* 58). Third, because revelation has at least part of its origin in the "collective unconscious," Knitter believes that different dogmas in each religion represent attempts to express symbolically the same "ineffable experience" so that while they differ they are in fact "rooted in the same archetypes" (*No Other Name?* 60). Fourth, "Jesus is called Christ because he represents the completion of the process of individuation, the realization of the self" (*No Other Name?* 61). Jesus therefore should be seen as one of the best symbols of the Christ but not the only one. When the NT says "one and only" it really means the symbol works, take it seriously. Yet for Jung and for Knitter other symbols work just as effectively. And according to Knitter that convinces many of the "essential sameness of all religions and the contemporary need for interreligious dialogue" (*No Other Name?* 63). Fifth, Knitter thus concludes that "As mystics in all the religions have asserted (in varying terminology), we are divine!" (*No Other Name?* 67). Sixth, "if deity has its being within our unconscious, it is not dependent on extraordinary events to reveal itself; it does not have to 'step down' and enter history here and there . . . the divine is *already there*" (*No Other Name?* 68). And since deity is "already there" Knitter insists that special revelation in Christ can be no more and no less than an instance of general revelation, namely, that revelation which arises from universal religious experience and can be discerned in all religions. This, for Knitter, is the basis for interreligious dialogue. Hence, "Jesus saves not by 'doing' or 'repairing' anything, but by showing, revealing what is already here" (*No Other Name?* 118). Do we not have in this reasoning what could be characterized as the triumph of Gnosticism in twenty-first-century guise with the equation of salvation with self-knowledge, the idea that we are divine and the complete irrelevance of the historical Jesus as the Word of God incarnate?

It is easy to see that the Ebionite starting point for Knitter's analysis (psychological experience) leads him to ascribe what was supposed to have happened once and for all in the history of the man Jesus to everyone's collective unconscious so that instead of looking exclusively to Jesus as the source of all truth, he now must conduct his search among the various religions. This sounds so very inclusive in today's pluralistic environment. But it is in fact more than a little exclusivist because, while Knitter insists that he will enhance and not compromise the uniqueness of Jesus Christ by this procedure, his starting point leads him to do exactly that. For Knitter, Jesus' uniqueness is not his identity as the eternally begotten Son but instead is the fact that he lived a uniquely human life as does everyone else. As he frequently notes, what happened to Jesus could have happened to other religious leaders and their followers. Thus, it is his Ebionite starting point in experience that leads Knitter to assume that Jesus is called Christ because he completes the psychological process of individuation. He cannot therefore admit that Jesus is who he is simply because he is. Jesus has lost his uniqueness as confessed at Nicaea and Chalcedon because Knitter's Ebionite starting point led him to the Docetic conclusion that Jesus is one revealer and one savior among others. It is precisely Knitter's theocentrism, grounded in his "unitive pluralism," that forces him to deny the very nature of Christ's uniqueness as confessed by the Christian church. Jesus can no longer be the one and only savior and revealer because he is no more and no less than a symbol of the revelation that arises from universal human experience. And that is not the end of it. Knitter's universalism leads him to embrace the rather overt pantheism espoused by Raimundo Panikkar.

While Panikkar believes that there is a "fundamental religious fact" that unites all religions, he also wishes to take religious differences seriously. Hence,

> It is not simply that there are different ways leading to the peak, but that the summit itself would collapse if all the paths disappeared. The peak is in a certain sense the result of the slopes leading to it. . . . It is not that this reality [the ultimate mystery] has many names as if there were a reality outside the name. This reality *is* the many names and each name is a new aspect. . . . The purpose of the new ecumenical ecumenism is to deepen one's grasp and living of this mystery. (*No Other Name?* 153)

Here Panikkar has identified God with each religious depiction of him so that he can argue that God would not in fact exist if the different religious expressions of "ultimate reality" did not exist. God's existence we are told is, in a certain sense, the result of the experiences leading to him. This God is certainly not the Christian God who exists self-sufficiently and eternally as Father, Son and Holy Spirit, and so can be recognized as God in distinction from the world. No wonder Panikkar believes that

> Jesus is the ultimate form of Christ. . . . Though a Christian believes that 'Jesus is the Christ' . . . this sentence is not identical to 'the Christ is Jesus.' . . . Jesus, therefore, is a concrete historical name for the 'Supername' — that is, the Christ which is always 'the name above every name.' . . . The name above all names — the Christ — can go by many historical names: Rama, Krishna, Isvara, Purusha, Tathagata. . . . Jesus . . . would be one of the names of the cosmotheandric principle. (*No Other Name?* 156)

This is a classic expression of what Barth identified as Docetic Christology because it sees Jesus as a particular instance of a "cosmotheandric" principle which Panikkar assumes to be operative in the world. As a result, it is not the man Jesus from Nazareth who is the Christ. Rather, he is one of many histori-cal embodiments of the Christ and the Christ is, for Panikkar, a living symbol of the "totality of reality: human, divine, cosmic" (*No Other Name?* 154). That of course is what cosmotheandric reality is: it is the blending together of hu-man, divine and cosmic reality. What is espoused here is unitarian and not trinitarian theology, and for that very reason it expresses a pantheistic mix-ture of human, divine and cosmic reality instead of a clear understanding of Jesus as one in being with the Father and with us.

And Knitter does not stop here either. Based on this understanding, he decides to re-define the very nature of truth itself. Apart from interreligious dialogue Knitter argues one might hold to an Aristotelian view of truth that defines the truth of religion through exclusion as a matter of either-or. Such an understanding, according to Knitter, has led Catholics in particular to den-igrate the truth of other religions and has led them toward legalism, supersti-tion and to the reduction of faith to doctrine (*No Other Name?* 218). But Knit-ter's new model, based on his belief that there is something common to all religions and is expressed in universal religious experience, is inclusive and not exclusive, we are told. And this leads to his new understanding of truth:

> truth will no longer be identified by its ability to exclude or absorb others. *Rather, what is true will reveal itself mainly by its ability to relate to other ex-pressions of truth and to grow through these relationships* — truth defined not by exclusion but by relation. . . . The new model reflects what our plu-ralistic world is discovering: no truth can stand alone; no truth can be to-tally unchangeable. Truth, by its very nature, needs other truth. . . . Truth, without 'other' truth, cannot be unique, it cannot exist . . . the model of truth-through-relationship allows each religion to be unique. (*No Other Name?* 219; most emphases mine)[29]

This supposedly inclusivist view of truth, however, can only work if the truth of Christianity is excluded from the relationship. So it is not as inclusive as it may seem at first blush. This thinking denies the main point of the doctrine of the immanent Trinity, namely, that the triune God exists from all eternity in self-sufficient freedom as one who loves. This God can and does "stand alone" and is indeed unchangeable, not in the sense that he is impassible and cannot act for us in the particular way he did on the cross, but in the sense that in all his changes his nature remains unalterably his nature as one who loves in freedom. And he would have continued to so exist even if he never decided to create, reconcile and redeem the world. For Knitter's view of truth, however, God, who is truth itself, needs other truth to exist. It is precisely the pantheistic perspective of Panikkar that leads Knitter to advocate a view of truth that makes God dependent on the world for his existence.

Salvation in Christ vs. Self-Justification

And it is just this thinking that sees Jesus as one revealer and one savior among many others that causes Knitter to espouse a rather unambiguous form of self-justification in his understanding of ethics. Instead of beginning his dialogue with other religions with Jesus Christ in his actual uniqueness in order to convey a genuine understanding of Christ's uniqueness to others, Knitter contends that he will not start with the question of whether there is "one savior/incarnation or many" but "how Christians and others can struggle, together, against those things that threaten their common humanity. Only in the praxis of such struggle can clarity on universal truths emerge" (*No Other Name?* 194).[30] The very assumption that truth will emerge from our common struggle against the threats to our common humanity suggests first that salvation can and should be equated with the success of that struggle, and second it suggests that such salvation is dependent on our working together with people of other religions to accomplish this "salvation." This is an essentially Pelagian view of salvation that ignores the need for Jesus and not only converts our justification by faith into our justification by works, but changes the meaning of justification and sanctification from an act of God in the history of Jesus Christ and the Holy Spirit, which includes us through faith and by grace, to the human accomplishment of our overcoming perceived threats to our humanity. How and why does this happen?

It happens because Knitter follows what he calls the liberation theological method of "doing before knowing."

> For liberation theology, the one thing necessary to be a Christian and to carry on the job of theology is commitment to the kingdom vision of liberating, redemptive action. . . . Jesus of Nazareth *is* a means for liberation from injustice and oppression. . . . Not knowing whether Jesus is unique, whether he is inclusive or normative for all others, does not interfere with commitment to the praxis of following him. (*No Other Name?* 196)

In Knitter's estimation "liberation christology allows, even requires, that Christians recognize the possibility of other liberators or saviors, other incarnations" (*No Other Name?* 196). Perhaps. But the problem here is that Knitter, following the method of liberation theology as he understands it, separates the kingdom from Jesus and then argues that we cannot claim that the kingdom was fulfilled in Jesus because Israel's hope was for the kingdom. Indeed, following Knitter's own words, the commitment of which he speaks is to a "vision of liberating, redemptive action" and not to Jesus Christ himself.[31]

But it makes a difference from within a Christian perspective how and why one is liberated. Here is where the doctrine of the atonement is tied to the doctrines of the incarnation and resurrection. It is exactly because Jesus Christ is God himself in the flesh that there is, as Torrance noted above, an atoning exchange within human history, so that God in Christ has done for us what we cannot do for ourselves. He freed us from the self-will (sin) that would lead us to think that we could detach his kingdom from him and then obey our vision in order to create a better world by working together with others against those things that threaten our common humanity. In the history of Jesus Christ, he took away from us the possibility and the burden of our self-justification exemplified by any attempt on our part to be faithful to our own visions of how we think things should be. Salvation for Christians actually means that in Christ, God has fulfilled his covenant with Israel so that salvation is exclusively an act of God in Christ while at the same time it is inclusive of everyone because it is an act of God exercised for the benefit of the entire human race and not just for a select group.

By contrast Knitter's view of freedom replicates the biblical notion of sin because it places salvation in human hands and explicitly does so because it renounces the idea that Jesus himself must be the one who sets us free. He renounces the idea that we must acknowledge and therefore know that there is but one savior of the world because the one God who is Father, Son and Spirit has acted and continues to act as our savior, helper and friend in Jesus Christ himself. The view of salvation offered by both Barth and Torrance shows that true liberation, the liberation from sin that occurs in Christ, frees us from the need to rely on our own vision to create a better world. Those who obey Christ will of course be working for a better world. But they will be doing so in the knowledge that they have been freed for that task by the risen Lord who has already overcome sin, suffering, evil and death in his own life history on our behalf. And they will recognize that the burden of actually making the world more human does not rest on what they do but on what Christ has done and is doing through them in the power of his Holy Spirit. They will be genuinely free for others because Christ has freed them from the idea that they can or must work with others to determine what universal truth is in the first instance and then to set about creating the conditions necessary to fulfill that truth. Because Jesus himself is the way, the truth and the life, there really is no way to the Father, except through the Son and by and in the Holy Spirit.[32] This kind of thinking is far less likely to produce the kind of anxiety that comes from supposing that the survival of humanity somehow depends on us exactly because it will always point away from us in prayer to the Holy Spirit as the first and final guarantee of our holiness.

One more point. It is interesting to note that Knitter's insistence on dialogue with people of other religions in order to understand Jesus' uniqueness is predicated on his assumption that there is a *common ground and goal for all religions* so that "I can never understand another's position as he does . . . unless I share his view; in a word, unless I judge it to be true" (*No Other Name?* 208). Consequently, according to Knitter "there must be the same ultimate reality, the same divine presence . . . the same God — animating all religions" (*No Other Name?* 209). In contrast to this, it is important to recognize that in a Christian doctrine of God and of revelation, God alone defines truth. Authentic freedom consists in obeying the Word heard and believed. But this Word is the act of God himself in the history of Jesus and the essence of the church in its preaching, teaching, sacraments and theology. Obeying any other word will not mean that we may possibly be led to a deeper apprehension of truth; rather it will mean that we are necessarily led away from the truth. Thus, to judge another religion as true even though it is in conflict with Christianity by virtue of the fact that its adherents will not begin thinking about God with Jesus himself as the first and final word of God acting for us within history, simply misses the fact that there is no other source of revelation and salvation than the one unique savior and revealer himself, Jesus, the God-man. Moreover, an "authentic" dialogue would be one where some actual recognition of truth took place. To ground this in religious experience (Christian or non-Christian) would deprive one or both dialogue partners (Christian or non-Christian) of the very truth of the Gospel. By arguing that we cannot step outside our own tradition Knitter appears to maintain the uniqueness of Christianity. Yet because it is our experience which makes it true, he is forced to say exactly what the theology of the NT does not say, namely, that there is another revealer or savior besides Jesus.

Rejecting Jesus' uniqueness as Christians have always understood it, he substitutes his definition of universal revelation for the truth revealed in Christ. Conversion no longer means repentance and belief in Jesus but "conversion to God's truth, as it is made known in dialogue" (*No Other Name?* 212). But dialogue means accepting a definition of ultimate reality based upon the common essence of religions, which by definition cannot allow Jesus to be the sole revealer or savior. Here Knitter appeals to Panikkar and to John Dunne's idea of "passing over."

Passing over is a shifting of standpoint, a going over to the standpoint of another culture, another way of life, another religion. It is followed by an equal and opposite process we might call 'coming back,' coming back with new insight to one's own culture, one's own way of life, one's own religion. . . . If I keep in mind the relativity of standpoints as I pass over from one standpoint to another, therefore, I effectively hold myself open toward mystery. (*No Other Name?* 214-15; see also 211 and 216)

While every human standpoint is indeed relative, the question raised by this analysis is this: can we equate the mystery of Christ with a common essence of religion which we imagine exists and can be attained by passing over from one religion to another? Must we not admit that we have no existential method by which to hold ourselves open to God because there is only one foundation which none of us has laid?[33] It is Christ himself who keeps us open to God; in him our lives were re-created and are continually renewed as signified by baptism and the eucharist.[34] There is an epistemological message here. Liberation theology, as depicted by Knitter, and Knitter's own method of doing before knowing, purport to separate praxis from knowledge of the truth in order to distinguish the culturally conditioned from the essential in the world religions. But the truth is that no one can express an idea of practice, ethical or otherwise, except by conceptualizing it in relation to some view of the truth. Thus, the notion of pure praxis appears as the consummate myth which was contrived in order to circumvent the truth of Christianity. Instead of allowing the kingdom of God and religious practice to be dictated by the person and work of Jesus Christ, these thinkers focus on a view of the kingdom and on religious practice in an effort to find a universally recognizable truth which avoids the scandal of the Gospel.[35]

Paul Knitter's theology thus provides an instructive example of how intimately connected the doctrines of incarnation, resurrection, atonement and the Trinity really are. It is precisely because he refused to begin his understanding of these doctrines with the man Jesus himself as attested in the NT, that is, with the incarnate Word, that Knitter embraced versions of Ebionite and Docetic Christology that led to his belief that it is we who are the real saviors of the world to the extent that we work with others for a better world and to the extent that the truth of Christology must be judged by our behavior. Yet, for Christians, as seen above in Chapter One, hope is tied exclusively to Christ's promise of eternal life and so those who live by faith know that they do not have to re-create who Jesus is to achieve a salvation of their own making. And their behavior stands under the sign of God's own judgment and grace as it was disclosed and is active in Jesus Christ himself. Hence the success of their work as witnesses to Christ's saving grace is really not their concern. It always is and remains God's concern — a concern he freely took upon himself in the incarnation and fulfilled in Christ's resurrection from the dead. For Christians, salvation already is in effect in Jesus himself and is universally available through faith in him. In light of this, Knitter's nonnormative Christology therefore is exposed as an ideological attempt to create a Christianity without Christ by undermining his Lordship in the interest of finding some humanly agreeable approach to God. In view of the intrinsic connection between Christ's incarnation and resurrection, however, this attempt represents the ultimate form of self-justification and thus necessarily falsifies any ethics that might follow from such thinking.

6. Incarnation and Resurrection in the Theology of Gordon Kaufman and Sallie McFague

Gordon Kaufman and Sallie McFague do not intend to maintain the uniqueness of Jesus Christ in the Nicene and Chalcedonian sense precisely because they use his "story" and "ministry" to advance their particular visions of how theology should function today. This is not to say that they do not understand the traditional Christologies. There are times when both theologians understand the traditional Christologies quite well in fact. Gordon Kaufman even tried to present his theology in a way that would harmonize with the tradition in his earlier work, *Systematic Theology: A Historicist Perspective.* There he presented the traditional Christologies pretty accurately and expended much energy explaining the traditional doctrines of the Trinity and incarnation. Even then, however, there was a marked tendency to undercut the actual meaning of those doctrines, as we shall see. Nonetheless Kaufman now rejects the traditional doctrines because he regards them as unfeasible in today's pluralistic society. And his criterion is not a more accurate view of Jesus' person and work, but our contemporary experience of ourselves in an evolutionary context, together with our experience of the threat of nuclear destruction. It is "our sense of living in a truly new situation"[1] that Kaufman believes requires us drastically to reconstruct traditional Christian claims.

Like Gordon Kaufman, his former student Sallie McFague rejects the traditional understanding of the doctrine of the incarnation and regards the doctrine as a myth that needs to be remythologized by perceiving that the world is God's body and that God now can be killed in this body as he was once killed in human form in the man Jesus.[2] Her criteria are quite similar to those advocated by Kaufman with the exception that she wishes to use those personal experiences that mean the most to her as her norm for speaking about God and God's relations with us. So instead of describing God impersonally as an "ecological reality" or a "serendipitous creativity" at work in the evolutionary process, she prefers to describe God as mother, lover and friend of the universe which is understood to be the expression of God in accordance with the idea that the world is God's body. I chose to explore the thought of Kaufman and McFague in this chapter because their visions are extremely popular among many contemporary Catholic and Protestant theologians and because they are prime examples of what happens when theological thinking does not begin with the risen Lord himself in his uniqueness as the incarnate Word, but rather begins from some social, religious or political agenda and then tries to fit Jesus into that agenda in order to make it function. Let us begin then with Gordon Kaufman.

Gordon Kaufman

Kaufman's View of the Resurrection

Gordon Kaufman presents his most sustained treatment of the resurrection in his book *Systematic Theology: A Historicist Perspective.* He begins acknowledging that the "resurrection-event" was crucial for the development of the Christian faith — far more crucial in fact than the "alleged virgin birth" — which he regards as an unfortunate confusion because it attempts to combine human interpretation with theological interpretation in an inappropriate way.[3] Interestingly, it is just this attitude, however, that demonstrates that Kaufman can only offer what David Fergusson called a "liberal" interpretation of the resurrection which collapses back into the "radical" view which reduces the resurrection to an event in the lives of the believers, thus undercutting the actual basis of the Christian faith. It will be recalled that one of the reasons offered by Fergusson for the liberal/radical approach to the resurrection was a suspicion of the concept of miracle.

This is important because, as we have seen, Barth insisted that the virgin birth and the empty tomb were linked since they were signs indicating the miracles of the incarnation on the one hand and of the resurrection on the other. "These two miracles belong together" wrote Barth, because together they

> mark out the existence of Jesus Christ, amid the many other existences in human history, as that human historical existence in which God is Himself, God is alone, God is directly the Subject. . . . The Virgin birth at the open-

ing and the empty tomb at the close of Jesus' life bear witness that this life is a fact marked off from all the rest of human life . . . not by our understanding or our interpretation, but by itself. (*CD* I/2, 182)

By contrast, for Kaufman, the virgin birth cannot be accepted as a miracle in that sense at all and so must be dismissed as a "biological" interpretation of a theological fact. Of course Barth was well aware of this manner of interpretation as can be illustrated by his dismissal of Brunner's "queer objection that the doctrine of the Virgin birth means a 'biological interpretation of the miracle' (meaning the miracle of the incarnation), and is in fact an expression of 'biological inquisitiveness'" (*CD* I/2, 183).[4] Barth insisted that the dogma of the virgin birth "denotes not so much the christological reality of revelation [the *vere Deus vere homo*] as the mystery of that reality, the inconceivability of it, its character as a fact in which God has acted solely through God and in which God can likewise be known solely through God" (*CD* I/2, 177). For that reason the virgin birth signifies that in response to all questions of Why? Whence? and How? "we can only answer that here God does it all Himself. . . . It eliminates the last surviving possibility of understanding the *vere Deus vere homo* intellectually, as an idea or an arbitrary interpretation in the sense of docetic or ebionite Christology" (*CD* I/2, 177). The real question to be asked with respect to the virgin birth, according to Barth, is when two theologians with

> apparently the same conviction confess the mystery of Christmas, do they mean the same thing by that mystery, if one acknowledges and confesses the Virgin birth to be the sign of the mystery while the other denies it as a mere externality or is ready to leave it an open question? (*CD* I/2, 179)

Of course Kaufman does not leave it as an open question. And my point here is that his confused rejection of the dogma indicates his inability to accept both the mystery of revelation and the incarnation, and that affects his view of the resurrection as we shall presently see.

There is enough ambiguity in Kaufman's presentation to suggest that perhaps he actually affirms the resurrection in the traditional sense. Hence he writes "The term 'resurrection of Jesus' thus points to the historical event which gave birth to the Christian faith" (*Systematic Theology*, 414). The resurrection, then, according to Kaufman was the answer to the question as to why Christians came to believe "that in Jesus Christ God himself is encountered" (*Systematic Theology*, 414). Indeed, according to Kaufman, *"There would have been no Christian faith had this event not happened"* (*Systematic Theology*, 415;

emphasis in original). Whatever it was, Kaufman says, this event followed the despair that resulted from Jesus' crucifixion and engendered in the disciples a new hope from out of their original despair. Hence, "It was in the conviction of Jesus' resurrection that the church was founded and the Gospel preached to all nations" (*Systematic Theology*, 415). Accordingly, Kaufman insists that "Unlike the 'virgin birth' which is a peripheral and dispensable symbol, 'resurrection' points to the heart of the Christian faith" (*Systematic Theology*, 416). He even cites the famous Pauline text that if Christ has not been raised, then our faith is without substance and we are still in our sins (1 Cor. 15:14ff.). With the exception of his attitude toward the virgin birth, his belief that it was "the conviction of Jesus' resurrection" on which the church was founded and the suggestion that the resurrection is a symbol, everything said here by Kaufman could be taken in a perfectly orthodox sense to be suggesting the centrality of the resurrection for the Christian faith.

But no less than everything depends upon the interpretation of what exactly happened that gave rise to that resurrection faith. If it is merely a description of the disciples' religious experience or their convictions and ours then, despite his citation of 1 Cor. 15, Christian faith is indeed without substance and we are still in our sins because we would then be alone with our faith; and the resurrection would be no more than a Docetic description of Jesus' religious significance for what we envision to be the important task or tasks that need to be accomplished by society in its attempts to create a more humane civilization. So what exactly does Kaufman mean when he speaks of Christ's resurrection from the dead?

Kaufman begins his explanation by noting that Paul could not have meant that Jesus' resurrection was simply "the raising of his physical body" although, for Paul, there was a continuity between the one who was resurrected with his new spiritual body and the historical Jesus of Nazareth (*Systematic Theology*, 418). Neither did it mean that a "bodiless" Jesus appeared. Rather, "Paul believed Jesus was alive again but in some nonphysical mode of being" (*Systematic Theology*, 418). Paul's concept of a "spiritual body" together with his reference to a series of "appearances" suggest that for Paul the risen Lord was manifested through what we would call "visions" (*Systematic Theology*, 419). So, Kaufman equates the resurrection appearances with a series of "visions" (*Systematic Theology*, 420). And he argues that the resurrection faith most likely did not begin with the discovery of an empty tomb which itself was an extrapolation from the appearances or visions.

Note that Kaufman has here laid the groundwork for an interpretation of the resurrection only in the subjectivist sense that the disciples were describing their visions rather than an event in the life of Jesus that enabled their faith. Here the objective event is already confused with the subjective experience by means of the category of vision. And it should be noted that, as seen in Chapter One, Karl Barth properly rejected any attempt to explain the resurrection using the category of a vision exactly because he believed that such an approach represented an apologetic concern to explain away the mystery and miracle attested in the event.[5] Hence Barth quite properly insisted that

> The texts do not speak primarily of the formation of the Easter faith as such but of its foundation by Jesus Christ Himself, who met and talked with His disciples after His death as One who is alive (not outside the world but within it), who by this act of life convinced them incontrovertibly of the fact that He is alive and therefore of the fact that His death was the redemptive happening willed by God . . . its objectivity, not taking place in their faith but in conflict with their lack of faith, overcoming and removing their lack of faith and creating their faith. (*CD* IV/1, 340-41)

What then does Kaufman make of the appearances? What is to be designated by the term "resurrection"? "*It does not refer to anything directly experienced by the disciples;* what was experienced were 'appearances' (and possibly an 'empty tomb')" (*Systematic Theology,* 421; emphasis in original). Hence, when the early Christians spoke of Christ's resurrection they were merely explaining these "experiences." In Kaufman's words,

> That is, on the basis of events directly known to them in which, as they believed, they encountered Jesus after his death, *they inferred* that another event had occurred after his death which they had not witnessed: Jesus' being awakened from the dead. (Nowhere in the canon is the claim made that someone directly witnessed the reawakening of Jesus.) (*Systematic Theology,* 421)

For Kaufman then belief in the resurrection was "*belief in the truth of a historical hypothesis* necessary (as they believed) to account for certain experiences which remade their lives" (*Systematic Theology,* 422; emphasis in original). According to Kaufman the Easter-event was seen by the early Christians as a "resurrection" mainly because it was "interpreted in terms of certain Jewish apocalyptic conceptions" (*Systematic Theology,* 422). Consequently, "The Easter-event in and of itself, then, did not give rise to the belief Jesus was risen: it was susceptible of a variety of interpretations" (*Systematic Theology,* 422). Because the disciples interpreted this experience in terms of Jewish apocalyptic they assumed "their master was again alive" (*Systematic Theology,*

422). For contemporary faith, however, Kaufman contends this interpretation will no longer do. And we must therefore interpret the founding event of Christian faith differently. How should we proceed?

Kaufman proceeds by explaining the appearances as "hallucinations" and expends much energy to justify this category against those who might suppose that such a conception could reduce the objective event of the resurrection to the subjective experience of the disciples. Nonetheless, Kaufman believes this is the most reasonable conjecture about what happened on Easter from a human point of view. Still, he insists we must add another level to our interpretation: that "through these events — however understood on the human level — God himself was acting" (*Systematic Theology,* 423). He even cites Bultmann who suggested that "'if it is possible for the historian to see nothing more [in Jesus' resurrection] than visionary experiences of fanatical persons, then we are simply asked whether we believe that God acts in such things, as they themselves believed and as the proclamation maintains'" (*Systematic Theology,* 423).

Of course God *could* act in such things. But in reality the NT testifies to the fact that God *has acted* in the actual life of the historical Jesus precisely by raising him from the dead. Naturally enough both Kaufman and Bultmann have missed the point of the NT proclamation exactly because of their Docetic perspectives. For both theologians, the resurrection cannot be an event in the very life of the historical Jesus that objectively gives rise to the disciples' faith. Rather, God's actions are seen and described without reference to Jesus himself as the incarnate Word so that the term God is not defined by who Jesus was and is, as the Word of God incarnate, but by their respective prior conceptions of God. And since Kaufman views God as *our* ultimate point of reference for interpreting human experience, his idea of God, as we shall see, is no more than a regulative idea deliberately constructed in such a way as to obviate any *homoousial* relation between the Son and the Father. Hence, his very starting point for thinking about God determines his views of God, Christ and the resurrection itself. That starting point of course is the idea that we must begin our thinking with God *rather than* with Christ; this, as we shall see, undercuts the fact that Christ is *homoousion* with the Father as Son from all eternity. Had Kaufman acknowledged the *homoousion* he would have insisted that we must begin our thinking about God with Christ who *is* God himself incarnate in history in the man Jesus of Nazareth. This is what happens when the content of revelation is separated from its form. This is why Barth rightly insisted: "The form here is essential to the content, i.e., God is unknown as our Father, as the Creator, to the degree that He is not made known by Jesus."[6] And the ultimate difficulty here is that because the resurrection and incarnation are intrinsically related, any Docetic view of the incarnation leads not only to a distortion of the resurrection itself and its meaning for Christian faith but to a distortion in the Christian understanding of God himself.

In any case, since Kaufman has detached revelation from Jesus himself and located it in the experience of the disciples he argues that "it *was* the experience of these appearances that gave birth to the faith that in and through the crucified Jesus God was acting decisively in human history" (*Systematic Theology*, 423; emphasis in original). Thus, for Kaufman two levels of interpretation of this experience are necessary: (1) the disciples knew themselves to be going through a "radical transformation" that was humanly intelligible as a hallucination and (2) this same event was understood as a divine act. So the decisive question, as Kaufman sees it, is: "Can it be believed that through these 'hallucinations' God was acting to bring his kingdom powerfully into human history?" (*Systematic Theology*, 424-25). Faith will answer yes, he says, while unbelief will answer no. But there can be little doubt that Kaufman has mishandled the actual question posed by the NT. For the NT, as we have seen already, the question concerned whether or not one would accept the risen Lord himself as the foundation of faith. For Kaufman this question has been transposed to a question about the disciples' visions or hallucinations and so Christian faith now becomes a description of a divine action that no longer is bound to the specific form of the revelation attested in the NT. As Kaufman himself notes, when he uses the expression "resurrection of Jesus," he is referring to *"the appearances theologically interpreted"* (*Systematic Theology*, 425; emphasis in original). But for him the appearances are no more than experiences of the disciples, theologically interpreted. It is at this decisive point that Kaufman demonstrates that he holds the liberal position as portrayed by David Fergusson and it is this position, as we have seen, that inevitably collapses back into the radical view espoused by Bultmann and others.[7]

Here Kaufman's own "modern" prejudice is on display since he argues that it was easier for a group of "first-century Galilean fisherman" than for us today, with our "naive skepticism," to be convinced that Jesus was really raised from the dead by means of "hallucinations" (*Systematic Theology*, 425-26). Hence,

> Contemporary belief . . . will not necessarily involve the conviction that the crucified Jesus became personally alive again; rather, it will see the events of Jesus' ministry and death — especially as appropriated through that strange event called the 'resurrection' — as the actual establishment of the kingdom of God. (*Systematic Theology*, 426)

But why would it have been easier for a group of first-century fishermen than for us to accept the fact that Jesus actually rose bodily from the dead? Here T. F. Torrance clearly had the more accurate view. On the one hand, as we have seen, Torrance properly insists that the resurrection was an absolutely new event that would be seen as utterly incredible from the human perspective. Hence, Torrance explained

> That God himself had become man was an offence to the Jew and folly to the Greek; that Jesus rose from the dead was deemed to be utterly incredible. Yet the incarnation and the resurrection forced themselves upon the mind of the Church against the grain of people's convictions. (STR, 17)[8]

Instead of admitting this truth, Kaufman dismisses the event by changing it to a description of Jesus' prior history in theological terms defined by the disciples' hallucinatory experiences. On the other hand, as we have just noted, Torrance rightly stresses that accepting the resurrection was no easier for the early Christians than for us because they were well aware of the fact that such belief went completely against the grain.

At this point in his discussion Kaufman presents what can only be described as a beguiling but in the end Docetic portrait of how he wishes to maintain the all-important continuity between the historical Jesus and the resurrection appearances. He is even unable to grasp the traditional view here arguing that "According to the traditional view, the continuity was, so to speak, the personality of Jesus: it was the same Jesus they had known before who was now risen from the dead" (Systematic Theology, 427). While I agree that it was the same Jesus who was now risen, I maintain that the continuity was not just to be found in Jesus' personality but in his person as the Word of God incarnate. This distinction makes all the difference in the world as we have been seeing throughout this book.

In any case, what Kaufman proposes here is that it is what Jesus' resurrection "signified for the disciples that was the crucial dimension of that event" (Systematic Theology, 428; emphasis in original). In other words, more important than Jesus' rising from the dead was the fact that something was revealed "through their belief: that God really had broken into history through Jesus of Nazareth . . . that God's presence in history in Jesus of Nazareth was continuous with his presence subsequently" (Systematic Theology, 428; emphasis in original). That God had broken into history then and now is indicated by the fact that they were "new men" who had experienced community, love, forgiveness, freedom and compassion then and now. In other words what was decisively important for the disciples' communal experience of faith was their "consciousness" of God's continuing activity in their history and "not the re-suscitation of their former friend and leader" (*Systematic Theology*, 429). And it is this that they apprehended through and by means of their "hallucina-tions." While these hallucinations and the disciples' interpretation of them as the "real presence of Jesus" may have been necessary epistemologically for the birth of the Christian faith, these "historically relative necessities" are no lon-ger relevant to us who live in quite different historical and epistemological circumstances! Therefore,

> The theologically important fact both for the first Christians and for us . . .
> was not that this *finite man* as such lives again, but that *God's act begun in*
> *him* was a *genuine historical act* which *still continues*, that the love, mercy,
> and forgiveness present in their midst with Jesus . . . was still present with
> them . . . in this sense, as the biblical writers claimed, Christ himself was
> raised from the dead. (*Systematic Theology*, 429; emphasis in original)

Since this is the continuity that for Kaufman is expressed by the biblical wit-ness to the resurrection of Jesus, he forthrightly insists that *"The question whether Jesus was alive again or not does not bear directly on this issue"* (*Systematic Theology*, 430; emphasis in original). Hence the difference between his "new" interpretation and the biblical witness is unimportant, he says.

But this thinking cannot disguise the fact that it is in reality Docetic be-cause it is not Jesus, the man from Nazareth who dictates what Kaufman thinks and says here, but Jesus interpreted in light of a series of divine actions supposedly occurring in the experience of the disciples. In other words the unique incarnation of the Word in the flesh of Jesus is detached from the his-torical Jesus and located within the community of belief in such a way that God can now be recognized and described without taking cognizance of Je-sus' bodily resurrection from the dead. This thinking of course would explain why Kaufman also misconstrues the nature of the incarnation itself by con-tending that God cannot be said to have become incarnate exclusively in the man Jesus but rather that he became incarnate in the spirit of love, freedom, forgiveness and mutual sharing of the community.[9]

Interestingly, however, Kaufman defends himself against Docetism by ar-guing that he has not detached God's action from history; he has merely sub-stituted the new community of love and forgiveness for the risen Lord him-self. The disciples' interpretation of their hallucinations, Kaufman believes, was not merely subjective but was objectively historical because it was "rooted in the experienced new quality of community" which they attributed to God's activity (*Systematic Theology*, 430). But this explanation is fatally flawed since in actuality he has changed the objective witness of the NT itself from witness to an event in the life of Jesus that gave meaning to their faith and to ours, to an event within the life of the community. This represents a classic collapse of the objective reality of revelation into the subjective experience of the community. And it was made possible precisely by Kaufman's Docetic Christology which itself resulted from his idealist understanding of the incarnation.

He cannot allow Jesus, the incarnate Word, to be the starting point of his reflections about God's activity within history just because Jesus, for him, is only the historical focal point for a series of new experiences which the community had after his death; Jesus is a paradigm for understanding God and humanity. Because Kaufman will not accept the fact that Jesus *is* the Son of God incarnate simply because he is (Barth's view discussed above in Chapter One),[10] he is forced to an Ebionite view contending that the "early Christians clearly were overwhelmed by the way in which their relation to God was rooted in the person-event Jesus Christ" (*Systematic Theology*, 178).[11] According to Kaufman, this is what led to their assertions that he was the only savior (Acts 4:12) and that he was the way, the truth and the life (Jn. 14:6). Indeed it was this experience that led to the statement in Matt. 11:27 and Lk. 10:22 that "no one knows the Father except the Son and anyone to whom the Son chooses to reveal him" (*Systematic Theology*, 178). And it is this Ebionite starting point that gives rise to his Docetic Christology.

Hence for Kaufman, God is a symbol used by the community as its ultimate point of reference to order its existence in ways that will make people more humane and peaceful. It has the function of humanizing and relativizing us and so should never be seen as fixed or finished by tying it too closely to any particular image (*TNA*, 33ff. and 25).[12] This thinking sheds light on Kaufman's later argument that the resurrection merely represented a kind of imperialism and triumphalism on the part of the community,[13] and it is just this thinking that demonstrates that it is Kaufman's idea of God that leads him to see Jesus as only one instance among others of God's revelatory and salvific activity within history. That is in fact the Docetic Christology which Barth and Torrance rightly rejected and which Rahner himself intended to avoid, but could not consistently escape, because of his own presuppositions. One does not avoid Docetism merely by emphasizing history. One avoids Docetism by acknowledging that the historical Jesus was and is the unique Word of God who, as such, not only revealed God to us and reconciled us to God but who rose from the dead and now lives as the risen Lord of the church and world history itself. Hence the foundation of the community cannot be found in the community's experiences of love, forgiveness, freedom and mutual sharing but must be continually sought and found exclusively in Jesus Christ himself who is present now in the power of his Spirit enabling the community to live as his body on earth. One cannot then begin to think about God apart from faith in Jesus of Nazareth and then try to redefine Jesus in light of the idea of God discovered in that way. As we shall see, this is the hallmark of Kaufman's theology and it subverts the humanity of Jesus by confusing his uniqueness with the experiences of the community itself. In fact Kaufman's thinking exemplifies just the dualism he thinks he overcomes because he will not allow God himself to be incarnate in the man Jesus and as the man Jesus.

It is no wonder then that Kaufman ultimately argues that the resurrection was the event "through which the real meaning of Jesus' career and death — and thus of all human history — broke into human history" (*Systematic Theology*, 431). Hence "The resurrection . . . was not primarily an odd physical event that happened two thousand years ago. . . . The resurrection was preeminently an event in the *history of meaning*" (*Systematic Theology*, 433; emphasis in original). And Kaufman once again attempts to defend himself against the charge of Docetism by arguing that its referent is actual history. But the point of this book is that it makes a difference which history one is referring to when one describes the incarnation and resurrection in their intrinsic unity. Is it the history of the Word of God incarnate in the man Jesus who reconciled the world to himself and destroyed sin and death in and through his life, death and resurrection? Or is it the community with its idea of divinity that re-interprets the historical "career" of Jesus so that it finds a new meaning in his life after his death than it did during his lifetime?

In the former case the community is what it is by virtue of its relationship with the risen Lord himself in specific historical circumstances such as the forty days after Easter. In the latter case the community itself becomes the locus of divine activity, so that it is and remains the community that must become the reconciler and redeemer in its ethical behavior as it strives to become a community of peace and reconciliation. But such a community is in fact lost because it is acting on its own and therefore unspiritually (without the Holy Spirit) trying to create something that not only does not and cannot be created, but it is also substituting itself for the risen Lord himself. As long as that occurs the community is making it impossible for the risen Lord himself to act in relation to it in decisive ways that would actually save it from its attempts at self-justification. What is needed is a return to faith and thus a reliance on the miraculous action of the Holy Spirit who alone creates and sustains faith in the risen Lord.

We have now seen how Gordon Kaufman envisions Christ's resurrection from the dead. Now let me briefly indicate that it is just because of his inadequate view of the incarnation and his confusion of the immanent and economic Trinity that he is led to this particular Docetic explanation of the resurrection. Finally, I will briefly illustrate the ethical implications of Kaufman's confusion of salvation with the activities of the community of faith.

Kaufman's View of the Incarnation and of the Trinity

As we have seen, it is precisely Kaufman's failure to accept the incarnation in the NT and traditional sense as an exclusive event in the life of the historical Jesus that causes him to shift the center of gravity away from Jesus' resurrection to the experience of the disciples and thus to subvert the real meaning of the Christian faith. What is it that leads Kaufman to confuse the incarnation of the Word in Jesus with experiences within the community of faith? Like many contemporary theologians Kaufman will not allow Jesus himself to be the starting point of his reflections. Instead, he insists that we must interpret Jesus' significance for faith in the terms we use to understand ourselves in our historically conscious contemporary world, that is, we must interpret who Jesus was and is in light of the evolutionary context within which we perceive ourselves today.

Kaufman's Enlightenment presupposition that it was easier for the people of Jesus' time to accept him as the unique savior of the world than it is for us today emerges here once more:

> When human life and its context was conceived almost exclusively in terms of familial and political models, it was natural and easy to think of human salvation as accomplished through the activities of a particular individual person, Jesus the Christ. (*TNA*, 56)

Here one must object once again, however, that it was no easier for the people of Jesus' time to accept him as he was, than it is for us today because, as T. F. Torrance rightly insists, the grace of God revealed in him requires an abandonment of self-reliance to complete reliance on Jesus himself. That is what Torrance calls "costly grace" because it costs us something to believe in Jesus today, just as it did in the time of the early church.[14] If it was easier then, why was Jesus crucified at all?

Why was he not hailed as the expected Messiah?[15] In any case, Kaufman believes that what determines Jesus' role as savior is not his person as the

Word incarnate but the models of reflection developed by the community in different historical epochs. Thus, because we today view ourselves in an evolutionary context, we can no longer accept the familial and political models that gave rise to this prior picture of Jesus: "in the biological and historico-cultural terms with which we now conceive human existence, no individual person can have this sort of absolute significance and cosmic efficacy for all others" (*TNA*, 56).[16] Of course T. F. Torrance suggests the right approach here by insisting that the work of Christ must be interpreted "from His Person rather than the other way round" and insists that "Unless we do that we will inevitably interpret both the work and the person of Christ from out of ourselves."[17] That is exactly Kaufman's error in his interpretation of the incarnation and it leads to the following four conclusions.

First, we must admit, according to Kaufman, that from early on Christian faith was characterized by a "deep ambivalence" which was symbolized by the cross and resurrection. The cross symbolized Jesus' life of self-sacrifice and suggested that suffering would be central to human life and that suffering itself would be seen as the "vehicle of human salvation" (*TNA*, 48; *GMD*, 114ff.). This is why the key figures of Christian history, such as Albert Schweitzer, Martin Luther King and Mother Teresa, are those who gave up much for others, perhaps even their lives (*TNA*, 49). The resurrection, on the other hand, symbolized a kind of triumphalism: even though people suffer, they will have a heavenly reward just as Jesus himself was exalted to the right hand of God (*GMD*, 114f.). Hence, it became a matter of self-interest for people to follow Christianity because no matter what happened in this world, life would be requited in the next. What at first seemed a "motif of absolute self-sacrifice for others in the Christian symbolism, turns out on close inspection to be rather an expression of prudential self-interest" (*TNA*, 49; *IFM*, 379). This understanding of the Christian symbolism, Kaufman claims, was rooted in "proclamation of the meaning of Jesus' crucifixion and what was called his resurrection" and was exemplified in Paul's thinking as recounted in Phil. 2:9-11 (*TNA*, 49; *IFM*, 378).

Without going into all the details of Kaufman's argument, it is important to realize that in his thinking it is not Jesus himself in his human life as the incarnate Word who gives meaning to the symbolism of cross and resurrection. Instead, it is the community using its mythic or historicist imagery that gives meaning to those symbols. That is why Kaufman insists that "The question . . . of who Jesus is (or was) and how we should interpret him theologically must be entirely and explicitly a matter of *our* decision" (*TI*, 125; emphasis in original). In fact then he argues that the triumphalist symbolism of the NT is a distortion of the true "story" of Jesus which was that he was a man who sacrificed himself for others (*TNA*, 54; *IFM*, 380ff.). Hence, according to Kaufman the symbolism of the cross and resurrection "laid the foundations for later Christian imperialism. Christians soon came to believe that Jesus was really the only one through whom God's grace and salvation were mediated" (*TNA*, 50; see also *GMD*, 115).

From Kaufman's point of view then when Christians thought of Jesus as the only Son of the Father they were absolutizing and reifying their own symbols, that is, they were turning their myths into things and mistakenly assuming that Jesus really was the unique Son of the Father and that he really was the only savior of the world.[18] Accordingly, this thinking led to such imperialistic activities on the part of the church as the Inquisition and Crusades. Enough has been said to realize that for Kaufman the incarnation is a myth used to interpret the man Jesus in his historical setting. But the man Jesus cannot *be* God himself incarnate among us. Of course that is why, when Kaufman begins thinking about God, he insists that he will "begin with God rather than, say, with Christ" because Christ, as all else that is created, is subordinate to the one ultimate God (*TNA*, 32).[19] This explains why his thinking about God is not and cannot be trinitarian in the proper sense. This starting point for thinking about God is essentially the Arian perspective that suggests that since Jesus is not one in being with the Father as Son from all eternity, therefore God too is the central focus of Jesus' life but cannot be conceived as identical with the man Jesus from Nazareth. Any such thought would violate Kaufman's above mentioned belief that our concept of God can never be fixed or finished! While Kaufman spends much time discussing how and why Christian experience is necessarily trinitarian in *Systematic Theology*, he explicitly denies the relevance of the immanent Trinity and undercuts the need to begin thinking about God the Father from the Son of God who was incarnate in Jesus himself.

This is why Kaufman insists that "we have no way of speaking or thinking of God-in-himself as somehow distinct from God-in-his-revelation-to-us" (*Systematic Theology*, 250-51).[20] Hence for Kaufman the distinction between the immanent and economic Trinity, "though seemingly of great importance, turns out to be a pseudo-distinction, arising from failure to grasp the relational character of our knowledge of God" (*Systematic Theology*, 251). Kaufman therefore argues that "We must . . . reject any attempt to speak of the inner-trinitarian relations, God as he is in and for himself" because our knowledge is analogical and symbolical (*Systematic Theology*, 251). And by that he means that our analogies only loosely describe God's personal being and will "in and through the personal being and will of Jesus" so that we can only know God's will for us and not what God is in himself. "God as he has made himself known is the trinitarian God: we cannot know, nor need we know, any more than this" (*Systematic Theology*, 251).

In my view this assertion amounts to a practical denial of God's existence because it reduces God to what we think God is for us. So Kaufman actually espouses a kind of agnosticism that avoids what he terms the "orthodox" and "modalist" positions, namely, the view that "God's inner essence is three-in-one" and "that it is a simple unity" (*Systematic Theology*, 100). His agnosticism is expressed as follows:

> the understanding of God given in his revelation . . . is his *true essence for us.* Since this is *what God really is in his relation to man,* it obviously is all we can ever know or need to know; and it is only confusing and misleading to inquire about some other essence (which by definition we cannot know) which God is in himself and to himself. . . . The doctrine of the trinity, then . . . expresses the structure of history (as apprehended in Christian faith) in relation to its ground, and, conversely, the way in which transcendent reality is bound up with history. (*Systematic Theology*, 101; emphasis in original)[21]

God, therefore, is known in a "special way through the point in history called Jesus Christ (and thus through the particular history of which Christ is the 'center')" (*Systematic Theology*, 101). Kaufman rejects the idea that the Trinity can be understood as three successive manifestations of God. Rather,

> at every point God's presence in history involves this threefoldness. The first person signifies God's transcendence . . . the second person refers to his special involvement in the person-event Jesus Christ . . . the third person designates his being in and with and under all events of history. (*Systematic Theology*, 101-2)

The doctrine of the Trinity then "is not a mysterious and esoteric item of information about the inner structure of some divine reality totally outside of and unconnected with our world and our experience" (*Systematic Theology*, 102). Here once again Kaufman re-iterates his agnosticism insisting that we have no access to the "innermost essence" of God in history or in revelation.

Second, because the symbols of the cross and resurrection receive their meaning from the community, Kaufman believes that what went wrong in Christology is not directly rooted in the story of Jesus but in the community's mythical concept of God as creator, Lord and Father. While Kaufman spent a great deal of time explaining how important it was to think of God as creator,

Lord and Father in his earlier work, *Systematic Theology: A Historicist Perspective*,[22] in his later work he argues that it was precisely the mythic framework that views God in this way that caused the later imperialism just mentioned. Hence, he argues that if we reconceive God as an ecological reality or serendipitous creativity at work within the process of evolution we will then be able to understand better the significance of Christology today. Traditional Christology therefore is deeply ambiguous. It presents us with a picture of a man who sacrificed himself for others; it shows us that in his suffering and death he experienced genuine weakness and that he was unwilling to use power to achieve his objectives. Yet it also presents us with the idea that this man triumphed and that the crucifixion was just one phase in God's working salvation for the human race from on high. We can no longer think of Christology along these lines according to Kaufman precisely because we can no longer accept Jesus Christ as the eternal Son of God.

Third, if we realize that theology is "essentially imaginative construction" and not an attempt to think about a real God existing independently of our symbols; if we take seriously our historical situation in which we could destroy the world by using nuclear weapons; if we realize that this situation is utterly new in history and could never have been anticipated by the tradition, then we will realize that no traditional understanding of God and Christ can be authoritative or binding for us. Truth becomes something we create instead of something we acknowledge.

Fourth, for these reasons Jesus' theological significance for us today can only be the extent to which we are able to make use of the symbol Christ to create a more peaceful and humane world. What sort of image then of the man Jesus comes through the NT witness according to Kaufman? We are presented there with a "man for others" (*TNA*, 55). Is this image or story to be seen as redemptive or salvific today? Kaufman insists that his question must not be understood in any traditional sense to imply that sin represents some type of "personal disobedience or violation of the divine will" (*TNA*, 55) or that salvation means being rescued from our condition of alienation and guilt. This thinking stems from the mythic view that sees God as a divine king and father and, as we have already seen, Kaufman has re-defined God as a serendipitous creativity at work in the process of evolution. So for Kaufman salvation can no longer be equated with an act of divine forgiveness somehow connected with Jesus' death on the cross. Such thinking arises from the old mythology and can no longer be helpful today, in Kaufman's view.

For Kaufman our most profound human problem today "is not estrangement from God . . . but rather the steady undermining of the conditions that make meaningful and fruitful human life possible" (*TNA*, 55).[23] Hence when we poison the ecosystem and oppress and dehumanize others through our social, political and economic arrangements, then we show that our most profound human problems are those aspects of life on earth that are most dehumanizing. With this re-definition of sin, Kaufman demonstrates that he has in fact failed to appreciate our deepest human need. According to Karl Barth, our deepest human need is for the "righteousness of God," a righteousness that can only come from God himself.[24] And because of our "world-will," because human sin in the biblical sense really means that we creatures in some way attempt to be God himself in our thinking (ideals), religious behavior and moral activity, therefore the most tragic aspect of human life, according to Barth, is expressed by the fact that although we yearn for God's righteousness on earth (as it is in heaven), we do not even dream of appealing beyond ourselves to solve this crucial predicament which is the root of all our other difficulties. This tragedy demonstrates that we are really seeking God without God and actually against God. And because the human situation is such that we really cannot extricate ourselves from this tragic predicament by relying on ourselves at all, any attempt to re-define sin in purely social, moral, political or environmental terms must necessarily miss the true meaning of sin and the actual meaning of salvation. And that is exactly what happens to Kaufman.

For Kaufman, God is powerless to act in relation to us because God, as he has conceived him, is indistinguishable from the evolutionary process itself. God, for Kaufman, is a symbol that we use to describe what is most important to us. It is a symbol of humanization and relativization going on in the universe. It cannot refer to an actually existing being who stands over against us with his own life, will and action because according to Kaufman's own belief, God's sovereignty is fundamentally irrelevant to us today. For that very reason Kaufman must insist that sin can no longer mean what it meant in the Bible, namely, our estrangement from God the creator due to our pride; an estrangement that arose precisely because, according to the Genesis story of Adam and Eve, the creature factually wanted to be the creator by going beyond the limits set by the creator which were meant for their preservation and not their alienation.

Rejection of the Immanent Trinity/Self-Justification

And because Kaufman has misunderstood who God is by confusing God with the evolutionary process, he then insists that in view of our contemporary understanding of ourselves in light of the evolutionary process, no individual human being can be viewed as the savior of the world (*TNA*, 56). Let it be noted very clearly that in this very way Kaufman has substituted his religious vision for the man Jesus from Nazareth whose sacrifice for us was, according to the NT, and according to Barth and Torrance, significant only because it was the sacrifice of the only begotten Son of God who was given for us that we might have life in his name.[25] Hence, it is his Docetic Christology which sees in Jesus only a vision of human self-sacrifice for others, and not the act of God who really became man for the sake of overcoming our "world-will" on our behalf, that leads him to reconceive salvation in purely social terms as well.[26] In fact then salvation also is re-defined in a purely social way to mean "all the activities and processes within human affairs which are helping to overcome the violence and disruptions and alienations . . . promoting personal and social deterioration and disintegration" (*TNA*, 57). Accordingly, "whenever a spirit of creativity and liberation and healing, of reconciliation and reconstruction, is at work in the world, there is to be seen a saving activity" (*TNA*, 57; see also *IFM*, 407ff.). This thinking about atonement of course is in perfect harmony with Kaufman's "wider Christology," which equates the meaning of the term Christ with the activity of the Christian community instead of acknowledging that its meaning is shaped exclusively by the person and work of Jesus himself. It is precisely because Kaufman has detached God's unique action in the incarnation from the historical Jesus that he then argues that salvation can no longer be seen as "a singular process or activity, a unilateral action from on high coming down to earth and working primarily in and through the church" (*TNA*, 57). But it is just this thinking that necessarily leads to the idea that salvation is a human act or a series of human actions; this in my view is precisely the self-justification that is excluded by any genuine Christology and soteriology.

What then is Jesus' role in all of this? According to Kaufman, Jesus can be viewed as the "paradigmatic exemplification" of various dispositions and virtues listed in Galatians 5 such as "'love, joy, peace, patience, kindness, goodness' and the like" (*TNA*, 58; *IFM*, 396ff.). And while Paul and John might have thought of these dispositions and actions in a mythic way as a special kind of "supernatural working of the divine spirit in the Christian community" (*TNA*, 58) what they actually were describing were generally recognizable attitudes and virtues present in Hellenistic culture at that time. What makes Christian life possible then according to Kaufman is not some supernatural activity or "quality" made available only through Christ, but rather "the valuation as *normative for human life* of qualities and potentialities which make for reconciliation and loving community — those potentialities and qualities paradigmatically epitomised in the story of Jesus" (*TNA*, 58; emphasis in original). Salvation thus means to order one's life "in accord with this vision of human existence." Hence all activities of reconciliation and healing at work anywhere in the world should be equated with "the salvific divine spirit — the spirit of Christ — at work in the world" (*TNA*, 58).

At this point in his reflections Kaufman asks a very pertinent question. Given this understanding of salvation in which there is no special connection with Jesus himself "Why bother to be a Christian?" (*TNA*, 59). Kaufman argues that in the old "mythic" view there were strong reasons of self-interest to believe that salvation was in Jesus alone because people thought that forgiveness, happiness and eternal life, including fulfillment, could only be found in him. What does Kaufman's view of salvation offer? It does not offer a peaceful, happy life on earth or some reward in heaven, he asserts. It offers only the awareness one might have of giving up one's life "to help liberate men and women from the evils which presently enslave them" (*TNA*, 59). Our deepest satisfaction then comes from giving up ourselves for others. Kaufman maintains that any sort of self-interested vision is dangerous today in our interdependent world because such an attitude might lead to nuclear destruction as one group tries to preserve itself at the expense of others. What is the solution to such evils? It is, according to Kaufman, that we must learn to subordinate ourselves — our interests, desires, religions, values, social classes and nations "to this wider loyalty to ongoing life — both human and other." Without this "we shall certainly all perish" (*TNA*, 60).

The Christian "vision" thus receives a new pertinence: since we do not belong to ourselves but

> come from and belong to God, that wider stream of self-giving creativity and life . . . [Jesus' self-giving] is a paradigmatic image and symbol of something at the very heart of those foundations: the interdependence and self-giving which underlies and makes possible all creativity and life, the very structure or activity which Christians call God. (*TNA*, 60-61)

We are told that "The self-sacrificial Jesus is able to call us back to the foundations of our being" (*TNA*, 60). But of course Jesus cannot *do* anything in this vision presented to us by Kaufman exactly because he is nothing more than a symbol of what Kaufman thinks is a "wider stream of self-giving creativity" at work in the world that he calls God. And the God he knows as a serendipitous creativity at work in the evolutionary process that is supposedly evolving toward the human and the humane cannot actually be the eternal Father, Son and Holy Spirit of Christian confession because Kaufman's God cannot have

pre-existed the world's existence.[27] So, to claim that the Jesus of his understanding can act in relation to us at all is a meaningless assertion, since Jesus is
only useful to Kaufman as a symbol of human self-sacrifice. And, as seen
above, Jesus has not actually risen from the dead in Kaufman's view, so he no
longer lives and acts in a "supernatural" way through the Holy Spirit uniting
specific individuals to him to form a community of believers who draw their
life from him alone and who for that reason love God by seeking God in
Christ and also love their neighbors. In fact Kaufman insists that this vision
of self-sacrifice is what is offered to Christians if they are to find salvation and
fulfillment — if humanity is to survive. But, and here is the key to Kaufman's
view of salvation, "it is we ourselves who will have to find our way through
the enormously complex and difficult tangles and thickets which humankind
now faces, including the nuclear dilemma" (*TNA*, 62).

For Kaufman salvation means whatever humanization may result from
our activities in the interdependent world, and in the end we are left to ourselves to try to save the world. It turns out then that for all his talk about
Christian vision and about Jesus himself, Jesus Christ is completely dispensable for Kaufman when it comes to saving the world. All that is needed is a
symbol that will help us humanize the world and relativize us. But the truth
of that symbol is certainly not dictated by who Jesus is as the eternal Son or by
the Holy Spirit as the Lord and giver of life. In effect Kaufman argues that it
would be arrogant to believe that Christianity is the one true religion because
other religions and secular visions have much to offer as well.

> Buddhists and Hindus, Jews and Moslems, Africans and Chinese, Marxists
> and Freudians, liberals and conservatives, ordinary folk and sophisticated
> intellectuals, will all, doubtless, have their contributions to make. . . . None
> of us knows a sure way through our present moment in history: those dog-
> matists who think they do are the greatest danger to us all. We must, there-
> fore, work together toward the common goal and the common good,
> drawing upon whatever resources — religious or secular, philosophical or
> poetic, mythic or scientific — are available to us, and offering them to each
> other as we grope toward an unknown future. (*TNA*, 62-63)

Amazingly, although Kaufman argues that his "ecological" theology is more
open than past authoritarian theologies, his turns out to be authoritarian in
the end. Why? Because he will rely on all religions and on Marxists and
Freudians (and thus on none at all) in order to advance his view of self-
justification. Only one vision is excluded completely from his reconception of
God, Christ and salvation, and that is Christianity in its traditional self-

understanding. That is Kaufman's authoritarianism. For Christ, the eternal Son of the Father, who alone can set us free (Jn. 8:36), Kaufman has substituted a picture of humanity attempting to save itself by relying on its own vision of some vague process of creativity supposedly at work in the world that is somehow evolving toward greater humanization. And he tells us that we must work toward the common good, offering each other whatever religious, secular, poetic, mythic or scientific resources we can muster as we "grope toward an unknown future" (*TNA*, 63).

But in reality Christians live and move and have their being in Christ Jesus, the man from Nazareth. And because he has risen from the dead and ascended into heaven from where he now interacts with us through his Holy Spirit, Christians do not grope toward some unknown future but look forward toward his second coming with the joy of those who trust his promise of eternal life.[28] Christians cannot be arrogant by claiming to possess the truth, because they know that whatever work they do for the coming of the kingdom is only possible because Christ enables it in his free love. But Christians never detach the question of truth in theology from the form of their good works because they know that what makes their works good is the grace of God revealed and active in Christ himself. And they know they must receive that as a gift from him again and again; and because of that they also know that they cannot control their Christian life by reducing it to some vague sense of humanization they might imagine taking place in the ongoing stream of things.

Here Kaufman has presented us with a picture of a human community lost and godless; a community that is totally self-reliant and self-absorbed; a community that has so excluded the risen Lord from its midst that it now must explicitly substitute its own self-giving for the once-for-all actions of Jesus himself on the cross and in his resurrection from the dead. The fact is that Christians do not live in the kind of hopelessness that would have to grope toward an unknown future specifically because their faith is not tied exclusively to this world with the idea that saving this world from destruction can or should be equated with the kind of salvation that is a reality in Jesus Christ. Instead, Christians look forward to the second coming of Jesus Christ himself. As he was the one in whom they first believed, he too is the one in whom they now hope. That is the eschatological hope in which they live joyfully even now without having to worry about saving the world because they know the risen Lord himself is at work in the church and in the world through the Holy Spirit making all things work toward the good for those who believe in him.

While Christians certainly will be working for a better world in obedience to the command to love God in Jesus Christ and thus to love their neighbors, they will just as certainly realize that because God has taken the burden of their cares on himself in the incarnation, death and resurrection of his Son, salvation could never be equated with their own good works. Yet, self-justification appears to be the only option when the resurrection is denied and the community is then understood to be grounded in itself. Any form of self-justification, however, simply reflects the fact that the community has ceased to live by faith and by grace and has, to that extent, lost the true basis and meaning of Christian hope. It has ceased to love God in Christ and has closed itself to its Lord and Savior by substituting itself for the incarnate and risen Lord. It has become an unspiritual community, a community without the Holy Spirit. That is the great danger of those inclusive theologies that refuse to see that the starting point for theology must always be the incarnate Word who died on the cross and actually rose from the dead for the salvation of the world; in reality they are not inclusive at all because they exclude in principle (sometimes unwittingly or even unintentionally) the one who alone has already united all humanity in a common bond. What Jesus Christ did in his life, death and resurrection, he did for the entire human race. No one is excluded. But the problem of sin is that humanity still refuses to hear this good news either in the form of its indifference to the significance of Jesus himself or in the form of creating new visions by which it will seek to humanize society or by retreating to a pious existence within so that the church might be understood as a kind of safe territory from which it mistakenly believes threats of this kind cannot confront it. In each of these ways self-reliant theologies avoid the fact that the only real inclusiveness is the inclusiveness provided by God in Jesus Christ himself and extended to all by the Holy Spirit. Any other inclusiveness ends by excluding the truth which alone can set us free to be the creatures God intends us to be.

We have now seen how Gordon Kaufman's understanding of theology prohibits him from actually acknowledging the fact that Jesus' own personal resurrection is the foundation for the theological enterprise. This affected and was affected by his view of the incarnation and the Trinity and led him to embrace the hopeless endeavor of self-justification. Now let us explore how his former student Sallie McFague falls into similar difficulties. Because their views are so similar, despite McFague's criticism of Kaufman for not embracing metaphors for God that are personal,[29] I will not present a detailed version of her theology. I will only present enough to show that it is precisely because she will not allow the risen Lord himself, the incarnate Word, to dictate what she thinks and says that she ends up denying Jesus' uniqueness as the sole Savior of the world and then argues once more for a kind of self-justification precisely because of her agnostic view of God and her inability to conceptualize a God existing in and from himself from all eternity.[30] It is my contention in this book that any form of self-justification demonstrates the fact that one has missed the point of theology by substituting some form of social, political or religious activity for the all-important act of God in his Word and Spirit which alone can free us for the activity required of Christians. Any hint of self-justification means that Christian ethics has already been separated from dogmatics in an inappropriate way with the result that ethical activity is seen as a work we perform to save ourselves instead of our free and joyful obedience to God's own sovereign acts of justification and sanctification. And as we have just seen in Kaufman's thinking, it is exactly this failure that leads people to suppose that fighting for the survival of the human race is the only worthwhile enterprise today, so that our attempts to save humanity come to be equated with God's very own act in Jesus Christ and the Holy Spirit.

But of course my point in this book is that theologians must look away from their political, religious and social goals (however important they may be in themselves) and toward the risen Lord himself to realize that there is no need to be anxious about the survival of the human race because God has effected its renewal in Jesus Christ himself. And the risen Lord, whose authority is the sole foundation of the community's existence here and now, has promised that he will be with us always even to the end of the world (Matt. 28:20). The promise and the joy that follow from it are lost and obscured, however, when we fail to realize that it was a promise made by the risen Lord himself. Take away his bodily resurrection and any real hope for the human race is lost as well. Take away his bodily resurrection and Christian hope becomes little more than the projection of our hopes and wishes onto the historical figure of Jesus reconstructed in whatever terms we deem significant based on our experiences of love, friendship and parenthood. When this happens the only thing left for humanity is its anxious attempt to fight for survival at all costs by relying on its own theological reconstructions, even if that means substituting itself for the genuine Lordship of Jesus Christ himself. When our actual salvation in Christ is discounted (wittingly or unwittingly) then we are left to ourselves in our lost condition to try to comfort ourselves with a love of God that is baseless and a hope of the future that is vacuous. The only hope in such circumstances is to repent and believe once again in the risen Lord.

Sallie McFague

McFague's View of the Resurrection,
the Incarnation and the Trinity

Sallie McFague follows the thinking of Norman Perrin[31] who argues that the resurrection should be interpreted in the context of the appearances. Hence "the *continuing empowerment* of God, in light of various interpretations of salvation, is the meaning of the resurrection" (*Models,* 199; emphasis in original). Accordingly,

> What actually happened on that first Easter morning, according to the evangelists, is that it became possible to know Jesus as ultimacy in the historicality of the everyday (Mark), that it became possible to live the life of a Christian within the church (Matthew), that it became possible to imitate Jesus in the meaningful life in the world (Luke). (*Models,* 199)

Notice that the one thing missing from this account of the resurrection is the fact that Jesus himself actually rose from the dead and encountered the disciples enabling their faith and ours. That is no accident, since McFague's thinking is inherently Docetic: "The resurrected Christ is the cosmic Christ, the Christ freed from the body of Jesus of Nazareth, to be present in and to all bodies."[32]

Consider also the following description of the resurrection offered by McFague: "The resurrection is a way of speaking about an awareness that the presence of God in Jesus is a permanent presence in our present" (*Models,* 59). Instead of allowing the resurrection to describe an event in Jesus' life history that gives meaning to Christian faith, McFague changes the meaning of the NT witness to refer to "an awareness" of God's presence in Jesus that continues today so that she can say that "Whatever the resurrection is . . . it is inclusive; it takes place in every present; it is the presence of God to us, not our translation into God's presence" (*Models,* 60). This awareness, she believes, is "what 'really happened' in the resurrection" (*Models,* 59).[33] McFague therefore explicitly rejects the traditional understanding of the resurrection because she sees Jesus merely as a paradigmatic image of a vision of inclusive fulfillment for all creation. Her question is not what is it that happened in the life of Jesus as the incarnate Word that gives meaning to history. Rather her question is "How should one understand the presence of God to the world in order to empower that vision?" (*Models,* 60). Her vision of course is of a universal divine presence that is thoroughly worldly, as she says, instead of being other-worldly as in the traditional understanding.

And her Docetic view of the resurrection leads her to misunderstand the resurrection faith itself. She contends that for the traditional view of the resurrection some and not all are included, and salvation occurs principally in the past and the future and not in the present, that is, "every present." In other words salvation is not a completely worldly reality because the resurrection means that some individuals will be translated bodily to another world; such a view, she contends, is mythological and no longer credible to us. Here she misses the actual meaning of the resurrection as elaborated above in Chapters One and Three, with which I of course agree and which forms the basis of my argument in this book. According to the traditional view, all are included in Christ's death and resurrection since he did what he did for everyone. Thomas F. Torrance believes that the resurrection has corporate implications so that unbelievers are judged by the risen Lord and believers enjoy the fruits of the resurrection, namely, eternal life (*STR*, 32-37). And while salvation does occur once for all in the life history of Jesus Christ, it is precisely his particular resurrection from the dead that makes it effective here and now in the lives of individuals and communities, as Barth and Torrance argued. And yet according to the NT witness what is a reality in the lives of those who believe in Jesus and hope in him throughout different historical epochs will not become fully realized in their lives until Christ's second coming. So salvation is not principally past and future; rather since salvation is the reconciliation of the world with God himself by God's own action in his incarnate Son, therefore it is the same yesterday, today and tomorrow just as Jesus Christ is himself the same yesterday, today and tomorrow. But it is an act of God within history. The fact that Jesus actually appeared to the disciples enabling their faith "once upon a time" means that resurrection cannot be universalized by detaching it from the specific history of Jesus himself. For that very reason it cannot be equated with a totally this-worldly reality without stripping it of its meaning as a divine act.

McFague will have none of this because she thinks of Jesus as a paradigmatic image of God's love and refuses to acknowledge that he is the unique Son of God who acted in a unique way within history on our behalf. So instead of thinking of the incarnation as God's unique act of assuming flesh in the man Jesus so that Jesus himself could forgive our sins and live a life of perfect obedience to the Father in our place and on our behalf, she thinks of the incarnation and therefore also of the resurrection in idealist terms as God's bodily presence to us "in all places and times of our world" (*Models*, 60) in accordance with her understanding of the world as God's body (*The Body of God*, ch. 6). Accordingly, Jesus is *paradigmatic of God the lover but is not unique. This means that Jesus is not ontologically different from other paradigmatic figures. . . .* He is special to us as our foundational figure: he is our historical choice as the premier paradigm of God's love. (*Models*, 136; emphasis mine)

Here once more one can easily see that it is her Ebionite starting point in experience that leads McFague to believe that Jesus is foundational to Christianity because we chose to make him so. All forms of Ebionite Christology, as we have already seen several times, however, assume that Jesus' uniqueness is somehow contingent on the impression he makes on us or on our choices to make him significant in our vision of reality. But as we have also seen, any such view undercuts Jesus' historicity because it fails to acknowledge him the way he is. This is what leads to her Docetic view that Jesus is not ontologically different from other key figures who embody God's love among us. In fact she insists that Jn. 1:14 represented the absolutizing of the scandal of particularity with the claim that God was embodied in this one individual human being, Jesus of Nazareth. While she thinks such an ethnocentric idea might have been plausible at the time of the Roman Empire, McFague argues, "In its traditional form the claim is not only offensive to the integrity and value of other religions, but incredible, indeed, absurd, in light of postmodern cosmology" (*The Body of God*, 159).[34]

But it is just this thinking that necessarily leads her to embrace a deadly form of self-justification that not only makes Jesus irrelevant, but places her in the unenviable position of having to equate salvation with whatever we do to make the world a better place. To anyone who has ever thought seriously about the problem of sin and evil, this is truly bad news because if there is one thing that we know for certain from the revelation of God in the history of Jesus Christ, it is that whenever we rely on ourselves and not on grace alone, we actually try to accomplish the impossible and inevitably make things worse — while of course assuming we are making things better. We take the weight of the world on our own shoulders and act as if we ourselves were God. This is disastrous because the truth is that we can never deliver what we think we can when we engage in any form of self-justification. We will return to this important issue before we end this chapter. For now let me briefly explain exactly how McFague's denial of the incarnation is rooted in her denial of the immanent Trinity and her agnostic view of God's being and action.

McFague insists that metaphors or models are not descriptive of who God is, because if they were, we would have a complete understanding of what we are describing. Metaphors or models are thus partial and imaginative (*The Body of God*, 152ff.). What she means by this is that she cannot *know* who God actually is but she can and must use those experiences that matter most to her to construct an image of God who, as she puts it, is "on the side of life."[35] But there are major flaws in this reasoning. First, her view of God is essentially agnostic: "I do not *know* who God is, but I find some models better than others for constructing an image of God commensurate with my trust in a God as on the side of life" (*Models*, 192; emphasis in original). This is why she explicitly rejects a doctrine of the immanent Trinity. Her theology, she says, "makes no claims about the so-called immanent . . . trinity, for I see no way that assumptions concerning the inner nature of God are possible" (*Models*, 224).[36] Second, because she does not really *know* who God is and because she will not allow a proper understanding of the immanent Trinity to dictate her views, she is constrained to think of God in mythological terms:

> through remythologizing the doctrines of God and human beings in light of the picture of reality from contemporary science — through the use of the organic model as a way of reconceiving the relation of God and the world — the appropriate human stance vis-à-vis God and our planet will emerge. Remythologizing . . . is a form of embodied thought combining image and concept that calls forth both a feeling and a thinking response. . . . If one uses the model of the universe as God's body . . . one would, or at least might, act differently toward it than if one used the model of creation as a work of art (one possible model from the Genesis story). (*The Body of God*, 81)

Third, this leads her to believe that "The transcendence of God frees us to model God in terms of what is most significant to us" (*The Body of God*, 193). Fourth, our human experience therefore becomes both starting point and norm for theology. Our understanding of the God-world relationship "must come from a place deep within human experience" (*Models*, 80). Fifth, the imagery of mothers, lovers and friends allows us to conceive of God "on the model of the most complex part of the whole that is the universe — that is, on the model of ourselves" (*Models*, 82). McFague thus insists that the richest source of our knowledge of God is ourselves (*Models*, 83). Hence she argues: "To speak of God's saving presence in our present only with the help of images about rocks and wind, or with any other natural metaphors, is to overlook the richest source we have — ourselves" (*Models*, 83). Sixth, because her source and norm for theology is our human experience of motherhood, love, friendship and fatherhood, as long as this last metaphor or model is understood as parenting and not in any patriarchal sense, her theology is inherently pantheistic, though she prefers to describe it as panentheistic. But as Karl

Barth pointed out long ago, panentheism is really worse than pantheism, because it fails to recognize that it necessarily makes God identical with the world to the extent that it fosters the idea that God somehow needs the world and thus exists in a relation of mutual dependence with the world.[37]

She herself argues that we should think of the world as God's body and that if we do we will see that it "is not something alien to or other than God but is from the 'womb' of God, formed through 'gestation'" (*Models*, 110). Indeed, McFague contends,

> If the world is God's body, then nothing happens to the world that does not also happen to God . . . we do not have to leave God when we die, nor do we join God in heaven . . . we are with God whether we live or die . . . our bodies . . . are within the body of God. God is not somewhere else . . . but with us in the earth, the soil, that receives us at our death. (*The Body of God*, 176-77)

And thus she maintains that because human love needs another, we must also realize that God needs us: "If personhood is defined in terms of intrinsic relations with others, then to think of God as personal in no sense implies a being separate from other beings" (*Models*, 83). The very concept of the world as God's body then not only leads McFague to compromise the freedom of God implied in the *creatio ex nihilo* which she explicitly rejects as an invention of the early church (*The Body of God*, 151), but it encourages the very universalism that detaches God's actions from his Word and Spirit and locates them in the world itself. That is why McFague cannot accept the fact that the incarnation occurred as a unique act of God in the human history of Jesus Christ. That is why the Holy Spirit has no existence distinct from the world in her thinking. That is why she seeks salvation in the world and in whatever achievements of peace and ecological responsibility become visible here on earth. All of this became possible and necessary precisely because McFague's thinking was not governed by a clear doctrine of the immanent Trinity at the outset or at any point along the way.

One more point needs to be made before we proceed to discuss the ethical implications of this theology. That is, when McFague couples the idea that God is Mother with the idea of the world as God's body, her pantheist confusion of God with the world is complete. She is aware that the Genesis story does not suggest that the world is God's body, noting that in Genesis the world is seen as external to God and dependent on him (*The Body of God*, 151). However, she notes that many believe that dependence, rather than externality, should be stressed. And so she claims that the so-called "production model" stresses God's transcendence but makes it difficult to affirm his immanence while the "procreation model" that she advocates will suggest "that the world comes from, is formed from, God rather than out of 'nothing' or out of some material other than God" (*The Body of God*, 151).

But, of course it is just this idea that is inherently pantheistic. It is exactly this that is excluded by Christian belief in God the Father almighty, the creator of heaven and earth: "By *faith* we understand that the worlds were fashioned by the Word of God (Heb. 12:3)" (Barth, *Credo*, 29). And as Barth stressed, this very same Word must be spoken to us if we are to know it. The world then is not formed from God but created through his Word and in the Spirit. It is an *opus ad extra*, not the emanation of God's own being. This is where the concept of Mother confuses the matter even further. While McFague claims her panentheism does not identify God with the world or reduce God to the world (*The Body of God*, 152), the fact remains that once it is said or implied that creation is formed from God, then and to that extent it has already become impossible to distinguish God from what he has made. And this becomes explicit with the use of the category Mother: "A metaphor to express the source of all life is not the Architect who constructs a world, but the Mother who encloses reality in her womb, bodying it forth, generating all life from her being" (*The Body of God*, 152). Here she follows Grace Jantzen's idea expressed in her book on the universe as God's body and writes: "'God formed it [the world] quite literally 'out of himself' — that is, it is his self-formation — rather than out of nothing" (*The Body of God*, 255), even though she notes Jantzen's strange use of the male pronoun! Because McFague is not thinking of creation as a free act of the triune God, she actually believes she must make a choice between seeing God as "architect" or, in terms of "procreation," as "Mother" who gives birth to the world.

In reality no such choice is required or is possible. Because creation is a free action of the Father almighty that takes place as an expression of God's love in his Word and through the Spirit,

> Heaven and earth are *not themselves God*, are not anything in the nature of a divine emanation, are not, as the Gnostics or mystics would again and again have it, in some direct or indirect way, identical with the Son or Word of God . . . the creation of the world is not a movement of God in Himself, but a free *opus ad extra*, finding its necessity only in his love, but again not casting any doubt on His self-sufficiency: the world cannot exist without God, but if God were not love (as such inconceivable!), He could exist very well without the world. (Barth, *Credo*, 31-32; emphasis in original)

According to Barth, in the Bible, creation means

> Creation solely on the basis of God's own wisdom. It means, *creatio ex nihilo* (Rom. iv.17). It means creation by the word, which is indeed the eternal Son and therefore God Himself. If that is so, if there is no question of an identity of the created world with God . . . then it necessarily follows that the *meaning* and the *end* of the world of His creation is not to be sought in itself. (Barth, *Credo*, 32; emphasis in original)

But, against McFague's contrived belief that *creatio ex nihilo* prevents recognition of God's immanence, Barth had no problem insisting on God's immanence precisely because of his transcendence: "in the proposition, 'God is the Creator,' we recognise not only God's transcendence, but also the immanence of that God so completely transcendent to the world" (Barth, *Credo*, 34).

According to McFague the Genesis story is no more than one model among others that we use "from the perspective of postmodern science" to interpret Christian faith, "our own embodied experience, and the well being of our planet and all its life-forms" and models are not judged by whether they "correspond with God's being" (*The Body of God*, 152). Once again it is because McFague is agnostic about knowing God in truth that she adopts the pantheism Christians have always rejected: "A procreation model . . . sees creation as emerging from God, as a body . . . that grows and changes" (*The Body of God*, 152). She combines this model with the emanationist model and concludes: "God bodies forth the universe" (*The Body of God*, 153). Hence, creation is to be seen as "the continuing, dynamic, growing embodiment of God" (*The Body of God*, 156).

McFague herself asks whether or not the metaphor of the world as God's body is pantheistic and admits that "The metaphor does come far closer to pantheism than the king-realm model . . . but it does not totally identify God with the world" (*Models*, 71). She, however, opts for a type of panentheism that she believes is captured by Paul Tillich's definition of pantheism: "'Pantheism is the doctrine that God is the substance or essence of all things, not the meaningless assertion that God is the totality of all things'" (*Models*, 201). Following Tillich she argues that this type of pantheism does not simply identify the world with God "but intends, instead, to conceive of the 'all' of the world 'in' God as God's inner modification and appearance, even if God is not exhausted by the all" (*Models*, 201). Here, unfortunately, both Tillich and McFague have in fact fallen directly into pantheism despite their beliefs to the contrary. First, both of them ignored a crucial point in the doctrine of creation emphasized by Barth, that is, although the world can be said to exist within God, we must also admit that it simultaneously exists by God.[38] This point is systematically excluded from McFague's monistic panentheism, which can never acknowledge God's actual freedom either *in se* or in relation to the body he needs. Second, the very idea that God is the essence of all things fails to distinguish created essences from the essence of God which does not need creation to be an essence. Third, the actual idea that the world could be seen as an inner modification of God once more cannot distinguish the world from God and so conceptually fails to describe a genuine relationship between two unequal partners.

And, as Barth himself noted, any partial identification of the world with God is a myth that is based on a deception, namely, the idea that through such partial identification one can really escape pantheism.[39] McFague argues that with this model "God is not reduced to the world" (*Models,* 71), yet the following illustrates that her thinking is indeed pantheist: (1) she literally cannot distinguish God from the world as when she says God is not totally different from the world (*Models,* 110); (2) she says "God becomes dependent through being bodily" (*Models,* 72), even though she says God is not as dependent as we are, so that if the world were to be "blown up" then "Presumably . . . another could be formed" (*Models,* 72); (3) she believes that God is *intrinsically* related to the world (*Models,* 78, 83f.); and finally (4) she says we could no longer see "God as worldless" (*Models,* 77).

Nonetheless, McFague insists that the universe should be seen as the "self-expression of God — God's incarnation" (*Models,* 72) and thus vulnerability, shared responsibility and risk necessarily follow. Hence the world as God's body is to be seen "as a way to remythologize the inclusive, suffering love of the cross of Jesus of Nazareth" (*Models,* 72). In McFague's words,

> In both instances, God is at risk in human hands: just as once upon a time in a bygone mythology, human beings killed their God in the body of a man, so now we once again have that power, but, in a mythology more appropriate to our time, we would kill our God in the body of the world. Could we actually do this? To believe in the resurrection means we could not. God is not in our power to destroy, but the incarnate God is the God at risk: we have been given central responsibility to care for God's body, our world. (*Models,* 72-73)

Again, if God is incarnate in the entire universe, then it is clear that we no longer look to Jesus as the unique incarnate Son, as the unique savior and mediator, but rather we now look to the evolutionary process and to whatever mythologies might be available to us in any religion so that we can think of the world as special. Why? Because McFague believes that if we do so we may be able to treat the world better and thus save it from destruction.

What about the problem of evil on this view? According to McFague her monist position cannot avoid the conclusion that "Evil is not a power over against God; in a sense, it is God's 'responsibility,' part of God's being, if you will" (*Models*, 75). Is God, then, responsible for evil in the world? Dualism and Gnosticism have always answered this question with a resounding yes. And McFague agrees: "in some sense evil has its origin in God. In an evolutionary perspective . . . the issue of what is evil is so complex that to say that evil has its origin in God means something very different from what saying this means in nonevolutionary theologians" (*Models*, 201).

Not only is God "involved in evil" according to McFague but God is also involved in suffering that is caused by evil. Since the world is God's body, God feels the pain of creation in his body and thus "one does not suffer alone" (*Models*, 75). Hence God's suffering should no longer be seen as only a few hours on the cross (as in the old mythology) but "it is present and permanent. As the body of the world, God is forever 'nailed to the cross,' for as this body suffers, so God suffers" (*Models*, 75). Here McFague's panentheism compromises the very meaning of atonement and the heart of the Gospel. Because, for her, the resurrection is not an actual event in the life of Jesus that gives meaning to faith, she literally cannot accept the incarnation of God in Jesus Christ and so detaches the incarnation from Jesus and locates it in the world (within the process of evolution) so that we now no longer relate with God's transcendence and immanence in Christ as it is revealed through his Spirit, but with a god who created evil and suffers its consequences eternally with us. Since Jesus cannot represent us as Lord and Savior, we must then be able to save ourselves. So McFague not only argues that "the God who suffers with the world cannot wipe out evil . . . but its power depends also on us" (*Models*, 75), but she also believes that "Wherever in the universe there is new life . . . God experiences these pleasures and rejoices with each creature in its joy" (*Models*, 75). Accordingly, since we creatures have a special kind of freedom, namely, we have the ability to "participate self-consciously in the evolutionary process" (*Models*, 76), we thus have a special responsibility and a special status: "we are the ones like God; we are selves that possess bodies, and that is our glory" (*Models*, 76). That is our status. What is our responsibility? For McFague, "we alone can choose to become partners with God in the care of the world; we alone can — like God — mother, love, and befriend the world, the body that God has made available to us as both the divine presence and our home" (*Models*, 76).

Sin and Salvation — Self-Justification

Here McFague has transformed the Gospel of grace into a paradigmatic model of self-justification and this can be seen with great clarity in her re-definition of sin and salvation in purely social terms. Sin is no longer an act against God. It is now to be seen as an act "against the world" (*Models,* 77); sin is, in McFague's view, a refusal "to take responsibility for nurturing, loving, and befriending the body and all its parts" (*Models,* 77). And since the world is God's body, it is "an expression of God" and it is "necessary to the continuation of life" (*Models,* 77). As the body of God, the world is a "thou" we meet "where God is present to us always and in all times and in all places" (*Models,* 77). Indeed, for McFague the "resurrection becomes a worldly, present, inclusive reality, for this body is offered to all: 'This is my body'" (*Models,* 77).

This then is McFague's new sacramental understanding of God's relation with the world: no longer does God act exclusively in the particular history of Jesus Christ; no longer is a sacrament a specific act done in the church in obedience to a command and with the promise of Jesus himself; no longer is the resurrection a specific event in the history of Jesus of Nazareth; no longer do we have a specific relation with the Father through the Son and in the Spirit. In short, no longer do we need to believe in our salvation as an act of God in Jesus and through the Spirit. Rather, our relations with God are our relations with the world which is thought to be God's body. And resurrection simply means that the world is also God's body that is offered to everyone; it cannot mean that God, who alone is righteous and good, has destroyed evil, death and sin in the life history of Christ. Instead, we are told that God is powerless in face of evil. In fact God's act of justification in Christ is so thoroughly obviated in McFague's thinking that she argues that the earth will be delightful to us only if we "nurture it" (*Models,* 77). She insists that if we let this metaphor have its way in our thinking then that "would result in a different way of being in the world. There would be no way that we could any longer see God as worldless or the world as Godless. Nor could we expect God to take care of everything" (*Models,* 77).

McFague links her pantheist idea of the world as God's body with her model of God the lover to argue against the traditional understanding of sin as pride. From the perspective of her model of God the lover

> Sin is the turning-away not from a transcendent power but from interdependence with all other beings, including the matrix of being from whom all life comes. It is not pride or unbelief but the refusal of relationship — the refusal to be the beloved of our lover God and the refusal to be lover of

all God loves. . . . It is a horizontal refusal to be part of the body of God *rather than* a vertical refusal to be inferior to God. (*Models,* 139; emphasis mine)

She makes the same argument using the metaphor of God as mother: "In this view . . . sin is not 'against God,' the pride and rebellion of an inferior against a superior, but 'against the body,' the refusal to be part of an ecological whole" (*Models,* 114). Unfortunately, however, her very re-definition of sin in social and ecological terms as a purely horizontal refusal of relationship to the world and to others clearly demonstrates that pride still is the central sin. Pride means self-reliance. It means the refusal to acknowledge that God is God, that is, God is the creator and Lord of all that exists in dependence on him. He does not need the world. The world is not an expression of God's being. In reality there can be no relation of parity between God and us. And for those very reasons we can count on God to help us in a way no one and nothing else can.

Ignoring God's actual love for the world, and in typically Pelagian fashion, McFague contends, "Life is not worthless, nor is it made worthy only through divine forgiveness; as such, it is valuable and precious" (*Models,* 133). And we need to feel that value "if we are to have the will to work with the divine lover toward including all the beloved in the circle of valuing love. We need to value life and deeply desire all forms of life to survive and prosper if we are to have any hope of attaining an ecologically balanced, nuclear-free world" (*Models,* 133). Indeed, instead of actually relying on God's forgiving grace to discover the value of the world, McFague's goal is to invent a way of thinking about God and God's relation with the world that will enable us to act differently toward the world: "How would we . . . act differently if we imagined the world to be the body of God . . . ?"[40] It is clear, then, that her Pelagian assumption that the world is good in itself without divine forgiveness issues directly in her espousal of self-justification, with the idea that it is we who must save the world through using metaphors such as the world as God's body that will enable us to rescue the world from destruction.

But one cannot equate salvation with preserving the world from destruction and assume that the world is good in itself without compromising the Gospel at its root: any such assumptions must mean that the death and resurrection of Christ himself have become irrelevant in the extreme. And any idea that we are responsible for the salvation of the world confirms once more that the meaning of sin as pride in the Christian tradition is decisive. The very idea that God needs us to save the world is the ultimate expression of pride. As such this idea leaves us in the hopeless position of those who have no decisive reason to believe and to hope that God can or will destroy sin and evil and grant us eternal life. All of this follows her refusal to begin her thinking with the risen Lord himself. That is why she remythologizes the resurrection "as a worldly, present, inclusive event — the offering of the world, God's body to all: 'This is my body'" ("Imaging a Theology," 217). At the very heart of this mythology is her idea of self-justification: "were this metaphor to enter our consciousness . . . it would result in a different way of being in the world. There would be no way we could any longer see God as worldless or the world as Godless" ("Imaging a Theology," 217). Hence "we alone — like God — love, heal, befriend, and liberate the world, the body" ("Imaging a Theology," 217). And because evil is part of God's being in her panentheistic confusion of creation and reconciliation McFague ultimately has nothing to offer as a solution to our deepest human need which is, as we have noted several times, for a righteousness that can only come from God, that is, from beyond the dialectic of good and evil at work in human experience apart from faith in Christ and the Holy Spirit.[41]

In accordance with her basic confusion of creation and atonement then, salvation means "a destabilizing, inclusive, nonhierarchical vision" that stresses God's "interdependence with the world" (*Models*, 56 and 79). As we are faithful to our vision of how things should be, we become the saviors of the world. And this means "we shall understand salvation to be the making whole or uniting with what is attractive and valuable, rather than the rescuing of what is sinful and worthless" (*Models*, 130). This is why McFague explicitly rejects salvation by faith and grace: "if we see Jesus as 'fully God and fully man,' the substitutionary sacrifice who atoned for the sins of the world . . . we not only accept a salvation we do not need but weaken if not destroy our ability to understand and accept the salvation we do need" (*Models*, 54). In her vision, salvation cannot have taken place in one individual and salvation must be "the task of all human beings. . . . It is not what one individual did two thousand years ago" (*Models*, 54). Because Jesus is a paradigm of God's love and not the incarnate Word who acted on our behalf, McFague believes "Jesus of Nazareth . . . does not 'do something on our behalf' but . . . manifests in his own life and death that the heart of the universe is unqualified love working to befriend the needy, the outcast, the oppressed" (*Models*, 55).

This insight, of course, is the ultimate form of wishful thinking because it is a vision of a vaguely described love at work in the universe that is powerless to overcome evil (since evil is part of its very nature) and that literally cannot act in a decisive way because, whatever it may be, it can do nothing without us — it is dependent on us to exist. And it cannot be seen as a truly Christian understanding of reality because this view refuses to acknowledge that the love God has for the world is in fact identical with the love of God revealed and active in the man Jesus of Nazareth (Jn. 3:16). By seeing Jesus merely as a paradigm of God's love but not as the unique Word of God incarnate McFague espouses a Docetic Christology that undermines a true understanding of salvation and is grounded in a false perception of the nature of Christ's resurrection.

That is why McFague argues that "Life is not worthless, nor is it made worthy only through divine forgiveness; as such, it is valuable and precious, and we need to feel that value . . . if we are to have the will to work with the divine lover" (*Models,* 133). Life certainly is not worthless. But it is not worthless precisely because it receives its worth as grace from God. Because of sin, that grace takes the shape of the forgiveness of sins effected in and through Jesus himself. But, because for McFague, Jesus' ministry, parables and actions only represent a paradigm of her vision of salvation (which is equated with rescuing the world — God's body), she makes the overt Pelagian claim that forgiveness is not necessary for creatures to become worthy in spite of their sin. This opens the door directly to an unconcealed form of self-justification, i.e., if we can invent language that will make us feel that the earth and others who inhabit the earth have value then we will work to save the earth from destruction. Of course she does speak of us working with the divine love, as we have just seen, but since this love is in reality indistinguishable from our love for the world, it is in fact a meaningless and vacuous assertion.

Perhaps the hallmark example of self-justification in McFague's thinking is her belief that "unless we understand God as needing us, we will lack the will to take responsibility for the world" (*Models,* 134). On the one hand we are not responsible for the world. We are responsible to God and have been enabled to respond to God faithfully in and through Christ's reconciling life, death and resurrection. In that way, because we love God in Christ and thus love our neighbor, we will of course care for the world as a reality distinct from God and endowed with a goodness freely given and maintained by God in his grace. On the other hand any idea that God needs the world represents a blatant form of pantheism that actually undermines the fact that true human freedom comes only through the Son who sets us free to love God and our neighbors and to care for the earth as stewards. McFague will have none of this because for her we are the saviors of the world, not God. The God she envisions is in fact an idol — a dim reflection of the human will to power over God himself: "The model of God as lover, then, implies that God needs us to help save the world!" (*Models,* 135). But for McFague, salvation means simply the survival of this world, while for Christians salvation means the beginning of a new creation, namely, our beginning to live the eternal life that is the gift of God in raising Jesus from the dead. Equating salvation with survival can only increase human anxiety and arouse a sense of self-reliance and ultimately hopelessness, while perceiving salvation as an act of God in his Word and Spirit will mean joy based on an act of God that is full of promise because it is the promise of eternal life which is lived now by faith and hope in the coming of the Lord who alone can complete the salvation of the world in redeeming us and all creatures at his second coming.

Atonement

McFague contrasts the classical with the traditional view of salvation and argues that whereas in the former Jesus acts alone so that "the atoning act, takes place for all time and for all people in one individual who represents and includes all other individuals" (*Models,* 143), this thinking no longer makes sense for us primarily because she claims "substantialist Greek thinking" does not take into account the solidarity that is evident in an evolutionary and ecological perspective. In her mind the traditional view suggests that we can share in the atonement effected by one individual two thousand years ago because we all share a human substance. This of course is not quite the traditional view since that view actually holds that we can share in the atonement effected in Jesus' life, death and resurrection only through the power of the Holy Spirit uniting us to him in faith. Our humanity is transformed in his humanity because his humanity is the humanity of the Son of God himself and he makes himself our contemporary through the Spirit. So it is not just that we share a common humanity that is important; it is that God chose to become one with us in our sinful humanity in the man Jesus from Nazareth and heals our humanity in him. It is in this reconciled humanity that we share through the power of the resurrection as the Holy Spirit enables us to live in faith, love and hope from and in the risen Lord himself. It is precisely because Jesus himself rose from the dead that our humanity is no longer subject to sin, suffering evil and death in him. Our new humanity is hidden with Christ in God (Col. 3:4). That of course is what it means to live in faith, love and hope.

As seen above in Chapters One and Three, Karl Barth and T. F. Torrance accurately represent the Christian tradition when they insist that we are saved by grace and by faith because Jesus himself is the savior of the world. Hence reconciliation has taken place once for all in his life history for our benefit. And it took place as an act of God for us and an act of the man Jesus representing us. What is disclosed in Jesus' life history then is not only our salvation but the very nature of our sin as our refusal to acknowledge God's righteous judgment and grace as they have been exercised and revealed in Jesus himself. Any claim that our relations with God and others can be rectified without this particular action of God for us that took place in the history of Jesus Christ amounts to a Pelagian claim that God loves us because we are already beloved. And, as we have seen, that is exactly the claim advanced by Sallie McFague just because her criterion for understanding God's love is not the act of God in Jesus Christ but human love which needs another to be what it is meant to be. Therefore, McFague argues that "The work of salvation is, in this model [God the lover], the address not to a sinner but to the beloved" (*Models*, 144). What she failed to notice here is that we are God's beloved in Christ and not in ourselves! McFague will have none of this and so she argues that in this model of God the lover, where every part of God's body is interdependent, the work of salvation is "spread out, and it is work that must be done again and again" (*Models*, 143). Salvation cannot be a once and for all event that "someone else does for us. Rather, it is the ongoing healing of the divided body of our world which we, with God, work at together" (*Models*, 143). Although McFague claims that her models of God as mother, lover and friend actually provide a better understanding of Christianity today, here it is more than evident that she has changed the meaning of Christianity by changing the very nature of salvation itself.

In fact it is precisely because she refuses to acknowledge Jesus' ontological distinction from us as the unique Son of God that she re-defines salvation in purely social, political and ecological terms as our piecing together the body of God (the world). This is the works-righteousness that no Christian theologian would want to espouse because the very idea that salvation is somehow dependent on us is not good news but bad news since it is we who have disrupted our relations with God and other creatures in the first instance by our sinful self-reliance. And any attempt by us to rectify this situation will always result in the prideful substitution of our human vision of salvation and our actions in response to that vision for the actual salvific acts of God himself within the sphere of history. It must be remembered always, as Barth insisted, that when we actually rely on God as we do in prayer (at his command and in the freedom he gives us in his Son) then "It will be God's affair, and [we] can leave it confidently to God, to hear and understand. . . . On no account, however, can man take it upon himself to cease speaking with God because of his incapacity for what God wants of him" (*CD* III/4, 90).

Further, while she does say that we work at this together with God, the fact remains that McFague's concept of God, as we have already seen, is nothing other than a symbol describing those activities going on in the world that offer some vague suggestion of a power at work in the universe that is on the side of life. This is certainly not the God of Christian faith whose personal relations with us are quite distinct from anything that we may surmise to be going on in the universe.[42] This God is really able to act on our behalf in a way that is decisive and in a way that cannot be compared with any work we may be able to do in the freedom that arises as a result of these divine actions. Moreover, God's act of love for the world is his act of sending his Son so that whoever would believe in him would have eternal life (Jn. 3:16). And the only hope that the world has in face of the threat of death is Jesus Christ himself since he is the only one who can remove the final threat of death from us and who can give us hope: "I am the resurrection and the life" (Jn. 11:25). As Barth succinctly put it:

> He [Jesus Christ] is the beyond in whom man in his transience, to which departure also belongs, may see his temporal being, not extended (for that would not imply a true beyond), but clothed with eternal life. That is why we are told that 'he that heareth my word, and believeth . . . hath everlasting life' (Jn. 5:24). That is also why the command to consider that we must die means that we are forbidden to fear death. In place of this fear we do not put a substitute faith which postulates a false beyond or a false present, or which effaces the distinction between them. We put hope in God as He has revealed Himself in Jesus Christ to be the hope of man. (*CD* III/4, 594)

Indeed, it is the risen Lord himself who does this so that without his actual resurrection from the dead, we are still lost and hopeless in the face of death. Moreover, any attempt whatsoever by us to try to solve this problem of death by trying to remythologize who God is and what salvation is only illustrates our anxiety and our fear in the face of death itself; it represents what is perhaps hidden to us beneath our own grand schemes, namely, our own worry about our own death.[43] As seen above, McFague does not accept the resurrection of Jesus as an event in his life that gives meaning to our lives and it is this failure that opens the door to her belief that theology is mythology and not an attempt to understand the truth of who God is based on God's own revelation of himself in Christ and the Spirit.

It is McFague's attempt to understand the atonement, incarnation and resurrection in the context of her view of evolution then that leads her to reject the traditional Christian teaching. But in so doing she is forced to the rather hopeless conclusion that salvation should be reduced to human and ecological fulfillment while also advocating the polytheistic idea that there can and must be many saviors of the world.[44] McFague thus asks:

Who, then, are the healers and the liberators — the 'saviors' of the world?
... if the one thing needful is reunification of the shattered, divided world,
there must be many saviors. Jesus of Nazareth, as paradigmatic of God as
lover, reveals God's passionate, valuing love for the world. . . . But as revelatory and powerful as that life was and continues to be, it cannot stand
alone as accomplishing salvation if salvation is seen as the piecing together
of the fragmented body of the world. . . . That work must be done and done
again, by many minds, hearts, hands, and feet. (*Models,* 150)

But that is the question: should we or can we reduce salvation to the piecing
together of the world as God's body? In McFague's pantheistic identification
of God with his body and her denial of Jesus' uniqueness as the Word incarnate, the answer apparently must be yes. But if God is seen, as he should be, as
the creator of the world that is essentially different from him and a world that
went wrong through sin and needs to be reconciled to God by God himself,
then her view is exposed for what it is. Her view denies that salvation is an act
of God for us in his Word and Spirit and instead represents a misappropria-
tion of salvation by us as something that we accomplish as we work together
for a better world. In reality this is a form of dualism that refuses to acknowledge that in the incarnation of God in Jesus Christ, God himself has crossed
the divide between the creator and creature in order to reconcile us to himself; it denies that the reconciliation that took place in Jesus' history for all is
the only possible basis for humans to act freely and lovingly toward their
neighbors and in a responsible way toward creation. All of this is possible and
even necessary for McFague because she really believes that the stories of
other such people as Sojourner Truth, Dorothy Day, Mohandas Gandhi, John
Woolman and Dietrich Bonhoeffer all reveal God's love by their good works
and so they are "illustrative of the many saviors of the world: their stories
flesh out the paradigmatic story of Jesus of Nazareth" (*Models,* 152). It is, of
course, very doubtful that any one of these people just mentioned would see
themselves as saviors of the world. But it is just because McFague refuses to
acknowledge Jesus for who he really is that she is forced to undermine his action as the savior and helper of the world and the one who alone enables the
kind of selfless love of others required of Christians.

Why is McFague unable to accept the traditional view? She admits that it
makes a stronger claim and offers something more satisfying than what she
offers. But she insists that "it is simply irrelevant to an understanding of sin
and evil in an ecological, nuclear age" (*Models,* 144-45). And "It is also part of
an outmoded mythology" (*Models,* 145). In a manner reminiscent of Gordon
Kaufman, McFague argues that the model of God as lover "in an ecological,

evolutionary context does not allow the work of one individual to be effective for all space and time" (*Models*, 143). This is why we must be involved in the work of salvation which itself must be something that is done again and again: "We participate . . . in our own salvation" (*Models*, 145). Further, her model of God as friend is overtly pantheistic since it leads McFague to follow the Stoics and say "such identification [of God and the world] is precisely what an inclusive vision of the gospel in an ecological, nuclear age requires" (*Models*, 170). This identification leads her to think that salvation once again means faithfulness to our vision of reality, instead of our faithfulness to Jesus himself:

> To be friends of Jesus . . . means to stand with him and with all others united by and committed to the common vision embodied in the shared meal extended to the outsider. . . . What creates this friendship is the common vision: in this model of fellowship, God and human beings are both friends of the world. In an ecological, nuclear era, salvation must mean this. (*Models*, 175)

It is here then that McFague builds a Pelagian perspective directly into her theology by insisting that "salvation is not the forgiveness of sins. . . . Salvation . . . belongs intrinsically to the 'first work,' creation. Salvation is a deepening of creation" (*Models*, 146). We have seen why Barth quite rightly rejected this Schleiermacherian insight above. Any such view does not and cannot take seriously atonement as a special divine act within history on our behalf; it makes it impossible to see that the Word is the subject of the redeeming act and not one element in the evolution of creation itself. This thinking on the part of McFague necessarily follows from her view of Jesus as paradigmatic of God the lover but not unique; it follows from her unwillingness to allow Jesus to be the one he is proclaimed to be in the NT, namely, the only begotten Son of the Father who became incarnate to forgive our sins and thus to enable us to be free for God, our neighbors and the stewardship of the world; it follows from her transposition of the resurrection from an event in the life of Jesus to our perspective on the world as God's body. All of this results from her Ebionite starting point and her Docetic conclusions and all of it can be avoided only by beginning theology at the only possible beginning, namely, with Jesus himself as he really was and is, that is, as the Lord of the universe and as the Savior of the world.

Before proceeding to an exploration of the thinking of a far more serious theologian, Wolfhart Pannenberg, we shall see how two other popular contemporary attempts to reconstruct the Christian understanding of the resurrection and incarnation lead directly toward forms of self-justification that obscure rather than clarify human freedom. It will be instructive to see how and why Roger Haight in his recent and popular book *Jesus, Symbol of God* understands these issues and then to compare his approach to that of John Hick.

7. Incarnation and Resurrection in the Thought of Roger Haight and John Hick

Roger Haight

Let us begin with the thought of Roger Haight in his recent book *Jesus Symbol of God*. In his chapter on the resurrection he proposes "one way of understanding what it means to say that Jesus is risen."[1] While Haight argues that Christians generally agree that Jesus is risen, he also insists that there is no prevailing consensus about what that statement means. Hence, he asks what the object of this Christian belief might be and contends that the meaning of the "symbol" resurrection "cannot be decided cleanly by the New Testament witness" (*Jesus*, 121). While Haight admits that the early disciples did indeed believe that Jesus had been raised from the dead, he also believes that "it is better to say that Jesus' resurrection is not an historical fact because the idea of an historical fact suggests an empirical event which could have been witnessed and can now be imaginatively construed" (*Jesus*, 124). Such thinking, for Haight, would undermine "the fundamental nature of the resurrection as a transcendent object of faith" (*Jesus*, 124).

So, within the context of the categories developed by David Fergusson, the question immediately arises: was the resurrection an event in the life of Jesus, or was it created within or realized by the faith of the disciples? While Haight thinks it is important that there be continuity between the historical and risen Jesus, he also believes that Jesus' resurrection

> need not entail the assumption of his physical corpse . . . the idea of the disappearance of Jesus' body is a way of signifying that the integral person, Jesus of Nazareth, was resurrected. . . . But the resurrection . . . does not re-

quire the disappearance of Jesus' corpse. Identifying the resurrection with the empirical disappearance of the body of Jesus may be seen as a category mistake that tends to distort the symbol. (*Jesus*, 125)

What then does the symbol describe, if it does not describe the fact that Jesus actually rose bodily from the grave and appeared to his disciples awakening their faith? According to Haight the resurrection "is an object of faith-hope," that is, faith means commitment to "the reality symbolized in the story of Jesus" while hope means "openness to the future . . . involving concern about one's own destiny" (*Jesus*, 125). Here it becomes abundantly clear that, despite his claim to present a mediating position between the radical and traditional (fundamentalist, in his opinion) view, Haight adopts what Fergusson characterized as the liberal view of the resurrection which inevitably collapses back into the radical view. For Haight insists that the origin of this symbol's meaning is the imagination of the human spirit; hence

> faith-hope in the resurrection gains expression as a function of the creative imagination. . . . The resurrection is not a datum lying on the surface of history, or in the region where dead bodies are buried. As a transcendent reality resurrection can only be appreciated by faith-hope. (*Jesus*, 125)

Certainly it is true that the resurrection is an event in history that cannot be verified by ordinary methods of historical investigation; it is also true that the resurrection cannot be understood without faith. But the questions raised by Haight's analysis in this context are whether or not the resurrection actually occurred as an event in history independent of the disciples' faith and whether or not the risen Lord actually exists now independently of our faith. The key question to be raised to Haight's analysis is whether the resurrection simply expresses our experience of faith-hope or instead describes an actually existing person, Jesus of Nazareth raised from the dead who encountered the disciples again in the Easter history of the forty days and who now interacts with us in the power of his Spirit.

The Nature of the Resurrection

What then is the nature of the resurrection? According to Haight, "we can approach the resurrection obliquely on the basis of the New Testament witness to this faith-hope and its object by means of an inquiry into the human experience that generated the initial conviction that Jesus was alive with God" (*Jesus*,

129). Here there is a subtle shift away from the actual faith of the New Testament to the liberal position. Hence, that which generated the initial belief in Christ's resurrection was not Christ's bodily resurrection from the dead and his actual appearances to the disciples. Indeed, Haight insists that his understanding of the resurrection "does not support the necessity of an empty tomb in principle" (*Jesus*, 134) because he sincerely believes that what generated the initial conviction that Jesus was risen was a human experience of faith-hope.

Nothing, however, could be further from the truth from within the traditional view as mentioned above by Fergusson and as we have been seeing throughout this book. The truth is that it was the risen Lord himself who appeared to the disciples and who enabled their faith and hope. And once the liberal position, which is more than a little ambivalent with regard to Christ's actual resurrection from the dead, is espoused, it is only a short distance to the radical position that there is nothing more to the resurrection than the faith-hope of those who believed in the historical Jesus and his cause. This thinking is not far removed from Bultmann's view that the Easter event was simply the rise of faith on the part of the disciples. Thus, Haight can argue that "One cannot know concretely how the disciples experienced Jesus as risen. . . . The stories of the apparitions . . . are not reports of events as they happened. . . . They were created afterwards as expressions of faith" (*Jesus*, 136). Indeed, Haight reasons that "it is not the case that the affirmation 'Jesus is risen' could only be true if Jesus were 'physically' encountered or the tomb were really empty" (*Jesus*, 145-46).

Haight relies on Rahner's transcendental analysis of the experience of hope to assert that hope, "as the fundamental posture of the openness of the human spirit to being itself . . . is the ground out of which faith arises. . . . This faith-hope has transcendental roots; its origin is an element of human existence as such" (*Jesus*, 140-41) and thus forms the horizon for understanding the meaning of the resurrection. There is no need to explore the details of how Rahner's method causes him to distort the meaning of the resurrection here. We have already discussed that in Chapter Two.[2] The important point here is to note that for all Haight's insistence that it should be Jesus himself who gives meaning to Christology (and he does insist upon this), his very method prevents that from happening. It is our transcendental experience of faith-hope that confers meaning on Jesus himself and on his resurrection. Therefore, precisely because the affirmation that Christ is risen is an object of faith-hope, it cannot be "a piece of objective information" (*Jesus*, 141) according to Haight. Because it is revealed to us, Haight takes that to mean that it is disclosed to us through our religious experience, which clearly is the element that determines the meaning and content of what is revealed.

What was it then that objectively mediated this religious experience for the disciples? It was, according to Haight, "Jesus himself during his ministry . . . after his death, the disciples' memory of Jesus filled this role" (*Jesus*, 141). At this decisive point in his argument, instead of pointing us to the risen Lord himself, Haight refers us to the disciples' memory. His interpretation of the resurrection is thus self-contained within the experience of faith-hope. We need not concern ourselves with the details that Haight provides as to how he believes the disciples' memory of Jesus led to their belief in his resurrection. It is enough to realize that he has presented a view of the resurrection that is at variance with the traditional one that sees the resurrection as an event in the life of Jesus that gives meaning to the disciples' faith and to ours. His thinking is incurably subjectivist. In the end he actually believes that Christian faith would be the same even if there "had been no explicit experience of resurrection." This is the case because "Jesus' life, what he said and did, is the center of faith. Jesus' ministry and message mediate a revelation of God" (*Jesus*, 150). But of course that is exactly the problem. In the NT Jesus did not mediate *a* revelation of God. He was not a symbol of God because if he were then we could argue as Haight indeed does that there are other symbols of God as well.[3] He was, as the Word incarnate, the Revealer of God. He was the one Mediator. Haight's very thinking, which claims to be historical, is not shaped by the Jesus of the NT but is instead shaped by his Nestorian separation of Jesus' divinity and humanity at exactly the point where faith would require that they be seen as one. And that is the perennial problem of defining Jesus' history in historicist fashion.

Resurrection and Incarnation

That leads us to the connection between the resurrection and the incarnation in the thought of Roger Haight. My thesis is that when the meaning of the resurrection is not dictated by Jesus himself, risen from the dead, but is instead dictated by the experience of faith-hope or any other experience, then the meaning of the NT faith is undermined precisely because such thinking presents a rather weak understanding of the incarnation and inevitably ignores or subverts the importance of a doctrine of the immanent Trinity. Let us briefly explore these issues.

Roger Haight's Christology from below is a Spirit Christology. Instead of beginning his reflections with a belief in Jesus as the incarnate Word he claims that "The recognition of Jesus' divinity is a function of an experience that he is the bearer of a salvation which is from God" (*Jesus*, 429). He thus presents his Spirit Christology by contrasting it with his understanding of Rahner's Logos Christology which he believes is, in many respects, a Christology from above that unfolds within the context of the immanent Trinity. The chief difficulty Haight has with this Christology is that it appears to compromise Jesus' consubstantiality with us. If Jesus' humanity is the humanity of the Logos, Haight wonders, how can we say that Jesus is one of us, when plainly he is also different from us? Haight also objects to Rahner's belief that the incarnation only happened once and thus asks: "Why is Jesus not one of many symbolic actualizations of God's loving presence to humankind? Cannot 'more' of God be revealed in other 'incarnations'?" (*Jesus*, 433). Haight's answer of course is that "it is not necessary to think that God as Spirit can be incarnated only once in history" (*Jesus*, 456).

How then does Haight understand the incarnation? First, it is "not literal language in which the referent is an object of this worldly knowledge and definition. We do not *know* God as Logos; God is an object of belief, which is an expression of faith-hope" (*Jesus*, 439). Second, the symbols God and Logos thus arise from religious experience which is itself the source of their meaning. Third, Haight recasts Rahner's theology of the symbol in the context of an incarnational Christology from below so that the human Jesus "is the concrete symbol expressing the presence in history of God as Logos" (*Jesus*, 439). Haight is thus able to adapt Rahner's theology of the symbol in order to say "Jesus is the symbolic self-expression of the Logos" (*Jesus*, 441). Since all language about God is symbolic, the "*conceptual* symbol 'Logos' does not refer to an objectified entity independent of or distinct from God . . . incarnation should not be parodied by a literal three-stage descent and ascent narrative involving a divine being" (*Jesus*, 441). As symbol of God, Jesus must therefore be understood dialectically, i.e., as a human person in whom God is present and revealed.

Haight intends to correct Rahner's Christology from above with his own Christology from below by stressing that "the human being Jesus is the symbol and expression of God as Logos present to him" (*Jesus*, 442). In other words, instead of adopting what he takes to be Rahner's Alexandrian emphasis on the hypostatic union, Haight will present a more Antiochene view of "divine indwelling" (*Jesus*, 443). Haight believes that Rahner's Christology is intelligible in a modern context precisely because it "appeals to the utopian dimension of human yearning in all human beings. . . . It understands Jesus as the historical symbol for faith-hope in a theistic vision that seeks to give meaning to all existence" (*Jesus*, 444). Haight, however, intends to shift Rahner's incarnational theology to an "indwelling" Christology in order to adjust it to the postmodern situation. For him "Jesus is the symbol of where human existence is headed and a parable of transcendent values . . ." (*Jesus,* 445). What then is the meaning of the incarnation in Haight's Spirit Christology, which emphasizes at once the historical Jesus, various historical interpretations of him, and appeals to "Christian experience and the language of grace as an analogy for understanding what is going on in christology" (*Jesus,* 447)?

We cannot go into all the details of Haight's Spirit Christology, but must instead ask what the incarnation looks like in light of his method. Haight wishes to stress that Jesus is divine and human. But in his Spirit Christology this means that "God, and not less than God [his paraphrase of Nicaea], is really present to and at work in Jesus, and that this is so in such a manner that Jesus is a manifestation and embodiment of the reality of God" (*Jesus,* 462). Haight wishes to retain Jesus' uniqueness, but "a Spirit christology may or may not hold a qualitative difference between the union of God with Jesus and the union of God with other human beings" (*Jesus,* 463). Any such qualitative difference according to Haight would mean that Jesus could not be consubstantial with us. Yet, in Haight's view, this language does suggest that something important here needs to be preserved and he proposes to do that with his "degree" Christology.

> If one says that the Spirit of God, which is God, is present to Jesus in a complete way, or in a fully effective way, in a most intense manner, need one say more? In short, one may understand that God as Spirit was present to Jesus in a superlative degree, and this is sufficient to convey all that was intended by a qualitative difference. (*Jesus,* 463-64)[4]

Haight complements this reasoning with the idea that Jesus' vocation, mission, and appointment by God to be firstborn of many also indicates his uniqueness while maintaining his consubstantiality with us. What then is the basis of this Spirit Christology? It is, according to Haight, experience: "There must be analogies in our experience if we are to appropriate the truth of past affirmations. Therefore Spirit christology appeals to the Christian experience of the internal working of God's grace as an analogy of how God was at work in Jesus" (*Jesus,* 464). Because Jesus is a human being like us in all things but sin "one can be inspired by and imitate Jesus. There is no gap between him and us. One can project upon him all the weaknesses of human existence in order to retrieve from him the inspiration of the power of his earthly life" (*Jesus,* 465).

There can be no disguising the fact that it is indeed human religious experience and not Jesus of Nazareth that determines Haight's view of both the incarnation and resurrection. Clearly, the liberal/radical view of the resurrection affects his view of the incarnation; and his view of the incarnation, as determined by his method, which refuses to acknowledge Jesus' pre-existence[5] affects his view of the resurrection. Since Jesus is not actually risen from the dead and since resurrection language expresses merely our faith-hope and that of his disciples, therefore incarnation cannot mean that Jesus *is* God incarnate. Rather, it symbolizes the fact that Jesus reflects God's love to a higher degree than others. Not only does Jesus have no independent significance as the one who initiates and sustains faith, but that which determines his uniqueness is the experience of the disciples and our transcendental experience.

There can be little doubt that, as we have already seen with respect to the Christology of Rahner and Macquarrie, the error of degree Christology stems from its failure to acknowledge that Jesus is antecedently the Son of God before all worlds, namely, that he is begotten and not made. This surely is the central belief of Nicaea, and this is what is denied and subverted by Haight's interpretation of the resurrection and incarnation. Whereas Paul argued that our faith is without substance if Christ has not actually risen from the dead, and Athanasius insisted that Jesus is both *homoousion* with the Father and with us and that, as we have seen a number of times, "It would be more godly and true to signify God from the Son and call him Father, than to name God from his works alone and call him Unoriginate,"[6] Haight uses our own experiences of ourselves and sees Jesus as one symbol among others. Indeed Haight is adamantly consistent in maintaining that what gives validity to Christology is not the reality of Jesus as truly God and truly human, but whatever in human experience we value and project upon Jesus in order to "retrieve from him the inspiration of the power of his earthly life" (*Jesus,* 465). But Jesus is not the inspiration here. The inspiration clearly stems from whatever we consider significant and whatever we then project upon Jesus in order to read back from him our own prior understanding of ourselves and God. Clearly this kind of self-justification is essential to Haight's theological method. But it is certainly excluded from a method that begins and ends its thinking with Jesus himself.

Resurrection and the Trinity

Thus, two points need to be noted here. First, Haight's denial that the resurrection is an event in the life of Jesus that gives meaning to faith is closely connected with his denial that Jesus is in fact God incarnate. Second, both of these views are consistent with his confusion regarding a proper doctrine of the immanent Trinity. For Haight "Trinitarian language cannot be taken as providing objective information about God . . ." (*Jesus,* 473). That certainly would have been news to Athanasius. T. F. Torrance rightly notes that it was the Arians who projected images of human relations into God mythologically in an attempt to understand God, and he rejects this, saying,

> To think of God like that, in terms of the creaturely content of images pro-
> jected out of ourselves, inevitably gives rise to anthropomorphic and poly-
> morphic notions of deity and in fact to polytheism and idolatry. However,
> if we think from a centre in God as he reveals himself to us through his
> Word incarnate in Jesus Christ, then we know him as Father in himself in
> an utterly unique and incomparable way which then becomes the control-
> ling standard by reference to which all notions of creaturely fatherhood
> and sonship are to be understood. (*TF,* 69)

For Haight there is no doctrine of an immanent Trinity in the New Testament and no such doctrine should be read into the New Testament. While it
is commonly accepted that there is no doctrine of the Trinity *per se* in the
New Testament, that does not mean that every doctrine of the immanent
Trinity represents something that is read back into the New Testament. In fact
a proper doctrine of the immanent Trinity is one which is faithful to the New
Testament witness concerning the Son's unique relation with the Father recounted in Matt. 11:27, Lk. 10:22, Jn. 17 and elsewhere.[7] The truth of the doctrine is grounded in the truth that the Son and Spirit who meet us in the
economy are antecedently and eternally God *in se.*

What then is the point of the doctrine of the Trinity for Haight? The doc-
trine is dependent on the "experience of Jesus as God's bringer of salvation"
(*Jesus,* 479). Not only that, but according to Haight "being a salvation bringer
makes Jesus the Christ" (*Jesus,* 400). Accordingly, for Haight there is a deeper
Christian experience and conviction that gives meaning to the doctrine of the
Trinity. What is it? It is the experience of salvation.

> The point of the doctrine of the trinity is therefore soteriological. The doc-
> trine that rests on and derives from the experience of salvation has as its
> point to assert and protect the economy of that experience of salvation. . . .
> The doctrine is not intended to provide information about the internal life
> of God, but is about how God relates to human beings. (*Jesus,* 485)

The only problem with this reasoning, and it is indeed a most serious problem, is that unless we know God in truth, we cannot say anything meaningful

about how God relates with human beings. In Haight's thinking the doctrine of the Trinity becomes a description of our experience of salvation (faith) and is in fact determined by it; to that extent his view of the Trinity remains agnostic — he rejects the idea that we can say anything accurate about God in himself. But in reality the doctrine is or should be a description of who God is who meets us in our experiences of salvation and faith. As Karl Barth once put it,

> the content of the doctrine of the Trinity . . . is not that God in His relation to man is Creator, Mediator and Redeemer, but that God in Himself is eternally God the Father, Son and Holy Spirit. . . . [God acting as Emmanuel] cannot be dissolved into His work and activity. (*CD* I/2, 878-79)[8]

When the doctrine of the Trinity is reduced to a description of our experiences of salvation then that is one more indication that the immanent Trinity has been confused with or collapsed into the economic Trinity. Such thinking reduces God to God's relation with the world precisely because it denies his freedom to exist eternally as the Father, Son and Holy Spirit.[9]

Resurrection and Atonement

This faulty understanding of the Trinity, incarnation and resurrection affects Haight's view of atonement and leaves him with a Pelagian understanding of salvation. This is why Haight speaks of Christ's mediation of salvation "as something that is a function of conscious awareness. One encounters God in Jesus. But the foundation of this experience is God and God's loving presence to human beings" (*Jesus,* 415). Here Haight separates the Son from the Father and the Holy Spirit in order to advance his idealist and ultimately unitarian view of salvation, which is determined by a vague notion of God as Spirit that he then presents as a universal that is to be found within all human experience. Salvation then is not an act of the triune God for our benefit; instead it is that which takes place wherever humans actualize their own self-transcendence. Not surprisingly then salvation and the kingdom are not identified with Jesus' person and work. There is no genuine need for repentance and belief in Jesus in the sense of John's Gospel, which identifies Jesus as the way, the truth and the life and insists that no one can come to the Father except through the Son (Jn. 14:4). Salvation and the kingdom certainly are not found in the mysterious unity of the Father, Son and Spirit in eternity and in history for Haight. Rather they are found in the universal experience of self-transcendence; they are something "that has been going on from the beginning, before and outside of Jesus' own influence" (*Jesus*, 422). This is why Haight follows Shubert Ogden and claims, in typically Docetist fashion, that "no event in time and history, including the event of Jesus Christ, can be the cause of salvation in the sense of the necessary condition of its possibility" (*Jesus*, 405). This thinking is in marked contrast to the message of Mk. 2:1-12 in the story of the paralytic cured by Jesus after Jesus forgave his sins.

There is an important train of thought here. First, Haight asserts that the doctrine of the Trinity describes only our experiences of salvation, then he insists that Jesus is not the unique savior of the world and finally he advances the idea that salvation really means our humanization through our own acts of self-transcendence. With this idea there are obvious correspondences with the thought of Gordon Kaufman and Sallie McFague despite the fact that they do not intend to maintain Christ's uniqueness while Haight does. But the point of this book is to emphasize that when Christ ceases to be the incarnate Word who alone justifies and sanctifies sinners, then salvation must be found in the human religious quest for meaning and salvation; and then Pelagianism becomes the only viable alternative. It is important to realize, however, as Barth pointed out and as we have already had occasion to note, that humanity's deepest need is for the righteousness of God — a righteousness that does not belong to us but that can only come from God himself. Indeed, according to Barth, the most tragic aspect of humanity is exemplified in the fact that we humans are seeking the righteousness that we cannot live without, through religious, moral and political ideals. This means that, as we have already seen, we are seeking God's righteousness without God and even against God by creating for ourselves an idol, a reflection of our own human righteousness writ large. And this is a tragedy because so long as this happens, then our deepest human need will not be recognized and the solution to this need cannot take place in our lives here and now.[10] This is the practical problem with those theologies that tend to equate salvation with human self-realization and then undercut our genuine human need for the revelation and grace of God revealed and active in Jesus Christ himself and through his Holy Spirit.

Roger Haight exemplifies precisely how the liberal/radical view of the resurrection undercuts the fact that it is and must always be the object of faith that determines what can and cannot be said about the historical Jesus and his interaction with us in history. By reducing the resurrection to the content of the human experience of faith/hope Haight compromised the truth of the incarnation and collapsed the immanent into the economic Trinity. And it is just this thinking that led him to believe that *we* can *use* Jesus as a way of experiencing the salvation that is open to any religious person in their experiences of self-transcendence. But it is precisely this thinking that separates us humanly and religiously from the justification that took place in Jesus himself because it denies him the freedom, as the risen Lord, to be the only one who justifies and sanctifies our faith through the Holy Spirit. And the situation thus created places the burden of salvation on us; instead of offering us the good news that nothing can separate us from the love of God in Jesus Christ, we are offered merely the ethical imperative and ethical ideal of humanity working for a better world. In the process we are in fact thrown back upon ourselves in such a way that we must then use Christ as an image to help us work out our own salvation. This form of self-justification not only obscures the triumph of God's grace in Jesus Christ, but it effectively leaves us locked within ourselves and isolated from the God of Christian faith. Any Christian ethics built upon this foundation is bound to be a failure because it will always equate salvation with our ethical achievements implying that God somehow requires and needs our good behavior to be able to act in history. In this situation Jesus himself becomes dispensable and righteousness can no longer mean obedience to Jesus Christ; instead it must mean obedience to our own ethical ideals. But the truth is that humanity has never been able to live righteously by positing ethical ideals and then following them. That is the whole point of Christianity: Christ promises to share his perfect obedience with us and thus enable us to do what we cannot do on our own morally speaking.

John Hick

Now let us explore the thought of one more prominent contemporary theologian whose attempt to think about both the incarnation and the resurrection from the vantage of "religious pluralism" has been widely influential. Unlike Roger Haight, John Hick makes no attempt to defend the thinking developed at Nicaea and Chalcedon and actually argues that we must reject what was taught by these councils in order to come to a more adequate grasp of Christianity as one religion among many others that are acceptable ways of "salvation/liberation." It would be rather easy to dismiss Hick's view that the incarnation is a myth and that Christian doctrine must be changed under the pressure of a contemporary explanation of theology from a "global" perspective simply because it explicitly rejects the teaching of the Christian church at Nicaea and Chalcedon. But Hick claims that his new interpretation of the Christian faith is actually a better construal than had been offered in the past.

For this reason his thinking must be presented and criticized for what it is: a deconstruction and reconstruction of the Christian faith based on Hick's Kantian interpretation of religious experience, his own peculiar view of inter-religious dialogue and his understanding of contemporary religious plural-ism. Because Hick intends to change the very nature of Christian faith, he does not spend a great deal of time investigating individual doctrines such as the doctrine of the resurrection in a scientific way; but it will certainly be clear from what is presented here that his interpretation of the resurrection is shaped by his mythological understanding of the incarnation and ultimately by his unitarian view of God. And it will be shown that his view of ethics rep-resents a rather blatant form of self-justification precisely because he is un-able to acknowledge Jesus' actual uniqueness as the Word of God incarnate. Not only does Hick's understanding of Christian ethics equate salvation with right ethical behavior, but he uses such behavior as his criterion for religious truth, thus compromising the very heart of the Christian faith, namely, that Jesus himself is the way, the truth and the life and that no one comes to the Father, except through him. Therein, we must stress once again, rests the sig-nificance of the doctrine of justification for Christian ethics. Let us begin then with Hick's interpretation of Jesus' resurrection.

Hick on Jesus' Resurrection

In *The Myth of God Incarnate* John Hick considers the resurrection in the context of comparing Christology and "Buddhology" contending that Chris-tians justify "ascription" of "divine attributes" to Jesus and not to Gautama because Jesus actually rose from the dead. While it is his resurrection, Hick says, that sets him apart from others and shows that he is God incarnate, Hick also believes that this argument is hard to sustain. Nonetheless, Hick asserts that there was some sort of experience of "seeing" Jesus after his death: "an appearance or appearances which came to be known as his resurrection, seems virtually certain in view of the survival and growth of the tiny original Jesus movement."[11] But, according to Hick, "we cannot ascertain today in what this resurrection-event consisted" (*Myth*, 170).[12] While possible expla-nations of the resurrection range from "resuscitation" to visions, Hick says it is doubtful that the resurrection (whatever its nature) was seen by people at the time as guaranteeing Jesus' divinity because the raising of the dead at that time was not as earth-shaking or incredible as it might be today. In this vein Hick refers to the raising of Lazarus, Jairus' daughter and the report in Matt. 11:5 that the dead are being raised up; further, there is the report in Matt.

27:52-53 that at Jesus' crucifixion tombs opened and many were raised from the dead. Hick is at pains to stress that the claim that Jesus had been raised did not "automatically put him in a quite unique category" (*Myth*, 171).

This is an interesting line of argument when weighed against Barth's assertion that the NT was not interested in other resurrections;[13] the NT was interested in the death and resurrection of this particular man because the kingdom of God is identical with his person and work. For the NT there was no separating the incarnate Word from the risen Lord. So the very idea that one could or should compare Jesus' resurrection with others who were reported to have been brought back from the dead essentially misses the point of the NT, namely, that Jesus' resurrection is unique because he himself, as the Word of God incarnate is unique — there really was and is no other human being who was and is the Word of God. Further, and unlike other resurrections, Jesus was not simply resuscitated only to die again, but he was raised by God bodily from the dead and as such was exalted to the right hand of God as Lord of the church and the world. He had a new spiritual body, that is, a body enlivened by the Holy Spirit and no longer subject to sin, suffering, evil and death. With Hick it is quite true to say that the resurrection did not prove his divinity; but it certainly revealed his divinity in the sense that it disclosed who it was who claimed to forgive sins and said he would come again to judge the living and the dead.

Moreover, the very notion that it was easier for those who lived during Jesus' time to accept the idea of a resurrection was quite properly contested by both T. F. Torrance and Karl Barth, as seen above. For Torrance, as for Barth, Jesus' resurrection was something completely unexpected and quite incredible; people did not automatically believe it during Jesus' lifetime any more than they would automatically believe it today. And in fact the Gnostics ridiculed Christian belief in Christ's bodily resurrection.[14] It is something completely new and can be known only from within the parameters set by the incarnation itself. Quite clearly, Hick's understanding of the resurrection is shaped by his mythological conception of the incarnation which we will return to in a moment. And it is that mythological comprehension that leads him to suppose falsely that it was easier for people to believe in the resurrection in Jesus' lifetime than it is for us today.

Here it is also worth noting that Hick insists that Jesus was raised by God and not "in virtue of a divine nature which he himself possessed" (*Myth*, 171). This leads Hick to believe that the earliest Christian preachers did not conclude that this man was God but that he was a man chosen by God for a special task "and declared by his resurrection to be Messiah and Lord (Acts 2.22 and 36)" (*Myth*, 171). But of course everything depends upon how one understands the earliest NT Christologies. Hick follows the thinking of John Knox and believes that the earliest NT Christologies were in fact adoptionistic. But, as we have seen above, both Barth and Torrance correctly insist that Jesus Christ was the Word of God incarnate simply because he was and not because he was a mere human being who was transformed into a heavenly figure by the community's faith. Because the object determining their thought about the resurrection is the unique man Jesus who was the Word of God incarnate, neither Barth nor Torrance posits an early adoptionist Christology that then supposedly developed into a Christology from above. This is precisely why both Barth and Torrance rejected any sort of Ebionite or Docetic Christology or any Christology reconstructed along Ebionite or Docetic lines.

This is an extremely basic point in Christology. And it marks a major dividing line between allowing the unique object of the Christian faith to dictate the possibilities and limits of what is said and the view held by Hick and many others that Jesus was a historical figure who was transformed into an exalted figure by the writers of the NT and ultimately by the early church in the creeds of Nicaea and Chalcedon. Interestingly, as we shall see, it is Hick's starting point in experience that leads to his conclusions which are essentially Docetic because it is not the historical Jesus who dictates his understanding here, but his view of God which will only allow him to see in Jesus one of several embodiments of deity. Here it is important to note that, unlike Hick, Torrance can argue that there is indeed a sense in which Jesus raised himself in perfect Amen to the Father;[15] if there is an unbroken unity of being between the Father and Son, then this idea espoused by Torrance would actually make perfect sense. The fact that God raises Jesus from the dead is not opposed to the fact that Jesus himself as the Son of God incarnate can also act from within history in response to God the Father. And it would not rule out the idea that the Holy Spirit could also be seen as acting here in raising Jesus from the dead.

Hick's position on the resurrection then is that "it is less easy to accept stories of a physical resurrection" today because we are so far removed from the event and the evidence is full of conflict and hard to decipher (*Myth*, 171). But he contends that even if we were to accept the idea of a physical resurrection of Jesus that would hardly prove that he was divine. What about the empty tomb? Since the earliest strata of the NT "do not include any reference either to the empty tomb or to a visible or tangible body of the risen Jesus" Hick contends that belief in the resurrection and ascension arose "prior to and independently of the later physical resurrection stories with which we are familiar in the Gospels" (*The Metaphor*, 23-24). What then about Hick's view of the resurrection event itself? We have already seen that for Hick "resurrection" refers "to the transitional event or events in virtue of which the Jesus movement survived the death of its founder" (*The Metaphor*, 23); he also believes that we cannot know exactly what that event was with any certainty. But he does offer some suggestions.

There can be little doubt that Hick's liberal interpretation of the resurrection and his Ebionite view of the incarnation are inextricably intertwined. On the one hand, Hick rather naively believes, in typical Ebionite fashion, that the man Jesus was deified by the Christian community: "In John . . . there is an elaborate narrative expressing the virtual deification of Jesus in the mind of his part of the church" (*The Metaphor*, 25). Instead of acknowledging that Jesus was the Son of God incarnate simply because he was and instead of allowing the witness of John and Paul *together with* the witness of the Synoptics to dictate his theology here, Hick separates John and Paul from the Synoptics with his belief that John and Paul are "unhistorical" and clearly insists that Jesus' sonship results from the community's conferral of divine status upon him based on its experiences of faith. On the other hand he offers a psychological explanation of the resurrection that falls squarely within what Fergusson characterized as the liberal view that collapses back into the radical view by grounding it in the disciples' experience: "the tradition developed from the remembrance of a numinous and transforming experience into a story of miraculous physical events. This pattern suggests that the original happening is more likely to have been in the realm of inner spiritual experience than in that of outer sense experience" (*The Metaphor*, 25). This Docetic conclusion results from Hick's Ebionite starting point. It is of course Docetic because it explains resurrection by abstracting from the particular resurrection of Jesus of Nazareth. For Hick, the resurrection cannot be understood as an event in the life of Jesus himself that gives meaning to the disciples' faith and to ours; rather resurrection language describes a numinous transforming experience and cannot in reality describe an "outer sense experience." This amounts to a denial of the NT witness to Jesus' bodily resurrection. In any case Hick notes that whatever it was that happened, it can never be completely verified from a historical point of view. No one would disagree with that. However, the question left unanswered with that assertion is whether or not the acts of God within history in the incarnation and resurrection could be verified by historical analysis at all. Of course Barth and Torrance would agree that God's actions within history cannot be verified by ordinary historical analysis because if they could, they would not be actions of God coming into history from outside. What is needed is theology and history. Any one-sided emphasis on theology leads to mythology while any one-sided emphasis on history leads to historicism and rationalism.

Notice, however, how Hick's presuppositions in this context preclude allowing the object of the Christian faith to determine what is thought and said in both instances. With respect to the resurrection he cannot imagine that Jesus actually rose bodily from the dead and enabled the faith of his disciples because he prefers to understand the NT attestations by reference to his understanding of Paul's experience on the road to Damascus. This experience, according to Hick, was of a blinding light and a voice, but no bodily presence. Hence, in Hick's view, the original experience of the resurrection was an experience "of a supernatural light around them within which they were conscious of the glorified presence of Jesus" in a manner similar to the way "near-death experiences" are described today (*The Metaphor,* 24). It does not seem to concern Hick that in 1 Cor. 15 Paul insists that unless Christ had been raised bodily from the dead Christian faith was without substance, people were still in their sins and he himself would have proven to be a liar for attesting the risen Lord's appearances to Cephas and the five hundred others. Hick's conclusions are consistent with his presuppositions: behind the NT testimonies is

> a man, Jesus, whose immensely powerful God-consciousness made God . . . intensely and startlingly real . . . he was so transparently open to the divine presence that his life and teaching have a universal significance which can still help to guide our lives today. (*The Metaphor,* 26)

There can be little doubt that this is a contemporary version of Ebionite Christology that grounds Jesus' uniqueness in the impression he made on the community with the result that, for Hick, Jesus was and is an ordinary man who was deified by the community because they ascribed deity to him on the basis of his extraordinary life. Hick himself forthrightly indicates that his picture of Jesus falls within the tradition of liberal theology "established by Schleiermacher, Strauss, Harnack and others" (*The Metaphor,* 18).

In this context, it is worth recounting that D. F. Strauss, who went to Berlin to study with Hegel, submitted a "prize essay" to the Catholic faculty of theology at Tübingen on the subject of "The Resurrection of the Dead."[16] In Strauss's words,

> A Catholic prize essay which I worked upon in 1828 was perhaps the first turning point in a critical direction. I proved the resurrection of the dead with full conviction, both exegetically and also from a natural-philosophical point of view, and as I made the last full stop, it was clear to me that there was nothing in the whole idea of the resurrection.[17]

Hick does not go quite that far. But he might as well have since he substitutes for the resurrection of Jesus of Nazareth the inner experience of St. Paul and the near death experiences of the present day. In other words, it is quite clear that Hick does not believe that Jesus actually rose bodily from the dead and appeared to the disciples enabling their faith; to that extent one could say, with D. F. Strauss, that there is nothing in the whole idea. What becomes of the idea in Hick's hands is that it is made to represent the mythology that Jesus lived an extraordinary human life for others and so was deified by the community.

Resurrection and Incarnation

As already intimated, it is exactly because Hick understands the incarnation as a myth that he is unable to take seriously the resurrection as an event in the life of Jesus himself that gives meaning to Christian faith. What does Hick mean by referring to the incarnation as a myth? For Hick,

> a myth is a story which is told but which is not literally true, or an idea or image which is applied to someone or something but which does not literally apply, but which invites a particular attitude in its hearers. Thus the truth of a myth is a kind of practical truth consisting in the appropriateness of the attitude to its object. That Jesus was God the Son incarnate is not literally true, since it has no literal meaning, but it is an application to Jesus of a mythical concept whose function is analogous to that of the notion of divine sonship ascribed in the ancient world to a king. (*Myth,* 178)

Applying this thinking to the incarnation, Hick therefore argues that "the real point and value of the incarnational doctrine is not indicative but expressive, not to assert a metaphysical fact but to express a valuation and evoke an attitude" (*Myth,* 178). In this thinking Hick has transferred the center of gravity from Jesus of Nazareth to the community suggesting that the doctrine of the incarnation does not describe a real event that took place in the life of Jesus of Nazareth; instead it describes people's subjective reaction to the man Jesus: they valued him and attempted to get others to do the same. Such thinking, however, fails to address the real point of the doctrine which is that Jesus is the Word of God simply because he is and not because the community began to think of him in a certain way based on the impression he made as a human being who was God-conscious.

Thinking mythologically Hick has apparently fallen prey to subjectivism by allowing only that the doctrine describes people's reactions to Jesus and not allowing for the fact that Jesus' actual uniqueness led them to think about him as they did. In fact Hick comes dangerously close to embracing Feuerbach's projection theory because he believes that in the first instance Jesus was an ordinary man who was exalted into a divine figure by virtue of the community's imagination. He can even say "Clearly, Feuerbach's account of the idea of God as a projection of human ideals has a certain application here" (*Myth,* 168). That is why for him Jesus was a "charismatic man, filled with the divine Spirit, [who] was gradually exalted and magnified by human piety into the pre-existent Christ, the eternal Logos."[18]

Hick therefore argues for what he calls an "Inspiration Christology" which holds that because Jesus was not really the incarnate Word, he was in reality only a higher degree of human being than the rest of us: "the union of divine and human action that occurs whenever God's grace works effectively in a man's or a woman's life was operating to a total extent in the life of Jesus" (*Disputed Questions,* 52).[19] In other words "Before Jesus became deified in the Christian mind and the trinitarian doctrine developed to locate him within the Godhead, the earthly Lord was thought of as a man filled with the Spirit" (*Disputed Questions,* 53). Hick therefore thinks that "a number of different beings . . . have been worshipped under the name of Jesus or under the title Christ" (*Myth,* 167). And in a manner not unlike that of Roger Haight, who argued that we project our weaknesses onto Jesus to retrieve from him the inspiration of his earthly life, Hick believes that

> communal or individual imagination has projected its own ideal upon as much of the New Testament data as will sustain it, producing a Christ-figure who meets the spiritual needs of his devotees; while behind this gallery of ideal portraits lies the largely unknown man of Nazareth. (*Myth,* 167-68)

It is this assumption that distorts the NT witness at the outset and produces just the dualistic picture of Jesus that Torrance and Barth quite properly argued against. It is here that decisions must be made. Either we accept the truth of the NT witness that the man Jesus of Nazareth is who he is as the Word of God incarnate simply because he is: the truth of the Gospel portraits rests on the truth of who Jesus really was and is so that there is no human Jesus to be found behind the Gospel confessions of him as the Word of God he was. Or we ascribe truth mythologically to the community. Then we no longer have the NT picture of Jesus but the picture of a historical figure read back into the NT by those who refuse to believe in Jesus with the rest of the

NT. In other words the assumption that there is a historical figure, a supposedly real Jesus, behind the Jesus of the NT who is presented as Messiah and Lord amounts to a separation of Jesus' humanity and divinity at the outset and represents the projection into the NT of a picture that is at variance with the NT faith itself. Has Hick fallen head long into subjectivism?

Paul Knitter defends Hick against the charge of subjectivism arguing that Hick does not intend to say that there is no reality outside people's personal response. He claims that for Hick there are facts that constitute the myth:

> If people began to talk about God incarnate in Jesus it was because they experienced him to be 'so powerfully God-conscious that his life vibrated, as it were, to the divine life; . . . he was so totally conscious of God that . . . [others] could catch something of the consciousness by spiritual contagion.' . . . Incarnation language refers not just to something that happens in us, but to something that happened in Jesus.[20]

Not exactly: incarnation describes a miraculous event that took place in Jesus' own life as he was conceived by the Holy Spirit and born of the Virgin Mary — that is the objective event that was attested in the NT and at Nicaea and Chalcedon. In a manner reminiscent of Schleiermacher, Hick and Knitter have both changed that ontological reality into the content of a mythological expression based on their view of the disciples' experiences that transforms Jesus into one who is more God-conscious than others. In that way they present him as different from us in degree but not in kind. But in reality they have changed Jesus from being the incarnate Word attested in scripture and at Nicaea and Chalcedon into a man with a powerful God-consciousness. In other words what determines their thought about Jesus is their mythological thinking, not Jesus himself. And that in the end is the subjectivism that is overcome by and called into question by the incarnation itself.

It is no secret that Hick rejects the teaching of Nicaea and Chalcedon because he thinks that the teaching of these councils represented a "supreme example of this projection upon Jesus of ideals to answer our spiritual needs" (*Myth*, 168). For this reason he argues that the Nicene understanding of Jesus as "God-the-Son-incarnate is only one way of conceptualizing the lordship of Jesus" (*Myth*, 168). In our new age of "world ecumenism," however, it is now proper "for Christians to become conscious of both the optional and the mythological character of this traditional language" (*Myth*, 168; also *Theology of Religions*, 101ff.). This thinking stands in radical contrast to the critical point of the *homoousion* affirmed at Nicaea and Chalcedon which is that the whole of the Christian faith turns on the truth of Jesus' consubstantiality with the Father and with us. Any arbitrary change in language amounts to an arbitrary change in the nature of the object of reflection. It is because Jesus is who he is that the language of Nicaea and Chalcedon is neither optional nor mythological. It is not optional because the language was deliberately chosen to describe the mystery of revelation and faith in opposition to Arian views that saw Jesus merely as a creature of God. It is not mythological because its truth is determined by the extent to which that language actually describes the mystery that Jesus himself is. As T. F. Torrance repeatedly insists, the thinking of the NT authors was constrained by the unique object they had encountered, i.e., Jesus Christ himself. Hick's thinking is not determined by Jesus himself but by a view of the incarnation that sees it as "taking place whenever and wherever God's will is freely done" (*Theology of Religions*, 136).[21] This is his metaphorical understanding of the incarnation: it is a way of speaking about people's obedience to God so that incarnation takes place wherever anyone freely does God's will on earth.

Hick changes the traditional teaching of Nicaea and Chalcedon not because he has a better understanding of the truth of Christianity but because he insists on seeing Christianity as one religion among others.[22] He contends that there was merely a functional value to the Nicene/Chalcedonian definitions because they were needed by a persecuted church to achieve some prestige in the world:

> It could well be that its deification of Jesus helped the early Christian community to survive its period of intermittent persecutions and that subsequently, if the church was to be spiritual, moral and cultural director of the Roman Empire, and thus of Western civilisation, it needed the prestige of a founder who was none other than God, in the person of the eternal Son. (*Disputed Questions*, 47-48)

But now Hick insists we live in a very different historical period and Christianity is no longer a small persecuted minority; hence "It is now seen as one religion among others in a manifestly pluralistic world" (*Disputed Questions*, 48). And Hick thinks this way because he embraces a version of Ebionite Christology: "The Christian gift to the world is Jesus, the 'largely unknown man of Nazareth' whose impact has nevertheless created such powerful images in men's minds that he is for millions the way, the truth and the life" (*Myth*, 182).[23] This, together with his belief that Jesus was "deified" by the community, makes it clear that the truth of Christology for him is grounded in the impression Jesus made on the community so that Jesus was then viewed as a god. Yet, as I have been arguing throughout this book, for the NT

Jesus' uniqueness is not grounded in the community's reaction to him but in his eternal relation with the Father. It is at this point that we see that Hick's mythological understanding of the incarnation is intimately tied to his mythological understanding of God. Not only does Hick misconstrue the meaning of the Christian doctrine of the Trinity, but his Kantian thinking makes it impossible for us to say anything about a really existing immanent Trinity.

Trinity and Incarnation in Hick's Thought

Consistent with his Kantian presuppositions, Hick proffers an idea of what incarnation and the Trinity might look like if his suggested reconstruction of Christian faith is carried out by the year 2056. And his idea is instructive. For Hick, "Jesus' life is seen as an outstanding occasion of divine incarnation" (*Theology of Religions,* 136). And by that Hick unquestionably means that Jesus' incarnation is one among many and that none is uniquely different from or superior to the others.[24] Closely connected with this Docetic view of the incarnation (Docetic because what is important is Hick's idea of incarnation and not Jesus of Nazareth who is God incarnate) is Hick's agnostic and idealistic view of the Trinity:

> The idea of the Trinity no longer involves three mysteriously inter-related centres of divine consciousness and will, but is a symbol for the three-fold character of our human awareness of God — as the creative source of all life, as the transforming salvific power, and as the divine spirit living within us. (*Theology of Religions,* 136)[25]

This thinking eliminates the very possibility affirmed in a properly understood doctrine of the immanent Trinity because for Hick trinitarian language describes nothing more than our human awareness of God. But the critical question facing Christian theologians is whether and to what extent their supposed awareness of God has a *terminus ad quem* that transcends that awareness itself and actually describes a genuinely existing immanent Trinity. For unless the Christian God made known in Jesus Christ and through the Holy Spirit is eternally the Father, Son and Holy Spirit and would be that eternal God even if he never created, reconciled and redeemed the world in his actions *ad extra,* then trinitarian theology becomes little more than the human use of religious language to speak with ourselves about our experiences in the economy of salvation.

It is Hick's refusal to acknowledge the truth of the incarnation that both undermines the Christian doctrine of the Trinity and leaves him with an essentially unitarian idea of God. In the end, it is his Arian starting point that insists we begin with God *rather than* with Christ that causes him to reject the incarnation itself in its uniqueness and it is his failure to accept the incarnation in its historicity as an act of God within history that forces him to insist that Jesus cannot be utterly unique as the Word of God incarnate. This is why he can hope that when the church re-defines its doctrines from within his pluralistic vision "worship [will be] explicitly directed to God, rather than to Jesus . . . we [will be] taught to address God directly as our heavenly Father, and not through any mediator" (*Theology of Religions*, 136). By contrast, according to Athanasius as we have had occasion to note more than once, "It would be more godly and true to signify God from the Son and call him Father, than to name God from his works alone and call him Unoriginate."[26]

Because Hick's conception of God is agnostic to start with, he prefers to think of God as "The real in itself" (*Theology of Religions*, 27). And he thinks of the Trinity as one possible description of the Real among others which include Allah, Adonai and Vishnu because, in typically Kantian fashion, he posits the noumenal existence of the Real in order to avoid sheer projectionism. But, at the same time, he contends that we can never know it; the most we can know are the appearances of the Real within the history of experience. In Hick's own words:

> we don't worship the noumenal Real in itself. We worship one or other of its personae — Allah, the Holy Trinity, Adonai, Vishnu, and so on. Or we orient ourselves in meditation towards one of its impersonae — the Tao, Brahman, the Dharma, Sunyata, and so on. But in doing so we are responding to the Real which, so to speak, lies behind its different manifestations to humankind. (*Theology of Religions*, 65)

Two false assumptions underlie this reasoning. First, Hick assumes that what he calls "the Real" is a genuine description of the Christian God so that he can actually equate the reality that is described as the Holy Trinity with Allah, Vishnu or the Tao as different manifestations of the same reality. Second, because of this assumption Hick concludes that, since the Real is never actually worshipped in itself, we only worship its personae or impersonae which take different forms. The forms, however, are irrelevant to the content, since no matter how different they may be, they all represent attempts to relate to "the Real."

Yet, the most basic question facing Christian theologians is subverted by this reasoning because, as Torrance and Barth never cease reminding us:

(1) what God is toward us in Jesus Christ he is eternally in himself, and (2) the form of revelation (Jesus of Nazareth and the witnesses to him) cannot be separated from its content (the eternally pre-existent Word who became flesh). For Christians, then, the form of revelation is Jesus Christ himself and the prophetic and apostolic witness to him. Therefore, given the fact that Jesus really is God incarnate, it is impossible to equate God with some noumenal reality thought to exist behind his back, a noumenal reality that can actually be detached from the revelation of God that took place in Jesus' life, death and resurrection and then equated with whatever we depict as divine by virtue of our relation to some *personae* or *impersonae*. The very fact that Hick thinks he can equate the reality "behind" the Trinity with the reality "behind" Allah and the Tao shows that his thinking is not at all dictated by who God really is in Jesus Christ. Instead, his thinking is dictated by his mythological interpretation of what can only be deemed his nominalist construal of experience with the result that the question of the truth of God's existence is left hanging in mid-air. Hick's idea of the Real represents a universalistic attempt to subvert the Christian understanding of the reality of God *in se* and *ad extra* (in revelation) and it thus turns out to be Hick's own mythological invention that was created to avoid acknowledging who God really was and is in Jesus Christ himself. And this has ethical implications.

Ethical Implications of Hick's Agnosticism

Since Jesus is only one inspired religious figure among others, salvation must be something we accomplish by using him as a model.[27] But other models work just as effectively, if not better, because for Hick salvation/liberation is equated with our moral behavior as well:

> Suppose, then, we define salvation in a very concrete way, as an actual change in human beings, a change which can be identified — when it *can* be identified — by its moral fruits. We then find that we are talking about something that is of central concern to each of the great world faiths. (*Theology of Religions*, 17)

Hick explicitly rejects what he construes as the traditional understanding of salvation "as being forgiven and accepted by God because of the atoning death of Jesus" (*Theology of Religions*, 16) in order to affirm a salvation, that is, a transformation/liberation that can be recognized and described within and without the Christian church.[28] Of course this is not a proper view of atonement because Jesus' death should not be understood as "causing" our forgiveness. Jesus himself forgives us because he alone, as the Word of God incarnate, has the power to forgive. And atonement means that he lived a life of obedience in relation to God on our behalf thus enabling us to do humanly what we in ourselves are incapable of doing, namely, obeying the one, true and ever living God. For this very reason salvation is not an observable phenomenon. And it certainly cannot be equated either with our moral behavior, with our moral ideals or with any human transformation thought to underlie such moral behavior and ideals. Hick has transposed all of this into our general relation with what he calls the Real and then sees Jesus as one instance of transformative moral activity among others. But the main point to be made here is that Hick equates salvation with human transformation that takes place by our practice of the Golden Rule: "Many have responded — again, in their varying degrees — to the moral claim of love/compassion mediated by the great traditions and widely formulated as the Golden Rule" ("The Non-Absoluteness of Christianity," 29).[29]

Here we see the fundamental confusion in Hick's perspective. It is because he confuses who Christ really was and is as the incarnate and risen Lord with a "Christ-idea" based on our ethical ideals that he argues that

> If centuries of Christian influence had sufficiently modified our human greed, acquisitiveness and propensity to cruelty, the absoluteness of Christ could not have operated to justify ruthless aggression and persecution. But in fact human savagery has too often found Christian dogma tailored to its own self-justification. And this entire situation, consisting in the combination of an absolute claim together with a moral powerlessness which belies that claim, adds to the problematic character of the traditional dogma. In the light of this we should, surely, carefully re-examine it to see whether it really is an essential part of Christianity. And I have been arguing that it not only lacks a secure historical grounding in the teaching of Jesus but also lacks any clear literal meaning. (*Theology of Religions,* 100-101)

Hick honestly believes that the truth of Christology and therefore of soteriology is determined by the validity of our ethical behavior insisting that "it doesn't seem to be the case that Christians have in general been morally and spiritually superior to Jews in general, or Muslims in general, or Buddhists, Hindus, Sikhs, Taoists, Confucianists, Baha'is, or the peoples of the primal religions" (*Theology of Religions,* 113). While there is good and evil in all religions, including Christianity, the criterion of truth lies in the extent to which religious traditions foster love of neighbor in the sense of the Golden

Rule. For him the ethical fruits embodied in the Golden Rule are not merely a sign of the truth of Christian witness, but are the criterion of universal truth. His question is not: what has the true God done for us within history in the history of Jesus Christ and his Holy Spirit? His question is: how can Christian thinking today effectively promote our "salvific transformation"? (*Theology of Religions,* 76). Hence, Hick argues that "No one, for example, would think of Jesus as a son of God if they also thought that he was selfish, deceitful, exploitative and malicious. We all operate with an implicit or explicit moral criterion. Sam Keen vividly calls it our 'spiritual bullshit detector'" (*Theology of Religions,* 77).

My point here is simply this: if and to the extent it is thought that we have a spiritual criterion which can be equated with a moral principle by which to judge the truth of the person and work of Jesus Christ, then and to that extent we have fallen head-long into a type of self-justification from which there can be no escape without a return to faith in Jesus himself. But that is just the problem. As long as it is thought that we have a moral criterion by which to judge the truth of Christology, we will always confuse salvation with human morality and then argue for some universalist position such as the idea that wherever people of any religion obey the Golden Rule, there we have salvation in the proper religious sense. What I have tried to argue in this book, however, is that because the resurrection and incarnation are intimately and ontologically related, therefore we have no spiritual criterion by which to judge the truth either of Christology or of soteriology. It is precisely this that has been taken out of our controlling hands by Jesus Christ himself because he has taken responsibility for us before God and humanity. And it is just this fact that can never be accepted by those who refuse to accept Jesus' Lordship as his actual Lordship. For those reasons we can and must turn to the risen Lord himself to recognize our justification and sanctification by faith. When we do this we discover that the truth of Christianity cannot in reality be discerned by exploring human transformations and ethical imperatives. The most Christians can do, and it is something they must do in virtue of their true freedom given and received in Christ himself and through his Spirit, is to witness to the fact that the risen Lord is alive and active both within and without the church enabling people to live responsibly in obedience to him. He really is the truth — not in the inappropriate sense that Christians can take that truth and control it or impose it on others. Any such idea would immediately betray its failure to perceive our justification by faith.

To be justified by faith means to recognize that Christians are not better than other people in other religions. Rather it is to recognize that, like everyone else, Christians stand completely in need of the grace of God revealed and active in Jesus' resurrection and in the outpouring of his Holy Spirit. Christians recognize the grace of God in its identity with Jesus Christ. Others do not. But that does not mean that God's grace cannot be effective for them and will not be effective for them. It can and it will, but only as the risen Lord himself acts on them and in them in his own way and in his own good time. That is the triumph of God's grace in Jesus Christ. All of this is lost by Hick's universalism. By making the incarnation a general occurrence within universal human experience, Hick not only denies the particular power of the risen Lord, but he equates the power of salvation with the human activity of loving one's neighbors as one loves oneself. Here we are presented with a picture of religious people mythologically accounting for their experiences in particular religious traditions but all ultimately describing the same ultimate reality, namely, the Real. And yet, if Jesus Christ really is the Son of the Father from all eternity and if it is he who has come down from heaven for us and our salvation, then it is not possible to recognize and respect the true God agnostically by positing the Real which can never truly be known, and then to harmonize all the different religions which do not as a matter of fact respect the triune God, with the claim that all religions are the same in that they all represent our "pilgrim's progress," that is, "our life-response to the Real" (*Theology of Religions*, 27).[30] It is just because self-justification is built into Hick's theology that he claims that

> The great world faiths orient us in this journey, and in so far as they are, as we may say, in soteriological alignment with the Real, to follow their path will relate us rightly to the Real, opening us to what, in different conceptualities, we will call divine grace or supernatural enlightenment that will in turn bear visible fruit in our lives. (*Theology of Religions*, 27)[31]

But that is just the problem. Any genuine recognition of the Lordship of Jesus Christ necessarily means acknowledgment that we cannot become righteous with the righteousness that comes from God alone and thus be in right relation with the triune God simply by following a religious path, Christian or other. That is the ultimate form of religious self-justification. It is not following a religious path that is thought to be in harmony with what we think is real that determines our righteousness. Only God can do that. And that is what he has in reality done in Jesus Christ. It is at this point that Christians must say: hands off. We cannot claim that if we follow some religious path we will be rightly related with the triune God. In fact we may find ourselves questioning some of the paths offered by our religious traditions and not following them precisely because we are following the good Shepherd, Jesus himself.

Only in obedience to Christ do we live our justification and sanctification. And for that very reason one cannot define sanctity as a universal human possession in the form of those who live ethically good lives and then reach the inappropriate conclusion that all religions enable people to become saints to the extent that they live the Golden Rule. A saint is one who is called by Christ and enabled by the Holy Spirit to renounce any ethical attempt to identify salvation with the good that is done to and for others. Christians of course will do the good. But that will be sign of their faith in the risen Lord and for that reason could never become a general means to a righteousness that could be defined apart from the historical Jesus who was and is the incarnate Word and who lives now in the power of his Spirit.

In this chapter we have seen that when Jesus' resurrection is not seen as the actual foundation of Christian theology not only does the truth of who Jesus was within the immanent Trinity become questionable, but who he is as the incarnate Word becomes questionable as well. Even though Roger Haight still wishes to maintain some sort of uniqueness for Jesus in his thinking, he nevertheless concludes that Jesus must be seen as one savior among others exactly because he could not imagine that the source of Christian truth could be the actual fact that Jesus himself rose from the dead and ascended into heaven. And this thinking issues in a form of self-justification which illustrates the fact that where the saving grace of faith is ignored, we are in reality left to ourselves to save the world using theology as a means toward that end. This, in my view, leaves us in a hopeless position and truly without freedom because it is just our thinking that keeps us from allowing the actual righteousness of God manifested in Jesus Christ to enter the picture. We have also seen that John Hick's religious pluralism explicitly refuses to begin with Jesus' resurrection precisely because he thinks the doctrine of the incarnation is a myth or metaphor that we use to express our valuation of him as an important example of love and goodness in our world. Unlike Haight, Hick has no intention of maintaining any sort of uniqueness for Jesus Christ in the traditional sense because he sees him as one among many. But it is precisely in so doing that Hick undermines the truth of the Christian faith and offers in its place a rather overt form of self-justification in the form of a Christology that advocates little more than encouraging our human attempts to live the Golden Rule and get along with people in other religions who are attempting to do the same. This thinking, however, completely ignores the issue of truth by transforming the nature of religious truth from its proper ground within the immanent Trinity and thus within the incarnate and risen Lord to a ground within human religious consciousness and ethical practice universally accessible to humanity without faith in Jesus Christ himself. In spite of their differences, the thinking of Roger Haight and John Hick coincides in their adoptionist perspectives and in their subsequent espousal of a type of self-justification. In the end the real Jesus of the NT and classical Christian faith has been transformed into an ideal of human behavior they intend to espouse. In this fashion they have, in their own ways, wittingly and unwittingly made Jesus himself completely irrelevant to Christianity and thus undermined any possible true understanding of Christian freedom. These are instructive examples of what happens when theology does not in point of fact begin with Jesus himself as attested in the NT. They illustrate how important it is to recognize that, as T. F. Torrance insists, the resurrection and incarnation must be interpreted in light of each other because it is Jesus himself, God incarnate, who alone gives meaning to Christian faith and practice. Now let us move forward from these more universalist and overtly unsuccessful attempts at Christology to explore one of the most important and far more serious attempts to present the Christian faith as grounded in the risen Lord with a view toward seeing just how the connection between the resurrection and the incarnation plays itself out in the thinking of Wolfhart Pannenberg.

8. Incarnation and Resurrection in the Theology of Wolfhart Pannenberg

Without offering anything like a full treatment of Wolfhart Pannenberg's Christology, this chapter will explore how the thinking of this important representative of contemporary Christology about the resurrection and incarnation differs from the thinking of his teacher Karl Barth and what those differences might mean for a theology that attempts to hold the two doctrines together both theoretically and practically.

Two cautionary notes are in order before we begin. First, Pannenberg's theology is magisterial in nature and seeks to place Christ and therefore the Trinity in the center with a seriousness that is quite clearly lacking in some of the presentations already considered such as Gordon Kaufman, John Macquarrie, Sallie McFague, Roger Haight, John Hick and Paul Knitter, even though they, too, attempted to explain the resurrection and incarnation in their own ways. For that reason we must recognize that, unlike those theologians who are trying to water down Jesus' significance in a pluralist environment, Pannenberg cannot be considered within that same class in any sense at all. He clearly seeks to accord priority not only to revelation but to the Trinity and to the risen Lord himself with at least the same seriousness with which Barth, Torrance and Rahner did.

Second, while we might readily admit that Pannenberg's thinking has changed between the time of his writing *Jesus — God and Man* and his three-volume *Systematic Theology,* in this chapter I hope to show that, because his basic method as elaborated in his earlier writing was never abandoned, there remain in his thinking certain critical difficulties that will alert us to the importance of never separating, theoretically or practically, the doctrines of the resurrection and incarnation in their essential connection. While the emphasis between Pannenberg's early and later writings may have shifted from stressing the historical verifiability of the resurrection as the prolepsis of the end of history to seeing that the meaning of reality is given in "subjective anticipations" that must be validated intersubjectively,[1] still, in both instances, his Christology from below remains decisive and his view of the resurrection as determining Jesus' person remains determinative both for his Christology and for his doctrine of the Trinity. And while his later work does indeed attempt to offer a trinitarian theological perspective, certain methodological difficulties such as his unwillingness to begin theology in faith are still in evidence. I believe the chief reason for these difficulties is traceable to Pannenberg's desire to present an apologetic public theology that can be grasped without assenting to the authority of Christ as the Word incarnate at the outset. That would explain why, as opposed to Barth, he will not begin thinking about God with the reality of God acknowledged by faith but rather with the idea of the infinite as we shall see and as he himself contends in Volume 1 of his *Systematic Theology*. What I hope to accomplish then in this chapter is to offer a close reading of key points in *Jesus — God and Man*, explaining how and why Barth reacted to Pannenberg's thinking; then I intend to show how and why those issues are still with us today.

Pannenberg's Christology

Early in his career Pannenberg would not begin his Christology explicitly with Jesus himself as the Word of God incarnate and because of that he found himself opposed to Barth's method and conclusions in certain decisive ways. This is no small matter and cannot simply be glossed over since, as I have just indicated, Pannenberg did not abandon this methodology in his later work. If Barth is right, and I believe he is, and if Torrance is correct in following Barth on the important connection between the incarnation and resurrection, then there can be no other starting point for Christology or for the doctrine of the Trinity than Jesus himself as attested in the NT and as confessed at Nicaea and Chalcedon. Yet it is not simply a matter of Barth and Torrance opposing Pannenberg here; instead it is a matter of who Jesus was and is. Hence, the issue here concerns the truth of the Christian faith which is identical with Jesus himself as the Word of God incarnate. Because his uniqueness prescribes the nature of the theological task, contemporary theology cannot go behind the NT confessions in search of a historical Jesus or some historical set of circumstances that might form the foundation for Christology today without making Jesus himself superfluous in a very real sense and without then suggesting some form of self-justification as well. That will be the thesis that I will try to develop in this chapter by comparing Pannenberg with Barth and Torrance. Again, the issue here seems to be one of apologetics as Barth himself recognized long ago. Pannenberg wants to go behind the NT confessions in order to establish who Jesus was historically as a basis for confessing his divinity and thus as a basis for affirming the incarnation, and he believes that Jesus' human activity needs future confirmation to validate his earthly claims and activity. It is that attempt to go behind the NT confessions to verify who Jesus was that in and of itself undercuts his own desire to affirm and maintain Christ's uniqueness as the eternal Son of the Father.

We have already seen how John Macquarrie and Karl Rahner argue, in very different ways of course, that the incarnation cannot be presupposed in contemporary Christology but rather must be seen as the conclusion of one's christological inquiries. In fact, as noted above in Chapter Five, John Macquarrie explicitly appeals to Wolfhart Pannenberg's Christology "from below" with the assertion that the incarnation cannot be the starting point but can only be the conclusion of Christology in order to explicate his own view of the matter. Pannenberg's methodological assertion bears repeating here:

> Methodological reasons do not permit us to work in this way with the in- carnation as a theological presupposition. To do so would be to make the humanity of Jesus' life problematic from the very beginning. To be sure, all Christological considerations tend toward the idea of the incarnation; it can, however, only constitute the conclusion of Christology. If it is put in- stead at the beginning, all Christological concepts, including that of penal suffering, are given a mythological tone. (*Jesus — God and Man*, 279)[2]

And, as we noted there, Karl Barth offered a rather negative assessment of Pannenberg's Christology from below as expressed in his important book *Je- sus — God and Man* in a letter to him in 1964. It might be worth repeating Barth's objections so that the issues may be seen plainly. After noting that the method Pannenberg chose for his Christology separated them theologically Barth wrote:

> My first reaction on reading your book was one of horror when on the very first page I found you rejecting M. Kähler in a way which led me to suspect that, like others, you — and you with particular resolution and with an ori- entation toward a Jesus who may be found historically — intended to pur- sue a path from below to above. Obviously your intention did not offer you

occasion to reflect that our common friend H. Vogel stopped at his admittedly very substantial analysis of the below, and never gave us the second
part of his christology [H. Vogel, *Christologie*, vol. 1 (Munich, 1949)] which
was to deal with the above reached from the below. I wrestle in vain with
the question by what right you manage to rest the doctrine of the revelation of God enacted in Jesus, indeed the very existence and life of God and
Jesus' identity with him, on the basis of the figure of your historical Jesus
and his message and commitment to God, confirmed by his resurrection
from the dead — all of which is much weaker in substance than Vogel's historical Jesus. As Biedermann already saw and said [A. E. Biedermann,
1869], we know that the resurrection may be reduced historically to objective visions of the disciples and the brute fact of the empty tomb. Is not this
to build a house on the sand — the shifting sand of historical probabilities
moving one way yesterday and another today? And if you think you are not
dealing here with sand but with solid rock, does this not consist finally and
properly of Jewish apocalyptic, in whose context you think we can explain
both the pre-Easter Jesus and the risen Lord? Is it in the light of this that
you explain the recognition and acknowledgment of a general ordination
of man to a being that transcends his life and death? In its positive content
is your christology — after the practice of so many modern fathers — anything other than the outstanding example and symbol of a presupposed
general anthropology, cosmology, and ontology?[3]

This lengthy quote raises a number of issues that, in my view, decisively show
how and why Pannenberg's interpretation of the resurrection is linked with
his Christology from below and ultimately shapes his view of the incarnation
and of the Trinity. Pannenberg's thinking is extremely popular today and
while he has attempted to offer a more trinitarian account of Christology in
his *Systematic Theology* there can be little doubt that key elements of his
Christology and trinitarian theology are every bit as problematic as Barth
suspected over forty years ago. Of course, Pannenberg never did intend his
Christology from below to stand without some version of the above or he
never would have insisted from early on that some idea of the incarnation
must follow from Christology from below. And while he did finally offer a
type of Christology from above to complement his Christology from below in
his *Systematic Theology,* his methodological commitment to Christology
from below, as we have already noted, was never abandoned and so the difficulties that arose in connection with *Jesus — God and Man* remain in evidence in his later work as well.

By seeing how Christology from below, even one that emphasizes the importance of Jesus' resurrection as Pannenberg actually does, correlates the incarnation and resurrection, it is hoped that the thesis of this book will become clearer: Christology must begin with Jesus himself as the Word of God incarnate and therefore in faith. The starting point for Christology therefore cannot be the early church's experience of Jesus or its ideas about Jesus; and the starting point cannot be history either, if it is thought that we can or must go behind the faith of the NT to a historical Jesus who in any sense (theoretically or practically) is not yet the eternal Word who was with God and who was God from all eternity. It is the fact that Pannenberg thinks Jesus' history needs confirmation that gives his Christology the appearance of the adoptionism he clearly and explicit rejects.[4] And it is his refusal to begin his theology in faith because of his fear of authoritarianism and subjectivism that forces him to look to history rather than to the incarnate Word and to the Holy Spirit (as the one who enables faith) to validate his Christology.

Christological Issues

Returning then to the issues raised in Barth's letter, we may note the following points that will be developed and discussed in this chapter. First, Pannenberg explicitly rejects what he calls "Christology from above" in order to pursue his Christology from below.[5] And he therefore explicitly rejects Barth's idea that Christology must begin from the man Jesus who was God incarnate (*Jesus — God and Man*, 33ff.).[6] For Pannenberg,

> A Christology from above presupposes the divinity of Jesus. The most important task of Christology is, however, precisely to present the reasons for the confession of Jesus' divinity. Instead of presupposing it, we must first inquire about how Jesus' appearance in history led to the recognition of his divinity. (*Jesus — God and Man*, 34)[7]

Further, Pannenberg believes that in a Christology from above "the historical man Jesus in his historical singularity does not come properly into view" (*Jesus — God and Man*, 35). And finally, according to Pannenberg, if we were to pursue Christology from above then we "would have to stand in the position of God himself in order to follow the way of God's Son into the world" (*Jesus — God and Man*, 35). Since it is impossible to escape our historical context which is determined by our human situation we are unable to overcome this limitation. As we have been seeing in this book, one's starting point for Christology is a most decisive issue — so decisive in fact that the decisions made at this point form one's view not only of the incarnation but of the resurrection, the Trinity and ultimately of ethics itself. Here the question quite obviously is whether one actually can explain how Jesus' historical appearance led to the recognition of his divinity without actually displacing the miraculous action of the Holy Spirit in the process. In addition, if Christology *can* give reasons for confessing Jesus' divinity then the crucial question becomes why anyone would actually *need* Jesus himself who, because he really is divine can only be the starting point for one's reflections.

Second, Pannenberg then argues that

> The confession of Christ cannot be presupposed already and simply inter-preted. Christology cannot take its point of departure from the confessions of the Reformation . . . or from the Christological formula of the Council of Chalcedon, nor can it simply develop the oldest primitive Christian con-fession, the sentence *Iēsous (Christos) Kyrios* ("Jesus is Lord," Rom. 1:4; 10:9; I Cor. 12:3). This confession itself must be grounded by Christology. (*Jesus — God and Man,* 28-29)

And yet it is just here that Paul insisted that no one can say Jesus is Lord ex-cept by the Holy Spirit so that if Paul's statement is true, then the ultimate ground of our confession of Jesus' Lordship is not something that can be proven historically as Pannenberg thinks (it cannot be grounded by Christol-ogy), but is in reality established as a miracle, namely, as an act of the Holy Spirit. The Holy Spirit is noticeably absent from Pannenberg's reflections on this particular issue.

Third, Pannenberg insists that it is only the historical Jesus who can and must be discerned by going behind the Gospel confessions that is the founda-tion for Christology:

> dogmatic Christology must go behind the New Testament to the base to which it points and which supports faith in Jesus, that is, to the history of Jesus. Christology has to ask and show the extent to which this history sub-stantiates faith in Jesus. (*Jesus — God and Man,* 29)

And he insists that this historical Jesus must be seen within the context of Jewish apocalyptic in such a way that it is this context that actually explains who he is and the meaning of his resurrection (see *Jesus — God and Man,* 32f.).

We have already seen that T. F. Torrance objected to this interpretation of the resurrection above because such interpretation failed to acknowledge that what happened in Jesus' resurrection was *utterly new* and *inexplicable* from any prior knowledge or experience, Jewish or other. And of course Barth's objection in his letter to Pannenberg is based on the fact that what happened in Jesus was offensive to his contemporaries and to us precisely because it is its own explanation: "this was not a self-evident truth [for the disciples], nor a discovery of their own, but a conviction that went utterly against the grain" (*CD* III/2, 449). In other words, as Torrance insists, the incarnation and resurrection are *ultimates* that carry their meaning in themselves and can only be known out of themselves.[8] If that is correct, and I think it is, then to suppose, even momentarily, that there is a Jesus behind the confessions is to embrace immediately, albeit perhaps inadvertently, some sort of Nestorian separation of the two natures so that any attempt to reunite them will inevitably be grounded in a view of history, apocalyptic, anthropology or theology. The determining element in one's thought will no longer be Jesus in his actual uniqueness. This is especially problematic when coupled with Pannenberg's idea that Jesus' resurrection *retroactively* decides not only our knowledge that Jesus is the Son of God, but that he *was* the Son of God on the level of being.

No doubt Pannenberg is inconsistent here. On the one hand he claims that because only the future will decide who or what a person is:

> To that extent it is not a special case that Jesus' essence is established retroactively from the perspective of the end of his life, from his resurrection, not only for our knowledge but in its being . . . through his resurrection it is decided, *not only so far as our knowledge is concerned, but with respect to reality,* that Jesus is one with God and retroactively that he was also already one with God previously. (*Jesus — God and Man*, 136; emphasis mine)

It is important to note here once again that, despite claims that Pannenberg later changed his views as offered in his earlier work, *Jesus — God and Man*, his statements in Volume 2 of his *Systematic Theology* seem very close indeed to what he just said. Hence, Pannenberg explains that Jesus' earthly claims are confirmed by his resurrection. But for him this means that

> Confirmation is more than disclosure of a meaning that the person and history of Jesus already had on his way to the cross, so that it was his even without the Easter event, though in hidden form. The Easter event certainly shed a new light on the death of Jesus, on his earthly ministry, and therefore on his person. But that does not mean that even without the event of the resurrection these would have been what they are when seen in this light. We depreciate the Easter event if we construe it only as a disclo-

sure or revelation of the meaning that the crucifixion and the earthly history of Jesus already had in themselves. Only the Easter event determines
what the meaning was of the pre-Easter history of Jesus and who he was in
his relation to God. (*Systematic Theology,* 2: 345)

On the other hand, Pannenberg seems to modify this view by agreeing with
Jürgen Moltmann's statement that "Whereas Jesus is not recognizable as the
Son of God until his death on the cross and his resurrection, in the order of
being he is the Son of God before his history takes place" (Moltmann, *The
Crucified God,* cited in *Jesus — God and Man,* 405). Does this imply that Jesus'
resurrection simply enables us to know the truth of who Jesus always was?
And if that is what he is saying, how does this square with his previously
stated belief that the resurrection decides who Jesus was and establishes his
essence not only for our knowledge (noetically) but also with respect to reality (ontologically)?

Pannenberg explains the matter by saying that we perceive Jesus' "eternal
Sonship as dialectically identical with his humanity" and that this is "based
noetically upon the particularity of just this human being in his relation to
the divine Father" (*Jesus — God and Man,* 337). Pannenberg adds, of course,
that ontologically "the divine Sonship designates the ontological root in
which Jesus' human existence, connected with the Father and nevertheless
distinguished from him, has the ground of its unity and of its meaning" (*Jesus
— God and Man,* 337). This rather vague statement of Jesus' divinity is repeated in his later work when Pannenberg says of Jesus' Sonship that it

precedes his historical existence on earth and must be regarded as the creative basis of his human existence. If the human history of Jesus is the revelation of his eternal sonship, we must be able to perceive the latter in the reality of the human life. The deity is not an addition to this reality. It is the
reflection that the human relation of Jesus to God the Father casts on his
existence, even as it also illumines the eternal being of God. (*Systematic
Theology,* 2: 325)[9]

What is missing here is a clear statement of the distinction in unity of Jesus'
humanity and divinity, a statement that is difficult for Pannenberg to make
because of his aversion to the Chalcedonian position. And the problem is
methodological. Because Pannenberg is unwilling to begin with the incarnate
Word, he is unable to allow the Word of God to be the subject of the events of
incarnation or of revelation in any decisive way. Rather, incarnation and revelation for Pannenberg result from our placing the events of Jesus' life into

their proper historical context and then drawing the only possible conclusion with the idea of the incarnation developed in light of the event of the resurrection. Serious questions however remain: Is our knowledge of Jesus' Sonship really attained in this way? Does this not eliminate the need for a present action of the Holy Spirit to disclose his being and action to us?[10] Does this not obscure the fact that, as the living Lord, Jesus himself, the Word incarnate speaks to us now and enlightens us through his Spirit about who he is and what his significance is within our history? To argue that our perception of Jesus' eternal Sonship is based on his human relation to the Father is, in my view, to undercut the fact we need to learn of Jesus' Sonship from God himself in his present actions in his Word and Spirit and thus through faith.

Yet there is another question that must be considered: if Jesus really was one with God previously, as Pannenberg claims, then how and why would he begin his thinking about Jesus as a mere man with his assertion noted above that he would "inquire about how Jesus' appearance in history led to the recognition of his divinity"? That very starting point conflicts with the assertion that Jesus was already "one" with God previously. Further, why then would Pannenberg insist that Jesus "was not only unrecognizable before Easter, but he would not have been who he was without the Easter event" (*Jesus — God and Man*, 137)? Why would he say that

> Apart from Jesus' resurrection, it would not be true that from the very beginning of his earthly way God was one with this man. That is true from all eternity *because* of Jesus' resurrection. Until his resurrection, Jesus' unity with God was hidden not only to other men but above all . . . for Jesus himself also. (*Jesus — God and Man*, 321; emphasis in original)

And note, too, Pannenberg's talk of Jesus' oneness or unity with God — is it a oneness or unity in being that exists prior to creation and prior to his historical existence? And if not, to what extent does Pannenberg really believe that Jesus, as Son of the Father is one in *being* with the Father from all eternity? These are important questions because Pannenberg's historical approach to these doctrines leaves little room for real divine action. For instance while Barth quite properly argued that only the risen Lord acting miraculously in his Spirit can enable us to grasp Christ's divinity as well as the meaning of the incarnation and resurrection in their essential unity, Pannenberg claims that the basis for statements about Jesus' divinity is an integrated view of the end along with Jesus' fate. The possibility for understanding then comes not from an act of the risen Lord himself through faith and in the power of his Holy Spirit, but from the way in which we integrate certain events recounted in scripture.

Only an integrated view of the Easter event together with the coming end, a view originally based on the expectation of the eschatological imminent end, made it possible to understand Jesus' activity and fate as God's revelation. (*Jesus — God and Man*, 185)

No, what made it possible to understand Jesus' activity and "fate" as God's revelation was the revealer himself speaking his Word through the power of the Holy Spirit and thus through the witnesses to these events.[11]

Fourth, Pannenberg thus begins his Christology from below asserting that one cannot simply relate the title *Christos* to the divinity of Jesus but rather one must discover "how this man is God. This involves the legitimacy of the transformation in the understanding of Jesus that took place in the transition from the Jewish into the Gentile sphere of tradition" (*Jesus — God and Man*, 31f.). Given this last point, it is not at all surprising that Barth would have reacted to Pannenberg's Christology with horror since Barth himself had identified that very starting point and view of the task of Christology as Ebionite or Docetic in orientation and design quite early in his *Church Dogmatics*.[12] This is no small issue today.

In *CD* I/1, Barth begins by noting that "What God reveals in Jesus and how He reveals it, namely, in Jesus, must not be separated from one another according to the New Testament" (*CD* I/1, 399). Without denying Jesus' distinction from the Father, Barth considers "the unity of the Son with the Father attested . . . and therefore the deity of Jesus Christ . . . as definitive, authentic and essential" (*CD* I/1, 400). For this reason and unlike Bultmann in his book *Jesus*, Barth insists that we cannot understand the Jesus of the New Testament one-sidedly by focusing only on his sayings and excluding his miraculous actions. Both must be seen together as is evidenced in Mk. 2:1-12 in the story of the paralytic. If the two are seen together, then Jesus will be acknowledged in his essential and authentic deity as the eternally begotten Son of the Father. Thus, for Barth,

The New Testament statement about the unity of the Son with the Father, i.e., the deity of Christ, cannot possibly be understood in terms of the presupposition that the original view and declaration of the New Testament witnesses was that a human being was either exalted as such to deity or appeared among us as the personification and symbol of a divine being. (*CD* I/1, 402)

This statement is a direct rejection of the manner in which M. Dibelius formulated the problem of New Testament Christology, that is, "as the way in which 'knowledge of the historical figure of Jesus was so quickly transformed into faith in a heavenly Son of God'" (*CD* I/1, 402). Barth rejects this thinking because it leads to a blind alley; it leads to modern historical versions of what he calls Ebionite and Docetic Christology. It leads to the idea that there really was a historical Jesus who was "transformed" into the Son of God on the basis of the community's reaction to him (Ebionite Christology) and it leads to the idea that the historical Jesus can be discerned because of some prior understanding of God that is seen to be fulfilled in him (Docetic Christology). Barth insists that we must begin with Jesus who *was* God incarnate simply because he was. And if we think that we must establish his divinity through Christology as Pannenberg clearly does then we have already discounted his authentic divinity and have begun traveling down the road of Ebionite and Docetic Christology, a road that leads to a dead end.[13]

Fifth, Barth objected to Pannenberg's attempt to understand Jesus' humanity, with Rahner, in the context of a "general ordination of man to a being that transcends his life and death." This is an extremely important point. Pannenberg believes that humanity has a certain *obediential potency* for God and that somehow our knowledge of God must be related to and even judged by the God of Philosophy.[14] This is why Pannenberg insists that Jesus' humanity is a particular instance of what happens generally within anthropology. This is the motor that runs his belief that it is only through future confirmation of events that they become what they are. And this thinking is what leads to Pannenberg's assertion that the resurrection not only discloses Jesus' eternal Sonship but in a real sense constitutes it. But it is just this thinking that claims too much for humanity marked by sin because it assumes that, since the fall, humanity is in some sense open for God when in fact, from Barth's perspective, humanity is closed to God and must become open through the miraculous action of the Holy Spirit. We shall return to this thought later in our discussion of the ethical implications of Pannenberg's Christology.

These then are the decisive differences between Barth and Pannenberg that Barth expressed in his letter to Pannenberg in 1964. And they are still decisive differences today that affect all aspects of theology precisely because Pannenberg honestly believes the task of Christology is to prove from history the uniqueness of Jesus as the incarnate Lord, while Barth thinks that no such proof from history is possible or necessary because the proof itself is and remains an *act* of God actually entering history from outside. But let us not suppose that I am simply saying that Pannenberg is mistaken because he does not agree with Barth. That would completely misunderstand my intentions. I am saying that the truth recognized by Barth is decisive and must be maintained in any serious Christology because it is a truth that is identical with the being and activity of the triune God himself. There is something really true about the Christian faith which Barth recognized and which I think we cannot discard if we are to speak seriously about the meaning of Christ's incarnation and resurrection in their essential unity.

At the beginning of this book and throughout I have followed David Fergusson's categories of radical, liberal and traditional to explore how contemporary theologians understand the resurrection and then to see how their views were shaped by a strong or weak doctrine of the incarnation and of the doctrine of the immanent Trinity. I then briefly indicated that wherever Christ's uniqueness is not acknowledged as the starting point for reflection on the resurrection, this led to some form of self-justification — sometimes overt and other times rather subtle. How does Pannenberg's thinking fit within these categories? First, Pannenberg certainly rejects the radical view of the resurrection because he most definitely does not want to reduce the Easter event to the rise of faith on the part of the disciples. Second, Pannenberg does not exactly hold to the liberal view either to the extent that he does not ground the resurrection in the disciples' experiences of faith. Third, yet Pannenberg does not quite hold to the traditional view because while he does say the resurrection was an event in the life of Jesus, he does not believe that it is the risen Lord *alone* who gives meaning to faith. Instead he contends that the historical event of the resurrection, when placed within its proper eschatological context, gives meaning to faith.

So, Pannenberg holds what could be deemed a hybrid of the liberal and traditional views because on the one hand it is not the risen Lord himself, but the community's experience of him in history, that gives meaning to faith and on the other hand, he insists that the resurrection was a historical event in a very real sense and that it cannot therefore be reduced to something merely subjective. Nonetheless, to the extent that Pannenberg can be said to embrace a liberal view of the resurrection at all, his thinking finally reduces the resurrection to a principle that is then used to substantiate all aspects of Christology and theology. I hope to show that this problem arises exactly because Pannenberg refuses to hold the resurrection and incarnation together at the start of his Christology; instead he separates them methodologically and then tries to reunite them on the basis of his analysis of history. Let us briefly explore exactly how Pannenberg understands the resurrection and then see what view of the incarnation and of the Trinity underlies this.

Pannenberg's View of the Resurrection

What was the original significance of the resurrection for Pannenberg? He believes the earthly Jesus most likely did not expect "a privately experienced resurrection" but "the imminent universal resurrection" so that when he did appear to his disciples they perceived that appearance as the start of the universal resurrection of the dead and the end of history. It was only with the second generation of NT witnesses (Mark, Matthew, Luke, John and the authors of the Deutero-Pauline epistles and of Hebrews) that the resurrection was understood as a "special event that happened to Jesus alone" (*Jesus — God and Man*, 66). The significance inherent in Jesus' resurrection, according to Pannenberg, from within "the horizon of the apocalyptic expectation for the future" was that "the resurrection did not first need to be interpreted, but for them it spoke meaningfully in itself: If such a thing happened, one could no longer doubt what it meant" (*Jesus — God and Man*, 67).[15] What then did it mean?

It meant several things. (1) The end of the world had begun so that the same Spirit who raised Jesus from the dead now dwelt in Christians. The word "Spirit" "designated nothing else than the presence of the resurrection life in the Christians" (*Jesus — God and Man*, 67). (2) For a Jew this could only mean *"that God himself has confirmed the pre-Easter activity of Jesus"* (*Jesus — God and Man*, 67; emphasis in original). (3) Through his resurrection Jesus was so closely connected with the Son of Man that he was then seen as the Son of Man. While the pre-Easter Jesus proclaimed "a correspondence in function between his own attitude toward men and the future attitude of the Son of man" so that there was a distinction between the man Jesus who visibly walked the earth and the Son of Man who would come on the clouds of heaven in the future, this distinction disappeared with the resurrection. "As the one who has been taken away to God, Jesus is a heavenly being." Hence, "By virtue of the resurrection, Jesus had moved into the role of the Son of Man" (*Jesus — God and Man*, 68-69). (4) If Jesus has been raised and ascended, then the end has begun and God would be ultimately revealed in Jesus: "Only because the end of the world is already present in Jesus' resurrection is God himself revealed in him" (*Jesus — God and Man*, 69). According to Pannenberg, translating these apocalyptic ideas into Hellenistic conceptuality means "in Jesus, God himself has appeared on earth. God himself — or God's revelatory figure, the Logos, the Son — has been among us as a man in the figure of Jesus." Consequently "This Hellenistic concept of revelation prepared the basic pattern for the subsequent doctrine of the incarnation" (*Jesus — God and*

Man, 69). This may also have been the path to the "thesis of the true divinity of Jesus" since "Jesus' divinity is already implied in some way in the conception of God's appearance in him, even though not with the later orthodox precision" (*Jesus — God and Man,* 69). (5) The transition to the Gentile mission was motivated by the resurrection; Jesus' message was the starting point. (6) The community's presentation of the words of the risen Jesus must be understood in content as the explication of the significance inherent in the resurrection itself so that Paul's Gospel is the exegesis of the appearances of the risen Jesus he experienced. What then was it that happened at the resurrection?

According to Pannenberg, it was not just a random miracle but something very particular "expected by postexilic Judaism in connection with the end of history" (*Jesus — God and Man,* 74). In essence it is a metaphorical way of speaking about "an event that is still hidden to us in its true essence" (*Jesus — God and Man,* 75).[16] According to Pannenberg, Paul got his information regarding Jesus' resurrection from the tradition of expectation in which he stood, and not just from Jesus' appearances: "Thus Paul did not arrive at his concept of the resurrection as transformation for the first time because of the impression made by his encounter with the risen Jesus" (*Jesus — God and Man,* 81). Accordingly, "Only the traditional expectation of the end of history rooted in apocalyptic gave Paul the opportunity of designating the particular event that he experienced . . . as an event belonging to the category of resurrection life" (*Jesus — God and Man,* 81). Therefore, in Pannenberg's view, Paul's "presupposition" for recognizing Jesus' resurrection was "the expectation of a resurrection of the dead." So, Pannenberg interprets Paul's statement in 1 Cor. 15:16 that "If the dead are not raised, then Christ has not been raised" as the precondition for grasping Christ's particular resurrection from the dead, and he argues: "Admittedly, the general concept of the resurrection cannot altogether be established from Jesus' resurrection alone" (*Jesus — God and Man,* 81).[17] Hence, the key to interpreting Jesus' resurrection and indeed the starting point for doing so is a prior expectation that can be established anthropologically:

> The expectation of resurrection must already be presupposed as a truth that is given by tradition or anthropologically or is established philosophically when one speaks about Jesus' resurrection. That this expectation has already become an event in Jesus can strengthen ex post facto the truth of the expectation, but cannot establish it for the first time. To be sure, only Jesus' resurrection guarantees to the individual his own future participation in salvation. (*Jesus — God and Man,* 81)

Here is where Barth and Torrance on the one side and Pannenberg and Rahner on the other are separated theologically. And not just Barth and Torrance and Pannenberg and Rahner, because I believe that Barth himself recognized a genuine truth, namely, that unless the *risen Lord himself* is the starting point for Christology, then Christology will be grounded in something other than Jesus, thereby stripping him of his essential Lordship and subjectivity at the outset. This, in my view, is in keeping with Paul's statement in 1 Cor. 15:14 that "if Christ has not been raised, then our preaching is without substance, and so is your faith." And certainly this is in accord with 1 Pet. 1:3: "Blessed be God the Father of our Lord Jesus Christ, who in his great mercy has given us a new birth into a living hope through the resurrection of Jesus Christ from the dead." It is the particular resurrection of Jesus Christ that gives meaning to faith and hope and not some generally demonstrable anthropological expectation. Thus, while Pannenberg here begins his interpretation of the resurrection with an anthropologically demonstrable horizon of expectation found within Judaism in the first instance, he is compelled to argue that that which gives meaning to Christ's resurrection is not exclusively Jesus himself risen from the dead, but a generally and even historically demonstrable apocalyptic horizon within which Jesus' resurrection is then given meaning by us.[18] While Pannenberg certainly insists that only Jesus' resurrection can guarantee individual salvation, this assertion is void of force precisely because of his prior claim that expectation of resurrection and not Jesus' own unique resurrection is the basis for affirming the meaning of Christ's resurrection.

This difference of starting points highlights the theme of this book. I believe Barth and Torrance are faithful to the NT insistence that it is the incarnate Lord *alone* who gives meaning to faith at all times and places. It was the risen Lord himself who enabled the faith of the disciples in his encounter with them during the forty days. This was not just a metaphorical way of speaking about a set of resurrection visions as Pannenberg thinks. And it was not in any way anticipated philosophically or theologically by any prior expectation.[19] It was something that happened in conflict with all previous knowledge and experience. It was a way of depicting the miraculous fact that Jesus alone, as the only man who was and is God incarnate, is the criterion for the truth of all theological reflection. Just as the earthly Jesus' authority is traced by Barth and Torrance to the fact that Jesus is himself the incarnate Word, so they believe that the risen Lord alone can be the starting point and criterion for dogmatic theology itself. But of course in their thinking this means that one cannot separate the incarnation and resurrection even for an instant without distorting the message of the NT and without negating the truth of Christology itself. It is in this rather subtle way that Pannenberg's thinking can be seen to fit within what David Fergusson labeled the liberal interpretation of the resurrection — instead of allowing the risen Lord himself to be his starting point, Pannenberg starts with the experience of apocalyptic expectation. In any case it is this starting point that leads Pannenberg to assert that "the primitive Christian motivation for faith in Jesus as the Christ of God, in his exaltation, in his identification with the Son of Man, is essentially bound to the apocalyptic expectation for the end of history" (*Jesus — God and Man*, 82) and

> Why the man Jesus can be the ultimate revelation of God, why in him and only in him God is supposed to have appeared, remains incomprehensible apart from the horizon of the apocalyptic expectation. . . . If this horizon is eliminated, the basis of faith is lost; then Christology becomes mythology and no longer has true continuity with Jesus himself and with the witness of the apostles. (*Jesus — God and Man*, 83)

Notice that the basis for faith here is the horizon of apocalyptic expectation and not the risen Jesus himself. And for Pannenberg the continuity with Jesus and the apostolic witness is not provided by the risen Lord himself speaking his Word through the apostolic witness in the power of his Spirit; it is instead the horizon of apocalyptic expectation. My suggestion is that this difficulty arises in Pannenberg's thought exactly because he did not hold the doctrines of the incarnation and resurrection together in the way that Barth and Torrance did and so his very method compelled him to base faith on an apocalyptic horizon rather than on the incarnate and risen Word of God.

The Nature of the Resurrection Event

Pannenberg thinks the resurrection is a historical event explaining that, if that were not so, then we would not be justified in believing that it actually happened. Our certainty that the resurrection is a historical event nonetheless does not stem from faith but only from "historical research, to the extent that certainty can be attained at all about questions of this kind" (*Jesus — God and Man*, 99). He insists that the risen Lord only could be designated by an extraordinary mode of experience, the vision, and only in metaphorical language (*Jesus — God and Man*, 99).[20] Using Paul's experience as analogy, Pannenberg asserts that all the witnesses "recognized Jesus of Nazareth in the appearance."[21] But the appearances could only be explained, according to

Pannenberg, "from the presupposition of a particular form of the apocalyptic expectation of the resurrection of the dead" (*Jesus — God and Man*, 93). The character of this event

> may have involved an extraordinary vision, not an event that was visible to everyone. . . . If someone sees something that others present are not able to see, then it involves a vision. . . . It involves extraordinary sights that were not imparted to all and also (in any event in the case of Paul) were not perceived by all present. (*Jesus — God and Man*, 93)

Pannenberg insists that this does not mean that what was experienced was therefore purely imaginary contending that "The Easter appearances are not to be explained from the Easter faith of the disciples; rather, conversely, the Easter faith of the disciples is to be explained from the appearances" (*Jesus — God and Man*, 96). So what about the appearances?

They are real, but must be described metaphorically. Jesus' resurrection is a historical event then in the sense that it can be understood "in the light of the eschatological hope for a resurrection from the dead" (*Jesus — God and Man*, 98). Because the risen Lord is not "perceptible as one object among others in this world; therefore, he could only be experienced and designated by an extraordinary mode of experience, the vision, and only in metaphorical language" (*Jesus — God and Man*, 99). And while Pannenberg admits that the resurrection cannot be seen as an isolated event, this leads him to think "It must be understood in the context of the Jewish expectation and above all of the appearance of Jesus on earth" (*Jesus — God and Man*, 111).[22] This is how Jesus made himself known in a very definite time and place and under definite historical circumstances. But it is to be noted that the way Pannenberg thinks the risen Lord makes himself known is not as the *subject* of the events of incarnation and resurrection but as the one who is identified by the community by means of its historical investigations relying on the horizon of apocalyptic expectation. This is why Pannenberg claims that it is only figuratively possible to say that God speaks (*Jesus — God and Man*, 167) while Barth insists that this is not to be understood metaphorically or figuratively but in a strictly realistic sense.[23]

What about the empty tomb? Pannenberg thinks that the fact that both Jewish polemic and Christian opponents agreed that Christ's tomb was empty offers strong historical support to the fact of the empty tomb.[24] He believes that the proclamation of Jesus' resurrection in Jerusalem presupposes the empty tomb, and he stresses that even if Mark's account of the empty tomb should prove to be legendary, the weight of the arguments presented there would remain (*Jesus — God and Man*, 101). Because the empty tomb tradition and the appearance tradition developed independently and yet also complement each other, Pannenberg believes that "they let the assertion of the reality of Jesus' resurrection, in the sense explained above, appear as historically very probable, and that always means in historical inquiry that it is to be presupposed until contrary evidence appears" (*Jesus — God and Man*, 105).

The Function of the Resurrection for Pannenberg

Pannenberg distinguishes his Christology from below from other such approaches by stressing that "Jesus' resurrection is the basis for the perception of his divinity" (*Jesus — God and Man*, 108). It "means above all God's revelation in him." Hence, he contests Werner Elert's attempt to base Jesus' divinity on his "Pre-Easter" claim to be the Son of God; this, in Pannenberg's reckoning, would undermine the fact that "only Jesus' resurrection has become the basis of faith in Christ" (*Jesus — God and Man*, 108). Elert's view calls into question the fact that Jesus' death brought the validity of his claims to authority into question. Following his own peculiar historical approach to theology Pannenberg insists that such an approach "always takes place from an already given context of meaning, out of a preunderstanding of the object of inquiry" which is then corrected in the process of research (*Jesus — God and Man*, 109).

But therein lies the predicament of Pannenberg's approach to both the incarnation and the resurrection. According to Barth and Torrance what happened in those events is utterly unique and cannot be compared to any events before or after precisely because Jesus himself is unique as true God and true man. The events of incarnation and resurrection must be understood from the risen Lord alone because of the unique nature of the incarnate Word himself. That is why both Barth and Torrance unequivocally reject any *a priori* attempt to integrate incarnation and resurrection into some prior historical, theological or other context. This would amount to a denial of Jesus' actual Lordship as the subject of the incarnation and as the living Lord acting in unison with the Holy Spirit after his resurrection.[25] It also would mean that knowledge of God, like knowledge of Christ, is something that can be accomplished through historical research without actually depending on a present revelation of Christ himself through the Holy Spirit as an act of God himself.[26] Pannenberg insists that if "historical study declares itself unable to establish what 'really' happened on Easter, then all the more, faith is not able to do so; for faith cannot ascertain anything certain about events of the past that would perhaps be inaccessible to the historian" (*Jesus — God and Man,* 109).[27] This reasoning unfortunately places history above theology since what is discovered theologically in Jesus' resurrection by definition cannot be established by means of historical study. It is in this vein that Pannenberg believes that knowledge, in the prophetic tradition, means that present claims must be confirmed or verified by future events. Hence, Jesus' whole pre-Easter appearance depended upon "a confirmation by God himself in the beginning of the end of history," namely, in the resurrection of Jesus (*Jesus — God and Man,* 112). There is an enormous difference between the views of Pannenberg and Barth here. Barth insists that

> It was because God Himself, the Creator, who was first hidden in the lowliness of this creature, in the death of this man, was now manifested in His resurrection, that it was absolutely necessary for this event genuinely and apprehensibly to include nature, and therefore to be physical. This was the mystery before which the apostolic community could adore. It was not interested in any resurrection or actuality of resurrection in general, but in the resurrection of this man, and the resurrection of all men inaugurated by it. (*CD* III/2, 451)

Since Barth never detaches the incarnation from the resurrection but sees them as intrinsically connected from the outset, he will not say that who Jesus was before Easter depended upon some future event that would confirm this; instead he argued that God himself was incarnate in Jesus and therefore the resurrection manifested who Jesus was as the incarnate Word.[28] This, of course, is the proper view of the matter that I have adopted in this book because it respects Jesus' uniqueness materially and methodologically. With this insight in place, we now must consider Pannenberg's understanding of the incarnation.

Pannenberg on the Incarnation

Pannenberg's Christology from below shapes his view of the incarnation in a way that leaves him open to the charge of adoptionism which he makes every effort to avoid theoretically but cannot actually escape conceptually; it causes him to present a view of the Trinity which obscures God's freedom rather than clarifying it.[29] The key differences between Pannenberg and Barth over such issues as the virgin birth, two-stage Christology, the *logos asarkos* and divine subjectivity will illuminate some of the differences and show why it is so important to hold together the doctrines of the incarnation and resurrection in a way that Pannenberg cannot because of his starting point.

As noted above Pannenberg's starting point for Christology is "the man Jesus" (*Jesus — God and Man,* 186). He deliberately contrasts his starting point with what he regards as the mythological starting point which, in his mind, is the basis of Christology from above:

> While myth conceives a prototypal, divine reality as the origin of every-thing earthly and human, Christology finds God *in* the man Jesus. Where mythical thought focuses on the relation of the deity to man and to the world, this corresponds to its structure of thinking from the perspective of the prototypal divine, from 'above' to 'below.' (*Jesus — God and Man,* 186; emphasis in original)

According to Pannenberg "primitive Christianity" did not make a sharp dis-tinction here as he thinks we must today and so they unashamedly spoke of the pre-existent Son of God coming into the world. But Pannenberg insists that even such statements are in reality intended to "unfold the significance of what happened in the earthly history of Jesus. Even they have their begin-ning in historical occurrences" (*Jesus — God and Man,* 186). And so the idea of incarnation, according to Pannenberg, was the inescapable *conclusion* in a line of thought from the appearance of the historical Jesus to his resurrection.

But here we face fundamental questions. We may freely admit that the early church's statement of Jesus' pre-existence began with the historical oc-currences in Jesus' life history as Pannenberg says, but can we thereby suppose that the origin of their truth is historically defined? Put another way, if Jesus really is the Word of God incarnate, then is it possible to say that the initial significance of the incarnation is to be found in the history of Jesus? Is it not to be found in the fact, confessed by faith, that Jesus is antecedently God in himself so that, with Barth, we must admit theoretically and practically that it is his antecedent existence that creates revelation and not revelation that cre-ates his existence? The matter may be simply expressed as follows:

> [W]e have to accept the simple presupposition on which the New Testa-ment statement rests, namely, that Jesus Christ is the Son because He is (not because He makes this impression on us, not because He does what we think is to be expected of a God, but because He is). With this presup-position all thinking about Jesus, which means at once all thinking about God, must begin and end. (*CD* I/1, 415)

For Barth it is impossible to consider the historical Jesus, even momentarily, from within the NT faith as anyone other than who he was, namely, the Word of God incarnate. This is the statement conveyed by the witness of John and Paul and it cannot be played off against statements offered in the Synoptics. There is a delicacy of detail here that must be clarified. On the one hand Barth stresses, as does Pannenberg, that the Synoptics start with the fact that the man Jesus (the carpenter's son) "shows Himself in His resurrection from the dead to be the Messiah and the Son of God" (*CD* I/2, 22). In light of that they look back and interpret his life, actions and sayings. In that sense they start from his human life before the resurrection. According to John's Gospel, "the great mystery is that God assumed humanity in Jesus" (*CD* I/2, 22). Barth contends, however, that "This pointing out, or discovery, or revelation, of the Son of God in the Jesus of Nazareth who appears first as one man with all other men, is the decisive presupposition from which the Evangelists (as witnesses of the resurrection) always start" (*CD* I/2, 22). It is the solution which they always seek to attest and proclaim. For Barth the problem before them is the humanity of Jesus; the solution is his divinity. In Barth's estimation,

> The content of this New Testament witness is the message of the resurrection and ascension which runs through all the Gospels and Epistles and is the mainstay of everything. He who died on the cross and thereby clearly showed Himself to be a man, He who completed His incarnation on the cross and was thereby veiled in His divinity, rose again the third day from the dead, and sits on the right hand of the Father — was exalted from the earth, went to the Father, as the Fourth Gospel puts it — that is the solution of the problem of Jesus, to which even the miracles could only point as Messianic signs. *It belongs to the incarnation itself as a mighty counterpart to it — the decisive contradiction to any ebionite Christology.* (*CD* I/2, 23; emphasis mine)

Put simply, it is because the man Jesus who rose from the dead was God incarnate that his life, death and resurrection was not only utterly unique but was the very act of God's salvation among us. The NT confession "made the definite claim that in Him alone, for the first time, and fully, they had found the Godhead" (*CD* I/2, 18).

But unless the miracle of the incarnation preceded Jesus' resurrection from the dead, some form of adoptionism will be implied and the ground will be pulled out from under the witness of the NT and from the saving significance of Jesus' human life on earth. Barth therefore insists that it is in the nature of the case that no proof of the fact that the risen Christ is the divine Son can be offered, "except in the form of an exposition of Jesus of Nazareth the Crucified, who in His humanity is at the same time the authentic witness to His divinity" (*CD* I/2, 23). Barth thus insists that the Johannine/Pauline statement that "God's Son or Word is the man Jesus of Nazareth" while the Synoptic statement that "Jesus of Nazareth is God's Son or Word" cannot be synthesized because the former is anti-docetic in emphasis while the latter is anti-ebionite in emphasis and both attest the reality of Jesus himself as truly divine and human. But, and here is the key, the fact that Jesus is the Son of God incarnate cannot be the conclusion of some historical, religious or existential study because Jesus Christ really *is* the Word incarnate simply because he *is* the Son of the Father from all eternity who became flesh for us and our salvation. This is not mythology but in the strictest sense it is a reality. This is where Barth and Pannenberg stand most opposed. And the position I have taken in this book is that because incarnation and resurrection are connected essentially because of the nature of God's very own actions in history, any attempt to see the incarnation as the conclusion rather than as the starting point for Christology necessarily invalidates that Christology. This matter is made even more complex by the fact that Pannenberg himself recognized the need for some sort of Christology from above as he developed his full doctrine of the Trinity. Still, the problems that follow his Christology from below are not completely eliminated as we shall see.

For Barth, "He is the Son of God who has come to us or the Word of God that has been spoken to us, because He is so antecedently in Himself as the Son or Word of God the Father" (*CD* I/1, 399). Hence "revelation and reconciliation do not create His deity. His deity creates revelation and reconciliation" (*CD* I/1, 415). This is why Barth insists that "all thinking about Jesus, which means at once all thinking about God, must begin and end" (*CD* I/1, 415) with the fact that Jesus is the Son simply because he *is*. "All reflection can only start with it and return to it" because "the statement about Christ's deity is to be regarded as a basic and not a derivative statement" (*CD* I/1, 415). And that is why "the knowledge of Christ's deity can only be the beginning and not the result of our thought" (*CD* I/1, 422). Any other starting point would call into question Christ's Lordship from the outset. By contrast, Pannenberg contends that "for the first Christians it was in no sense self-evident that God was in Jesus" (*Jesus — God and Man,* 132).

Two-Stage Christology

Since Pannenberg will not begin with the incarnation, he adopts a form of two-stage Christology. Initially, Pannenberg contends that Rom. 1:3f. represents a "special" two-stage Christology in which Jesus' divine Sonship "that is established by the divine Spirit has not yet been accorded to the earthly Jesus (although as the Son of David he already has been chosen for it), only to the exalted Lord" (*Jesus — God and Man*, 117-18).[30] In Pannenberg's view this is connected by Paul with Jesus' pre-existence (Phil. 2:5ff.) which suggests that Jesus was already the pre-existent Son of God (also Gal. 4:4; Rom. 8:3). Pannenberg insists that although the idea that Jesus was installed as Son of God through the resurrection has been termed "adoptionism," Paul was not an adoptionist in the sense of the second-century heresy (*Jesus — God and Man*, 119). Pannenberg actually argues against those who would suggest that Jesus receives his divine Sonship only as a consequence of the resurrection insisting that "Jesus was already the Son of God previously" (*Jesus — God and Man*, 135). Here Pannenberg strongly and correctly opposes any sort of adoptionism: "Jesus did not simply become something that he previously had not been, but his pre-Easter claim was confirmed by God. This confirmation, the manifestation of Jesus' 'divine Sonship' by God, is the new thing brought by the Easter event" (*Jesus — God and Man*, 135).[31] This sounds good as far as it goes. But when placed within Pannenberg's historical perspective, this idea of confirmation becomes problematic because he asserts that as confirmation the resurrection has "retroactive force for Jesus' pre-Easter activity." What does this mean and why is it problematic?

As seen at the beginning of this chapter in relation to Barth's criticism of him, this means to Pannenberg that Jesus' human life must be seen within a perspective which he takes to be that of Hebrew thought over against Hellenistic thought. According to the former, an essence is only what it is by virtue of its future which is unpredictably open, while for the latter an essence always is what it is. Within this context Pannenberg insists that Jesus' essence is what it is "retroactively from the perspective of the end of his life, from his resurrection, not only for our knowledge but in its being" (*Jesus — God and Man*, 136). That is where the problem arises, however. Jesus' resurrection (or rather the risen Lord) certainly disclosed who he was before Easter as the incarnate Lord, but just as certainly it did not make him the Lord in his being. It is this idea of Pannenberg's that is inherently adoptionistic and undercuts the reality of his divine Sonship. Pannenberg insists that the resurrection makes it true that Jesus is one with God "and retroactively that he was also already one with God previously" (*Jesus — God and Man*, 136). But the truth is that because he was really one with God previously, it is impossible to contend, as Pannenberg does, that the resurrection decides that Jesus was in reality the Son of God. According to Pannenberg, Jesus "would not have been who he was without the Easter event" (*Jesus — God and Man*, 137). Consider the following remark by Pannenberg offered in Volume 1 of his *Systematic Theology:*

> The eternal Son is first . . . an aspect of the human person. . . . Hence self-distinction from the Father is constitutive for the eternal Son in his relation to the Father. The transition from the relation of Jesus to the Father to the thought of the eternal Son, and consequently the difference between Father and Son in God's eternal essence, *depend* upon, and take place in, the fact that God as Father is manifest in the relation of Jesus to him. . . . [Furthermore] The self-distinction of the Father from the Son is not just that he begets the Son but that he hands over all things to him, so that his kingdom and *his own deity are now dependent upon the Son.*[32]

How can the eternal Son first be an aspect of the human person, Jesus of Nazareth, without reversing the relation between creator and creature and in fact making God's own being somehow dependent on history? That Pannenberg understands God as a dependent deity is, according to Ted Peters, one of the merits of his thinking.[33] But from my perspective any idea that God depends upon creation necessarily means that God has not been recognized at all since the Christian God does not abandon his Lordship by becoming incarnate but rather he exercises it in that way.

However, no genuine Lordship is recognized if God is thought to be constituted by his relations with us in history so that it might be suggested that Jesus' human relation with the Father is what constitutes his divine Sonship. No doubt Pannenberg clearly wishes to assert the Son's eternal self-distinction from the Father as the basis of what occurs in salvation history. But the problem is that, because of his method, Pannenberg blurs the distinction between the immanent and economic Trinity by the way he focuses on Jesus' human self-distinction from the Father as that which, at least in part, constitutes his eternal Sonship. It is this idea of Pannenberg's that represents a subtle form of adoptionism and therefore represents a practical denial of Jesus' eternal Sonship that precedes his life on earth. Of course, Pannenberg makes every effort to avoid this, especially when he says that Jesus' divinity or Sonship precedes his incarnate life on earth,[34] and also when he contends that "If Jesus as a person is 'the Son of God,' as becomes clear retroactively from his resurrection, then he has always been the Son of God . . . the idea of Jesus' adoption by God says too little" (*Jesus — God and Man*, 141).[35] But because he mistakenly thinks Barth rejected *any* idea of a *logos asarkos* he affirms (with Barth he believes) that somehow the Logos comes into existence within history itself.[36] It will be remembered that Barth affirms the *logos asarkos* in his doctrine of the Trinity and Christology only to stress that the God who meets us in history is not defined by history or dependent upon it. And so he argues that God in Christ is at once *logos ensarkos* and *logos asarkos*.[37] Importantly, then, Pannenberg's peculiar idea of the incarnation is what leads him to emphasize Jesus' resurrection as *the* determining element in his life on earth in such a way as to assert that it is this event that actually *constitutes* his divinity. And this idea, which is certainly opposed to Barth's conception of the immanent Trinity, has definite trinitarian implications as we are beginning to see.

This thinking leads Pannenberg to affirm an early "two-stage Christology" in order to uphold the idea that the earthly Jesus did not yet hold the office of King (*Jesus — God and Man,* 219). By contrast, of course, Barth rejected any two-stage Christology by insisting that the apostles spoke as those who had behind them the empty tomb and had in front of them the living Jesus. Hence,

> *apart from* Jesus' history as the mighty Word in which God's reconciling act was revealed, the apostles lacked all interest in any other aspect of his history. They ignored any reality that might have preceded this history of salvation and revelation. There *was* simply no such reality; therefore they could not know or be concerned with any such hypothetical reality. Jesus' history was real, and real to *them,* pre-eminently as a history of salvation and revelation. For them, Jesus' reality was exclusively linked to their proclamation and based on his self-proclamation as *Kurios,* Son of God and son of man. It was neither a 'historical Jesus' nor a 'Christ of faith' which they knew and proclaimed, neither the abstract image of one in whom they did not yet believe nor the equally abstract image of one in whom they afterward believed. Instead, they proclaimed concretely the one Jesus Christ who had encountered them as the one who he was, even when they did not yet believe in him. Having their eyes opened by his resurrection, they were able to tell who he was who had made himself known to them *before* the resurrection. A twofold Jesus Christ, one who existed *before* and another who existed *after* Easter, can be deduced from New Testament texts only after he has been arbitrarily read into them.[38]

Here Barth clearly indicates that the resurrection enables the disciples to understand who the pre-Easter Jesus was. But there is no hint in this thinking that Jesus is somehow constituted in his unity with God by the resurrection because Barth insists, correctly, that there is only one Jesus Christ who was the Word incarnate. Hence his Lordship or kingship is not something that accrued to him but something that stemmed from his person and work. For

Pannenberg, it is Jesus' message and actions that are repeatedly substituted for his person and work by virtue of the historical perspective he imposes on the NT.[39]

Two-stage Christology fails to acknowledge that the starting point for Christology is and always remains Jesus himself as the Word of God in the flesh; when this starting point is respected it will be understood that Christology can never begin with a view of history, apocalyptic expectation or a supposed openness of humanity for the divine without calling into question Jesus' actual Lordship from the outset. Here, of course, there is a major difference over how to understand Jesus' reconciling work. By speaking of a pre- and post-Easter Jesus, Pannenberg insists that Jesus' death *befell* him so that he endured it, with the result that it is not so much part of his *work* as something that happened to him, that is, his fate (*Jesus — God and Man*, 220). This is why Pannenberg insists that "Neither the crucifixion nor the resurrection was actively accomplished by Jesus" (*Jesus — God and Man*, 245).[40] Yet, if Jesus was and remains truly the Word of God incarnate then he *alone* was and remains the subject of his reconciling and sacrificial activity as a sovereign work of grace. Pannenberg says that when Paul refers to Christ as the subject of his sacrifice to the Father, he is no longer thinking of the pre-Easter Jesus. In the Synoptics, too, Pannenberg contends the picture of Jesus "as the acting agent results only from transferring the Messianic office of the exalted Lord back into the path of Jesus to the cross" (*Jesus — God and Man*, 220). Here Pannenberg's two-stage Christology strips the earthly Jesus of the power to *be* the reconciler in the priestly office of his incarnate life in order to affirm that it was the community which apparently conferred this status upon him by reading his earthly fate from the perspective of later events. And this happens because he separates Jesus' person and work at exactly the point where Christology must see them united.

This is where Pannenberg's adoptionism comes to the fore and returns to haunt him. He rejects the "orthodox Protestant" view that Christ's office must be understood in light of "the divine-human person" who bears that office. This thinking, in his mind, bypasses the historical reality of Jesus. What then is Pannenberg's solution here? For Pannenberg, "Jesus appeared at the beginning not as a God-man but as a man. . . ." And because Jesus was the bearer of an office simply as a man in the first instance, "this statement is a presupposition for the discussion of his divinity. Precisely the confirmation of Jesus in his earthly mission through his resurrection was the basis for the confession of his divinity" (*Jesus — God and Man*, 223). And here he returns once again to his belief that, in light of the resurrection, while we can say Jesus was always one with God even before Easter, we cannot allow that pre-Easter life actually to *be* "divine-human" in any direct sense because that is sheer mythology. Therefore,

> Jesus' resurrection is not only constitutive for our perception of his divinity, but it is ontologically constitutive for that divinity. Apart from the resurrection from the dead, Jesus would not be God, even though from the perspective of the resurrection, he is retrospectively one with God in his whole pre-Easter life. (*Jesus — God and Man,* 224)

Simply put, any claim whatsoever that Jesus' divinity is *constituted* by his resurrection amounts to a denial of Jesus' divinity, not an affirmation of it.[41] Pannenberg's assertion that Jesus is "retrospectively" one with God can only mean that the community *regards* him as one with God in his pre-Easter life. But it can never mean that he *really was* one with God in that pre-Easter life because it if did, our thinking would have to acknowledge that by stressing that no historical event, including the resurrection, constitutes Jesus' divinity; it discloses it, or better, he discloses himself in it, but it cannot constitute it, because by definition his divinity was his eternal Sonship which is grounded antecedently in his relation to the Father "before all worlds." It is, as Barth insisted a basic and not a derivative statement, and as T. F. Torrance rightly insisted, it is an ultimate, from which there can be no abstracting. Moreover, whenever Jesus was disclosed to the faith of the disciples and whenever he is disclosed to us now, it is he, the living Lord himself, who enables us to know and love him in the power of his Holy Spirit. Thus, history does not disclose his uniqueness to us; it is rather the Word acting in history that continually does so according to God's promise. And to perceive this, of course, faith as a gift of that same Spirit is necessary.

According to Pannenberg, "For Luther, the immediate object of all statements about Jesus was the God-man Jesus Christ. In our approach, on the contrary, Jesus appears first as a human being; the claim of his unity with God requires more exact proof" (*Jesus — God and Man,* 221).[42] The proof Pannenberg offers is not the person and work of Jesus Christ, the Word of God incarnate, but the history that he thinks he has discovered first in the apocalyptic expectation of Judaism and then ultimately in an anthropology that sees humanity as fundamentally open to God so that Jesus can finally be seen as the savior insofar as he fulfils humanity's basic openness to God that is part and parcel of what it means to be human.[43] That is why he can say that

> The real line of connection [for grasping Christ's offices] is in the apocalyptic transformations of prophetic traditions. Because of the significance

of his activity and fate, the figure of Jesus attracted to itself all of Israel's traditions. Here resides the truth of the typological pattern of his threefold office. (*Jesus — God and Man*, 225)

Make no mistake — by refusing to allow that the Word is the subject of the event of incarnation, Pannenberg substitutes the community's activity of recognition for the risen Lord's subjective activity as well. No longer can Jesus, in his uniqueness as priest and king (Pannenberg thinks he may have exercised his office as prophet during his earthly life), be the one who *alone* reconciles us with God. Here, with the notion of human openness to God, Pannenberg flirts with the Pelagian idea that humanity is somehow intrinsically aligned toward God in spite of the fall so that instead of truly *needing* to rely on Jesus *alone* at this point, Christology must prove his divinity from such historical events as his message, authority and resurrection.[44] Yet none of these factors proves Jesus' divinity because each can only disclose who he was both before and after Easter. Take away Jesus' pre-temporal divinity, or compromise it in any way, and the only option left, if one still wishes to be self-consciously Christian (and Pannenberg most certainly does), is to try to prove his divinity from history or anthropology thereby unfortunately proving only how much we truly *need* the incarnate Word as the sole starting point for Christology as well as for understanding the doctrine of atonement. This explains Pannenberg's downright antagonism toward the doctrine of the virgin birth.

The Virgin Birth

According to Pannenberg, the legend of the virgin birth stands in irreconcilable contradiction with the Christology of John and Paul because, in his view, it suggests that "Jesus first *became* God's Son through Mary's conception" (*Jesus — God and Man*, 143; emphasis in original). Pannenberg insists that "The Biblical legend seeks to express that from his birth onward Jesus has been God's Son because *through* his birth he is God's Son. It is, thus, directed toward Jesus, not toward Mary" (*Jesus — God and Man*, 144; emphasis in original). Here he rejects Barth's view that the virgin birth is a sign pointing to Jesus' eternal Sonship so that, in Barth's view, there is ultimately no conflict between the presentations of Matthew and Luke on the one side and John and Paul on the other. In other words Barth does not think the virgin birth signifies any sort of adoptionism but a miracle, namely, a special new direct act of God within history that cannot be traced to anything within history itself.[45] Against Barth, Pannenberg insists that the virgin birth does not point toward the miracle of Christmas, i.e., toward the "secret of the incarnation of the pre-existent Son" but "stands in contrast to it in its conceptual structure" (*Jesus — God and Man*, 143).

Curiously, Pannenberg asserts that, because Barth interprets the virgin birth as the negation of our human capacity for God by virtue of the fact that what is here accomplished is done through the sheer grace of the Holy Spirit, he is "already on the path of Roman Mariolatry" (*Jesus — God and Man*, 144).[46] "In Mariolatry," according to Pannenberg, "the church has not, as in Christology, pursued the inner logic of a historically given starting point, but has sought repeatedly to express its own essence in the figure of Mary" (*Jesus — God and Man*, 147). Yet this completely misses Barth's point. He argued decisively against an independent Mariology as "an excrescence, i.e., a diseased construct of theological thought" saying that "Excrescences must be excised" (*CD* I/2, 139),[47] insofar as any such thinking detached Mary's significance from its christological center. It is because Barth argued that the incarnation was not the result of human cooperation with God but only of God's grace and the human freedom engendered by grace that he explicitly rejected the Roman Catholic understanding of Mariology. Yet Barth did indeed insist on the importance of the virgin birth precisely because he quite properly wanted to hold the incarnation and resurrection together as miraculous actions of God within history.[48]

And it is because Pannenberg will not consider the incarnation as a starting point in his Christology that he is led to reject the virgin birth outright arguing that it would be better if it had not been made part of the Apostles' Creed (*Jesus — God and Man*, 149) and that Christianity's opposition to Gnosticism would be better served "by a normal birth" (*Jesus — God and Man*, 146).[49] This is also the basis of Pannenberg's belief that Christology can and should be grounded in the supposed anthropological openness of humanity toward God — a doctrine very clearly rejected by Barth for the same reasons he rejected an independent Mariology. Here then is the key difference between Barth and Pannenberg: Pannenberg will not begin Christology with the miracle of the incarnation but insists that the incarnation can be proven by placing the idea of it in the context of apocalyptic expectation and then showing how early Christianity had to think that way about the man Jesus *because* of the resurrection.

By contrast, Barth insisted that Jesus was conceived by the Holy Spirit and born of the virgin Mary and that what that meant was that the Son of God miraculously, i.e., in a way whose *how* could not be explained, assumed our sinful flesh from Mary precisely in order to redeem it in and through his entire incarnate life which culminated on the cross and in the resurrection.[50]

That is why Barth insisted that "What in fact makes revelation revelation and miracle miracle is that the Word of God did actually become a real man and that therefore the life of this real man was the object and theatre of the acts of God, the light of revelation entering the world" (*CD* I/2, 147). Hence for Barth, "By being called the work of the Holy Spirit the conception of Christ is actually withdrawn from any analogy save the analogy of faith and, like every genuine miracle, from any explanation of its How" (*CD* I/2, 201). Here then is Barth's chief point against Pannenberg, with which I fully agree:

> in the inconceivable act of creative omnipotence in which He imparts to human nature a capacity, a power for Himself, which it does not possess of itself and which it could not devise for itself; in the inconceivable act of reconciling love by which He justifies and sanctifies human nature in spite of its unrighteousness and unholiness to be a temple for His Word and so for His glory; in the inconceivable act of redeeming wisdom in which He completely assumes His creature in such a way that He imparts and bestows on it no less than His own existence. . . . Noetically, i.e., for us to whom this sign is given, who have to recognise it in and by this sign, the fact that Jesus Christ is the Son of God come in the flesh stands or falls with the truth of the *conceptio de Spiritu sancto*. But it could not be said that ontically, in itself, the mystery of Christmas stands or falls with this dogma. The man Jesus of Nazareth is not the true Son of God because He was conceived by the Holy Spirit and born of the Virgin Mary. On the contrary, because He is the true Son of God and because this is an inconceivable mystery intended to be acknowledged as such, therefore He is conceived by the Holy Spirit and born of the Virgin Mary. And because He is thus conceived and born, He has to be recognised and acknowledged as the One He is and in the mystery in which He is the One He is. (*CD* I/2, 201-2)

In their quite different conceptions of the virgin birth then lies the entire difference between Barth and Pannenberg concerning the proper relationship between the resurrection and incarnation. It is just because Pannenberg will not acknowledge the incarnation as a miraculous action of the Holy Spirit that is the very basis of the revelation completed in the resurrection that he constructs his Christology from below in a historical way that bypasses the need for faith at the outset and sees it only as a conclusion to his historical investigation. Importantly, it is for this reason that Pannenberg will not trace Jesus' sinlessness back to his divinity but only to his dedication to his Father and thus to the way he lived his life and to his "fate."[51] And that is why Pannenberg has great difficulty accepting the fact that from the moment of incarnation our reconciliation was a reality; for Pannenberg reconciliation could only be the result of the historical process of Christ's dedication to the Father that led to the cross and resurrection. For Barth of course incarnation meant reconciliation.[52] And for Torrance also the incarnation meant the healing of our human nature.[53] This has ramifications for Pannenberg's understanding of Chalcedon and ultimately shapes his view of the Trinity. Let us briefly explore Pannenberg's view of these matters along with their ethical implications.

Pannenberg on the Trinity and Chalcedon

Pannenberg believes the two-natures doctrine of Chalcedon creates an impasse from which there is no escape. Consistent with his method which refuses to begin with the incarnation, Pannenberg contends that the Chalcedonian "compromise" did not work precisely because it began with the incarnation. Of course the compromise of which he speaks is what he envisions as the compromise between the extremes of Alexandrian and Antiochene Christology, that is, Christology which either emphasizes too much Jesus' divinity (Alexandrian) or his humanity (Antiochene).[54] In Pannenberg's estimation, the Chalcedonian formula did not offer a solution to the problem of Christology by lifting it to a new plane of understanding, but instead it simply tried "to force together the theological antitheses on their own plane. But these antitheses are necessary results of a Christology that begins with the concept of incarnation" (*Jesus — God and Man*, 287). Nevertheless, one wonders whether or not Pannenberg acknowledges the real possibilities and limits of the doctrine in the first place since he argues that

> The formula of the true divinity and the true humanity of Jesus begins with the fact that one describes one and the same person, the man Jesus of Nazareth from different points of view. The unity of the concrete person Jesus of Nazareth is given, and both things are to be said about his one person: he is God and he is man. The formula about the two natures, on the contrary, does not take the concrete unity of the historical man Jesus as its given point of departure, but rather the difference between the divine and the human, creaturely being in general. (*Jesus — God and Man*, 284)

This understanding of the doctrine is flawed because Pannenberg refuses to begin where Chalcedon began.

First, the starting point for the Chalcedonian definition was not the relationship between divinity and humanity in general but the mystery of Jesus Christ himself. Second, Pannenberg will not accept the fact that the term person as used at Chalcedon referred to the eternal person of the Son who had become incarnate and so was the unique subject of the events of incarnation and resurrection. Pannenberg here equates person with the historical figure of the man Jesus who is not yet the eternal Son in accordance with his belief in two-stage Christology and his future-oriented grasp of reality. If the person of the Word has become incarnate in Jesus then we must say that the incarnate Word is both truly divine and truly human and that the two natures (divine and human) are "unconfused, unchangeable, undivided and inseparable." This recognizes the mystery of Jesus Christ, a mystery which simply cannot be explained from a human point of view, but can only be accepted or acknowledged as both Barth and T. F. Torrance repeatedly insisted. In other words, Chalcedon simply tried to recognize the mystery of faith and never tried to resolve the problem of Christology since any attempt to do so would then necessarily result in precisely the over-emphases that Pannenberg rightly thinks must be avoided. These over-emphases, however, do not result from the Chalcedonian formula, as Pannenberg assumes, but rather they result from any attempt to explain the mystery of revelation prior to accepting the reality of the incarnation as an act established and maintained by God alone in the history of Jesus of Nazareth. Once again we see that Pannenberg's opposition to Chalcedon results from his refusal to hold together the doctrines of the incarnation and resurrection in their essential unity. Just because he insists on seeing the incarnation as the result of his Christology from below he is led, with Schleiermacher, to suppose that we can actually explain *how* Jesus can be God and man at the same time. This goes beyond the limit recognized and articulated by the Council of Chalcedon and is the bane of contemporary Christologies from below.

Pannenberg accepts Schleiermacher's critique of the two-natures doctrine as it relates to the relation of nature and person when Schleiermacher says "here one person is supposed to participate in two wholly different natures" (*Jesus — God and Man*, 286). He claims that Schleiermacher thought that no real unity was possible without "one nature giving way to the other" (*Jesus — God and Man*, 287) with the result that Christology would always waver between separating the two natures or combining them into a third reality. Pannenberg claims that Schleiermacher's "penetrating insight" was formulated centuries earlier by Apollinaris of Laodicea when he held that "two beings complete in themselves cannot together form a single whole." Any attempt to think of a single "individual" in whom both natures remain distinct leads inevitably to an impasse from which there is no escape. If divinity and humanity as two substances are supposed to be united in the individuality of Jesus, then either the two will be mixed to form a third or the individuality, Jesus' concrete living unity, will be ruptured. (*Jesus — God and Man*, 287)

It is extremely important to realize that this whole contrived issue results from Pannenberg's refusal to admit at the outset that Jesus' person is the person of the Word and that on the basis of the inconceivable mystery of the incarnation he exists as *vere deus, vere homo*.[55]

There is in the person of the Son or Word a divine and a human nature. This is just the insight that is missed if Christology begins only with the man Jesus and not with the man Jesus who was and is God incarnate. Pannenberg mistakenly believes that the traditional view of the matter as explicated by "Alexandrian" Christology, according to which the pre-existent Word became flesh, meant that "Jesus could not be conceived as a real, individual man" (*Jesus — God and Man*, 290). Yet, long ago Barth recognized that those modern theologians who thought they had caught the ancient theologians in an error here actually misunderstood the traditional language which did not deny that Jesus was an individual man; instead it denied that his existence as man had any independence from the Word.[56] And of course it is that independence that is at issue in Pannenberg's Christology from below. Pannenberg contends that both Alexandrian and Antiochene Christology must lead to this impasse because they mistakenly begin with the incarnation. But as I have tried to show throughout this book, whenever Christology does not begin with Jesus as the incarnate Word, it must end in some form of adoptionism and must inevitably obscure the importance of the immanent Trinity. Such thinking tends to see the Trinity as somehow coming into existence in coordination with the events of history instead of seeing it properly in its pre-temporal, supra-temporal and post-temporal existence before, within and after the existence of this world.

While Pannenberg rejects the teaching of Chalcedon, he does insist that we must retain what he considers to be the inner truth of the doctrine, namely, the elements of truth in the extreme positions of Alexandrian and Antiochene Christology as exemplified by Apollinaris on the one side and Nestorius on the other. He formulates those elements of truth as follows: "neither the unity of God and man in Jesus Christ nor the truth of his humanity and his being God may be lost from view" (*Jesus — God and Man*, 292). But the problem with this thinking, as we have been seeing, is that one may speak of Jesus as God and one may speak of the unity of God and man in

Jesus Christ without actually allowing Jesus himself as the Word of God incarnate to dictate the meaning of what is said. That certainly should be the true criterion of Christology and it cannot come clearly into view when it is supposed that the incarnation must be the conclusion and not the starting point for Christology. Importantly, Pannenberg carries through his rejection of the Chalcedonian formulation by rejecting the later teaching of the church that there was not just one will in Christ (Monothelitism) but that there were two wills in Christ (Dyothelitism).[57] He believes that the church dogma of the two wills meant that the "vital unity of Jesus was basically lost" (*Jesus — God and Man*, 294). Pannenberg's thinking here is especially interesting in the context of our present discussion. He contends that

> the basis for affirming Jesus' divinity lies precisely in his unity of will with the Father in the execution of his mission. . . . The decision about Jesus' own divinity as the Son can be made only indirectly, through his unity of obedience and mission with the Father. (*Jesus — God and Man*, 294)

Once again, this thinking must be rejected because it misses the main point of Christology, namely, that the basis for affirming Jesus' divinity lies in the act of the Holy Spirit enabling believers to acknowledge the uniqueness of Jesus himself as the incarnate Word. It does not lie in his unity of will with the Father in executing his mission. The execution of his mission and unity of will with the Father instead were only possible because the man Jesus was already the Son of God while living out his incarnate life through his ministry, his death on the cross, his resurrection from the dead and his ascension into heaven and session at the right hand of the Father.[58] Further, *we* do not make the decision concerning Jesus' divinity at all — the most we can do is *acknowledge* what is a reality grounded within the immanent Trinity and executed according to God's eternal election of grace. Consequently, we cannot say that the decision about Jesus' divinity is made indirectly by our observing his obedience and mission in light of the resurrection. Jesus is God become man simply because he is and not because the community may or may not be able to trace his obedience and mission to the Father.

According to Pannenberg, the conflict between the Lutherans and Reformed over the *communicatio idiomatum* illustrates

> the inescapable dilemma of every Christology that begins with the statement of the incarnation in order to reproduce the uniting of the Son of God with the humanity of Jesus beginning with his birth rather than moving to the statement of the incarnation as the goal of Christology in order

to find Jesus' unity with God retroactively confirmed from his resurrection for the entirety of his existence. (*Jesus — God and Man,* 301)

Starting with the incarnation, according to Pannenberg, will require us either to deify Jesus' humanity and thus compromise his earthly life, or it will require us to conceive the unity of God with Jesus only very loosely. If there is a real *communicatio idiomatum,* then for Pannenberg, the unity of natures implies "a blending together" which compromises the human nature. In sum, according to Pannenberg the weakness of Chalcedonian Christology is that it does not resolve the problem of how to think about Jesus as God and man without dissolving his divinity into his humanity or making him into some third thing. Hence,

> If the incarnation is identical with the event of Jesus' creation in Mary, if it is concluded with the ending of Jesus' earthly life, Jesus was from the very first moment of his existence not a man in the same sense as all other men, if in fact divine and human are two different things. (*Jesus — God and Man,* 301)

There can be little doubt that Pannenberg is saying that if Jesus really is truly God and truly human at the same time and from the moment of his conception then he cannot really be human as we are. But why must this be so? According to the traditional teaching, it is precisely by virtue of the Word assuming flesh in Jesus of Nazareth that Jesus' humanity is fully and completely human in the same sense as we are, but without sin — even though it is our sinful flesh that he assumed. Why then would Pannenberg suppose that starting with the incarnation must undermine this truth? The answer seems to be that in Pannenberg's mind no genuinely existing human being simultaneously could be God because if he were, then he could not be truly and fully human. But this is a dilemma created by Pannenberg imposing his anthropology onto his Christology instead of allowing the unique man Jesus, in his unity with the Word, to dictate his thinking from the outset. Herein lies the chief problem of going behind the Gospel confessions to base Christology on the historical figure of Jesus the man in abstraction from the incarnation.[59] Perhaps the chief indication that it is his anthropology that is determining his Christology is the fact that Pannenberg adopts the term *dedication* from Hegel in order to explain Jesus' person.[60]

Jesus' Unity with God and the Doctrine of the Immanent Trinity

As we have seen, Pannenberg has an ambiguous understanding of Jesus' unity with God which results from his method that allows anthropology to define his Christology. He does not want to get into the difficulties associated with the idea of Jesus' consciousness of his own Sonship or of his being the Word. Rather, he wishes to establish Jesus' unity with God and thus his divinity by analyzing Jesus' human relation with his Father (*Jesus — God and Man*, 332). Pannenberg thinks it is difficult and possibly even impossible to decide whether the pre-Easter Jesus actually said what Jn. 10:30 claims, namely, that "I and the Father are one" (*Jesus — God and Man*, 334). But this is not a problem for him because Jesus was one with God's will *functionally* by virtue of his message and all his activity as determined by his message. Hence for Pannenberg,

> One cannot properly understand Jesus' Sonship without taking his relation to God the Father as the point of departure. The question of the unity of the man Jesus with the eternal Son of God cannot be put and answered directly. That is the common mistake of all theories that attempt to conceive the unity of God and man in Jesus on the basis of the concept of the incarnation of the Logos. (*Jesus — God and Man*, 334)[61]

Here is where his anthropology determines his Christology. Following Hegel, Pannenberg assumes that it is part of a person's character to transcend its isolation and "separatedness" through "dedication." For Hegel, "The truth of personality is just this, to win it through this submerging, being submerged in the other" (*Jesus — God and Man*, 336). Therefore, according to Pannenberg,

> The divinity of Jesus as Son is mediated, established through his dedication to the Father. In the execution of this dedication, Jesus is the Son. . . . The mutual dedication of Father and Son to one another, which constitutes the Trinitarian unity of God, also establishes thereby first of all the true divinity of the Son. (*Jesus — God and Man*, 336)[62]

But what exactly is it here that establishes Jesus' Sonship? Is it his eternal relation with the Father or is it his human dedication to the Father?

We get a clue about what he means when Pannenberg objects to Gogarten's belief that "Jesus' being as man is not indirectly, but directly identical with the divine Sonship" (*Jesus — God and Man*, 337). This makes his historical life unimportant for dogmatics Pannenberg asserts. So, Pannenberg claims that Gogarten has failed to see that the pre-Easter Jesus was not conscious of his identity with the Son of God since this happened only with his resurrection. This, because it is only the resurrection that "brings God's own confirmation of the meaning of Jesus' earthly life as *dedication* to God" (*Jesus — God and Man*, 337; emphasis mine). For Pannenberg, it is perfectly proper to designate Jesus' human existence as that of the Son from the perspective of this confirmation — but this is apparent only from the end; this, in Pannenberg's opinion, is the only way to maintain the true humanity of Jesus. This then is what Pannenberg offers in place of the Chalcedonian definition:

> His humanity is not synthesized with a divine essence, but it involves two complementary total aspects of his existence. These aspects are as different from one another as God and man are different. Nevertheless, with the special relation to the Father in the human historical aspect of Jesus' existence, his identity in the other aspect — that of the eternal Son of the eternal Father — is given. Thus the perception of Jesus' eternal Sonship as dialectically identical with his humanity is based noetically upon the particularity of just this human being in his relation to the divine Father; ontologically, the relation is inverted, for the divine Sonship designates the ontological root in which Jesus' human existence . . . has the ground of its unity and of its meaning. (*Jesus — God and Man*, 337)

We have already seen the inadequacy of this thinking above. One point needs to be added here, however, and that is that Jesus' eternal Sonship is not *dialectically* identical with his humanity but in fact is identical in the substantial sense indicated by Chalcedon.[63] Here it is important to see that it is the concept of *dedication* that Pannenberg has appropriated from Hegel that leads him to undermine the actual meaning of Jesus' eternal Sonship as well as the genuine basis of Jesus' uniqueness. Pannenberg argues that

> the dependence that was the reason for Jesus' human *dedication* to God is dependence upon the *Father*. Precisely in and because of this *dedication* to the Father, Jesus is identical with the person of the Son. 'Person' is a relational concept, and because the relation of Jesus to the Father in his *dedication* to him is identical with the relation to the Father intended by the designation 'the Son,' Jesus in his human *dedication* to the Father is identical with the eternal person of the Son of God. (*Jesus — God and Man*, 339; most emphases mine)

Here a proper doctrine of the immanent Trinity could have helped Pannenberg clearly affirm that it is not *because* of Jesus' human dedication to the Father that he is identical with the person of the Son;[64] it is because the eternally begotten Son of the Father who is one in being (of one substance) with the Father before all worlds became flesh by the power of the Holy Spirit through the virgin Mary that Jesus is the Son. Without this acknowledgment, Christology will always be on the verge of adoptionism and trinitarian theology will always be on the road toward a dependent deity. In his later theology Pannenberg certainly saw the issue here when he said "No matter how we reach the concept of the incarnation, however, its own logic demands that we think of the eternal Son as the basis of the earthly existence of Jesus" (*Systematic Theology*, 2: 384). Yet, once again, his method makes it virtually impossible for him to maintain the logic of this insight. So he also insists that "the constitution of the person of Jesus takes place in the whole process of this history [Jesus' life history]" (*Systematic Theology*, 2: 385).

Yet both adoptionism and any idea of a dependent deity were excluded by the early church precisely in order to affirm Jesus' true divinity and to preserve the divine freedom as the ground of human freedom. Pannenberg is forced to confuse history and eternity with his thinking as when he argues that "the man Jesus had his independence . . . as the Son . . . to the extent that he lived in self-sacrifice to the Father and in dependence upon him in the accomplishment of his existence" (*Jesus — God and Man*, 339). But that is just the problem. The Son actually existed prior to his human existence on earth and the fact that he condescended to live a sacrificial life for us gives meaning to his incarnate life, death and resurrection. While he theoretically admits to Christ's pre-existence, there is no practical room for such an existence in the traditional sense in Pannenberg's thought, because to him any such idea smacks of mythology. And indeed it is his very notion of a dependent deity that is catastrophic here because it implies that Jesus needed to accomplish his existence in his historical relation with the Father in order to be the eternal Son. In effect this is a denial rather than an affirmation of his eternal Sonship. This explains why Pannenberg describes the incarnation as a way of Jesus fulfilling his Sonship:

> The assuming of human existence by the eternal Son is not to be seen as the adding of a nature that is alien to his deity. It is the self-created medium of his extreme self-actualization in consequence of his free self-distinction from the Father, i.e., a way of fulfilling his eternal sonship. (*Systematic Theology*, 2: 325)

Here, in a manner similar to Rahner, Pannenberg implies that by virtue of his self-distinction from the Father, the Son's own "extreme self-actualization" involves the coming into being of Jesus' human existence. But where is the distinction between Christ's divinity and humanity to be drawn here if his humanity is not "alien to his deity"? And how are we to conceive of the incarnation as a special new direct act of God coming into history if it is envisioned as a way for the Son to fulfill his own Sonship. In a clear doctrine of the immanent Trinity we would have to acknowledge that his Sonship needs no fulfillment because it is fully divine in the Son's *perichoretic* relations with the Father and Spirit in eternity. What he fulfills is his election or free choice to be God for us.

More evidence that anthropology rather than Christology is dictating Pannenberg's thought can be seen in the following remarks: "If the history of a person is accomplished in the give-and-take of acting and receiving, the existence of Jesus is integrated into the person of the eternal Son precisely through the history of his earthly way in its reference to the Father" (*Jesus — God and Man,* 344). And Pannenberg thinks that

> The openness to God that characterizes Jesus' humanity in his dedication to the Father and shows him to be the Son constitutes his personal identity with the Son. This is not alien to the humanity of man as such. . . . Openness to God is the radical meaning of that human 'openness in relation to the world.' (*Jesus — God and Man,* 344)[65]

We will return to this thought momentarily to note the Pelagian overtones. But for the moment let us specify more precisely how Pannenberg's understanding of the Trinity is exactly that which inadvertently undermines his view not only of the relationship between the resurrection and incarnation, but of the very meaning of these doctrines.

First, Pannenberg repeatedly insists that any idea that the Son pre-exists his life on earth and then becomes incarnate is nothing but mythology. This is confirmed, as seen above, by his objections to the *logos asarkos*.[66] In his *Systematic Theology* Pannenberg appears to want to find a place for the *logos asarkos*. But his thinking does not seem to permit it. For instance, in speaking of the love of God and neighbor Pannenberg makes the following odd remark: "As there can be no immanent Trinity without the economic Trinity, so there can be no faith without works of neighborly love."[67] Of course there could be an immanent Trinity without the economic Trinity because, as Barth rightly insisted, the economic Trinity does not arise as a matter of course from the immanent Trinity. This statement suggests failure to distinguish the immanent and economic Trinity, even though Pannenberg is well aware of the fact that such distinction is vitally important in order to avoid collapsing the divine being into the processes of history.[68] While it is true that neighborly love is an expression of faith, it is false to suggest that there would be no immanent Trinity had God not freely acted externally as creator, reconciler and redeemer in the economy. Pannenberg's thinking here suggests that, despite statements that confirm his desire to distinguish the immanent and economic Trinity, his approach to theology does not allow for any such distinction in the traditional sense that asserts God's freedom precisely by indicating that God exists eternally and freely as Father, Son and Holy Spirit and would so have existed even if he had decided never to create and save the world. Again, it is not enough to just say this. Robert Jenson is perfectly willing to acknowledge this statement exactly as rendered but then goes on to insist on the identity of the immanent and economic Trinity understood eschatologically with the result that Jesus will not be the eternal Son until history is complete.[69] What is required is a type of theological thinking that is marked by the fact that God really did exist in full loving freedom before history and in no sense needs history to fulfill his existence because his entrance into history is an act of pure grace by which he establishes our freedom and then reestablishes it as reconciler and redeemer.

This explains why Pannenberg himself says:

> That God as economic trinity has a history is itself a facet of the abundance of the eternal life of the trinitarian God. In talking about the unity of economic and immanent trinity, however, one must never forget that the 'place' of such identity is in the eschatological consummation of history, *not in the past or present.*[70]

The problem here is this: if the place of the unity of the immanent and economic Trinity is not found within the immanent Trinity's pre-temporal existence and therefore in God's eternal election of grace, then the actual freedom of God to have existed without the world is denied. Then one must conclude, as Pannenberg does, against his own stated intentions, that the unity of the immanent and economic Trinity is somehow the result of God's involvement with history. Such thinking in reality compromises the pre-temporal existence of the immanent Trinity. In truth the unity of the immanent and economic Trinity is to be found in the incarnation and resurrection of Jesus Christ because it is in him that the eternal Word has become flesh and overcome sin and death once and for all. Because Pannenberg sees the incarnation as the end and not the starting point for Christology and since he believes that only the future determines the present in accordance with his idea of dedication taken from Hegel and his idea of anticipation taken from Heidegger, he conceives the identity of the immanent and economic Trinity only as a future event; this sense of futurity, rather than the miraculous actions of God within history, causes Pannenberg to begin his thinking with the resurrection and not with the incarnation. And that starting point, as we have seen, leads to many of the difficulties that arise in his Christology from below and his view of the Trinity.

Second, as Pannenberg himself notes and as we have been seeing throughout this chapter, "The trinitarian conception of God is based upon Christology . . . it is Jesus' relation to the 'Father' that *constitutes* his own identity as 'Son' of that Father as well as the impossibility of conceiving of the eternal Father otherwise than in relation to *this* Son."[71] Pannenberg recognizes that this historical thinking requires "extensive revisions" of traditional Christology and trinitarian theology. He believes he has provided that without losing "their essential content." But by refusing to allow the Word or Son of the Father actually to have an identifiable pre-existent history and truly to be the acting *subject* in relation to us within created time and history, Pannenberg is forced to conclude that the Son essentially comes into existence within history by virtue of Jesus' message being confirmed. This once again amounts to a denial of the traditional christological assertion of the Son's *homoousion* with the Father and a compromise of the eternal divine freedom with the suggestion that the Father somehow not only depends upon the Son within history for his existence but that the Father depends upon the Son within the immanent Trinity.

As already stressed, Pannenberg certainly does not wish to deny the importance of a doctrine of the immanent Trinity. Hence, he insists "The acts of the trinitarian persons in their mutual relations must be sharply differentiated from their common outward actions" (*Systematic Theology*, 2: 3). Indeed, "God does not need the world in order to be active. He is in himself the living God in the mutual relations of Father, Son and Spirit" (*Systematic Theology*, 2: 4-5). But the logic of his method does not allow these crucially important insights to structure his Christology and trinitarian thinking. Hence, instead of admitting that God is and remains free in relation to the world of his creation, Pannenberg presents a God who really needs to develop his being and nature in relation to history. As a result, Jesus' human differentiation from God the Father is seen as the basis for his eternal distinction as Son and Jesus' message and work actually tend to displace his being as God and man in the Chalcedonian sense.[72] And Pannenberg does not allow for the fact that the immanent Trinity comes into history from outside so that what we encounter in the incarnation and resurrection of Jesus Christ is something utterly un-imaginable and new — an act of God that must come to us.[73]

Ethical Implications

It is beyond the scope of this work to deal with specific ethical issues. But what is important to note is that the way we know God and Christ already signals the ethical problem and its only possible solution. For instance, if knowledge of God can only take place in obedience, because knowledge of God is not a work that is justified by or from human experience and through reason but only by God's grace, then quite obviously the same must be true about knowledge of Jesus Christ and his significance for faith.[74] If the basis and meaning of our life in Christ is the fact that the risen Lord is alive even now and interacting with us through the sphere of history in and through historical events such as our hearing a sermon or reading scripture or receiv-ing the sacraments or even through events that are purely secular and even outwardly anti-Christian as it is God's freedom to do, then all forms of self-justification are ruled out. We must continually rely on the risen and as-cended Lord in prayer and thanksgiving[75] and thus refrain from any attempt to justify our knowledge through reason or history.

One has only to peruse Barth's discussion of our knowledge of God to see that his thinking is shaped by his view that we are justified by faith and thus our knowledge of God can only take place in our free obedience which means our free acknowledgment that what God has revealed in Jesus Christ is right and that this puts us in the right. The difference between Barth and Pannenberg on this point is captured by Pannenberg's remark that "If Jesus' activity was so unique that it had to be considered as something without any analogy, then no one could have community with him. But having commu-nity with Jesus is the basis of being Christian" (*Jesus — God and Man*, 205).[76] By contrast, Barth insisted that community with Christ is established as a miracle by the very fact of his existence as Emmanuel, that is, his being as God for us.[77] And for this there is no analogy other than the analogy created by the miracles of the incarnation and resurrection in their unity. Hence, Pannenberg thinks the basis for community with Jesus is his universal rele-vance which can be established, at least in part, by exploring the hopes and desires of humanity.[78] Barth of course thinks that Jesus' universal relevance is grounded in his antecedent existence as the eternal Son of the Father and therefore in the election that is decided in pre-temporal eternity and exe-cuted within history in the incarnation, life, death and resurrection of Jesus himself. While Pannenberg is right to say that salvation is related to our needs, he is mistaken to suggest that our *true* needs can be understood apart from faith in the incarnate Word. Our deepest need, as Barth rightly stresses, is for the righteousness that can *only* come from God himself.[79] But if we suppose, even for a moment, that our needs can be discerned in some general way by exploring human longing and hope and then seeing Jesus as the one in whom our hopes and longings are fulfilled in an anticipatory way, then we have undercut our actual neediness.[80] Once again the issue here concerns God's activity within history. Pannenberg virtually excludes any action of a divine subject in relation to us: "Perception of Jesus' divinity was possible only from the consideration of his earthly work and of the claim contained in his whole activity on the one hand and of his fate in the cross and resurrection on the other" (*Jesus — God and Man,* 209). Here Jesus' divinity is discovered by our consideration of his earthly work instead of by a specific act God himself in the humanity of Jesus. But for Barth it is quite a different matter:

> God Himself is in the world, earthly, conceivable and visible, as He is this man. We have to do with God Himself as we have to do with this man. God Himself speaks when this man speaks in human speech. God Himself acts and suffers when this man acts and suffers as a man. God Himself triumphs when this One triumphs as man. The human speaking and acting and suffering and triumphing of this one man directly concerns us all, and His history is our history of salvation which changes the whole human situation, just because God Himself is its human subject in His Son, just because God Himself has assumed and made His own our human nature and kind in His Son, just because God Himself came into this world in His Son, and as one of us 'a guest this world of ours He trod.' (*CD* IV/2, 51)[81]

For Barth, however, we only perceive Jesus' divinity when, in a special new action, God unveils himself to us in the speech and action of the man Jesus. Hence, "Knowledge of it [God's majesty hidden in Christ's humanity] becomes real to men only in virtue of a special unveiling through Jesus' resurrection from the dead, or through all the sayings and acts of His life so far as they were signs of his resurrection" (*CD* I/2, 38).

So I would suggest that there is at least one crucial ethical implication of the fact that the incarnation and resurrection are defined only by the person and work of Jesus Christ himself as the incarnate Word. And that is that we must realize that *any* form of self-justification at all whether ontic or noetic actually represents a new form of legalism or the opening to some form of license in the sense that such self-justification suggests that humanity can reach God by a self-chosen method and then can and should assure itself that it has indeed reached God without actually relying in faith on the risen Lord himself. This then is the main issue that has arisen in Pannenberg's doctrine of God and Christology when we compare his views with the understanding of these doctrines offered by Barth and Torrance.

On the one hand, Pannenberg claims to base his thinking exclusively on Jesus Christ and explicitly opposes self-justification. But on the other hand, he does not allow Jesus Christ as attested in the NT to be his sole starting point because he insists on going behind the Gospel confessions to a historical Jesus who becomes the Christ through his dedication to his Father. And instead of admitting, with Barth and Torrance, that the *how* of Jesus' unique existence as God and man cannot be explained because it is a miracle and knowledge of it takes place as a miracle because God alone actively includes us in his trinitarian self-knowledge and love, Pannenberg attempts to explain it by showing how the Christian conviction that Jesus is divine arose and why it made sense in light of the historical developments he sees at work in the early church.

In a similar way in his *Systematic Theology*, Pannenberg adopts the concept of anticipation from Heidegger to argue that it is through our experiences of anticipation that we know God in such a way that this can and must be verified through a kind of natural theology.[82] From Barth's point of view we have seen that this procedure itself is the ultimate form of self-justification. We do not have the historical means to show how and why the conviction that Jesus was the Son of God arose because that conviction itself is grounded in the being and action of Jesus himself and is a possibility recognizable by us only because of a present action of the Holy Spirit. And we do not have the means to demonstrate true knowledge of God apart from the analogy of faith, that is, apart from the fact that it is an event enclosed within the mystery of the divine Trinity in such a way that when knowledge of God actually takes place it too is a miracle.

Perhaps the most obvious difference here between Barth and Torrance on one side and Pannenberg and Rahner on the other can be seen by observing that Barth and Torrance reject any idea of an obediential potency for revelation while Pannenberg and Rahner find such an idea not only plausible but necessary in the doctrine of God and Christology. We have already documented Rahner's thinking above in Chapter Two. Here we note that Pannenberg repeatedly asserts that human openness for God must form the context within which our knowledge of God then either is verified or called into question.[83] Take this one example. Pannenberg asserts:

> The openness to God that belongs to the structure of human existence as such (even when it is in fact lived in contradiction to God) and that finds its fulfillment only when human existence is personally integrated in dependence upon God is fulfilled in Jesus by the divine confirmation of his eschatological message (including its claim to authority) through his resurrection from the dead. (*Jesus — God and Man*, 348)

As Barth frequently emphasizes, what we know from the revelation of God in Jesus Christ is that we are not open to God but closed to him and in need of reconciliation so that we may be open to him only through the Holy Spirit and only through faith.[84] For this reason it is not our openness to God that is fulfilled in Jesus. Such thinking would indeed suggest that we could rely on our supposed openness to some extent and then see Jesus as the one who validates that openness. This would make us, rather than Jesus, the subjects of reconciliation and redemption. Against such thinking, it is important to realize that it is our opposition to God that is overcome in Jesus, not our supposed openness which is fulfilled, with the result that any claim to openness on our part is eliminated as a human possibility. This makes an enormous difference as to how one understands salvation. Because Pannenberg thinks of salvation within the context of our supposed openness to God, he believes that "Openness to God is the radical meaning of that human 'openness in relation to the world' that constitutes man's specific nature in distinction from all animals" (*Jesus — God and Man*, 344).[85] But such an understanding of salvation obscures the radical nature of our reconciliation with God in Christ. In light of the revelation of God in Jesus Christ one could not say that openness to the world is what makes us human because our humanity, which has its reality from and in Christ's humanity, is distinguished from the animals by the fact of God's covenant relation with humanity established and fulfilled in the life history of Jesus of Nazareth. What makes us human is God's gracious act of creation in and through his Word, his act of reconciliation in his Son and his act of redemption in his Spirit. We are human because of Jesus Christ himself. It is in him and from him alone that we know that our true human nature does not include sin but excludes it.

This explains why Pannenberg can see a convergence between our love for others and the kingdom: "We need to see more clearly," Pannenberg writes, "that love for fellowmen is participation in God's love; that is to say, love for fellowmen is participation in the coming Kingdom of God."[86] But exactly what role does Jesus play in this thinking and to what extent has Pannenberg blurred the distinction between the two commands to love God and neighbor? On the one hand, Pannenberg quite properly wishes to say that the relevance of Jesus' message was to show that Christian love for God does not mean escape from the world but affirmation and transformation of the world. This is good and important. On the other hand, Pannenberg comes dangerously close to collapsing the two loves when he writes:

> While preaching and theology have generally declared that true love for God leads to love for fellowmen, they have also given the impression that somehow these two loves are just that, namely, *two* loves. The mere fact that they have been distinguished in a way that makes it possible for people to separate love for God from love for fellowmen points to the real problem. (*Theology and the Kingdom,* 112)

Pannenberg therefore insists that the key to understanding the indissoluble connection between love for God and neighbor is to realize that God's *being* is identical with the coming of his kingdom which means that ethical failure is related to a faulty doctrine of God.

So Pannenberg suggests that we should not think of God as "an entity which has the definite mode of its being in some transcendent realm" because that might imply that "love for God moves in another direction than love for fellowmen" (*Theology and the Kingdom,* 112-13). And he agrees with Rahner when he answers his question: "And in the depth of turning to the cohuman Thou do we not also love God?" (*Systematic Theology,* 3: 187), insisting that Rahner did not reduce love of God to love of neighbor even though Rahner conceives God as the "silent incomprehensibility" at work in human love so that we love God in loving our fellow humans even without any specific advertence to God himself (*Systematic Theology,* 3: 187-88).[87] Hence Pannenberg rejects the distinction between a "vertical" love for God and a "horizontal" love for "fellowmen," fearing that we would then focus on another world and not on this world. Yet herein lies the problem we have been considering in this chapter. If God's love for us in Christ has priority here, as it must, since it is the enabling condition of our love for God and love of neighbor, then we must indeed maintain both the vertical and horizontal dimensions. Failure to do so would mean equating our love for neighbor with the presence of God's kingdom in such a way that we could speak of participating in the kingdom of God without actually relying on Jesus Christ himself who is the present and coming kingdom itself.[88]

Again the difference between Pannenberg and Barth is clear. Pannenberg speaks of the kingdom revealing itself "as still unrealized future that confronts every present and that will confront a, hopefully, better future situation" (*Theology and the Kingdom,* 115). And he also thinks that for a proper commitment to this world "a vision of the transcendent is necessary," that is, a transcendence that is "engaged in the dynamics of this world" (*Theology and the Kingdom,* 114). Yet this very thinking is not explicitly and materially dictated by the fact that the kingdom is identical with Jesus Christ himself. Thus, Pannenberg can say that "Jesus discovered the revelation of God's love in the very fact that the imminent Kingdom of God was announced before its coming in its fullness. . . . Men receive the opportunity to open themselves to God's future" (*Theology and the Kingdom,* 117).[89] And "If a particular action springs from the spirit of creative love and contributes to individual and social integration, unity, and peace, then that particular action expresses the spirit of God's Kingdom" (*Theology and the Kingdom,* 118). Finally, Pannenberg says,

> Jesus himself was only a forerunner. He revealed the redeeming love of God precisely as the forerunner and herald of God's still imminent Kingdom. His message was a preliminary and precisely in that way he participated in and revealed the ultimate reality, the love of God. To love the preliminary is no little thing. Christians are surely right to call for devotion to Jesus. He who despises the preliminary because he waits for the ultimate will not be able to recognize the ultimate in its coming. (*Theology and the Kingdom,* 126)

Here we may observe that the end result of a Christology from below is the separation of the present kingdom from Jesus himself. This becomes extremely clear when contrasted with Barth's vision.

> 'The kingdom of God is at hand' means 'the Word was made flesh and dwelt among us' (Jn. 1:14). In him the divine righteousness and order contest, defeat, overcome, and set aside human unrighteousness and disorder. The first disciples found themselves confronted already in their own lifetime with the kingdom of God as God revealed and declared Christ to be the One he was in his resurrection from the dead, as he, the Crucified and Slain, appeared and met them as the Living One, and as they thus found themselves confronted with Jesus. Similarly, people of all times find themselves confronted already with the mystery of the absolutely new and inconceivable and incomparable thing of the kingdom of God as in the power of his Holy Spirit they find themselves confronted with this Living One as their Lord, as the Lord of all lords [Rev. 17:14; 19:16]. (Barth, *The Christian Life,* 249)

And so Barth insists that there is in the NT no trace of an idea that God's kingdom has come or will be expected "apart from the history of Jesus

Christ." Consequently, for Barth, Jesus Christ is not just a manifestation of the kingdom of God or a copy of an original precisely because

> The proclamation of the kingdom of God by Jesus . . . is not the proclama-
> tion of a reality and truth differing from himself. . . . In the history of his
> prophecy, the reality and truth of the kingdom are not just indicated in the
> sense that there is a coming somewhere behind and above his own words
> and works and suffering and death, he himself being merely the precursor
> and herald of the kingdom . . . he himself is the Son of God, so that his per-
> son and work and word cannot be distinguished from the person and work
> and word of God; and God's kingdom is his, the kingdom of the Son no
> less than the Father. (Barth, *The Christian Life,* 249-50)

This is why Barth insists that whoever knew and loved Jesus, knew and loved the "imminent kingdom of God. Speaking about God's kingdom could only mean telling his story" (Barth, *The Christian Life,* 253). In this sense Barth in-
sists that the kingdom was both present and future in the history of Jesus so that in virtue of the Easter history, the disciples did not merely look back to what Jesus said, but now saw him "in the future of his completed history." They now saw him as the one who was hidden from cradle to grave as the eternal Son of the Father who is the Lord of heaven and earth. When they looked back to the coming of the kingdom in him, they immediately had to look forward to his future. All of this takes place in the gift and power of the Holy Spirit: "We are referred to the power of God to open blind eyes to see this light. This power of God is the Holy Spirit. The Holy Spirit certainly did and does make use of the eyewitnesses, but he is not limited to them or their mediating force" (Barth, *The Christian Life,* 256).

Further, in contrast to Barth's interpretation of the parable of the Good Samaritan which, as we saw above, insisted that our neighbor is one who demonstrates God's mercy to us and is often unexpected, Pannenberg, while partially agreeing with Barth, argues we should not just wait around for our neighbors to show up and make themselves known to us. "We should be going out to create new neighbors."[90] This thinking really goes too far in the di-
rection of usurping God's own activity in relation to our human love of God and neighbor. While Pannenberg is quite clear in Volume 3 of his *Systematic Theology* that any equating of love of God and neighbor would be problem-
atic (*Systematic Theology,* 3: 189), and while he very clearly insists that our love for God and neighbor must be grounded within the immanent Trinity as our participation in the works of the economic Trinity (*Systematic Theology,* 3: 193), he also causes difficulty at just that point with his remark discussed

above that "As there can be no immanent Trinity without the economic Trinity, so there can be no faith without works of neighborly love" (*Systematic Theology*, 3: 193). And he maintains that "in love of God and love of neighbor we do not have two wholly different realities but two aspects of human participation in one and the same love of God" (*Systematic Theology*, 3: 193). Yet with these remarks the suspicion remains that Pannenberg is suggesting that faith is somehow contingent on loving our neighbors just as the immanent Trinity is somehow contingent on the existence and activity of the economic Trinity. And such thinking has Pelagian overtones because it implies that we can, to some extent, rely on our own acts of love to participate in the kingdom of God.

Hence we may conclude this chapter with the remarks of Karl Barth that echo his statement in the Barmen Declaration:

> He is the one Word of God that we must hear, that we must trust and obey, both in life and in death. If the crucified Jesus Christ is alive, if His community is the company of those among whom this is seen and taken seriously, as the axiom of all axioms, then the community cannot take account of any other word that God might have spoken before or after or side by side with or outside this word. . . . It accepts and proclaims this one Jesus Christ as the one Word, the first and final Word, of the true God. In it it hears the Word of all God's comfort, commandment and power. It is altogether bound to this Word, and in it it is altogether free. It interprets creation and the course of the world and the nature of man, his greatness and his plight, wholly in the light of this Word and not *vice versa*. It does not need to accept as normative any other voice than this voice, for the authority of any other voice depends upon the extent to which it is or is not an echo of this voice. (*CD* IV/1, 346)

That, then, is the main issue as it concerns Pannenberg's theology. Is he really allowing Jesus Christ to be the first and final Word of God when he refuses to begin his Christology with the incarnate Word and then proceeds to understand Christ's resurrection by methodologically detaching it from its indissoluble connection with the incarnation? Does he not separate the kingdom from Jesus Christ when he says that Jesus is "only a forerunner . . . and herald of God's still imminent Kingdom"? Does Barth not have the better view, which unequivocally excludes Pelagian overtones, when he insists that the kingdom is inseparable from Jesus Christ himself as the Son of God acting for our salvation?

In this chapter I have explored the complex, interesting and revealing thinking of Wolfhart Pannenberg in some detail in order to show the kinds of difficulty that can arise when it is thought that one can or must separate the incarnation and the resurrection with the idea that the incarnation can only be the conclusion and not the starting point for a proper theology of the resurrection. And it must be noted once more that of the many theologians explored in this volume Pannenberg is to be seen as one who is very seriously and resolutely interested in recognizing and maintaining Christ's genuine uniqueness for Christian faith and practice. Yet his thinking stands as a clear warning that unless Christology begins and ends with Jesus Christ himself, truly divine and truly human in the Chalcedonian sense, it will inevitably have to spend time trying to find a place for him in its reflections. We have seen that whenever theologians have to "find a place for Jesus" they have already given up thinking theologically because Jesus himself is the way, the truth and the life and unless he actually is the starting point for a theology of the resurrection, his Lordship will have already been called into question practically and methodologically with the result that his necessity for theology and for our own salvation will be marginal at best.

9. Conclusion

What can be learned from this exploration of how a number of prominent contemporary theologians with wide-ranging viewpoints understand the meaning and importance of Jesus' resurrection from the dead in its intrinsic connection with his incarnation? The first and most important thing to be learned is that unless the resurrection is understood to be an event in the life of Jesus that gives meaning to Christian faith, the church is in danger of being left alone with its own faith. In other words unless Jesus really rose from the dead, appeared to his disciples and enabled their faith and unless he is alive now in his unique divine-human being and action as the ascended Lord acting as the One Mediator between us and the Father, Christian faith becomes little more than a matter of projecting subjective feelings and experiences onto reality and then describing them in religious terms appropriated from the Bible and the tradition. Then any talk of hope also becomes a matter of sheer conjecture and wishful thinking. Unless the hope of Christians is tied to one who can fulfill his promise of eternal life, we are of all people the most to be pitied (1 Cor. 15:19). But as the apostle Paul insisted we do not grieve as those who have no hope because Christ has indeed been raised from the dead (1 Thess. 4:13-14) and is alive now enabling the faith of those who acknowledge him by the power of his Holy Spirit.

Intimately connected with this first point is a second from which it is inseparable, namely, that whenever the starting point for Christology is not exclusively Jesus, the man from Nazareth as attested in the NT, then the starting point becomes, at least in part, the experience of his disciples and our present experiences of faith and hope. To the extent that this shift of focus away from Jesus himself and toward our experiences of faith and hope occurs, Jesus' actual Lordship — the fact that Jesus really was and is the only begotten Son of the Father who became flesh to atone for our sins and enable our justification and sanctification — becomes something that theologians must "find a place for" or if they cannot, then they must explain it according to their various world-views in such a way that they make Jesus irrelevant to Christian faith and practice. What follows, I have argued, is always some form of self-justification. And self-justification in any form is, in my view, a sure sign that the church has ceased to live by the promise of its own eternal life which is grounded in and remains effective in the one who alone is the way, the truth and the life. Any such thinking effectively leaves the church hopeless because it is still in search of its Lord in the form of its world-views. It is to that extent an unspiritual community — a community without the Holy Spirit.

Finally, the main thesis of this book is that a Christology that genuinely begins and ends with Jesus Christ himself as attested in the NT could never begin "from below" with the idea that the incarnation must be the conclusion and not the starting point for its reflections. Because it is the incarnate Word who meets us as the risen and ascended Lord in the power of his Holy Spirit, there can be no such theoretical or practical bracketing of Jesus' being into a historical Jesus who is thought to exist behind the NT faith confessions and the Christ of faith which is then thought to have arisen on account of the impression Jesus made upon the community then and now. Both of these alternatives detach the Holy Spirit from the Word and thus undermine the truth of Christology. Any proper Christology will necessarily hold the incarnation together with the resurrection because Jesus' divinity is, as Barth put it, authentic, definitive and essential. And recognition of his divinity can take place only in faith through the Holy Spirit himself (1 Cor. 12:3). As such, who Jesus is as the risen Lord and unique savior of the world is not in the least dependent on the choices of the community or its belief or unbelief. This can be the source of the greatest hope and strongest faith when it is acknowledged, as it ought to be. But when faith and hope are transmuted into faith and hope in something the community prescribes for itself as a belief or something the community must accomplish in its ethical behavior, then everything becomes uncertain once again and Christian faith becomes a matter of anxiety over how we must act and what we must do in order to be saved. What is needed is a return to faith which is itself enabled by the Holy Spirit uniting us to Christ and through him to the Father.

We have seen that variations of these erroneous views abound in contemporary theology. For instance, we have seen that John Macquarrie believed that modern Christology had a dual foundation, namely, the witness of the early church and contemporary experience. Exactly because he did not begin his Christology with Jesus himself and the events of his life — the resurrection in its essential unity with the incarnation — he blended together Jesus and the community into what he called the Christ-event and then claimed that we cannot think that when the NT referred to Christ's resurrection it actually meant that he rose bodily from the dead. Instead he argued that the historical event depicted by resurrection language was the rise of the church itself. For him it is clear that resurrection language primarily described the experience of the disciples and our experiences today.

But, of course, as I have argued, such thinking pulls the ground out from under Christian theology because it neither begins nor ends with the objective historical event that validates all Christian dogmatics, namely, the resurrection of the incarnate Word. Jesus, as Lord of the church and world is dissolved by Macquarrie into the experience of the community in such a way that he becomes little more than a focal point for discussing various viewpoints and activities. And this flawed thinking was made possible by the fact that Macquarrie did not take the incarnation seriously enough. The symptom of a weak doctrine of the incarnation (one that detaches the revelation of God from the man Jesus as the incarnate Word and locates it in a set of universally accessible experiences and ideas) is demonstrated in Macquarrie's suggestion that the whole fabric of the Christian faith would remain untouched if we omitted the "joyful mysteries" that came after the cross. Failing to allow Jesus Christ himself in his actual uniqueness as the Lord of the church to determine his thought, Macquarrie blended them together in the Christ-event and then concluded that the church, not the risen Lord himself, is the outward and visible aspect of the resurrection. The resurrection was not, Macquarrie thought, something in the "career" of Jesus. And for him the ascension is simply "an event in the consciousness of the disciples rather than in the career of Christ himself." For those very reasons Macquarrie depicts a church alone with itself using resurrection and incarnational language to organize its experiences. And of course a church alone with itself can only try to justify itself using theological language drawn from the Bible and the tradition; to that extent it cannot live its actual justification by faith until it turns or returns noetically and ontically to faith in Jesus, the risen and ascended Lord of the church and world; it must allow the Holy Spirit to empower it once again to accept the Lordship of Christ himself in his distinction from the church. And Macquarrie was not alone.

The major premise of Paul Knitter's nonnormative Christology is that while all religions can and should be theocentric but not Christocentric, Christians must admit that while Christ is normative for them as their savior figure, he is not normative for those in other religions who choose to believe in other savior figures. Jesus then cannot be the one and only savior of the world because in our pluralist society any such thinking would undermine the validity of other religions that do not accept him in his traditionally recognized uniqueness as the only Son of the Father.

In reality, of course, Christology and trinitarian theology are just as intimately connected as is the resurrection and incarnation. Hence, Knitter's nonnormative Christology severs the *homoousion* at its root because his very method not only prevents but excludes the fact that knowledge of the Father can only take place in and through the Son who reveals him in the power of his Holy Spirit. For Knitter, as for John Hick, the incarnation was a myth and not a metaphysical fact. That is why his thinking is not at all determined by who Jesus really was and is as the risen and ascended Lord, but rather by his theocentric ideal which he claims will allow all religions to be unique. The only problem, however, with this reasoning is that Knitter has changed the meaning of the incarnation itself by denying the one thing that makes it true and decisive, namely, the fact that Jesus really *is* the unique Son of the Father and as such is one in being with God and with us. And this thinking leads him to a unitarian view of God that refuses to acknowledge that Jesus, as Son is one in being with the Father from all eternity. It is a view that ignores the fact that the Holy Spirit is the Spirit of Christ himself and as such unites us to Christ and not to a theocentric ideal.

From this he is led to think that the resurrection was simply a mythological way of describing a series of conversion or faith or revelation experiences with the result that he sincerely believes that the object determining the resurrection accounts and the empty tomb tradition is nothing but a set of universally available faith experiences that can be had without specifically relating to Jesus himself as the risen Lord. In this way Knitter demonstrates that what gives meaning to his beliefs is not the risen Lord himself but a docetically reconstructed set of experiences that allows for his nonnormative Christology. He also equates the resurrection with religious experience instead of with something that took place in the life of the historical Jesus exactly because for him the incarnation was a myth and not a reality in the particular life of Jesus of Nazareth. By pulling the ground out from under the actual historical foundation of the church, Knitter is led into the most extreme form of self-justification by actually redefining the nature of truth itself to fit his panentheistic ideal of a truth that cannot exist without "other truth." But of course if Jesus is the way, the truth and the life, then it is clear that truth is really exclusive in the sense that only Jesus is unique as the Word of God incarnate and as the only savior of the world. But it is also inclusive in the sense that who Jesus is excludes no one and depends upon no one's acceptance or rejection to be valid as saving truth. The embodiment of Knitter's self-justification is his belief that Jesus is *a* means for liberation and that liberation means commitment to a vision of liberating action. For Knitter our commitment to our vision is substituted for obedience to Christ himself and that is why he must argue for some form of self-justification. His Christology, as he says, requires that there could be other liberators or saviors of the world because, at the outset, it denies to Jesus his true being as the incarnate and risen Lord. All of this thinking simply ignores the fact that no one can really say Jesus is Lord and mean it without the Holy Spirit.

And that, unfortunately, is not the end of the story. We saw the same thing happen time and again as we explored the thinking of theologians as different as Roger Haight, John Hick, Gordon Kaufman and Sallie McFague. Because Roger Haight could not and would not allow the risen Lord himself as the incarnate Word to be the starting point of his reflections, he concluded that if anyone were to suppose that the resurrection described an event in the history of Jesus himself and therefore in our history, such a person would have committed a category mistake. Similarly, for Haight it is a matter of principle that Jesus' tomb need not be empty and, as he insists, Christianity would be the same even if there were no resurrection faith. All of this is possible and even necessary because, for Haight, resurrection language describes people's experiences of faith/hope and as such it is a symbolic expression of such experiences.

This thinking excludes the idea that Jesus really *is* the eternal Son of the Father in the flesh because its concept of reality is walled up within the experiences of faith and hope and gains its expression as a function of the creative imagination and not from a genuine relationship with the risen and ascended Lord himself as empowered by the Holy Spirit. This is why Haight can say that the stories of the appearances cannot be reports of events that actually happened but rather "were created afterwards as expressions of faith." Not only does this beg the question about where the truth of Christian faith and hope come from, but it transmutes it into a soliloquy in which the disciples were left alone with their faith after the death of Jesus. Consequently, Haight substitutes the disciples' memory of Jesus' ministry for the risen Lord himself and he does this precisely because instead of allowing for the unique incarnation of the Son in the flesh of Jesus of Nazareth, he adopted a Spirit Christology according to which Jesus is indwelt by the Holy Spirit to a greater degree than that rest of us and is to that extent to be considered the incarnation of God.

Yet, the unmistakable error in this thinking is the notion that Jesus differs from us only in degree and not in kind. It can easily be seen that Haight's difficulty accepting the resurrection as an event in Jesus' life that gives meaning to Christian faith and hope results from his failure to acknowledge the incarnation as a unique event in the life of the historical Jesus. That is why for Haight, as for Macquarrie, Hick and Knitter, it is a matter of principle that there can be other incarnations and other savior figures. This widespread opinion is possible only for those who deny or ignore the reality of the incarnation in its essential unity with the resurrection of the man Jesus himself. And it is no accident that for the theologians just mentioned there is no properly functioning doctrine of the immanent Trinity.

All of them ignore or deny that we can know who God is in himself because some of them think of the doctrine of the Trinity more as a description of the experience of salvation than of who God really is as the eternal Father, Son and Spirit while others ignore the eternal Trinity by thinking of God in unitarian terms that undercut the essential union of the Son and Spirit with the Father from all eternity. Ignoring the Holy Spirit in particular in the Spirit's unity with the Son and Father, is what allows theologians to shift the focus of faith away from the risen and ascended Lord and toward their own experiences of faith and hope, thus ultimately confusing the Holy Spirit with the human spirit. It is for these reasons that, among other things, they all believe there can be many saviors of the world. I have shown how this thinking leads directly to the kind of self-justification that weakens Christian faith and hope by supposing that, in the words of Haight, we "can project upon him [Jesus] all the weaknesses of human existence in order to retrieve from him the inspiration of the power of his earthly life." If Jesus' function for faith and hope is merely as a model we use for our own inspiration, then once again we have a Christology that leaves us alone with ourselves using Jesus to inspire ourselves. No longer are we dependent upon the Holy Spirit as the Lord and giver of life. This kind of thinking can only create more anxiety instead of pointing us to the true comfort that comes from a knowledge of the truth that Jesus, the incarnate Word is risen from the dead and is coming again to complete the redemption that is a reality in his own life for our benefit.

While Roger Haight at least attempted to reconcile his views with traditional Nicaean and Chalcedonian Christology (unsuccessfully of course) we have seen that John Hick, Gordon Kaufman and Sallie McFague had no intention of allowing Nicaea or Chalcedon to determine their thinking. Like Haight, they all believe that theology is essentially a matter of employing our creative imaginations to solve the world's problems. One might even say that for these thinkers it is precisely because their driving motive is a rather unconcealed form of self-justification that they cannot accept the fact that theology is never self-grounded but can only be grounded in an act of God himself coming into history from outside. It is a matter of complete embarrassment for these theologians to think that a true theology of freedom might be inextricably tied to the fact that the resurrection was an actual event in the life of the historical Jesus which gives meaning to Christian faith and hope through the ages. This is the case for Kaufman and McFague because they insist that in light of evolution we can no longer imagine that salvation could come in the form of one individual, Jesus of Nazareth.

In his earlier theology Kaufman offered a "historicist" explanation of the resurrection by substituting for Jesus himself a set of hallucinations that he claimed escaped Docetism because it referred us to historical experiences on the part of the disciples. But we saw that his thinking was indeed Docetic because the NT did not refer primarily to the experiences of the disciples but to the event of the resurrection itself and thus to the risen Lord himself in his uniqueness as God incarnate as the one who enables faith and hope in the proper sense. In his later theology he regarded belief in the resurrection as an unfortunate form of triumphalism. And he believed the idea that God would be incarnate in one man, Jesus of Nazareth, was unintelligible while the idea that salvation took place exclusively in him represented a false form of reification of symbols. All of this we have seen, once again, illustrates with clarity the theme of this book. When Jesus himself as the incarnate Word is not the starting point for understanding the resurrection as the foundation for Christian theology, something else must take his place. For Kaufman that something else is the creative imagination, with the result that the theological task is equated with us using our religious imaginations to create a better world. Kaufman is so consistent in this that he eventually suggests that Christians made a serious mistake believing that Jesus was the only begotten Son of the Father and that Jews and Muslims were correct in criticizing them for compromising God's actual oneness (*GMD*, 119). In this way he enshrines the Arian heresy in place of the faith articulated at Nicaea and Chalcedon and he systematically excludes the idea that salvation is an act of God within history that cannot be equated with our working for a better world. As those who recognize and live their justification by faith Christians do, of course, work for a better world. But justification and salvation are acts of God that free them for this service of the present and coming kingdom and as such can never be reduced to these human activities of obedience without obviating genuine Christian faith and hope and plunging the church into confusion and anxiety about its own present and future. Again, the crucial weakness in this thinking is traceable to Kaufman's confusion of the Holy Spirit with the human spirit in the form of our creative imagination.

Sallie McFague, of course, thought of the resurrection more as a way of conceptualizing our experiences of God's presence than as an event in the life of Jesus. In fact the only way she could conceive of the resurrection in this scenario was to detach it from Jesus himself and argue that the resurrected Christ was "Christ freed from the body of Jesus of Nazareth." But the point of this book has been to show that because Jesus of Nazareth himself *is* the Word or Son of God incarnate, therefore, not only can we not think of the resurrection as referring to Christ freed from the body of Jesus, but we must direct our attention more specifically to Jesus himself in his true humanity (risen bodily from the dead) and now glorified and thus empowered by the Spirit and freed from sin, suffering evil and death. Jesus Christ himself lives. That is the testimony of the NT and it is quite specific with quite particular historical recollections feeding the memory of the church. For that reason our humanity and thus our bodiliness has a validity and meaning it cannot have in Gnostic-dualist forms of thought.

Because McFague's thinking is essentially universalist and thus Docetic (Gnostic-dualist), it is not Jesus Christ himself who gives meaning to her theological predilections, but rather her idea that God is mother, lover and friend of the world. When asked if these models are arbitrary as descriptions of who God really is McFague responded that because she does not know who God is, therefore she had to turn to those experiences that mattered most to her (motherhood, love and friendship) to explain who God is. But the problem with this, as we have seen, is that in her attempt to avoid being arbitrary, she could only respond arbitrarily by pointing us to our own experiences of ourselves in order to create God in our own image. As a result, she offers us the twin ideas that we can meet God in the ecological processes of creation (the world as God's body) and fight for the survival of the human race against potential nuclear and ecological destruction (salvation) by attempting to save the earth.

In her estimation Jesus cannot be ontologically different from other paradigmatic historical figures who manifest God's love for the world. He cannot be unique, she insists. Thus, in place of Jesus, the Son of God, who justifies and saves the godless, she substitutes her vague and agnostically determined view of a God who is on the side of life and its fulfillment. The only problem, as we have seen, is that, as McFague herself insists, we cannot really know who God is in his eternal nature, and so we are left with belief in a God who needs the world and is in reality indistinguishable from the world as his body. Like Knitter and Hick, McFague believes the incarnation is primarily a myth about the man Jesus so that today we must save the world by remythologizing the old story with a new one more in tune with the way we think today in terms of evolution. Hence for her, as for her mentor Gordon

Kaufman, the incarnation no longer can refer to a specific event in the life of Jesus. Rather it refers to the incarnation of God in his body the world. The result is that our faith is now sustained by our relation with the world around us rather than with our relation with the risen Lord himself. Here again the Holy Spirit in his essential union with the Word is ignored so that self-justification becomes the only viable option because everything depends on us. We are referred back to our own self-experience (because the Holy Spirit is confused with the human spirit once more) in order to re-define God, Christ and salvation. As we have seen, McFague goes so far as to claim that evil itself has its origin in God. And sin, she believes, can no longer be seen as an act against God but rather as an act against the world. All of this thinking reinforces the thesis of this book. Unless Jesus himself, the man from Nazareth, is acknowledged as the very Word of God incarnate in history, then the idea of his bodily resurrection will be an obstacle on the path toward self-justification with the result that incarnation and resurrection will simply become ways for us to speak about our relations with the world. Such thinking pays a dear price — by abstracting from the historical Jesus in his uniqueness — this approach leaves us alone and cut off from any objectively real transcendent divine action that could do for us what we cannot do for ourselves. It leaves us without the Holy Spirit once again as the Lord and giver of life and as the one who enables our faith in Christ himself.

We have already seen that John Hick and Paul Knitter agree with McFague that the incarnation and resurrection should be interpreted mythologically. In that way both theologians undermine the actual meaning of the NT as well as the meaning of Christology. We have already summarized Knitter's thinking. For Hick, Jesus' resurrection did not automatically put him in a unique category (as if it could!) so that it is easy for him to assume that the earliest Christologies were adoptionistic and argue that the meaning of the resurrection, insofar as it can be determined at all, refers "to the transitional event or events in virtue of which the Jesus movement survived the death of its founder." And Hick equates this transitional event or events with a numinous transforming experience rather than an outer sense experience.

Thinking mythologically, Hick literally is unable to acknowledge that what happened in the life of Jesus was something utterly new and inexplicable from outside a specific relationship with the unique God-man, Jesus himself — a relationship that we cannot create but that can arise only through the Holy Spirit miraculously enabling faith in the Word as the risen and ascended Lord himself encounters us and strengthens that faith. Instead he compares the disciples' transforming experiences with Paul's Damascus road experience and with near death experiences and concludes that Jesus was a man who was powerfully God-conscious and that as such he can still guide us in our lives today. It is clear that Hick's view of the incarnation shapes his view of the resurrection. Neither is to be conceived as a historical event in the life of Jesus giving meaning to Christian faith and hope. Instead both are seen as expressions of people's attitudes toward Jesus and as attempts to get other people to have similar positive attitudes. In no case can the incarnation or the resurrection refer to metaphysical facts, namely, to the truth that Jesus really was the incarnate Son of the Father and that Jesus really did rise bodily from the dead. It is not surprising then that Hick, like Macquarrie, espouses an inspiration or degree Christology according to which Jesus is really no different from anyone who lives a life of love and openness to the divine. In a manner similar to Roger Haight, Hick believes the community projected its own ideals onto Jesus and produced a "Christ-figure" who meets their spiritual needs. All of this is possible and even necessary for Hick because he assumes that the language of Nicaea was both optional and mythological.

It goes without saying that Hick's thinking sets the theme of this book into glaring relief. Thinking mythologically, as Hick does, means that Jesus' humanity can never be decisive in one's thinking because myth by its very nature embodies an idea of timeless non-historical truth. As such Jesus could never be acknowledged as uniquely divine and human, but can only be seen as one instance in the Docetic/pluralist ideal of God-consciousness espoused by Hick. Jesus is only one incarnation and one savior among many others. This is Hick's religious ideal; he wishes to invent a universalist religion in which a God-centered universe of faiths will no longer have to worry about whether there is one unique savior of the world. In his mind this will eliminate religious conflict and lead toward the peaceful co-existence of religions. And it is easy for him to think of God in an Arian universalist fashion precisely because for him the idea of the Trinity is just that, an idea symbolizing the "three-fold character of our human awareness of God" instead of an idea that corresponds to who God is as Father, Son and Spirit from all eternity as he has made himself known in and through his unique self-revelation in his Word and Spirit.

Hick's mythological universalism is both dualistic and agnostic. On the one hand Hick believes that the Holy Trinity, Allah, Vishnu and Tao are different manifestations of the same reality — what he calls "the Real." On the other hand he thinks we can never actually know "the Real" in itself. However, if we can never actually know "the Real," what is it that we are talking about when we refer to this "reality"? Clearly, in Hick's thinking it is his mythological unitarian-universalist idea of God that ignores the particularity of who God really is in Jesus Christ. While Christians believe they really know God in his inner reality as Father, Son and Holy Spirit through faith in Jesus Christ, his Son which is itself imparted by the Holy Spirit and thus is not under our control, Hick insists that in his new pluralist construction we can know the Father directly without the Son. In the end Hick cannot describe who God really is and what he does describe is inherently an Arian construct that severs the bond between the Father and Son and leaves us alone with ourselves. All of this occurs because Hick confuses the Holy Spirit with the human spirit. Hence, Hick's idea that the Holy Trinity, Allah, Vishnu and Tao are all different manifestations of the same reality is completely off the mark by virtue of the fact that Jesus is not the embodiment of an idea that can be described as "the Real." Rather Jesus himself is the incarnate Son of the Father and as such is the only man who is one in being with God and with us. The Trinity, then, is not one manifestation of some hidden reality among others. The Trinity is the one, true and eternal God himself existing in unapproachable light, but also the one who manifests himself in history as our Lord, Savior, Helper and Friend in the man Jesus and in his particular resurrection from the dead.

It is just this universalism in Hick's view of God that lays the groundwork for his particular form of self-justification. Instead of allowing Jesus himself as the Word incarnate, risen from the dead to justify and sanctify us in thought, word and deed through the Holy Spirit, Hick equates salvation with human observance of the Golden Rule and concludes that salvation cannot be the act of Jesus himself in his unity with the Father and Holy Spirit. Instead salvation takes place wherever anyone observes the Golden Rule. The only problem with this reasoning is that it fails to recognize the depth of human sin or the true meaning of salvation as an act of God. God himself, who is for us in Jesus Christ, has been so marginalized in Hick's thinking that God can be little more than the idea of human beings working together for a better world. But that is just the problem. The world into which the Word of God entered in Jesus of Nazareth rejected its savior quite explicitly at that particular time. It is not surprising that it continues to do so today. What, perhaps, is somewhat surprising is the fact that this rejection is now taking place in the form of those who still wish to call themselves Christians.

All of this thinking bears out the thesis of this book in a startling way. My point is simply this. We must begin Christian theology with Jesus Christ the man from Nazareth who was and is the Word of God incarnate because, as T. F. Torrance consistently recognized, he is an ultimate; he is *the ultimate* for Christian thinking and acting. We cannot bypass him because he himself is God among us and thus is our only entrée into a genuine knowledge of God and salvation. As Karl Barth also insisted, we really need Jesus, the Word of God incarnate, noetically and ontically at the outset of our reflections because he himself, the risen and ascended Lord, is the only one who can validate our reflections. Christian faith and hope are defined not by the way we believe and hope but by who Jesus Christ was and is as the incarnate, risen and ascended Lord. Because of that, any theoretical or practical departure from the faith of the church, namely, from the fact that the risen Jesus himself enables and maintains our faith and hope in and through the power of his Holy Spirit, necessarily means that we will confuse our justification and salvation with those social, political and religious activities that matter most to us.

Importantly, such thinking, as I have indicated throughout this book, is possible only because and to the extent that theologians believe that they can and must turn to those experiences that matter most to them to understand who God is, who we are and what we must do to create a better world. The point of this book then is really quite simple (with profound ramifications of course). And it is this. Whenever theologians do not begin thinking about God in faith, that is, in faith in Jesus Christ himself as the author and finisher of faith, they will necessarily begin thinking in a way which will have to substitute some other god and thus some other savior for the one true God (the immanent Trinity acting economically as our savior, helper and friend). This will never relieve the world's distress. It can only enhance it. And the only hope for the world is a return to Jesus Christ who came to save the world and not to condemn it.

That is why I chose to follow the thinking of Karl Barth and T. F. Torrance in order to hold together the resurrection and incarnation in their indissoluble unity as acts of the triune God within history that give meaning to Christian faith and practice on all levels. Both theologians help us realize that Christology must begin again and again with the risen Jesus who was and is the Word of God incarnate. This is the direction toward which we are pointed by the Holy Spirit. Neither theologian would allow for the idea that we might begin Christology from below with the notion that the incarnation was the conclusion and not the starting point of Christology. Because Jesus really is uniquely divine and human and because this is not a construct of Christian self-consciousness, Barth and Torrance rightly insisted that faith and hope are definitely defined by their relation to Jesus of Nazareth and to no one and nothing else.

There is no need to rehearse the important positive points made by Torrance and Barth about the inherent connection between the resurrection and the incarnation for all aspects of theology. That was already accomplished in Chapters One, Three and Four above. Here it is important to realize simply that the thinking of two important contemporary theologians,

Karl Rahner and Wolfhart Pannenberg, embodied just the proposal that Torrance and Barth rightly rejected with important consequences. There is no doubt that, unlike many of the other theologians who we saw in Chapters Five through Seven, Rahner and Pannenberg wished to maintain the sense of the traditional doctrines of incarnation and resurrection just as seriously as did Torrance and Barth. Both Rahner and Pannenberg, each in their own way, but in many ways in quite similar fashion, attempted to construct Christologies from below while at the same time maintaining the essential sense of Nicaea and Chalcedon. Both theologians, however, as we have seen in detail, ran into methodological and therefore theological difficulties because and to the extent that they did not in fact begin their thinking with Jesus Christ himself but rather tried to fit a historically reconstructed Jesus into their *a priori* anthropological views.

Rahner insisted that we could not begin thinking in a too narrowly christological way with Jesus himself because that was too simple an answer for contemporary theology and Jesus himself, he believed, had become a problem today. We must admit that our analysis has shown that for many contemporary theologians Jesus really is a problem in the sense that they can no longer accept him for who he truly is. In this Rahner is correct. But of course that is hardly a reason to abandon faith in him. One cannot change reality because one finds it disturbing and even offensive! Nonetheless, instead of beginning and ending his thinking exclusively with the incarnate and risen Lord himself, Rahner turned to transcendental experience to make sense of the resurrection and incarnation. Unlike many of the other thinkers we have considered, Rahner very seriously wanted to maintain the truth of the Christian faith and to affirm Jesus' once-for-all uniqueness. But his method kept him from doing so. We have seen that it was not Jesus himself, risen from the dead, who consistently shaped Rahner's thinking about the incarnation and the resurrection. Rather it was our transcendental experiences of faith and hope. In order to accomplish his reinterpretation of the resurrection and incarnation Rahner ascribed grace and revelation and thus also salvation directly to human being and action in the form of an obediential potency and a supernatural existential with disastrous results. Instead of pointing us to our constant need for Jesus himself and instead of allowing the Holy Spirit the freedom to unite us to Christ himself, Rahner argued that everyone experienced resurrection hope, anonymously perhaps, simply by having a transcendental experience of hope for some sort of life beyond death. And, ethically speaking, Rahner concluded that self-acceptance is the same as accepting Christ.

Our position, of course, is that any such thinking completely undermines the need for Jesus and obscures the fact that it is our relationship with Jesus himself, as attested in the NT, that shapes our thinking so that it is quite impossible to be an anonymous Christian or to have an anonymous knowledge of God or an anonymous experience of the risen Lord. Yes, indeed, the risen and ascended Lord is quite able to work outside the visible church to bring people to himself and enable behavior that is beneficial to society at large just as the Holy Spirit blows where he chooses. But that does not change the fact that a Christian is one who accepts the teaching of the apostles about Jesus himself. It is not an anonymous teaching with an amorphous content so that one could actually conclude, as Rahner does, that it is a matter of indifference whether or not the risen Lord had a head; or one could conclude, as Rahner does, that everyone has an unthematic and anonymous knowledge of God and of Christ. The apostolic teaching was a specific teaching with a very definite content, namely, that Christ has died and Christ has risen and Christ will come again. In the end Rahner's universalism is really not all that different from the more blatant forms of universalism advocated by others such as McFague, Kaufman and Knitter. Knitter himself, as we have seen, appealed to Rahner's transcendental method to validate his own universalism. And the culprit that allows for such universalism and even requires it is Rahner's starting point in transcendental experience. That is why I set Rahner's transcendental theology into relief against the background of the thinking offered by Barth and Torrance who unequivocally refused to begin theology with experience or ideas but instead insisted that theology must always begin with the risen Lord himself who was none other that the incarnate Word, Jesus of Nazareth. This is the direction to which we are driven by the Holy Spirit in its distinction from the human spirit. If only Rahner could have consistently maintained the important insight that contemporary theology must begin with Jesus himself because he alone is God's self-communication within history, much could have been different in his thought. And there could have been wide agreement between the Reformed theology of Torrance and Barth on the one side and the Roman Catholic theology of Rahner on the other.

Theoretically, Rahner could have begun there, given his belief in the identity of the immanent and economic Trinity. But he chose not to do so because instead he pursued a kind of correlation theology that sought to explain the meaning of Christian faith according to a set of experiences universally available and explicable without faith in Jesus himself. This opened the door for him to construct an *a priori* anthropology in order to explain Christology. And this, we have argued, following the thought of Torrance and Barth, is precisely the thinking that undermines Christology methodologically and materially by ignoring the actual uniqueness of Jesus and our need for him at the outset. It makes him unable to distinguish the Easter event as an event in the life of Jesus from the Easter faith of the disciples. Similarly it leads him to believe that Jesus rose into their faith and into ours as well in a way that allows his theology to bypass the historical testimony of the NT to insist that an anthropology constructed according to his method could explain the necessity of and meaning of the resurrection (and subsequently of the incarnation) without first acknowledging and believing the revealed Word itself. This ultimately led to Rahner's belief in the identity of love of God and love of neighbor and the idea that our choices of good or evil determine who we will become in such a way that very little, if any room, is left for Jesus Christ himself to be the ultimate arbiter of what we are and what we will become. Is it not ultimately a form of self-justification to claim, as Rahner does, that self-acceptance is the same as accepting Jesus and his Gospel? Does not such thinking once more sever the bond between the Word and Spirit?

The positive position adopted in this book was established by comparing Rahner's thinking with the positions offered by Torrance and Barth. It seems clear to me that both Barth and Torrance allow the incarnate and risen Jesus himself to determine what they have to say about the resurrection, incarnation, the Trinity and Christian ethics. Any Christian systematic theology must begin, as both Torrance and Barth insist, with Jesus himself as the risen Lord and thus with the testimony of the NT. There can be no going behind the faith of the NT in search of a historical Jesus or a more original experience of Jesus. There is no such phenomenon. The miracle of Christmas itself eliminated that approach to Christology root and branch. It is here that choices must be made. Either one can begin thinking christologically with Jesus himself as attested in the NT or one will begin with a set of experiences and ideas and think that somehow divinity was ascribed to Jesus by the community on the basis of its experiences (Ebionite Christology) or its ideas (Docetic Christology). There is no third option. And once that second choice is made, implicitly or explicitly, Christology is undermined and the door is opened for an Ebionite or Docetic explanation of Christ's resurrection and then for a kind of natural theology that universalizes the meaning of grace and revelation in such a way that it is thought that an *a priori* doctrine of the God-Man is not only possible but necessary. Yet, as we saw with Torrance and Barth, any such attempt at an *a priori* understanding of grace and revelation necessarily means a misunderstanding of Christian revelation in its identity with Jesus Christ himself.

Neither Barth nor Torrance would allow theologians to snoop around within their own experiences or among the inventory of their own ideas in order to find their justification because they both insisted, quite rightly in my view, that our justification was and is a reality only in Jesus Christ and there-fore only in faith in him (not ourselves). Justification is tied to the Holy Spirit acting to enable us to live from and in Christ himself. Both Barth and Torrance were able to insist in a way that Rahner could not that there is al-ways a specific content to the Christian confession, namely, we cannot sepa-rate the form and content of revelation and thus we cannot know the true meaning of Christ's bodily resurrection or the true meaning of the incarna-tion without acknowledging God's particular self-communication in the man Jesus from Nazareth. The form is the life of the historical Jesus as attested by both the OT and the NT. The content is the action of God in history in his Word and Spirit in its prophetic and apostolic forms. Both Barth and Torrance therefore would have nothing to do with any sort of anonymous knowledge of God or of Christ or of the resurrection because their thinking was decisively tied to the events of Christ's life recorded in scripture. This is the strength of a Christology that allows Jesus himself to shape one's under-standing of anthropology rather than the other way around. This strength is also the weakness of Christology in the sense that any theology that takes seri-ous account of Jesus Christ himself will never be self-grounded but will al-ways reckon with the fact that Jesus himself, in his distinction and union with Christians is the sole enabler of faith and hope through the present activity in history of his Holy Spirit which is inseparable from the Word of God incar-nate in Jesus himself.

As we have seen, in contrast to Rahner, Torrance and Barth quite rightly emphasized that Jesus' bodily resurrection was a matter of history. In no sense were the NT descriptions of the appearances or of the empty tomb simply ways of speaking of the disciples' experiences of faith. Torrance and Barth in-sisted that what happened in Jesus' life was something utterly new which could not be compared to any event before or after it. Almost no one today accepts this proviso. Yet, in my view, this is an important insight that must be retrieved if Christ's bodily resurrection is to be allowed to have its properly determinative place in Christology and trinitarian theology today. As we have seen throughout this book it is essential that Jesus, risen bodily from the dead and now ascended into heaven and coming again, be acknowledged as the Lord of the church and of the world. Such acknowledgment means that we cannot and must not attempt to think about God, Christ, the church or the sacraments in a way that bypasses history because it is in history that God himself became one of us and it is in and through history that God makes himself known and enables us to live our eternal life here below by faith and hope in the risen Lord, and when Christ comes again and redemption is com-plete, in a relationship with God that is not merely a vision but one in which we fully relate with God himself in new spiritual bodies (enlivened by the Holy Spirit) as those who will be raised to eternal life according to Christ's promise. But the security of our knowledge of our own eternal life, as it is grounded in the risen Lord, can only be found in the particular history attested in the NT and in the history of the church's teaching regarding the uniqueness of Jesus himself. In other words it is not found in history in general or in a set of experiences accessible to people generally speaking or even in a set of ideas that happens to be universally available. What is known in faith, which is itself enabled miraculously by the Holy Spirit, is that the particular history of Jesus himself makes a difference to history generally in such a way that it can neither be seen nor understood properly apart from a specific relationship with Jesus — a relationship that is never controlled by the church or by human individuals within or without the church. It is controlled rather by the Holy Spirit who is distinguished from all human spirits by the fact that he opposes our self-indulgence and our self-justification and enables us to live our new and righteous lives in and from Christ himself.

Finally, what can be said here about the thinking of Wolfhart Pannenberg? We have spent a great deal of time on the thought of Pannenberg because, among contemporary theologians, he is one who explicitly followed Barth while also diverging from Barth in a number of crucial ways. More than that, however, Pannenberg is a Christian theologian who is intensely interested in the truth of the Christian faith in a way that others such as John Hick, Roger Haight, Gordon Kaufman, Paul Knitter and Sallie McFague are not. His thinking represents a massive attempt to re-think Christology "from below" without losing the main confessions of Christianity concerning Christ's eternal Sonship and without in any way undermining the central importance of Christ's resurrection from the dead for Christian faith and practice. And, as we have seen, Pannenberg wishes to maintain the general sense of a properly conceived doctrine of the immanent Trinity in order to underscore God's freedom for us in Christ and through the Spirit.

Nevertheless, we found that Pannenberg's belief espoused in *Jesus — God and Man* and never abandoned even in his later work, that the incarnation must be seen as the conclusion and not the starting point for his Christology from below caused severe damage to his attempt to present Jesus himself in his authentic, definitive and essential deity. The appearance of adoptionism (in spite of his explicit rejection of it) ran throughout Pannenberg's thinking. And the main problem was identified early on directly by Barth himself. Pannenberg had allowed his thinking about Jesus of Nazareth to be shaped by a prior anthropology into which he then inserted the NT recollections in order to demonstrate apologetically how and why belief in Jesus' divinity arose.

But if Barth and Torrance are right, and I believe they are, then the only one who can demonstrate Jesus' true divinity and humanity is Jesus himself, the incarnate and risen Lord. And that is what he does in the power of his Holy Spirit even now as people are enabled to know the triune God in and through their union with Christ by grace and revelation. Pannenberg's method will not allow for this and that is what opens the door to his ideas that: (1) human beings are open to God; (2) Jesus is in the process of becoming who he will be eternally; (3) God himself is dependent on the outcome of history; (4) the resurrection itself constitutes Jesus' divinity; (5) the God of the philosophers can actually function as a criterion for knowledge of the true Christian God; (6) we cannot begin thinking about Jesus' resurrection in faith in the incarnate Word; (7) we cannot begin thinking about God today with the reality of God known in faith; and (8) we are the ones who have to work to create neighbors instead of allowing our neighbors to become visible in the present activity of the trinitarian God himself who alone can enable this in Spirit and in truth. All of these assumptions we have explored and found wanting because each, in its own way, separates the incarnation from the resurrection and then places the weight of emphasis on our approach to God rather than on God's approach to us in his Word and Spirit. There is no need to rehearse the details here. It is enough to realize that Pannenberg's extremely sophisticated Christology suffers from a major weakness: it refuses to begin and end with the simple fact that Jesus is the Son of God because he is and not for any other reason whatsoever, whether it be historical or theological.

In sum, the most important positive and negative points then to be noted with assistance of the theology of Barth and Torrance are: (1) Christology must begin with Jesus Christ himself and when it does it has the possibility of discovering something utterly new and different — something that could never be discovered in any other way — that is, that God is not locked up within himself but God has become incarnate to enable us to know the truth and to live eternal life in union with him in and through Christ himself and by the power of the Holy Spirit; (2) Christology must hold together the doctrines of the incarnation and resurrection because it is in the incarnate Word who lived a life of perfect obedience in order to represent us before the Father and overcome our sinful alienation from God in and through his entire life and then in and through his death and resurrection that we are saved. Any idea whatsoever that the incarnation should be seen as the result and not the starting point for theology necessarily means a compromise of Christ's true divinity which must be acknowledged as definitive, authentic and essential. That means Jesus' divinity cannot be seen as coming into being by virtue of his human relations with his Father — that would neither be authentic, definitive nor essential — it would be a dependent deity; (3) Christology must take seriously both Jesus' full divinity and his full humanity and therefore theologians may recognize that, while we seek God in Christ and therefore love God and our neighbors, all of this becomes a possibility of faith and grace as empowered by the Holy Spirit and therefore our human actions in service of the kingdom of God never become self-validating and always exclude even the slightest idea of self-justification both in the sphere of knowledge of God and of Christ and in the sphere of human behavior. Our Christian lives are never the guarantee that we are faithful Christians. Our Christian lives are always marked by sin and brokenness and always stand in need of God's grace and love. Hence Christians never look to themselves to understand the meaning of who Jesus Christ is today, but only toward the living Lord himself who is coming again to judge the living and the dead; (4) Christology can never detach the title Christ from Jesus himself and attempt to locate the meaning of the doctrine of the incarnation within the community or within the world at large; (5) Grace and revelation can never be detached from Jesus himself and located directly within our Christian experiences of faith and hope. Because Christ rose bodily from the dead, his unique divine-human representation of us before the Father as the ascended and advent Lord has not come to an end. That is why we must look to him and not to the Christian experience of faith for the comfort and truth of Christianity.

Endnotes

Notes to the Preface

1. David Fergusson, "Interpreting the Resurrection," *Scottish Journal of Theology* (hereafter: *SJT*) 38 (1985): 287-305, 287.

2. Rudolf Bultmann, "New Testament and Mythology," 1-44, at 42, in *Kerygma and Myth: A Theological Debate,* ed. Hans Werner Bartsch, trans. Reginald H. Fuller (London: SPCK, 1954). See also Fergusson, "Interpreting the Resurrection," 288. By contrast, of course, Karl Barth insisted that the Easter-narratives of the NT attested "the Lord Himself who is in the centre of the picture, and not the miracle of His appearing (although this is emphasised too). They do not attest only a miracle of believing. . . . They attest Jesus Himself, who, having come back to them miraculously, creates and kindles this recognition. They attest the miraculous consequence of the divine act of His awakening from the dead as it took place for Him and therefore for them. They attest His living presence." Karl Barth, *Church Dogmatics,* 4 vols. in 13 parts (hereafter referred to in text as *CD*), vol. 4, part 2: *The Doctrine of Reconciliation,* trans. G. W. Bromiley, ed. G. W. Bromiley and T. F. Torrance (Edinburgh: T&T Clark, 1970), 148.

3. Fergusson, "Interpreting the Resurrection," 294.

4. Fergusson, "Interpreting the Resurrection," 296.

5. Fergusson, "Interpreting the Resurrection," 297.

6. Fergusson, "Interpreting the Resurrection," 299-300.

7. Fergusson, "Interpreting the Resurrection," 292-93. This excellent statement of the traditional view is supported by Larry W. Hurtado, *Lord Jesus Christ: Devotion to Jesus in Earliest Christianity* (Grand Rapids: Eerdmans, 2003), 170, when he writes: "The reference . . . to Jesus' burial (1 Cor. 15:4) functions to indicate a real death, and to assert, thus, a real resurrection, not merely a postmortem apparition but a new and momentous eschatological event . . . what Paul is anxious to reaffirm as the tradition is that Jesus has been raised from death to glorious eschatological bodily existence (15:42-49), and that his resurrection is the unique pattern for, and proof of, the future resurrection of believers."

8. Fergusson, "Interpreting the Resurrection," 300.

9. Strangely, even though Bultmann is willing to admit that "When he suffered death, Jesus was already the Son of God . . ." ("New Testament and Mythology," 39), he was unwilling to admit that Jesus, as the Son of God, was the subject of the events of the cross and resurrection, but instead thought of the NT accounts of the resurrection as myth and, since he could not accept the notion of the miraculous, he removed the resurrection from the sphere of history as an event in the life of Jesus and placed it in the faith of the disciples. Hence for him "*faith in the resurrection is really the same thing as faith in the saving efficacy of the cross,* faith in the cross as the cross of Christ. . . . The saving efficacy of the cross is not derived from the fact that it is the cross of Christ: it is the cross of Christ because it has this saving efficacy" ("New Testament and Mythology," 41, emphasis in original). On the contrary, the saving efficacy of the cross is indeed derived from the fact that it is the cross of Christ because he is the Son of God who died for us and as the Son of God incarnate he was indeed raised from the dead, destroying death itself. This is where Barth's insistence that the saving efficacy of Christ's actions for us is grounded in his antecedent existence as the eternal Son of the Father is decisively important. Barth's proper view of the matter is instructive in this context: "Because and as the event of revelation participates in the majesty of the will and act of God, because it is itself a divine act of majesty as the revelation of God in the flesh, it necessarily has the character of a miracle . . . it is not because it is miraculous that it is majestic, but because it is majestic that it is miraculous. . . . It is the positive aspect and its acknowledgment — that it is the majesty of God, the Lord, who is at work in Him and gives Himself to be known in Him; Himself and His will and the act of reconciliation accomplished in the crucifixion of the Son of God and Son of Man. The miracle is unequivocal in itself and as such" (*CD* IV/2, 147).

10. That would indeed be the solution to the problems that I highlighted in *Justification: What's at Stake in the Current Debates,* ed. Mark Husbands and Daniel J. Treier (Downers Grove, IL: InterVarsity Press, 2004), ch. 9, "The Theology of Justification in Dogmatic Context."

Notes to Chapter 1

1. See Barth, *CD* I/2, 40f. and 151ff.

2. See Chapter Two below. As we shall see, Rahner argues that the human nature of Christ is the constitutive real symbol of the Logos. As such it is filled with the reality symbolized and stands in a mutual causal connection with that reality. The implications of this thinking will be discussed in detail in Chapter Four.

3. This is why Barth insists in *CD* IV/1 that "The historical actuality of Jesus Christ is not the highest evolutionary continuation, the crown and completion of the positing which God has willed and accomplished of a reality of the world and man which is distinct from Himself. It is not the immanent *telos* of such a reality" (49).

4. Hence "If it is true that God became man, then in this we have to recognise and respect His eternal will and purpose and resolve — His free and gracious will which He did not owe it either to Himself or to the world to have, by which He did not need to come to the decision to which He has in fact come, and behind which, in these circumstances, we

cannot go, behind which we do not have to reckon with any Son of God in Himself, with any λόγος ἄσαρκος, with any other Word of God than that which was made flesh" (*CD* IV/1, 52).

5. Cf. Barth, *CD* I/2, 63ff.

6. Barth, *CD* I/2, 159ff.

7. Barth, *CD* I/2, 161.

8. Arguing against Brunner's assertion that it is inconceivable that everyone, "'even those who lived thousands of years before Jesus,' should have their being in the history of Jesus, that the history of human existence should derive from that of the man Jesus" Barth asked pointedly: "is it so inconceivable, does it need such a great imagination to realise, is it not the simplest thing in the world, that if the history of Jesus is the event of atonement, if the atonement is real and effective because God Himself became man to be the subject of this event, if this is not concealed but revealed, if it is the factor which calls us irresistibly to faith and obedience, then how can it be otherwise than that in this factor, and therefore in the history of Jesus, we have to do with the reality which underlies and precedes all other reality as the first and eternal Word of God, that in this history we have actually to do with the ground and sphere, the atmosphere of the being of every man, whether they lived thousands of years before or after Jesus? Does not this question, this protest against the incarnate Word as the content of the eternal will of God, involve a retrogression even behind Schleiermacher . . . ?" (*CD* IV/1, 53).

9. Karl Barth, *Evangelical Theology: An Introduction* (hereafter referred to in text as *Evangelical Theology*), trans. Grover Foley (Grand Rapids: Eerdmans, 1963), 29-30. It will be important to see the difference here between Barth and Torrance on the one side and Rahner on the other. Rahner believes that the "pre-existence Christology" of John and Paul is not "a strictly original datum of revelation . . . but inspired theology, developed from Jesus' self-interpretation in connection with the experience of his resurrection" (Karl Rahner, *The Trinity* [hereafter: *Trinity*], trans. Joseph Donceel [New York: Herder and Herder, 1970], 66) while Barth and Torrance, as we shall see, insist that the resurrection, as an act of the living Lord, is the revelation by the risen Jesus, of who he was from the very beginning of his earthly way as this is in fact grounded in his antecedent existence as the begotten Son of the Father. For Barth and Torrance his pre-existence is thus an original datum of revelation because it is identical with the fact that this man Jesus was the Word who was with God and was God. Recognition of this truth must be grounded in who Jesus actually was and not simply in his "self-interpretation" and in light of the "experience of his resurrection." As we shall see in detail in Chapter Three this is why Torrance spends a great deal of time explaining why it is improper to separate theology from historical critical understanding of scripture. And much later we shall see how Wolfhart Pannenberg's Christology from below falters over this same issue. In *CD* IV/2, where Barth affirmed the importance of the historical in considering the resurrection, he also rejected any sort of two-stage Christology: "It will not be 'the historical facts' which we have to find (or think we have already found) somewhere behind the texts, and which we then claim as objective reality" (149). For Barth "The singularity of the event of revelation conditions the singularity of the knowledge which it awakens and underlies. Because it takes place in the majesty of the will and act of God, the knowledge of it cannot derive from the knowing man, but only from the One who is revealed in it" (*CD* IV/2, 149).

10. See Barth's account in the doctrine of reconciliation of the "resisting element in man" which he says can take three forms: (1) indifference, (2) the creation of "world-views" and (3) the apparent acceptance of grace "though only in its own way and with a view to rendering it finally innocuous" and thus ensuring that it will no longer give offense by creating unrest and thereby giving rest (CD IV/3, 258f.). Indifference of course means acting as though reconciliation had not in fact taken place in Jesus Christ; the creation of world-views represents an active human attempt to come to terms with revelation and reconciliation by incorporating God's act of grace into a view of reality which then becomes the criterion for the word of grace itself. "The Word of grace has the dangerous force of an offence which strikes man from without and from a superior height, and in virtue of which he must only try to understand himself, and can only understand himself, as he is understood. . . . It does not say No to him, but Yes, and indeed the most radical, warm and unconditional Yes that could ever be conceived. Hence it does not forbid him to say Yes to himself in his own place. . . . It allows him, however, to say to himself only the Yes which is an answer to the Yes said to him. This is its dangerous force. This is why it is an offence to him. A world-view is the glorious possibility of evading this offence, of fleeing from it. So long as man, viewing the world, is observer, constructor and manager, he is safe, or at any rate thinks he is safe from this offence" (CD IV/3, 257). In Barth's mind of course the problem here is one of pride: no world-views "can find any place for Jesus Christ. Of course, they can find room for an abstract God and an abstract man, but not for Him, the God-man. . . . They offer plenty of pictures, panoramas, generalities, doctrines, human attempts at self-understanding. But His voice . . . is not heard in any of them" (CD IV/3, 257).

11. Here it is to be noted that all charges against Barth of Christomonism are subverted by his emphasis on our union and distinction from Christ through the Holy Spirit. Hence, speaking of our responsibility to live in conformity with God's grace revealed in Christ, Barth insisted that "there can be no question of a conformity which means equality, of anything in the nature of a deification of man, of making him a second Christ. The correspondence which alone can be considered in this connexion cannot and will not mean abolition of 'the infinite qualitative difference' between God and man. It is a question of responsibility and therefore of a correspondence in which God and man are in clear and inflexible antithesis. . . . Whatever the action demanded of us may be, it will be our action, a human action. It will have to attest and confirm the great acts of God; but it will not be able to continue or repeat them. The covenant, the partnership remains, but there is no development of an identity between God and man" (CD II/2, 577).

12. Karl Barth, Credo, trans. Robert McAfee Brown (New York: Charles Scribner's Sons, 1962), 166-67. Underestimating Jesus' Lordship followed from depreciating the foundation of the community in his resurrection and a failure to perceive the "consolation of the Holy Spirit in whose work the community may find full satisfaction at every moment in its time of waiting" (CD III/2, 509). Barth rightly was suspicious of any anthropological attempt to ground and explain Christian hope because any such attempt meant ignoring our one possible hope which is Jesus Christ himself coming again: "Jesus Christ is also the content of the divine pledge, the One in whom the Christian is summoned to hope. It is a terrible thing if at this point, at the last moment, we ignore Him as though He were only a means or instrument or channel, and look to something different from Him, some general

gift mediated by Him, regarding this as the object of Christian hope. . . . If we look aside here, trying to understand the awaited and expected being of man and all creation in the service of God only as the manifestation of a general idea of man or of being, we shall betray the fact that for all our recalling and appealing to the name of Jesus Christ earlier — indeed from the very first in our discussion of the being of reconciled man — we have not really been thinking or answering in relation to Him but have been developing an anthropological concept which we have found elsewhere and to which we have simply given a christological superscription" (*CD* IV/1, 116). See also *CD* IV/3, 931, where Barth insists that Christians expect "The coming of Jesus Christ in glory, i.e., His consummating revelation of that which is still hidden, namely, that the will of God has been definitively, irrevocably and unassailably done by Him on earth as it is done in heaven."

13. It is worth noting that Catherine Mowry LaCugna, *God for Us: The Trinity and Christian Life* (hereafter: *God for Us*) (San Francisco: HarperSanFrancisco, 1991) actually allows theodicy to set her agenda with the idea that all critiques of "classical theism cry out for soteriology: Can we believe in God after Auschwitz? Can a male savior save women? . . ." (3). Precisely because of this, her trinitarian theology is not grounded in the truth described by Barth but in her belief that "Divine life is . . . *our* life" (1). Hence her ethics is essentially Pelagian: "The heart of the Christian life is to be united with the God of Jesus Christ by means of communion with one another" (1). "*Entering into divine life therefore is impossible unless we also enter into a life of love and communion with others*" (*God for Us*, 382, emphasis in original). Indeed "According to the doctrine of the Trinity, God lives as the mystery of love among persons" and we should ask "what forms of life best enable us to live as Christ lived" (*God for Us*, 378). It is just because she reduces God's eternal self-sufficient existence to God's existence for us that she substitutes our communion with each other for Jesus Christ himself acting for us through the Holy Spirit. Notice that she argues we are united with Christ "by means" of communion with one another; this makes our salvation contingent on what we do. That is what Barth is denying here in order to affirm that we are united with Christ by means of the Holy Spirit uniting us to the man Jesus who, as God incarnate, reconciled the world to God once and for all. Thus the means of union with Christ is not our communion with each other; it is instead the Holy Spirit. And the hallmark of Barth's theology is that the Holy Spirit cannot be separated from Jesus, the Word of God incarnate. Substituting our communion with each other for the Holy Spirit would imply some sort of self-justification and would make our relations with God and each other uncertain. Unfortunately, in response to the question of theodicy, LaCugna argues that "The only option is for Christian theology to start afresh from its original basis in the experience of being saved . . ." (3). LaCugna's confusion of the immanent and economic Trinity stems from her confusion about the basis for Christian theology. That basis, as Barth here correctly contends, is Jesus Christ himself as the Word of God incarnate.

14. In his doctrine of reconciliation Barth rejects the same thinking once again by rejecting the idea of conditional salvation:

> Were Christ a thousand times to Bethlehem come,
> And yet not born in thee, 'twould spell thy doom,
> Golgotha's cross, it cannot save from sin,

Except for thee that cross be raised within,
I say, it helps thee not that Christ is risen,
If thou thyself art still in death's dark prison. (*CD* IV/1, 287)

15. Wolfhart Pannenberg, *Systematic Theology, Volume 1* (hereafter: *Systematic Theology 1*), trans. Geoffrey W. Bromiley (Grand Rapids: Eerdmans, 1991), 430.

16. All of this is well documented in my book *Divine Freedom and the Doctrine of the Immanent Trinity: In Dialogue with Karl Barth and Contemporary Theology* (hereafter: *Divine Freedom*) (London and New York: T&T Clark, A Continuum Imprint, 2002), e.g., ch. 7, esp. 203 for Moltmann's thinking and 152f. for Pannenberg's.

17. See, e.g., Molnar, *Divine Freedom*, ch. 7. See also David Lauber, *Barth on the Descent into Hell: God, Atonement and the Christian Life* (Aldershot: Ashgate Publishing Limited, 2004), ch. 4.

18. See *CD* IV/1, 279ff., for how Barth understands Jesus' ministry and sacrifice as his unique and unrepeatable act of reconciliation of us with God. "That He has made a perfect sacrifice means primarily and comprehensively and decisively that He has fulfilled the will of God the doing of which the action of all human priests and all the sacrifices made by men could only proclaim and attest" (281).

19. Hence Barth insists that Christ's sacrifice is a human action "but in and with the human action it is also a divine action, in which there takes place that which all human offerings can only attest, in which the reservation under which all human offering takes place, and its character as merely representative, symbolical and significative are done away, in which the concept of sacrifice is fulfilled and the true and effective sacrifice is made. Our whole understanding depends upon our recognising that God's own activity and being, His presence and activity in the One who is His own Son, very and eternal God with the Father and the Holy Spirit, is the truth and power of that which takes place here as a history of human sacrificing and sacrifice" (*CD* IV/1, 280).

20. See Karl Barth, *The Göttingen Dogmatics: Instruction in the Christian Religion*, vol. 1, ed. Hannelotte Reiffen, trans. Geoffrey W. Bromiley (hereafter: *The Göttingen Dogmatics*) (Grand Rapids: Eerdmans, 1991), where Barth stresses that the incarnation and resurrection are miracles that cannot be explained but only believed or rejected. "Thus to make the conception by the Spirit plausible by referring to instances of parthogenesis [*sic*] in the lower plant and animal kingdoms makes no more sense than to defend the resurrection with the help of occultism and spiritism" (161).

21. Importantly, in this context Barth astutely rejects any attempt to explain Christ's bodily resurrection as a "vision" either objectively or subjectively considered because in his view any such explanation smacks of an apologetic being used to explain away the mystery and miracle attested in the event (*CD* IV/1, 340-41).

22. This is in accord with Barth's earlier emphasis in *CD* I/2 that in virtue of the incarnation Jesus Christ himself is our justification and our reconciliation with God. For Barth everything depends upon the fact that there never was a man Jesus who was not in fact the eternal Son of God (*CD* I/2, 348).

23. Cf. above and *Evangelical Theology*, 29-30. Cf. also Barth, *CD* I/1, 459-60.

24. For a similar idea see Barth, *CD* II/1, 51. Barth writes "God is who He is, the Father, Son and Holy Spirit, Creator, Reconciler and Redeemer, supreme, the one true Lord; and

He is known in this entirety or He is not known at all. There is no existence of God behind or beyond this entirety of His being."

25. Barth insists that "He is the man Jesus and no one else. He is not soul or spirit in the abstract, but soul of His body, and therefore body as well. To be an apostle of Jesus Christ means not only to have seen Him with one's eyes and to have heard Him with one's ears, but to have touched Him physically. . . . It is impossible to erase the bodily character of the resurrection of Jesus and His existence as the Resurrected" (*CD* III/2, 448).

26. Thus "He is the Son of God who has come to us or the Word of God that has been spoken to us, because He is so antecedently in Himself as the Son or Word of God the Father" (*CD* I/1, 399). Hence "revelation and reconciliation do not create His deity. His deity creates revelation and reconciliation" (*CD* I/1, 415). This is why Barth insists that "all thinking about Jesus, which means at once all thinking about God, must begin and end" (*CD* I/1, 415) with the fact that Jesus is the Son simply because he *is*. "All reflection can only start with it and return to it" because "the statement about Christ's deity is to be regarded as a basic and not a derivative statement" (*CD* I/1, 415). And that is why "the knowledge of Christ's deity can only be the beginning and not the result of our thought" (*CD* I/1, 422). We shall have occasion to note this extremely important point several times in this book especially in relation to those who believe the incarnation can only be the conclusion and not the starting point for Christology.

27. See Molnar, *Divine Freedom,* ch. 2.

28. Because Jesus Christ himself, the incarnate Word, is the source of knowledge here Barth insists "Such a starting point for the confession safeguards it from devotion to and suspicion of historism, false realism, deification of the creature, all of them characteristics of ebionite Christology" (*CD* I/2, 19). And it renders any Docetic interpretation of John and Paul equally problematic.

29. See esp. Barth, *CD* I/2, 149, 159f. and *CD* I/1, 323.

30. In *CD* IV/2, Barth describes the resurrection as the *terminus a quo* and the ascension as the *terminus ad quem* of Jesus' Easter history: they are, Barth says, "two distinct but inseparable moments in one and the same event" (150). They disclose the historicity of Jesus' self-revelation. What is decisively important for Barth is the fact that in Jesus, God humbled himself that we, in our humanity, might be exalted in him. So what is revealed is the fact of Jesus' exaltation "as it had already taken place in the pre-Easter life, and found fulfillment in His death on the cross." Indeed "it is the revelation of the exaltation of the Son of Man. If it took place in the glory of the Son of God who became and was also the Son of Man, it was His exaltation in the human essence assumed by Him. As the Son of God He did not need to be exalted. In fact, He could not be exalted. In His majesty as the Son of God, which He did not forfeit but exercised, He became man. The Lord became a servant. . . . But He was never greater as Lord than in this depth of His servanthood. And if He was and is revealed as the Son of God in His resurrection and ascension, it is in the power and glory of His unity with the man Jesus of Nazareth" (150).

31. It has been suggested that Barth has undervalued the ascension. For instance Oliver O'Donovan, *Resurrection and Moral Order: An Outline for Evangelical Ethics,* 2nd ed. (Grand Rapids: Eerdmans, 1994), 57 believes that when Barth wrote in *CD* I/2 that the empty tomb and ascension were "merely signs" of Easter as the Virgin Birth was the sign of Christmas, he needed to make amends in *CD* IV/2 by describing them as "inseparable mo-

ments in one and the same event." But a careful reading of these texts does not disclose the problem O'Donovan thinks he has found. When Barth referred to the empty tomb and ascension as signs, he clearly meant to say that we do not believe in the empty tomb, *per se,* any more than we believe in the ascension, *per se,* as the disappearance of Jesus from visible human history. What he wanted to stress was the fact that both the empty tomb and Jesus' disappearance into heaven signified that the man Jesus, as Son of God, was alive and indeed active as the risen and ascended Lord who would be with us always even to the end of the world. Even in *CD* I/2 Barth was quite clear that the risen Jesus was actively alive and that there was an intrinsic unity of the resurrected and ascended Lord. In *CD* IV/2 Barth rightly stresses the unity of these two moments as our justification as O'Donovan himself notes. O'Donovan accuses Barth of subordinating his doctrine of creation to Christology which he claims led to Apollinarianism in his Christology. According to Alan Torrance, *Persons in Communion: Trinitarian Description and Human Participation* (hereafter: *Persons in Communion*) (Edinburgh: T&T Clark, 1996), 193, there was an Apollinarian tendency in *CD* I/1. And according to Douglas Farrow, *Ascension and Ecclesia: On the Significance of the Doctrine of the Ascension for Ecclesiology and Christian Cosmology* (hereafter: *Ascension and Ecclesia*) (Grand Rapids: Eerdmans, 1999), Barth is guilty of a kind of Christomonism because he too strongly emphasizes God's pre-temporality, God's unity over his triunity and did not pay enough attention to the Holy Spirit. The reality is, however, that Barth understood creation from revelation and thus in and through the doctrines of the incarnation and reconciliation. That is precisely why Barth was able to stress the realm of creation as grounded in the covenant of grace which he saw as the internal basis of creation. And in *CD* I/1 Barth very clearly maintained what George Hunsinger calls the Chalcedonian pattern without overemphasizing either Jesus' humanity or his divinity. The criticisms offered by Farrow are addressed in Molnar, *Divine Freedom,* chs. 3 and 9. Aside from Barth's constant and explicit disavowals of any Ebionite or Docetic understanding of Jesus Christ or the church, Barth's entire Christology is decidedly anti-docetic as for instance when he says "The concept of the true humanity of Jesus Christ is therefore primarily and finally basic — an absolutely necessary concept — in exactly the same and not a lesser sense than that of His true deity. The humanity of Jesus Christ is not a secondary moment in the Christ-event. It is not something which happens later, and later again will pass and disappear. It is not merely for the purpose of mediation. Like His deity, it is integral to the whole event" (*CD* IV/2, 35). With regard to Christomonism, Barth consistently argued for our distinction in union with Christ: "for all the intimacy and intensity of the connexion between them [Jesus Christ and the man called by him] there can be no question of an identification of the follower with his preceding leader . . . [of] the life of the one awakened by the Holy Spirit with the One who gives him this Spirit. There can be no question of an identification of the Christian with Christ" (*CD* IV/3, 539).

32. This is an extremely important point that sets Barth's thinking off decisively from Karl Rahner's anonymous Christianity. While Rahner contends that all are Christians anonymously to the extent that they live lives of faith and hope even in a general sense of accepting their own transcendental dynamisms and living lives in obedience to conscience without any explicit acknowledgment of Jesus Christ, Barth argues that one cannot be a Christian without specifically acknowledging Jesus Christ through the Holy Spirit. None of this is under our control. All depends upon God's free actions of grace in his Word and Spirit.

33. For a detailed discussion of the differences between Barth and Rahner over how to understand the relationship between love of God and love of neighbor see Paul D. Molnar, "Love of God and Love of Neighbor in the Theology of Karl Rahner and Karl Barth," *Modern Theology* 20, no. 4 (October 2004): 567-99.

34. Cf. also Barth, *CD* IV/3, 902-42.

35. In answer to the question of what happens to those who have never heard the Gospel Barth writes: "Jesus Christ has risen for each and every one of this majority too" so that "the same Holy Spirit who has been strong enough to enlighten his [a Christian's] own dark heart will perhaps one day find a little less trouble with them; and decisively that when the day of the coming of Jesus Christ in consummating revelation does at last dawn . . . the One whom he expects as a Christian, will know how to reach them" (*CD* IV/3, 918). Instead of resolving Christian hope into the universal of all those who have some definitive hope, Barth allows hope to be defined by the object of faith and love who is the subject coming again, namely, the risen and ascended Lord himself. This, of course, is why Barth can say that the will of God is done in all ages outside the church and often better outside, to the shame of the church. However, the difference between Barth's assertion and any sort of anonymous Christianity is that Barth adds: "This is not in virtue of a natural goodness of man. It is because Jesus, as the One who has risen from the dead and sits at the right hand of God, is in fact the Lord of the whole world, who has His servants even where His name is not yet or no longer known and praised" (*CD* II/2, 569).

36. It is important to realize that for Barth hope is not a "quality of the soul" that needs practice to be made strong (*CD* IV/3, 913). This would imply some sort of self-justification (*CD* IV/3, 914, 920). Against this Barth writes: "He [the Christian] does not guarantee his future by hoping any more than he justifies himself by believing or sanctifies himself by loving" (*CD* IV/3, 914).

37. Barth spells this out brilliantly in *CD* IV/3 § 73.

38. Barth's thinking here is not only pneumatological but explicitly christological and trinitarian. Thus, he insists that we can discern the divine command only from Christ's obedience: "In what Jesus does, everything is permission, freedom, spontaneity. The will of God is His own will. To do it is the meat by which He lives. He is *the* Son of the Father. It is as we look at Him and only at Him . . . that others — we ourselves — can also be called and be free. Jesus is free as God Himself is free. . . . It is in freedom that God has turned and covenanted Himself to man, and it is in the same freedom that the act of the covenant has been completed by Jesus. . . . All that Jesus does is, therefore, suffused and irradiated by the way in which He does it. He does it in the ἐξουσία of Him who is permitted to do what He is commanded, and commanded only what He is permitted. And this obedience of Jesus is the clear reflection of the unity of the Father and the Son by the bond of the Spirit in the being of the eternal God Himself, who is the fulness of all freedom" (*CD* II/2, 605).

39. For more details on this see Molnar, *Divine Freedom,* 129, 241ff., 255, 294.

40. This is why Barth was so opposed to any idea that we could know and obey God's will by following our "moral nature." In the next chapter it will be seen that this is the point at which Barth and Rahner differ most sharply because for Rahner this last presumption is the starting point of his theology and therefore also of his ethics.

41. This is why, for Barth, dogmatics itself is ethics. There can be no true understanding of ethics apart from faith in Christ and thus apart from revelation. And any true understand-

ing involves the fact that we are questioned by the Word of God incarnate in Jesus himself as to the rightness of our life's actions, including the obedience of our knowledge and behavior. Any attempt therefore to separate ethics from dogmatics or to consider it apart from dogmatics and thus independently and outside the context of faith would amount to using our own moral ideas as the criterion for who God is *in se* and *ad extra,* instead of allowing God to be the one who alone can do this in specific circumstances according to his promises and grace to be God for us in his Word and Spirit. See Barth, *CD* I/2, 782-96.

42. It is here that Barth rejects the idea that humanity has an aptitude on the basis of which it can cooperate with God in spite of the fall. The fall means that we utterly lack the capacity for God. But the *analogia entis* assumes that human nature is "merely sick, deranged and impotent" so that there can be "talk of a remnant of the original divine image and likeness which remains in spite of the fall" (*CD* II/2, 532). This thinking, with the idea of a *liberum arbitrium,* Barth insists misunderstands the seriousness of the human situation and creates a distraction by suggesting that God's loving kindness can be found in a metaphysics of being in which the original unity of heaven and earth can be found and neatly coordinated. This union Barth contends is precisely what was lost in the fall and restored by God's grace in the humanity of Jesus Christ. But because Jesus Christ is the grace of God's reconciliation, such grace can only be found by looking at him and not at all by looking at humanity in its moral life. See *CD* I/2, 793.

43. Cf. *CD* II/2, 585ff. Barth maintains that "The command of God sets man free" (*CD* II/2, 586). It does not compel us but frees us and that is why it does not appeal to our fear like other commands which are not the divine command. Still, the command of God involves a command to do this and not to do that. But Barth insists this command is grounded in the freedom given by God in Christ to do it. Hence the command not to do something is grounded in the permission granted to do it: "Do not do this — not because you again hear an outer or inner voice which seeks to make it doubtful or dreadful for you, not because there is any power in heaven or on earth to prevent or spoil or for some reason forbid it. No, but: Do not do this, because it would be a continuation of the fall of Adam . . . because you, the free man, are exempted from the necessity of doing it — really exempted by the fact that you have been made righteous and glorious in the resurrection of Jesus Christ. . . . The command of God orders us to be free" (*CD* II/2, 587-88).

44. This is why Barth rejects any form of self-justification in all areas of his theology. See, e.g., *CD* IV/1, 615-18. Hence, Barth maintains that "Faith . . . is not the way which — another Hercules at the crossroads — man can equally well choose and enter, which he can choose and enter by the same capacity by which he might go any other way" (*CD* IV/1, 616). This, because as sinners we cannot justify ourselves but only recognize that we are justified by God himself who awakens in us the ability to do good works. Faith itself as a human work does not justify us either since we need justification here too. "Faith is not at all the supreme and true and finally successful form of self-justification" (*CD* IV/1, 617). Also, in connection with hope, Barth rightly argues that "it is not the sincerity or drive of this Christian hope which constitutes the light of the community sent out to witness. Only the Holy Spirit of Jesus Christ active within it is this light" (*CD* IV/1, 152). Nor is it by obedience, our free actions or by our love that the church is built up because "It [the church] lives wholly in the power of its Lord and His Spirit" (*CD* IV/1, 152). See also *CD* III/1, 264f. for the same ideas in relation to free obedience as a choice that corresponds to God's will in creation.

Notes to Chapter 2

1. Karl Rahner, *Foundations of Christian Faith: An Introduction to the Idea of Christianity* (hereafter referred to in text as *FCF*), trans. William V. Dych (New York: Seabury, 1978), 11ff.

2. Richard P. McBrien, *Catholicism Completely Revised and Updated* (San Francisco: HarperSanFrancisco, 1994), 1240.

3. See *FCF*, 8, where Rahner notes that fundamental theology should present arguments of credibility but without claiming to establish Christian faith in its properly theological sense as assent to revelation. Rahner sees his task as one which reflects on the faith and gives an account of it "in an intellectually honest way" (*FCF*, 9). See also Karl Rahner, "The Foundation of Belief Today," *Theological Investigations*, 23 vols. (hereafter referred to in text as *TI*), vol. 16, trans. David Morland, O.S.B. (New York: A Crossroad Book, Seabury Press, 1979), 3ff., where Rahner links apologetic and fundamental theology.

4. Ultimately this thinking leads Rahner to say that even though Catholic theology sees miracles and Jesus' resurrection as object and ground of faith these do not justify faith "from outside" (*FCF*, 239). Rather, according to Rahner, the ground of faith is reached only in faith and is therefore not extrinsic to faith itself. Hence, Rahner will even say that a miracle is a call that presupposes a person who is willing to allow himself to be called in the depths of his existence. And human willingness to believe is a "precondition for the experience of a miracle" (*FCF*, 263). First, unless the object and ground of faith justify faith from outside, then there will always be the suspicion that it is the experience of faith itself that has become the object of faith. Second, while it is true to say that we cannot experience the ground and object of faith outside of faith, it is false to imply that our faith is a precondition for any miracle, much less the miracle of the resurrection. This thinking follows from the mutual conditioning that characterizes Rahner's thought, but as we shall see, fails to acknowledge grace as free grace and the resurrection as an event in Jesus' life that gives meaning to faith. Finally, it is precisely Rahner's methodological appeal to the depths of human existence for his interpretation of theology that causes this mutually conditioned view of faith and the object and ground of faith.

5. In his important article on theological method Rahner writes: "The *a priori* transcendental subjectivity of the knower on the one hand and the object of knowledge (and freedom) on the other are related to one another in such a way that they mutually condition one another" (*TI* 11: 68-114, "Reflections on Methodology in Theology," 87).

6. Rahner writes: "anthropology and Christology mutually determine each other within Christian dogmatics if they are both correctly understood" (*TI* 9: 28-45, "Theology and Anthropology," 28).

7. Rahner writes: "the revealed Word and natural knowledge of God mutually condition each other" (*TI* 1: 79-148, "Theos in the New Testament," 98). This is also why Rahner insists that "A 'transcendental Christology' presupposes an understanding of the relationship of *mutual* conditioning and mediation in human existence between what is transcendentally necessary and what is concretely and contingently historical. . . . Transcendental Christology appeals to a person who . . . already has at least unthematically a finality and a dynamism imparted by God himself towards God's self-communication" (*FCF*, 208). See William V. Dych, S.J., *Karl Rahner* (Collegeville: The Liturgical Press, 1992), 58, where he

notes that the relation between our faith and Jesus' resurrection must be seen in "the circle of the mutual dependence of the objective and subjective elements in our experience."

8. *TI* 18: 143-56, "What Does It Mean Today to Believe in Jesus Christ?" 145. While Rahner does not start with the fact that "Jesus is God" he insists that his "questing Christology," which begins with transcendental experience, will present the "classical Christologies" in a different formulation. Of course the question I am raising is whether or not the truth of the classical Christologies is undercut precisely by beginning with a Jesus behind the faith that acknowledges his divinity.

9. *Karl Rahner in Dialogue: Conversations and Interviews 1965-1982*, ed. Paul Imhof and Hubert Biallowons, trans. Harvey D. Egan (hereafter referred to in text as *Rahner in Dialogue*) (New York: Crossroad, 1986), 76. What exactly does Rahner mean by grace? Rahner says, "what we call God's grace is primarily something that means basically the self-communication of God in the depth of the person's spiritual existence . . . it is something that is, as a matter of course, given always and everywhere to all human beings, whether they freely accept or reject it. . . . God is the innermost dynamism of the world and of the person's spirit . . . the grace of this self-communication of God is, as a matter of course, given in their spiritual reality. And this is the most fundamental, the most original element of what we call revelation" (*Rahner in Dialogue*, 75). Having said this, it is interesting to note that Rahner describes his earlier theology as "almost pantheistic," stressing that, in his mind, it was only "almost" pantheistic (*Rahner in Dialogue*, 124). This assessment would apply to his later theology perhaps even more. See Karl Rahner and Wilhelm Thüsing, *A New Christology* (New York: A Crossroad Book/Seabury Press, 1980), 4ff., and *FCF*, 295ff.

10. Significantly, Rahner defines freedom as "the freedom of self-understanding, the possibility of saying yes or no to oneself, the possibility of deciding for or against oneself, which corresponds to the knowing self-possession, the understanding subject-nature of man" (*TI* 6: 185).

11. Hence when Rahner considers the meaning of the incarnation he writes "We are still moving within the framework of an essential [or transcendental] Christology, that is, we are not yet asking the question whether there has already existed in history a saviour as we are understanding the term, nor who he is concretely" (*FCF*, 212-13). And, strangely, Rahner insists that in carrying his transcendental Christology further and "prior to the question about an encounter with the historical, concrete Jesus, it makes sense to ask what is really meant when Christianity speaks of an *incarnation of God*" (*FCF*, 212). That is the ambiguity in Rahner's thought. He *says* his transcendental Christology develops only after an actual encounter with Jesus, the God-Man, but in reality and methodologically it develops without allowing Jesus to determine its truth content at the outset. This disastrous thinking results from Rahner's belief that the incarnation is the end but not the beginning of Christology today. This same ambiguity can be seen at *FCF*, 228-29, where Rahner says he was after the idea of a God-Man "prescinding from the question whether and where this idea has been realized" and that he's doing this "only because in fact we believe . . . we have found this God-Man in Jesus Christ." If he believes he has found this in Jesus then, according to his own view of Christianity, he cannot prescind from Jesus himself and still develop a proper Christology. Rahner's Christology leaves one with the impression once again that what he finds in Jesus is little more than the *idea* he originally constructed *a pri-*

ori from evolution and human experience. Since Jesus is not determining his thought here, it is not surprising that Rahner can later say self-acceptance is the same as accepting Christ.

12. See Rahner and Thüsing, *A New Christology*, 4ff., and *FCF*, 295ff.

13. Consistent with his "searching Christology" and in line with his own apologetic concerns Rahner believes that those outside Christianity have already uttered "an interior and unreflexive 'yes' to Christ" (*FCF*, 294). Why? Because it is to be assumed, Rahner says, that the person addressed is a "person of morally good will, and hence . . . existing in the interior grace of God and in Christ" (*FCF*, 294). Thus Rahner says fundamental theology today can appeal in three ways [through an appeal to love of neighbor, to the readiness for death and to hope in the future] to this "global understanding of existence which is already 'Christian' because of antecedent grace" to work out the content of a part of transcendental Christology. What all three appeals have in common is "the supposition that if a person accepts his existence resolutely, he is really already living out in his existence something like a 'searching Christology'" as a kind of "anonymous Christology" (*FCF*, 295). Rahner insists that this appeal to one's "searching Christology" must be accompanied by the conviction that only in Jesus of Nazareth and not "someone who is to come" does one find what one is searching for. But the problem with this reasoning is that if a person of good will is already searching for what can only be found in Jesus even prior to hearing the Gospel preached and taught then it cannot be Jesus himself who alone gives meaning to what is thought and said simply because Jesus himself is necessary only as that historical embodiment of what one discovers by accepting oneself in the experiences of love, death and hope. This, then, would be an almost classic case of Docetic Christology in which the ideas of the absolute savior and God-Man determine who Jesus is as a particular instance of transcendental experience.

14. This is why Rahner believes that, strictly speaking, although the "pre-existence" Christology of John and Paul should be considered revelation, "it is not a strictly original datum of revelation" (Rahner, *The Trinity*, 66).

15. Rahner insists that transcendental Christology's attempt to develop "the 'idea' of a bringer of salvation in the absolute" can never be "a substitute for the historical experience of Jesus of Nazareth — in other words of that reality in which this 'idea' has been made real, and only precisely in virtue of this permits the idea as such to become real in history" (*TI* 11: 95-96). But given the fact that Rahner believes this idea must be developed *a priori*, and given what we have already identified as an ambiguity in Rahner's thought, it is reasonable to wonder what exactly confers reality on Jesus. Is it the idea or Jesus himself as the Word incarnate? Or is it perhaps some combination of the two? Rahner clearly wants to say it is the reality of Jesus. But his method causes him to describe the reality of Jesus as little more than the historical embodiment of the idea that people are in search of by virtue of their transcendental dynamisms. And to protect against Docetism, Rahner ascribes this dynamism to grace and revelation, which, as we shall see, only compounds the ambiguity.

16. See, e.g., *TI* 16: 199-224, "The One Christ and the Universality of Salvation," 220ff. In accord with this belief Rahner frequently argues that self-acceptance is the same as accepting God: "If a man freely accepts himself as he is . . . then it is God he is accepting" (*TI* 16: 67). He claims this as the teaching of Vatican II which, he says, teaches that salvation is possible for all people: "It can be found in people who consciously believe they are and

must be atheists, as long as they are completely obedient to the absolute demands of conscience, that is ... they accept themselves unconditionally ... fulfilling that primordial capacity of freedom" (*TI* 16: 60-78, "Faith Between Rationality and Emotion," 67). By universalizing faith and identifying it with freedom Rahner can then identify the human quest for meaning with his "questing" Christology. All of this undercuts our actual need for Christ and for faith in him prior to understanding who God is and who we are.

17. *TI* 4: 221-52, "The Theology of the Symbol," 224.

18. See Molnar, *Divine Freedom*, chs. 4, 5 and 6. It is precisely the *vice versa* of Rahner's axiom that is required by his symbolic ontology that causes much of the difficulty here. And because being as such is the limit of all knowledge for Rahner he writes: "Our statement about the intelligibility of being in itself derived from the fact that, always and also in the first question about being every possible object of knowledge is already viewed by anticipation under the general aspect of being as such. Hence there can be no being that does not, by itself, positively range itself in the context of being as such. This is precisely the reason why it is intelligible." Karl Rahner, *Hearer of the Word: Laying the Foundation for a Philosophy of Religion*, trans. Joseph Donceel, ed. Andrew Tallon (New York: Continuum, 1994), 78. The same ideas are expressed in *FCF*, 24ff.

19. See *FCF*, 280, for Rahner's rejection of adoptionism.

20. For more on this see Molnar, *Divine Freedom*, chs. 2 and 4.

21. See, e.g., *TI* 4: 105-20, "On the Theology of the Incarnation," 115, 116; *TI* 11: 215-29, "Christology in the Setting of Modern Man's Understanding of Himself and of His World," 225; *TI* 5: 157-92, "Christology within an Evolutionary View of the World," 177-78. Compare to *TI* 4: 231ff.

22. In his book on the Trinity, Rahner writes "He who *sees* me, sees *me*" (32) in order to stress that when we encounter the humanity of Jesus we encounter the Logos itself because it is "expressed" in it and is thus full of the thing symbolized, essentially related to it in a mutually causal way. A lot hinges here on the fact that Rahner interprets creation and incarnation with the idea that the Father expresses himself in his Word and thus freely empties "himself into the non-divine; because, when this happens, that precisely is born which we call human nature ... human nature is not a mask ... from behind which the Logos hides to act things out in the world. From the start it is the constitutive, real symbol of the Logos himself" (*The Trinity*, 33).

23. In accordance with his preference for what he calls "neo-Chalcedonism" over a "pure Chalcedonism" Rahner wishes to see Christ's humanity as "that which comes into being when the Logos ex-presses himself into the non-divine" (*The Trinity*, 31) so that he can say "the relation which exists between the two is more essential and more intimate" (*The Trinity*, 32).

24. Rahner, *The Trinity*, 33.

25. See David Coffey, "The Theandric Nature of Christ," in *Theological Studies* (hereafter: *TS*) 60, no. 3 (September 1999): 411ff.: "For Rahner, human nature, though created, is potentially divine, and in the case of Christ actually so" (412). It is important to note that Coffey's belief that Christ's human nature as "theandric," i.e., "human in a divine way, or, equally, divine in a human way" is "inevitable once human nature is defined in terms of orientation to God" (413). Such a definition, as we have seen, is intrinsic to Rahner's tran-

scendental method and from my point of view it necessarily confuses nature and grace and reason and revelation.

26. Joseph H. P. Wong, *Logos-Symbol in the Christology of Karl Rahner* (Rome: Las-Roma, 1984), 193. Cf. also *TI* 4: 251 and 239. Similarly, Ted Peters, *God as Trinity: Relationality and Temporality in Divine Life* (hereafter: *Trinity*) (Louisville: Westminster/John Knox Press, 1993), presses Rahner's axiom "to its extreme consequence" (192); thus "the loving relationship between the Father and the Son within the Trinity *is* the loving relationship between the Father and Jesus . . . [hence] when we look at Jesus we see the real thing [the Son]" (22).

27. For Rahner formal causality means "(a taking up *into* the ground [*forma*], 'ein In-den-Grund [forma] — *Hinein*nehmen')." *TI* 1: 319-46, "Some Implications of the Scholastic Concept of Uncreated Grace" (329). God relates with the creature in revelation via quasi-formal causality, that is, by entitatively modifying the knowing subject so that God is experienced in the experience of self-transcendence as the term of our transcendental dynamisms. That is the basis for Rahner's belief in a supernatural existential.

28. Rahner, *Trinity,* 40; emphasis mine.

29. Rahner, *FCF,* 12. See *TI* 11: 101ff., *TI* 4: 108; and "The Concept of Mystery in Catholic Theology," 36-73.

30. Rahner, *TI* 11: 102.

31. John P. Galvin, "The Invitation of Grace," in *A World of Grace,* ed. Leo O'Donovan (New York: Crossroad, 1981), 64-75, 72.

32. Galvin, "The Invitation of Grace," 71-73.

33. Rahner, *FCF,* 12.

34. William V. Dych, S.J., "Theology in a New Key," in O'Donovan, ed., *A World of Grace,* 13.

35. Dych, *Karl Rahner,* 36-37.

36. Stanley J. Grenz and Roger E. Olson, *Twentieth-Century Theology: God and the World in a Transitional Age* (Carlisle, UK: Paternoster Press, 1992), 246-47.

37. Rahner, *TI* 11: 185-214, "The Position of Christology in the Church Between Exegesis and Dogmatics," 210.

38. Rahner, *TI* 4: 121-33, "Dogmatic Questions on Easter," 132.

39. Here Stephen T. Davis, "'Seeing' the Risen Jesus," in *The Resurrection: An Interdisciplinary Symposium on the Resurrection of Jesus,* ed. Stephen T. Davis, Daniel Kendall, S.J., and Gerald O'Collins, S.J. (New York: Oxford University Press, 1998), 126-47, properly insists against this kind of thinking, that "a glorified body *(soma)* is still a body — that is, still a material object that can be seen" (140).

40. This is why Rahner argues that the Easter event "is still reaching completion in us" (*TI* 4: 133).

41. See also *TI* 17: 16-23, "Jesus' Resurrection," 22, where Rahner repeats this same insight. It is no accident that Rahner frequently refers to the resurrection of Jesus as "What we call the resurrection of Jesus" (Rahner and Thüsing, *A New Christology,* 26), since for him one cannot really describe precisely what that might mean based on experience. This is partially why Rahner says, "it is possible for us to say, with Willi Marxsen, in a positive, though not exclusive sense that Jesus had to rise again in the faith of those who believed in him. This cannot, however, be claimed in the sense that Jesus would only exist in that faith.

On the other hand, if there were no community of faith . . . there would be no permanent presence of God in the world and Jesus would not be present as God's promise of himself. . . . Jesus would not have been Jesus, if there had not been such a Church" (Rahner and Thüsing, *A New Christology*, 26).

42. Rahner can even say, "We dare to believe, in hope, in our own history and this enables us to believe in the resurrection of Jesus" (Rahner and Thüsing, *A New Christology*, 13).

43. Rahner, *TI* 7: 159-68, "Experiencing Easter," 164; emphasis mine.

44. Because Rahner thinks this way, he actually maintains that "God confers on man the power to make a genuine answer to his Word, and so makes his own further Word dependent upon the way in which man does in fact freely answer" (*TI* 1: 111).

45. Of course, this is why Rahner can also say, "The experience of Jesus gives us, in so far as we freely commit ourselves to our own hope, the strength and the heart to affirm from the centre of our own experience, and from the hope that lies within it, that he is risen. The basic human hope and the historical experience of Jesus are bound together for a Christian as a unity" (*TI* 16: 17).

46. *TI* 13: 152-68, "Theological Observations on the Concept of 'Witness,'" 165-66.

47. Karl Rahner and Karl-Heinz Weger, *Our Christian Faith: Answers for the Future*, trans. Francis McDonagh (hereafter referred to in text as *Our Christian Faith*) (New York: Crossroad, 1981), 113.

48. See *TI* 4: 347-54, "The Life of the Dead," 352, where Rahner equates the doctrine of the "immorality of the soul" with that of the "resurrection of the flesh" although he does wish to reject any philosophical dualism of body and soul.

49. *TI* 17: 16-23, "Jesus' Resurrection: Some Observations Drawn from Systematic Theology," 16.

50. This is why Rahner argues that "Anyone who has ever made a morally good decision in a matter of life and death, radically and uncompromisingly . . . has already experienced in this decision the eternity which we mean here" (*FCF*, 272). And unfortunately, it is just this thinking that leads Rahner to conclude that self-acceptance is the same as accepting God and Christ. See, e.g., *TI* 16: 59.

51. It should be noted that in *Foundations* Rahner says he will "prescind here from the question to which stratum in the tradition of the resurrection of Jesus the empty tomb belongs, and what significance it has in this tradition. Resurrection does not mean to begin with a salvifically neutral survival of human existence, but means its salvation and its acceptance by God" (*FCF*, 267).

52. Colin E. Gunton, *Yesterday and Today: A Study of Continuities in Christology* (Grand Rapids: Eerdmans, 1983), 15ff. For Gunton, "There are, in Rahner's work, traces of what has come to be known as 'degree' Christology" (15). It is, according to Gunton, more correct to see degree Christology as Christology from below and it generally operates without Rahner's "counterbalancing emphasis on the eternal Logos" (15).

53. Quoted in Gunton, *Yesterday and Today*, 15.

54. Gunton, *Yesterday and Today*, 16.

55. Gunton, *Yesterday and Today*, 16.

56. Gunton, *Yesterday and Today*, 17.

57. See Rahner, *TI* 4: 125f.

58. This same thinking appears in Rahner, *TI* 4: 109-10.

59. See *FCF*, 218, and *TI* 4: 109-10. After explaining how Rahner's theology of the symbol influences his view of the incarnation, William V. Dych actually writes, "In the light of Rahner's evolutionary view of Christology, this process wherein the Word becomes flesh is identical with the process wherein flesh becomes the Word of God" (Dych, *Karl Rahner*, 79).

60. This is in accord with the basic principles of Rahner's theology of the symbol according to which he believes that in Christ "the finite itself has received infinite depths" and "is no longer in opposition to the infinite, but is that which the infinite himself has become, that in which he expresses himself as the question which he himself answers. He does this . . . in order to make himself the portal and the passage" into the infinite (*FCF*, 226). Cf. also *TI* 4: 239f. and *TI* 4: 117.

61. Rahner equates the experience of our innermost dynamism of spirit with what we call God and calls this experience a grace (*Rahner in Dialogue*, 76). Indeed Rahner insists that "grace is primarily something that means basically the self-communication of God in the depth of the person's spiritual existence. . . . God is the innermost dynamism of the world and of the person's spirit . . . the grace of this self-communication of God is, as a matter of course, given in their spiritual reality. And this is the most fundamental, the most original element of what we call revelation" (*Rahner in Dialogue*, 75). Hence, "When and where this innermost self-communication of God, which is already revelation is wholly and correctly reflected in consciousness, and is objectivated in words, there we have that which one calls . . . in the common (and correctly common) theological sense revelation . . . the original self-communication of God and at the same time the reflective awareness of this original self-communication as it occurs in the history of humankind" (*Rahner in Dialogue*, 76).

62. Rahner, *TI* 6: "Reflections on the Unity of the Love of Neighbour and the Love of God," 231-49, 236.

63. James F. Bresnahan, "An Ethics of Faith," in O'Donovan, ed., *A World of Grace*, 169-84, 172.

64. The predicament that I have identified here can be illustrated clearly by noting two important remarks made by James F. Bresnahan: (1) "Christ is the appearance within human history of a person who sums up the moral ideal which believers also recognize by reflection on their own moral experience" (*A World of Grace*, 180) and (2) "If all humanity can be understood as moving towards the full truth about itself in Christ, then the consciousness of freedom and of the basic moral ideal is part of that movement in the grace of Christ" (*A World of Grace*, 181). First, the very notion that believers could suppose that they might equate Christ with a moral ideal gleaned from their own moral experience shows that the ethical criterion has been shifted from Jesus Christ himself as our justification and sanctification to our moral ideals and the experiences which support those ideals. This thinking is docetic in origin and outcome because this morality is not centered in and dictated by an encounter with the historical Jesus but rather is centered in an ideal which Christ is thought to confirm. Moreover, this thinking opens the door to self-justification precisely because the very notion of moral goodness advanced within this perspective is one which suggests that we can actually rely on our moral experience and moral ideals to love God and neighbor and thus to live out our justification. It leads to this conclusion:

"every human person who reaches awareness of the basic moral ideal of love knows Christ, the exemplar of this ideal, even if not by name" (*A World of Grace*, 181). Second, can all humanity be understood as moving towards that truth about itself in Christ? The answer is no if it is the historical Jesus that we have in mind, because if that were true, Jesus would not have been crucified but would have been acknowledged by all as the Messiah of Israel. The answer could only be yes if Christ is no more than an exemplar of the moral behavior we think should be advanced within a Christian perspective. But if this is the case, then it is clear that the incarnate Word has in fact been reduced to a moral ideal in the form of a degree Christology which refuses to begin by allowing the risen Lord himself to be the starting point as well as the conclusion of our christological reflections.

65. Aside from Rahner's own frequent assertion that self-acceptance is the same as accepting Christ, note the following remark by Bresnahan: "the mission of Christian natural law . . . will be an effort in all humility to announce the full meaning of what non-Christians already aspire to in their moral life and, if they are truly persons of good will, what they are already achieving — love of God and love of neighbor in unity, fashioned in the likeness of Christ" (*A World of Grace*, 182). For an example of Rahner's thinking, consider this remark: "freedom is not originally the capacity of choosing any object whatsoever or the ability of adopting an individual attitude toward this or that; it is rather the freedom of self-understanding, the possibility of saying yes or no to oneself, the possibility of deciding for or against oneself, which corresponds to the knowing self-possession, the understanding subject-nature of man" (*TI* 6: 178-96, "Theology of Freedom," 185).

66. For a full discussion of these issues and how they relate to Barth's theology see Molnar, "Love of God and Love of Neighbor in the Theology of Karl Rahner and Karl Barth," and Molnar, "The Theology of Justification in Dogmatic Context," in *Justification: What's at Stake in the Current Debates*. Rahner's theory of anonymous Christianity is the logical outworking of a theology that does not begin with the incarnation of God in Jesus Christ but with our experiences of self-transcendence.

Notes to Chapter 3

1. Thomas F. Torrance, *Space, Time and Resurrection* (hereafter referred to in text as *STR*) (Edinburgh: T&T Clark, 1998), 71.

2. Thomas F. Torrance, *The Trinitarian Faith: The Evangelical Theology of the Ancient Catholic Church* (hereafter referred to in text as *TF*) (Edinburgh: T&T Clark, 1988), 60f. and esp. 111-125. See also T. F. Torrance, *Reality and Evangelical Theology* (Philadelphia: Westminster Press, 1982), 59.

3. In another context Torrance notes that while some of Barth's former students professed agreement with Barth on this, they, like Ernst Käsemann, had in reality developed "a docetic view of the resurrection." Thomas F. Torrance, *Karl Barth: Biblical and Evangelical Theologian* (hereafter: *Karl Barth*) (Edinburgh: T&T Clark, 1990), 133. In order to avoid such a view, Torrance insists that "a much closer relation between the resurrection and the incarnation in space and time had to be thought out in our theology" (133). And Torrance indicates that Barth agreed with him.

4. Torrance therefore insists quite rightly that "what Christ united to himself in this way he redeemed and saved, for from beginning to end, from his birth of the Virgin Mary to his resurrection from the empty tomb, the whole incarnational assumption of our human nature was at the same time a reconciling, healing, sanctifying and recreating activity" (*TF*, 162).

5. See, e.g., Thomas F. Torrance, *God and Rationality* (hereafter referred to in text as *God and Rationality*) (Edinburgh: T&T Clark, 1997), 133f. Torrance asserts that "the rational structure of knowledge of God cannot be scientifically studied except on the ground of actual knowledge where 'natural' theology is *natural* to the material content of that knowledge and developed in accordance with the nature of God as He revealed Himself in His Word and Acts." See also Thomas F. Torrance, *The Ground and Grammar of Theology* (Charlottesville: University Press of Virginia, 1980), ch. 4.

6. See Torrance, *The Ground and Grammar of Theology,* 91ff. and *Reality and Evangelical Theology,* 33.

7. Thomas F. Torrance, *Reality and Scientific Theology* (hereafter referred to in text as *RST*) (Eugene, OR: Wipf and Stock Publishers, 2001), 59.

8. For Barth, "What is 'God' to the natural man, and what he also certainly calls his 'God,' is a false god" (*CD* II/1, 86). Barth does concede the vitality of natural theology, but not in the way Torrance presumes: "It cannot be denied that there are gods who are in fact knowable to us there. But it is very much to be denied that we have the right to identify any of them with the real God" (*CD* II/1, 90). For a thorough discussion of how Barth's understanding of natural theology actually relates to Torrance's "new natural theology" see Paul D. Molnar, "Natural Theology Revisited: A Comparison of T. F. Torrance and Karl Barth," *Zeitschrift für dialektische Theologie* 1 (2005): 1-31.

9. Torrance explains that the "'trinitarian character' in our knowing of God" corresponds "to the trinity of relations in God himself" and thus since God is triune in his nature as Father, Son and Holy Spirit therefore "we must know him in accordance with his triune nature from the start" (*The Ground and Grammar of Theology,* 148).

10. See T. F. Torrance, "The Problem of Natural Theology in the Thought of Karl Barth," *Religious Studies* 6 (1970): 121-35, 126ff. See also Thomas F. Torrance, *Theology in Reconstruction* (London: SCM Press, Ltd, 1965), 162f. Hence, "Justification by the grace of Christ alone, does not mean that there is no natural knowledge — what natural man is there who does not know something of God even if he holds it down in unrighteousness or turns the truth into a lie? But it does mean that the whole of that natural knowledge is called in question by Christ who when he comes to us says: 'If any man will come after me, let him deny himself, take up his cross and follow me' . . . man is summoned to look away from all that he is and knows or thinks he knows to Christ who is the Way the Truth and the Life; no one goes to the Father but by him. The theology of Barth can be described, then, as the application of justification to the whole realm of man's life, to the realm of his knowing as well as the realm of his doing." For similar ideas see Thomas F. Torrance, *Theological Science* (Oxford: Oxford University Press, 1978), 102f.

11. Indeed, according to Torrance "there strikes at us through the blank face of the universe a mysterious intelligibility which takes us under its command in such a way that we feel we have to do with an undeniable and irreducibly transcendent reality" (*RST,* 58). How can the universe cry silently for an explanation? How can we speak of a mysterious

intelligibility from the "blank face" of the universe? Do not those questions come from those who are reflecting on the universe rather than from the universe? And if so, are those not the perennial questions of natural theology? The only difference here between Torrance and the more traditional natural theologies, and it is an important one, is that Torrance here refuses to build a logical bridge from the contingent universe to God the creator.

12. Torrance, *Theological Science*, 101.

13. Thomas F. Torrance, *Divine and Contingent Order* (Edinburgh: T&T Clark, 1998), 73. While Torrance here seems to think that the contingent order of the universe itself points us to a place beyond empirical reality, the truth of the matter is that this is an interpretation of the universe that anyone who already believes in the doctrine of creation would offer. So it is not really a natural theology and the idea that God's signature is in created being would seem to be in conflict with Torrance's belief that we can't rely on the world to disclose the transcendent God. Such an idea is reminiscent of the old-style natural theology Torrance rejects.

14. *The School of Faith: The Catechisms of the Reformed Church*, trans. and ed. with an introduction by Thomas F. Torrance (Eugene and Pasadena: Wipf and Stock Publishers, 1996), liii. Hence Torrance writes, "We cannot understand the almightiness or creatorship of God in terms of abstract possibilities and vague generalities — from what we imagine God is not, or from examining what God has brought into being in complete difference from himself" (*TF*, 78).

15. See *RST*, 42-43. Torrance here insists that natural theology can and should be "*artificially* bracketed off from the material content of actual knowledge of God, and could be accepted only as a *temporary* methodological device for purposes of clarification" (*RST*, 42). But what could possibly be clarified if, according to Torrance's own understanding of scientific theology, we artificially separate our thinking from the unique object that alone can enable true understanding in this matter? Here, however, the cat is let out of the bag because Torrance argues that such a bracketed natural theology "still retains the imprint of its empirical origins and foundations, which means . . . we cannot in truthfulness forget its correlation with revealed theology" (*RST*, 42-43). But this suggestion itself, according to Barth's analysis, must imply that revelation is no longer normative as long as one assumes theology can be separated from its object even momentarily without falling into idolatry. It is Torrance's aim in chapter 2 of *Reality and Scientific Theology* to explore natural theology by means of this abstraction. Yet it seems clear that what he really wants to do is to say that humanity needs to think scientifically both within natural science and theological science. And he does admit that the universe itself is "dumb" and cannot reveal anything. It is we, as the priests of creation, who enable it to reveal its secrets and who bring it to intelligibility ultimately in light of its contingence originally disclosed to faith. See Torrance, *The Ground and Grammar of Theology*, 111, 153.

16. See, e.g., Thomas F. Torrance, *The Ground and Grammar of Theology*, 99f. See also Torrance, *Reality and Evangelical Theology*, 32.

17. See Torrance, *The Ground and Grammar of Theology*, 94, 106ff. See also Torrance, *Divine and Contingent Order*, ch. 3.

18. See, e.g., Torrance, *The Christian Doctrine of God*, 114f.

19. Torrance therefore rejects Paul Tillich's symbolic view of our relation with God as a symbolic relation which means that the "cognitive content in what is called knowledge of God derives, not from faith in God, but from some aspect of human culture." *The Ground and Grammar of Theology*, 150. Such thinking would make Jesus Christ "a mere symbol, some representation of God detached from God" thus undercutting the *homoousion* which for Torrance is the "ontological and epistemological linchpin of Christian theology." *The Ground and Grammar of Theology*, 160-61.

20. Torrance, *God and Rationality*, 170.

21. Thomas F. Torrance, *Space, Time and Incarnation* (hereafter referred to in text as *STI*) (Edinburgh: T&T Clark, 1997) 52-53.

22. Torrance describes the incarnation as a "staggering doctrine" because "the Son of God has become man without ceasing to be the God he ever was."

23. Torrance brilliantly shows how this receptacle notion of space affected both Lutheran and Reformed Christology and conceptions of Christ's real presence in the Eucharist (*STI*, 30ff.). Torrance insists on holding together, with proper distinctions, Christ's real presence in the Eucharist and his real presence in history and on the last day at the *parousia*. He insists that the receptacle notion does not allow for these distinctions and so cannot see Christ's Eucharistic presence as "active self-presentation of Christ to us in space and time that reaches out toward the consummation in the final *parousia*" (*STI*, 32). Torrance thus opposes any timeless view of Christ's real presence because it blurs these time distinctions by reducing Christ's real presence to a purely spatial presence unconditioned by time.

24. See *TF*, 87ff. "*While God was always Father, he was not always Creator or Maker....* God was always Father not always Creator, but now he is Creator as well as Father. It is in similar terms that we may speak of the eternal Son who *became* Man. The Son was always Son of God, but now he is Man as well as God.... If the Son or Word of God by whom he created all things was not always incarnate, but became man in the fullness of time, then God's communication of *himself* to us in Jesus Christ ... is something new to the eternal being of God ... he is free to do what he had never done before, and free to be other than he was eternally" (*TF*, 87-89).

25. For Torrance, of course, God's existence is not timeless since he argues that "we must think of the constancy of God which is his unchanging eternal Life as characterized by *time*, not of course our kind of time which is the time of finite created being ... but God's kind of time which is the time of his eternal Life without beginning and end ... the time of God's Life is defined by his everlasting uncreated Nature in which he transcends our temporality while nevertheless holding it within the embrace of his divine time ... we must distinguish between God's uncreated time and our created time ... we must think of our creaturely time as contingently grounded upon the eternal time of God ... far from being some kind of timeless eternity or eternal now that devalues or negates time, the real time of God's eternal Life gives reality and value to the created time of our life" (Torrance, *The Christian Doctrine of God*, 241).

26. See, e.g., Torrance, *The Ground and Grammar of Theology*, 161.

27. For a full discussion of this issue see Molnar, *Divine Freedom*. Torrance repeatedly and correctly insists that it is "strictly by reference to the Father-Son, Son-Father relation that the Nature of God's Being is to be defined, or rather that God defines his own Nature

for us. . . . It belongs to the epistemological significance of the incarnation that it has opened up for us knowledge of God in accordance with what he is in himself, but to know God . . . in his internal relations, makes the doctrine of the Trinity essential to the Christian understanding of God" (*The Christian Doctrine of God,* 117). It is in this context that Torrance constantly stresses Athanasius' controlling insight that "It would be more godly and true to signify God from the Son and call him Father, than to name God from his works alone and call him Unoriginate" (*The Christian Doctrine of God,* 117).

28. See, e.g., Torrance, *The Christian Doctrine of God,* 3, 8, 18, 21, 30, 32, 72, 79, 92, 97, 99, 107, 114, 116, 130, 142, 243. This crucial insight appears in every one of Torrance's works and structures his entire theology of God and salvation.

29. Torrance, *The Christian Doctrine of God,* 32.

30. Torrance therefore relies heavily on Matt. 11:27 and parallel passages here to assert that knowledge of God takes place from this center in God and not from any center in ourselves. See, e.g., Torrance, *TF,* 58f.; *The Christian Doctrine of God,* 57ff., 61f., 77f.; Thomas F. Torrance, *Trinitarian Perspectives: Toward Doctrinal Agreement* (hereafter: *Trinitarian Perspectives*) (Edinburgh: T&T Clark, 1994), 91f.; and *The Ground and Grammar of Theology,* 154.

31. Torrance calls Athanasius' statement unfortunate because, as Georges Florovsky rightly admitted: "The term *theosis* is indeed embarrassing, if we would think of it in 'ontological categories.' Indeed, man simply cannot become 'god.' But the Fathers were thinking in 'personal' terms, and the mystery of personal communion was involved at this point. Theosis means a personal encounter. It is the ultimate intercourse with God, in which the whole of human existence is, as it were, permeated by the Divine Presence" (*The Christian Doctrine of God,* 96).

32. "The Platonising translation of θέωσις as 'deification' is rather misleading, for there can be no suggestion that the *nature* of human being is deified through what might be called *theotic* activity in the renewing and sanctifying presence of God. 2 Pet. 1.4" (*The Christian Doctrine of God,* 95). In this context Torrance says this should be understood to imply we are "partners of the Deity" and not "partakers of divine nature."

33. Thomas F. Torrance, *Preaching Christ Today: The Gospel and Scientific Thinking* (hereafter referred to in text as *PCT*) (Grand Rapids: Eerdmans, 1994), 36.

34. See also *PCT,* 37.

35. In this context Torrance astutely links the doctrine of justification by faith to Bultmann's mishandling of the NT contending that for Bultmann we have to give the NT a meaning for ourselves today in our contemporary situation and thus we should not concentrate on something that took place in the past since that would destroy faith. For Bultmann we must abandon the idea that we can find security in "an objective act of God in history" but instead we must "take the road of radical decision in which [we] work out the meaning for [ourselves] in the present" (*God and Rationality,* 59). Bultmann thus loses the objective meaning of justification which gives meaning to our faith.

36. That was Bultmann's error. Bultmann clearly expounded the difference between the Jewish ethic which was concerned with the commandments instead of their content and Christian ethics which is concerned with radical obedience to Jesus so that we are forced out of our hiding place behind the law and formal authority and "made fully responsible for [our] actions" (*God and Rationality,* 61). But he ultimately distorted the Gos-

pel by throwing us back completely on our own resources, thus ignoring the fact that God in Christ made himself responsible for us.

37. That is why Torrance insists, against Bultmann, that we not only should not exclude the "supernatural message as academically unthinkable for 'modern man'" but that we must interpret the Bible "in the light of the *logos* of God's self-revelation which it conveys and which . . . created the historical community of reciprocity between God and ancient Israel and God and the apostolic Church, within which the Old and New Testaments arose and took shape as the media through which that *logos* continues to be heard in the obedience of faith" (*STR*, 5).

38. Torrance quite properly rejects detaching space from time as he believes happens in much modern theology because it one-sidedly emphasizes history so that faith then is separated from any involvement in space and associated only with time. For Torrance "This goes far to account for the current debâcle of what is called the historico-critical method in biblical interpretation, in its failure to grapple with the spatio-temporal reality of the historical Jesus, not to mention the incarnate presence and redemptive activity of God in our world of space and time" (*Divine and Contingent Order*, 64).

39. It will be remembered that Barth insisted that theology could never be done properly unless Hilary's dictum in *De Trin.* 4 *para.* 14 that words must be understood from the realities signified rather than subjecting the realities to the words. Barth wrote: "*Intelligentia dictorum ex causis est assumenda dicendi, quia non sermoni res, sed rei sermo subjectus est.* Without having this statement before us, we cannot understand the point here [regarding the unique oneness of the Trinity], and he who does not adopt this statement as his own methodological axiom is no theologian and never will be" (*CD* I/1, 354). This is why Torrance argues that "terms are not prior to realities but realities come first and terms second" (*The Christian Doctrine of God*, 117).

40. What Torrance rejects then is the kind of source, form or redaction criticism that operates with the assumptions of "observationalism and phenomenalism. Thus they assume that theoretical elements can only have a later origin and have to be put down to the creative spirituality of the early Christian community rather than to Jesus himself" (*Reality and Evangelical Theology*, 80). Torrance opposes the idea that John's Gospel should be given a late date because of the "Greek theological ideas" scholars claim to find in it. In his view "the Fourth Gospel is probably the most 'Hebraic' book in the New Testament" as exemplified in the report of Jesus' statement "to the half-Jewish woman of Samaria: 'You worship what you do not know; we worship what we do know, for salvation is of the Jews'" (Thomas F. Torrance, *The Mediation of Christ* [Grand Rapids: Eerdmans, 1983], 29).

41. This thinking is supported by the view of Walter Künneth, *The Theology of the Resurrection* (St. Louis: Concordia Publishing House, 1965), who insists that the apostolate is *"founded by the appearance of the Risen One"* with the result that "the Risen One's own statements during the appearances acquire special importance" (90). Künneth cites Schlatter to stress that the risen Lord's own statement seemed to be the focus of Matt. 28:18ff. and Luke 24:46ff., and he writes: "incidentally the suggestion that the words of the Easter story could or must only have come from a later age is worthless" (90).

42. See Torrance, *Reality and Evangelical Theology*, 15ff.

43. For a discussion of Einstein's method of interrelating levels of knowledge and reality see Torrance, *The Ground and Grammar of Theology*, ch. 5.

44. Torrance thus interprets Einstein's saying that God does not wear his heart on his sleeve to mean that "we cannot deduce from appearances the deep structure of reality" (*The Ground and Grammar of Theology*, 119). Such thinking would be dualistic and would prevent a genuine knowledge of the historical Jesus since it would only interpret him according to his appearance and not according to his deeper reality as the Word incarnate. See *The Ground and Grammar of Theology*, 121ff.

45. It is extremely important to note that Torrance insists that theology is not concerned with "Jesus' own private religious understanding of God" because it is interested in "what he means us to have through his vicarious life and activity, i.e. the understanding which redeemed sinners have of the God and Father of Jesus Christ" (*STR*, 13). This is why Paul did not expend much effort attempting to ground his teaching about God which was mediated through Christ and the Spirit "upon the *ipsissima verba* or private religion of Jesus" (*STR*, 13).

46. See Torrance, *Divine and Contingent Order*, 26ff.

47. Torrance criticizes Pannenberg for not taking into account the fact that Judaism "did not anticipate resurrection as a *decisive event* in history" and "the fact that in its happening the resurrection of Jesus radically transformed the whole concept of the resurrection" (*STR*, 35). Pannenberg's Christology will be explored in detail in a later chapter.

48. See, e.g., Torrance, *The Ground and Grammar of Theology*, 117f.

49. See, e.g., Torrance, *The Ground and Grammar of Theology*, 118, 157f., 161, 164 and 166.

50. Torrance insists "we must take the *empty tomb* in the Gospel reports quite seriously — the body of Jesus Christ was raised, certainly a spiritual body, but it was not less body because it was a body healed and quickened by the Spirit" (*STR*, 141).

51. See, e.g., Torrance, *Reality and Evangelical Theology*, 124-25. This is why Torrance insists that because the incarnation has now taken place "we must think of it as the decisive action of God in Christ which invalidates all other possibilities and makes all other conceivable roads within space and time to God actually unthinkable" (*STI*, 68). "Since in Jesus Christ the eternal Son has entered within the contingence of the created order, making it his own, He may be known only in and through its creaturely freedom and spontaneity, and therefore not in any *a priori* manner" (*STI*, 74).

52. See also *TF*, 154ff. for how this relates to Torrance's view of the atonement. See also *The Christian Doctrine of God*, 215, where Torrance writes: "God crucified dies our death, descends into the chasm or abyss of our alienation from him in order to effect atonement and propitiation. This is the act whereby God gives *himself*, his all in the sacrifice of Christ on the Cross. . . . This is an act of incredible divine omnipotence in which God reveals that he loves us more than he loves himself." For Torrance, Christ's passion "belongs to the very Being of God" (*The Christian Doctrine of God*, 246). "Through his resurrection and ascension all that Christ Jesus has done for us in his historical life and death in offering himself for the sins of mankind has not only been accepted by the Father but has been taken up into God and is anchored in his eternal unchangeable reality. Unless that is the case, unless the atoning exchange effected through the suffering and death of Christ was indeed the vicarious act of God himself . . . then what took place in his crucifixion would have been in

vain" (*The Christian Doctrine of God*, 246-47). Hence for Torrance "God is certainly impassible in the sense that he is not subject to the passions that characterise our human and creaturely existence, and it is certainly true that God is opposed to all suffering and pain. He is, moreover, intrinsically impassible" (*The Christian Doctrine of God*, 248). Nonetheless, in light of God's act of salvation in the history of Jesus himself, God does not remain aloof from us but suffers for us in order to save us and redeem us. Hence, following Athanasius, Torrance notes that while suffering and death are not "'natural to the Godhead . . . they *came to belong to God by nature*, when it pleased the Word to undergo human birth and to reconstitute in himself, as in a new image, that what he himself had made but which had been disorganised by sin, corruption and death'" (*The Christian Doctrine of God*, 248; emphasis in original). Hence for Torrance "What Christ felt, did and suffered in himself in his body and soul for our forgiveness was felt, done, and suffered by God in his innermost Being for our sake" (*The Christian Doctrine of God*, 249). Therefore for Torrance when we understand the suffering and dying of God soteriologically and not logically (logically God could only be impassible or passible) we must acknowledge that God always is and remains impassible in the sense that he remains eternally who he was and is, but that we must also acknowledge that he is passible in the sense that he took on the form of a servant for our sakes (*The Christian Doctrine of God*, 250). The "conjunction" of passibility and impassibility in the incarnation "is as incomprehensible as the mode of the union of God and man in Christ. Just as in creation and incarnation God acted in entirely new ways while remaining unchanged in his divine nature, just as he became man without ceasing to be God and became a creature without ceasing to be the Creator, so he became passible (παθητός) in one sense without ceasing to be impassible (ἀπαθής) in another sense" (*The Christian Doctrine of God*, 250).

53. Torrance notes that, for Cyril of Alexandria, Jesus took food not to nourish his body but to nourish the disciples' faith.

Notes to Chapter 4

1. See Molnar, "Natural Theology Revisited," in *Zeitschrift für dialektische Theologie*.

2. See *CD* IV/2, 126. Barth writes: "He is the *doctor veritatis*. He is the finger of God . . . which causes the reason of man . . . to receive the truth. . . . Wherever there is Christian *gnosis* it is His work. That is why it has no other sources or norms. That is why it can be had without any demonstration of its origin." See also Barth, *Evangelical Theology*, 6: "The separation and distinction of this one true God from all the others can only be continually his own deed."

3. See above Chapter One and *CD* I/2, 40f. and 151ff.

4. See above Chapter Two. This thinking represents a clear contemporary application of the container concept of time and space to the incarnation and as we shall see it is just this that leads to the difficulties in Rahner's Christology because he sees Christ's human nature as the constitutive real symbol of the Logos that is filled with the reality symbolized and stands in a mutual causal connection with that reality.

5. Cf. *CD* I/2, 63ff. For an especially clear explanation of this see also Barth, *The Göttingen Dogmatics*, 152-67, esp. 156ff. On Barth's view of miracle see 161.

6. Even as early as *The Göttingen Dogmatics* Barth rejected this idea: "The humanity of Christ, although it is body and soul, and an individual, is nothing subsistent or real in itself. Thus it did not exist prior to its union with the Logos. It has no independent existence alongside or apart from him. Those who want to see revelation in the idea of humanity as such are grasping at something that in itself is not just meaningless but nonexistent . . . the idea of humanity, and this individual who incorporates it [Christ], cannot for a single moment be abstracted from their assumption into the person of the Logos. The divine subject who unites himself with them makes them revelation. The human nature of Christ has no personhood of its own" (157).

7. In *CD* IV/4 *Lecture Fragments, The Christian Life*, trans. Geoffrey W. Bromiley (hereafter: *The Christian Life*) (Grand Rapids: Eerdmans, 1981), Barth puts the matter bluntly in connection with the petitions of the Lord's Prayer: "In its concrete content and compass, what is prayed for [the coming of the kingdom] is not like any other event . . . it is absolutely unexpected and inconceivable. It comes down directly from above. . . . It thus demands and creates freedom for human thought and volition in a new dimension. . . . It also opposes the kingdom of demons. . . . The Lord does not reason and discuss or debate with either demons or the men to whose help he hastens. . . . He does not concur or collaborate with them. He simply goes his own way, the way of his own honor and our salvation" (235).

8. Karl Rahner and Joseph Ratzinger, *Revelation and Tradition*, Quaestiones Disputatae, 17, trans. W. J. O'Hara (New York: Herder & Herder, 1966); Karl Rahner, "Observations on the Concept of Revelation," 9-25, 16.

9. *FCF*, 173.

10. *TI* 9: 253-57, "Self-Realisation and Taking Up One's Cross," 256.

11. *TI* 18: 143-56, "What Does It Mean to Believe In Jesus Christ?" 145.

12. As seen above, Torrance describes the incarnation as a "staggering doctrine" because "the Son of God has become man without ceasing to be the God he ever was" (*STI*, 53).

13. Joseph Cardinal Ratzinger, *Principles of Catholic Theology: Building Stones for a Fundamental Theology*, trans. Sister Mary Frances McCarthy, S.N.D. (San Francisco: Ignatius Press, 1987), astutely argues that this very thinking compromises the newness of Christianity by resolving the particular into the universal and by reducing "Christian liberation into pseudoliberation. . . . Self-acceptance — just being human — is all that is required [to be a Christian]" (167). Ratzinger properly rejects this kind of thinking as a type of rationalism that fails to come to grips with the particularity of Christianity that calls for conversion and not self-acceptance.

14. Hence, Rahner can say, as seen above, that "the symbol is the reality, constituted by the thing symbolized as an inner moment of moment of itself, which reveals and proclaims the thing symbolized, and is itself full of the thing symbolized, being its concrete form of existence" (*TI* 4: 251). And this leads to the idea that "what Jesus is and does as man reveals the Logos himself; it is the reality of the Logos as our salvation amidst us . . . here the Logos with God and the Logos with us, the immanent and the economic Logos, are strictly the same" (*Trinity*, 33). Clearly it is the container concept of space and time that governs Rahner's thinking at this sensitive point and allows him to formulate a mutually conditioned concept of revelation itself because for him the symbol brings about

what is symbolized and is its very reality. This thinking necessarily blurs the distinction between Christ's humanity and his divinity here and elsewhere. Here the Word has lost its sovereignty.

15. That is why Barth asks: "Does the divine sonship of Jesus Christ mean that God's revealing has now been transmitted as it were to the existence of the man Jesus of Nazareth, that this has thus become identical with it?" In other words, "Is the *humanitas Christi* as such the revelation?" (*CD* I/1, 323). Barth rejects this thinking because he insists that it is evidence that we have taken control of revelation by means of certain conceptions deriving from humanity itself. The question here is from where does the power of continuity come in which Jesus stood as the revealer. And Barth's answer is that it did not come from Jesus' humanity as such but from the action of the Word in that humanity. Why? Because his humanity was given up to death on the cross and it is "from death, from this frontier, since the Crucified was raised again, that He is manifested as the Son of God. Nor is His resurrection described as an operation proper to the *humanitas Christi* but rather as something done to it, as a being raised from the dead by God (frequently, cf. Gal. 1:1; Rom. 6:4; Eph. 1:20 expressly by God the Father)" (*CD* I/1, 323). Of course Rahner's answer to this question is that the power does come from his humanity as such because that is now filled with the reality symbolized (his divinity) and because the finite has been given an infinite extension by virtue of the incarnation. Here is *the* crucial difference between Rahner and Barth that separates them in their interpretation of the resurrection. As we have seen, Rahner thinks he can understand the meaning of the resurrection by exploring our transcendental experiences of hope while Barth insists that the resurrection can only be understood from and in Christ himself as the risen Lord. For Barth, therefore, hope is defined exclusively by who Jesus was and is and not by our hope itself.

16. Rahner and Thüsing, *A New Christology*, 13. Unfortunately, confusing the disciples' experience of faith with the risen Lord, then appealing to experience to explain the resurrection and finally denying that what is discovered in the encounter with the risen Lord is utterly new is widespread among those who are influenced by Rahner. Thus, Dermot A. Lane, *The Reality of Jesus* (New York: Paulist Press, 1975), 60-61, explains the meaning of the resurrection using an "interpersonal model" of personal relations and blends resurrection and faith together arguing that resurrection and faith "are *intrinsically* related dimensions of the *same transforming experience*" (61, emphasis mine). Then he claims that because we have hope, therefore "the resurrection appears not as some exception . . . [but] as the full realisation and actual fulfilment of those seeds of indestructibility which exist within the heart of every individual" (64). And Gerald O'Collins, *Jesus Risen: An Historical, Fundamental and Systematic Examination of Christ's Resurrection* (New York: Paulist Press, 1987), 56, conceding too much to Bultmann, argues that while Bultmann was overly subjective and Barth overly objective, Bultmann nonetheless "rightly acknowledged the human questioning which can and should make the Easter kerygma vitally significant." This leads O'Collins to contend that our prior beliefs about God shed light on the claim about Jesus' resurrection so that it is incorrect to think that it is absolutely and utterly new (139). But it is not our human questioning that makes the Easter kerygma vitally significant; it is the risen Lord himself who does that in the power of his Holy Spirit. And unless the event is acknowledged as utterly new, then to that extent, we no longer need to rely on Jesus himself to make sense of the kerygma. A choice is required here between relying on our human

experience and the Holy Spirit who enables us to experience the power of the risen Lord as a power distinguishable from our experience of faith. For a full critique of Lane's thinking on this issue see Molnar, *Divine Freedom,* 53-54.

17. See Rahner, *TI* 4: 240f. and *The Church and the Sacraments,* Quaestiones Disputatae, 9, trans. W. J. O'Hara (New York: Herder and Herder, 1968), 38.

18. The importance of this issue is captured nicely in an imaginary dialogue among Barth, Bultmann, a follower of Pannenberg and a follower of Moltmann, when the follower of Moltmann noted that there was "big news" in the Sunday *New York Times:* "Archaeologists have uncovered the skeleton of a young man crucified and buried outside the walls of Jerusalem some two thousand years ago." Daniel L. Migliore, *Faith Seeking Understanding: An Introduction to Christian Theology* (Grand Rapids: Eerdmans, 1991), 270. Bultmann responded that since the reporters were wondering whether this might be "You-Know-Who" he was glad he had demythologized the event some years earlier. It is just that disregard of the empirical correlate that leads to the subjectivism Torrance here rejects. N. T. Wright, *The Resurrection of the Son of God* (Minneapolis: Fortress Press, 2003), 321, captures this nicely when he says "neither Paul nor any other early Christian could have conceived of a 'resurrection from the dead' which left a body in the tomb."

19. Torrance does not here appeal to a biblical text but rather to Cyril of Alexandria. See *STR,* 32, n. 7. For a possible biblical warrant see below, Chapter Eight, n. 40. Torrance also refers to the fact that Calvin did not hesitate to state that, in addition to his being raised by the Father "He rose again Himself as Conqueror." And he mentions that *The Larger Catechism* unambiguously says "He rose again from the dead the third day by His own power" (Torrance, *The School of Faith,* lxxvi-lxxvii). For Torrance it is important to say that Christ also rose by his own power to avoid any suggestion of Nestorian separation of his divinity and humanity in the act of atonement.

20. A. Katherine Grieb, "Last Things First: Karl Barth's Theological Exegesis of 1 Corinthians in *The Resurrection of the Dead,*" *SJT* 56, no. 1 (2003): 49-64, 61.

21. These issues are discussed in detail in Molnar, *Divine Freedom.*

22. See, e.g., Torrance, *Karl Barth,* 110.

23. See, e.g., *TI* 9: 117-26, "The Need for a 'Short-Formula' of Christian Faith," 123, where Rahner expresses his belief that we are "divinised" in the ground of our existence and so we seek the God-man "not expressly but in reality all the same, in wishing the ultimate question (of one's own being and of one's destiny in death) and the ultimate acceptance (of this question by God) to appear together. . . . To this extent every man who is true to his conscience is for us an Advent Christian, looking forward to the *one* Man in whom his own question (we do not merely *put* questions; we *are* questions) and God's acceptance have become one and have finally appeared in one person. As Christians we have the courage to believe that this looked-for one is found. He is Jesus of Nazareth."

24. For a full discussion of this issue see Molnar, "Natural Theology Revisited," in *Zeitschrift für dialektische Theologie.*

25. For a full discussion of how the commands to love God and neighbor disclose the differences in the theologies of Barth and Rahner see Molnar, "Love of God and Love of Neighbor in the Theology of Karl Rahner and Karl Barth."

Notes to Chapter 5

1. In fact, Macquarrie actually believes that his thinking has avoided adoptionism and Pelagianism and is faithful to the teaching of Chalcedon. See John Macquarrie, *Jesus Christ in Modern Thought* (hereafter referred to in text as *Jesus Christ*) (Philadelphia: Trinity Press International, 1990), 382f. In his more recent book *Christology Revisited* (Harrisburg, PA: Trinity Press International, 1998), Macquarrie claims that he has been "unjustly" called an adoptionist (23). But his own description of his degree Christology in the same volume confirms the fact that his Christology really is an adoptionist Christology, because he refuses to acknowledge that Jesus is the Word of God incarnate simply because he is. Instead of following the path of Chalcedon, which he claims began with the Logos, Macquarrie begins by asking "How does a man become God?" (*Jesus Christ,* 360). For him therefore the presence of God in the man Jesus is something that occurs subsequent to his human appearance on earth. This leads him to assert that "if we speak of an incarnation, this cannot mean a simple identity of God with Christ" (*Christology Revisited,* 76); "Adoptionism . . . need not in any way impugn the unique status of Jesus Christ" (*Christology Revisited,* 77); and, following John Knox and Karl Rahner, "the unitary person, leading edge, or *hypostasis* of Jesus was not the *hypostasis* of the divine Logos . . . but was the human *hypostasis* transfigured by a constant immersion in the divine Spirit" (*Christology Revisited,* 79). That is adoptionist Christology classically illustrated by Barth in his rejection of Ebionite Christology and clearly and rightly rejected by Thomas F. Torrance, who insisted, with Barth, that Jesus' humanity was posited in the Person of the Logos and had no existence separate from that.

2. *CD* 1/1, 400 and Torrance, *TF,* 124-25. Torrance writes: "any detraction from the Son cannot but be a detraction from the Father, for to deny the divine nature of the Son is to deny that God is eternally and intrinsically Father, and to deny the divine reality of the Word is to say that in himself God is essentially wordless and wisdomless. . . . The *homoousion* was . . . a bulwark against Sabellianism and Arianism, against unitarianism and polytheism, alike."

3. See *Jesus Christ,* 62, where Macquarrie sums up his version of Paul's thinking by saying: "one way of defining resurrection would be to say that it is the lifting of human life on to a new level," and in Macquarrie's reading of 1 Cor. 15:45-49 he expresses his belief that for Paul "the man from heaven is not there at the beginning of the story, he is not the primal man, but comes at the end. He emerges at the resurrection . . . he is sent or destined or called by God to bring to light the true nature of man — a nature which was concealed as a potentiality even in the first Adam" (*Jesus Christ,* 62-63). This interpretation is in keeping with Macquarrie's explanation of Phil. 2:6ff., following J. D. G. Dunn, to mean that the divine intention for humanity was fulfilled "in the one who became Lord" (*Jesus Christ,* 57). And this means that Jesus humanly accomplished what Adam did not by laying aside all desire to displace God. It was Adam's grasping at equality with God that Jesus did not choose. This grasping at equality did not refer to a pre-existent situation in which Jesus, as Son, was equal to God and indeed was God himself. So instead of holding that a pre-existent personal agent became man and acted on our behalf in the incarnation, Macquarrie dismisses any notion of personal pre-existence on the part of Jesus as the Son as mythological and as something that would compromise belief in his au-

thentic humanity. The adoptionist overtones to all of this are pretty clear and indeed they are clear enough that Macquarrie is compelled to assert that he does not wish his Christology to end there but he desires to bring it to a conclusion in some form of incarnational Christology. As we shall see, however, that does not even come close to presenting the actual NT view of the matter. It goes without saying that this interpretation of the NT is completely wide of the mark, first, because it does not deal with the plain sense of Phil. 2:6ff. as expounded with clarity for example by Gordon D. Fee ("St Paul and the Incarnation: A Reassessment of the Data," in *The Incarnation: An Interdisciplinary Symposium on the Incarnation of the Son of God,* ed. Stephen T. Davis, Daniel Kendall, S.J., and Gerald O'Collins, S.J. [Oxford: Oxford University Press, 2002], 62-92, 80), and second, because it uses a notion of metaphor or myth that refuses to allow the reality being discussed to determine its meaning. Hence for Macquarrie "God's metaphorical 'sending' of his metaphorical 'son' can be understood in ways that do not imply pre-existence, once we accept that the language is metaphorical and not literal" (*Jesus Christ,* 56). Here Macquarrie's denial of Jesus' actual pre-existence as the eternal Son of the Father has important trinitarian implications because this denial fosters exactly the kind of Christology from below that is in fact adoptionistic and thus pulls the ground out from under the actual meaning of both the incarnation and the resurrection. By contrast, Gordon Fee argues that "the one who as a man humbled himself to the point of death on the cross had previous existence as God, and as such 'poured himself out' by becoming human" (*Incarnation,* 80) and refutes Dunn's interpretation point by point. And it is worth noting that, among other things in his commentary on Phil. 2:6ff., Barth argues that "This equality of Christ with God is, so to speak, the fixed *ultimate* background from which his road sets out and to which it returns. . . . He is so much God's Equal that he does not by any means have to make of his equality with God a thing to be asserted tooth and nail — not because he could also give it up, but because his possession of it . . . is beyond dispute" (Karl Barth, *The Epistle to the Philippians,* 40th Anniversary Edition, trans. James W. Leitch, intro. Bruce L. McCormack and Francis B. Watson [Louisville/London: Westminster/ John Knox Press, 2002], 61-62). This is why Barth argues that Jesus remains fully divine in humbling himself but that his divinity is concealed in his humanity: "That means that he exists in such a way that to any direct, immediate way of regarding him — for example, to the historical and psychological approach — he does not present the picture of his proper, original, divine Being, but solely the picture of a human being. That is the way it is now with the heavenly Head of the church. . . . Is he not equal with God? He is. But where, then, do we see any sign of that? Where is the glittering crown of his Godhead? The *humilitas carnis* (humility of the flesh) covers the *divina majestas* (divine majesty) like a curtain, says Calvin. . . . He emptied himself of the form of God in taking on our form. It is God's Equal himself, in all his freedom and his entirely royal sovereignty, who is the ground of this *incognito*. . . . Flesh and blood cannot, may not, and will not reveal to us who this is" (*The Epistle to the Philippians,* 63-64).

4. *Jesus Christ,* 363, 370.

5. As seen above in Chapter One, Barth argued that it is only by the resurrection itself that faith in the risen Lord became possible. Hence he also argued that it was not easier for them to accept because of the prevailing "mythical world-view" since even then "the Easter message seems to be utterly 'incredible'" (*CD* III/2, 447). And as seen in Chapter

Three, Torrance makes the same point contending that the resurrection was utterly incredible both then (in the time of the NT) and now. See Torrance, *STR*, 17.

6. Following J. D. G. Dunn, Macquarrie echoes the thinking of M. Dibelius which Barth specifically and properly rejected. Dibelius held that the problem of Christology arose because of the "way in which 'knowledge of the historical figure of Jesus was so quickly transformed into faith in a heavenly Son of God'" (*CD* I/1, 402). Barth correctly judged that this thinking leads directly to Ebionite and Docetic Christology because it fails to begin with Jesus himself as the Word of God incarnate and thus within faith. Macquarrie himself seeks a "unifying idea amid the diversity of the New Testament, an idea which he [Dunn] expresses as the conviction that the historical figure, Jesus the Jew, becomes an 'exalted being'" (*Jesus Christ*, 12).

7. Resurrection for Macquarrie does not refer to an event in the life of Jesus that gives meaning to faith. Rather it refers to "the lifting of human life on to a new level" (*Jesus Christ*, 62). And that means that Jesus was not some "superhuman" but that because he brought "to light the true nature of man — a nature concealed as a potentiality even in the first Adam" he can be considered the "man from heaven" (*Jesus Christ*, 63).

8. Thus Macquarrie writes "I have never myself understood why theologians have maintained that there could be only one incarnation and it had to happen exactly as it did" (*Jesus Christ*, 170). And Macquarrie insists that the idea of many savior figures makes sense as long as "incarnation is not supposed to be an isolated event in Jesus Christ alone, but is seen to have been a continuous process of incarnation that began with creation, reached its climax in Christ and continues even today" (*Jesus Christ*, 421).

9. See Wolfhart Pannenberg, *Jesus — God and Man*, 2nd ed., trans. Lewis L. Wilkins and Duane A. Priebe (hereafter referred to in text as *Jesus — God and Man*) (Philadelphia: Westminster Press, 1977), 279. Given what has been said already in this book, it is not at all surprising that Barth's reaction to this work by Pannenberg was rather negative. Barth wrote to Pannenberg: "My first reaction on reading your book was one of horror when . . . I found you rejecting M. Kähler in a way which led me to suspect that, like others, you . . . intended to pursue a path from below to above. . . . Is not this to build a house on the sand — the shifting sand of historical probabilities. . . . *In its positive content is your christology — after the practice of so many modern fathers — anything other than the outstanding example and symbol of a presupposed general anthropology, cosmology, and ontology?*" (*Karl Barth Letters 1961-1968*, ed. Jürgen Fangmeier and Hinrich Stoevesandt, trans. and ed. Geoffrey W. Bromiley [Grand Rapids: Eerdmans, 1981], 178, emphasis mine). We shall consider this in greater detail in Chapter Eight.

10. That is why he believes that "The idea that there is an implacable conflict between adoptionist and incarnational christologies is quite mistaken. Each of these approaches needs the other" (*Jesus Christ*, 373). Macquarrie pursues the same argument in his more recent book *Christology Revisited*, ch. 4.

11. Interestingly, in *Christology Revisited* (31ff.) Macquarrie claims that Barth's interpretation of the Virgin Birth is the most adequate for contemporary theology. But he completely misinterprets and ignores Barth's most important points which were that the Virgin Birth is a sign indicating the miracle of Christmas and that because this is a miracle, the incarnation must be the starting point and not just the conclusion of one's theology. Unlike Barth, Macquarrie is opposed to "nature miracles," while Barth insisted that since

God became incarnate in Jesus of Nazareth, any denial of "nature miracles" such as his bodily resurrection or the incarnation itself would amount to a denial of revelation. This does not mean that one has to accept every miracle in the NT exactly as recounted, Barth says, but one cannot play off spirit and nature in order to argue, as Macquarrie does, that "there are good reasons for doubting whether any nature miracles were ever performed by Jesus" (*Christology Revisited*, 37-38).

12. Macquarrie continues to argue for his degree Christology in *Christology Revisited:* "we must understand the difference between Christ and the rest of humanity as one of degree, rather than of kind" (*Christology Revisited*, 59). And he defends Norman Pittenger's Christology against the charge of adoptionism leveled by Eric Mascall (correctly, I think) by saying: "It is true that more than once in his writings, he declares that the difference between Jesus Christ and other human beings is one of degree, rather than of kind, but in saying this I think he is simply claiming that the distinctiveness of Christ is conceivable within the category of humanity" (*Christology Revisited*, 74).

13. See *Jesus Christ*, 204ff. Macquarrie says: "I think he [Schleiermacher] was right in claiming that what we may call a union with the divine was possible for Jesus of Nazareth only because this is a potency that is present in all human nature. Christ did not, so to speak, begin with a supernatural endowment that put him in a different category from all other human beings — then he would not be one of us and would have no significance for human life" (*Jesus Christ*, 203). This thinking leads to the Docetic idea that "incarnation did not take place on a particular date but was a process that had been going on during a very long period of preparation" (*Jesus Christ*, 205). Indeed, Macquarrie believes that "this earth, the human race, yes, Jesus Christ himself were already latent, already predestined, in the primaeval swirling cloud of particles. Schleiermacher understood this when he wrote that 'Christ, *even as a human person,* was ever coming to be simultaneously with the world itself'" (*Jesus Christ*, 392). Incarnation therefore for Macquarrie means "the progressive presencing and self-manifestation of the Logos in the physical and historical world. For the Christian, this process reaches its climax in Jesus Christ" (*Jesus Christ*, 392). Barth, of course, was correct when he wrote: "It was Schleiermacher who, after the example of many a Gnostic in the 2nd century, after the example of John Scotus Erigena and of Duns Scotus, taught that the appearance of Jesus Christ was to be regarded as the 'creation (in Schleiermacher equivalent to 'preservation') of human nature now completed for the first time' — so far, i.e., as there is to be found in it the preservation 'of the receptivity implanted in human nature from the beginning and continuously evolving, a receptivity which enables it to take up into itself such an absolute potency of the God-consciousness'" (*CD* I/2, 134). It is because Schleiermacher did not take sin seriously enough as a compromise of communion between God and creatures that he could not conceive the unity of God and us in Christ as a new creation. Instead, Christ was no more than the continuation of human nature "which was originally good and unbroken in its God-consciousness" (*CD* I/2, 134). Unless Christ is really seen as the "new man," reconciliation, redemption and incarnation will not be seen as free acts of divine Lordship. Hence, as Barth correctly put it: "The Word of God is not seriously regarded by him as the Subject of the redeeming act, but as one of the factors in the world-process" (*CD* I/2, 135). Macquarrie's thinking suffers from this exact same weakness. It is even worth mentioning that Macquarrie explicitly appeals to "The Celtic philosopher Eriguena" (*Jesus Christ*, 381) to espouse his own

Pelagianism: "I believe that to some extent God's image remains vestigially in every human being, but the Christian claim is that in Jesus Christ that image has clearly shone forth. But . . . the difference between Christ and other human beings is one of degree, rather than of kind" (*Jesus Christ,* 382).

14. Of course this is why Macquarrie argues that "There is a sense in which all natural theology is revealed theology . . . there is also a sense in which all revealed theology is natural theology" (John Macquarrie, *In Search of Deity: An Essay in Dialectical Theism* [New York: Crossroad, 1987], 12-13). Macquarrie's "Dialectical Theism" is a version of panentheism that attempts to "find a path between theism and pantheism" (*In Search of Deity,* 15). And, confirming the fact that panentheism always collapses back into pantheism, it is this search that leads him to think that God really cannot exist without being immanent in the world: "Dialectic requires us to say that if God is transcendent, he must also be immanent" (*In Search of Deity,* 28). The point of the doctrine of the immanent Trinity, by contrast, is that God's transcendence does not require him to become immanent within the world. That he does become immanent in his Word and Spirit is a free act of love neither necessitated by his nature nor by any principle of dialectic. Not surprisingly Macquarrie actually believes that "It may be the case . . . that any dialectical theism must eventually come to think of God in a threefold way, and this would explain why triune deities appear in many unrelated forms of religion" (*In Search of Deity,* 69). But as I have argued in *Divine Freedom,* just thinking of God in a threefold way does not necessarily mean that one is thinking of the Christian God.

15. This explains why Macquarrie literally holds what Barth called an Ebionite view of Jesus: "Just as there was a tendency to ascribe, if not actually omnipotence, at least supernatural powers to Jesus in his earthly human life, there was a similar tendency to ascribe to him omniscience" (*Christology Revisited,* 39). And he explicitly embraces John Knox's belief that the earliest Christologies were adoptionist, but that such adoptionist Christology did not last long since it inevitably led to the ideas of pre-existence and incarnation (*Christology Revisited,* 64ff.). The only problem with this thinking is that it is inescapably Ebionite. As Barth noted, it was just this thinking that was advanced by Martin Dibelius that he rejected, and that in my view must still be rejected today, because it implied and implies that Jesus was the Lord based on the community's reaction (faith) to him: "The New Testament statement about the unity of the Son with the Father, i.e., the deity of Christ, cannot possibly be understood in terms of the presupposition that the original view and declaration of the New Testament witnesses was that a human being was either exalted as such to deity or appeared among us as the personification and symbol of a divine being" (*CD* I/1, 402).

16. Eduard Schweizer, *Jesus,* trans. David E. Green (Atlanta: John Knox Press, 1971), 21-22.

17. Macquarrie admits that his position sounds Hegelian since for Hegel "the Absolute Spirit has from all eternity been going out into the realm of the finite" (*Jesus Christ,* 111). And this, Macquarrie insists, should not be surprising since Hegel's view of the Spirit developed from his reflections on the doctrine of the Trinity. This is why Macquarrie actually believes that "distinctions within God arise almost necessarily from reflection on what God, if there is a God, must be" (*Jesus Christ,* 111). There is a note of unreality in this view of the Trinity. And it stems from Macquarrie's failure to acknowledge that the God who meets us in the incarna-

tion and resurrection is the God who existed from all eternity as Father, Son and Holy Spirit and the God who would have been the self-same God even if he never decided to create, reconcile and redeem the world. The fact that Macquarrie can even wonder if there is a God when speaking about the Trinity shows the nature of his speculations. He believes the distinctions within God arise from human speculation about what God must be, if there is a God. Any serious discussion of the Trinity, however, arises on the ground of God's revelation of himself in his Word and Spirit and thus acknowledges that revelation is the expression of God's antecedent existence before all worlds as the eternal Father, Son and Spirit. All theology turns on acknowledging this. Macquarrie cannot do so because from the outset of his reflections Jesus is a mere man who is different in degree and not in kind from the rest of us. This denial of the doctrine of the immanent Trinity leads to his unitarian and modalist conception of the Christian God. It is interesting to note that the only way Macquarrie seems able to conceive of Jesus being different in kind from us is to envision some *tertium quid* which, as Barth rightly noted, manifested the supreme misunderstanding of the Chalcedonian position. See *Christology Revisited*, 58. Macquarrie conceptualizes this by saying that in Jesus a "new species" had appeared. Strangely, Macquarrie's explicit rejection of the Patristic notion of *anhypostasis* reflects a basic misunderstanding of Christology noted by Barth decades ago. Macquarrie thinks it deprives Jesus of human personhood. But in fact, according to Barth, the doctrine merely intended to say that Jesus' human personhood had no existence apart from the Word (*CD* I/2, 163ff.). Since Macquarrie's starting point precludes this idea from the beginning, he then presents the doctrine of *enhypostasis* and *anhypostasis* as "as a conceptual jungle" in order to advance his degree Christology (*Christology Revisited*, ch. 3). And he embraces monothelitism, which was condemned by the Third Council of Constantinople in 680, insisting that "Two wills in one person would be a pathological condition" (*Jesus Christ*, 167). By contrast, Barth astutely wrote: "In recent times the doctrine of the *anhypostasis* and *enhypostasis* of Christ's human nature has occasionally been combated by the primitive argument, that if the human nature of Christ is without personality of its own, it is all up with the true humanity of Christ and the Docetism of early Christology holds the field. . . . This argument is primitive because it rests simply upon a misunderstanding of the Latin term *impersonalitas* used occasionally for *anhypostasis*. But what Christ's human nature lacks according to the early doctrine is not what we call personality. This the early writers called *individualitas*, and they never taught that Christ's human nature lacked this, but rather that this qualification actually belonged to true human being. *Personalitas* was their name for what we call existence or being. Their negative position asserted that Christ's flesh in itself has no existence, and this was asserted in the interests of their positive position that Christ's flesh has its existence through the Word and in the Word, who is God Himself acting as Revealer and Reconciler" (*CD* I/2, 164).

18. It is worth noting the similarity between this notion and Rahner's "searching Christology" here.

19. Paul F. Knitter, *No Other Name? A Critical Survey of Christian Attitudes Toward the World Religions* (hereafter referred to in text as *No Other Name?*) (Maryknoll, NY: Orbis Books, 1985), 197.

20. Colin Gunton, "And in One Lord, Jesus Christ . . . Begotten, Not Made," in *Nicene Christianity: The Future for a New Ecumenism*, ed. Christopher R. Seitz (Grand Rapids: Brazos Press, 2001), 35-48, 35.

21. Paul F. Knitter, *Introducing Theologies of Religions* (hereafter referred to in text as *Theologies of Religions*) (Maryknoll, NY: Orbis Books, 2002), 153, emphasis in original.

22. See *Theologies of Religions*, 119-20, where Knitter, following the thinking of John Hick, asserts: "The early Christians . . . were trying to put into words what they had experienced in and through him. . . . They were talking about matters of the heart, not conclusions of the head." This Ebionite starting point leads Knitter to conclude that when the NT refers to Jesus as the Son of God "It indicated specialness, not exclusivity" (*Theologies of Religions*, 120). Because this NT language is poetic, symbolic and metaphoric it cannot be taken to mean literally that Jesus is the unique Son of the Father, according to Knitter. It is instead what he calls "love language" (*Theologies of Religions*, 152). Such language is one way, Knitter says, that theologians today reinterpret the "one-and-onlys" of the NT. It affirms "the meaning of Jesus" without denying that of others and thus there can be "many 'one-and-onlys'" (*Theologies of Religions*, 152).

23. See Molnar, *Divine Freedom.*

24. Walter Kasper, *The God of Jesus Christ*, trans. Matthew J. O'Connell (New York: Crossroad, 1986), 294, citing Gregory of Nazianzus.

25. For a detailed exploration of these difficulties see Molnar, *Divine Freedom*, chs. 4, 5 and 6 and Chapter Two above.

26. For a thorough critique of Knitter's unitarian theocentrism see Paul D. Molnar, "Some Dogmatic Consequences of Paul F. Knitter's Unitarian Theocentrism," *The Thomist*, 55, no. 3 (July 1991): 449-95.

27. Knitter reemphasizes dialogue as the key to presenting a feasible theology of religions in his latest book. But this very procedure undermines the *homoousial* relation between Jesus, the Son with God the Father, separates the Spirit from the Word and therefore undercuts the very substance of the Christian faith. Knitter weaves together various statements from Vatican II and from Pope John Paul II in order to assert that because salvation can be found in and through other religions, therefore one must be open to the possibility not only "of a Buddhist becoming a Christian but of a Christian becoming a Buddhist. This is dialogue in the fullest sense" (*Theologies of Religions*, 83). This is reminiscent of his belief, following John Macquarrie, that one can be totally committed to Jesus Christ and yet look for revelations beyond him (*No Other Name?* 157). If, however, one really were committed to Jesus Christ who is the Word of God incarnate then one would recognize that there is no revelation beyond or apart from him, the revealer of God. And Knitter repeatedly separates the Spirit from the Word arguing that the Spirit is alive and active in other religious communities (*Theologies of Religions*, 90). But it makes a difference which Spirit one is speaking about. If Knitter had been speaking of the Holy Spirit, then that Spirit would have pointed us to Jesus Christ as the foundation and source of our knowledge of God and of salvation. But for Knitter, following Jacques Dupuis, "what the Spirit is about in other religions may be genuinely different from what one finds in God's Word in Jesus — never *contradictory to*, but really *different from*" (*Theologies of Religions*, 90). Hence "To affirm the Spirit within other cultures and religions implies, therefore, that God has more to say to humanity than what God has said in Jesus. . . . God does not intend all people to find their fulfillment in the Christian church" (*Theologies of Religions*, 90-91). And this thinking leads directly to Dupuis' apparent degree Christology: "'This plenitude [the fullness of God's truth in Jesus] . . . is not . . . one of extension and all-comprehension,

but of intensity. . . . It does not — it cannot — exhaust the mystery of the Divine'" (*Theologies of Religions*, 92). And this leads both Dupuis and Knitter to the very contradiction of God's Word in Jesus that they think they have avoided: "Dupuis," Knitter writes, "therefore explicitly admits that the fullness of God's truth in Jesus is 'relative' (that is, limited — a word that few Christian theologians would dare to use)" (*Theologies of Religions*, 92). Hence "Christians have to *relate* what they have in Jesus to what the Spirit is doing in other religions. Indeed, Christians don't really know the fullness of God's message in Christ unless they talk with others" (*Theologies of Religions*, 92). This familiar refrain in Knitter's thought is based on a denial of Christ's uniqueness as the one eternal Word of the Father, beside whom there is no other exactly because it has detached the Spirit from the Word and located that Spirit within other religions so that Knitter and Dupuis can then look beyond Jesus Christ for the revelation and salvation of God within history. Not only is this a brand of Docetic Christology, but this very procedure calls into question the actual foundation of the Christian faith, which is none other than Jesus Christ himself. The very idea that Christians should consult with those who do not believe in Jesus to understand him as the revealer and savior demonstrates that Knitter and Dupuis are not thinking of the Jesus of the NT and of Chalcedon. For that Jesus can be understood only through faith in him which comes from the Holy Spirit uniting people to him in specific historical circumstances. It may also be noted here that Dupuis' attempt to universalize Christ's particular saving work by categorizing it as the "Christic mystery" based on "religious experience" allows him to locate the "Christic mystery" in those who do not believe in Jesus himself (Jacques Dupuis, S.J., *Jesus Christ at the Encounter of World Religions* [hereafter: *World Religions*], trans. Robert R. Barr [Maryknoll, NY: Orbis Books, 1991], 144ff.). But it is just this thinking that makes experience the criterion of truth and leads to a form of self-justification. On the one hand, Dupuis argues: "Salvation depends on the manner, on the intensity with which each person responds in his or her concrete situation, to the Christic mystery of salvation present and active in each one, whether consciously or unconsciously" (*World Religions*, 146). On the other hand, Dupuis contends that because other religions contain and signify God's presence to humanity in Christ, therefore "their own religious practice is the reality that gives expression to their experience of God and of the mystery of Christ. It is the visible element, the sign, the sacrament of that experience" (*World Religions*, 147). The first statement by Dupuis clearly espouses conditional salvation. And as we have seen, any notion of conditional salvation means uncertainty and anxiety and thus obscures our true freedom which comes by faith in Christ and therefore by grace alone. The second statement by Dupuis clearly substitutes religious experience for the act of the Holy Spirit which unites us to Christ in and through our experiences of faith. It is precisely this Ebionite procedure which allows him to find the "Christic mystery" within everyone's religious experience and thus apart from faith in Jesus of Nazareth.

28. Athanasius, *Contra Ar.* 1.34, in *A Select Library of Nicene and Post-Nicene Fathers of the Christian Church, Second Series,* trans. and ed. Philip Schaff and Henry Wace (Edinburgh: T&T Clark, 1987), 326.

29. In his most recent book Knitter continues to employ this argument: "maybe, instead of concluding that 'many absolutes' equal 'no absolutes,' it would be better to say that the 'many absolutes' among the religions of the world are in need of each other and have to connect in dialogue with each other. There is — or there might be — a *complementarity of*

absolutes" (*Theologies of Religions*, 234). In so doing he unwittingly opens the door to polytheism.

30. Knitter repeats this agenda in *Theologies of Religions*, 134ff.

31. Knitter has not made up this approach of liberation theology out of whole cloth. He has in mind Rosemary Ruether's idea that the truth of Christology should be judged by the ethical behavior of Christians. See Paul F. Knitter, "Theocentric Christology," *Theology Today* 40, no. 2 (July 1983): 130-49, 141. According to Knitter, this means that "we must judge the truth of any Christological statement by its ethical fruits, that is, by the praxis to which it leads" ("Theocentric Christology," 141). Based on this criterion, the idea that the incarnation happened only in Jesus of Nazareth is the "immoral factor in the 'scandal of particularity,'" according to Tom Driver, because if the incarnation happened only once in history then all other human history is "nil" or at least inferior ("Theocentric Christology," 142). And according to Dorothee Soelle much Christology is a kind of "Christofascism" because it allows and requires Christians to impose themselves on other cultures ("Theocentric Christology," 142). If, however, we keep clearly in mind the theme of this book, then we can easily see how misguided this thinking really is. It is not our behavior as Christians that determines the truth of who Christ was and is from all eternity. He is who he is whether we believe or not and whether we act well or badly as Christians. Any notion that our behavior could or should be the norm for the truth of Christology has already confused Christ with Christians and undermined our justification in him alone. Where Christians have behaved and do behave as absolutists (unethically), it is not because of their belief in the actual Lordship of Jesus Christ, but such behavior results from their failure to acknowledge his true Lordship by attempting to impose their will on others in the form of anti-Semitism or by confusing Christianity and culture. Obedience to Christ himself always means allowing him the first and final Word and thus could never mean imposing Christianity on others. It must be admitted that such imposition has happened. But the claim that this results from traditional Christology is false. In the context of our present discussion it is important to see that it is just because self-justification is built into the thinking of Ruether and Knitter that they wish to move Christ from the center and put their "kingdom vision" in his place with the idea that all are saved by working together for a better world. But salvation cannot be equated with our ethical behavior as we have already noted several times without denying both divine and human freedom. Further, one of the key difficulties of liberation theology is precisely its praxis-based method. Hence, Knitter cites Gustavo Gutiérrez to make his point: "the subject of liberation theology is not theology but liberation" so that the ultimate arbiter of truth is "the transformative response of Christian praxis" (*No Other Name?* 194). Here we may simply note that when liberation and not knowledge of God in Christ occupies center stage, then God has really been displaced by the human attempt to fashion God in our own creaturely image. This thinking necessarily leads to the collapse of theology into an anthropology based on liberation and not on God's liberation of the human race in Christ and through the Spirit. Whenever the ultimate arbiter of truth becomes praxis (Christian or other) then self-justification has triumphed and Christianity has collapsed. For the connection between this liberationist thinking and the feminist attempt to re-define God see Molnar, *Divine Freedom*, ch. 1. The same difficulties are captured in the remarks of Jon Sobrino that "the only way to get to know Jesus is to follow after him in one's own life; to try to identify one-

self with his own historical concerns; and to try to fashion his kingdom in our midst. In other words, only through Christian praxis is it possible for us to draw close to Jesus. Following Jesus is the precondition for knowing Jesus" (Jon Sobrino, *Jesus the Liberator* [Maryknoll, NY: Orbis Books, 1993], 84). First, as seen above in connection with our rejection of Rahner's "Searching Christology," one can follow Jesus only by obeying the Christ of the apostolic witness and not by supposedly searching *a priori* for a savior within one's own experience apart from faith in Jesus of Nazareth. Second, the fact that one identifies with Jesus' historical concerns is no guarantee that one is actually relying on Jesus himself — one may well be using Jesus merely as a model to achieve a certain kind of human behavior, like liberation. Third, the very idea that we could or should "fashion his kingdom in our midst" illustrates that self-justification follows necessarily from the failure to allow Jesus himself to be the way, the truth and the life. Fourth, it is certainly not only through Christian praxis, as Sobrino contends, that one draws close to Jesus but only through his Holy Spirit and thus by faith alone. Finally, because it is only through the Spirit that we may know Jesus as the incarnate Word who is the Savior and Helper of all, one could never say that following Jesus is the precondition for knowing him. One can only follow someone or something that one knows already. Any idea that we could follow Christ without knowing him is a sure sign of a Docetic Christology because it has to mean that we would first be following an idea of Jesus and only then would we supposedly come to know him as our practice coincided with our ideal of human liberation. Any such thinking, however, strips Jesus of his actual Lordship by placing the human struggle for liberation in the center so that Jesus merely becomes a means to an end. We have already discussed at length the weakness of such thinking in light of the fact that incarnation and resurrection are inseparably united in the person and work of Jesus himself.

32. At this point both in *No Other Name?* and in *Theologies of Religions* Knitter argues that our ethical behavior should be the criterion for Christology itself. He follows Rosemary Radford Ruether's opinion that "Anti-Judaism was the negative side of the Christian affirmation that Jesus was the Christ" (*Theologies of Religions,* 136; *No Other Name?* 164ff.). But of course this thinking not only represents a distinct kind of works-righteousness but misses the point of Christology itself. Any genuine confession of Jesus as the Christ would have to include both Jews and Gentiles just as did the apostle Paul in Romans 9–11. It is not the Christology of the church that leads to anti-Semitism, but those who fail to accept Jesus as the only Lord of all who do so.

33. Cf. 1 Cor. 3, esp. v. 11: "For the foundation, nobody can lay any other than the one which has already been laid, that is Jesus Christ."

34. Cf. Acts 2:37-38 and compare Col. 2:6ff. and Rom. 6:3-4. Also, "He who eats my flesh and drinks my blood abides in me and I in him" (Jn. 6:53-56).

35. It is imperative to realize, as Barth does, that "Jesus Christ is Himself the established kingdom of God" (*CD* II/2, 177).

Notes to Chapter 6

1. Gordon D. Kaufman, *Theology for a Nuclear Age* (hereafter referred to in text as *TNA*) (Philadelphia: Westminster Press, 1985), x.

2. Sallie McFague, *Models of God: Theology for an Ecological, Nuclear Age* (hereafter referred to in text as *Models*) (Philadelphia: Fortress Press, 1987), 72-73.

3. Gordon D. Kaufman, *Systematic Theology: A Historicist Perspective* (New York: Charles Scribner's Sons, 1968) (hereafter referred to in text as *Systematic Theology*), 413. See also *Systematic Theology*, 203f. Kaufman claims that the "so-called virgin birth" actually threatens the Christian faith because it suggests that Jesus is half God and half man so that he is taken by many contemporaries to be "a piece of fantastic and incredible mythology" (*Systematic Theology*, 203). The virgin birth should therefore be rejected "on both theological and historical grounds" (*Systematic Theology*, 204). According to Kaufman it offers a "biological" interpretation of a theological fact and so represents a confusion of categories. And the historical evidence offered by the NT is very scant indeed. While Barth, for instance, acknowledges that the NT evidence is scant and even problematic at times, he insists that it is precisely the dogma of the virgin birth that affirms the *vere Deus vere homo*, that is, that Jesus is fully God and fully human and that the incarnation cannot be understood in a Gnostic or Docetic sense: the "*natus ex Maria* had without doubt already acquired the sense and at least the practical significance of a protection against gnostic and docetic ideas like those of Valentinus, according to whom Christ had received nothing from His human mother, but had assumed a heavenly body newly created for this purpose, had thus passed through Mary merely as water through an aqueduct, in other words had only apparently been born and become man. The Church was right to reject the doctrine of this Valentinian miracle" (*CD* I/2, 185-86).

4. Following M. Dibelius, Barth correctly insists that neither in the NT nor in the creed has the doctrine been offered as a "biological" explanation of the incarnation. What happens in the sphere of biology is only a sign of the reality of revelation, namely, of that act of God taking place in the history of Jesus at his birth and again at his resurrection. It is a sign that here we have Jesus, *vere Deus vere homo*. Responding to Brunner's analysis, he wrote, "Brunner's denial of the Virgin birth is a bad business . . . it throws an ambiguous light over the whole of his Christology. . . . Brunner's contribution to this matter in his more recent book, *Man in Revolt*, is so bad that my only possible attitude to it is silence" (*CD* I/2, 184).

5. See above, Chapter One, and *CD* IV/1, 340-41.

6. *CD* I/1, 390. While Kaufman apparently is willing to admit just this point (*Systematic Theology*, 112ff.), his explanation of revelation illustrates that by that category he means to suggest that the "person-event Jesus Christ" (*Systematic Theology*, 114) is interpreted by us in a theological way and as "paradigmatic" of who God is (*Systematic Theology*, 331), but not in such a way that he alone actually discloses something to us that we could not know elsewhere. This thinking develops in Kaufman's later theology to the point where he insists that to believe in the resurrection and to call Jesus the second person of the Trinity is to reify our concepts and thus to make the man Jesus something that he was not. Such reification, according to Kaufman, is the result of our triumphalist and imperialist tendencies. On this issue see, e.g., *TNA*, 50; and Gordon D. Kaufman, *In Face of Mystery: A Constructive Theology* (hereafter referred to in text as *IFM*) (Cambridge, MA: Harvard University Press, 1993), 390-91.

7. Kaufman is not unaware of the change he has wrought since he offers a word about the "linguistic propriety" of designating the "*experienced appearances*" by the expression

NOTES TO PAGES 197-99

"Jesus' resurrection" when they themselves designated by it "the *prior event of Jesus' raising,* which they believed made possible the appearances" (*Systematic Theology,* 425, emphasis in original). His usage, he notes, is a bit out of accord with the traditional "literal" usage. Here Kaufman argues that a choice is required: either one must use the historically more precise term "appearance" or "hallucination" and completely dispense with the word "resurrection" or if one retains the expression "resurrection," then one will have to realize that a modern understanding of that event "is somewhat different from the first-century view, as well as from what 'resurrection' literally suggests. It is this second alternative that I prefer . . . though the literal referent for the term is changed in my interpretation, its theological meaning is not essentially altered . . . it still refers to the event making possible the birth of Christian faith, i.e., to God's decisive act, and that is what is crucial" (*Systematic Theology,* 425). But that is precisely the question raised in this book. Can Kaufman's interpretation still refer to the event that made possible the birth of Christian faith if it transforms the actual historical event in the life of Jesus that gave rise to faith to an experience on the part of the disciples that can then be described as a divine action without faith in Jesus himself? My answer is an emphatic no. Unless the risen Lord himself actually encountered the disciples after his death and burial as the one who personally enabled their faith, Christian faith no longer has a personal object distinct from itself that can act in relation to Christians making possible their forgiveness and eternal life itself. Such a misconstrual of the resurrection is tied to a distorted view of the incarnation and ultimately to a unitarian view of God. Further, whenever the meaning of the resurrection as an act of God is detached from Jesus himself as the incarnate Word, then the only option left for the theologian is to espouse some form of ethical self-justification and thus obscure the true meaning of the atonement and human freedom as well. This, as we shall see, is exactly what happens to Kaufman in the end. For he argues that salvation should be equated with our attempts to humanize the world rather than with God's act of reconciling the world in Jesus Christ. In fact, in his later theology Kaufman insists that to tie God's act of reconciling to the man Jesus is incompatible with a contemporary evolutionary view of the world. See Kaufman, *TNA,* 56ff.

8. See T. F. Torrance, *STR,* 175ff., and Chapter Three above. Torrance rightly insisted against Bultmann that "It just will not do to claim . . . that 'the objective form' in which the New Testament and early Christian presentation of Christ, with respect to the incarnation, atonement, resurrection and ascension, was cast, was the result of mythological objectifying shaped by a primitive and unscientific world-view, as if the early Christians were not deeply aware of the profound conflict between the Gospel and the prevailing world-view! On the contrary, it is apparently his own world-view, with its dualist, obsolete, scientific preconceptions, which make him 'mythologize' the New Testament in this way, and then 'demythologize' it in terms of his own mistaken exaltation of self-understanding which transfers the centre of reference away from the action of God in the historical Jesus to some spiritual event of 'resurrection in man's experience'" (*STR,* 17-18).

9. See Kaufman, *IFM,* 383, where he writes, "To say God is incarnate in Christ, then, is not to say simply and directly that God is incarnate in Jesus; rather, God is incarnate in that larger, more complex human reality, surrounding and including and following upon the man Jesus: the new Christian community, with its spirit of love and freedom, of mutual sharing and forgiveness of one another. It is in this new order of interpersonal rela-

370

tionships that the incarnation of God is to be found." This confusion of Jesus as the uniquely incarnate Son of the Father with the community is similar to John Macquarrie's confusion of Jesus and the community under the category "Christ-event" as discussed above. Indeed, like Macquarrie, Kaufman mistakenly follows the thinking of John Knox in his book, *The Humanity and Divinity of Christ: A Study of Pattern in Christology* (Cambridge: Cambridge University Press, 1967), to make just this point. See also Gordon Kaufman, *The Theological Imagination: Constructing the Concept of God* (hereafter referred to in text as *TI*) (Philadelphia: Westminster Press, 1981), 124.

10. For a detailed explanation of how a proper Christology should avoid both Ebionite and Docetic viewpoints see Molnar, *Divine Freedom*, ch. 2.

11. Kaufman offers the same Ebionite starting point in *TI*, arguing that, "to the degree and in the respects that Jesus impresses us as the proper paradigm for grasping the normatively human, he can also serve as a concrete model for working out our conception of God" (*TI*, 144). The same thing happens in *God — Mystery — Diversity: Christian Theology in a Pluralistic World* (hereafter referred to in text as *GMD*) (Minneapolis: Fortress Press, 1996): "From the very beginning Christians were so impressed by the power and significance of salvation through Jesus Christ that they were led to make highly exclusivistic claims: There is salvation in no one else. . . . No one knows the Father except the Son" (*GMD*, 17). It should be stressed here that for Christian theology Jesus is not a concrete model for working out our concept of God and his uniqueness cannot be equated with the impression he makes on us insofar as we wish to see him as a paradigm of some sort. Rather, he himself (not the impression he makes on us) must be the starting point for Christology and trinitarian theology simply because he *is* God himself present among us; he really is the Word of God spoken to us and he really is the man who answers for us representatively. For that reason we may, as T. F. Torrance frequently and rightly insists, think from a center in God by allowing Jesus to be our starting point rather than attempting to think from a center in ourselves. These two different ways of thinking represent the difference between our self-justification and our justification by faith. Ebionite Christology always begins from a center in us and not from a center in God provided by God himself in Christ and through the Holy Spirit. In a similar way and in connection with the limits of our knowledge of God, Barth insists that we do not have the last word and cannot use Jesus as the last word to guarantee the truth of our knowledge of God. "Jesus Christ is really too good to let Himself be introduced and used as the last word of our self-substantiation" (*CD* II/1, 250) wrote Barth. It is in this sense that Barth maintained that "we are not referring to the articles of Christology. . . . We are referring, christologically speaking, to Jesus Christ Himself" (*CD* II/1, 251). Because grace is not a general possibility, Barth argued that there is and must always remain a vacuum within us that we cannot fill: "in this vacuum of our action and line of thought, stands Jesus Christ: not a Christological article which we can now utilise as a key to turn this last lock . . . but Jesus Christ Himself as the preeminent Judge and Saviour of our action" (*CD* II/1, 251).

12. Because the symbol "God" is a metaphor or analogy drawn from human experience and history, it is "never applicable literally," and "Our concept of God, thus . . . will never be finished or fixed in some particular form or image" (*TNA*, 25). "The theologically significant function of the symbol 'God,' we noted, is not that it names an entity or being which we might otherwise ignore or overlook, but rather that it focuses our consciousness

and attention on that which humanises and relativises us," writes Kaufman (*TNA*, 37). And it is just this thinking which clearly does not begin with Jesus Christ in his historical reality as the Word of God incarnate that leads directly to Kaufman's pantheistic confusion of God with the evolutionary process: "There is a hidden creativity at work in the historico-cultural process" (*TNA*, 41) and thus "The symbol 'God' suggests a reality, an ultimate tendency or power, which is working itself out in an evolutionary process" (*TNA*, 43). "God — this whole grand cosmic evolutionary movement — is giving birth, after many millennia, to finite freedom and self-consciousness in and through our human history, in *us*" (*TNA*, 44). For similar ideas see *IFM*, 348ff. Consider also the following: "I have attempted to hold together the mythic and the metaphysical dimensions in the concept of God and to show how they are related to each other. By *identifying God with the mundane cosmic, vital, and historical powers* which have given rise to our humanity and which undergird all our efforts to achieve a fully humane society, I have attempted to provide a metaphysically plausible referent for a religiously significant symbol" (*TI*, 54, emphasis mine). The problem with this reasoning, and it is an enormous problem, is that the Christian God really is not identical with any cosmic, vital or historical powers; hence these created forces are not a plausible referent for the Christian concept of God which is constructed on the basis of God's self-revelation in his Word and Spirit and so describes the creator as the Father who created the world through his Son and in his Holy Spirit. In his later work Kaufman describes God as a "serendipitous creativity": "The symbol 'God' refers to the ultimate reality with which we humans have to do; today, I have argued, this should be understood as that cosmic serendipitous creativity which manifests itself in the evolutionary-historical trajectory that has brought humanity into being and continues to sustain it in being" (*IFM*, 375). For more on how Kaufman developed this pantheistic concept of God see *IFM*, 275ff.

13. See Kaufman, *TNA*, 49ff. Since the resurrection is not a genuinely historical event in the life of Jesus therefore for Kaufman it must reflect the community's triumphant desires. See also *IFM*, 378ff.

14. Torrance, *God and Rationality*, ch. 3.

15. In contrast to Kaufman, Torrance gets it just right: "By bringing the Kingdom of divine grace to bear directly upon their lives He revealed the vast chasm between the heart of man and the Will of God, for it provoked the bitter hostility of man to God and brought Jesus to the Cross. Yet in His suffering and passion He launched God's supreme attack upon man's self-centredness, self-concern, self-security, self-seeking, and self-will" (*God and Rationality*, 65-66).

16. Hence Kaufman writes: "tying the incarnation . . . to a single individual renders it not only paradoxical almost to the point of unintelligibility; it also opens it to criticisms . . . of . . . parochialism . . . sexism . . . and . . . chauvinism" (*IFM*, 386).

17. Torrance, *God and Rationality*, 65.

18. What does Kaufman mean by reification? "It is taking the content of a symbol (or image or word) to be a proper description or exact representation of a particular reality or being; in Kant's apt phrase, it is 'treating our thoughts as things.' We reify the symbols 'creator' and 'lord' and 'father' when we take them to mean that God *really is* a creator/lord/father. (The literal meaning of the word 'reify' is simply 'to make into a thing.')" (*IFM*, 330, emphasis in original). Amazingly, Kaufman is quite literally unable to imagine reality in the scientific sense as understood by T. F. Torrance and Karl Barth. For them our thinking

is accurate to the extent that the unique nature of the object in question is allowed to dictate meaning. For Kaufman there is no unique object distinct from the symbol that we use and invest with meaning in particular circumstances. That, of course, does not mean there is no object. It means the object (in the case of Jesus) is not seen in its true depth but only as an aspect of history or evolution, so that for Kaufman, the real Jesus is a mere man and not the Son of God incarnate. Kaufman's thinking is thus subjectivist to the extent that he is unable to imagine that Jesus actually exists as the pre-existent and incarnate Son and that God actually exists independent of our symbols as the eternal Father, Son and Holy Spirit who encounters us in the economy as our savior, helper and Lord. The point he misses is that when Christians think of God as creator, Lord and Father they are not making something out of their symbols; rather, *through* their symbols, they are recognizing something, or rather someone, that actually exists independently in its own right. At times of course Kaufman is ambiguous about this as when he insists that his idea of God does indeed have objective content and is not simply a projection. Unfortunately, however, because he believes that the concept has mythological as well as metaphysical content he identifies that objective content with the process of evolution itself and therefore misses the real objectivity of the triune God.

19. Hence "Theology is first and foremost 'thinking about God,' not 'thinking about Christ'" (*GMD*, 11).

20. Kaufman therefore reduces the doctrine of the Trinity to a practical notion that helps us focus on humane ways of ordering our existence. It is therefore "not a speculative concept pretending to set forth the inner structure of the divine being — something about which we can have no knowledge" (*IFM*, 457).

21. While it is true to say that there is no other essence of God behind the God revealed in the economy, it is completely false to say or to imply that there is no more to God than what God reveals. It is the other way around: the only reason God is for us is because he is free and thus exists in himself without needing us from all eternity. For more on this see Molnar, *Divine Freedom*, chs. 1, 2 and 5.

22. See *Systematic Theology*, chs. 7-14 and 18-22.

23. In *IFM*, Kaufman suggests that the biblical story of the fall teaches us "that the knowledge of good and evil belongs to God, not to us; that is, that the ultimate norms, values, and meanings of life always escape us, remaining a matter of profound mystery. To suppose that we know them is to *sin* — to fall away from God" (368). On the surface it would seem that here Kaufman accepts the traditional view of sin. But he does not. On the one hand, although Kaufman is quite right to insist that none of our views is identical with the truth itself, he mistakenly adopts a form of agnosticism suggesting we can never actually know good and evil or apply ultimate norms to human behavior. The biblical story says we cannot know good and evil as God knows them. It does not say we cannot know good and evil. On the other hand, since Kaufman confuses God with the evolutionary process, when he argues that the symbol God is a limit idea intended to remind us that God transcends us and stands over us, he literally cannot refer us to the living God. He thus insists that "God's truth" is not a particular content that *"we know"* (*IFM*, 370, emphasis in original). It is rather a "symbol to remind us that we do not in fact possess ultimate truth" (*IFM*, 370). Hence God's will must be a symbol of "a cosmic trajectory of which we are part" (*IFM*, 371). But if God's will cannot be distinguished from a cosmic trajectory, as it

cannot when God is seen as a serendipitous creativity, then Kaufman is not speaking of the God who can and does act as Lord and Savior in his Word and Spirit.

24. See Karl Barth, "The Righteousness of God," *The Word of God and the Word of Man,* trans. Douglas Horton (Gloucester, MA: Peter Smith, 1978), 14-16 and 22.

25. That is why Kaufman really believes that today we must make a choice between an understanding of Christian faith primarily as "the presentation of certain indispensable *truth (s)* to humanity so that 'whoever believes . . . should not perish but have eternal life' (John 3:16)" or as "a 'ministry of reconciliation' . . . inspired by the love of God manifested in Christ (2 Cor. 5:17-20)" (*TI,* 202-3). Kaufman insists that the second of these must be given priority over the first, that is, the primary focus of the church should not be on presenting truth-claims but on building community with others. And Kaufman insists he has not shortchanged or sold out Christianity in any fundamental way by advocating this choice. But of course it is quite clear from what we have presented in this chapter that by not seeing the issue of truth together with that of reconciliation he has detached God's act of reconciliation from God's act in the history of Jesus and located it in our human attempts at reconciliation using Jesus' human life as a paradigm for how we should behave toward others. Beyond that he has pulled the ground out from under the very existence of a community reconciled with God, and demonstrating that reconciliation in its work toward and with the world, exactly because he has collapsed the truth of the resurrection into the subjective experiences of the disciples and us, thus losing the objective foundation of the church's continued existence in history. And by insisting that the world could not be reconciled in the individual, Jesus of Nazareth, Kaufman has completely lost the true basis for any Christian activity in this world. Further, by thinking of God as an ecological reality working within the process of evolution he was led to deny the very identity of the Christian God as a reality, namely, the eternal Father, Son and Holy Spirit existing from all eternity in his own right over against the world as well as within the world in his Word and Spirit. In these ways there can be no doubt that Kaufman has indeed shortchanged and sold out Christianity in the most fundamental ways possible by confusing God with the world, denying Christ's actual uniqueness as the eternal Son, distorting the incarnation and then using the images of God, Christ and salvation to argue that it is up to us alone to create a more humane world. This is the ultimate form of self-justification that necessarily follows any attempt to relegate issues of truth to a secondary status in Christian theology. After all it is the truth (Jesus himself) who alone can set us free from sin and enable our ministry of reconciliation. Kaufman's confusion on this issue results from his belief that it is our love for one another that is the criterion of our love for God (*IFM,* 333). Of course it is the other way around for the NT. Kaufman argues that truth, goodness and beauty are grounded in the overflowing creativity of the cosmic process and for that reason our striving for humane values is not merely a human activity (*IFM,* 338).

26. Of course that is why Kaufman insists that the claim that God is incarnate in Jesus is a confession of faith and not a statement of fact (*Systematic Theology,* 180-81). Naturally, as Barth and Torrance both argue and as Rahner himself intends to argue, any confession of faith that is not an acknowledgment of fact is simply a projection of faith and not a recognition of Christian truth.

27. "God will no longer be pictured or conceived as a personal being in the heavens above who 'before the foundation of the world' . . . devised a detailed divine plan . . . we

will no longer . . . be able to imagine ourselves as in direct personal interaction with this divine being" (*IFM*, 332).

28. For an apt description of Christian hope see Chapter One above.

29. See *Models*, 80; and above, 191-92.

30. Consider this remark by McFague: "when people are attempting to express the in-expressible, they use what is nearest and dearest to them: they invoke the most important human relationships" (*Models*, 84). Hence she believes there is no access to an immanent Trinity and will only speak of an economic Trinity. Of course nothing could be further from the truth because, as Hilary insisted, we cannot measure God's nature by our human nature. It is the other way around. Because God is revealed and active in the incarnation of God in Christ and through the Spirit we may know God from within God's own activity in history. But we have no secure knowledge of God apart from Jesus himself as the incarnate Word and the Holy Spirit who unites us to him in faith (see Molnar, *Divine Freedom*, ch. 1). By detaching knowledge of God from God's Word and Spirit which exist inherently in God from all eternity, McFague commits exactly the same error as the Arians. She projects her images of God from human experience, defining the creator by the creature and thus collapsing theology into anthropology by reducing our God-talk to the social functioning of our concepts.

31. See Norman Perrin, *Resurrection according to Matthew, Mark, and Luke* (Philadel-phia: Fortress Press, 1977).

32. Sallie McFague, *The Body of God: An Ecological Theology* (hereafter referred to in text as *The Body of God*) (Minneapolis: Fortress Press, 1993), 179.

33. In a manner similar to Kaufman, McFague's thinking is, at times, ambiguous enough to suggest that perhaps she actually believes in the resurrection as an event in Je-sus' personal history: "The death and resurrection of Jesus," she writes, "are paradigmatic of a mode of change and growth" (*The Body of God*, 191). But when she writes "Often that pattern has been absolutized as occurring completely and only in Jesus of Nazareth: his death and resurrection are the answer to the world's woes. In his death all creation dies, in his resurrection all arise to new life. The absolutism, optimism, and universalism of this way of interpreting the ancient and recurring relationship between death and new life — a relationship honored in most religious traditions as well as in evolutionary biology — are problematic in a postmodern, ecological, and highly diverse cultural and religious era" (*The Body of God*, 191). It is more than evident that for McFague the resurrection describes nothing more than the faith and hope evident in all religions that there is a "basic trust-worthiness at the heart of existence" and that "life, not death, is the last word" (*The Body of God*, 191). Yet, for her, this faith and hope are only wagers (*The Body of God*, 181) that we make that "the source and power of the universe is on the side of life and its fulfillment" (*The Body of God*, 191). Hence "The 'risen Christ' is the Christian way of speaking of this faith and hope" (*The Body of God*, 191).

34. It will be remembered that T. F. Torrance has indicated correctly that the idea of the incarnation of God in the man Jesus was no less incredible to the people of Jesus' time than it is today. The only question is: will they or we allow our thinking to be shaped by him or by our postmodern or ancient cosmology?

35. McFague writes: "The transcendence of God is . . . that aspect or dimension that we never see, never know. It is what God is when God is not 'being God'" (*The Body of*

God, 192). And "the transcendence of God frees us to model God in terms of what is most significant to us" (*The Body of God,* 193).

36. McFague explicitly rejects any idea of a God who does not need the world, arguing that "this is a sterile and unattractive view of divine love that most of us would not settle for even as a description of human love. If, among ourselves, we want to be loved not in spite of who we are but because in some sense we are valuable, desirable, and needed, then is this not the case also with divine love?" (*Models,* 102). The answer of course is no, because the hallmark of divine love is that it is free. A God who needs anything outside himself to be God is clearly not God; even a God who needs his own being to be God is not God. The Christian God exists as the one he is from all eternity in full loving freedom and not out of any need. It is this perception that allows us to distinguish God from us so that we may then see that the God who loves us in Christ, even though we are sinners, actually does so in a way that is recognizably divine; that is, his acts of creation, reconciliation and redemption are acts of divine Lordship even though they involve his own suffering and death in the humanity of Christ himself for our benefit. I have made a case for this in my book *Divine Freedom* relying on Barth's understanding of God as one who loves in freedom. And, as noted above, Walter Kasper, too, expresses God's freedom with clarity: "if God needs the world in order to be able to be the one God, then he is not really God at all. The transcendence and freedom of God are perceived only if the world is not necessary for God to be himself" (Kasper, *The God of Jesus Christ,* 293f.). But the key here is that God's transcendence and freedom are not properly perceived if they are perceived at all apart from Christ: "If the freedom of divine immanence is sought and supposedly found apart from Jesus Christ, it can signify in practice only our enslavement to a false God. . . . The freedom of God must be recognized as His own freedom . . . as it consists in God and as God has exercised it" (*CD* II/1, 319f.).

37. See *CD* II/1, 312-13; and Molnar, *Divine Freedom,* 202ff.

38. See *CD* II/1, 499ff., for Barth's very interesting discussion of God's freedom in this regard. Barth insists quite properly that because God is really free in himself he does not need any "improvement or enlargement of Himself" by creating the world. Indeed "Creation cannot bring Him any increase, decrease or alteration of His divine being and essence by reason of its existence. . . . It cannot do this because it is His creation, the creation of His free love, which has its existence and essence by Him while what God has in Himself is the ground of its existence and essence and not that existence and essence itself" (*CD* II/1, 499). This leads Barth to reject both monism and dualism because "while the world certainly exists in God, it does so by Him" (*CD* II/1, 500). Barth insists, against dualism, that there is a real participation of God in the existence of his creatures and of the creatures' participation in his immutability because just as "the world certainly is by God it is for that very reason in God" (*CD* II/1, 501).

39. See *CD* II/1, 312f. This is why Barth rejects panentheism as a "worse case" than "undiluted pantheism." It is, he says, in its materialist or spiritualist form, "more crass than crass pantheism" (312).

40. Sallie McFague, "Imaging a Theology of Nature: The World as God's Body," in *Liberating Life: Contemporary Approaches to Ecological Theology,* ed. Charles Birch, William Eakin, and Jay B. McDaniel (hereafter referred to in text as "Imaging a Theology") (Maryknoll, NY: Orbis Books, 1990), 201-27, 203. This is why she believes "we have been given central respon-

sibility to care for God's body, our world" ("Imaging a Theology," 214). This chapter presents many of the themes that appear in *Models of God* in a useful summary fashion.

41. Thus McFague writes, "Evil is not a power over against God; in a sense, it is . . . part of God's being" ("Imaging a Theology," 215).

42. Indeed, in a manner similar to Kaufman, McFague's idea of God is really the equivalent of what C. S. Lewis once characterized as the God of the "Life-Force Philosophy." It is a conceptual combination of a type of materialism and religion so that it presents us with a God who is somewhere between the two and who is in fact indistinguishable from the processes of evolution in the end. Such a God is in reality powerless to act for us because this is a tame God that we control based on our need to feel good in the face of evolution itself. Such a view, according to Lewis, is produced by those who seek the comfort of religion without its truth. See C. S. Lewis, *Mere Christianity* (New York: Simon & Schuster, 1996), 34-35.

43. See *CD* III/4, 588ff. As Barth insisted: "God is the hope of man — the God who took such an interest in him that He Himself became man in Jesus Christ, that in Jesus Christ He died with us and for us, and that in the resurrection of this man Jesus Christ, He then revealed Himself to be the hope of man, to be the manifest hope of all those who look to Jesus Christ and are ready to live by faith in Him" (*CD* III/4, 594).

44. The work of salvation, McFague insists, "need not be seen as special or religious; rather, it is ordinary secular work oriented toward healing the world's divisions and freeing the world's oppressed" (*Models,* 153). This insight fits with McFague's aversion to the idea that salvation could be a miracle (see *Models,* 148).

Notes to Chapter 7

1. Roger Haight, S.J., *Jesus, Symbol of God* (hereafter referred to in text as *Jesus*) (Maryknoll, NY: Orbis Books, 1999), 120.

2. See also Molnar, *Divine Freedom,* ch. 6, "Karl Rahner and Thomas F. Torrance: God's Self-Communication in Christ with Special Emphasis on Interpreting Christ's Resurrection."

3. It is important to realize that even thinking of Jesus as the symbol of God in the Rahnerian sense is more than a little problematic because, among other things, it suggests that the incarnation was necessary for God to be God, it tends to confuse Jesus' divinity and humanity and it also leads Rahner to separate revelation from the specific actions of God in his Word and Spirit and locate them within our experience in the form of the supernatural existential. All of this is discussed above in Chapter Two. For more on this see Molnar, *Divine Freedom,* chs. 4 and 5.

4. See Gunton, *Yesterday and Today,* 15ff., and Chapters Two and Five above, for an understanding of the problems involved in any sort of degree Christology. The main problem of course is that it fails to acknowledge Jesus as the one he is, but instead makes him a higher instance of what all of us are.

5. In light of historical consciousness Haight believes "One cannot really think of a pre-existence of Jesus . . . what is pre-existent to Jesus is God, the God who became incarnate in Jesus" (Haight, *Jesus,* 458-59).

6. Athanasius, *Contra Ar.* 1.34.

7. Cf. Arthur W. Wainwright, *The Trinity in the New Testament* (London: SPCK, 1980), and Torrance, *TF.*

8. Cf. also *CD* I/2, 35-37, and *CD* II/1, 309, 313.

9. For more on this problem see Paul D. Molnar "Experience and Knowledge of the Trinity in the Theology of Ted Peters: Occasion for Clarity or Confusion?" *Irish Theological Quarterly* 64 (1999): 219-43.

10. See Barth, "The Righteousness of God," in *The Word of God and the Word of Man,* 9-27.

11. John Hick, ed., *The Myth of God Incarnate* (hereafter referred to in text as *Myth*) (Philadelphia: Westminster Press, 1977), ch. 9, "Jesus and the World Religions," 167-85, 170.

12. See John Hick, *Disputed Questions in Theology and the Philosophy of Religion* (New Haven: Yale University Press, 1993), where he claims that "It is impossible for us today to know the precise nature of the resurrection event" (41); and John Hick, *The Metaphor of God Incarnate: Christology in a Pluralistic Age* (hereafter referred to in text as *The Metaphor*) (Louisville: Westminster/John Knox Press, 1993), where he claims that "The term 'resurrection' has been used throughout Christian history to refer to the transitional event or events in virtue of which the Jesus movement survived the death of its founder. . . . Precisely what this transitional event was we cannot now discern with confidence" (23).

13. See Chapter One above, 26-27 and Chapter Eight below, 279.

14. Elaine Pagels, in her University Lecture in Religion at Arizona State University entitled "The Gnostic Jesus and Early Christian Politics," January 28, 1982, 4, states: "At a time when other Christians insisted that Jesus rose bodily from the grave, gnostic Christians tended to ridicule that view as naïve, or, in their words, the 'faith of fools.' The *Treatise on Resurrection,* discovered at Naj Hammadi, offers instead a symbolic interpretation of resurrection . . . resurrection symbolizes the moment of enlightenment: 'It is . . . the revelation of what truly exists, and a transition into newness.' Whoever grasps this, the author suggests, becomes spiritually alive."

15. That is why Torrance insists that both the ideas of the virgin birth and the empty tomb were not invented but forced themselves upon the early church against its current beliefs. And this reflected the fact that the resurrection unveiled "the mystery of the incarnation: the birth and resurrection of Jesus belong inseparably together and have to be understood in light of each other" (*STR,* 56). Because the resurrection of our human nature is the goal of the atonement, Torrance can also say, in light of the concepts of "perichoresis" and "enhypostasis," that "the resurrection also means that the steadfastness of the Son of Man is such that it held on its way in utter obedience to the Father in the spirit of holiness in the midst of judgment, death and hell, and in spite of them, so that he raised himself up from the dead in perfect Amen to the Father's Will, acquiescing in his verdict upon our sin but responding in complete trust and love to the Father. The resurrection is the goal of the steadfast obedience of the Son of Man in answer to the steadfast love of the Father . . . the resurrection is the complete Amen of the Son to the Father as of the Father to the Son. . . . It is with the resurrection that the *I am* of God is fully actualized among us — the *Ego eimi* of God to man, of God in man, and so of man in Christ to God" (*STR,* 67-68). For more on the idea that Jesus raised himself see above, Chapter Four, n. 19 and below, Chapter Eight, n. 40.

16. See Horton Harris, *David Friedrich Strauss and His Theology* (Cambridge: Cambridge University Press, 1973), 19.

17. Harris, *David Friedrich Strauss,* 19.

18. John Hick, *A Christian Theology of Religions: The Rainbow of Faiths* (hereafter referred to in text as *Theology of Religions*) (Louisville: Westminster/John Knox Press, 1995), 96.

19. Hick insists that if we hold to an "inspiration Christology" we will return to the "original understanding of Jesus in the very early church" and this will allow us to realize that the intersection of divine and human that took place in Jesus did not take place uniquely in him; rather it is "one that occurs in different ways and degrees in all human openness and response to the divine initiative" (Hick, *Disputed Questions,* 54). Of course the reason Hick thinks this way is that he is judging what is presented by the NT and the early church both historically and theologically by history alone and reaches the conclusion that history itself cannot allow us to affirm Jesus' uniqueness as traditionally understood. And when he fails to receive historical confirmation that Jesus is uniquely God's Son, he resorts to mythology in order to explain the Christian confession of Jesus' Lordship. See also Hick, *Theology of Religions,* 91f., for more on Hick's view of Jesus as a "Spirit-filled man."

20. Paul F. Knitter, "Theocentric Christology," *Theology Today* 40, no. 2 (July 1983): 130-49, at 133.

21. In "The Non-Absoluteness of Christianity" (in *The Myth of Christian Uniqueness: Toward a Pluralistic Theology of Religions,* ed. John Hick and Paul F. Knitter [Maryknoll, NY: Orbis Books, 1987], 16-36 [hereafter referred to in text as "The Non-Absoluteness of Christianity"]), John Hick asserts that the incarnation "has occurred and is occurring in many different ways and degrees in many different persons," with the result that one must, but cannot, actually determine from a historical perspective that God's inspiration and grace (incarnation in Hick's thought) were "more fully" or even "absolutely" present in Jesus (32).

22. See Hick, *Theology of Religions,* 87; Hick, "The Non-Absoluteness of Christianity," 33.

23. See also Hick's classically Ebionite remark that Jesus "was transformed in the mind of the church from the eschatological prophet of Israel into a semi-divine Son of God and then eventually into the fully divine God the Son, second person of the Holy Trinity" (Hick, *Theology of Religions,* 93).

24. Hick clearly wishes to argue that "Christianity is seen in a pluralistic context as *one* of the great world faiths, *one* of the streams of religious life through which human beings can be savingly related to that ultimate Reality Christians know as the heavenly Father" (Hick, "The Non-Absoluteness of Christianity," 22).

25. Indeed, Hick argues that "We cannot, then, meaningfully attribute personality to the infinite and eternal existence of God *a se*" (John Hick, *God Has Many Names* [Philadelphia: Westminster Press, 1982], 108). And, carrying through the logic of his "inspiration" Christology, Hick contends on the one hand that we ought not to speak of the three divine persons "in the modern sense" as distinct centers of consciousness, will and emotion. That would seem to place his thinking in harmony with the traditional trinitarian opposition to modalism. But it does not because, on the other hand, Hick claims that this thinking al-

lows one to "speak of the Father, the Son and the Holy Spirit as loving one another within the eternal family of the trinity, and of the Son coming down to earth to make atonement on behalf of human beings to his Father. An inspiration christology is, however, fully compatible with the conception of the trinity as affirming three distinguishable ways in which the one God is experienced as acting in relation to, and is accordingly known by, us — namely as, creator, redeemer, and inspirer. On this interpretation, the three persons are not three different centers of consciousness but three major aspects of one divine nature. . . . Such an 'economic' understanding of the trinity is as orthodox as a 'social' one and would seem to represent the direction that trinitarian thought is likely to follow in theologies that accept a pluralistic understanding of the human religious situation." Hick, "The Non-Absoluteness of Christianity" (32). The only problem with this view is that it is thoroughly modalistic because such thinking is "purely economic" and is not at all grounded in God's eternal existence as one God, three persons. The persons only refer to the way the one God is experienced by us, not the way God exists from all eternity in himself.

26. See Athanasius, *Contra Ar.* 1.34.

27. For Hick it is not the case that "The God of universal love at the centre [of all major religions] cannot be spoken of or recognized without Jesus" because the idea of universal "divine goodness/love/compassion is common to Judaism, Islam, theistic Hinduism, Sikhism, Jainism, as well as Christianity. These are theistic forms of what I call the 'cosmic optimism' of the great post-axial traditions" (*Theology of Religions*, 104-5). That is why Hick explicitly rejects the Christian view of atonement. When the questioner in the imaginary dialogue suggests that Christians affirm that God was incarnate in Jesus revealing himself in Jesus' words and in his atoning death and asks if that is something Hick denies, he responds: "Yes, it is. Surely one doesn't have to believe that Jesus was the second person of a divine Trinity in order to accept his teaching about the love of God" (*Theology of Religions*, 105-6). Why? Because Buddhists, Muslims and Sikhs can follow their leaders without believing they are God incarnate. Here it is clear that Hick literally cannot begin Christology with Jesus as he really was but begins by assuming that he was an ordinary man upon whom the community conferred divinity and from whom they may remove it according to their pluralistic vision of divine love. This thinking represents an almost classic case of subjectivism.

28. Of course, since "the fruits of the Spirit seem to be as much (and as little) evident outside the church as within it," Hick suggests "that we should continue to follow the clue provided by these fruits." And that leads him to the conclusion that people's ethical behavior or ethical ideals should be the criterion for religious truth (*Theology of Religions*, 16f.). And that view represents an inherent form of self-justification because by it Hick assumes that we have the ability to decide the truth of who Jesus was by means of our own ethical ideals. This is a blatant form of self-justification because it assumes that we have a capacity not only to transform ourselves and our world by our ethical behavior using religious categories, but it presumes that it is we who decide the truth of who Jesus was and is by means of our ethical instincts. Yet, the whole point of the NT was to insist that we must repent of the attempt to define truth according to any human standard, including the ethical, and simply rely on Jesus himself as the way, the truth and the life because of who he was and is. It is here that Hick's Ebionite starting point leads to his Docetic Christology. Hick rejects traditional Chalcedonian Christology because he sees no way that we can rationally affirm

Jesus' true divinity and true humanity simultaneously. He rejects the idea that in the end the fact that Jesus is the "God-Man" can only be accepted as a mystery because "it's a mystery created by human beings through a process that we can trace historically, and in fact it's only a mystery in the sense of a form of words which has no clear literal meaning!" (*Theology of Religions,* 98). Here once again the main theme of this book comes to light: if Jesus is not accepted as the one he is from all eternity and the one he became for us in the incarnation, then his person and work will be grounded in human religious experience and the truth of the resurrection and incarnation will be undermined by a combination of Ebionite and Docetic Christology and soteriology. That is why Hick believes that the mystery of the God-Man is a mystery created by human beings whereas in fact, for Christians, it is a mystery grounded in God's eternal election of us in his Son to be his covenant partners; and that is, as Barth insisted, a covenant of grace that can in no way be understood or assessed in light of our ethical ideals.

29. The Golden Rule is the "ideal" taught by all the great religious traditions and therefore is the true "universal" salvation (*Theology of Religions,* 77-78; see also John Hick, *An Interpretation of Religion: Human Responses to the Transcendent* [New Haven: Yale University Press, 1989], 316ff.). Salvation/liberation for Hick means the transformation of human existence "from self-centredness to a new centring in the Real . . . the criterion by which to judge both a tradition as a whole and its constituent elements, including its doctrines, is soteriological. The question is how effectively they promote this salvific transformation" (*Theology of Religions,* 76). One should not be deceived by Hick's claim that his criterion is soteriological. It certainly is not soteriological in the Christian sense because his thinking is dualistic — it will not allow for the fact that in Jesus' life, death and resurrection God himself was uniquely incarnate and active as the one who saves us from sin, suffering, evil and ultimately from death. Christian soteriology then means freedom to serve God in Jesus Christ and can never be equated with any transformation taking place within humanity that can be universally identified. This same idea of the Golden Rule as the universal ideal is seen by Hick to be generated by the "inter-personal nature of personality" because "its basic principle is mutuality, or acceptance of the other as another person. . . . The fundamental moral claim is accordingly to treat others as having the same value as myself. This is in effect a transcription of the Golden Rule found in the Hindu, Buddhist, Confucian, Taoist, Zoroastrian, Jain and Christian scriptures and in the Jewish *Talmud* and the Muslim *Hadith* . . . and is likewise a translation of Kant's concepts of a rational rationality" (*An Interpretation of Religion,* 149).

30. It will be remembered that Hick's understanding of the Real cannot be equated with the triune God precisely because, as he puts it, "the Real in itself cannot properly be said to be personal or impersonal, purposive or non-purposive, good or evil, substance or process, even one or many" (*Theology of Religions,* 27). When compared to the triune God this idea of the Real is truly agnostic because it denies to the triune God what Christianity has always insisted is pivotal, namely, that God is three-personal, that he alone is good and that he is one being, three persons and thus one and many simultaneously.

31. That is why Hick prefers to follow the "liberating" Buddhist teaching that religious doctrines should be seen as "'skillful means' *(upaya)* enabling people to move in different ways towards the salvific transformation of enlightenment or awakening" (*Theology of Religions,* 114). The problem with applying this thinking to Christian doctrine is that Chris-

tians think true doctrine is a description of truth and cannot be changed or used by people as a means to attain enlightenment because true doctrine points us to Jesus himself as the light of the world. The very notion that it is a means of enlightenment shows how deeply Hick's own thinking is entangled in a form of self-justification.

Notes to Chapter 8

1. See Christoph Schwöbel, *Wolfhart Pannenberg, The Modern Theologians: An Introduction to Christian Theology in the Twentieth Century*, vol. 1, ed. David F. Ford (Oxford: Blackwell, 1989), 257-92, 283.

2. Pannenberg insists that both Nestorianism and Monophysitism are the only options "so long as Christology is developed from the concept of the incarnation, instead of culminating in the assertion of the incarnation as its concluding statement" (*Jesus — God and Man*, 291). Later in volume 2 of his *Systematic Theology* (3 vols., trans. Geoffrey W. Bromiley [Grand Rapids: Eerdmans, 1991-98; hereafter referred to in text as *Systematic Theology* with volume and page number), Pannenberg attempts to clarify this thinking by asserting that the Antiochene (Nestorian) or Alexandrian (Monophysite) dilemma "is insuperable as long as we think that the event of the incarnation was complete with the birth of Jesus" (*Systematic Theology*, 2: 384). He refers to his earlier view espoused in *Jesus — God and Man*, saying that he had himself related the incarnation "exclusively to the beginning of the earthly course of Jesus as the basis of his individual life" (*Systematic Theology*, 2: 384), and concludes that no matter how we reach the concept of incarnation, the doctrine demands that "we think of the eternal Son as the basis of the earthly existence of Jesus" (*Systematic Theology*, 2: 384). And he says that he did not do this in *Jesus — God and Man*, but rather based it on Jesus' relationship of obedience with the Father. Still, Pannenberg insists that Jesus' creaturely independence "as the medium of the incarnation," must imply that "the constitution of the person of Jesus takes place in the whole process of this history" (*Systematic Theology*, 2: 385). Here two problems that arose in *Jesus — God and Man* remain: (1) Pannenberg believes that Jesus' person is constituted at least in part by his human relation to his Father and (2) while Pannenberg quite properly asserts that we must think that the eternal Son is the basis of Jesus' earthly existence, his own method which begins with his human history in order to validate that claim undermines this assertion. Is Jesus' person constituted by his human relation to the Father or is his person the eternal person of the Son which alone gives meaning and existence to Jesus' humanity? My contention is that we must acknowledge that the incarnation is the starting point because that act of God in Christ alone and not any historical or theological conclusion of ours determines the validity of Christology. And we may also note that Pannenberg's own assessment of his earlier method does not escape this ambiguity either because he says his belief that Christology should not begin with the incarnation was in keeping with the idea that pre-existence and incarnation were "mediated by the kerygma of the resurrection of the Crucified and grounded in it" (*Systematic Theology*, 2: 384). Pre-existence and incarnation, however, are not grounded in the kerygma or in Christ's resurrection; in reality the kerygma is grounded in Christ's pre-existence and incarnation as the eternal Son of the Father, as is the resurrection.

3. *Karl Barth Letters 1961-1968*, ed. Jürgen Fangmeier and Hinrich Stoevesandt, trans. Geoffrey W. Bromiley (Grand Rapids: Eerdmans, 1981), 178.

4. See, e.g., below, 291ff.

5. *Jesus — God and Man*, 36-37.

6. While Pannenberg later modifies his "Christology from below" by placing it in what he calls a broader context so that the Son is conceived both as at work in the world generally and also incarnate in Jesus alone, he still does not abandon the basic methodological principles of his Christology from below. Thus Pannenberg writes "The emerging synthesis is no more what I earlier called 'a christology from below.' But it presupposes and integrates that methodical approach" (Wolfhart Pannenberg, *An Introduction to Systematic Theology* [Grand Rapids: Eerdmans, 1991], 67). He integrates it with his trinitarian approach to theology. And this leads to several problematic assertions: (1) "the incarnation of the Son cannot be properly conceived as a completely exceptional and supernatural event"; (2) "there must exist a special relation of the aim and destiny of human existence in general to the eternal Son of God"; (3) "the concept of divine sonship becomes a comprehensive category without losing its special relation to Jesus of Nazareth" (*An Introduction to Systematic Theology*, 65-66). With these three ideas Pannenberg draws the crucial conclusion drawn before him by Schleiermacher: "From the point of view of such a broader approach to the concept of the Son of God as eternal correlate of the Father, his incarnation and the advent of the second Adam coincide, because the *incarnation of the Son is now seen as the completion of the creation of humanity in the image of God*" (*An Introduction to Systematic Theology*, 66, emphasis mine). It is critical to realize that Barth rejects all of these assertions exactly because he regards the incarnation and resurrection as interconnected miracles that cannot be explained simply by contextualizing them. It will also be remembered that Barth categorically rejected Schleiermacher's idea that the incarnation represented the completion of creation precisely because it obscured the real meaning of reconciliation, opened the door to the Pelagian idea that humanity is somehow open to God in spite of the fall and failed to acknowledge that the Son was the subject of the redeeming act. See *CD* I/2, 134ff.; and Chapter Five, n. 13, above.

7. This is why Pannenberg insists that "the task of Christology is to establish the true understanding of Jesus' significance from his history, which can be described comprehensively by saying that in this man God is revealed" (*Jesus — God and Man*, 30). Of course it is my contention that a true understanding of Jesus' history cannot be historically derived; it must come as a revelation of God himself and thus as an act of God's Word and Spirit that comes to us miraculously through faith. But this means that a true understanding of Jesus' significance would not simply say God is revealed in this man but that this man is the Revealer because he is the Word of God incarnate. I agree with Pannenberg that this is hidden in Christ's human life. I disagree that it is constituted by his life history and ultimately by his resurrection because that suggests a dependent deity which in my view does not recognize Jesus' true eternal divinity but makes it the outcome of the historical process. In his later thinking, which tried to explain this more in terms of trinitarian doctrine, Pannenberg claimed to base his doctrine of the Trinity on the content of revelation by insisting we "begin with the relation of Jesus to the Father as it came to expression in his message of the divine rule. The NT statements about the deity of Jesus all presuppose his divine sonship and are ultimately grounded in his relation to the Father. The relation of

his message and work to the Father forms the foundation of the confession of the divine sonship of Jesus by the Christian community in the light of the divine confirmation of his fulness of power by the Easter event" (*Systematic Theology,* 1: 304). Here it will be seen that there is no major difference between what Pannenberg thinks in *Jesus — God and Man* and his later *Systematic Theology* because the key assertion remains that the foundation for asserting Jesus' divinity is not his antecedent existence as the eternal Son of the Father, now become incarnate for us and our salvation, that is, the person of Jesus Christ as the incarnate Word, but rather it is his message and work and thus his human relation to the Father. And Pannenberg still thinks the Easter event in a real sense makes Jesus the Son of the Father "retroactively." So Pannenberg can say that "The relations between the person of Jesus, the Father, and the Spirit might well prove to be not just historical or economic but relations which characterize the eternal divine essence" (*Systematic Theology,* 1: 307). My point is that you cannot begin Christology in its essential connection with the doctrine of the Trinity unless you first *acknowledge* that the relations between the eternal Father, Son and Spirit are the basis of the historical actions of Jesus, the incarnate Word, and the Holy Spirit acting within the economy. In light of who Jesus actually was and is it can never be an open question about whether his relation to the Father is merely economic! And the ultimate problem here is that Pannenberg is thinking of Jesus in the first instance merely as a man: "The self-distinction of Jesus as man from the Father is *constitutive* not merely for his fellowship with the eternal God . . . he himself . . . is so at one with the Father that God in eternity is Father only in relation to him. . . . The eternal Son is first . . . an aspect of the human person. . . . Hence self-distinction from the Father is *constitutive* for the eternal Son in his relation to the Father" (*Systematic Theology,* 1: 310, emphasis mine).

8. See above, Chapter Three, 109, 111. Cf. also 279.

9. Chapter 10 concerns the deity of Christ. Pannenberg puts it this way: "As the one who corresponds to the fatherhood of God, Jesus is the Son, and because the eternal God is revealed herein as Father, and is Father everywhere only as he is so in relation to the Son, the Son shares his deity as the eternal counterpart of the Father. We have here an aspect of the reality of the person of Jesus which is his as the eternal correlate of the deity of the Father and which precedes his human birth. The eternal Son is first, however, an aspect of the human person. . . . Hence self-distinction from the Father is constitutive for the eternal Son in his relation to the Father" (*Systematic Theology,* 1: 310). How can the eternal Son who is begotten of the Father *before* all worlds *first* be an aspect of the human Jesus? Here Pannenberg gives the impression that Jesus' Sonship is merely a description of his human relation with his Father. Pannenberg insists that it is by Jesus subjecting himself to the will of the Father that his Sonship is disclosed. But the NT stresses that he, as the eternal Son who became flesh for us and our salvation, actively discloses himself to his disciples and to us (e.g., Matt. 11:27).

10. Is it not the case that by describing the Spirit's action in terms of the "field" theory Pannenberg strips the Spirit of his ability to act as the sole divine subject in relation to us?

11. This very same difficulty is in evidence in Pannenberg's view of how we know God by means of the experience of anticipation. See Paul D. Molnar, "Some Problems with Pannenberg's Solution to Barth's 'Faith Subjectivism,'" *SJT* 48, no. 3 (1995): 315-39.

12. For a full discussion of how Barth's understanding of Ebionite and Docetic Christology relate to contemporary Christology see Molnar, *Divine Freedom,* ch. 2.

13. It is important to note that, as we saw above, John Macquarrie in his book, *Jesus Christ in Modern Thought,* echoes the very perspective that Barth here rejects when he claims to find, following J. D. G. Dunn, "a unifying idea amid the diversity of the New Testament, an idea which he [Dunn] expresses as the conviction that the historical figure, Jesus the Jew, becomes an 'exalted being'" (*Jesus Christ in Modern Thought,* 12). And it must be stressed that when Pannenberg thinks the problem of Christology consists in "the legitimacy of the transformation in the understanding of Jesus that took place in the transition from the Jewish into the Gentile sphere of tradition" his thinking is similar to the view of Dibelius that Barth rejected, namely, that the problem of Christology concerns "the way in which 'knowledge of the historical figure of Jesus was so quickly transformed into faith in a heavenly Son of God.'"

14. See *Systematic Theology,* 1: 79, where he argues that Christian theology had to meet the criterion of natural theology if it were to have credibility. And this is why Pannenberg repeatedly speaks of our human openness to God as the anthropological basis for understanding revelation. In *Jesus — God and Man* Pannenberg specifically approves Rahner's idea that it is "the open transcendence of man to God's absolute being that constitutes the particular structure of being human as such and comes to fulfillment in the event of the incarnation of God in man" (*Systematic Theology,* 1: 317).

15. And so in Volume 2 of his *Systematic Theology* Pannenberg says "in the context of Jewish experience the meaning of the event was so clear that no one to whom the Lord appeared could acknowledge the event and remain an unbeliever" (345).

16. See G. E. Michalson, Jr., "Pannenberg on the Resurrection and Historical Method," *SJT* 33, no. 4 (1980): 345-59. He concludes that "in explaining what he means by resurrection as a 'metaphor,' Pannenberg reveals that his proof really refers to the experiences of the first Christians and not to the object of their experience, a result he had explicitly set out to avoid. . . . Pannenberg's conception of the resurrection turns out to be as vague, indeterminate, and unhelpful as the Bultmannian notion of the 'rise of faith in the disciples'" (358). Importantly, Pannenberg still thinks of the resurrection as a metaphor in *Systematic Theology,* 2: 346ff.

17. For a similar idea see *Systematic Theology,* 2: 350-51.

18. As seen above Rahner's argument that it is our horizon of expectation that gives meaning to the resurrection in accordance with his transcendental method is quite similar to Pannenberg's thinking here and Pannenberg himself notes the correspondences with Rahner at a number of places in his thinking. For Pannenberg, "The phenomenology of hope indicates that it belongs to the essence of conscious human existence to hope beyond death" (*Jesus — God and Man,* 85). It is in this context that Pannenberg argues that "the expectation of a resurrection from the dead need not appear meaningless from the presuppositions of modern thought, but rather it is to be established as a philosophically appropriate expression for human destiny" (*Jesus — God and Man,* 88). This, of course, is in complete contrast with Torrance's insistence that the resurrection is something *utterly new* that cannot be established philosophically at all because it forces itself on us in conflict with all our prior ideas and experiences. Barth thinks the same way when he argues that belief in the resurrection went utterly against the grain. And suggesting that the resurrec-

tion is a philosophically appropriate expression for human destiny ignores the fact that it, as God's revelation to us who are sinners in need of reconciliation, it is in reality offensive to us and can only be grasped as a mystery and miracle in faith.

19. As C. E. B. Cranfield, *On Romans and Other New Testament Essays* (Edinburgh: T&T Clark, 1998) says, "there is no reason to believe that the Old Testament had suggested to the disciples, before the first Easter Day, any hope of this sort" (145). He is referring to hope for "their Master's being raised from the dead before the general eschatological resurrection" (145). In *Systematic Theology*, 2: 350, while Pannenberg agrees that "Jewish expectation of an eschatological resurrection . . . did not count on the resurrection of one individual before the end of this aeon," he also continues to maintain that "*Eschatological expectation of a resurrection from the dead provided linguistic expression and a conceptual framework for the Christian Easter message.* It made it possible for the disciples to identify the appearances of the crucified Lord to them" (348-49, emphasis in original). And so he argues that "for its final verification, the Christian message of the resurrection of Jesus needs the event of an eschatological resurrection of the dead. The enacting of this event is one of the conditions, if not the only condition, on which to maintain the truth of the resurrection of Jesus. Maintaining this truth implies a view of reality that rests on the anticipating of a fulfillment of human life and history that has not yet taken place. Hence the Christian Easter message will be contested as long as the general resurrection of the dead and the coming again of Jesus are still future" (*Systematic Theology*, 2: 350-51). Pannenberg seems to think that hope for the general resurrection and hope for Jesus' particular resurrection are interchangeable. For Pannenberg, Jesus' resurrection is explained within the context of the general expectation of the resurrection of the dead: "The only point of importance here is that we cannot detach the conceptual content of the doctrine of the resurrection of Jesus from the more general expectation of an end-time resurrection of the dead. This is because it is only in this connection that the mode of the reality of the life of Jesus that the Easter event proclaims can be upheld in contrast to mere hallucinations or ghostly apparitions" (*Systematic Theology*, 2: 350).

20. In *Systematic Theology*, 2: 354, Pannenberg still describes the appearances in terms of "visionary experiences." But he insists that this cannot mean that they are merely psychological projections insisting, against Schillebeeckx, that "We must begin with the fact that the Easter appearances formed the starting point for the kerygma of the resurrection of the Crucified" (356).

21. Pannenberg continues to use this same analogy in *Systematic Theology*, 2: 354f.

22. Interestingly, Pannenberg thinks that Barth allowed the incarnation to take the place of the resurrection as the foundation of Christology (*Jesus — God and Man*, 111) when in reality Barth's insistence, noted by Pannenberg, that the resurrection was the revelation of Jesus's history consummated on the cross (*CD* IV/2, 122ff. and 140ff.) illustrated that for Barth one could not separate resurrection and incarnation with the methodological assumption that the incarnation could only be the conclusion and not the starting point for Christology. Pannenberg claims that for Barth "Jesus' resurrection is not a completely new event with its own decisive importance" (*Jesus — God and Man*, 111). Yet Barth actually asks regarding John's Gospel "Why is it that for him too the Easter-story is not merely a confirmation but a new thing, and as such the pre-condition of the witness of the Holy Spirit which is the basis of the community?" (*CD* IV/2, 140). And Barth insists that

"The resurrection and ascension are this once for all and all-sufficient event of revelation — the event of His self-declaration, and therefore the event in which the basis of the knowledge of Jesus Christ which we seek was laid and is laid. This is the objective basis from which alone, by the witness of the Holy Spirit, all subjective knowledge of Jesus Christ can derive. . . . It is the basis on which this knowledge is unconditional and completely trustworthy because it is grounded in its subject-matter" (*CD* IV/2, 142). This revelation is not in competition or conflict with the revelation that was hidden in Jesus' life and activity before Easter. It is the same Jesus, true God and true man who is revealed before and after.

23. Thus for Barth "we have no reason not to take the concept of God's Word primarily in its literal sense. God's Word means that God speaks. Speaking is not a 'symbol' (as P. Tillich . . . thinks). . . . We shall have to regard God's speech as also God's act, and God's act as also God's mystery. But as only God's act is really God's mystery . . . so only God's speech is really God's act" (*CD* I/1, 132-33). Compare this to Pannenberg: "This [Barth's] understanding of the divine Word [taken from Ignatius] has, however hardly any other value than that of a metaphor. It is only figuratively possible to say that the invisible God speaks. . . . Jesus' resurrection means that God has claimed as his own the promise of salvation made by the pre-Easter Jesus and thus recognized Jesus' word in a definite sense as his own word. . . . it is still only a figurative expression when the event of God's revelation in Jesus' fate is designated as God's 'Word,' an expression that — in order to be true — presupposes a substantiation outside itself for the fact that God is revealed in the person of Jesus" (*Jesus — God and Man*, 167). This is why Pannenberg argues that "Today the idea of revelation must take the place of the Logos concept as the point of departure for Christology" (168). In reality the point of departure for Christology is Jesus Christ, the Word of God incarnate. But because Pannenberg will not start his Christology with the incarnation he replaces the risen Lord with the idea of revelation and then concludes that we cannot literally envision God's speaking his word in Jesus. This explains why in Volume 1 of his *Systematic Theology* Pannenberg denies that God is always the content of his Word and refuses to equate the Word with Jesus himself (243, 235ff.). For Pannenberg, "Jesus Christ as the direct Word of God is to be integrated into this [saving] plan and understood in light of it" (236). Yet, if Jesus *is* the Word, then, as Barth correctly insisted, he cannot be integrated into any plan; the plan is understood from the light which comes from him. Pannenberg is willing to think of the Son as "the Mediator of the words of God (cf. Matt. 11:25-27) and not himself the Word" (235, cf. 251) just because he is unwilling to allow the logic of Jn. 1:14 to be dictated by the being of the Word described in Jn. 1:1-2. In other words, in Jn. 1:1-2 Jesus as the Word *is* God; it is the *Word* which became flesh and it is Jesus, the Word who gives meaning to salvation. Pannenberg cannot admit this because "the various experiences of revelation . . . do not have God as their direct content. . . . All of these contribute to God's making himself known in his deity, and to that extent they are all factors in the history of the divine action" (243).

24. See *Systematic Theology*, 2: 358-59: "Though primitive Christian conviction as to the resurrection of Jesus rests not on the finding of his empty tomb but on the appearances, the tomb tradition is significant for the total witness to the Easter event" (359). Without the empty tomb there is danger of subjectivism or some sort of superficial spiritualizing of the Easter message.

25. For a superb recognition of how Jesus' uniqueness precludes any attempt to include Jesus in a context see John Webster, *Word and Church: Essays in Christian Dogmatics* (Edinburgh & New York: T&T Clark, 2001), Chapter Four, on the incarnation. Webster's view of the incarnation moves in exactly the opposite direction from Pannenberg's: "it is not a matter of engaging in a struggle to establish the conditions under which an event of incarnation might be considered a possible object of confession. The rule for theological (indeed, for all) reasoning is: thought follows reality. . . . The incarnation is thus that *from which* theology moves, rather than that *toward which* it moves" (118, emphasis in original). Indeed, "uniqueness is not predicated of Christian conviction but acknowledged in the object of confession who, as Lord is absolutely unique. Thus Christian theology speaks of *the* incarnation, of the *one* Lord" (134, emphasis in original). And the personal union of natures which is affirmed by Chalcedon "is utterly unique, an instance of itself, and in no sense a complement, completion or parallel to any other realities" (146).

26. This is one of the principal reasons I objected to Pannenberg's methodical attempt to ground theology in the experience of anticipation. See Molnar, "Some Problems with Pannenberg's Solution to Barth's 'Faith Subjectivism,'" esp. 322ff.

27. This is in harmony with Pannenberg's refusal to begin theology in faith as Barth does with the reality of God. See Molnar, "Some Problems with Pannenberg's Solution to Barth's 'Faith Subjectivism,'" 316f.

28. Quite a lot of the difficulty here stems from Pannenberg's methodological assumption that "all designations of essential contents [*Sachbenennungen*] whatever, depend upon anticipations of a future that has not yet appeared." Hence, "what is present in its appearance is essentially a fore-conception [*Vorgriff*] of its future" (Wolfhart Pannenberg, *Basic Questions in Theology: Collected Essays*, vol. 1, trans. George H. Kehm [Philadelphia: Fortress Press, 1970], 168-69). Following this line of logic, Pannenberg assumes that the possibility of naming essences lies in the experience of anticipation. Consequently Pannenberg understands the incarnation within this perspective: "Judged from the perspective of eschatology, this anticipation [of a future general resurrection] takes on the character of an incarnation of God himself in the person of Jesus" (Wolfhart Pannenberg, *Metaphysics and the Idea of God*, trans. Philip Clayton [Grand Rapids: Eerdmans, 1990], ch. 5, 91-109, "Concept and Anticipation," 96). Of course my point is that any thought of the incarnation of God in Jesus Christ must be grounded in the miraculous act of God assuming flesh from the virgin Mary at the start of Jesus' life on earth and completing that history in the resurrection of Jesus from the dead. But that means that the incarnation cannot be explained at all as an instance of anticipation that must be verified by future events but can only be accepted in faith as the starting point for Christology and theology in general.

29. The situation here is complex. There is no doubt that Pannenberg wishes to affirm a doctrine of the immanent Trinity. But his method causes him to be unable to allow the doctrine of the immanent Trinity to inform key elements of his thinking, as we shall see.

30. This same insight is repeated in *Jesus — God and Man*, 134-35.

31. See also *Systematic Theology*, 2: 319, where Pannenberg writes: "The incarnation of the Son in the figure of Jesus means that this man is the Son of God in person and that he was so throughout his life." This argument against adoptionism, however, becomes less convincing when seen in the context of Pannenberg's assertion that a person's identity takes shape in one's history and that this applies to Jesus as the Son of God. Hence "The

Easter event definitively decided the personal identity of Jesus as the Son of God, but in the light of that event he was the Son of God from the very beginning of his earthly course, and even from eternity." The problem here of course is that history does not shape or determine the eternal existence of the Son in relation to the Father because the immanent Trinity is fully existent from all eternity. And Easter did not decide Jesus' personal identity as the eternal Son; rather the risen Lord disclosed his identity in that history.

32. *Systematic Theology*, 1: 310-11, 313 and 322, emphasis mine. Cf. also *Systematic Theology*, 2: 391.

33. See Ted Peters, *God as Trinity: Relationality and Temporality in Divine Life* (Louisville: Westminster/John Knox Press, 1993), 135ff. According to Peters, "Pannenberg believes that the reciprocity in the relationship of the divine persons makes room for the constitutive significance of the central events of salvation history for the Godhead of God" and that "Without this kingdom, God could not be God. The existence of God as Trinity depends upon the future of God's coming kingdom" (135). Peters also notes that, for Pannenberg, "the divinity of the eternal God is in the process of being determined and defined in the historical events of Jesus' destiny. The eternal nature of God is at least in part dependent upon temporal events" (137). And finally, Peters explains that in Pannenberg's view "Jesus subordinated himself totally to God, and in so doing placed himself in total communion with the Father. By submitting himself to the Father, he thereby becomes the eternal Son. . . . This self-distinction constitutes his unity in God" (142). All of this leads Peters to conclude that we no longer have any reason on the basis of scripture to affirm the existence of "such a thing as a divine substance or nature. There is simply God. God is God. It is God who defines what divinity is. . . . If in the process of historical self-expression God becomes one who is in relationship to the world . . . then so be it. And this is just the claim made by doctrines such as the incarnation in Jesus, the indwelling of the Holy Spirit, and the *resulting* Trinity. God is in the process of constituting himself as a God who is in relationship with what is other than God" (145, emphasis mine). By contrast John Webster quite properly insists that when the Nicene creed speaks of the Word or Son as of one substance *(homoousios)* with the Father this should alert us to the fact that the bond between Jesus and God is not just moral but ontological and that what takes place in Jesus is "a direct and immediate" divine act and "not a mere symbolization of a god whose identity lies elsewhere. 'Substance' thus provides a conceptual blockade against subordinationism, in which the status of Jesus Christ is relegated to that of being first among creatures" (Webster, *Word and Church,* 143). The thinking of both Peters and Pannenberg undermines the proper sense of a doctrine of the immanent Trinity by making God dependent on events within history and because of that it necessarily embraces a form of adoptionism that also destabilizes the doctrine of the incarnation so that Jesus as Son is no longer seen as one in being with the Father before all worlds. For an illuminating discussion of these issues see Stanley J. Grenz, *Rediscovering the Triune God: The Trinity in Contemporary Theology* (Minneapolis: Fortress Press, 2004), 88-106.

34. Thus, "While it was to be said with regard to Jesus' divinity, looking backward from his resurrection from the dead, that it always existed even before the beginning of his earthly existence, the effect of his unity with God upon the human course of Jesus' life went through a process of development" (*Jesus — God and Man,* 195). This explains why Grenz can say that for Pannenberg the divine unity is "bound up with the work of the

three persons in the world (the economic Trinity), which work — and hence which unity — is completed only eschatologically" (Grenz, 100). Of course the problem with this reasoning is that God's unity is an eternal unity that exists within the immanent Trinity and does not come into being in coordination with his sovereign acts of love within history on our behalf.

35. Even though, as we have seen, Pannenberg insists that Jesus "would not have been who he was without the Easter event" he also claims that because this confirmed his pre-Easter claim to authority "Jesus' unity with God, established in the Easter event, does not begin only with this event — it comes into force retroactively from the perspective of this event . . . the pre-Easter Jesus' claim to authority is to be understood as an anticipation of his unity with God that was shown by the Easter event" (*Jesus — God and Man*, 137). But, of course, that is exactly the problem: if Jesus really *was* one in being with the Father from all eternity then any allegation whatsoever that his pre-Easter claim to authority was only an *anticipation* of his unity with God actually severs his eternal oneness in being with the Father by implying that it is a reality yet to be achieved in an event within history, namely, the resurrection. So, while Pannenberg thinks he avoids adoptionism with this idea of Jesus' retroactive unity with God, in reality he does not, precisely because and to the extent that he conceives it as something yet to be achieved in the Easter event.

36. The idea of a *logos asarkos* is certainly the main object of attack in Pannenberg's rejection of Christology from above in *Jesus — God and Man*. Such an idea, he believes, would allow one to see "Jesus of Nazareth only as the earthly appearance of this divine Logos instead of seeking in the historical and resurrected Jesus himself the power in which the world intrinsically coheres" (*Jesus — God and Man*, 394). And of course such a thought would undercut Pannenberg's Christology from below, which seeks to validate Christ's divinity from his experiences within history. For Pannenberg, "the concept of the *logos asarkos* must be judged as an expression of the fact that the assimilation of Hellenistic and Hellenistic-Jewish cosmology by Christian theology did not lead to a total melting down of the alien substance" (*Jesus — God and Man*, 394). Still, in a much later context Pannenberg insists, against Robert Jenson, that "There was . . . the divine logos before he became flesh, the *logos asarkos*. But this logos, the eternal Son of God, was always to become incarnate . . . and therefore his incarnation was not accidental to his eternal identity as Logos and Son of the Father. . . . The sending of the Son belongs to the eternal identity of the Father, if the Father is seen as determined from eternity to complete his creation" (Wolfhart Pannenberg, "Eternity, Time and the Trinitarian God," *CTI Reflections* [published by the Center of Theological Inquiry, Princeton], 3 [1999]: 43-61, 56). We might say that while Pannenberg here gives with one hand he takes away with his other. While it is correct to say that his incarnation was not an accident, the implication that incarnation constitutes his identity as Son of the Father is precisely the issue at stake in any genuine acknowledgment of God's eternal freedom. As Barth himself correctly observed, it is not accurate to think of the incarnation as the completion of creation because such a view underestimates the problem of sin and instead of thinking the incarnation as a free new act of God which is not necessitated by his essence or any other constraining factor, it tends to subvert the fact that the Word is the subject of the redeeming acts of God in history. Instead it tends to envision the Word as part of the process of history itself. And since Pannenberg continues to believe that the kingdom of God is somehow dependent upon

our recognition of it ("Eternity, Time and the Trinitarian God," 54) and that God's own identity depends upon his kingship over his creation so that "with the manifestation and recognition of his kingship his divine nature itself is at stake" (54) it seems clear that his actual position with respect to God's freedom has not changed very much. While Pannenberg indeed argues for a distinction between the immanent and economic Trinity, this thinking, which introduces a type of mutual conditioning into the relation between the immanent and economic Trinity, undercuts any truly positive affirmation of God's continued freedom. This can be seen in his idea that "the eternal identity of the triune God [is] conditioned by events in time like the incarnation" (55) and in his idea that the biblical notion of time is similar to the idea espoused by Plotinus (52ff.). God's eternal identity is not conditioned by the incarnation and consummation; rather it is revealed in these historical events to be the identity of one who eternally exists as Father, Son and Spirit and thus as one who loves in freedom. By contrast, Pannenberg thinks God's "future action seems to constitute his identity" (53).

37. See Molnar, *Divine Freedom,* ch. 3.

38. Barth, *Evangelical Theology,* 29-30, emphasis in original. See also Barth's remark: "If we try to bypass this decision [Jesus' resurrection], concentrating our attention upon a human Jesus who is not the *Kyrios* because He is not risen, we simply show that we have failed to take note of what they [the Gospels] really say, and intend to say" (*CD* III/2, 450).

39. See *Systematic Theology,* 1: 263ff., and *Jesus — God and Man,* 354. See also Paul D. Molnar, "Reflections on Pannenberg's *Systematic Theology Volume 1:* A Review Discussion," *The Thomist* 58, no. 3 (July 1994): 669-93.

40. It will be remembered, of course, that for T. F. Torrance, following Cyril of Alexandria, it was imperative that we admit that Jesus actively arose from the dead because Christ's activity in the resurrection "is essential to the unity of his person as Mediator." Since it was the whole Christ who died for us and who now lives forever, he came to redeem not just a part of us but us in our entirety so that we cannot have contempt for the body which has been saved by God in and through Christ's death and resurrection. See Chapter Four above, 142. Torrance may well have a point here. But in general the NT references to Jesus' resurrection invariably refer to God the Father or the Holy Spirit in unity with the Father (Rom. 8:11) raising Jesus from the dead. See, e.g., Arthur Wainwright, *The Trinity in the New Testament,* 185: "The resurrection itself was the act not of Christ but of the Father." Still, in virtue of the fact that the whole Trinity is involved in the economic actions *ad extra (opera trinitatis ad extra sunt indivisa),* it might well be appropriate to hold the view espoused by Torrance and Cyril. And there can be little doubt that Cyril had in mind Jn. 2:19-22 where Jesus' reference to destroying the temple and raising it up in three days is interpreted to refer to his resurrection. Hence Jesus says: "Destroy this Temple, and in three days I will raise it up . . . he was speaking of the Temple that was his body, and when Jesus rose from the dead, his disciples remembered that he had said this, and they believed the scripture and what he had said." In fact Cyril says, referring to the incarnate Word that "as God he is life and life-giver, and so he raised up his own temple" (St. Cyril of Alexandria, *On the Unity of Christ,* trans. and intro. John Anthony McGuckin [Crestwood, NY: St. Vladimir's Press, 1995], 118), and in a direct reference to Jn. 2:19 on the very next page, Cyril describes Christ's actions as the "life-giving power of the Father" (119). There

seems no reason to ignore this as a biblical warrant for including Christ's own activity in the resurrection.

41. As seen above in Chapter One, it is just because Barth insisted that our recognition of Jesus' divinity is not a derivative statement that he also quite properly insisted that "the knowledge of Christ's deity can only be the beginning and not the result of our thought" (*CD* I/1, 422). Pannenberg's belief that it must be the result of our thought spoils any genuine recognition of Jesus' divinity because it will not allow him alone to be the subject who actively validates our Christology through the action of the Holy Spirit.

42. Pannenberg carries this thinking to its logical conclusion in connection with the atonement arguing that Luther justified Jesus' substitution "not from the human course of the event but on the basis of the incarnation" (*Jesus — God and Man,* 278) with the result that "Luther did not clearly see that all statements about Jesus' cross are only possible in the light of his resurrection. This is probably again related to the fact that Luther understood the substitutionary character of Jesus' death in the light of the incarnation, not on the basis of the resurrection. In this he shared the perspective of the entire patristic and medieval tradition that was only shaken by the Enlightenment" (*Jesus — God and Man,* 279). Here, of course, Luther, Torrance and Barth all agree against Pannenberg that the incarnation and resurrection must be held together intrinsically precisely because it is Jesus' person and work that give meaning to the atonement and not history or our supposed anthropological openness to God. In my view the answer to the Enlightenment is not to place Jesus within a historical perspective that is then supposed to make him relevant to contemporary thought. Instead, the answer must be found precisely in Jesus' person and work so that it is not his resurrection as an event in history that confers meaning on his message and fate; rather it is his resurrection in union with his entire incarnate life that indicates who the subject here is who once lived and now lives as the Lord of history and Lord of the church. This can only happen as a statement of faith in the power of the Holy Spirit.

43. That is why Pannenberg can follow Bultmann by assuming "the validity of the formal attitude of openness for the future in general as its decisive aspect in order thus to save it for modern understanding" (*Jesus — God and Man,* 241). Hence while the imminent expectation of the kingdom determined Jesus' life history, it is no longer applicable for us since it was fulfilled in him. It was the original condition which made Jesus' message possible; but it could never arise today. What remains valid today, however, is the fact that "It confronts men with the coming Kingdom of God, which is nothing else than the nearness of the Creator for whom man inquires in the openness of his existence" (*Jesus — God and Man,* 243). That unfortunately is the problem. In light of revelation we know that we are not open to the God made known in Jesus Christ; we are in fact closed to God and in need of repentance to become open. This thinking allows Pannenberg to substitute Jesus' message for his person as we have already noted.

44. Pannenberg expressly appeals to Rahner's Christology to support this thinking (*Jesus — God and Man,* 344ff.; see also 226ff. and 262). This is why Pannenberg insists that "If substitution is not a universal phenomenon in human social relationships . . . then it is not possible to speak meaningfully of a vicarious character of the fate of Jesus Christ. Substitution as such cannot be a miraculously supernatural uniqueness of Jesus. The particular vicarious significance of Jesus' fate 'for us' can be defended only on the basis of an understanding of human behavior generally which — as in ancient Israel — sees individuals

interwoven with one another in their actions and in the results of their actions and certainly also in the ethical problem" (*Jesus — God and Man,* 268). Hence, "Under the presupposition that there is an element of substitution active in all social relationships, one is permitted to understand Jesus' death as a vicarious event" (*Jesus — God and Man,* 269). Of course, as seen above, particularly with the help of T. F. Torrance, this very thinking undermines the actual meaning of Jesus' vicarious action on our behalf precisely because it ignores his actual significance for faith which is to be found not in his "fate" but in his *action* as the man Jesus who *was* the Son of God representing us before the Father.

45. This is why Barth quite properly insists that the actual becoming flesh of the Word of God is a miracle and that this means "it is an event in this world of ours, yet such that it is not grounded upon the continuity of events in this world nor is it to be understood in terms of it" (*CD* I/2, 187). This last point is especially important with regard to Pannenberg because it is just here that their disagreement has its root. Barth insists that "An explained miracle is obviously a miracle no longer. It is no longer exposed to rejection. It no longer has to be believed. Those who explain a miracle . . . are simply showing thereby that they do not want to have to decide between rejection and belief. No less than everything depends on our seeing that on the height of the incarnation (as of every Christian doctrine) we have to declare that miracle cannot be set aside or toned down" (*The Göttingen Dogmatics,* 161). This is why Barth also insists, correctly, that "A miracle is an event that one can only reject, only declare to be impossible and absurd, or only believe. Anything that softens or removes this either/or disrupts the concept of miracle" (*The Göttingen Dogmatics,* 161).

46. This is an amazing statement in light of Barth's assertion that Evangelical and Roman Catholic theology differ most over their respective conceptions of grace and that this divergence can be seen in connection with "the latest doctrine in relation to the Virgin Mary (1950) [the assumption], the proclamation of which has shed a new and garish light on the situation, we can only say that, humanly speaking, they have diverged hopelessly. The heart and guiding principle of the Romanist doctrine of grace is the negation of the unity of grace as always God's grace to man, as His sovereign act which is everywhere new and strange and free. It is the negation of the unity of grace as His grace in Jesus Christ. It is the division of grace by which it is first of all His, but then — and this is where the emphasis falls — effected and empowered by His grace, it is also our grace" (*CD* IV/1, 84).

47. Among other things Barth objected to the idea that Mary's role in salvation history could usurp Christ's role as the one Mediator. He certainly realized that the figure of Mary "is an indispensable factor in Bible proclamation." But whenever she becomes "the object of special attention, which ascribes to her what is even a relatively independent part in the drama of salvation [it] is an attack upon the miracle of revelation, because it is, after all, an attempt to illumine and to substantiate this miracle from the side of man or of his receptivity" (*CD* I/2, 140). Of course Barth accepted the fact that Mary was *Theotokos* and that she had a proper role to play in salvation history christologically speaking. And in that regard, unlike Pannenberg, he accepted the doctrine of the virgin birth as a sign of the miracle of Christmas. What he objected to was any idea that Mary could be seen as interceding for us before God on her own as "the mother of all graces." Barth opposed statements such as the one exhibited in the Offertory of the Feast of the Rosary where Mary "is made to say of herself: *In me gratia omnis viae et veritatis in me omnis spes vitae et virtutis*"

(*CD* I/2, 142). This illustrates that Barth objects to any compromise of Christ's unique mediation with the idea that Mary too might be considered the mediatrix of grace and hope. In Barth's view there is in reality no Reformed position "which has proved so illuminating even to a child as the simple No uttered from the standpoint of Reformed knowledge in answer to the whole doctrine and worship of Mary, an answer which in every circumstance must be uttered inexorably. In the doctrine and worship of Mary there is disclosed the one heresy of the Roman Catholic Church which explains all the rest. The 'mother of God' of Roman Catholic Marian dogma is quite simply the principle, type and essence of the human creature co-operating servantlike . . . in its own redemption on the basis of prevenient grace, and to that extent the principle, type and essence of the Church" (*CD* I/2, 143). Clearly what Barth objects to here, among other things, is the idea that "Man is capable, by prevenient grace, of preparing himself for genuine sanctifying grace, by uttering this *fiat*" (*CD* I/2, 144). Hence even Przywara could claim to give the true meaning of the *analogia entis* by speaking of the possibilities of an "incarnational cosmos, including body and soul . . . because in their totality . . . they are 'open' to God" in the sense that there is a "receptive readiness for Him" within creation (*CD* I/2, 144). The corresponding view of the church is also objectionable from Barth's perspective: "It, too, vies with Christ in the infinite distance, it is true, between creature and Creator, yet in such a way that not only is it born of Christ but, particularly in the Eucharistic centre of its life, Christ is also born of it. Not only does it need Christ, but in all seriousness Christ also needs it. As Mary inevitably co-operates in man's redemption as an 'intercessory power,' so does the Church in consummating the sacraments" (*CD* I/2, 146). To this thinking Barth connects the 1854 doctrine of the immaculate conception, papal infallibility (1870) and "the canonization" of natural theology saying that "The Church in which Mary is venerated is bound to regard itself as it has done in the Vatican decree; just as the same Church must be the Church of the man who co-operates with grace on the basis of grace" (*CD* I/2, 146). Against this Barth insists "Jesus Christ, the Word of God, exists, reigns and rules in as sovereign a way within the created world as He does from eternity with the Father, no doubt over and in man, no doubt in His Church and by it, but in such a way that at every point He is always Himself the Lord, and man, like the Church, can give honour only to Him and never, however indirectly, to himself as well. . . . Faith in particular is not an act of reciprocity, but the act of renouncing all reciprocity, the act of acknowledging the one Mediator, beside whom there is no other" (*CD* I/2, 146).

48. T. F. Torrance followed Barth's thinking on the virgin birth. See, e.g., Thomas F. Torrance, *The Doctrine of Jesus Christ* (Eugene, OR: Wipf and Stock Publishers, 2002), 115ff. That is why, in contrast to the thinking of Pannenberg, Torrance insists that "in a real sense the Resurrection might well be said to be the completion of the Incarnation. . . . We must not think of the Incarnation as the peak of history, the flowering of the race, the height of civilization and all that!" (78).

49. Again it must be stressed that the difference between Barth and Pannenberg here is extremely significant because, following Barth's thinking, one would have to conclude that Pannenberg was simply trying to explain the mysteries of the incarnation and resurrection and thus was refusing to make the required decision to accept or reject these events as miracles. We might also add that in his *Systematic Theology,* 2: 318, Pannenberg still rejects the virgin birth because he says the story is legendary and is not historical and factual

as is the resurrection. He takes the same position in *The Apostles' Creed: In the Light of To-day's Questions,* trans. Margaret Kohl (Eugene, OR: Wipf and Stock Publishers, 2000), 71ff. Here, however, Pannenberg no longer promotes removing this from the creed; instead he thinks Christians today can assent to the intention "which prompted the story of Jesus' virgin birth" even though that has grown beyond the nativity legend to include "the idea of the pre-existence of the sonship of Jesus in the eternal nature of God" (76-77). That intention was to stress that the Son of God is identical with the historical person, Jesus and that Jesus did not become God's Son at some point in time. In that sense the formula of the virgin birth expresses the nature of God's final revelation in Jesus. Still Pannenberg believes that most Christians today "would personally look for a different way of expressing this intention from the one offered by the story of the virgin birth" (77).

50. It is interesting to note that T. F. Torrance, following Barth in this, insisted that any attempt to explain the *how* of the incarnation amounted to a failure to accept its reality as an act of God coming into history from outside. See Torrance, *The Doctrine of Jesus Christ,* 108, 110-14. Torrance rejected any attempt to find an analogy for the incarnation because Jesus himself is unique as the incarnate Word. Obviously that is the position I have adopted in this book.

51. See *Jesus — God and Man,* 360ff. While Pannenberg notes that the older dogmatics derived Jesus' sinlessness from his divinity, he cannot. How then did Jesus overcome sin? In Pannenberg's view it is through his resurrection, so that without the resurrection this would not have become a reality (363). So Pannenberg insists that Jesus' sinlessness "results" only from the process of his entire life.

52. Thus "The positive fact which fills the space marked off by the *natus ex virgine* is God Himself, i.e., in the inconceivable act of creative omnipotence in which He imparts to human nature a capacity, a power for Himself, which it does not possess of itself" (*CD* I/2, 201). See *CD* I/2, 156ff., for more on sinlessness.

53. See Torrance, *TF,* 162, and above, Chapter Two.

54. See *Systematic Theology,* 2: 384ff. for his most recent discussion of these issues. While it is clear that he now wishes to take the incarnation seriously in a way that he did not in *Jesus — God and Man,* it is also clear the he still objects to the Chalcedonian formula for the same reasons he gave early on and he still will not allow the incarnation itself to be his starting point.

55. T. F. Torrance certainly identifies the issue when he writes: "When it is realised that the Person of Christ is divine and not just human, but nevertheless divine Person incarnate in human form, it will be obvious that we can find no analogy whatsoever to enable us to understand what took place in the event of the Incarnation" (*The Doctrine of Jesus Christ,* 108). This is in accord with Barth's similar insistence that there is no fixed and general analogy for the union of God and man in Christ because we have no *a priori* by which to grasp such an event (*CD* IV/2, 53). That is why the union of natures achieved in the incarnation can only be its own analogy (*CD* IV/2, 58). Both Christology and the Trinity depend upon a proper acknowledgment of Christ's pre-existence: "The whole discussion of the pre-existence of Christ hinges on the fact that Christ manifestly, antecedently and therefore is eternally in himself what he is in his revelation and saving activity. This of course does not mean that his humanity is eternal, but that his Person is eternal, and that his divine *Person* is not human but Divine . . . we do not say that God is Father, Son, and

Holy Spirit, because he becomes Father, Son, and Holy Spirit to us, but while we only know him because he becomes so to us, he only becomes Father, Son, and Holy Spirit to us precisely because he *is* first and eternally Father, Son, and Holy Spirit in himself alone" (*The Doctrine of Jesus Christ,* 107, emphasis in original).

56. See *CD* I/2, 164-65. Barth notes that the doctrine of *anhypostasis* and *enhypostasis* is sometimes rejected by those who insist that if Christ does not have a personality of his own he would not be truly human. Barth claims this is based on confusion resulting from the fact that the term *impersonalitas* was used to translate the term *anhypostasis* so that it was claimed that for the ancient Christologies Jesus did not have a personality. In reality Barth insists the ancient Christologies did indeed insist that Christ had a full human personality but that his humanity had no existence at all or at any time apart from the Word: "It is in virtue of the eternal Word that Jesus Christ exists as a man of flesh and blood in our sphere, as a man like us, as an historical phenomenon. But it is only in virtue of the divine Word that He exists as such" (*CD* I/2, 165). For a fuller discussion of this issue see above, Chapter Five, n. 17.

57. Monothelitism was condemned at the Third General Council of Constantinople in 680-81 as follows: "we preach, according to the doctrine of the holy Fathers *two natural wills* and two natural active principles inseparably, immovably, undividedly, and unconfusedly in him *(Christ)* . . . as blessed Athanasius says, the human will had to be moved to submit to the divine will. For, as his flesh is called, and is, the flesh of the Word of God, so his natural will is called, and is, the real will of the Word of God, as he himself says: 'Because I came down from heaven, not to do my own will, but the will of him who sent me' *(John 6:38),* calling his own will the will of his flesh. For the flesh, too, was his own. . . . Nor do we in any way admit one natural active principle of God and the creature, so as neither to raise what is created into the divine nature nor lower what is higher in the divine nature to suit the place of created things. For we ascribe both the miracles and the suffering to one and the same, according to the natures in and of which he consists, as Cyril so admirably says" (Josef Neuner, S.J., and Heinrich Roos, S.J., *The Teaching of the Catholic Church,* ed. Karl Rahner, S.J. [Cork: The Mercier Press, 1967], 169-70). Barth, of course, approved the fact that there was a true human will "different from the will of God although never independent of it" (*CD* I/2, 158) because for him Jesus took upon himself our fallen state and lived it in solidarity with us as the eternal Son of God.

58. That one of the key issues here was the problem of adoptionism was captured in a statement of the creed of the Council of Friaul in 796: "Nor did that human and temporal birth take anything from the divine and timeless birth, but in the one Person of Jesus Christ there is the true Son of God and the true Son of Man, not a different Son of God and a different Son of Man, but one and the same Son of God and man, in both natures, that is, divine and human, true God and true man, not apparently the Son of God but truly, not adoptive but real, for he was never separated from the Father on account of the man *(human nature)* he assumed . . . we confess him in both natures as the real and not adoptive Son of God, because, having taken human nature, one and the same is the Son of God and of man. Naturally Son of the Father in his divinity, and naturally Son of his Mother in his humanity" (*The Teaching of the Catholic Church,* 171).

59. It is here of course that Pannenberg criticizes Barth once again for beginning with the incarnation so that Barth too is unable to escape this contrived dilemma (*Jesus — God*

and Man, 302f.). He claims that Barth avoids but does not solve the problem of the *communicatio idiomatum.* Yet Barth was quite clear that any communication of attributes could not compromise the priority and thus the divinity of the Word. Hence one could not simply conceive of the divinity and humanity of Christ as mutually conditioning factors in mutual relationship (Cf. *CD* I/2, 164ff., and *CD* IV/2, 53). For Barth, "The Son of God does not need any completion, any concretion, any form which perhaps He lacks." "He is not," Barth says, "like Hegel's absolute spirit who can develop to a synthesis only in thesis and antithesis. He is actual in Himself — the One who is originally and properly actual. . . . He is the Creator and Lord of heaven and earth. And it is as such that He makes His existence that of another, of the man who is bound by all these antitheses and concerned to bridge them" (*CD* IV/2, 53-54). This is why Barth insists that the hypostatic union cannot under any circumstances be understood by comparing it with anything else at all. Indeed, while other antithetical concepts such as form and matter or soul and body are "mutually necessary," the same cannot be said of the divinity and humanity of Christ because the Logos remains the divine subject of the events of Jesus' life not only without compromising his human self-determination but in and with the Spirit, actually enabling it. Importantly, Barth insists "The divine nature in the existence of God the Son is indispensable to the human, but the human is not indispensable to God the Son and therefore to the divine nature" (*CD* IV/2, 54).

60. Another indication is the fact that when Pannenberg considers the notion of substitution, he does not want to say that *everything* Jesus did "was done in our place" because this would compromise the historical uniqueness of Jesus which he thinks means more than just substitution. But Pannenberg says that even if he were to accept such an idea, it cannot preserve the particularities of his humanity and divinity. Then he asks "How could a man who knew himself to be God, who interceded in our place, still be man as we are?" (*Jesus — God and Man,* 317). It is just because he thinks he can and must explain how this can be so that Pannenberg illustrates that anthropology and not Christology dictates his understanding here. From an anthropological perspective it would be absurd to think of a man who, as God, interceded in our place before God. But from a Christological perspective, it makes perfect sense because we cannot explain *how* Jesus can be God and man. That is just what faith acknowledges but cannot prove without resolving the mystery into something that can be explained and thus explained away.

61. It is important to realize here that Pannenberg holds essentially this same view in Volume 2 of his *Systematic Theology.* See text above, 268. In a very similar way Pannenberg contends we cannot begin thinking about God today with the reality of God, but must instead establish theology's truth claims by showing how its truth is grounded in the truth of all that is true in human experience. See *Systematic Theology,* 1: 42ff., and Molnar, "Some Problems with Pannenberg's Solution to Barth's Faith Subjectivism," 316ff.

62. Again Pannenberg's thinking here is remarkably similar to his thinking in *Systematic Theology,* 1: 310, where he says, "The eternal Son is first, however, an aspect of the human person. . . . Hence self-distinction from the Father is constitutive for the eternal Son in his relation to the Father." For more on this see Molnar, "Reflections on Pannenberg's Systematic Theology," 511, and above in this chapter.

63. Pannenberg insists upon the dialectical nature of Jesus' identity with the eternal Son in an effort to show that it is not a general understanding of *dedication* that is dictat-

ing what he has to say here: "Only in the situation of his urgent expectation does his dedication to the Father have its eschatological character and show him, in distinction to all others, to be the eternal Son. Thus Jesus' identity with the eternal Son of God is dialectical: the understanding of this man, in his humanity changed into its opposite, leads to the confession of his eternal divinity" (*Jesus — God and Man*, 342-43). It cannot be stressed too strongly, however, that this very thinking is an instance of what Barth quite properly identified as Ebionite Christology just because it assumes that a man was changed into something in the incarnation when in reality Jesus' humanity was posited as a miraculous act of the Word in union with the Holy Spirit. None of this can disguise the fact that it is indeed the concept of *dedication* that is Pannenberg's anthropological key to explaining and thus resolving the mystery that Chalcedon refused to resolve or explain. While Pannenberg is careful to insist that it is not Jesus' dedication as such that was the divine in him, he still thinks that it is Jesus' human dedication to the Father that establishes his Sonship.

64. Clearly, Pannenberg is aware of difficulties here because he insists that it is not Jesus' "dedication as such" in contrast to other aspects of his existence that "was the divine in him" (*Jesus — God and Man*, 342). It is the whole significance of his historical existence together with his dedication that distinguishes Jesus from all others. That is why he insists that Jesus' humanity and divinity are related dialectically.

65. In this thinking Pannenberg is in harmony with some of Rahner's most basic anthropological assumptions. See, e.g., Wolfhart Pannenberg, *Anthropology in Theological Perspective*, trans. Matthew J. O'Connell (Philadelphia: Westminster Press, 1985), 68ff. Pannenberg thus can say, "The exocentric structure of human living has therefore an openness that is not restricted to the things of this world. The openness of the step which first makes possible the very perception of an object reaches beyond the totality of all given and possible objects of perception, that is, beyond the world" (68). In this sense Pannenberg agrees with Transcendental Thomism that a "'preapprehension' of being in general [is] a condition for the knowledge of an individual object" (68 n. 68). This, Pannenberg notes, is what he had in mind in 1962 when he wrote that "the so-called openness of the human being to the world signifies ultimately an openness to what is beyond the world, so that the real meaning of this openness to the world might be better described as an openness to God" (69).

66. See text above, n. 36.

67. Pannenberg, *Systematic Theology*, 3: 193.

68. See, e.g., Pannenberg's criticism of Robert Jenson for failing to distinguish the immanent and economic Trinity properly and insisting that "Without that distinction, the reality of the one God tends to be dissolved into the process of the world" (Wolfhart Pannenberg, "A Trinitarian Synthesis," *First Things* 103 [May 2000]: 50).

69. See Molnar, *Divine Freedom*, ch. 3.

70. Wolfhart Pannenberg, "A Response to My American Friends," in *The Theology of Wolfhart Pannenberg: Twelve American Critiques, with an Autobiographical Essay and Response*, ed. Carl E. Braaten and Philip Clayton (Minneapolis: Augsburg Publishing House, 1988), 323, emphasis mine.

71. "A Response to My American Friends," 326, emphasis mine.

72. See *Systematic Theology*, 1: 263ff. This leads to the adoptionist idea that "the difference between Father and Son in God's eternal essence, depend upon, and take place in, the

fact that God as Father is manifest in the relation of Jesus to him" (311). Most of the difficulty here is caused by the fact that the mutuality between the Father and Son that Pannenberg wishes to emphasize is a mutuality dictated not by the free loving exchange between the Father and Son within the immanent Trinity but by a notion of mutuality that requires that the Father be dependent on the Son and therefore on whatever is realized by the Son within history. This is why it is important to realize that the order within the immanent Trinity cannot be trifled with even though it is perfectly proper to affirm with Pannenberg a genuine mutuality within the Trinity.

73. For more on this thinking, along with my analysis and critique, see Molnar, "Some Problems with Pannenberg's Solution to Barth's 'Faith Subjectivism,'" 315ff. Part of the difficulty is that Pannenberg really allows the experience of anticipation to set the parameters for theological discussion.

74. As John Webster rightly points out: "Barth negotiates the passage from objective to subjective, not through a theory of spirituality, experience, or morality, but through the doctrines of resurrection and Holy Spirit in which the outgoing, self-realising character of reconciliation is articulated. Reconciliation is not a mere possibility awaiting realization; it is, as Barth puts it later, 'the only reality' which 'can alone lay claim to the term'" (John Webster, *Barth's Ethics of Reconciliation* [Cambridge: Cambridge University Press, 1995], 97).

75. Webster, *Barth's Ethics of Reconciliation,* 27 and 189. See also Barth, *The Christian Life,* 245-46: for Barth, prayer is necessary because "the Father in heaven frees his children — and therefore imperiously summons them — to turn to him with this prayer [the Lord's prayer] . . . those who call upon God with it do not venture it because they snatch at it as a last resort in face of the confusion and distress of the human situation. They venture it in the freedom of obedience to pray to God thus. . . . The prayer for the coming of the kingdom, however, looks directly and exclusively beyond all that people can and should do for the betterment of the human situation to the change, which it can be God's business alone to effect . . . as it is made in obedience to God's command as a prayer for the new thing which is to be expected from God alone, it has an objectively and subjectively solid basis that is protected against all doubt."

76. The contrast between Pannenberg and Barth could not be clearer: Pannenberg thinks "the designation of Yahweh as God and the Christian attributing of deity to Jesus Christ make sense only on the condition of an established pre-Christian and extra-Christian use of the word 'God'" (*Systematic Theology,* 1: 68), while Barth insists that no idea of Lordship can lead to the fact that God really is the Lord (*CD* II/1, 75). Hence, for Barth, "If we know about God as the Lord, it is not because we also know about other lords and lordships. It is not even partly because of this previous knowledge and partly because of God's revelation. It is in consequence of God's revelation alone" (*CD* II/1, 76). And contrary to Pannenberg, Barth insists: "If we know about God the Reconciler it is not even partly because we know about other reconciliations. It is simply and solely because God Himself has revealed Himself as the Reconciler. . . . All that we can do is to be grateful that He is this God, and therefore God among us and for us. We certainly cannot boast that we have contributed to this knowledge with the help of what we know elsewhere about reconciliation" (*CD* II/1, 78).

77. See, e.g., *CD* IV/2, 100f., where Barth writes: "Already in the eternal will and decree of God He was not to be, nor did He will to be, God only, but Emmanuel, God with man, and, in fulfillment of this 'with,' according to the free choice of His grace, this man, Jesus of Nazareth. And in the act of God in time which corresponds to this eternal decree, when the Son of God became this man, He ceased to all eternity to be God only, receiving and having and maintaining to all eternity human essence as well. Thus the human essence of Jesus Christ, without becoming divine, in its very creatureliness, is placed at the side of the Creator.... It is the form which He does not lose.... He is God in the flesh" (*CD* IV/2, 100-101).

78. Hence Pannenberg can say, "The saving character of the universal relevance that belongs to Jesus' figure is determined by whether Jesus is to be understood as the *fulfillment* of the hopes and deep longing of humanity" (*Jesus — God and Man*, 205, emphasis in original). No, the saving character that belongs to Jesus is determined by the fact that he himself is the Word of God incarnate who has the power, hidden in the cross and revealed in his resurrection, to fulfill God's covenant promises to be a savior to Israel and thus to the world. This is why Barth rightly says, "The Son of God does not need any completion, any concretion, any form which perhaps He lacks. He is not an abstraction which follows something real and is attained by the interpretation of it.... He does not need the action of another to be who He is in reaction to it, nor the reaction of another to be who He is in His own action" (*CD* IV/2, 53).

79. "The righteousness of his kingdom is something totally inconceivable from man's standpoint. What takes place with it is for man something absolutely new and unexpected" (Barth, *The Christian Life*, 16). "He comes and creates righteousness, zealous for his honor as Creator and burning with love for his creature.... The kingdom of God defies expression. It is real only as God himself comes as King and Lord, establishes righteousness in our relationship to him and to one another, and thus creates peace on earth" (*The Christian Life*, 237).

80. Thus, for Pannenberg, "the judgment is justified that Jesus fulfills the hopes of the peoples because with his activity the fulfillment of the promises of Israel begins. Both are essentially associated: only as the fulfillment of the longing of the peoples is Jesus really the fulfillment of Israel's eschatological promises" (*Jesus — God and Man*, 207). It is the other way around. Because Jesus, as the incarnate Word, fulfills God's promises to Abraham and his descendents, therefore the hopes of the peoples are fulfilled.

81. While Barth rightly insists that the incarnation means that God really becomes man in Jesus of Nazareth so that we really meet God in meeting him, he has no intention of confusing his divinity and humanity with the idea that the divine and human essence of the incarnate Word could be considered equal. Hence Barth insists "He [the Son who is equal to the Father] is not of equal being and essence with the humanity assumed by Him" (*CD* IV/1, 52). And among a number of key distinctions that Barth makes to illustrate that Jesus, in his uniqueness cannot be understood by analogy with anyone or anything else we already know, Barth further insists that we cannot try to grasp the hypostatic union by the analogy of soul and body since both are mutually necessary and Christ's humanity is not necessary for the Son to be the divine Son. Any such thinking would end equating humanity and divinity. Thus, for Barth, "The divine nature in the existence of God the Son is in-

dispensable to the human, but the human is not indispensable to God the Son and there-fore to the divine nature."

82. See Molnar, "Some Problems with Pannenberg's Solution to Barth's 'Faith Subjec-tivism.'"

83. It is for this reason that in his *Systematic Theology,* 1: 79, Pannenberg can say that the natural theology of the philosophers actually is a criterion which must be met by the-ology: "The natural theology of the philosophers had formulated a criterion for judging whether any God could be seriously considered as the author of the whole cosmos, and Christian theology had to meet this criterion if its claim could be taken seriously." And Pannenberg, like Rahner, embraces an unthematic knowledge of God as infinite as the context within which knowledge of the Trinity takes place (*Systematic Theology,* 1: 114ff.).

84. This is why Barth insists that in the speaking and receiving of God's Word we are not just referring to an act of God generally, "and not just an act of God in creaturely real-ity as such, but an act of God in the reality which contradicts God, which conceals Him, and in which His revelation is not just His act but His miraculous act" (*CD* I/1, 168). Be-cause the incarnation means God's entry into the sinful secularity of the world, this cannot be evaded and so we must admit that we have "no organ or capacity for God" and that we are at "enmity" with God and "powerless to be obedient to Him." Still, this seemingly ab-surd obstacle to our relation with God that God himself seems to have put in our way is re-ally the way he has chosen to come to us. God reveals himself precisely in this concealment and not without it.

85. Here Pannenberg specifically approves of Rahner's thinking citing Rahner as fol-lows: "If the essence of man generally is understood existentially-ontologically as open . . . transcendence toward God's absolute being, then the incarnation can appear as the (surely free, unmerited, and singular) absolutely highest fulfillment of what 'man' as such means" (*Jesus — God and Man,* 345). While Pannenberg thinks that Rahner's belief that this idea of self-transcendence was already fully developed in Thomas Aquinas is not convincing, he does note that the general idea is rooted "in the Thomistic idea of the *potential obedientialis* of the humanly natural toward the Creator" and does not oppose this al-though he believes the sharp distinction between nature and super-nature obstructs a proper view of the process of human openness. Hence Pannenberg actually can say that "In fact one must understand Jesus' unity with God as the fulfillment of the openness to the world that is constitutive for man as such" (*Jesus — God and Man,* 199-200). And based on a phenomenology of hope Pannenberg thinks "that it belongs to the essence of con-scious human existence to hope beyond death" so that "To surrender oneself to such ques-tioning [beyond death] is the condition for man's full humanness" (*Jesus — God and Man,* 85-86). Yet, it is not our openness to the world that constitutes us as humans, but God's ac-tivity for us in Jesus Christ. And the condition for our full "humanness" is not the fact that we surrender to such questions but that we surrender to Jesus himself who alone can make us truly human. Any such thinking clearly allows anthropology to determine Christology rather than the other way around. Once again this is an issue of self-justification.

86. Wolfhart Pannenberg, *Theology and the Kingdom of God* (hereafter referred to in text as *Theology and the Kingdom*), ed. Richard John Neuhaus (Philadelphia: Westminster Press, 1969), 113.

87. Pannenberg is clearly not completely convinced by Rahner's presentation because

he wonders why love of God has to become thematic in and for itself in Rahner's analysis. For a different perspective and a comparison of Rahner and Barth on the subject of love of God and neighbor that argues that Rahner has indeed confused the two commands, see Molnar, "Love of God and Love of Neighbor in the Theology of Karl Rahner and Karl Barth," *Modern Theology* (October 2004).

88. The corollary to this thinking is Pannenberg's tendency to think of God as a "dependent" deity: "it is necessary to say that, in a restricted but important sense, God does not yet exist. Since his rule and his being are inseparable, God's being is still in the process of coming to be" (*Theology and the Kingdom,* 56).

89. Compare this to Barth's statement that "He does not come with a purpose whose execution depends, if not totally, then at least partially on the action, or at any rate the co-operation of Christians" (Barth, *The Christian Life,* 237).

90. Ted Peters, "Pannenberg's Eschatological Ethics," in Braaten and Clayton, eds., *The Theology of Wolfhart Pannenberg,* 243, citing Pannenberg's *Ethics,* trans. Keith Crim (Philadelphia: Westminster Press, 1981). This interpretation seems valid in light of the fact that Pannenberg says that, since we become a person's neighbor through a free act of love, "It is to such free acts of love which create neighbors that Jesus calls us when he says, 'Go and do likewise'" (Pannenberg, *Ethics,* 65). The dubious point here of course is the idea that our love creates neighbors. And in this context, instead of appealing to Christ himself as the sole enabling condition of our love of neighbors, Pannenberg appeals to our creative imagination: "Only the creative imagination of love discovers in a situation a need and at the same time the means for meeting it. . . . Christian ethics is the opposite of . . . situation ethics, because its starting point is not the situation but the creative imagination of love" (*Ethics,* 65). My point is that the starting point for Christian ethics is neither the situation nor the creative imagination but the command and promise of Jesus Christ himself (the risen Lord) calling us, equipping us and enabling us through his Holy Spirit to live the righteousness already enacted in his own life history on our behalf. He promises to share his perfect obedience with us and then enables us, through our free obedience to him, to live it.

Selected Bibliography

Athanasius. *Against the Arians.* 1.34. *A Select Library of Nicene and Post-Nicene Fathers of the Christian Church, Second Series.* Translated and edited by Philip Schaff and Henry Wace. Edinburgh: T&T Clark, 1987.

Barth, Karl. *Church Dogmatics.* 4 volumes in 13 parts.

> Vol. 1, pt. 1: *The Doctrine of the Word of God.* Edited by G. W. Bromiley and T. F. Torrance. Translated by G. W. Bromiley. Edinburgh: T&T Clark, 1975.

> Vol. 1, pt. 2: *The Doctrine of the Word of God.* Edited by G. W. Bromiley and T. F. Torrance. Translated by G. T. Thomson and Harold Knight. Edinburgh: T&T Clark, 1970.

> Vol. 2, pt. 1: *The Doctrine of God.* Edited by G. W. Bromiley and T. F. Torrance. Translated by T. H. L. Parker, W. B. Johnston, H. Knight, and J. L. M. Harie. Edinburgh: T&T Clark, 1964.

> Vol. 2, pt. 2: *The Doctrine of God.* Edited by G. W. Bromiley and T. F. Torrance. Translated by G. W. Bromiley, J. C. Campbell, Iain Wilson, J. Strathearn McNab, Harold Knight, and R. A. Stewart. Edinburgh: T&T Clark, 1967.

> Vol. 3, pt. 1: *The Doctrine of Creation.* Edited by G. W. Bromiley and T. F. Torrance. Translated by J. W. Edwards, O. Bussey, and Harold Knight. Edinburgh: T&T Clark, 1970.

> Vol. 3, pt. 2: *The Doctrine of Creation.* Edited by G. W. Bromiley and T. F. Torrance. Translated by Harold Knight, G. W. Bromiley, J. K. S. Reid, and R. H. Fuller. Edinburgh: T&T Clark, 1968.

> Vol. 3, pt. 4: *The Doctrine of Creation.* Edited by G. W. Bromiley and T. F. Torrance. Translated by A. T. MacKay, T. H. L. Parker, Harold Knight, Henry A. Kennedy, and John Marks. Edinburgh: T&T Clark, 1969.

> Vol. 4, pt. 1: *The Doctrine of Reconciliation.* Edited by G. W. Bromiley and T. F. Torrance. Translated by G. W. Bromiley. Edinburgh: T&T Clark, 1974.

Vol. 4, pt. 2: *The Doctrine of Reconciliation.* Edited by G. W. Bromiley and T. F. Torrance. Translated by G. W. Bromiley. Edinburgh: T&T Clark, 1967.

Vol. 4, pt. 3: *The Doctrine of Reconciliation.* First Half. Edited by G. W. Bromiley and T. F. Torrance. Translated by G. W. Bromiley. Edinburgh: T&T Clark, 1976.

Vol. 4, pt. 3: *The Doctrine of Reconciliation.* Second Half. Edited by G. W. Bromiley and T. F. Torrance. Translated by G. W. Bromiley. Edinburgh: T&T Clark, 1969.

Vol. 4, pt. 4: *The Christian Life. Lecture Fragments.* Translated by Geoffrey W. Bromiley. Grand Rapids: Eerdmans, 1981.

———. *Credo.* Translated by Robert McAfee Brown. New York: Charles Scribner's Sons, 1962.

———. *The Epistle to the Philippians 40th Anniversary Edition.* Translated by James W. Leitch. Introduction by Bruce L. McCormack and Francis B. Watson. Louisville/London: Westminster/John Knox Press, 2002.

———. *Evangelical Theology: An Introduction.* Translated by Grover Foley. Grand Rapids: Eerdmans, 1963.

———. *The Göttingen Dogmatics: Instruction in the Christian Religion Volume One.* Translated by Geoffrey W. Bromiley. Grand Rapids: Eerdmans, 1991.

———. *Letters 1961-1968.* Edited by Jürgen Fangemeier and Hinrich Stoevesandt. Translated and edited by Geoffrey W. Bromiley. Grand Rapids: Eerdmans, 1981.

———. *The Word of God and the Word of Man.* Translated by Douglas Horton. Gloucester, MA: Peter Smith, 1978.

Braaten, Carl E., and Philip Clayton, eds. *The Theology of Wolfhart Pannenberg: Twelve American Critiques, with an Autobiographical Essay and Response.* Minneapolis: Augsburg Publishing House, 1988.

Bresnahan, James F. "An Ethics of Faith." In *A World of Grace,* edited by Leo J. O'Donovan. New York: Crossroad, 1981.

Bultmann, Rudolf. "New Testament and Mythology." In *Kerygma and Myth: A Theological Debate,* edited by Hans Werner Bartsch, translated by Reginald H. Fuller, 1-44. London: SPCK, 1954.

Coffey, David. "The Theandric Nature of Christ." *Theological Studies* 60, no. 3 (September 1999).

Cranfield, C. E. B. *On Romans and Other New Testament Essays.* Edinburgh: T&T Clark, 1998.

St. Cyril of Alexandria. *On the Unity of Christ.* Translated and introduced by John Anthony McGuckin. Crestwood, NY: St. Vladimir's Press, 1995.

Davis, Stephen T. "'Seeing' the Risen Jesus." In *The Resurrection: An Interdisciplinary Symposium on the Resurrection of Jesus,* edited by Stephen T. Davis, Daniel Kendall, S.J., and Gerald O'Collins, S.J., 126-47. New York: Oxford University Press, 1998.

Dupuis, Jacques, S.J. *Jesus Christ at the Encounter of World Religions.* Translated by Robert R. Barr. Maryknoll, NY: Orbis, 1991.

Dych, William V., S.J. *Karl Rahner.* Collegeville: The Liturgical Press, 1992.

———. "Theology in a New Key." In *A World of Grace,* edited by Leo J. O'Donovan. New York: Crossroad, 1981.

Farrow, Douglas. *Ascension and Ecclesia: On the Significance of the Doctrine of the Ascension for Ecclesiology and Christian Cosmology.* Grand Rapids: Eerdmans, 1999.

Fee, Gordon D. "St Paul and the Incarnation: A Reassessment of the Data." In *The Incarnation: An Interdisciplinary Symposium on the Incarnation of the Son of God,* edited by Stephen T. Davis, Daniel Kendall, S.J., and Gerald O'Collins, S.J. Oxford: Oxford University Press, 2002.

Fergusson, David. "Interpreting the Resurrection." *Scottish Journal of Theology* 38 (1985): 287-305.

Galvin, John P. "The Invitation of Grace." In *A World of Grace,* edited by Leo J. O'Donovan. New York: Crossroad, 1981.

Grenz, Stanley J. *Rediscovering the Triune God: The Trinity in Contemporary Theology.* Minneapolis: Fortress Press, 2004.

———, and Roger E. Olson. *Twentieth-Century Theology: God and the World in a Transitional Age.* Carlisle, UK: Paternoster Press, 1992.

Grieb, A. Katherine. "Last Things First: Karl Barth's Theological Exegesis of 1 Corinthians in *The Resurrection of the Dead.*" *Scottish Journal of Theology* 56 (2003): 49-64.

Gunton, Colin E. "And in One Lord, Jesus Christ . . . Begotten, Not Made." In *Nicene Christianity: The Future for a New Ecumenism,* edited by Christopher R. Seitz. Grand Rapids: Brazos Press, 2001.

———. *Yesterday and Today: A Study of Continuities in Christology.* Grand Rapids: Eerdmans, 1983.

Haight, Roger, S.J. *Jesus: Symbol of God.* Maryknoll, NY: Orbis, 1999.

Harris, Horton. *David Friedrich Strauss and His Theology.* Cambridge: Cambridge University Press, 1973.

Hick, John. *A Christian Theology of Religions: The Rainbow of Faiths.* Louisville: Westminster/John Knox Press, 1995.

———. *Disputed Questions in Theology and the Philosophy of Religion.* New Haven: Yale University Press, 1993.

———. *God Has Many Names.* Philadelphia: Westminster Press, 1982.

———. *An Interpretation of Religion: Human Responses to the Transcendent.* New Haven: Yale University Press, 1989.

———. "Jesus and the World Religions." In *The Myth of God Incarnate,* edited by John Hick. Philadelphia: Westminster Press, 1977.

———. *The Metaphor of God Incarnate: Christology in a Pluralistic Age.* Louisville: Westminster/John Knox Press, 1993.

———. "The Non-Absoluteness of Christianity." In *The Myth of Christian Uniqueness: Toward a Pluralistic Theology of Religions,* edited by John Hick and Paul F. Knitter. Maryknoll, NY: Orbis, 1987.

Hunsinger, George. *How to Read Karl Barth: The Shape of His Theology*. New York: Oxford University Press, 1991.

Hurtado, Larry W. *Lord Jesus Christ: Devotion to Jesus in Earliest Christianity*. Grand Rapids: Eerdmans, 2003.

Imhof, Paul, and Hubert Biallowons, eds. *Karl Rahner in Dialogue: Conversations and Interviews 1965-1982*. Translated by Harvey D. Egan. New York: Crossroad, 1986.

Kasper, Walter. *The God of Jesus Christ*. Translated by Matthew J. O'Connell. New York: Crossroad, 1986.

Kaufman, Gordon D. *God — Mystery — Diversity: Christian Theology in a Pluralistic World*. Minneapolis: Fortress Press, 1996.

—————. *In Face of Mystery: A Constructive Theology*. Cambridge, MA: Harvard University Press, 1993.

—————. *Systematic Theology: A Historicist Perspective*. New York: Charles Scribner's Sons, 1968.

—————. *The Theological Imagination: Constructing the Concept of God*. Philadelphia: Westminster Press, 1981.

—————. *Theology for a Nuclear Age*. Philadelphia: Westminster Press, 1985.

Knitter, Paul F. *Introducing Theologies of Religions*. Maryknoll, NY: Orbis, 2002.

—————. *No Other Name? A Critical Survey of Christian Attitudes Toward the World Religions*. Maryknoll, NY: Orbis, 1985.

—————. "Theocentric Christology." *Theology Today* 40, no. 2 (July 1983): 130-49.

Knox, John. *The Humanity and Divinity of Christ: A Study of Pattern in Christology*. New York: Cambridge University Press, 1967.

Künneth, Walter. *The Theology of the Resurrection*. St. Louis: Concordia Publishing House, 1965.

LaCugna, Catherine Mowry. *God for Us: The Trinity and Christian Life*. San Francisco: HarperSanFrancisco, 1991.

Lane, Dermot A. *The Reality of Jesus*. New York: Paulist Press, 1975.

Lauber, David. *Barth on the Descent into Hell: God, Atonement and the Christian Life*. Aldershot: Ashgate Publishing Limited, 2004.

Lewis, C. S. *Mere Christianity*. New York: Simon & Schuster, 1996.

McBrien, Richard P. *Catholicism Completely Revised and Updated*. San Francisco: HarperSanFrancisco, 1994.

McFague, Sallie. *The Body of God: An Ecological Theology*. Minneapolis: Fortress Press, 1993.

—————. "Imaging a Theology of Nature: The World as God's Body." In *Liberating Life: Contemporary Approaches to Ecological Theology*, edited by Charles Birch, William Eakin, and Jay B. McDaniel. Maryknoll, NY: Orbis, 1990.

—————. *Models of God: Theology for an Ecological Nuclear Age*. Philadelphia: Fortress Press, 1987.

Macquarrie, John. *Christology Revisited*. Harrisburg, PA: Trinity Press International, 1998.

—————. *In Search of Deity: An Essay in Dialectical Theism*. New York: Crossroad, 1987.

———. *Jesus Christ in Modern Thought*. Philadelphia: Trinity Press International, 1990.

Michalson, G. E., Jr. "Pannenberg on the Resurrection and Historical Method." *Scottish Journal of Theology* 33, no. 4 (1980): 345-59.

Migliore, Daniel L. *Faith Seeking Understanding: An Introduction to Christian Theology*. Grand Rapids: Eerdmans, 1991.

Molnar, Paul D. *Divine Freedom and the Doctrine of the Immanent Trinity: In Dialogue with Karl Barth and Contemporary Theology*. New York and London: T&T Clark/Continuum, 2002.

———. "Experience and Knowledge of the Trinity in the Theology of Ted Peters: Occasion for Clarity or Confusion?" *Irish Theological Quarterly* 64 (1999): 219-43.

———. "Love of God and Love of Neighbor in the Theology of Karl Rahner and Karl Barth." *Modern Theology* 20, no. 4 (October 2004): 567-99.

———. "Natural Theology Revisited: A Comparison of T. F. Torrance and Karl Barth." *Zeitschrift für dialektische Theologie* 1 (2005): 1-31.

———. "Reflections on Pannenberg's Systematic Theology Volume I: A Review Discussion." *The Thomist* 58 (1994): 501-12.

———. "Some Dogmatic Consequences of Paul F. Knitter's Unitarian Theocentrism." *The Thomist* 55 (1991): 449-95.

———. "Some Problems with Pannenberg's Solution to Barth's 'Faith Subjectivism.'" *Scottish Journal of Theology* 48 (1995): 315-39.

———. "The Theology of Justification in Dogmatic Context." In *Justification: What's at Stake in the Current Debates*, edited by Mark Husbands and Daniel Treier. Downers Grove, IL: InterVarsity Press, 2004.

Neuner, Josef, S.J., Heinrich Roos, S.J., and Karl Rahner, S.J., eds. *The Teaching of the Catholic Church*. Cork: Mercier Press, 1967.

O'Collins, Gerald. *Jesus Risen: An Historical, Fundamental and Systematic Examination of Christ's Resurrection*. New York: Paulist Press, 1987.

O'Donovan, Oliver. *Resurrection and Moral Order: An Outline for Evangelical Ethics*. Second edition. Grand Rapids: Eerdmans, 1994.

Pagels, Elaine. "The Gnostic Jesus and Early Christian Politics." University Lecture in Religion at Arizona State University, January 28, 1982.

Pannenberg, Wolfhart. *Anthropology in Theological Perspective*. Translated by Matthew J. O'Connell. Philadelphia: Westminster Press, 1985.

———. *The Apostles' Creed: In the Light of Today's Questions*. Translated by Margaret Kohl. Eugene, OR: Wipf and Stock Publishers, 2000.

———. *Basic Questions in Theology. Collected Essays*, Volume 1. Translated by George H. Kehm. Philadelphia: Fortress Press, 1970.

———. *Ethics*. Translated by Keith Crim. Philadelphia: Westminster Press, 1981.

———. "Eternity, Time and the Trinitarian God." *CTI Reflections* (published by Center of Theological Inquiry, Princeton) 3 (1999): 43-61.

———. *An Introduction to Systematic Theology*. Grand Rapids: Eerdmans, 1991.

———. *Jesus — God and Man*. Second edition. Translated by Lewis L. Wilkins and Duane A. Priebe. Philadelphia: Westminster Press, 1977.

———. *Metaphysics and the Idea of God*. Translated by Philip Clayton. Grand Rapids: Eerdmans, 1990.

———. "A Response to My American Friends." In *The Theology of Wolfhart Pannenberg: Twelve American Critiques, with an Autobiographical Essay and Response*, edited by Carl E. Braaten and Philip Clayton. Minneapolis: Augsburg Publishing House, 1988.

———. *Systematic Theology, Volume 1*. Translated by Geoffrey W. Bromiley. Grand Rapids: Eerdmans, 1991.

———. *Systematic Theology, Volume 2*. Translated by Geoffrey W. Bromiley. Grand Rapids: Eerdmans, 1994.

———. *Systematic Theology, Volume 3*. Translated by Geoffrey W. Bromiley. Grand Rapids: Eerdmans, 1998.

———. *Theology and the Kingdom of God*. Edited by Richard John Neuhaus. Philadelphia: Westminster Press, 1969.

———. "A Trinitarian Synthesis." *First Things* 103 (May 2000).

Perrin, Norman. *Resurrection according to Matthew, Mark, and Luke*. Philadelphia: Fortress Press, 1977.

Peters, Ted. *God as Trinity: Relationality and Temporality in Divine Life*. Louisville: Westminster/John Knox Press, 1993.

———. "Pannenberg's Eschatological Ethics" In *The Theology of Wolfhart Pannenberg: Twelve American Critiques, with an Autobiographical Essay and Response*, edited by Carl E. Braaten and Philip Clayton. Minneapolis: Augsburg Publishing House, 1988.

Rahner, Karl, S.J. *The Church and the Sacraments*, Quaestiones Disputatae 9. Translated by W. J. O'Hara. New York: Herder and Herder, 1968.

———. *Foundations of Christian Faith: An Introduction to the Idea of Christianity*. Translated by William V. Dych. New York: Seabury Press, 1978.

———. *Hearer of the Word: Laying the Foundation for a Philosophy of Religion*. Translated by Joseph Donceel. Edited by Andrew Tallon. New York: Continuum, 1994.

———. *Theological Investigations*. 23 volumes.

Vol. 1: *God, Christ, Mary and Grace*. Translated by Cornelius Ernst, O.P. Baltimore: Helicon Press, 1961.

Vol. 4: *More Recent Writings*. Translated by Kevin Smyth. Baltimore: Helicon Press, 1966.

Vol. 5: *Later Writings*. Translated by Karl-H. Kruger. Baltimore: Helicon Press, 1966.

Vol. 6: *Concerning Vatican Council II*. Translated by Karl-H. and Boniface Kruger. Baltimore: Helicon Press, 1969.

Vol. 7: *Further Theology of the Spiritual Life 1*. Translated by David Bourke. New York: Herder and Herder, 1971.

Vol. 9: *Writings of 1965-1967 1*. Translated by Graham Harrison. New York: Herder and Herder, 1972.

Vol. 11: *Confrontations 1*. Translated by David Bourke. New York: Seabury Press, 1974.

Vol. 13: *Theology, Anthropology, Christology*. Translated by David Bourke. London: Darton, Longman & Todd, 1975.

Vol. 16: *Experience of the Spirit: Source of Theology*. Translated by David Morland. New York: Seabury Press, 1976.

Vol. 17: *Jesus, Man, and the Church*. Translated by Margaret Kohl. New York: Crossroad, 1981.

Vol. 18: *God and Revelation*. Translated by Edward Quinn. New York: Crossroad, 1983.

————. *The Trinity*. Translated by Joseph Donceel. New York: Herder and Herder, 1970.

————, and Joseph Ratzinger. *Revelation and Tradition*. Quaestiones Disputatae, 17. Translated by W. J. O'Hara. New York: Herder and Herder, 1966.

————, and Karl-Heinz Weger. *Our Christian Faith: Answers for the Future*. Translated by Francis McDonagh. New York: Crossroad, 1981.

————, and Wilhelm Thüsing. *A New Christology*. New York: A Crossroad Book/Seabury Press, 1980.

Ratzinger, Joseph Cardinal. *Principles of Catholic Theology: Building Stones for a Fundamental Theology*. Translated by Sister Mary Frances McCarthy, S.N.D. San Francisco: Ignatius Press, 1987.

Schweizer, Eduard. *Jesus*. Translated by David E. Green. Atlanta: John Knox Press, 1971.

Schwöbel, Christoph. *Wolfhart Pannenberg, The Modern Theologians: An Introduction to Christian Theology in the Twentieth Century Volume I*, edited by David F. Ford, 257-92. Oxford: Blackwell, 1989.

Sobrino, Jon. *Jesus the Liberator*. Maryknoll, NY: Orbis, 1993.

Torrance, Alan. *Persons in Communion: Trinitarian Description and Human Participation*. Edinburgh: T&T Clark, 1996.

Torrance, Thomas F. *The Christian Doctrine of God, One Being Three Persons*. Edinburgh: T&T Clark, 1996.

————. *Divine and Contingent Order*. Edinburgh: T&T Clark, 1998.

————. *The Doctrine of Jesus Christ*. Eugene, OR: Wipf and Stock Publishers, 2002.

————. *God and Rationality*. Edinburgh: T&T Clark, 1997.

————. *The Ground and Grammar of Theology*. Charlottesville: The University Press of Virginia, 1980.

————. *Karl Barth, Biblical and Evangelical Theologian*. Edinburgh: T&T Clark, 1990.

————. *The Mediation of Christ*. Grand Rapids: Eerdmans, 1983.

————. *Preaching Christ Today: The Gospel and Scientific Thinking*. Grand Rapids: Eerdmans, 1994.

————. "The Problem of Natural Theology in the Thought of Karl Barth." *Religious Studies* 6 (1970): 121-35.

————. *Reality and Evangelical Theology*. Philadelphia: Westminster Press, 1982.

————. *Reality and Scientific Theology*. Eugene, OR: Wipf and Stock Publishers, 2001.

————. *The School of Faith: The Catechisms of the Reformed Church*. Translated and edited with an introduction by Thomas F. Torrance. Eugene and Pasadena: Wipf and Stock Publishers, 1996.

————. *Space, Time and Incarnation*. London: Oxford University Press, 1978.

————. *Space, Time and Resurrection*. Edinburgh: T&T Clark, 1998.

————. *Theological Science*. Oxford: Oxford University Press, 1978.

————. *Theology in Reconciliation*. London: Geoffrey Chapman, 1975.

————. *Theology in Reconstruction*. London: SCM, 1965.

————. *The Trinitarian Faith: The Evangelical Theology of the Ancient Catholic Church*. Edinburgh: T&T Clark, 1988.

————. *Trinitarian Perspectives: Toward Doctrinal Agreement*. Edinburgh: T&T Clark, 1994.

Wainwright, Arthur W. *The Trinity in the New Testament*. London: SPCK, 1980.

Webster, John. *Barth's Ethics of Reconciliation*. Cambridge: Cambridge University Press, 1995.

————. *Word and Church: Essays in Christian Dogmatics*. Edinburgh and New York: T&T Clark, 2001.

Wong, Joseph H. P. *Logos-Symbol in the Christology of Karl Rahner*. Rome: Las-Roma, 1984.

Wright, N. T. *The Resurrection of the Son of God*. Minneapolis: Fortress Press, 2003.

Name Index

Subject Index

Advent Lord, 155, 329. *See also* Parousia; Second coming

Agnosticism (agnostic), 97, 123, 138, 205, 213, 216-17, 220, 241, 253-55, 258, 318, 320

Analogy, 41, 84, 238, 276, 290, 302, 304, 395nn.50 and 55, 400n.81
Analogia entis (analogy of being), 40, 52, 340n.42, 394n.47
Analogia fidei (analogy of faith), 39

Anonymous Christianity, 49, 125, 150, 338n.33, 339n.36
Anonymous Christian, 51, 324
Anonymous Christology, 343n.13
Anonymous experience of the risen Lord, 63, 113, 141, 323-24, 326
Anonymous faith, 62, 129

Anthropology, 22, 47, 49, 61, 75-76, 124, 129, 191-92, 137, 157, 165, 264, 267, 271, 287-88, 295-96, 299, 324-27, 361n.9, 367n.31, 401n.85
philosophical, 64, 165
theological, 7, 157, 162, 165
transcendental, 69, 71, 137

Apollinarianism, 82, 338n.32

Apologetic, 46, 47, 50, 127, 195, 262, 263, 327

Arianism, 95, 171, 176, 359n.2

Ascension, 8, 18, 27-29, 35, 38, 79-80, 91, 93, 100, 104, 116, 134, 141, 158, 160-61, 246, 281, 294, 313, 337n.32

Atonement, 5, 7-8, 15, 19, 23, 29, 36-37, 43, 47, 83, 85, 89, 100, 102, 108-9, 112, 115-16, 121-23, 130, 134, 144, 164, 159-70, 187, 189, 208, 222, 225, 227, 229, 231, 241, 256, 288, 354n.52, 370n.7, 392n.42
Anselm's satisfaction view, 37
cross ix, 3, 8, 10-12, 14, 16, 26, 36-37, 39, 41, 80, 97, 101, 103, 126, 133, 158, 161, 185, 203-6, 211-12, 221-22, 230, 267, 268, 281, 286, 289, 291, 294, 303, 313, 332n.9
forgiveness, x, 101-2, 173, 198-99, 201, 206, 208, 224, 226, 231, 256, 355n.52, 370n.7
punishment, 37
reconciliation, 5, 8-10, 12, 14-16, 31, 33, 36, 98, 102, 104, 130, 132, 134, 152, 158, 173, 201, 208-9, 215, 225, 227, 230, 282, 291, 305, 346n.10, 374n.25, 399n.74
salvation, xi-xii, 5, 7, 12, 15, 18, 22, 24, 36, 38, 43, 46-47, 49, 51, 54-58, 67, 69, 74-77, 79-83, 89, 100-103, 123, 131, 134, 144, 146-48, 150-52, 161-63, 169-71, 177, 182-83, 186-90, 202-4, 206-16, 218, 223-31, 236, 240-44, 253, 255-59, 274-75, 281-82, 284-85, 303, 305, 309-10, 316-19, 321-23, 365-66n.27, 367n.31

413